ESSAYS

ON THE

PROGRESS OF NATIONS,

IN CIVILIZATION, PRODUCTIVE INDUSTRY, WEALTH AND POPULATION.

ILLUSTRATED BY

STATISTICS OF MINING, AGRICULTURE, MANUFACTURES, COMMERCE, COIN, BANKING, INTERNAL IMPROVEMENTS, EMIGRATION AND POPULATION.

BY EZRA C. SEAMAN.

NEW YORK:
CHARLES SCRIBNER, 145 NASSAU STREET.
1853.

Stereotyped and Printed by
C. W. BENEDICT,
201 William Street, N. Y.

TO THE REV. GEORGE DUFFIELD, D.D.

SIR,—

THE kind interest taken by you in the prosecution of my inquiries, and in the first publication of a portion of these Essays—the profound attention you have given to many of the subjects treated in them, and the deep interest you have taken in the diffusion of useful knowledge, have induced me to inscribe this volume of Essays to you, as a token of the high respect which is entertained for your character and services, as a great moral and religious teacher, by the

AUTHOR.

PREFACE

A PORTION of these Essays were published in the year 1846; a supplement to the original work was published in 1847, and a second supplement in 1848. The tariff of 1846 having been passed since the original work was published; great changes having been made in the commercial policy of Great Britain; California and New Mexico having been ceded to the United States by treaty; a new census having been taken by the United States, and also by several countries of Europe; the work has been revised and enlarged in view of these changes.

The population of the countries of Europe and America, is given according to the most recent enumerations, with the progressive increase; the amount of the commerce of the United States, and of the principal commercial nations of Europe, at different periods, is stated according to the latest commercial reports which have been published; and the productive industry of the United States, and of several countries of Europe, is stated and compared together, as far as is practicable in such a work, with the information at present attainable. The most of the matter contained in the original work and the supplements, has been condensed, corrected, and re-arranged; the chapters divided into sections for convenience of reference; a large amount of new matter added, and many branches of the subject treated of not contained in the former work, making it, in a great degree, a new work, rather than a new edition of the former work.

It is more theoretical than the former work, with fewer details of statistics; though it contains the results—the mere aggregates—

of a much greater amount of facts and statistics. It comprises the leading principles of political economy and social philosophy, and the facts from which they are deduced, united in a systematic series of essays, logically arranged, showing the connection of the whole, and the bearing of each upon the development of the faculties of man, upon productive industry, civilization and the progress of nations.

The object of the Author has been to connect political economy with statistics; to bring the rules and principles of the former, to the test of the established facts of the latter; and to try them, as far as practicable, by the severe test, and certain standard, of the principles of mathematics. This is the only mode by which they can be reduced to certainty, and by which errors, false assumptions, fallacious reasoning, and erroneous conclusions, can be detected and corrected.

Political economy is claimed to be a science, but it is in a very unsettled and imperfect condition at present. The rules laid down as principles are inconsistent with each other, and many of them are founded on assumptions which are erroneous and untrue. Modern society and its institutions are so complicated, and so many causes operate at the same time to produce effects, that it is often very difficult to determine what causes have contributed most to produce them. The whole subject of political economy is so complicated, that the only mode of even approximating to the truth, is to observe and collect carefully the facts showing the progress of nations during a series of ages; to note their condition at different periods, and their relative progress; to apply the inductive system of philosophy, and from the effects observed, endeavor to deduce the causes which produced them. Such is the mode in which almost all scientific truths have been discovered—that is, by observation, experiment, and the deductions of reason. The course of events in different countries, under different institutions, and various systems of policy, are but experiments, which should be carefully observed and noted, to enable us to learn from the experience of other nations, as well as our own. Until that mode is pursued to ascertain the principles of political economy, statesmen and nations will continue to grope their way in uncertainty and error, and be often misled by rules laid down as principles which are founded on false assumptions.

The Author has endeavored to show the effect on the progress of man and of nations, of civil, political, and religious liberty; of the development of the intellect; of educating the whole people; of the general diffusion of knowledge and science; of the discoveries, inventions, machinery, and improvements of modern times; of the use and necessity of immaterial as well as material capital; of adapting the division of employments to the condition and wants of the country; of making production free, but regulating the foreign commerce of a country in such a manner as to secure to its citizens a field of employment, to encourage and promote their industry; of the use of the precious metals, and of banking institutions and paper money; of foreign debts and colonial bondage; of associations, municipal and other corporations, local powers, and confederated systems of government; of associating, uniting, and organizing numerous individuals, their capital and labor, by means of corporations, for great enterprises and undertakings, which a few persons are incapable of accomplishing; of the union of civil and ecclesiastical power; of despotism in any form; of ecclesiastical hierarchies, and all attempts to enforce uniformity of opinion in matters of religion or government; of large standing armies, the centralization of power, and its concentration in the hands of one man, or of an aristocratic few. The object has been, to inquire into the causes and principal elements of individual and national progress, and the institutions which tend to promote it, as well as those which have a contrary tendency. How far the Author has been successful in his efforts, it is submitted to the judgment of an intelligent and generous public to determine.

Nearly all the works on political economy used in the schools, advocate the free-trade side of the question; and though there are many reports, addresses, and speeches, and some substantial works, which controvert those doctrines with great ability, yet there is no complete work on the subject of political economy, taking that view of the question, and presenting the leading facts from which its principles are deduced. This work is designed for common school libraries, for mechanics' and other public libraries, and for all classes of learners and inquirers into industrial, social, and political questions. It is hoped it may be found useful as a text-book, in connection with other works on political economy, for students in academies and colleges, who should be made acquainted with all the views and phases in which the subject can be presented. They should examine both sides of every question.

To express an opinion in favor of discrimination for the benefit of American industry, in laying duties on imports, is said by the advocates of free-trade to have a political bearing, and to involve partisan politics. On the contrary, they claim that the doctrines of free-trade are scientific, and the expressions of opinions in accordance with them are proper, and not subject to a similar charge. To discuss one side of the question is claimed to be scientific and proper; but a cry is raised against the discussion of the other side of the same question, as involving party politics, which they allege should be kept out of the schools, out of all agricultural conventions, and out of all other conventions and meetings of the people, except those of a purely partisan character. They seem to think that the schools and students should be supplied with books inculcating the doctrines of free-trade: that is esteemed proper; but to supply them with books on the other side of the question, would be promoting partisan politics, and therefore pernicious. It is to be hoped that such sophistry will soon be discarded, and that both sides of every industrial, political, and economical question, will be examined with equal care. Accurate information upon the subjects treated in this volume, is necessary to every statesman, as a guide to enlightened legislation.

The most of the work was prepared for publication during the years 1850 and 1851, and much of it stereotyped previous to the reception of the information relative to the *coup d'état* of Louis Napoleon of December 2d, 1851. This accounts for what is said in the fifth chapter, in relation to the constitution of France. The publication has been delayed in order to obtain the principal results of the late census of 1850. Through the kindness of Mr. Kennedy, the superintendent of the census, and of Mr. Irving, his chief clerk, the Author has been favored with much information collected with the census. He has also been favored during the progress of the work, with important information from several other officers of the government, who have greatly facilitated his inquiries. The works most frequently consulted, in addition to official documents and reports, have been "Hunt's Merchants' Magazine," "The American Almanac," "British Almanac and Companion," "Annuaire of France," "McCulloch's Statistics," "Commercial Dictionary and Universal Gazetteer," "Porter's Progress of the Nation," "Hallam's Middle Ages," "Jacob on the Precious Metals," "Brande's Encyclopædia of Science and Art," "Gibbon's Rome," "Mosheim's Church History," and "Murray's Geography."

The facts and statistics have been collected and arranged, and the estimates and deductions made with great labor, care, and attention; and the Author hopes and trusts, that they may be useful to the public, and that the statistics, in the form in which they are condensed and combined, may comprise information valuable to the reading community of all parties and sects, whether they do or do not agree with the Author in his deductions and estimates.

WASHINGTON, *July*, 1852.

TABLE OF CONTENTS.

CHAPTER I.

CHAPTER II.

CHAPTER III.

CHAPTER IV.

CHAPTER V.

CHAPTER VI.

ON THE NATURE AND CONSTITUENTS OF WEALTH, AND HOW ACCUMULATED; ON VALUE, EXCHANGEABLE VALUE AND PRICE; CAPITAL AND MATERIALS, AS DISTINGUISHED FROM PRODUCTS FOR CONSUMPTION; PRODUCTION, THE RESULT OF THE COMBINED ACTION OF LABOR AND CAPITAL, BOTH MATERIAL AND IMMATERIAL, UPON RAW MATERIALS; WEALTH ACCUMULATED BY INDUSTRY AND FRUGALITY; PURSUITS PERSONIFIED, THEIR RELATIVE IMPORTANCE, 125–151.

CHAPTER VII.

CHAPTER VIII.

CHAPTER IX.

CHAPTER X.

ON THE PRECIOUS METALS, COIN, AND BANK NOTES, 240–271.

CHAPTER XI.

ON SUPPLY AND DEMAND, THE WANTS OF MAN, AND A PROPER DIVISION OF EMPLOYMENTS, 272–299.

CHAPTER XII.

CHAPTER XIII.

CHAPTER XIV.

CHAPTER XV.

CHAPTER XVI.

CHAPTER XVII.

CHAPTER XVIII.

CHAPTER XIX.

CHAPTER XX.

On the population of the new world, 578.

CHAPTER XXI.

On the property and productive industry of the United States, (continued from chapter xiv,) 614.

CHAPTER I.

ON THE LAWS OF NATURE, AND THEIR OPERATIONS AND EFFECTS UPON THE CONDITION, TRANSACTIONS, AND WELFARE OF INDIVIDUALS; AND UPON THE PROGRESS OF NATIONS.

SEC. 1. *Importance of understanding the Laws of Nature.*

INASMUCH as the destiny of man and the progress of nations are in a great measure shaped and controlled by the laws of nature, or, in other words, by the general providences of God, it becomes necessary to inquire into, and to study these laws. That climate, and the situation, condition, and resources of a country in regard to soil, mines, mountains, timber, navigable waters, and small streams and springs, have a great influence upon man, and upon the progress of communities and nations, is obvious to every intelligent mind. Large bodies of water are not only convenient as aids to commerce, but they are absolutely necessary to produce a constant and sufficient quantity of evaporation to furnish with regularity clouds, rains, and dews to moisten the earth, render it fit for vegetation, and enable it to support animal life; and hence the central portions of large continents, lying at a great distance from seas and lakes, are very generally barren wastes. It is necessary to study all these things and conditions, in order to learn their influences upon the health, means of subsistence, comfort, and wants of individuals and communities; and upon their progress in productive industry, commerce, civilization, wealth, numbers, and power. In no other mode can we account for the different degrees of advancement which have been made by the nations of the earth respectively in different ages. Man should study and understand the laws of nature, to enable him to use to the best advantage, and to improve his faculties and the physical advantages which surround him; to use dame nature and her laws and products, as well as all the elements of the material world, as instruments to furnish himself with the necessaries, comforts, and enjoyments of life, and to protect himself, as far as possible, from the physical evils and ills to which he is subject. A knowledge of the laws of nature is necessary to enable him to direct his industry in such manner as to render it effective and useful, in order to supply his wants, promote his comforts, and secure his well-being.

As man by the use of the telescope and other mechanical aids, can see objects which are beyond the reach of the natural vision, so, by the aid of science, he can extend his intellectual vision to things, laws, and results, beyond the most distant conceptions of the uncultivated mind. A complete knowledge of the laws of nature, and of all their principles, comprises the whole circle of the sciences—intellectual, moral, social, and political, as well as natural. The study and knowledge of the laws of nature, or many of them, including all the physical, and mechanical, and a portion of the mental sciences, lie at the very foundation of all human improvement and progress.

SEC. 2. *The Laws of Nature deduced from the elements of the material and intellectual worlds; and defined.*

The series of worlds comprising the Universe, are composed of matter of various kinds; each possessing distinct properties, affinities, and powers, by which the several kinds act and react upon each other with perfect uniformity, form combinations, and produce dissolutions, and cause the motion of the heavenly bodies, and the action of what we usually term the elements, upon the face of the earth. Man was constituted by the Supreme Being mostly of the same materials as the material world, partakes of its properties, and is subject to, and adapted to the same general laws; and while some things are congenial to his nature, and necessary to sustain life, others are destructive to his existence as an organized being. There seems to be a living principle pervading organized beings, which is the basis of life, and the active agent which is the builder of all organic structures, vegetable as well as animal; and in addition to this, man is endowed by his Creator with an intellect, adapted to his physical and organic constitution and nature. Though the intellect or mind is an intelligent and active principle of itself, capable of originating action, possessing freedom of action, or freedom of will, as it is usually termed, yet it is perfectly dependent upon, and can act through the medium of physical organs only.

The earth and all its products are spread before mankind, to be equally enjoyed by all; this constitutes a community of interest among the whole human family; hence equality to some extent, of natural, not acquired rights, such as a right to life, liberty, and to pursue one's own happiness in a proper manner, lies at the foundation of justice; and hence the duty of each to respect the rights of his fellow beings. This community of interest, and the moral duty of man to man, would form but a feeble bond of union among mankind, if the Deity, in the formation of man, had not placed in him a desire of conjugal union, and fixed in his constitution a principle of sympathy for his fellow beings, and his family and associates, in particular, which acts as an instinctive propensity of his nature, impelling him to social intercourse as a means of enjoyment; also impelling him to do good and relieve distress. This sympathy is the source, if not the very essence of what some call moral sense; and constitutes the basis of the domestic affections, of our social feelings, and of every feeling of benevolence, charity, and philanthropy. This instinctive propensity, or feeling of sympathy, results partly from our intellectual, and partly from our physical or organic constitution and nature; or more probably from the intimate union and combination of the two, and constitutes our moral nature and the principal bond of union between man and man. Certain relations, therefore, exist between man and his Maker, between man and man; between man and the material world, of which he constitutes a part, and between the intellectual and physical, or organic part of man. All these relations, and the properties and powers of matter and of spirit upon which they depend, have been nicely adapted to each other by the infinite wisdom and benevolence of the Deity; *they comprise the physical, organic, spiritual, and moral laws of the universe, and constitute what are usually called the laws of nature.* The laws which govern the living principle (including both animal and vegetable life) being fixed, certain, uniform in their operations, and analogous to the laws which govern grosser matter, will be generally included in these essays under the terms *physical law of nature.*

SEC. 3. *Necessity of intellect, and the importance of its development and cultivation.*

All natural laws and physical agencies being governed by powers and properties inherent in matter, and not by intelligence, their constant tendency in action is to change and vibrate from one extreme to another—from heat to cold, and from cold to heat; from wet to dry, and from dry to wet, etc., etc.; one extreme tending to produce the opposite extreme. These constant changes are necessary to furnish a sufficiency of water upon all parts of the surface of the earth to promote vegetation; and though some of the direct effects of these changes are prejudicial to the health of man when he is much exposed to them, yet they are equally necessary to the life of man as to vegetables, by reason of their supplying him with water as well as with vegetation. Man needs the benefits resulting to him from these frequent changes produced by natural laws; but in order to secure his health, he finds it necessary to resist, as much as possible, the direct effects of these changes upon his system, and to maintain by means of clothing, dwellings, and fires, a uniform temperature, a uniform and dry atmosphere, and uniformity, to a considerable extent, in his diet, drink, exercise, sleep, and all his habits.

Mind or intellect is therefore necessary to direct all the movements of man, to enable him not only to avoid and resist the pernicious effects upon him of the elements of the material world, and to use these elements as instruments and agents to promote his comforts; but also to prevent the appetites and passions of his physical nature from running into excesses, and eventually undermining his health and constitution, bringing on debility and disease, or leading him into vice and crime. A just medium, which can be maintained only by a constant exertion of intellect, avoiding extremes in all cases, un juste milieu, as the French express it, is not only the path of virtue, but it is the only mode to secure the general welfare and happiness of man.

Intellect of a high order, comparatively speaking, (or capable of becoming so by cultivation,) was given to man to restrain, regulate, and give direction to his appetites, and to stimulate him to activity and industry, as well as to direct and govern all his actions. Intellect is not only the balance-wheel which regulates all his movements, but when cultivated, it is one of the great mainsprings which propels him on to activity, industry, and enterprise. Though literary men are often indolent and inefficient, the mazes of literature seemingly serving to bewilder and distract their minds, yet men of science are generally very active and enterprising.

The mind of man is constituted with capacities for development and improvement to an almost unlimited extent, by means of its own activity; and it is generally supposed that he is placed in this world as a state of probation, to exercise and develope his faculties, and fit him for a higher and more important state of existence. Longevity to a certain extent, is necessary to effect this object; and in order to promote longevity, it is necessary for man to develope his physical as well as his mental faculties, and to provide himself with all the physical comforts in his power, to secure him against the diseases and ills of life as far as practicable.

Man should study the constitution and nature of things, and the laws of the material world, so as to make them instruments and agents to promote his welfare, and not become the victim of their operation, and be swept by them down the current of time, without much influence over his own destiny; as is the case with every savage and barbarous people. He should study them in order to avoid natural causes and agencies which he cannot control, and to learn to use material things, not only for food, clothing, dwellings, and fuel, but also to make use of them, and of the laws of nature, as instruments and agents to aid him in his labors to increase the fruits and products of the earth, and enable him to supply himself with all the necessaries and comforts of life, which tend to promote his health, physical welfare, and happiness.

It has been stated, that while some things are congenial to the nature of man, and necessary to sustain life, others are destructive to his existence as an organized being. Caloric is necessary to the existence of animal as well as vegetable life, but too much of it, causing an excessive degree of heat, will destroy life. Some combinations of matter, and conditions of the atmosphere, so filled with carbonic acid gas and heated with caloric, as to be prejudicial to health, and destructive to animal life, tend in a high degree to promote the growth of vegetation, and indirectly, and in the final result, promote animal life and the welfare of man. Thus, even those elements and laws of nature, whose immediate effect is to destroy the life of man when exposed to them, in their general and ultimate effects, tend to provide the materials to furnish him with food, clothing, fuel, and a shelter, and to promote his general welfare.

Man's intellect and understanding was given to him to enable him to judge of, learn from experience, and understand, the properties, tendencies, and effects of all the elements of matter, and of all their various combinations; that he might avoid such elements, combinations, and qualities as are injurious and dangerous to him, and whose evil tendencies he cannot control, and use such materials, and in such combinations and quantities, and in such mode and conditions of the human system, as to promote his health and general good. In hot climates, he promotes and secures his general health and welfare, and that of his family, by planting shade trees, and building a house to protect them from the burning heat of the sun during the day. In very cold climates, he is constantly struggling with the cold instead of the heat, and is obliged to build a house or hut as warm as possible, and to provide himself with a large amount of fuel and of clothing, of leather, furs, and skins, or of cloth made of wool, to protect himself from the severity of the cold. In changeable, and what are usually termed temperate climates, he finds it necessary to resort to all these means, and to use these and many others, some to protect himself from the excessive heats of summer, and others to defend him against the cold of winter: and in all climates, he must use means to protect himself against rains, storms, dews, winds, and bad air; and must also provide himself with a sufficiency for every day's use of wholesome water as well as food.

Man is born in perfect helplessness and ignorance, and yet he is required to conform to the laws of God as unfolded in the volume of nature; and must learn them before he can do so. His whole life should therefore be a constant effort to learn these laws; to prevent the physical appetites and propensities of his nature from running into excess and vice; to resist and avoid the influence of the elements and combinations of matter which are dangerous, or injurious to him; to subdue and regulate properly his own appetites and passions; and to subdue the earth, and convert its products into useful instruments and materials for securing and promoting his health, enjoyment, and general welfare. Hence one of the first and most important duties of parents, is to give their children as much instruction as is in their power, and adapted to their station and condition, to fit them in the best manner to discharge their duties, provide for and satisfy their own wants, and for the great business and duties of life upon which they have entered.

Sec. 4. *Moral Law of Nature distinguished from the Physical Laws of Nature.*

It must have been designed by the Deity, and probably forms the basis of His moral law and government, that man should be subject to a constant struggle with the physical laws of nature, and required to make great efforts to support life and satisfy his own wants, and provide for his own comforts, as a suitable discipline to develope his faculties, and fit him for a higher state of existence. *The moral law and government of God may be called the moral law of nature.* It requires man to develope his faculties; to struggle against the physical laws of nature; to use natural agents as a means of providing for his own wants and comforts; and to act under all circumstances in such a manner as to promote his own general welfare and happiness and that of his fellow beings, and particularly of those depending upon him, to the greatest extent possible. This conclusion is deduced from the consideration, that the Deity, being an omniscient and benevolent being, must have established all the physical, as well as the spiritual and moral laws of the universe which comprise the law of nature, in such a manner as to promote the general welfare and happiness of man, when he conforms to them, as far as is in his power. *Moral virtue may therefore be defined, perfect obedience to the moral laws of nature, or in other words to the will of God; and the distinction between right or wrong lies in conform-*

ity, or non-conformity, to this great rule. By acting in accordance with the moral laws of nature, mankind will not only avoid many evils, but promote their own welfare and happiness to the greatest extent of which their constitution and nature will admit. The principle of sympathy for his fellow beings was implanted in the organic and physical constitution of man, in order to give him a physical propensity to act in accordance with the moral law and government of God, so far as to do his duty to his fellow beings.

SEC. 5. *Utility the principal test to determine the Moral Law of Nature.*

The word Utility implies active agency, or effective means to produce some result, or promote some end or object; and hence the different senses in which it is used by different persons and authors. Some use it in a very loose and vague sense; calling that useful which may be used as an effective means to advance their selfish and temporary ends and objects, and gratify their passions and sensual appetites, even at the expense of their own ultimate good and general welfare, and of the rights and welfare of their fellow beings. To use the word in this loose and vague sense, is an abuse of language. It is generally used in common parlance to designate the capacity of things to satisfy the wants of man, without reference to the character of those wants—whether natural, or artificial and factitious. It is sometimes used in a limited and more strict and philosophical sense, and applied only to means which tend to promote either the general welfare and happiness of the human family, or the well-being of one or more individuals, in a manner entirely consistent with the ultimate end and object for which they were created, and with the rights and general welfare of others. In this strict and philosophical sense (which is the only one that is accurate), it always designates an active agency, effective means or capacity, that is real and substantial; while in its ordinary use in common parlance, it often designates utility that is factitious only. In this strict and philosophical sense, the utility of an act, thing, custom, habit, institution, or law, consists in its natural tendency to promote the general welfare and happiness of man, or of some particular individual class or community, without injuring or infringing the rights of others. In this sense, no act or thing can be useful any farther than it is in accordance with the moral laws of nature, as explained in the last section. Utility, in this strict and philosophical sense, is a test of the moral quality of actions, because it is evidence that they are in accordance with the moral laws of nature. It is also one of the chief tests of the character and value of all human laws and institutions. The words expedient and expediency should be used in the same strict and philosophical sense. Whatever act, course of policy, custom, institution, or law, is useful in this sense, is also expedient, and whatever is not useful, is not expedient.

To determine the utility or expediency of an act, institution, custom, or law, we should look to its general tendency, and to its ultimate natural consequences; and not to any partial or temporary tendency or effects, which may be the result of peculiar circumstances. We should also look to its general effects upon the community, or upon all the persons affected by it; and should not call that useful which necessarily injures one by benefiting another; like the traffic in intoxicating drinks, and keeping gambling-houses, and places of vicious amusement. A murderer is executed by the government in pursuance of a general law; not because the execution is or can be of any utility to the criminal, but it is done for the protection of the community, to deter others from committing like crimes; but although the sole tendency of the execution may be to protect and benefit the community, yet the general tendency of the general law upon the subject, was to protect the person who became a murderer, just as much as to protect any other member of the community. The rule is similar in relation to the acts of individuals; utility, general utility, is the test; which is never inconsistent with the rights of any individual, nor with equal justice to all. It comprises whatever promotes the general welfare and happiness in the aggregate, of any one or more persons, and is not injurious to the community, nor to the rights of any individual. In this view of the subject, an act may be in accordance with the law of nature, and with the will of God, and therefore a good act, though all its direct utility and benefit is confined to the actor, or to him, his family and friends; even in this case the act may be said to promote, in a remote degree, the general welfare and happiness of the community in the aggregate, inasmuch as the welfare and happiness of the community comprises that of each and every member of the community.

SEC. 6. *Illustrations of the importance of understanding the Laws of Nature.*

In order to promote health, vigor, and activity, to secure his system from disease and his person from accidents which may endanger his limbs or destroy his life, it is necessary for man to study and understand the laws of nature; as is well illustrated in Combe's treatise on the Constitution of Man. In order to be eminently successful in any department of industry or business, whether agricultural, mechanical, manufacturing, mining, or commercial, or the transportation of property or persons, it is necessary to observe carefully the laws of nature; and to conform strictly to the nature of things and of man, as well as to the tendencies of business.

The farmer should not only look carefully to the markets to see what products are in demand and bring the best price, but he should attend carefully to the climate in which he lives, and to the situation and soil of his farm, and to what crops and what mode of cultivation it is best adapted. The mechanic also, and manufacturer of every kind and character, should thoroughly understand the nature, properties, strength, and durability of the materials he works in, as well as the climate of the country in which they are to be used, in order to adapt them to the use of man, and make them promote his comforts and physical well being to the greatest extent possible. The physician also should study nature and her laws, as his only guides in the management and cure of diseases; and every person who has a proper regard for his own health, should follow the same guides, and observe carefully the effect of every kind of food and drink upon his own health and constitution, in order to regulate his diet in the manner most conducive to health and activity of both body and mind.

Theology also derives aid from the laws of nature, and particularly from psychology, or the nature and capacities of mind, which constitutes a branch or department of the law of nature; and whether we regard John Calvin, Dr. Paley, or Bishop Butler of England, the late Dr. Edwards of Massachusetts, or many other eminent divines, their permanent influence over the doctrines and creeds of their respective Churches for ages, depends much on the extent and accuracy of their knowledge of the laws of nature, and their capacity to use such knowledge to aid them in understanding and expounding the Holy Scriptures. The following is an extract from a work of Samuel F. B. Morse, A. M., a professor in the University of the city of New York: "Upon this freedom to choose according to the dictates of reason and conscience, granted to man by his Maker, denied by Roman Catholics and claimed by Protestants, is built the fabric of religious liberty. Difference of opinion being allowed, controversy of course ensues, and converts are made, not by force of arms, but by force of truth, supported by appeals to reason and conscience. Zealous according to the strength of his belief in the dogmas of his sect, the Protestant calls to his aid the treasures of science. He believes that the divine author of truth in the BIBLE, is also the AUTHOR OF TRUTH in NATURE; the Protestant is therefore the consistent encourager of all learning, of all investigation. Every discovery in science, he feels, brings to religious truths fresh treasures. Free inquiry and discussion, all intellectual activity, legitimately belong to Protestantism. It is by thus opening wide the doors of knowledge, and letting in the LIGHT of NATURAL SCIENCE upon what it believes to be the *revealed truth of the Bible*, that Protestantism has been able gradually to bring out the principle of *religious liberty*, and in its train, the invaluable blessing of *civil liberty*."

The learned jurists who reported the CODE NAPOLEON, in their preliminary discourse, make the following remark: "Le droit est la raison universelle, la supreme raison fondé sur la nature même des choses. Les lois sont, ou ne doivent étre que le droit réduit en regles positives, en preceptes particuliers."* In accordance with this wise precept, the principal part of the LAWS OF NATIONS, and also the Roman civil law, from which our principles of equity jurisprudence are borrowed, are deduced from and founded on the laws of nature; on the nature of things, and the nature and condition of man. In the absence of revelation on this subject, this is the only proper and safe foundation on which to found human laws and human institutions. Unfortunately for the Anglo-American, as well as the British people, the foundations, and great leading principles and characteristics of the common law of England, were established upon the usages and customs of feudalism, and the decisions and precedents of courts of justice in an ignorant and semi-barbarous age; and during the last five centuries it has undergone very little change, except what has been effected by judicial legislation, constantly resorting to subtle distinctions and ingenious sophisms, to obviate some evil, or supposed evil, and without professing to make or acknowledging any change whatever, new principles have been constantly introduced, as the wisdom, the prejudices, or the weakness of influential judges dictated, until it has become a stupendous fabric of discordant materials, in which the law of nature is often entirely disregarded.

The learned Sir James Mackintosh, in the third chapter of his History of England, makes the following remarks in reference to the common law: "A proneness to uninstructive acuteness, and to distinctions purely verbal, tainted it from the cradle. It has been the ancient and unremitted complaint of the most learned lawyers, that it has been overloaded with vain and unprofitable subtleties, which, in the eager pursuit of an ostentatious precision, has plunged it into darkness and confusion." This has resulted from a disregard of the laws of nature.†

* Natural right is universal reason, founded on the nature of things. Laws should be natural right reduced to positive rules and precepts.

† See this subject of the Common Law in sec. 6 of Chap. V.

Sec. 7. *On the General and Special Providences of God; and the use of Natural Causes to effect his purposes.*

The general providences of God are generally understood to be, the natural and necessary sequences and effects produced by the action and re-action of the elements of matter and of spirit, in accordance with a system of laws established by Him, which constitute the laws of nature. So far as the mind of man is governed by causes external to itself, it is subject to those general laws; but so far as it acts from its own inherent impulses and powers, it appears to be a free agent, and to act according to its own habits and caprices, exempt from those general laws.

The special providences of God, on the contrary, are supposed to be, effects produced by special interpositions of His power, different from what would have been produced by the undisturbed operation of his general laws. Special providences may be used as a means of rewarding or punishing individuals or nations for obedience or disobedience of his moral laws and government; and also to save man in particular instances from the evil consequences which would otherwise result to him from his violation, ignorantly, of the laws of nature; or to save him from the violence of the elements beyond his control. But however strongly we may believe in special providences in particular cases, if we look at the history of man, and contemplate his ignorance, his vices, follies, and crimes, we must come to the conclusion, that almost all action is directed and governed, as well as originated either by natural causes and physical agents, in pursuance of fixed laws, or by the free agency of man, influenced by, and to some extent, subject to, physical laws and impulses; and that the Deity himself generally uses human agents and natural means, not supernatural ones, to effect his purposes. This is made still more evident by the fact of his using a visible Church and human agents as his ministers to spread the gospel and propagate Christianity, instead of doing it by the direct and supernatural agency of inspiration.

Were it not for the free agency of man, whereby he has power to contravene the physical as well as the moral laws of nature, special providences would seem to be unnecessary. Everything in the universe might be governed by general laws. The general laws and providences of God, we can, to a limited extent, inquire into and learn; but the special interpositions of divine power are beyond the scrutiny of man. That the Deity acts principally by and through the means of natural causes and physical agents, and thereby governs mankind, not only physically, but morally and spiritually, as well as the whole material world, has been shown pretty clearly, if not demonstrated, by the learned and philosophical Dr. Edwards.

SEC. 8. *Inherent weakness of the human mind, and the influences upon it of external causes.*

To maintain the position I have stated, of the general use of natural causes and agents as the means of action, it is not necessary to carry the doctrine so far as has been done by Dr. Edwards, and many others of the necessitarian school; who maintain that the mind and the will of man has no self-determining power, and cannot originate action, and do any particular act of itself, without being directed and governed by some motive or cause external to the mind itself; that belief of anything must be the effect of evidence, and every act of the mind must be produced by causes external to the mind itself, acting upon it; that all human actions, and all the operations of the human mind, are directed and governed by a chain of causes that produce a physical necessity, from which it cannot escape; and that all these causes are brought into operation by the ordinary working of the laws of nature established by the Deity, and were, and must have been, designed by him at the time of the creation. In this mode they deduce the philosophical conclusion, that every act of man, as well as every occurrence in the physical world, is the necessary result of the ordinary operation of God's laws, and must have been not only foreseen, but foreordained by him.

This is nearly the same as the doctrine of fatalism, and is carrying the effect of physical causes to a very great length; so far as not only to annihilate entirely the freedom of the human will, and of the human mind; but to destroy also nearly all the faculties of the mind, and render it utterly incapable of either determining, directing, or controlling its own action. If this view of the subject is correct, the mind possesses only the power of communicating or transmitting the impressions it may have received from external causes (which is nothing more than the resisting or reacting power of matter); and even admitting it to be an active principle or agent, if it cannot act without being excited to action by external causes, its powers of action would seem to be no greater than those of electricity, magnetism, caloric, or any of the imponderable substances which pervade the universe. If this is true, man is but a machine, and can act only as he is excited by natural causes; he can move only in the direction given to him by such causes; and can hardly be called, with propriety, a free or moral agent.

If we were to confine our attention to the torpid state of the human mind in Mahometan countries, and in all Asia, and the isles of the ocean, except China and Japan, and reflect that scarcely any change has been made in those countries for more than thirteen centuries, except those which have been the result and effect of the opinions, principles, religious creeds and doctrines that originated with Mahomet in the seventh century; and that the manners, customs, castes, opinions, prejudices, habits, pursuits, and condition of the mass of the people have been the same from age to age, for nearly two thousand years, we might be inclined to believe the most extreme doctrines of the necessitarian school of divines. Such facts are calculated to lead men to the conclusion that the human mind possesses no independence; no freedom of will, no inherent powers of action; no self-determining power; that it is directed and governed entirely by a chain of external causes, and by a physical necessity from which there is no escape; and that the extraordinary capacity of Mahomet was the effect of a supernatural agency and power, conferred upon him by some evil spirit.

But if we turn our attention to the northern and western parts of modern Europe, and particularly to Great Britain, France, Germany, Netherlands, and to the Anglo-American States, and contemplate the reformation commenced by Martin Luther, the writings of Grotius, and many others, the career of Columbus, of Peter the Great of Russia, and of Napoleon Bonaparte, the many valuable discoveries and inventions, and the vast improvements made within the last four centuries, and more particularly during the last century, *we shall find a mass of evidence of the great power and capacity of the human mind; of its independence, its freedom, and power of originating action, of determining, guiding, and directing its own movements; and even of resisting the influence of external causes and agents, of inquiring after original truths; and acting according to its own ideas of duty, propriety, justice, or expediency.*

It is very certain, however, that man has comparatively little control over the operations of his own mind and the formation of his own opinions. While the ignorant and the weak-minded (who are unable to weigh evidence with accuracy) are the sport of circumstances, and may believe or disbelieve anything according as the mind may be influenced by interest, passion, prejudice, education, or superstition; a well cultivated and well balanced mind, can neither believe without evidence, nor disbelieve what is attested by competent proofs. In any view which may be taken of this subject, conceding to men of eminent ability the largest amount of intellectual power, capacity, freedom of will, and ability to act and reason independent of, and free from the control of external causes which can be reasonably claimed for them; yet, inasmuch as the mind can act only by and through the medium of physical organs, as its agents or instruments and informants; as it is dependent on the brain as a physical organ, in and by which it thinks, reflects, compares, judges, reasons, and wills; and as it is dependent on the nervous system as a physical organ, by means of which it acquires a knowledge of the external world, as well as of the wants, sufferings, and appetites of the body; it is very certain that the greater portion of the human family are almost entirely directed and governed by wants, appetites, and causes of a physical character, by motives and passions not originating in the mind, and by the circumstances and conditions in which they are placed; and that they possess very little power to resist such appetites, passions, and motives, and to change by invention and well directed industry, their condition and circumstances in life. Perhaps it would not be extravagant to say, such is the power and influence of circumstances, and of external causes over the mind of man, and the operation of the metaphysical laws of suggestion and association, that nine-tenths of the mental action of the most original minds, and ninety-nine hundredths of that of inferior and uncultivated minds, is not only originated, but determined, directed, and governed by causes external to the mind itself; which even the most powerful and best informed minds are often too feeble to resist. How important, therefore, that young persons should be kept from vicious associations and the formation of bad habits, that their minds should be developed and strengthened by cultivation and exercise, well filled with proper and correct principles, opinions, and ideas, by which they may be constantly influenced and guided, and may not be subjected to the sole control of physical appetites, and the current opinions and prejudices of the ignorant, the harangues of demagogues and fanatics, and other accidental circumstances and extraneous influences.

SEC. 9. *Means used to form the opinions and govern the people.*

The great mass of mankind never seem to learn anything, (except the most simple truths,) from either experience or observation: but learn from, and are mostly guided, by imitation, precedent, and the instruction of others. They do not seem to possess the power of learning causes by analyzing, nor of combining facts, generalizing, and deducing new truths from their own experience, or from facts which have come within their own observation or reading; and hence, in most countries, they follow on by imitation from father to son, from generation to generation, for thousands of years, in the same track and routine, without change or improvement; and are seemingly impelled by circumstances, and wafted on like the clouds of the air, without exercising much, if any influence, over their own destiny. And this perfect submission to circumstances, under the impression that they must fulfil the same destiny as their ancestors, and have no power to improve their condition by any efforts of their own; this abject devotion to ancient customs and precedents, is often dignified with the title of conservatism.

There is scarcely one in a hundred of the uneducated classes, of any age or country, who can reason at all, except to an extremely limited extent. Inasmuch as they have no knowledge of even the elements of any science; no clear conceptions of even the nature of numbers and quantities, in an abstract point of view; and have never been taught to reason correctly; they learn from imitation, precedent, and instruction only; and have scarcely any ideas, except what they derive directly from and through the senses, together with some vague opinions which they have learned from tradition and the oral instructions of their priests. Such people in all countries, are under the influence and control of the educated classes; of the aristocracy, the clergy, the members of the learned professions, and the military and civil officers of government, who literally think for them, and form and guide their opinions, and direct their movements; whether they are slaves, serfs, villains, or dependent and poor tenants, peasants, or poor artizans. Hence the policy of Austria, Russia, and other arbitrary governments is to keep their subjects in ignorance, and to endeavor to think for them, and form their opinions, as the most effectual mode of making them submissive, quiet, contented, and obedient, in bearing all the burthens, and performing all the duties which their masters impose on them. The same policy is pursued by the American slaveholders towards their slaves, and for the same purposes; and the policy of the Pope and the Catholic priesthood towards the mass of the people, is not materially different. The Bible is kept from them; they are denied the right to read and exercise their own individual judgments in matters of religion, but must allow their priests to read, think, and judge for them, and to form their opinions; and no efforts are made by the priests to establish common schools, or to teach the common people anything beyond the catechism, and the ceremonies and dogmas of religion, and absolute unconditional submission in all things to their priests and rulers. Their whole efforts in matters of education are directed to founding colleges, and high schools, for training up young men for the priesthood, and instructing and breathing their opinions into the children and youth of the aristocracy, and the wealthy classes, in order to form their opinions, and govern them, and through them, to govern the mass of the people.

The conduct and acts of such a people are not directed by the independent operations of their own minds, nor are their opinions formed by the operation of their own reasoning powers, but all their acts and opinions are the result of causes external to their own minds, operating upon them; hence they are governed in part by natural causes, by their own physical appetites and passions, and partly by the educated classes, who infuse opinions into their minds, and thus influence and direct them.

SEC. 10. *Causes of the Revolution of France of* 1789, *and the means used to excite the people.*

After the commencement of the French revolution of 1789, the prostration of the nobility and clergy, and the confiscation of their property, the people were as utterly unable to think for themselves, and to reason correctly, as they were before, and were henceforth governed by the Jacobin clubs, and other affiliated clubs and societies. These clubs and societies were organized at Paris to discuss political questions, and had their branches and auxiliary societies in almost every province; by means of which they communicated their opinions and proceedings throughout the kingdom with great rapidity; and thus formed the opinions of nearly the whole nation, and in some measure thought for them. These clubs at Paris were governed by a few men of learning, talents, address, and eloquence; mostly needy youngish professional men, aspiring to place and power; who had nothing to lose, as they supposed, by revolution, or any kind of excess. Robespierre, Danton, Marat, and some other ambitious demagogues, were the great master-spirits of the clubs, and the prime movers of the bloody scenes of the reign of terror of the revolution. When the National Assembly suppressed the Jacobin clubs, mobocracy soon ceased.

Among the principal causes of the commencement of this mighty revolution, were the privileges of the nobility and clergy, the extravagance of the government, the embarrassment of the national finances, and the necessity of imposing on the people new taxes and still heavier burthens. These causes were entirely natural, but not sufficient of themselves to produce any material effect upon the minds of an illiterate and unthinking multitude. They, however, gave occasion and furnished the means for the Abbé Sieyes, and other talented political writers, to excite the minds of the people by their writings and discussions, and to move them to collect together in tumultuous assemblies, rise in mobs, and act in concert, in order to obtain what their advisers and leaders taught them were their rights. The great mass of mankind have been oppressed with heavy burthens and taxes, imposed on them by their rulers and priests, in all ages of the world, and in almost every country; but they have generally submitted quietly to their masters, and have never rebelled, or combined to overthrow or change the government, except when aroused and excited to action by some of the educated classes. The officers and soldiers of the French army, which served in the American revolution, acted, on their return home, as instructors of their fellow-citizens, to teach them their rights, or what they supposed to be their rights. And, inasmuch as the people were illiterate, ignorant, and almost incapable of reasoning, and were governed entirely by their own appetites and passions, and the exciting opinions of the leaders of the Jacobin clubs, when their passions were once aroused, they could not be influenced by any opinions of even their leaders or favorites, not in accordance with their own passions; and hence their leaders were suspected of treachery, whenever they counselled moderation, and were cried down, condemned, and guillotined, one after another.

Many of the historians of the French revolution, including M. Thiers, have attempted to apologise for all its horrors and crimes, by representing them as the inevitable result of natural causes, which no human exertions could avert or prevent; that even such spirits as Robespierre, Danton, Marat, and their vilest and most violent and bloodthirsty associates, were the mere instruments of fate, and in the commission of their crimes, only obeyed the laws of necessity, the laws of nature, and submitted to impulses which they had no power to resist. If this apology were true, they were not free, and therefore not moral agents, and the whole responsibility of all their crimes would rest with the Author of all things, who thus fixed their fate, and imposed on them this stern necessity. This mode of reasoning, in accordance with the doctrines of fatalism, and the extreme portion of the necessitarian school, annihilates the independence, freedom, and power of the human mind, and reduces man to a mere machine, moved and directed entirely by external causes; and therefore it cannot be true to its fullest extent; though nine tenths of it perhaps is true to the letter.

The people had been kept in ignorance and been oppressed for centuries; the American revolution, and the impulse its history, its result, and the condition and institutions of the Americans, gave to many of the authors and political writers of France, soon caused a diffusion among the people of a few leading ideas and opinions about liberty, equality, and a republican form of government, the purport and effect of which they did not fully understand. They then realized, for the first time, that they were wronged and oppressed; and were taught by their leaders, the orators of the clubs, that extreme measures were necessary to rid themselves of the nobility and clergy, and finally of the king and royalists, who, they were told, were their oppressors and natural enemies. The great mass of the revolutionists and anarchists believed these principles and measures of their leaders to be just and necessary; I may say, honestly and sincerely believed them, and felt that such things as mobs, insurrections, violence, banishment, confiscations, revolutionary committees, trials, and executions, were necessary and just, under the circumstances in which they were placed. These new political ideas excited a strange delusion; a sort of political fanaticism in the minds of nearly all the lower classes of the nation, which lasted for years, and seemed to hurry them on to the commission of every kind of excess. The mass of the people were governed solely by this spirit of delusion, and the passions engendered by it; a small portion were governed by avarice and a desire to plunder; and even the leaders, the worst of them, did not fully understand the tendency and final effect of their measures, and were governed partly by this spirit of delusion, and partly by ambition for place and power.

In this view of the subject, the French revolution, with all its civil contests, mobs, excesses, and horrors, and all the wars growing out of it, except the wars of Napoleon, were wars of opinion; wars of principle; as strictly so as the American revolution, or the wars growing out of the Reformation of the sixteenth century; and though the opinions and principles for which the French revolutionists contended were in many respects false, delusive, dangerous, and pernicious in their tendency, yet they arose mostly from natural causes, operating on the human mind.

If opinions alone can have such a wonderful influence over the conduct and acts of men, how extremely important, in a republican form of government, that all the people who exercise the elective franchise should be properly educated; and that their opinions should be correct on all subjects connected with government and the good order of society? The condition and history of Mexico, and of all the Spanish American Republics, during the last twenty-five years, furnish evidence, that an elective government, approximating to a democracy, cannot be sustained in a country where the great mass of the voters are illiterate, ignorant, incapable of reasoning upon the subject of government; and who depend on priests, office-holders, and aspirants to place and power, to instruct them and think for them.

SEC. 11. *Effect of Habits, Pursuits, Exercise, &c. upon the Constitution of Man.*

It has been frequently remarked, *that habit is a sort of second nature; it actually modifies and in some measure changes the organic structure and constitution of man.* Climate, mode of living, diet, pursuits and habits, all have an influence not only upon the health, strength, activity, and longevity of man, but they actually change the formation and constitution of his physical organs. The pursuits of a blacksmith, shoemaker, and almost every other, when followed for a series of years, by exercising some organs and muscles more than others, tend to enlarge them, to change their formation and structure, and cause others to dwindle for want of sufficient exercise. (*Vide Sec.* 11 *of Chap.* 2.) The mind acts not only as a guide and governor, but also as a stimulant to the body; and ideas and opinions existing in the mind act as stimulants to excite it to action; so that the activity of every person's intellect is increased, as the aggregate amount of his knowledge increases. As the mind acts by and through the brain and nervous system as physical organs, the more active particular faculties of the mind may be, the more it exercises and increases in size and power the particular organs on which its action depends.

Man is not only influenced in all his acts and career through life, by his opinions, habits, pursuits, worldly condition and circumstances, but the physical structure and formation of the organs of his material frame, and his moral and intellectual as well as physical nature, are all in some measure changed by the same causes. By the laws of the animal economy, all these physical peculiarities, and to some extent, the mental and moral qualities which depend upon them, are transmitted from parents to children, through successive generations. And this, together with uniformity of climate, similarity of education, diet, and modes of living, is the reason why the people of every nation, not only have a general similarity of features and complexion, but also acquire what is usually called a national character. (*See on this subject Sec.* 2 *of Chap.* 2.) In this mode, causes which originated in the human mind, have produced physical effects, at first, perhaps, simple in their character, which have in their turn been the efficient cause of other effects; and have thus been the original cause of a chain of effects, or of antecedents and consequents, which have had a very important influence upon the welfare of a large portion of the human family for centuries; and will continue to produce their effects until the end of time.

Sec. 12. *Effects of Gunpowder, Fire-arms, and the Arts, in changing the character of War.*

Gunpowder and firearms have changed the whole character and operations of war. The precise time when they were invented does not appear to be known with certainty. Gunpowder was in use in some parts of Europe in the latter part of the thirteenth century; cannon were invented and in use soon after, between the years 1313 and 1350; though small arms were unknown until nearly two centuries afterwards, and were first used by the Spaniards about the year 1521. The use of cannon alone, without small arms, enabled Cortez, with a little handful of soldiers, to conquer the natives of Mexico, the most civilized and powerful of all the nations then on the Western continent.

In ancient times, when men fought with spears, javelins, and other weapons wielded by hand, very little science was necessary to command and marshal an army in the field of battle; but great physical strength, experience, skill, and bravery, in the rank and file of the army, were necessary to ensure success. Maximin, an ignorant Thracian peasant, without any knowledge of science of any kind, but a giant in size and strength, (being about eight feet high,) by reason of his great strength, activity, and valor, gained the confidence of the Roman Emperor, Severus, and of the army; was raised to the highest military command; was an efficient general; and was finally, in the year A. D. 235, proclaimed by the army Emperor of the Roman world. His acquirements would fit him for only the lowest grade of military command at the present age of the world; and he influenced his army in battle more by his personal example in attacking the enemy furiously, and slaying them with his own powerful arm, than by any great efforts of mind, or exercise of military science in conducting or marshalling them. What a wonderful contrast between him and Napoleon Buonaparte as military commanders! The former used physical power, and the force of example to influence his men, and was unfit for a commander in modern times; the latter, by his mighty intellect, and accurate military science, directed all the movements of his men with as much precision as an architect can plan and frame a building, and, when not overwhelmed with superior numbers, he conducted them to certain victory.

In ancient warfare, the party on the defensive could not gain much advantage over his antagonist by choosing his ground, and attacking his enemy from hills and heights, and from behind breastworks, trees, fences, buildings, or cotton-bags; but when they fought hand to hand both parties were nearly on an equality, so far as situation was concerned, and everything depended on physical strength, skill, experience, and personal bravery. In modern warfare, with the use of fire-arms and heavy ordnance, the party on the defensive, having an opportunity to fortify heights, hill sides, and the mouths of rivers and harbors, and to throw up breastworks to shelter themselves from the enemy's fire, can select their ground, occupy narrow passes, defiles, and commanding positions, and have great advantage over their assailants, which they did not, and could not possess, when men fought hand to hand, with swords, pikes, battle-axes, javelins, arrows,&c. Much also now depends on fleets and vessels, not only as powerful movable engines to assail the enemy, but also to transport troops, provisions, arms, and munitions of war, to act in concert with, aid, and support land forces. All the operations of war are now very complicated and expensive, depend mostly on mechanical power, require vast expenditures on the part of the government, and great science, experience, and ability, in the commanding officer, and in all the superior officers; but no very great skill, experience, or extraordinary physical power, on the part of the rank and file of the army, is necessary. In ancient times it required as many years as it apparently now does months to make an efficient soldier. All the operations of ancient warfare, on the contrary, were simple; and veteran troops engaged in an offensive war, maintained themselves mostly by booty, contributions levied on, and plunder taken from the enemy. Hannibal, the Carthaginian general, maintained his army in the Roman territories seventeen years, without any aid from Carthage, during nearly all the time; this cannot be done in modern times. Napoleon attempted it, and thereby excited the hatred and indignation against him of nearly all Europe, and finally failed in the attempt. The military power of a nation in these days, depends more on their wealth, and power to equip fleets and to support fleets and armies, than on the number of its citizens capable of bearing arms.

In ancient times, war was waged entirely by muscular power, but at present mostly by mechanical power. It formerly required great physical strength, long experience, and skill, in the soldiery, now it depends much more on the science and ability of the officers. It was formerly maintained by plunder, but now by money; formerly when men fought hand to hand, situation gave little advantage to assail the enemy, and the aggressor had nearly equal advantages with the defender, to assail his antagonists; but now, the use of fire-arms gives the party on the defensive, a great advantage over his antagonist. Offensive warfare is now much more difficult, hazardous, and expensive, than in ancient times, and defensive warfare much less so.

As the success of war formerly depended on muscular strength, skill, and experience in war, qualities which savages and barbarians usually possess, the barbarians of Northern Europe were enabled to overrun and overturn the western Roman empire in the fifth century; and the hordes of barbarian Tartars have frequently conquered the more civilized nations of southern Asia; but the history of the last century shows the influence of the mechanic arts, of machinery, productive industry and wealth, as well as the use of gunpowder, and fire-arms, upon war, and furnishes evidence that civilized nations can never be again conquered by savages or barbarians.

As mechanical power is now chiefly used in war as a substitute for muscular power, and wealth and productive industry are necessary to supply it, great monied capitalists have, for half a century past, exerted more influence upon questions of war and peace, than great military chieftains; and the peaceful farmer, mechanic, and artisan, and the lords of the spindle and loom, have more influence upon the power, as well as over the destinies of nations, than Prætorian guards and standing armies.

Gunpowder is also of great practical utility, and has produced very important results as a mechanical power, in aiding man to blast rocks, and work in quarries of stone, mines, &c. Its benefits in these particulars, cannot be easily calculated. Without its aid, the progress of man in cutting canals, mill races, and railroads through ledges of rocks and solid stone, and working in stone quarries and mining operations, would not probably be more than one tenth part as great as it is at present.

Sec. 13. *Nations like individuals, with but little industry, seem to be impelled by fate.*

Nations much more than individuals are seemingly impelled by the hand of fate; by a succession and chain of natural causes; by circumstances for the most part beyond their immediate control. By industry, economy, frugality and enterprise, guided by good judgment and wisdom during a long succession of years, if attended with good fortune, individuals may materially alter and improve their condition, and overcome the adverse circumstances which may have surrounded them during the early part of their lives; but even then, the principal part of their lives must be a scene of toil and anxiety; and they really improve the condition of their posterity, much more than they do their own. Though individuals are occasionally elevated suddenly by a concurrence of circumstances, or natural causes; by some freak of fortune, of fate or accident; yet they can usually do very little to elevate themselves, or change their condition in life, and station in society, except by the constant toil and vigilance of years. Nations being made up of individuals, the great mass of whom in most countries are very ignorant, and have comparatively little wisdom, sagacity, prudence, or economy, and a great many of them not much industry or energy, must necessarily make much slower progress in improvement, wealth, and power, than some portions and classes of the community, who compose them. Hence the pursuits and habits of industry, and the modes of doing business and performing every species of labor, as well as the modes of living, and the customs and condition of the people, remain the same, unchanged, in some countries, for centuries in succession ; and the people seem impelled, by the hand of fate ; by a succession of natural causes ; by the circumstances and condition in which they are placed, and over which they can exercise very little immediate influence.

SEC. 14. *Effect of Inventions and Machinery upon the industry, power, and population of Great Britain.*

Though the laws of nature are uniform in their operation, yet man by his inventive powers and his own efforts and industry during a series of years, can alter the face of nature, and convert the ores and mineral substances in the bowels of the earth, and other material things, and nature's products, as well as nature's laws, into instruments and mechanical powers, to augment the productiveness of his own industry, and the products of the earth. The more labor saving machinery he can invent and bring into use, the more easily he can subdue the earth ; convert its resources and products to his use ; increase the products of agricultural as well as mechanical industry, and facilitate their transportation and exchange ; and the more capital he can accumulate ; and this again aids him, in rendering his industry still more and more productive, and enables him to increase his capital and wealth, and to multiply his comforts with still greater and greater rapidity. Capital is not only wealth of itself, but it is one of the principal elements, instruments and agents, by which man makes his industry productive, whereby he creates value, produces what is necessary to supply his own wants, and accumulates wealth.

When great labor-saving machines, like the Spinning Jenny, Steam Engine, and Power Loom, are invented, which increase the productive industry of man ten or twenty fold ; and such inventions come into general use in a nation, and without consuming any food or clothing, accomplish as much labor as several millions of persons could by hand ; what an immense change it will produce in half a century, in augmenting the products of industry ; multiplying the comforts and diminishing the diseases and ills of life; developing the resources, and increasing the capital, wealth, and power of the nation! Such and similar causes, and inventions acting and reacting upon the British nation for about three quarters of a century, have increased the comforts of the British people; decreased their ills of life; diminished the ratio of mortality; and been the principal causes of doubling the population; and augmenting their capital, productive industry, commerce, wealth, revenues, naval and military power, about five fold, during that period. The inhabitants of Great Britain did not double in five centuries, from the year 1000 to the year 1500; they scarcely doubled during the next 250 years, from 1500 to 1750; but since the year 1790, they have doubled in 50 years, and sent out swarms of emigrants beside, to people other countries. The laws of nature have not changed, but the inventive genius and industry of the British people have materially changed their condition, and thereby diminished the ratio of mortality, while the condition of three quarters of the human family has remained unchanged. The strong contrast between the condition of Great Britain and Ireland at this day, is owing mostly to the fact that the Irish have continued to be an agricultural people, in consequence partly of the physical condition of the country, the want of fuel, minerals, and water power, and the character and ignorance of the people; and partly by reason of the selfish and tyrannical restrictions imposed upon their manufactures, by the British Parliament.

Every yard of cloth made prior to the year 1738, and nearly every one made before the year 1767, was made of materials picked and carded by hand, spun by hand with a distaff and spindle, or on a one thread wheel, and woven in a hand-loom. In that year, James Hargreaves, of England, invented the Spinning Jenny, which was a great improvement upon the Spinning Machine invented by Wyatt and Paul in 1738, and enabled one person to spin, at first eight, then sixteen, and finally, one hundred and twenty threads of cotton weft, or filling, at once; but it was not fitted to spin warp. The genius of Sir Richard Arkwright soon supplied the deficiency, and in 1769, invented the Spinning Frame; that wonderful piece of machinery, which spins any number of threads at once of any degree of fineness and hardness; leaving to the person tending it, only the labor of filling the machine with cotton, and joining the threads when they break. This machine in its present improved state, and also the mule, enables a person to spin cotton, about thirty times as fast, taking all numbers, coarse and fine, as could be done with the old one thread wheel.

In 1785, Dr. Cartwright, of England, invented the power loom-to weave by water, or steam power, by means of which and the improvements made thereon, a person can now weave about twelve or fifteen times as fast as with the old fashioned hand loom, in use before the invention of the fly shuttle in 1738.

The original machine for carding with cylinders was invented by Lewis Paul, and patented in 1748; but it was very imperfect, and of but little practical value, and not much used, until it was improved in 1772 by John Lees, and soon afterwards by Sir Richard Arkwright, who constructed it in pretty nearly the same form and mode as the carding machines now in use. In 1775 Mr. Arkwright took out a second patent for a series of machines, comprising the carding, drawing, and roving machines, all used in preparing silk, cotton, flax, and wool for spinning. The machinery for spinning was much improved by the invention by Samuel Crompton in 1779, of the Mule; which combined the advantages of the Spinning Jenny of Hargreaves and the Spinning Frame of Arkwright. Other machines were invented prior to the year 1800, for opening, cleaning, picking, and spreading the cotton, and fitting it for carding; and all these series of machines were improved, brought to a tolerable state of perfection, and in general use among the manufacturers of Great Britain before the year 1806, and the most of them before the year 1790. To use the clear and forcible language of Mr. Baine in his history of the cotton manufacture, "It is by iron fingers, teeth, and wheels, moving with exhaustless energy, and devouring speed, that the cotton is opened, cleaned, picked, spread, carded, drawn, roved, spun, wound, warped, dressed, and woven."

The same number of persons, including those engaged in the manufacture and repair of the machinery used, can at this time make about twenty times as much cotton cloth per year, as they could have done by the old process in use prior to these inventions, and prior to the invention of the fly shuttle in 1738. All these great inventions, together with that of the Steam Engine, and the Cotton Gin, were made and brought into use during the eighteenth century; and though many of them have been gradually improved and perfected during the present century, yet no very great improvement or alteration has been made in the machinery and mode of making cloth in Great Britain during that time, and it may be safely asserted that before the year 1806, the same number of persons could make at least three fourths as much cloth, cotton, woollen, linen or silk per annum, as they can at this time, (1845,) and fifteen times as much as they could have done prior to the year 1738.

The Steam Engine was greatly improved and adapted to ordinary use as a motive power, by James Watt, about the year

1767. It came into pretty general use in Great Britain prior to the year 1790, and has been of incalculable service and value to mankind; and more especially so to Great Britain, in working her mines, and particularly in raising coal from the mines; as well as in moving machinery to manufacture cotton, wool, silk, linen, iron, cutlery, &c.

The continental nations of Europe, being the most of the time from 1790 to the close of the year 1815, involved in the wars growing out of the French revolution, did but little to introduce the use of machinery, and to improve their system of manufacture, until after the end of those wars; so that Great Britain enjoyed the full benefit of the monopoly of the markets of the greater part of the commercial world for her manufactures, with scarcely a competitor, for more than a quarter of a century, and at higher prices than before the invention and introduction of machinery. The immense advantage derived by the British people from the use of machinery, high prices, and this great monopoly, gave such activity to their industry of all kinds, and made it so productive and profitable, as to enable all classes, the commercial and agricultural as well as the manufacturing and mining, to pay high wages for labor, and yet to create and accumulate capital and wealth from 1790 to 1816, with a rapidity unknown in any other age of the world; notwithstanding the enormous burthens imposed on them to support the war.

The number of persons, including their families, engaged in the cotton manufacture in Great Britain in all its branches, in 1840, including those engaged in making and keeping in repair the machinery used, has been estimated by McCulloch at about one million five hundred thousand; and if their labor is twenty times as productive as the labor of the same number of persons prior to 1767, it is equal to the industry of thirty million persons, including their families and children, without the aid of modern machinery. The saving is therefore equal to the labor of a population of twenty-eight millions five hundred thousand. The labor saved by machinery and the Steam Engine in the manufacture of wool, silk, linen, mining, raising coal, making iron and cutlery in Great Britain and Ireland, is probably as much more, or equal to a population of twenty-eight millions five hundred thousand; making the total saving in the United Kingdom in 1840, by means of machinery of recent invention, equal to the productive labor of a population of fifty-seven millions.

The quantity of cotton manufactured in Great Britain in 1840, was a little over four hundred million pounds; and from 1810 to 1815, during the last struggle with Napoleon, about one hundred million pounds, annually. If we estimate the saving by means of machinery, at three fourths as much for each laborer from 1810 to 1815, as from 1840 to 1845, it would, from 1810 to 1815, be equal to the labor of three fourths of one fourth of fifty-seven millions of inhabitants, or more than ten millions.

Let it be remembered that I have taken into the account the labor of making the machinery, and keeping it in repair; and that it labors for man unceasingly, without fatigue; consumes nothing but a little oil; eats nothing, drinks nothing, and requires no clothing; that it is the most valuable servant man ever had, and requires no expensive comforts to be provided for it. If a people who have not the use of machinery are taxed to support the government, and carry on war, to the amount of one eighth part of their gross earnings and incomes, it is the largest amount that can possibly be collected of them for a series of years in succession; and it takes at least seven eighths of all their earnings and incomes, in the aggregate, to support them from year to year; while a people, having machinery and extensive manufactures, like Great Britain, Massachusetts, Rhode Island, and some other states and countries, produce so much, that they are able to live on less than three fourths of their earnings and incomes, in the aggregate; and may contribute one fourth, and even more than that, in case of necessity, to the support of the government. Inasmuch as the productive power of the machinery of Great Britain and Ireland, from 1810 to 1815, was equal to that of ten million persons, and yet consumed nothing; it enabled the nation to levy and collect taxes, to support the war as much as if the population had been increased 80,000,000, or eight times the ten millions, without the machinery.

To give the reader an idea of the effect of the machinery, and productive industry, upon the wealth, power, and revenues of Great Britain, and the ability of the nation to wage war, at different periods, I have made the following table, showing the population, national debt, and annual public revenues of the United Kingdom, at several different periods from the year 1600 to 1815. The statements of the revenues are mostly taken from Mr. Alison's History of Europe, and are made in pounds sterling:

Date.	Population.	National Debt.	Puplic Revenues.
1600	6,500,000		£480,000
1688	7,850,000	£664,263	2,001,885
1748	10,350,000	78,293,312	6,923,000
1783	12,600,000	283,484,870	11,962,000
1801	15,370,000	528,839,277	34,113,146
1815	19,000,000	864,822,441	72,210,512

Mr. Alison states the public revenues from taxation, directly and indirectly, at over £68,000,000 sterling for each of the years 1813 and 1814. Such enormous taxes as the people of Great Britain paid from 1800 to 1815, were never paid, and never could have been paid by any other people. Nothing but the great and unrivalled power of their machinery, their extensive manufactures and commerce, the monopoly of the markets of half the world for their manufactures, and high prices enabled them to do it; and to loan to the government about £20,000,000 annually, beside, to carry on the war. And in spite of these immense burthens, which would have crushed any other people to the earth, and reduced the people as well as the government to bankruptcy, they flourished and increased in wealth as well as in population faster than during any other fifteen years in their whole history as a nation.

One of the principal causes which led to, and produced the French revolution, and the fall of the monarchy, was the heavy debt of France, and the financial embarrassments of the government. Napoleon, President Jefferson, and many other statesmen of that day, looking upon the immense and rapidly accumulating debt of the British nation under the policy of Mr. Pitt, and the enormous burthens imposed on the people, thought it impossible for them to sustain themselves very long under such burthens, and that a revolution, and dissolution of the British government within a short time, was inevitable. They regarded the government as upon the brink of ruin; as impelled forward by natural causes, from which there was no escape; and looked upon its ruin as certain. They reasoned from the experience and history of other nations, and their reasoning, if applied to any other nation, in any age of the world, would have been correct. Their only error was, in not properly calculating and appreciating the power and productive energy of the machinery of Great Britain; equal, as I have estimated it, so far as ability to pay taxes, and support war, was concerned, to eighty millions of inhabitants.

As the people were accumulating wealth and capital, by their manufacturing and mining industry, and their commerce, with unexampled rapidity; nearly all the loans to the government were made by British capitalists, to whom nearly the whole national debt was due, and the stability of the government was not affected by it. The only effect of it was, to give to the capitalists a perpetual mortgage upon the productive industry of the laboring classes, which was then less oppressive, while they enjoyed a monopoly of the use of machinery, and of the cotton manufacture, and wages were high, than it has been during the last twenty years, since the introduction of machinery into France, the United States, and into all the nations of central and northern Europe.

SEC. 15. *Population, Revenues, and Power of France from* 1789 *to* 1815, *compared with those of Great Britain.*

Let us now take a summary view of the condition of France, and see the extent of her population, revenues, and power, compared with Great Britain. In 1789 her population was about 25,500,000, and her annual revenue a trifle less than £20,000,000 sterling. Prior to 1806 her territory had been increased, and her population amounted to about 28,000,000, beside the Netherlands which had also been added to the French empire and swelled its population to 34,000,000, while that of Great Britain and Ireland was then less than half as great. The whole revenues of the vast Empire of France in 1802 were but £22,942,000 sterling; in 1803 £23,062,000; in 1804 £23,342,000; in 1808 £26,500,000; in 1809, £29,000,000; in 1810 £29,700,000; and including the revenues derived from the Roman States, they amounted in 1811 to £36,200,000; in 1812 to £35,300,000, and in 1813 to but £33,000,000 sterling. It appears, that the revenues of the French nation, during the whole war, from 1800 to 1815, were only about one fourth part as great as those of the British, in proportion to the population; and yet the French people were exhausted and impoverished by the war, while the British were growing rich, and accumulating capital, with great rapidity.

Napoleon counted up his millions of subjects, and reasoned in this way; the Empire has over 34,000,000 of inhabitants, besides its dependencies, and the British Isles less than 17,000,000; the French people are valiant, warlike, and ambitious of military glory, while the British have been pretty uniformly unsuccessful in all their military campaigns in America as well as in Europe, during the last forty years, and have been successful only in fighting the enervated and half civilized inhabitants of India; and surely, under such circumstances, over 34,000,000 of people with my superior talents as a military commander and conqueror, can overcome half that number who are only a nation of shop-keepers. His error was, in not understanding and not taking into account the power of machinery, and its immense effect in increasing the productive industry and power of the British people. Nearly all his ideas of government, and of war, (except so far as the use of gunpowder and fire-arms had modified and changed military operations,) were drawn from the history of the ancient Romans, and the wars of the Cæsars; he did not, nor did any statesman of that period, seem to understand the prodigious influence which the machinery invented during the previous fifty years, had, in increasing the power of the British nation. His calculations were all founded on the assumption that he was contending with about sixteen or seventeen millions of people, in no respect superior in power in proportion to their numbers to the French; when in fact he was contending with a people, whose actual revenues, from taxation, were more than twice as great as those of France, and whose ability to raise means, by loans and taxation, to maintain fleets and armies, and to carry on military operations, were about three times as great.

Alison, in the 77th chapter of his history of Europe, says the expenditures of the British nation, during the year 1815, the last year of their great struggle with Napoleon, reached the unparalleled sum of £110,000,000 sterling; about £38,000,000 of which was raised by loans, and no less than £11,035,232 of it paid in the shape of subsidies, to other nations of Europe, to aid them in carrying on the war; that "such was the exhaustion of the finances of the great powers of Europe, from the unparalleled efforts they had made during the two previous years, (1813 and 1814,) that they were unable to put their armies in motion without this pecuniary assistance; and that it might truly be said, that the whole military force of Europe was this year arrayed in British pay against France." Large subsidies had also been granted by the British to other nations of Europe, during previous years, to aid them in carrying on the general war against Napoleon; and all these subsidies, and three quarters of the revenues and loans of the British nation, were furnished by means of the machinery, and the increase of the products of manufacturing industry, and the commerce of the British people, in consequence of their machinery.

Sec. 16. *Inventions and Machinery produced the overthrow of Napoleon.*

The effects of the inventions of Sir Richard Arkwright, James Watt, James Hargreaves, Samuel Crompton, and Edmund Cartwright, and some others of Great Britain, and of Eli Whitney of Massachusetts, upon the productive powers of man and upon the manufacturing industry, commerce, and increase of wealth and power of Great Britain, were the natural and ordinary physical effects of natural causes; and in the great chain of causes and effects which operated upon and controlled the destinies of Europe, and produced the final overthrow of Napoleon at Waterloo, the inventions of each of those celebrated men probably had more influence than the genius and the military talents and efforts of the Duke of Wellington. Their effects will be felt throughout the civilized world, as long as civilization shall last. They have been the principal, yea almost the sole means of so increasing the comforts of life, as to reduce the ratio of mortality of Great Britain nearly one third, and to reduce it very sensibly in almost every country of Europe, as well as in America. They enabled the British people to monopolize for a long period, nearly half the commerce of the civilized world; to involve almost every nation in debt to them, and to make them in some measure dependent upon them, and tributary to them, for their manufactured goods and fabrics. *The same causes continue, and by their natural operation, tend to throw the balance of trade in favor of Great Britain, and against every other nation and people; and to involve them more and more in debt to the British manufacturers and merchants, to drain them of the precious metals to pay the interest on their debts; and to impoverish them as debtors, and to enrich the British as creditors. The same causes have produced a very great increase of the population of the British Isles.* During the period of twenty-five years from 1750 to 1775, they did not increase over 10 per cent., and they never increased as much as that during any prior twenty-five years, in their whole history; but during the last fifty years, they have increased from 15 to 18 per cent., every ten years. In 1775, the whole population of Great Britain and Ireland was only about 11,700,000; in 1841, it amounted to over 26,500,000, and is now (1845) about twenty-eight millions; while if none of these inventions had been made, it would not at this day, have amounted to over fifteen and a half, or sixteen millions; and the revenues, wealth, and power of the British nation would probably have been about one fourth part as great as they are now.

What would have been the effect upon Europe, and the civilized world, if these inventions had been made a quarter of a century later, and their effects had not been developed, until after the close of the career of Napoleon? Is it not probable, yea almost certain, that he would have conquered the British Isles, established an universal empire in Europe, and extended it over the principal part of the civilized world? On the other hand, what would have been the effects upon the United States of America, if these splendid inventions had been made in England, and had developed their effects upon the productive industry, commerce, population, wealth, and power of the British Isles, half a century sooner? Is it probable that we should have gained our independence when we did? Or should we have been held in subjection as colonies by the power of Great Britain, until, in the progress of time, her government is revolutionized, that we might take advantage of her anarchy, confusion, and weakness, to throw off the yoke of bondage, and establish our independence?

SEC. 17. *The physical laws of nature, constitute the basis of the laws of trade.*

When Mr. Biddle and his associates by very adroit management, and profuse promises, obtained in (1835,) from the legislature of Pennsylvania, a charter for his misnamed United States Bank, with a capital of $35,000,000, free from the control of Congress, and from the inquisitive and troublesome investigations of government directors, and Congressional committees; he established a son in the cotton trade in Liverpool; launched out millions annually to buy up cotton and state stocks; and apparently expected to control the money, stock, and cotton markets of the United States, and the exchanges between the new and the old world; to raise and depress cotton and stocks at pleasure; and to compel the British and French, and others to pay such prices for cotton as he might dictate. But unfortunately for Mr. Biddle's calculations, on the one hand, the Southern planters had been for years turning nearly all their attention to the culture of cotton, and had increased its production beyond the wants of the civilized world, and a rapid decline in price was a natural and necessary consequence; and on the other hand, many of the States had projected great and visionary schemes of internal improvement, and embarked in expensive works, which could yield very little income in the then existing state of the country, and had made large loans to carry into effect their projected schemes, the interest on which it was impossible for them to pay, and a shock of the public credit, and fall of state stocks was a necessary and unavoidable consequence. In addition to these natural causes, the large importation of foreign goods under the free trade compromise act of 1833, the accumulation of a foreign debt of over $200,000,000, and a rapid exportation of specie to pay the heavy balances of trade against our country, and the interest on our debt, contributed also as natural causes to excite alarm, to depress the prices of cotton, state stocks, lands and other property, to drain the banks and the country of specie, and to create a panic; and in the final result, not only the cotton and state stocks owned by Mr. Biddle's bank fell in price, but hundreds of its heavy borrowers and debtors, who had speculated in cotton, stocks, and lands, were ruined, and the Bank itself, with its immense capital, was prostrated as quickly and easily as any country bank of an hundred thousand dollars capital.

The same causes produced the suspension of nearly all the banks of the United States, in May, 1837; and similar causes, that is, excessive importations and large exports of coin to pay the balance of trade against Great Britain in 1847, caused the most severe commercial crisis, and the greatest amount of bankruptcy in that country, which ever occurred in any country, in a single year.

Such are the tendencies of the physical laws of nature, which aid the industry of man, have a powerful influence upon the prices of commodities, and form the basis of the laws of trade. In fact, commerce is so far governed by the laws of nature, that its tendencies and effects are irresistible; and the only way to escape its effects, when they are injurious, is to avoid the causes which produce them.

The only practicable mode of avoiding the injurious effects of a balance of trade against a country, is to prevent such balance, by regulating its foreign imports, with a view to adapt them to the condition of the country, to the wants of the people, and to the value of their exports, and means of payment.

All these questions have been discussed, and these facts alluded to, as illustrations, to show the effect of the laws of nature upon the destiny of nations as well as of individuals; to show that nature's laws aid the diligent, the industrious, the frugal, the saving, and the intelligent, and make the capital accumulated by industry and frugality, a powerful agent and engine to increase still further the productive industry of man; and to show how man can influence his own destiny, and change his own condition, and how far he is governed by the stern laws of physical necessity, over which he can exercise no influence whatever.

CHAPTER II.

Laws of nature continued.—On the constitution and nature of man, and the end or purpose for which he was created—education and exercise necessary to develope and improve his mental and moral as well as his physical faculties, and to fit him for the final end of his existence.

Sec. 1. *Education, Habits, and Government of a People, have an influence upon their improvement.*

As the mind which controls the body, is constantly influenced by its opinions, as well as by the education, habits, passions, and pursuits of the individual; and by the institutions, form of government, and social system under which he has been bred—it is obvious that all these things have an influence upon the development and improvement of the mind, and upon the progress of communities and nations in productive industry, civilization, and wealth. This influence is in accordance with, and produced by the ordinary operation of the laws of nature. The term civilization, in fact, comprises the intellectual, moral, and physical education of man, and the improvement of the social system and government under which he lives. It is, therefore, appropriate to discuss all these topics as introductory to the general subject of these essays. It is also appropriate to their general object, to examine and treat of the constitution and nature of man, and the end or purpose for which he was created, in order to determine the true end and aim of education, as well as to ascertain what is in accordance with the moral laws of nature, and therefore useful, expedient, and virtuous.

Sec. 2. *The Mind being dependent on physical organs, its capacity depends on the perfection and discipline of those organs.*

To constitute man, both a living principle and an intellectual principle have been superadded to the grosser matter of the material world—as explained in section 2 of Chapter I. This living principle is the basis of all organization, and of all living organs. The mind, as has been remarked, depends upon physical organs, that is, upon the brain and nervous system, as instruments, in, through, and by means of which it acts. These physical organs are not only the medium through which the mind receives impressions from, and ideas of external objects, and by which it conveys its influence by volition to the muscular system, but the brain is also the vehicle in and by the aid of which the mind thinks, wills, recalls previous impressions and ideas, compares, judges, deduces conclusions, and goes through with any complicated process of reasoning. This being the case, *the capacity, power, and fertility of the intellect; its quickness of perception and of action, retentiveness of memory, and power of comparing, judging, and reasoning with accuracy, depend upon the physical organs and instruments, by means of which it acts.* Though ideas, principles, sensations, and truths are not innate or inherent in the mind, yet the faculties and capacities by means of which it acts, becomes conscious of sensations, conceives ideas, and deduces principles and truths by a process of reasoning, are innate; that is, inherent in the mind itself, in connection with its physical organs; and cannot be developed without organs of some kind, as instruments of action. Hence the necessity of a spiritual body at the resurrection; and hence the power and peculiar characteristics of every man's intellect, depend upon the organization, and the greater or less degree of perfection of the physical organs of the mind, by means of which it acts; and hence also the importance of education and exercise to develope those organs, and to improve the mind.

SEC. 3. *Mind not the result of organization—its faculties and power.*

The atheist, and many physiologists insist that the mind and all its faculties not only depend upon organization, but are the direct result and effect of organization, and cannot have an existence without it; or, in other words, that we have no mind, and that the faculties usually called mental faculties, are the result and effect of an organized compound of the material substances composing the body. Now the whole comprises all its parts, and a compound comprises all the properties of each, and all of the simple elements of which it is composed. All the substances composing the body, and all matter with which we are acquainted, except light, caloric, electricity, and magnetism, which are called imponderable substances, possess the property of gravitation, and also the properties of the chemical affinities, and these properties are uniformly the same under all circumstances, whether in a simple or compound state. The gravitating principle of matter is neither increased nor diminished, by compounding or combining it in any mode or manner whatever. Man, however, and all animals, possess not only the power of resisting the action of gravitation, but also the power, by means of the mind, by the faculty of volition acting upon the muscular system, of raising from the ground and carrying great weights, in opposition to the principle of gravitation and the laws of the material world. This is equivalent to demonstrative proof, that mind cannot be composed of the matter of the material world, nor the result or effect of the organization of such matter, *for all nature's laws are uniform, and cannot act inconsistent with themselves ; but man acts inconsistent with the laws of matter, and therefore he must have a principle, spirit, or power within him, not derived from this matter, with which his acts are inconsistent.*

Another class of reasoners start up and say, that mind is the same as caloric, light, electricity, magnetism, or a compound of two or more of those imponderable substances, and thus attempt to evade the argument, that mind acts inconsistent with such matter, and therefore cannot be composed of it. Let us examine this argument. Caloric, light, electricity, &c., though not possessed of the principle of gravitation, are governed by fixed laws, and operated upon by external substances ; by the laws of affinity, or attraction, and the more general law of a tendency to establish an equilibrium. It is impossible for any of these substances to act in and of itself, without being excited to action by some affinity, or attraction, external to itself; and when it acts, it always acts in conformity with laws fixed and certain in themselves, and in a uniform manner, under the same circumstances. *Mind, on the contrary, is endowed by the Creator with self-acting power, or power to originate action in and of itself, and to act without being put in motion by any cause, or motive external to itself*; *and it can act arbitrarily, and according to its own whims or caprice, and is not subject in its acts and movements to fixed laws, like caloric, electricity, and other imponderable substances. God has made it after his own image, and made it a cause in and of itself, and thus it has the power of originating action, and acting according to its own free will. In this consists its freedom of will, and in fact its entire will, including the self-determining power of the will.* There is in chemistry a principle called elective affinity, and double-elective affinity; and in each case, a simple substance is attracted towards two other substances at the same time, and is uniformly governed by the strongest affinity, and never by the weakest; but I presume no man ever thought of calling this elective affinity, freedom of action, or freedom of will, and being governed by the strongest motive; and yet if the mind is governed by a physical necessity from which it cannot escape, and which makes all its acts certain, because subject to fixed laws, and external causes operating upon it, its freedom of action and of will is no greater than that of two substances which are attracted to each other by the chemical laws of elective affinity. The mind also compares, judges, reasons, and deduces conclusions, but two minds rarely reason alike. Some reason with great accuracy, and are seldom led into error, while others are constantly led astray by their passions and prejudices, as well as by their weakness, and can scarcely deduce the most trifling conclusion without danger of falling into error. Can electricity or magnetism judge, compare, or reason; and does it not uniformly act by the same laws, and always with the same accuracy, and if it could reason with accuracy in one case, would it not do so in every case? These views seem conclusive to my mind, that the intellect or mind of man is of a higher origin, and possesses more inherent powers and capacities than any of the matter or elements of matter of this material universe; and yet it may be a mere centre of action, or an organ builder by means of its own powers of attraction, and unable to act to any extent without organs, as its instrument of action, which may be developed and improved by education and exercise.

SEC. 4. *Physical organs and condition transmitted from parent to child, which tends to form national character.*

It seems to be a law of the animal as well as the vegetable economy, that like shall reproduce its like, subject to slight modifications of climate, and other circumstances, which have an indirect influence. Hence if we plant Indian corn, we do not expect to reap wheat, nor vice versa. Grains and vegetables do however partially change their character by being cultivated for years, in a different climate and different soil. So with man, he not only reproduces his kind, *but hands down to his posterity his peculiar physical organization, his form, strength, and even his weaknesses and diseases; and also the form and organization of his brain and nervous system, and his peculiar characteristics of mind, and traits of character depending upon them.* Many of man's diseases and weaknesses are brought upon himself by misconduct, licentiousness, intemperance, luxury, and indolence, or violating the natural laws of God in some other mode; and the physical evils resulting are handed down to his posterity. Hence we read in Scripture that the sins of the father are visited upon his children even unto the third and fourth generation.

The climate, mode of life, pursuits, habits, and customs of any people, have an effect upon their physical constitution, upon the organs of sense, and the brain and nervous system, or organs of the mind, as well as upon the shape of the head and features of the face, and formation of the limbs and body. *The more active the minds of a people, the greater and more perfect will be the de-*

velopment of the brain, and it will be adapted to the character of their pursuits, and the kind of mental exercise they usually have. All these physical peculiarities are more or less handed down to posterity from generation to generation, affect the national mind, and constitute the national character. Hence we observe that the leading characteristics of almost every nation, in the progress of time, no matter what or whence their origin, have become assimilated to each other, and constitute what is called national character. Some, like the Arabs and Tartars, have been entirely stationary, and suffered scarcely any change in their national character and condition for many centuries; others, like the Turks, have degenerated, and been actually sinking in the scale of civilization; whilst many other nations have been developing their mental and physical capacities, as well as the resources of their country, and making rapid strides in the high career of civilization, towards that state of perfection of our constitution, designed by the Deity. (*See on this subject Sec. 2 of Chap. I.*)

SEC. 5. *The pain and evil to which man is subject, arise from his constitution, and from the mode of his existence.*

Mankind were designed by an all-wise and benevolent Creator, for as much happiness in this world, as is consistent with their constitution and nature, being made subject to physical as well as moral evil, pain and death, and placed here in a state of probation, trial and discipline, for another state of existence. God could have created man otherwise, but as maintained by the great and learned Burlamaqui, in his natural and political law, the Deity being all-wise, could not do, that is, there was a moral, if not a physical impossibility, in his doing, what was inconsistent with itself; he could not desire to effect an object, without using the most fit means to attain it; and could not use means inconsistent with the object in view; nor inconsistent with other parts of his works, and the framework of his moral government, which is carried into effect mostly by means of the general operation of physical laws. He might have created man a spiritual being, and not subject to death, but he could not make him a free agent, a rational being, partly spiritual and partly corporeal, subject to the physical laws of the earth, to the reproduction of his kind, and to the dissolution or separation of the soul and body, and give him the necessary senses and sensibility to effect the end in view, without at the same time subjecting him to pain and suffering, both physical and mental; and to both physical and moral evil. The evils, however, to which the nature and constitution of man are incident in this life, are aggravated by reason of his faculties, and the capacities of the earth to maintain him, not being completely developed, and in consequence of his ignorance, indolence, vicious habits and passions, and failure to act in all cases in accordance with the constitution of his nature and the laws of the material world.

SEC. 6. *Man was designed for an industrious, rational, social, moral, religious, and selfish being.*

It was evidently intended by the Creator, that man should be an industrious being; that he should subdue and cultivate the earth, and develope its resources, in order to supply himself with all that is necessary to preserve life, promote health, strength, activity and longevity, and to multiply and people the earth; and as an incentive to do so, he was created with physical appetites, and mental passions. It is universally admitted that *he was designed as a rational being*, but of what use would reason be to him, if he were so far governed by natural causes, that he could not be influenced in the least by his own reason? *It is also evident that he was designed as a social being, a moral being, and a religious being;* and that he should fulfil all the requirements of the law of nature. The natural propensity of man to seek the society of his fellow man, and to sympathise with and participate in the pleasures of his associates, is conclusive evidence that he is by nature a social being; his propensity to sympathise with and participate in the sufferings and misfortunes of his fellow man, even though strangers to him, and his instinctive inclination to relieve them, is evidence that he is a moral being; the whole history of the human family, in all ages, and almost all countries, shows that next to avarice, religious feeling has influenced a larger proportion of mankind, than any other mental passion; this proves that he is a religious being.

That he is a selfish being, arises from his own sensations, appetites, and wants, and the impulses of nature to gratify them. Pope says,—

Self-love the spring of action moves the soul,
Reason's comparing balance rules the whole.
Man, but for that, no action could attend,
And, but for this, were active to no end.

All these capacities and propensities of his nature are given him to be employed, exercised, and gratified, partly as a means to develope his faculties and fit him for a higher state of existence, as the final end of his being, and partly as an incentive to action, to exercise, and industry, as the principal means of attaining this great final end and object of his existence.

SEC. 7. *The leading passions enumerated and described.*

Physical appetites and passions have more or less influence

over every individual, during every day of his life, from birth to the grave; but when his appetites are satisfied, he is freed in some measure from their dominion, and his mental passions have time and opportunity to operate.

After the gratification of the physical wants and appetites, the *domestic affections* are the first, most constant and powerful passions which occupy and influence the human mind; and incite the individual to action, industry, and enterprise, for the purpose of providing for his family the luxuries, as well as the wants and comforts of life. They are founded on moral and social sympathy, but mostly on the former. Secondly, *social sympathy*, or a desire for social intercourse, is one of the most universal passions which influences the human mind. Thirdly, *vanity*, or a *desire* for *display* and *ostentation;* such as a display of personal beauty, fine dress, ornaments, acquirements in the fine arts, science, rank and family lineage, official power and station, valor, strength, agility, or other superiority, either mental or physical. Vanity is the motive; fashion and display the objects of this passion. The Olympic and other games among the Greeks, excited the people of all the Grecian States, and became fashionable among all classes, high and low; as it gave the youth an opportunity to display their physical strength and superiority. War among savage and barbarous nations is almost the only mode by which individuals, and the young in particular, can display their superiority. This is the reason why war is so much more exciting and popular among savage, barbarous, and half civilized nations, than it is among those that are enlightened, whose vanity and ambition can be sufficiently gratified by acquirements, objects and pursuits of a civil nature. This is the same passion which led the French, during the revolution, as well as the legions of Napoleon, the Greeks and Romans, and every other warlike people, in search of what is usually called glory, or military fame.

Fourthly, *avarice*, or the desire for the possession and accumulation of property, is the next in order, the most engrossing passion which occupies and controls the human mind.

It is associated with the desire of gratifying hunger, thirst, and other physical wants. It is in some respects a mere handmaid to the passion for display, fashion or vanity, among civilized and highly cultivated nations. This is evident from the fact that, though savages have physical wants as well as civilized men, yet they seem to be entirely destitute of every thing like avarice, or a desire to accumulate property, beyond their immediate wants. Avarice is the motive; wealth, display and power, are the objects of this passion.

Fifthly, the natural inclination, as evidenced by the practice of all nations and people, to worship the Supreme Being. The source or cause of this natural impulse, or religious instinct, must be the same in all mankind, whether Christians, Jews, Mahometans, or Pagans; the difference in its manifestation arising from education, habit, or accident. There is no reason to doubt that the Jews, Mahometans and Pagans are often as sincere and devoted to their religious creeds, dogmas, and opinions, as the Christians are to the doctrines and precepts of the holy scriptures. When this passion is carried to excess, it begets bigotry, enthusiasm, fanaticism, intolerance, and a spirit of persecution. Religious feeling is the steadiest and strongest passion which can operate upon the mind through life. No other will lead a person so readily to sacrifice his interest, or his life. It has had the greatest and most permanent influence upon the nations of the earth, of any passion whatever. The Jews exhibit the most remarkable examples of its constant and permanent influence. It is now over 2,500 years since the ten tribes of Israel were conquered, and carried into captivity by the Assyrians; for nearly two thousand years they have been dispersed among all the nations of the earth, an oppressed and often a persecuted people ; yet they have in all countries and in all climates preserved themselves a separate and distinct race, and have not sacrificed their religious opinions and ceremonies for the gratification of avarice, ambition, vanity, love, or any other passion, but are essentially the same people they were over two thousand years since.

Sixthly, a desire for power and dominion, usually called *ambition.* This passion seems to spring from, and be founded upon, the desire of the mind for freedom of action, freedom of will, and freedom from all restraint, together with a desire of the necessary power and means of carrying into effect one's will in all cases. But this kind of liberty and freedom of action in one person, implies subjection and subserviency, if not perfect slavery, in the person thus subjected to his will. A desire for power and dominion over property, is the same as the passion of avarice, and a desire to exhibit and display the extent of one's property or power, is mere personal vanity. The leading motive with many if not most persons, in acquiring either property or power, is to enable them to make a great display, and to exhibit what they think their superiority over their fellow beings.

The great lawgivers, savans, writers, statesmen, and conquerors of the world, who have struggled to acquire, or increase their power and influence, have done so for one or more of the following reasons; first, to gratify their vanity ; secondly, for fame, present or future, on account of great achievements, exhibiting their superiority over their fellow beings ; or thirdly and lastly, for the purpose of directing and controlling their fellow beings in order to improve their condition, and promote their happiness. Personal vanity is often connected with national glory, and I fear there are ten aspirants for power to gratify mere personal vanity for display, where there is one ambitious of fame; and ten ambitious of fame, where there is one who seeks and strives to improve the condition and promote the happiness of his fellow beings.

Seventhly, a desire for *revenge*. This is a passion which rages in its full violence only in the minds of savages. It is not only the most powerful, but almost the only powerful mental passion which operates upon the great mass of savages; who have not much ambition for power or fame, not any, or scarce any avarice, and very little social sympathy. Revenge is so neutralized and softened, among a civilized people, by avarice, ambition, vanity, and other mental passions, that its influence need seldom be taken into the account, in estimating human motive.

The excessive gratification of physical appetites generally tends to blunt the mind, render it torpid, and incline both body and mind to inactivity and sleep; *but the gratification, as well as the operation upon the mind of mental passions, usually render it more active and acute, and the person more wakeful and energetic. Mental passions thus act as powerful stimulants; most persons are wakeful, energetic and enterprising, and their minds active in proportion to the strength of their passions;* and if by means of misfortune they become discouraged on the one hand, or on the other, accumulate sufficient to satisfy their wants and their avarice, they henceforward lose their enterprise, and much of their activity and energy, of mind as well as body.

If man had no intellectual passions, nothing but physical appetites to stimulate him, when his immediate wants were gratified, he would relapse into indolence and inertness; and be reduced to a state of degradation, nearly as low as that of many of the brute creation: and never could have made the least progress in civilization or improvement in his condition, above that of the lowest grade of savages.

Sec. 8. *A moderate gratification of the natural passions is in accordance with the object of creation.*

All the natural propensities, instincts, appetites, and passions of man, were given to him by the Creator, for good and wise purposes; and the gratification of them in a proper manner, and within moderate and rational limits, must be consistent with his nature, and intended to promote his happiness and well-being; but no one can be carried to excess, without weakening and eventually destroying some other faculty of his nature, and injuring his physical constitution. It was designed that all his natural, not his artificial appetites and passions, should be gratified to a moderate extent, and not that one or two should engross his whole mind or attention, to the sacrifice of all the others, and to the sacrifice eventually of his health, constitution, and mental powers on all other subjects. Excessive indulgence for a considerable length of time in innocent amusements, and even the excitement of gay society, relaxes the tone and energy both of the mind and the physical system, and unfits them for the sober, rational, and necessary employments of life. Moderation is consistent with the exercise of all the faculties of man, and with the gratification of all the appetites and passions of his nature; but excessive indulgence in one or more, necessarily produces the neglect and decline of others. The necessary tendency of moderation, is to produce good consequences; on the contrary, the necessary tendency of excess, is to produce evil consequences. Moderation is almost a necessary accompaniment of virtue; vice can scarcely exist, without either excess, or the wrong direction of a passion, which might otherwise be deemed virtuous. For instance, to desire the punishment of a criminal, is certainly a virtuous feeling, though it might be deemed malevolence, by persons sympathizing with the criminal; but to desire the punishment of good and innocent persons, is of itself a vicious and wicked feeling.

Even avarice, when it exists in a moderate degree, is consistent with the nature and end of man, and becomes a vice, only when it is in excess, and leads to covetousness and oppression. The same may be said of ambition; it is laudable as long as its ends and objects are good; and vicious when its ends and objects are evil. So of dislike, abhorrence, indignation, anger and hatred: they are virtues, when excited by vice, misconduct and crime, and become vices only when excited by conduct which is correct and innocent.

Hence the importance of a proper education, to regulate the intellectual passions, and give them such direction as to make them useful stimulants to both body and mind. Monarchs, Priests, and Chieftains, have made great use of the passions, to control the mind, and to govern and enslave mankind.

SEC. 9. *On Education—its different kinds, history, and importance.*

Education consists of the development and discipline of the intellectual and physical faculties, and of the social, moral, and religious feelings, propensities, and passions of man, as well as the acquisition of knowledge and science.

It may be divided into six kinds:

1st. Intellectual education, or the development and discipline of the brain and the intellectual faculties; consisting of the instruction and discipline of the schools, that of books, and that derived from observation, examination, comparison, reflection, and reasoning.

2nd. Industrial education;—which consists of the exercise of training the muscles, brain, and nerves of the human system to habits of industry, in some particular employment or pursuit, whereby any physical effort may be made with greater facility and skill.

3rd. Social education;—which consists of the manners and habits of every individual, in his intercourse with his fellow-beings; comprising his powers of conversation, practical knowledge of vocal and instrumental music, dancing, and other matters of amusement.

4th. Moral education;—consisting of a development of proper feelings of charity and sympathy for persons in distress; and of the acquisition of principles of justice, and of propriety of conduct, in the intercourse of man with his fellow-beings.

5th. Religious education; and

6th. Professional and business education.

The first, second, fourth, and fifth kinds of education, as above enumerated, should be extended to the whole community. The great mass of the people will acquire, without much effort or expense, all of the third, which is necessary for their purposes. The sixth may be confined to the professional classes, merchants and business men, and persons who conduct great and difficult enterprises and pursuits, in which great numbers of laborers and large amounts of capital are employed. Books and the education of the schools not only furnish the symbols of thought, and the tools or means to exercise, improve, and expand the mind, but they also place before it ideas, subjects, and questions for consideration; they arouse it from its lethargy, excite it to action, discipline it, and induce it to think, examine, compare, analyse, reason, and judge for itself. A school education, however, so far as it teaches language only, merely communicates to the mind the symbols of ideas, and the tools or instruments by which to acquire knowledge; but so far as it teaches the true principles of natural, mechanical, moral, political, mental, or theological science, it communicates the very essence of knowledge itself;—and so far as it teaches the learner penmanship and the use of numbers, it instructs him in the art of doing business, and preserving a memorial of his acts.

Letters and a written language are necessary to fix in a definite form, and to preserve and communicate ideas, knowledge, experience, memorials of experiments, and discoveries in science; and of inventions, and improvements in the useful arts. It is impossible for a nation or community to emerge from barbarism, and make any considerable progress in civilization, without a knowledge of letters.

Until a comparatively recent period, education by means of schools and books, was confined to the wealthy classes; and such is the case now in all Roman Catholic, Mohammedan, and Pagan countries. In 1494, it was enacted by the Parliament of Scotland, *that every baron and substantial freeholder should send his eldest son and heir to school from the age of six to nine years; and afterwards to a grammar school.* This was in accordance with the practice at that period, of all the western and central countries of Europe, where Catholicism prevailed. The idea was, that it was important to educate the heir, who was to inherit the estate and be the head of the family, but the younger sons and the mass of the people who were to be mere laborers, did not need any education.

The first General Assembly of the Reformed Church of Scotland, met on the 20th December, 1560. They determined that it was necessary to have a school in every parish, for THE INSTRUCTION OF YOUTH IN THE PRINCIPLES OF RELIGION, GRAMMAR, AND THE LATIN TONGUE.

It is stated by the Rev. Mr. Hetherington, in his History of the Church of Scotland, that the compilers of the Book of Discipline in 1561, proposed that the patrimony of the Church should be appropriated to the support of the new Ecclesiastical Establishment, under which designation they included the ministry, the SCHOOLS, AND THE POOR.

The Presbyterian, and some of the other Reformed Churches at an early day, determined, *that the rights of private judgment, in all matters that respect religion, are universal and inalienable*; that every one should search the Scriptures, and be governed by them and by his own conscience,—that is, that every one should search and interpret the Scriptures for himself, and act in accordance with his own understanding, interpretation, and private judgment of their import. They thus *treated education, so far as respects reading, as necessary to the performance of a religious duty; and made the schools a part of the new religious Establishment in Scotland, and equally important and necessary as the ministry.* These opinions have been entertained and acted upon by that Church ever since that time, and by Congregational and some other Protestant Churches for more than two centuries past.

In 1616, the Privy Council of Scotland enacted, "that in every parish where convenient means could be had for entertaining a school, one be established, and a fit person appointed to teach the same, at the expense of the parishioners;" and in 1633 this Act of the Council was ratified in Parliament.

But this act was only permissive and not mandatory, and was very defective. In 1638, the General Assembly of the Presbyterian Church of Scotland "*directed the Presbyteries to see that schools were provided in every landward parish, and such support secured to schoolmasters as should render education easily accessible to the whole population of the kingdom.*" During the civil wars in 1646 a more enlightened Act of Parliament was passed than that of 1633 just referred to, which, though rescinded at the restoration (in 1660) was adopted almost verbatim in the celebrated Act of William and Mary, in the year 1696. That statute is the foundation of the present parochial system of education in Scotland.

As remarked by Mr. Hetherington, that statute provided for what had been long and earnestly sought by the Presbyterian Church of Scotland—a school in every parish throughout the whole kingdom, so far supported by the public funds as to render education accessible to even the poorest in the community.

Thus we see that the influences of the Church operated upon the government, until the latter, acting from time to time in accordance with impulses received from the former, passed Acts for the establishment and support of schools for the education of the whole people.

In 1647 the Plymouth Colony of Massachusetts passed an Act "that every township of fifty householders should appoint a person to teach all the children to read and write, and that every township of one hundred families should support a grammar school."

In the following year (1648) the Legislative Assembly of the Colony of Connecticut, passed a statute in relation to education of very nearly the same purport as that passed in Massachusetts. The Puritans or Congregationalists of Massachusetts and Connecticut entertained the same opinion as the Presbyterians of Scotland—that education is necessary to the performance of religious duty;—and the former seem to have borrowed their ideas and system of education substantially from the latter. This was the foundation of the system of common school education in New England, which was adopted in the state of New York in the early part of the nineteenth century, and has been more recently adopted, and is now in successful operation, in nearly all the free states of the Union.

The Episcopalians of England took a different course. In this particular, they adhered to the tenets of the Catholic Church—denied the right of each person to interpret the Scriptures for himself, and to act in accordance with his own private judgment; and claimed that every one should yield his own private judgment, and receive the interpretation of the Church (that is, of the clergy) as correct in all cases. Inasmuch as laymen were required to yield the interpretation of the Scriptures to the clergy, the church of England have regarded education as unnecessary for the laboring classes; and hence they have made no efforts to extend a common school education to the whole people. Such being the opinions of the Episcopalians, who constitute about three fifths of the population of England, no Act has ever been passed by the British Parliament to provide for the establishment and maintenance of common schools, by the government, or by tax on property. The result is that no effort has been made to give the whole population of England a common school education.

While in Scotland and many of our free states, about one in four of the whole population attend school a portion of the year, in England only about one in eleven attend, and among the Episcopal population of England only about one in twenty attend; in the Roman Catholic countries of southern Europe, perhaps one in an hundred of the population attend school, in Russia only one in two hundred and fifty, and in Mohammedan countries a still smaller proportion.

Sec. 10. *On School District Libraries — their origin and importance.*

On the 20th of April, 1837, the Legislature of Massachusetts passed an act authorizing each legally constituted school district in the State, to raise by tax for the purchase of a library and apparatus, a sum not exceeding thirty dollars for the first year, and ten dollars for any succeeding year. Any town in its corporate capacity, and by virtue of its general authority to maintain schools, may raise whatever sum it pleases for the same object. By an Act of the 3d of March, 1842, the Legislature granted from the State Treasury, the sum of fifteen dollars to every school district, which should raise and appropriate an equal amount for the purchase of a district school library; and if that sum is raised by subscription or donation, and appropriated to that object, it entitles the district to the bounty of the State.

The Legislature of New York passed a similar act about the same time, or very soon afterwards, to provide for a school district library, in every district within the State. In 1838, the Legislature of Michigan passed an act authorizing each school district to raise by tax, ten dollars per annum, to buy books for a district library—and the proceeds of certain fines were appropriated to the same object. In 1843, an act was passed providing for township libraries in the State of Michigan, to be divided every three months among the several school districts of the town; so that one library, by means of the quarterly distribution of books among the several districts, may answer for all the inhabitants of the township.

The whole number of volumes in the school district libraries of the State of New York, on the 1st day of January 1844, was 1,038,396—and on the 1st day of January 1847, 1,310,986—amounting at the latter period to about 118 volumes to each district, the districts then numbering 11,052.

The late superintendent of common schools of the State of New York, says in his report, "The object of the law for procuring district libraries is to diffuse information not only, or even chiefly, among children or minors, but among adults, and those who have finished their common school education. The books, therefore, should be such as will be useful for circulation among the inhabitants generally. They should not be children's books, or of a juvenile character, or light and frivolous tales and romances; but works conveying solid information, which will excite a thirst for knowledge, and also gratify it, as far as such library can."

"Books are here found suited to every age, and almost every grade of intellect; and the instruction and information afforded by them to our citizens of adult age, are of incalculable benefit."

As language of itself does not constitute knowledge, but only the symbols of knowledge, and the medium by which it may be acquired, the common schools do very little except to communicate to the learner the key and the instruments, by means of which he may acquire knowledge from books.

Books and libraries are therefore necessary to complete that system of education which is commenced only in the common school—and the *establishment of school district libraries may be regarded as an era in the history and progress of popular education, second only in importance to the establishment of common schools themselves.* These libraries will unfold to the poor as well as to the middle classes, vast sources of valuable information, which will tend to expand their minds, to increase intelligence, and the productiveness of their industry, and to elevate their character.

SEC. 11. *Education and exercise are necessary to develope the faculties of man.*

The mind, as well as the body, is developed and strengthened, and all the muscles and organs of the system are increased in size, and rendered more perfect by frequent exercise. This is verified in the case of the blacksmith, whose right arm, by the daily use of heavy hammers, in forging and working iron, becomes larger and stronger than the arms of any other class of men. It is a general rule, applying to all classes of persons, that the limbs and organs, or part of the system most exercised, become the strongest. But the greater part of employments give a healthy exercise to nearly all parts of the human system, and tend to increase their strength and activity.

Even the senses are rendered more acute and accurate by exercise, attention, and practice. An experienced banker, accustomed to examine critically the execution of bank notes and drafts, can readily see and detect defects, omissions and differences in the execution, or engraving, too minute and slight to be perceived by a person of less experience; and sailors can often perceive distinctly vessels and objects at a distance upon the water, which are beyond the reach of the vision of landsmen. A skilful musician, whose organs of hearing have been disciplined for years, will be put in pain by slight discords, which would not be observed by ordinary hearers. Perhaps this increased skill depends as much on the mind, as it does on the senses. It arises from the attention given by the mind to the subject, as well as to the operation of the senses.

The more a person exercises his memory, judgment, or reasoning faculties, upon any particular subject, the more acute, accurate, and active, the faculty exercised becomes. In as much as all the operations of the mind are carried on by means of the brain and nervous system, which consists of physical organs, when the mind has dwelt long upon any particular subject, the succession of ideas in the mind, from frequent occurrence and repetition, become associated together and form trains of thought, so that when the same subject is again introduced to the mind, the same succession of ideas and trains of thought will be suggessed to it, and follow each other in their accustomed order. This association of ideas in the mind depends on the same cause, and is governed by the same laws, as the characteristic of the muscular and organic system usually called habit. No man can be a great general in modern times, since war has been reduced to a system, and become a very complicated science, unless his mind has been thoroughly disciplined by active service in the field, as well as by extensive reading and learning in mathematics, fortification, and military tactics. Nor can a man become a distinguished diplomatist, lawyer, orator, debater or tactician, as a leader of a political party, without experience as well as learning in those several departments; learning alone is not sufficient; practice also is necessary. To make a great statesman, legislator, or judge, more mature judgment, and more various and extensive acquirements, observation, and reflection are necessary, but experience in either of those particular departments, is not so important. In those great departments of life and some others, *extensive acquirements, science, observation, reflection, and practical experience in some other department of business, seem to supply the place of experience in those in question.* The science of government can only be acquired by many years of intense mental labor.

The mind as well as the body, can be fully developed and strengthened by exercise, and exercise only, and neither of them can be fitted for any of the higher employments of civilized life, without many years of training, and intense application. The muscles of the body, as well as the current of thought, and succession of ideas in the mind, must be adapted, by practice and discipline, to their respective ends, before any high degree of excellence can be attained in any useful employment of life. Everything must become habitual, before it can be performed skilfully. How infinitely superior is civilized man to savages and barbarians, not only in the development and cultivation of his intellectual and moral powers and faculties; but also in physical developments, and the adaptation of the muscular system, to some useful and productive industry, or business, to which he may have been bred! He may not be superior in strength or agility for the chace, or for warlike operations, but superior in adaptation to useful labor, in any employment which will enable him to provide himself with the necessaries and comforts of life, and to fill the station for which he was apparently designed by the Supreme Being.

It is a common adage, that there is no royal road to science; nor is there any short and easy path to attain it. It can only be acquired by many long years of patient and toilsome labor, diligence and attention. The remark has often been made, that the sons of great and eminent men, who have raised themselves to distinction, by patient industry and energy of character, do not generally possess the talents and abilities of their fathers. Being generally bred in luxury and comparative indolence, which serves to stimulate their pride, vanity, and passion for amusement and pleasure, they seldom exert themselves sufficiently to acquire much vigor either of body or mind; and they are often led on by the specious attractions of frivolous amusements, until their passions for amusement become so strong, that they cannot be resisted; and the mind becomes unfitted to enjoy the sober realities of life.

Luxury and indolence are the grave of talent. A person may be born with as much native talent as Julius Cæsar, Cicero, or Napoleon Bonaparte, and if cradled in luxury, and bred in indolence, unless he makes a total change of his habits, (which is almost impossible,) he must necessarily remain through life, comparatively feeble and inefficient. He may, by means of his native genius, elegance of manners and general information, acquired without reasoning much, be able to make a speech or address, upon the mere surface of things, that may tickle the fancy of a popular audience, and be effective for the moment; but to discuss great principles with ability, point out their tendencies, trace them to their ultimate results, and warn the public of the dangers attending them; or to originate and mature great and important measures for the benefit of their country, requires an enlarged wisdom, acquired by attentively observing the current of human events, much learning, deep reflection, and a well-balanced, and well disciplined mind.

Nor is discipline of mind in one department of science or business, of as much importance in other departments, which are very different in their character, as many of the schools and schoolmen pretend. To play chess, many games of cards, and some other games of amusement well, requires science and discipline of mind as well as experience; and yet the science and discipline of mind thus acquired, serve only to intoxicate the mind, and to divert it from, and unfit it for any rational and useful employment. If these reflections are correct, they show the importance of "training up a child in the way he should go," and forming his habits of mind and body, and adapting them not only to the paths of virtue, but to the pursuits which he is to follow through life. They show also the reason of the great difficulty and hazard of a man's changing his pursuits, after he has attained the middle age of life.

The same course of reasoning will apply to our moral, benevolent, and social feelings. They are quickened, increased, and strengthened by frequent exercise, in the same manner as our physical and intellectual faculties. Frequent attention to the wants and sufferings of the poor and unfortunate, serves to awaken, increase, and strengthen our benevolent feelings and sympathies, for persons in distress, and to render them more quick and active. In order to cultivate the moral faculties, however, it is necessary to restrain our selfish as well as our malevolent passions. Moderation, and the restraint of violent passions and appetites, lie at the foundation of all virtue. A person of violent and unrestrained passions, may have certain generous impulses, which may be called instincts, or propensities, but cannot be properly dignified with the title of virtues. One of the noblest acquirements of man, consists in the power, which may become a fixed habit, of restraining his own passions, and giving a proper direction to his moral and social feelings. Even conscience can be cultivated, and generally depends upon the education, habits, and opinions of the person.

The frequent gratification of feelings and desires, increases their force, and is accompanied by an impulse of nature, which is greatly strengthened and increased in violence by repetition, until it becomes an habitual attendant upon its associated feeling, or desire, and soon becomes so powerful as not to be easily overcome, or restrained. Though passion is essentially physical in its character, yet it is so dependent upon the will, and upon habit, and the principle of association, that it may be disciplined and controlled by the mind. *Passion may therefore be defined an impulse of nature, arising by the force of habit, from any feeling or desire with which it is associated.* The very source or origin from whence violent passions arise, consists in the repeated and habitual indulgence of feelings and desires, which were at first moderate, and easily controlled. *Indulgence is the source of passion and vice; and self restraint, and a proper direction and exercise of moral feelings and sympathies, lie at the foundation of virtue.* Proper exercise and discipline are therefore as necessary to the development of our moral, as of our intellectual and physical faculties.

Exercise and discipline being necessary to develope, strengthen, and bring to perfection all the moral, as well as the intellectual and physical faculties of man, industry, in which I would include both mental and physical labor, may be regarded as one of the first and greatest of virtues. Indeed, it would seem from the very nature and constitution of man, as well as from the original command to him, that he should eat bread in the sweat of his face, to have been imposed upon every well person as a duty, to attend to some business or employment, either of utility to himself or his fellow beings, which may serve to exercise, develope, and discipline his organs and faculties. *The necessity of industry in this view of the subject, seems to have been imposed upon man by the Deity for a two-fold object; first, to develope and discipline his physical and intellectual organs and faculties, to enable him to provide himself with the necessaries and comforts of life, and to maintain his offspring, and to people, replenish, and subdue the earth;*

Secondly, to develope his intellectual and moral faculties, to fit him for living in a state of society in this world, and for a higher state of existence in the world to come. That this life is but a state of probation, to develope the faculties of man, and fit him for another and better world, is believed not only by Christians, but by a large proportion of the Pagan nations of the earth.

Liberty, industry, and conformity to the moral laws of nature, and the perfect development and proper direction and exercise of all the faculties of man, are necessary to promote the highest degree of happiness in this world, as well as the world to come, to which his nature is adapted. This great and important end, so far as this world is concerned, consists in civilization; in the highest degree of civilization of which the nature of man is capable.

CHAPTER III.

ON CIVILIZATION—DEFINITION AND SUCCESSIVE STEPS IN THE PROGRESS OF CIVILIZATION—GRAZING, MINING, MECHANISM, AGRICULTURE AND COMMERCE—DEPENDENCE OF AGRICULTURE—INVENTIONS AND IMPROVEMENTS.

Sec. 2. *Civilization is progressive.*

It is not a new doctrine, that the constitution, including not only the physical, but so much of the mental faculties and capacities of man, as depend on the formation of the brain and other physical organs, may be in a state of development and progressive improvement from generation to generation, and from age to age. It is partly from this source, and partly from the fact that knowledge is rapidly increasing in the civilized world, that some politicians of our country have borrowed the idea of progressive democracy. That civilization in the aggregate is progressive in this and many other countries, is beyond a doubt; but in as much as it embraces an immense number and variety of faculties, powers, principles, and elements variously combined, it may improve in some respects, and be at the same time declining in others. That the principles of the political parties of our country are undergoing great changes from time to time, is beyond a doubt; but whether they are improving, or verging towards corruption and tyranny, admits of different opinions; the developments of the future can alone determine this question to the satisfaction of all. My object is to analyze the elements and principles of civilization, together with the elements and principles of our social system, habits, customs, institutions, government, and national policy, both foreign and domestic; and to ascertain, as far as practicable, what parts of our system, institutions, customs and policy tend to advance, and what tend to retard us in the progress of civilization.

Sec. 2. *Civilization defined.*

Civilization consists in the development and melioration of the intellectual, physical, and moral faculties, constitution and condition of man; and in the improvement of the social system and government of the society in which he lives. The highest degree of civilization for which man was designed by his Creator, consists in such a development and improvement of his faculties, constitution and condition, and such an organization and improvement of the social system, and system of government under which he lives, as tend to secure his rights, and promote his health, activity and general welfare and happines, to the greatest extent in the aggregate, of which his nature is susceptible. The institutions of religion are included under the term social system; and the development of the resources of the country, together with the accumulation of capital and of the comforts of life, are included under the terms physical condition. This definition is a condensation of the statement and definition of civilization given by M. Guizot, the learned French scholar and statesman, in his lectures on the general history of the civilization of Europe; except that less importance is attached by him to the physical condition of man.

SEC. 3. *Industry, property and education, lie at the foundation of civilization.*

Wandering tribes of shepherds are always either savages or barbarians, ignorant and degraded; with the exception of the chiefs, they are very poor and destitute; and the condition of wandering hunter is still worse. The latter are generally poorer, more destitute, and enjoy less of the comforts of life, than the former. Degradation of morals usually goes hand in hand with destitution, misery and ignorance. Though it is not universal, yet in most cases, long-continued physical suffering, arising from destitution, hardens the feelings and produces moral degradation. There is no reason to doubt, that physical comforts tend to promote good morals; though luxury usually produces more or less social vice. No people can become civilized without fixed habitations and regular industry, to provide themselves with the comforts of life. Fixed habitations constitute property; and nearly all the property in the world, as well as the necessaries and comforts of life, are produced by the labor and attention of man. Though the greatest amount of wealth is not necessary to a high degree of civilization, yet civilization and wealth generally advance together. *Industry and property therefore lie at the very foundation of civilization; without which it cannot exist;* and it progresses in proportion to the advance a people make in productive industry, in cultivation of mind, and in the application of the natural sciences to the production of whatever is necessary to supply the wants of man.

The Spartans, Romans, and all the warlike nations of antiquity, despised labor, and looked upon it as degrading, and fit only for slaves. Christianity has in a measure sanctified industry, and made it respectable. As the Christian religion is a spiritual matter, it cannot be understood and realized by a people who have not made considerable advancement in the cultivation of their minds. It cannot be propagated among savages, and can exist in its purity only among a highly civilized people. This is verified by the history of the various attempts to Christianize the North American Indians, as well as by the whole history of Europe during the dark ages. It is impossible to elevate man in the scale of existence, and raise him in the grade of civilization, in any mode, or by any means, except by improving at the same time, both his mental and physical condition. To improve his morals, and give him a knowledge of the spiritual religion of Christianity, without first raising both his mental and physical condition above that of a savage or barbarian, is impracticable.

Industry and business not only afford the principal means of exercising the mind; but they supply the sole means of supporting schools, scholars and students devoted to the acquisition of learning and science, and of supporting a Christian ministry. *Regular industry may therefore be regarded, as one of the chief corner-stones of both civilization and Christianity; and industry and education lie at the foundation of all improvement and progress in the world.* Industry cannot be rendered very effective without education, and the application of the natural sciences. Whatever course of policy tends to promote the cause of education and science, to diffuse useful knowledge, and increase productive industry, must therefore promote improvement, and the great cause of civilization. Hence monasteries, nunneries, and all the institutions of the mendicant orders, are contrary to the spirit of civilization and Christianity, and tend to impede their progress.

SEC. 4. *Successive steps in the progress of civilization.*

The primary wants of man consist of food, drink, clothing, fuel, lodging, and a house, hut, or tent to shelter him from the elements. The two first, and the last, are absolutely necessary, without which he cannot long exist in any climate; clothing and fuel are equally necessary in cold climates, though not so much so in warm countries, and in the torrid zone. The first end to be attained by man in his progress towards civilization, consists in such a development and exercise of his intellectual and physical faculties, as will enable him to provide himself with whatever is necessary to sustain life, and promote health, strength, activity and longevity; to provide himself with food, clothing of some kind, lodging, fuel, and a house, hut, or tent to shelter and protect him from rains, dews and storms, cold, heat and dampness, and the changes of the weather; frequent exposures to any of which affect his health, and shorten his life.

The first step in his progress, is to tame, domesticate, and subject to his use, such animals as will furnish him food and clothing, or either, or be useful as beasts of burden and labor, in subduing the earth. The wandering tribes of Arabs and Tartars of Asia, and of ancient Muscovy, (now Russia,) and Poland, who subsisted mostly on the milk and flesh of their cattle and camels, and were clothed and sheltered with their skins, were elevated far above the lowest grade of savages, who subsist entirely on game, fish, and the spontaneous productions of the earth, having no domestic animals but the dog, which is useful to them in hunting only.

The second step in the progress of civilization, is to learn to make iron, and to work it into edge tools, and other tools and instruments of mechanism, to enable him to work in wood, stone, and other materials, and to convert them to his use. This is so universally admitted, that most authors and philosophers have regarded the knowledge and use of iron, as the principal test of civilization. The inhabitants of Mexico and Peru, at the time of the discovery of America by Columbus, used agricultural implements, tools and instruments to work in wood and stone, made of hardened copper. This was a tolerable substitute for iron.

The natives of America north of Mexico, had some knowledge of the Art of Pottery, of shaping clay, and converting it into articles of domestic use by burning; and some of them made rough axes and tools of stone with which they could hack rather than cut down trees, make bows and arrows for hunting, and dig up the earth, make mounds and huts, and cultivate to a trifling extent, maize or Indian corn, and a few vegetables; but none of them appear to have had any knowledge of iron, or any other metal suitable for edge tools, or for instruments of agriculture, and the mechanic arts.

The next and third step in his progress, is to invent and make ploughs, hoes, spades, and other instruments and utensils for digging up and cultivating the earth; to invent and make spinning wheels and looms, to spin, weave, and convert flax, wool, cotton, hemp, and silk into cloth; and to invent and make wheeled carriages, wagons or carts of some description, and rough dwelling houses partly of wood, but mostly of stone, brick, or clay.

It appears from the Scriptures, that the Egyptians, Phœnicians, Israelites, and the neighboring nations, had the art of making flax and wool into cloth at a very early period. A rude species of house-building, and the art of making cloth, were invented in most countries in very early ages of the world, when little or no use was made of the earth except for supporting their flocks and herds, and producing a few vegetables and fruits, which grew spontaneously.

Sec. 5. *On the Metals—they precede both Agriculture, and a Division of Employments.*

A division of employments cannot take place, until man has made some progress in making tools and instruments to work with, and in the mechanic arts; for up to this period, he clothes himself in furs and skins, subsists upon the products of his flocks, and the spontaneous productions of the earth, fish, and game. *It is impossible for him to cultivate grain or vegetables to any extent, until he has learned to make iron or copper, and to work it into something like ploughs, spades, shovels, hoes, and pick-axes, to dig up, and subdue the earth, and fit it for the reception of seed, and the production of crops.* After he has learned to make iron, or copper, and work it into tools and instruments of industry; some turn their attention to mining and making iron; others forge it, and make it into diverse instruments and edge tools; others use the tools to work in wood, and make utensils and instruments of industry; some engage in house-building, of stone, clay or brick, with a very little wood for doors; some build entirely of wood; and others make wheels and looms, with which the female part of the community spin and weave cloth. It is my intention to distinguish agriculture from grazing, and to confine the term agriculture to its strict sense and meaning, of cultivation of the ground in fields, raising grain, vegetables, &c. As agriculture cannot by any possible means be carried on, except to a very trifling extent, without various tools and instruments, made partly of iron and copper, and partly of wood, the wood part of which cannot be made without edge tools made of iron, or hardened copper, *it follows as a necessary consequence, that not only the art of making iron or copper, but the mechanism required to make the tools and implements of agriculture, must precede the practice itself of agriculture. Some portion of the mechanic arts, therefore, necessarily precede agriculture, which is entirely dependent upon them, and cannot exist without them.*

Subsequent to the division of employments, which follows, and cannot precede the mechanic arts, the art of cultivating the ground, or agriculture in its strict sense, is resorted to by man, to provide himself with a more regular and certain supply of vegetable food than he could procure from the spontaneous productions of the earth. The famines we read of in Scripture were at a very early period, when the cultivation of the earth in Palestine was very rare and trifling; though much more common and extensive in Egypt, Assyria, and some other countries. Attention is not given to agriculture by any people, until they settle down and establish themselves in fixed habitations; while they remain in tents, and remove from place to place to find pasture and water for their herds and flocks, they do not usually acquire or claim any permanent or vested interest in any particular portion of soil, and do not remain stationary long enough to cultivate crops and harvest them. Not only Abraham and Lot, but all the Israelites, before they went to Egypt, as well as while in the wilderness, and until after their return to the land of Canaan, dwelt in tents, and lived a pastoral, not an agricultural life; they must have understood the art of spinning and weaving, even at that early period, and made cloth for clothing, as well as for their tents. See on this subject, Gen. ix: 23. do. iv: 19 and 22—do. xli: 42.—do. xxxvii: 4, 23, 31, 34—do. xxxviii: 14—do. xxxv: 3, and 21—do. xxxi: 33. It is evident from these and many other passages in the book of Genesis, that the Israelites had a knowledge of metals, and kept sheep on account of their wool, and made cloth of various kinds, while they dwelt in tents, and did not cultivate the ground, but lived on the flesh of their flocks, and the spontaneous productions of the earth.

All grains, vegetables, and plants, as well as fruits, grew at first spontaneously in some climates and countries, and have been transplanted by man from one climate and country to another, and improved by cultivation. The cotton plant appears to have been a native, and to have grown spontaneously in India, China, Egypt, Madagascar, Mexico, and many other countries, and flax in Egypt, Palestine, and all the countries of southern and central Europe. Man must have learned the use of cotton and flax, and to spin and weave them into cloth, before the thought could have been suggested to him of cultivating them; for they are not fit for food, of either man or beast, and are valuable only for clothing and the oil obtained from their seed. The use and manufacture of cotton and flax must therefore have preceded the cultivation of these plants; so necessary to the comforts and to the very existence of civilized man. Previous to their cultivation also, man must have had the use of iron, and learned to make some rough species of plough, spade, or hoe, with which to dig up and subdue the earth.

A similar course of reasoning applies to every species of grain, vegetable, and plant cultivated by man. He must have found them, in the first instance, growing spontaneously, appropriated them to his own use, and thus learned their utility and value; and after he acquired a knowledge of iron, and the art of making it, together with a sufficient knowledge of mechanism to forge and work the iron, and make edge tools, and work in wood; and had also invented and learned to make some rough species of agricultural instruments, he first began to raise by cultivation the several species of grain, vegetables, and plants which had been found useful to him. As he increased in knowledge of the mechanic arts, a division of employments took place; his employments became more and more diversified, and barter, or an exchange between man and man of the products of their respective employments, was introduced. As he acquired more knowledge of the mechanic arts, and learned to make more instruments and tools necessary to cultivate the earth, and to convert its products into food, clothing, and utensils of use, convenience, and comfort; he acquired the means of extending the cultivation, and improving in the mode of cultivating it. As population increased, the demand for agricultural, as well as mechanical products, increased, which acted as a stimulant to agriculture, and also to the mechanic arts and commerce. One improvement and discovery has led to another; and every useful and valuable invention in the mechanic arts, has not only increased the comforts of man, but contributed to promote his health, increase his longevity, and multiply population, and contributed, directly or indirectly, to an improved mode of cultivating the earth, an extension of agriculture, and an increase of its products, in quantity, quality, and value.

Agriculture is therefore directly dependent upon the mechanic arts, not only for its origin, but also for every step of its progress in the march of improvement. It follows the mechanic arts, and cannot precede them, and may be said to be the fourth step in the progress of civilization.

Sec. 6. *Origin, basis, and advantages of Commerce.*

While man remains in a state of native simplicity and ignorance, the whole of a tribe being engaged in the same employments and mode of life, there is little or no occasion for exchange, barter, or commerce of any kind; but as soon as the mechanic arts and the cultivation of the earth are introduced, then comes a division of employments, which is immediately followed by a mutual interchange of the products of labor, or barter, and this is the beginning of regular commerce. *Commerce is thus completely dependent upon the mechanic arts, and the division of employments, and cannot exist without them, except to a very limited extent. Agricultural products alone cannot furnish the materials of an active commerce; and two nations almost exclusively agricultural, have seldom much intercourse with each other.* Commerce is generally carried on between two parties, of one of the three following characters: first between the farmer, or grower of the raw produce on one side, who exchanges a portion of his surplus produce with a mechanic or manufacturer in his vicinity, for the products and fabrics of mechanism, which he needs for the use of himself or his family; secondly, between two mechanics in the vicinity who mutually exchange the surplus products of each other's labor, and part with what they do not need, in exchange for what they do need for their own use and consumption; and thirdly, between parties, one or both of whom is a merchant, who buys to sell again, and make gain, or sells what he has previously purchased, for the purpose of making a profit by its sale. *The two first species of commerce, or barter, are much the most profitable to the consumers, and to all the laboring classes, as they thereby acquire what they need for their own use and comfort, without paying anything for transportation, or anything for expenses and profits of merchants, factors, agents, &c.:* on the contrary, the last species of commerce loads down its products with the costs of transportation, and generally with two or three, and often with four or five profits and expenses, of merchants and commercial agencies, beside interest on commercial capital, amounting in the whole, to be paid by the consumer, to from twenty to two or three hundred per cent, on the original cost of the article. The wisdom of Mr. Jefferson's remark, in his letter to Mr. Austin, is most manifest, that the manufacturer should be placed by the side of the farmer.

There is very little occasion for commerce or barter between agriculturists, or between two agricultural nations; the most natural and profitable foreign commerce, is between two nations of different climates, or in different states of improvement and condition, where one party exchanges the produce of the earth with the other for the products of mechanical and manufacturing industry, whereby each party acquires what he wants directly, and in exchange for the products of his own industry. Tyre, Carthage, and Athens, in ancient, and Venice, Florence, Genoa, and the Netherlands, in more modern times, were the greatest of commercial nations at their respective eras, as Great Britain is now; *because they were also in advance of all other nations in the mechanic arts and manufactures; and their commerce was based on their mechanism and manufacturing industry, which furnished the principal subject matter and materials for making exchanges, and carrying on commerce with foreign nations.*

Sec. 7. *Successive steps in the progress of civilization recapitulated.*

Of the five great divisions and departments of human employment and industry, all of which and many others seem necessary to man, before he can attain a very high state of civilization, the most simple, and the first attained in his progress towards civilization, is the pastoral or nomade state; in which he lives as a shepherd, raising and tending his flocks and herds, subsisting upon their milk and flesh, and the spontaneous productions of the earth, and clothing himself in their skins and wool. *His second step in the progress of civilization*, is to learn the business of mining, smelting ores, forging and making iron, and working it into edge tools, and other tools and instruments, to work in wood, stone, &c. *His third step* is to learn a rude system of house-building, and to invent spinning-wheels, and looms, and to learn the art of spinning, weaving, and making cloth; and of making ploughs, and other tools, and implements of agriculture. It thus embraces nearly the whole circle of the mechanic arts, and of manufactures. *His fourth step* consists in learning to plough, or dig up and cultivate the earth, as an agriculturist. *Lastly comes commerce, the connecting link in the chain, between all the other employments. Though commerce is entirely dependent upon the mechanic arts, and upon agriculture, to supply its materials, yet it is the very life-blood of civilization, and seems necessary to stimulate and render active all the arts and employments of civilized life; and civilization to any great extent cannot exist without it. All these several employments, together with the necessary instruction in the knowledge and science required for pursuing them advantageously, mutually act and react upon each other; and each contributes to promote, sustain, and increase the productive energy of the others; to multiply the comforts, and promote the welfare of mankind.*

SEC. 8. *Effects of science, the mechanic arts, inventions and discoveries, on the progress of civilization.*

Progressive improvement and advancement in civilization, depend on industry, on productive industry, and the application of the natural sciences to labor; productive industry depends mostly on the rewards and compensations of labor, and the activity of commerce, which act as stimulants to the mind of man; and these again are based and depend upon the mechanic arts, and machinery. It may therefore be truly said, that a *division of employments, agriculture, commerce, and the whole fabric of civilization, all depend upon the mechanic arts, and cannot exist without them; and that as a general rule, no nation or people can advance in civilization any faster than they make progress in the mechanic arts, and the sciences on which they are based.*

The history of civilization is the history of the triumphs of man over the material world, and over the physical laws of nature. He has not only subdued a large portion of the earth; but all the metals, all kinds of wood and timber, nearly every species and product of vegetation, all the earths and gases, coal, stone, and salt, as well as a large portion of the animal creation, and the winds and waters upon the surface of the earth, have all been subjected to the use and control of man, and made subsidiary to his comforts, enjoyments, and general welfare. By these means, he can overcome the wants and evils of hunger, thirst, cold, heat, storms, and wind; and not only render himself comfortable, but resist the causes of disease, and has actually increased his ordinary period of life, in every highly civilized country on the earth.

The arts of smelting ores, and of hammering and forging iron, and other metals, and converting them into utensils, edge tools, and other instruments, were discovered at a very early period of history, and were in a measure the inceptive steps of civilization among Pagan nations. Man soon arrived at a point of civilization, at or near which he seemed to pause for many centuries, as if it were a barrier which he could not pass. At length clocks were invented, the art of making glass windows was invented, chimneys were invented, and the art of making cotton and linen rags into paper was invented; all these inventions came into use in Europe in the 11th, 12th, and 13th centuries. Then came the invention of gunpowder and its application to mechanical purposes for blasting rocks and ores, and working in mines, as well as for warlike purposes, and also the invention of the mariner's compass, the great handmaid of navigation, in the 14th century. The 15th century produced and introduced the great inventions of printing, and the sawmill, for sawing lumber, and near its close, the discovery of America. During the forepart of the 16th century, the use and culture of maize or Indian corn, and potatoes, were introduced into Europe from the New World. Many other inventions and discoveries of less importance were made and introduced between the 12th and the middle of the 16th century; and during that period, the art of spinning, weaving, and working silk, cotton, hemp, and flax, as well as wool, into cloth, was introduced into many countries, partly by means of the crusades to the Holy Land; and in all the countries of Europe, the manufacture of those articles into cloth was greatly increased. When compared with his condition in the 11th and 12th centuries, the comforts of man were greatly increased, the ratio of mortality diminished, and his condition much improved by all these causes, which were in full operation from the middle of the 16th century to the time of the invention of the Spinning Jenny in 1767; and yet the paralyzing influence of the religious persecutions, and the civil wars growing out of the reformation of the 16th century, together with the use of ardent spirits, greatly retarded the progress of improvement; and the ratio of mortality, as well as of the increase of population, was nearly the same in almost every country of Europe and America, during the last ten years of that period, as it was during the first ten. The revocation of the Edict of Nantes, by Louis XIV., in 1685, had such an effect upon France, by driving out of the kingdom half a million or more of her most skilful mechanics and artisans, that the kingdom was less flourishing, and the condition of the people not much better in 1785, than in 1685; and this cause, which depressed France, is one of the principal causes of the progress and improvement of Great Britain during that period.

The thermometer, barometer, and telescope, were all invented the forepart of the seventeenth century. They have been of great advantage to the progress of the useful arts, as well as to the prosecution of inquiries and discoveries in the natural sciences.

Paper money was invented in England the latter part of the 17th century, and soon afterwards introduced into France, where it produced the famous Mississippi scheme in 1719; but the *great facilities it gives to gambling speculations, extravagance, deception, and fraud, of every kind and character, seem to render it probable that it has been rather a curse than a blessing to the human family.* Though the Moors introduced the art of distillation and use of distilled liquors into Europe in the 12th or 13th century, yet their use was comparatively trifling, until after the discovery of America, the introduction of African slaves into the West India Islands, and the extensive cultivation of the sugar cane; which led to the increased distillation and supply of rum, and its more general use among all classes of people. This evil of itself, was sufficient to balance nearly all the benefits derived from improvements made during the two centuries previous to the invention of the Spinning Jenny. The discovery of the benefits of inoculation for the small pox, the forepart of the 18th century, and of the efficacy of vaccination for the kine pox as a preventive and check to the spread of the small pox about the year 1798, have probably had more effect in diminishing the ratio of mortality, than all other discoveries in medicine from the commencement of the 16th, to the close of the 18th century. During the religious wars and persecutions of the 16th and 17th centuries, a large portion of the Protestant mechanics and artisans, who could emigrate with more facility than agriculturists, fled to Great Britain and Holland for an asylum; which is the principal cause of the rapid improvement of those nations from the commencement of those persecutions and wars, to the invention of the Spinning Jenny; while the march of improvement, and the progress of civilization seemed to have been arrested, and nearly stationary, in all the remaining part of the world, except the Anglo-American colonies,

Russia, the protestant part of Europe, and perhaps the isles of Japan and China.

The flying shuttle for weaving, which was invented about the year 1738, the improvement of the steam-engine, the invention of the Spinning-Jenny, Spinning-Frame, Spinning-Mule, Power-Loom, Carding-Machine, Cast-iron stove, Iron Railway, Saw-Gin for cleaning cotton, and machinery for rolling iron, during the last half of the 18th century; and the invention of Steam-Boats, Locomotives, or Steam-Carriages, Iron Ploughs, and many other mechanical inventions, including electro-magnetic Telegraphs, during the present century, together with the discoveries and improvements in the medical, natural, and political sciences, have improved the condition of the people, and advanced the cause of civilization more during the last hundred years, than it advanced during any previous five centuries, since the creation of the world.

The discussion of this subject will be continued in the next two chapters on government, and ecclesiastical government; in order to show the impediments in the progress of civilization, as well as the causes of its advancement.

CHAPTER IV.

ON THE PRIESTHOOD, AND ECCLESIASTICAL GOVERNMENT; AND THE INFLUENCE OF PROTESTANTISM, CATHOLICISM—MAHOMETAN FATALISM AND MORMONISM, UPON THE HUMAN MIND—AND UPON CIVIL GOVERNMENT, THE PROGRESS OF IMPROVEMENT, AND CIVILIZATION.

SEC. 1. *Influence of the Priesthood—Ecclesiastical tyranny.*

A PART, and one of the most efficient parts of government in all civilized countries, consists in the education of the people; so as to restrain their passions, form their minds, direct their opinions, and teach them obedience and submission to the government. Education in this view of the subject, is not confined to instruction in the schools, but includes all public executions, military exhibitions and amusements, addresses, lectures, religious instruction and ceremonies, auricular confessions and examinations, auto da fés, &c., &c.; as well as mental and physical training in some useful employment or business. From the beginning of the fifth century, until the diffusion of learning by means of the art of printing in the 15th century, nearly all the learning of Europe was confined to the clergy; very few laymen could read and write, and fewer still were qualified for high and important offices; and hence the bishops and higher order of the clergy engrossed nearly all the civil offices of government. Such being the condition of the Christian world, the clergy necessarily became almost exclusively the teachers of letters, science, philosophy and political principles, as well as morals and religion; and *thereby they formed, fashioned and moulded, after their own views and wishes, the minds and opinions of youth; and in a great measure formed and controlled public opinion; and literally thought for the people, and infused their opinions into them.* The schools and the pulpit were then much more efficient engines of power than they are now; in-as-much as they were then the principal means of disseminating opinions of all kinds, political and philosophical, as well as moral and religious; they accomplished what is now done by the press in all Protestant countries, and wherever freedom of opinion is tolerated.

As the clergy were politicians and teachers, as well as ministers of the gospel, the dividing line between religion and politics, between morals and philosophy, was lost, or overlooked; they forgot, or seemed to forget, that the sole object of divine revelation was to teach religion and morals, and not to teach politics, natural science, or philosophy; and thus the church gradually encroached upon the domain of philosophy and science, as well as of politics.

From the time of the Emperor Constantine to the Reformation, the church usurped the whole domain of metaphysics and philosophy, and held the human mind in subjection in nearly all matters of science, as well as in religion. The consequence was, that, scarcely any advancement was made in either science or the useful arts, except what was purely the result of accident. The art of making glass-windows, paper, chimneys, the mariner's compass, gun powder and fire-arms, watches and saw-mills, and of printing with moveable types, comprise nearly all the inventions of importance during this long interval of twelve centuries; all of which were made during the last four centuries of that period; and several of them were partially borrowed from, or suggested by, information obtained from the Mahomedans during the crusades. We have no evidence of any advancement or discovery in science or the useful arts during the first eight centuries of that period.

The church made more efforts to form, guide, restrain and control the opinions of men, than to influence their moral conduct. To promote obedience to the church, faith, and the observance of the ceremonies and ordinances of the church, with a view to an atonement for sin, appeared to be the principal end and aim of the clergy; and it seems as though many of them scarcely regarded the subject of morals as within the domain and objects of Christianity. Hence the shameless profligacy existing among the clergy as well as laity, during the whole of this period—the most of which is known by the significant appellation—THE DARK AGES. During several centuries heresy was more severely punished than vice or crime. Men charged and convicted of what were deemed heretical opinions in matters of religion, were burned at the stake, however moral, pious, and devoted, they might be; while the most shameful profligates were not even reproved for their vices, and the perpetrators of the most awful villanies and cold blooded murders, went unpunished, provided they had the means of buying the necessary indulgences, and paying the pecuniary penalties for their crimes.

During that period, the scriptures were in the possession of those only who were learned in the dead languages. They had never been translated into any of the modern languages. All the prayers and chants were made, and the ceremonies of the church conducted in a language unknown to the people ; and very little effort was made to instruct the people in morals, except by means of auricular confession. The whole system of fasts and penances, was to atone for sin. The monasteries and nunneries, and all the mendicant orders, were for the same purpose, to promote the piety, and effect an atonement for the sins of the inmates ; and not to promote either the morals, piety or intelligence of the great mass of the people.

The influence of the Catholic priesthood is brought to bear upon the lay members, mostly by means of auricular confession. John Rogers, Esq., a Counsellor at Law, of London, and a Friend, published a work some years since entitled Anti-Popery, which was reprinted in New York in 1841. The following is an abstract of his views, of the effects of Auricular Confession.

1st. It has lowered the people, and raised the priesthood ; thereby filling the former with degradation, and the latter with pride.

2d. By making the priesthood acquainted with the secrets of the lay members of the church, it has increased their power at the expense of the people ; it has made them strong and the people weak ; it has made them tyrannical lords, and the people fearful and trembling slaves.

3d. By acquainting the priesthood with the business and property of the people, and their intentions in bequeathing it, it has enabled them to exercise an improper influence over the minds of the people, and the sick in particular ; and to induce them to give large legacies and bequests to the church (that is to the clergy), at the cost of comparative poverty to the wife and children ; making the clergy opulent, and the wife and children indigent.

4th. It gives an unmarried clergy an opportunity to exercise a dangerous influence over females, and thereby enables them in many instances to triumph over their virtue.

5th. By giving the clergy great and undue influence with kings and ministers of state, it has enabled the former to wield an unhappy influence over the minds of the latter ; and to plan and promote political intrigue, to the ruin of many an individual and family ; to the injury of the state ; and to the dishonor of religion.

It has been estimated by many writers, that in the 12th and 13th centuries, more than one-third of all the property of all Catholic countries, including nearly all Europe, was held by the clergy and the monks. This fact strongly confirms the third position taken by Mr. Rogers, as before stated.

How can the church, during the dark ages, be regarded otherwise than as a system of ecclesiastical government, devised to enable the Pope, Cardinals and Bishops to mould the minds, form the opinions, and govern the people ?

When Galileo taught in Italy the Copernican system of Astronomy, as late as the year 1633, it was decided by the POPE and a COUNCIL OF CATHOLIC CARDINALS AND BISHOPS, "that to maintain the sun to be immovable, and without local motion in the centre of the solar system, is an *absurd proposition—false in philosophy*, HERETICAL *in religion*, and CONTRARY TO THE TESTIMONY OF SCRIPTURE ;" and he was consigned to the *dungeons* of the INQUISITION, and compelled to recant and abjure his opinions, in order to save his life.

Mr. Ranke, in his History of the Popes, in treating of the intellectual tendency of the age from the year 1572 to 1590, says, "Philosophy and science in general, now passed through a very important epoch. After the genuine Aristotle had been restored, men began in philosophy too (as well as in other departments, and with other ancient writers) to cast themselves loose from his authority, and to enter upon a free investigation of the highest problems. It was not in the nature of things, that the church should favor this tendency, SHE HERSELF HAD PRESCRIBED THE HIGHEST PRINCIPLES IN A MANNER THAT FORBADE ALL DOUBT. Now, whereas, Aristotle's adherents had frequently avowed opinions at variance with the church, savoring of naturalism, something similar might be apprehended on the part of his opponents. They wished, as one of them expressed himself, to compare the dogmas of the existing race of teachers with God's original handwriting, the world and nature ; a project, the issue of which could not be foreseen, though whether it led to discoveries or to errors, it could not fail to be highly perilous ; THE CHURCH, THEREFORE, SET ITS VETO UPON IT.

"Telesius, though he never ventured beyond the strict domain of science, was nevertheless all his life CONFINED TO HIS LITTLE NATIVE TOWN ; CAMPANELLEA WAS FOR EVER TO LIVE AN EXILE, AND FINALLY TO ENDURE THE TORTURE ; the most profound of them all, Giordano Bruno, a true philosopher, after many persecutions and long wanderings, fell at last under the censure of the Inquisition, was arrested, carried to Rome, and SENTENCED TO BE BURNED, NOT ONLY AS A HERETIC, BUT AS A HERESIARCH, who had written some things affecting religion, and that were not seemly. He was charged with having composed diverse books, in which, besides *praising not a little the Queen of England, and other heretical sovereigns*, he had written things concerning religion which were not becoming, even though he spoke philosophically. After such examples, where was the man who would venture upon the free exercise of his understanding !"

"The investigations of physics and of natural history, were in those times almost inseparably connected with those of philosophy. The whole system of opinion that had hitherto prevailed, was called in question. In fact, the Italians of that epoch manifested a grand tendency to searching thought, to vigorous prosecution of truth, and lofty forecasting speculation. Who can say at what they might have arrived! But the *Church marked out a line for them, that they were not to overstep. Woe to him who ventured beyond it.*"

It was the Christian clergy of Europe who conceived and matured the doctrine of the divine right of kings and princes, and the duty of absolute submission on the part of the people. This tyrannical and despotic doctrine was not borrowed from ancient Rome, for the Roman Emperors as well as the Popes were elected, and were not hereditary. It is the work of the clergy of a comparatively modern period; and as late as the year 1682, "the University of Oxford in England, adopted it, and ordered the political works of Buchanan, Milton, and Baxter, to be publicly burned in the court of the schools."*

Since the commencement of the present century, the truths discovered and taught by geologists in relation to the creation of the world, were thought by many of even the Protestant clergy, to be contrary to the Bible, and therefore impious, and rank infidelity; and had it not been for the progress of intelligence, freedom, and toleration of opinion, during the last century and a half, and if the same spirit had prevailed that was predominant in the colony of Massachusetts in the 17th century, it is by no means certain that the geologists would not have been compelled to retract and renounce their opinions, or be banished, even in this 19th century.

Such is the restraining and depressing influence which the clergy have exercised over the progress of physical science! Such have been the effects of religious opinions, honestly and sincerely entertained by many devoted disciples of the Christian religion, in exciting a spirit of intolerance and persecution! This tendency to restrain, confine and control the human mind by means of the decisions of synods and councils, creeds, confessions, and forms, commenced as early as the third century, and continued to increase until the time of the crusades, when it was probably at its height; but it did not diminish very sensibly, until after the invention of the art of printing, and the reformation, commenced by Martin Luther in the 16th century. What an immense effect this tendency of the church, (to restrain and

[* See Macaulay's History of England, Chap. I and II.]

control the human mind,) together with religious schisms and persecutions, must have had on the spirit of the Roman people, in producing the decline of the Roman power and empire; and preparing it for the yoke of the barbarians in the west and north, and of the Saracens in the south!

After the victory of Augustus Cæsar over Mark Antony at Actium, he became nearly absolute master of the whole Roman world, and from that time forward, to the end of his long reign, the Roman people increased in number, improvements and wealth, as rapidly as during any period of the republic. They continued to improve during the first two centuries and a half of the empire, after they had lost their civil liberties, while the people still enjoyed their religious freedom. But after the union of Church and State under Constantine in the fourth century, and the attempt was made to establish religious creeds and doctrines by law, to silence and punish what was deemed heresy, and thus restrain the human mind, and limit its inquiries, the public mind soon sunk into a sort of lethargy, from which it did not recover until the reformation in the sixteenth century.

Mr. Macaulay describes the condition of the Roman Empire during its decline, when subject to the despotism of Church and State united, as having schools in which nothing was taught, but what had been known for ages; a polished society, in which a most elaborate system of jurisprudence was established, in which the arts of luxury were well understood—in which the works of the great ancient writers were preserved and studied—and which existed for nearly a thousand years, without making one great discovery in science, or producing one book which is read by any but curious inquirers. The human mind had fallen into a state of stupefaction, which he likens to the condition of the people of China; where, during many centuries, nothing has been learned or unlearned; where government, education, and the whole system of life, are in accordance with set forms and precedents, and appear like matters of ceremony.

Such is substantially the intellectual condition of the people of Russia, and of Catholic and Mahomedan countries at the present day; and such has ever been the intellectual condition of the people in all countries and in all ages, where their education has been controlled by an absolute monarch, or an ecclesiastical hierarchy. Nearly all the activity of the human mind among such a people is produced by a state of war; and all the improvements made by them, are by means of borrowing from, and copying, the inventions and improvements of other nations.

Nearly all the inventions, valuable discoveries, and improvements made among ancient nations, were made by manufacturing and commercial states, where Polytheism prevailed, and whose institutions were more or less popular in their character; where the human mind enjoyed perfect freedom of opinion, and was stimulated by commerce, and a mechanical spirit.

Every valuable invention, discovery and improvement, made during the last three centuries and a half, has been made in Protestant communities, where the spirit of Protestantism prevailed more or less; and not one, that I am aware of, has originated where the human mind has been subject to Catholicism, Mahomedanism, Brahmanism, or any other system of ecclesiastical despotism. The same may be said of jurisprudence, government and science, as well as the useful arts: advances have been made in them only where the human mind has been comparatively free, and unshackled, by either monarchical, ecclesiastical, feudal, or military despotism.

In the early stages of civilization, man must commence his industry in ignorance; and until he acquires some knowledge of the sciences to aid and guide him, he soon attains the end, and utmost limits of his progress. It is only by studying and yielding to the guidances of science, that he can make any considerable advancement. As he discovers the principles of natural science and applies them more and more to industry and the useful arts, he makes his labor more and more productive, and thereby improves his condition.

Physical science is necessary to direct all the operations of mining, and working in the metals; and the use of the metals, together with mechanical philosophy, lie at the foundation of mechanism; which is the great main-spring and chief instrument of agriculture, and of that kind of productive industry, which prepares all raw materials for use and for commerce. I am not aware that any temporal prince or sovereign, however despotic and absolute his power, ever attempted to prevent or check the prosecution of physical science, or its dissemination among the people, under any pretence whatever. But on the contrary, it has been generally encouraged by sovereigns in all ages of the world, as a means of increasing the prosperity of their people, and their own power, and they have exhibited their fears only of political and moral science. *The Catholic clergy were the first, in the order of time, to restrain the human mind from the prosecution of new discoveries in natural science, under pretence that the new opinions propagated were contrary to scripture, and therefore impious and heretical.*

Ancient Egypt, Assyria, Greece, Tyre, Carthage, and Rome, all flourished under the free toleration of Polytheism; and Rome began to decline as soon as the religious persecutions commenced, after the church became the established religion, and was united with the state, in the 4th century.

Ancient Egypt, Assyria, Persia, and modern China, as well as Russia and Prussia, and many other countries, have all improved and increased in population, wealth, productive industry and power, under governments nearly or quite absolute and despotic. Peter the Great of Russia, by introducing ship building and many other useful arts and branches of mechanism into his dominions, and encouraging the mechanic arts, manufactures, mining, navigation and commerce, raised his people from semi-barbarism, and laid the foundation of the improvement, civilization, and the present power and great increase in population and wealth of the nation.

Much of the ancient world flourished under Polytheism, and many portions of the modern world have flourished under Protestantism ; but I apprehend that *no instance can be found upon the pages of history, where any people, whose minds were moulded, formed, restrained and controlled by an ecclesiastical hierarchy of any kind, have ever increased very rapidly, either in numbers, science, improvements, wealth, or physical comforts.* Whether we look to the influence of the religious castes and the hierarchy of India; to Mahometan countries during the last twelve centuries; to Europe, while it was subject to the spiritual dominion of the church, acting in concert with temporal governments from the beginning of the 4th to the middle of the 16th century ; or to Italy, Spain, Portugal, Mexico and South America at the present day, the picture in these particulars, is substantially the same ; the paralyzing effects of ecclesiastical dominion appear to be similar in all countries subject to it, and under all creeds and religious systems.

SEC. 2. *Supposed end and object of the Scriptures, of Christianity, and of Church Government.*

What it may be asked, can be inferred from all this ? Can it be inferred that Christianity itself is an evil ? Certainly not ; but that *the evil results from the union of temporal and spiritual power in the same person or persons ; and that church government should be wholly disconnected from the civil and political power of State.* I cannot doubt that one of the ends and purposes of Christianity, is to enlighten, moralize, and civilize mankind ; and hence we have a written word, a preached gospel, and organized churches, with their rules of moral discipline ; but their power to punish should be confined to reproofs, censures, and excommunication from the church as members (as is the case in the United States), without any power to touch the property of their members, or to restrain, or inflict any punishment whatever upon their persons.

And in matters of education, as the clergy in Protestant as well as Catholic countries are almost the only teachers in colleges and the higher seminaries of learning, they should bear in mind, that the records of divine revelation were not given to teach philosophy, politics, or natural science, but religion and morals; and that when they teach philosophy and science, whether physical or metaphysical, they should teach them as matters of human reason, and not as things of divine revelation; as matters of individual opinion, which may or may not be correct, and not as religious tenets; they should teach them as humble individuals, liable to err, and not as Vicars of Christ, claiming to be infallible; they should address the understanding, and endeavor to convince the judgment, and not alarm the fears by denunciations of heresy, or threats of the Inquisition; and finally, they should inculcate a spirit of free enquiry, and not one of absolute submission to authority.

It should be remembered that divine revelation as contained in the scriptures, consists entirely of language, which was either communicated to the writers by the Deity, or else the matters to which the language relates, was communicated by inspiration, and was clothed in words by the writers, the prophets, and apostles; the words are but representatives of acts, principles, and things, which have, or have had a real existence; that words have no real meaning unless they truly represent acts, principles, and things to which they are applied; that man is so constituted, that he can learn only through the medium of the senses, the understanding, or divine inspiration; that it is impossible in the nature of things for man to understand words, or the language of the scripture, unless he has a knowledge of the things which the words represent; and hence it would seem to be impossible even for the Deity, to teach man without inspiration, and by revelation, or words only, the mysteries of nature and of physical and metaphysical science; and that he could do so only by inspiring him with a knowledge of the things which the words represent; that is, by teaching those things to him in detail, by exhibiting to his senses or to his understanding, by inspiration, all the elementary atoms of matter, and their various properties, powers, attractions, and combinations, and showing the application of the words and language to them; and thus teaching him all the details of chemistry, natural philosophy, astronomy, physiology, botany, geology, and metaphysics. It is, therefore, impossible for man to understand the language even of scripture, explaining the mode of creation, and the essence and mode of existence of the Deity, and of the things and beings in the world of spirits; because he cannot, except by means of divine inspiration, understand the subject matter which the language represents. Hence we may conclude, that the sole object of divine revelation was to teach man such general truths as he is capable of understanding; such as the existence, and some of the principal attributes of a Supreme Omniscient, and Omnipotent Creator, of the immortality of the soul, a future life and world, and his moral and religious duties in this world. If these views are correct, the Scriptures cannot be relied on to disprove any theory or system of philosophy or science, either physical or metaphysical, which recognizes the existence of the Supreme Being, and the immortality of the soul.

The Scriptures were never intended to teach or explain, the principles of natural science, and cannot be relied upon for that purpose; but on the contrary, the discoveries and truths of natural science, may often be used advantageously, to explain the general and mysterious truths announced in the holy scriptures.

These illustrations are intended to show how the clergy have often travelled out of the path of their duty, in denouncing discoveries in science as contrary to Scripture; and what evils have been the consequence.

Sec. 3. *Origin and progress of Ecclesiastical Government.*

The patriarchal system of government grew up among all the pastoral nations of western Asia, and among the Israelites also, from the earliest period of history. Each great family of the Israelites had its head, and each tribe its prince or leader, chosen for life out of the several heads of the families it contained. These were called the Elders of Israel, and together with judges, officers, and high priests of the several tribes, comprised the great national councils of the Israelites. Our Saviour prescribed no definite form of church government to his followers (at least no form is prescribed in the New Testament); and in as much as the church recognized the authority of the Old Testament, as well as the New, they very naturally adopted in substance, the system of government of the Jewish church. Each church was substantially independent of every other, during the first century and an half after the Christian era; the people had a voice in the election of bishops, presbyters or priests, and deacons; yet the government of the churches, legislative, executive, and judicial, was mostly exercised by the clergy, the mass of the people having very little participation in it. After the middle of the second century, the system of government was for several centuries an ecclesiastical aristocracy; nearly all its powers were exercised by the bishops, and by Synods and Councils of the Bishops and higher orders of the clergy; but it finally degenerated into an absolute monarchy, and the whole power vested in the Pope.

This was the natural and necessary consequence of the ignorance of the great mass of the people, before the invention of the art of printing, and the general diffusion of learning and intelligence, by means of common schools and the press. If the ignorant masses of those days had participated in the affairs of church government, it might have led to confusion, anarchy, and violence, equal to those of Athens, and of Rome in the time of the republic. The government of the Jewish church was a clerical aristocracy, and the Christian church fell into substantially the same form; which was the best adapted to the condition of the civilized world, and the ignorance of the great mass of mankind at that age, otherwise it would not have been adopted; but the simple fact that no form of government was authoritatively prescribed for the church, is evidence that no one form was fitted for, or should be adopted by, the church, in all countries, and in all subsequent ages and conditions of intelligence among the people.

SEC. 4. *Government of Protestant churches.*

That religious feelings and propensities have been seized upon by priests, rulers, and ambitious aspirants to power, perverted from their proper end and object, and converted into the most powerful and effective means of enslaving mankind, is proven by the history, during the last twelve centuries, of almost all the nations of the earth, Christian and Pagan, as well as Mahometan.

It is not my intention to discuss the doctrines, religious principles, morals, ceremonies or usages of the Catholic church, or of any other church; but simply to state the leading features of ecclesiastical government, peculiar to that and other churches, in order to deduce some conclusions of their probable effects upon the general policy, and upon the civil and political governments, and civilization, of the nations of the earth. As a general rule, which may admit of some few exceptions, it may be said that, there is no necessary connection between the great body of doctrines, creeds, religious principles, and ceremonies of a church, and its form of ecclesiastical government. The government of churches may be either purely monarchical, aristocratic, or democratic, or a mixture of all three of these forms, or any two of them, and two churches may adopt different forms of government, and still profess identically the same doctrine and religious principles. This is evident from the circumstance, that the government of the Congregational and Baptist churches in all their departments, are pure democracies; while the government of every other Protestant church, is more or less leavened with the principles of aristocracy; not hereditary aristocracy, but the aristocracy of official station; an elective aristocracy; not elected for a year, or two years, but in many cases for life, or during good behavior.

The government of the Methodist Episcopal Church is a clerical aristocracy; all the branches of its government, elective, legislative, executive and judicial, being vested in the clergy. But as the clergy are comparatively poor, are removed from place to place frequently, generally have families, are constantly mingling with the people, and perfectly dependent upon them for the means of support, they never can have much *esprit de corps*, nor can their influence over the people ever become dangerous to civil liberty. This form of church government appears to be the nearest to that of the primitive church of the first and second centuries, of any now existing; and it is perhaps better adapted than any other, to secure order and harmony in the church, where the mass of the people have a very limited education. The assemblies of the Episcopal church of the United States consist of two separate houses; a house of bishops, and one intended to be composed equally of clerical and lay delegates, chosen by the people. This gives the church great stability. The assemblies of the Presbyterian, and most other Protestant churches, are composed of clerical and lay delegates, like that of the house of delegates of the Episcopal church. These churches seem better adapted than the Baptist, Methodist, Congregational and Catholic, to the condition of a mixed population, composed of many talented and well educated people, and great numbers whose minds are uncultivated —the former not being generally willing to submit to the democratic spirit of the majority on the one hand, nor to a clerical aristocracy on the other. In Catholic countries, the educated classes look with but little respect upon the popish ceremonies, and regard the church only as a useful engine to govern the laboring classes.

The Episcopal Hierarchy of England, is very different from the government of the Episcopal church of the United States. While the latter, and all the Protestant churches, have the spirit, and much of the forms of republicanism; the former retains much of the oppressive spirit of Popery; and is the mere half-way house between Popery and Protestantism.

SEC. 5. *On the Government of the Roman Church; its form and character.*

The government of the Roman Catholic church is an elective monarchy, based on an aristocracy, elected or appointed for life by the monarch; and they in turn elect his successor. The Pope is elected as the head of the church, as a monarch for life, by the college of Cardinals. When elected, he has almost supreme and absolute power over the church, legislative, elective, and judicial, as well as executive, and has no charter or constitution to limit his power; nothing but the general usages of the church to check or restrain him. Its laws he often changes without the aid of a council, and no general council can be convened without his order; and when assembled, he can veto all its proceedings, and prorogue it at pleasure. All the members of these councils, consist of cardinals and bishops appointed either by the Pope himself, or by his predecessors, and the people have no voice in the matter. No general council has been convened during many centuries, and all the legislation for the church, in the interval, has been by the Pope alone.

The Pope not only appoints the Cardinals, but all the Bishops, and higher orders of clergy throughout the church; not only in Europe, but in America. The bishops in their respective dioceses, select and train up young men for the ministry, and appoint and ordain all the lower orders of the clergy, send them wherever they please, to take charge of, and exercise ecclesiastical authority over the people, without consulting them, and without their consent; *and the priesthood claim and generally exercise the sole right, either by themselves or by their delegated agents, to instruct the people in all matters of education, in order to form and guide their opinions in all matters of morals and civil government, as well as in religion. And no effort has ever been made in any Catholic country, to educate the mass of the people, or any of the common classes, except some few selected by the priests, to be educated and trained for the ministry.* The whole of the zeal and exertions of the Bishops and Priests seem to be directed to train up young men for the priesthood, and to educate, mould the minds and views, and form the opinions of the noble and wealthy classes; who are to fill the learned professions, and the offices of the civil government; and to make agents and instruments of them, to manage and govern the people; and to leave the mass of the people in ignorance, that they may be the more easily directed and governed. There may be some exceptions to this in the United States, but it is true as a general rule.

Such are the general outlines of this stupendous fabric and machinery of ecclesiastical government, in which the people, including all the lay members of the church, have not the slightest participation. The papal power and government of Rome was founded entirely on usage and precedent; and under a very similar system to that of the common law and government of England, it was gradually expanding during a period of about ten centuries, before it became matured and perfected, and all the parts of its complicated machinery became adapted to each other, as they are at present. It has stood the shock of time, and the subversion of dynasties, and of nations, for more than twelve centuries; *and to secure uniformity, regularity and harmony in all its movements for centuries in succession; perfect submission in the people, and obedience to one directing head, it is perhaps the most perfect government that ever existed on earth.*

The college of cardinals by whom the Popes are elected, is a small body of men; only seventy in all; who have been educated as priests, gone through all the gradations of the priesthood, and been made cardinals by the pope at an advanced period in life; after their minds are matured by study, reflection, observation, and experience; after the soothing hand of time and the clerical discipline has cooled and exhausted their physical passions, and almost all sympathy for their kindred; and they have imbibed the *esprit de corps* of the priesthood, become absolutely devoted to it, and shown themselves men of a high order of intellectual capacity. They have generally elected one of their own number as Pope, and rarely elected one under sixty years of age. Pope Gregory XVI. was born September 18th, 1765; made a cardinal priest in March, 1826; and elected Pope, February 2d, 1831, in the 65th year of his age. In 1844, there were but 65 cardinals, and 5 vacancies; five of them were over 80 years old, 16 over 70 years old; 18 over 60 years old; 14 over 50 years old; and only 3 under 40 years of age. The church has also 12 Patriarchs, 684 Archbishops and Bishops, and several hundred thousand inferior clergy, all obedient to the direction of one head; a man of learning, maturity of mind, much experience and observation, and elected on account of his supposed superior talents, capacity, and devotion to the ecclesiastical polity of the church. No helpless child, no dissipated youth, and no person of feeble intellect ever obtains the papal crown, by hereditary right or otherwise. As the clergy are not allowed to marry, and have no legitimate children, or heirs whom they care anything about; the order of priesthood is their only heir; which increases their *esprit de corps*, strengthens the bond of union among them, makes them more devoted to their order, and rapidly dries up all feelings of sympathy for their kindred, and for the whole body of the people.

Such is the system of ecclesiastical polity, without one popular feature in it, which holds dominion over the minds of 160,000,000 of inhabitants; the great body of whom seem to be studiously kept in profound ignorance, that they may be managed and governed the more easily; that their leaders may think for them, and save them the trouble of thinking for themselves. It is not strange that such a combination of learning and talent, all obedient to one man, acting in concert, operating upon the hopes and fears of the mass of the people, and wielding their prejudices and passions at will, should enable the Pope to crown and dethrone kings at pleasure, and to require the proud monarchs of England and France to hold the stirrups of his saddle while he mounted his horse, as was done in the twelfth century.

It is claimed by the Papists, that Christ intended to establish, and did establish but one Church, to extend throughout the earth, as an Universal, or Catholic Church; that the Popes of Rome are successors of St. Peter, and invested as the vicars and vicegerents of Jesus Christ, with the supreme legislative, executive, judicial, and elective power over the whole church; that the government of the church is not only a monarchy, but an universal monarchy; and that the pope is not only absolutely *supreme*, but INFALLIBLE. It is insisted that infallibility necessarily results or arises from supremacy, or a right to make a final decision of every question, and from which there is no appeal; and that if any one had a right to say to the Pope that any of his decisions were erroneous, such person would have a right to disregard them;* which would destroy his supremacy. It is said the Pope judges, but cannot be judged.

On the subject of civil government, it is maintained, that man being necessarily associated, and necessarily governed, sovereignty and the powers of Government result directly from the nature of man, and not from the will or consent of the people; that sovereignty no more results from their will than society itself does; and hence the broad conclusion has been deduced, that Sovereigns do not depend on the choice, favor, or will of the people, but on the divine will, who has conferred the power on them on account of the necessity that man should be governed, and of the inability of mankind to govern themselves. This is the foundation of the doctrine of the legitimacy of Sovereigns, and of sovereignty; and of the DIVINE RIGHT of kings, as claimed in Europe for centuries. It also held that the people are in duty bound to submit to and obey passively the kings and emperors, their legitimate sovereigns, under all circumstances; that a monarch cannot forfeit his right to the throne; *and that no amount or continuance of oppression and tyranny can justify resistance or rebellion, in any case whatever.*

The following is a translation of an extract from the December number, 1844, of Mr. F. Berteau's "Revue Française," published in the city of New York, and exhibits in a clear light the character of the government of the Roman church. "It is a singular circumstance, *that the one of three (Gregoire VII., Saint François D'Assize, and St. Thomas D. Aquin) who ranked the highest and contributed most to the grandeur of the*

Church, owed this reputation to the employment of means, the least in harmony with the spirit of Christianity, that is to say, to the use of force, in its sense the most energetic and the most material. Gregory VII. founded the absolute power of the Popes, and consolidated, in this manner, the organization of the Church, by giving it the form of a monarchy, the most durable of all."

Again he says, " On ne peut s'empêcher d'en conclure, que dès le onziéme siécle du moins, le but de l'Englise fut la domination temporelle, bien plus qu'une suprematie purement spirituelle." That is to say, " One cannot avoid the conclusion, that from the eleventh century at least, the object of the Church was temporal dominion, much more than purely spiritual supremacy."

"In effect, the constant object of the pursuits of Gregory VII. even when he was only the monk Hildebrand, *was the subjection of the civil power to the authority of the Pope. He contemplated universal monarchy, with the sovereign pontiff for the supreme chief.*"

Perhaps it was at first with a view of pure ecclesiastical reform, in order to find a force capable of repressing the corruption, of which the clergy then afforded a deplorable example. But once engaged in the struggle, whether he was hurried on in his career by circumstances, or by ambition, he thought of nothing except to render the church of Rome all powerful, and to humble before it emperors and kings."

Such are the remarks of an intelligent French writer, and a friend to the Catholic church. The fact is well attested by many candid writers and historians, that the popes and great leaders of the church of Rome struggled during centuries for temporal dominion, as well as spiritual supremacy; to make the pope an universal monarch, temporal as well as spiritual; and it is probable that they did not give up this object, until they were humbled by the French revolution, and the power of Napoleon.

Not only the pope, but all the Catholic priesthood claimed perfect exemption from any subjection to the civil power. They insisted that the clergy could be tried only by the Church, that is, by brother members of the clerical profession, and could not be tried even for the highest crimes, such as murder, arson, &c., by the civil courts. They succeeded in carrying this doctrine into practice; and even in England, the plea of a criminal, charged with a crime of the highest character, that he was a clergyman, if true, was treated as a valid plea in abatement; and the culprit was discharged, to be tried, and perhaps only reprimanded by his brethren of the clergy. Such was the supremacy they gained over the civil government and laws throughout Europe; *and such the influence, like a spell of enchantment over the popular mind, that they not only thought for the mass of the people, and moulded their minds, views, and opinions according to their own wishes, and fitted them to submit quietly to the clerical yoke, but by enslaving their minds, they took away from them all desire for freedom and independence.*

It was not the object of the pope and clergy to enslave and tyrannize over the persons and property of their votaries by means of force; but to mould their minds and opinions in such a manner as to make them perfectly submissive, and capable of being led by advice and persuasion wherever, and in whatever manner they desired; force was however resorted to, when persuasion failed, and the Inquisition was finally devised, as the most effectual means of applying force, and accomplishing the object.

If meekness, humility, patience, and quiet submission to authority, are Christian virtues, the virtues of the Catholic population in the aggregate, are in these particulars greater than those of the Protestants. This remark, however, does not apply to the Catholics of Ireland, who have been oppressed and schooled in agitation and rebellion for centuries.

The mental passions of avarice, and ambition for power and display, are much the strongest and most predominant among the educated classes in all countries; and as education in Catholic countries is mostly confined to the clergy, nobility, and wealthy, these passions have but little influence upon the mass of the people who are poor, ignorant, and humble; but in Protestant countries, and more particularly in Scotland, New England, New York, and wherever all the people have a common school education, this serves as the leaven, and exciting cause to these passions, which pervade nearly the whole community. And so predominant are these passions in some communities, that Mammon, Fashion, and Power, are seemingly the principal deities which are worshipped. Hence we should not conclude that ignorance is an unmixed evil, nor knowledge, of itself, a pure and unalloyed good; for almost every community affords some striking examples, that learning often proves rather a curse than a blessing, unless moral education goes hand in hand with intellectual cultivation.

Such in the main are the doctrines of the Catholic church upon the subject of ecclesiastical and civil government, as well in the 19th, as from the 12th to the 16th century; and such have been their effects. Hence the pope, and higher orders of the priesthood of this church, have generally been the allies of kings in their contests with the people; hence they have been, and are at this day, the main support and pillars of the most absolute monarchies of Europe; and hence the anxiety of Napoleon to re-establish the Catholic church in France, and to induce the Pope to remove to Paris, in order to make the Church, the pope, and the Catholic priesthood, the chief props and pillars of his throne, next to the sword in importance.

The popes generally supported the kings of Europe in their claims to absolute power, in their struggles with the barons. The Pope absolved King John of England from his oath to observe and faithfully maintain *Magna Charta;* and also absolved Henry III. of England from a like oath, to observe and maintain the OXFORD ARTICLES, adopted in 1258, to reform the government, and restrain the absolute power of the King.*

It should be remarked, however, that Catholics bred in the United States, constantly mingling with Protestants, surrounded by the free institutions and free spirit of Protestantism, imbibe the spirit of free inquiry, and become partially Protestantized. The spirit and influence of the Catholic church and clergy are very different in the United States, and very different also (since the French Revolution of 1789) in France, Belgium, Germany, and Switzerland, from what they are in Spain, Portugal, Italy, Mexico, and South America.

SEC. 6. *Character and usages of the early Christians, and the changes which they underwent.*

As remarked by Gibbon, "The Christians (even prior to the time of the Emperor Constantine,) formed a numerous and disciplined society; and the jurisdiction of their laws and magistrates was strictly exercised over the minds of the faithful. The loose wanderings of the imagination were gradually confined by creeds and confessions; the freedom of private judgment submitted to the public wisdom of Synods and Councils; the authority of a theologian was determined by his ecclesiastical rank; and the episcopal successors of the apostles inflicted the censure of the church on those who deviated from the orthodox faith."

All this might be necessary before the invention of printing; when the expenses of obtaining books copied by hand were so great, that none but the wealthy and noble could procure them, or educate their children; when the middling classes as well as the poor were not only illiterate, and incapable of reading the holy Scriptures, or any other books, but unable to obtain them to read; when nearly all instruction was oral, by preaching, addresses and public lectures, or reading the Scriptures by the priests; when a moderate degree of knowledge of the Scriptures could be obtained only by a course of studies for years, and was mostly

* Vide M. Guizot's Essais sur l'Histoire de France, 310 and 341, and Sismondi's France, 291, 293, and 299, VOL V.

confined to the priesthood; when the people generally were too ignorant to be capable of reasoning much, and were required to have faith without proofs, and mental conviction of the great truths of the Bible, without sufficient learning and capacity to examine and understand the force and effect of the evidences upon which those truths are founded. In this mode, doctrines and usages not enjoined by the Scriptures, but which arose from the condition and ignorance of the people, have been sought to be perpetuated by the Pope and clergy of the Catholic church—as a means of keeping the laity in subjection, and in spiritual bondage, for centuries after the art of printing and the dissemination of learning have removed the causes upon which such doctrine and usages were founded.

Mr. Gibbon again remarks, that "Faithful to the doctrine of the apostle, who in the reign of Nero had preached the duty of unconditional submission, the Christians of the three first centuries preserved their consciences pure and innocent of the guilt of secret conspiracy, or open rebellion." While they experienced the rigor of persecution, they never sought revenge, or retaliation of any kind, but when one cheek was smote, they turned the other also. During all this period, the discipline of the church, and its government and treatment of its own members was equally mild and in accordance with the true spirit of Christianity. No physical punishment was inflicted; and none of any kind, except to reprove, inflict the censures of the church, and to expel disobedient and refractory members. After the conversion to Christianity of the Emperor Constantine, in the fourth century, and the union of church and state, and the church was raised from a weak and defenceless condition to great power, and became an arm of the government, it developed a new principle, not contained in the scriptures, nor consistent with the spirit of Christianity; that is, that the church had the power to inflict physical punishments, and even to take life, in order to check heresy, as well as to restrain the disobedience of its members. It was but a short time before the factions in the church became nearly as ambitious, turbulent, violent, persecuting and blood-thirsty, in accomplishing their purposes, as the factions of Rome were, in the days of Marius, Sylla, Mark Antony, and Augustus Cæsar.

Gibbon says (in the XXVII. and XXVIII. chapters of the Decline and Fall of the Roman Empire), that the Emperor Theodosius promulgated no less than fifteen severe edicts against the heretics and pagans, in the space of fifteen years, from A.D. 380 to 395. These edicts were directed first against any and all heretical preachers as well as pagan priests, who should presume to teach their respective tenets and opinions; secondly, against any and all persons who should dare to confer, receive, or promote an heretical ordination: *and it was reasonably expected, that if the race of pastors could be extinguished, their helpless flocks would be compelled, by ignorance and want of teachers and leaders, to return within the pale of the Catholic church.* Thirdly, against every sort of assembly, meeting, convention, conference or collection of persons, assembled for religious exercises, or worship, of any kind, not in accordance with the prescribed orthodox faith of the Catholic church. And fourthly, against pagan sacrifices, and practices of divination. The edicts were generally enforced by pecuniary penalties and forfeitures; sometimes by exile, and by death in but few cases. Certain lay-heretics were excommunicated by the church, and subjected to some civil disabilities; none of the edicts (according to Gibbon,) subjected laymen to punishment or the forfeiture of property, for entertaining heretical or pagan opinions, but for propagating their opinions, or assembling with others, for religious exercises and worship. He says (in chapter XXVIII.) while the imperial laws which prohibited the sacrifices and ceremonies of paganism were rigidly enforced, the palace, the schools, the army, and the senate, were filled with declared and devout pagans; and that they obtained without distinction, the civil and military honors of the empire.

Sec. 7. *Origin and character of Mahometanism, and of the Popish Inquisition.*

Though it is true, that as early as the fourth century, bishops of the church were charged, tried and convicted of heresy, and deposed from their clerical rank and station, and in some instances exiled, and in others put to death; yet I am not aware that Christian churches were ever in the habit of inflicting physical punishments on laymen, on account of their opinions only, prior to the establishment of the Inquisition. It is not improbable, however, that these tyrannical laws, and the practice under them in Christian countries, suggested to Mahomet the first idea of propagating his religion by the sword; they probably led the way, and suggested the idea of the Inquisition; which was first established by the pope in the south of France, about the year 1204, to root out and suppress what was deemed the heresies of the Albigenses.

Mahometanism (the greatest scourge and curse which ever afflicted the human family,) arose in the seventh century. Mahomet and his disciples and successors taught the two most pernicious principles, the most dangerous and destructive to morals and civilization, ever inculcated upon this earth; the first, that their religious doctrines should be propagated and extended by the power of the sword; the second, that the true church were not bound to keep faith, or any engagements with heretics. As the Mahometans, acting upon these vile principles, extended their conquests west, and had many bloody battles with the Christian nations of Europe, overrun the greater part of Spain, threatened and endangered the whole of Christendom, and finally overturned the eastern Roman empire, the Christians felt it necessary to adopt some portion of their treacherous and pernicious policy, in order to be able to meet and combat them with their own weapons.

The establishment of the Inquisition in the 13th century, appears to have been the first general and systematic attempt of the Christian church to propagate their doctrines and creeds by force; by using physical punishment to compel laymen to renounce their religious opinions which were not in accordance with those of the church, and to make a public profession of the orthodox opinions of the day. Many centuries previously, Mahomet had taught his followers the duty of extirpating idolatry, and propagating their doctrines and creeds by force, and of putting to the sword all persons in their power who would not receive and adopt them, or pay tribute as vassals.

The supreme court of Inquisition was established in Spain in 1478; and Dr. Morse says in his Geography (published in 1793), that, "besides the supreme court of Inquisition at Madrid, there are eighteen inferior tribunals in the several provinces of the monarchy, which entertain a numerous host of spies, or familiars, amounting to about 20,000 persons, who, on the slightest suspicion of heresy, denounce persons of every condition, sex and age."

It is estimated in Brande's Encyclopædia of Science and Art, that from the time of the establishment of the Inquisition in Spain, until it was abolished by Napoleon in 1808, no less than 340,000 persons had been punished by those tribunals in that country, of whom nearly 32,000 were burnt. Courts of Inquisition were also established in several of the states of Italy, in Portugal, and some other countries.

In the 14th century, statutes were enacted in England, authorizing the apprehension, trial, and execution by the barbarous practice of burning, of all persons convicted of heresy in matters of religion. These and similar statutes were in force in England for about two centuries; and during the short but bloody reign of Queen Mary, several hundred persons were burned in pursuance of them. Such were the intolerant opinions then prevailing, in all Catholic, as well as Mahometan countries.

The supreme ecclesiastical, civil, and military power was vested in Mahomet during his lifetime, and in his successors, the

Caliphs, after his death. The Koran inculcates but one single virtue, that of abstinence from the use of wine and intoxicating drinks; and allows the followers of the prophet four wives, as many concubines as they can support, and the indulgence of almost every other appetite of the flesh, and of every passion of a corrupt and ambitious mind. They were ordered to propagate his doctrines with the sword; allowed to plunder all heretics, and every country which they could subjugate; and the pleasures of a sensual paradise were promised to all his devoted followers, and to all who should die or be slain in attempting to spread his religious doctrines. The ambition for power, military glory, and conquest, of his followers, as well as their avarice, and their licentious appetites and passions, were all gratified by their wars, conquests, and the opportunities afforded for plunder, and to take captives. It is not at all wonderful, that such a system of religion, and of civil and military government united, should be rapidly extended, and more particularly in warm climates, where the appetites are strong, and the passions ardent.

The union of church and state under the Emperor Constantine—the spirit of intolerance produced by it—the attempt to establish by law, and to enforce uniformity of opinion and religious worship; and the practice of deposing and banishing bishops for alleged heresy; excited faction, insurrections, mobs, murders, and terrible massacres, by the multitude. Mahometanism overrun about half of the Christian world, and these dissensions among Christians are assigned by Mosheim in his Ecclesiastical History, as the principal cause of its progress. He says, "To these causes of the progress of Mahometanism, we may add the bitter dissensions and cruel animosities that reigned among the Christian sects, particularly the Greeks, Nestorians, Eutychians, and Monophysites; dissensions that filled a great part of the east with carnage, assassinations, and such detestable enormities, as rendered the very name of Christianity odious to many. We might add here, that the Monophysites and Nestorians, full of resentment against the Greeks, from whom they had suffered the bitterest and most injurious treatment, assisted the Arabians in the conquest of several provinces, into which the religion of Mahomet was afterwards introduced."*

SEC. 8. *On Fatalism, and its influence on the Mahometan character.*

The doctrines of fatalism inculcated by the Koran, had also a very great effect upon the minds of the followers of the prophet, and increased their military power, by inspiring them with the

* See Rees and also Dobson's Encyclopædia, title, Mahometanism.

ardor and zeal of fanaticism. The doctrine of fatalism, fate or destiny, as generally understood, implies that the operations of the human mind, as well as the action and changes of all material things, are governed by a chain of natural causes, which act with perfect uniformity, and produce effects which follow each other from absolute necessity; and that no human being can interrupt their connection, or avert their effects. It teaches that the human mind is utterly powerless, and can neither originate any action or idea, nor give any direction or guidance to its own action; but is entirely directed and governed by external causes operating upon it; and that every idea existing in the mind at any time, must have been suggested by some external cause. (See Sec. 8 of chap. I.) It thus inculcates the absolute necessity as well as duty of submission and obedience to every impulse of appetite, and to every idle thought, opinion, and passion, under the belief that they proceed from natural causes, from the fixed and uniform laws of God, or of fate, which cannot be resisted, and must be submitted to. As fatalists are inclined to follow all the impulses of passion and appetite, and all the idle thoughts and whims of the mind, as indications of fate which they cannot resist, they are not much inclined to daily labor, and to follow any regular industrial pursuit, for the reason that labor and industry are not in accordance with the passions and impulses of the mind. Such a process is too slow and tedious to be agreeable; the mind rejects it, and does not dwell upon it; and hence they do not often get the impression, that it is their fate to improve their condition by the toils of daily industry.

Wars, plunder, conquests, games of chance, gambling of every species, and sensual indulgences, are more generally suggested to the mind, because more exciting, than the drudgery of daily toil; and hence these pursuits enlisted the passions of the Mahometan fatalists, and they followed the impulse of these passions from a sense of duty, in some measure, as well as of necessity, believing them certain indications of the hand of fate, which they could not resist, and must obey. Hence they plunged into battle without any fear of danger, under the belief that they were subject to fate, and could not alter their destiny, or shorten their days by exposure to danger, and that if it was their fate to fall in battle, they should enjoy the pleasures of a sensual paradise.

Such feelings and principles of fanaticism had as much influence as any doctrines of the Koran upon the character, habits, and military success of the Mahometans. It made them fearless, fierce, and energetic soldiers, thirsting for plunder; but indolent, inert, quiet and inefficient citizens, content to live in idleness, upon the scanty means doled out to them by the hand of fate.

Hence they became successful warriors and conquerors; but in consequence of their indolence, every country which became subject to their dominion, soon languished, and declined in the arts, productive industry, and population; and since the Tartars and Turks gained the ascendency over the Saracens in the 14th and 15th centuries, they have exhibited a still greater degree of indolence, and an influence much more destructive and pernicious than the Arabs.

SEC. 9. *Origin and character of the sect of Mormons.*

If we turn our attention to the Mormons of our own country, we shall witness a people who profess to be governed by special revelations from the Deity, made from time to time, and by the operations of the Spirit, who have manifested in many respects a spirit very similar to that of the Mahometans; though much less honorable and honest, than has been generally exhibited by both Saracens and Turks.

Joe Smith, the prophet of Mormonism, before and when he commenced his impostures, resided at the village of Palmyra, in the county of Wayne and state of New York. He spent most of his time in bar-rooms, and was remarkable for nothing but indolence and scheming on a small scale. He had very little intelligence, was coarse in his manners, without expansion of mind, elevation of thought, or dignity of character; and finally became a drunkard.

About the year 1825 he obtained a manuscript, containing the reveries of a half-deranged clergyman. From this he manufactured the Mormon bible, and published it to the world, as containing a series of revelations made to him by the Deity. By this imposition, he deceived many persons, and formed the sect since known as Mormons.

The town or city of Nauvoo, in Illinois, was built by the Mormons. It became a den of adulterers and thieves, who emerged from the city, plundered the surrounding country, and on their return were secreted and protected by their brethren, and shielded from punishment. Many of them appeared to be deluded with the same religious fanaticism as the Mahometans, that it was right to plunder infidels and heretics.

They had been driven out of the state of Missouri, in consequence of their alleged misconduct and crimes, before they built Nauvoo; and the depredations charged upon them finally enraged the people of the vicinity to such a degree, that Joe Smith was killed by a mob in 1846, and they were driven out of the state of Illinois by force. It is to be hoped that their sufferings have taught them a salutary moral lesson, which may be of permanent use to them in their new homes in the desert.

The case of the Mormons is a memorable instance of the tendency of the human mind to superstition and to credulity in religious matters, even in this nineteenth century. Like Mahometanism, it is presented as an example of the impediments to the progress of civilization.

CHAPTER V.

ON THE MODE, MEANS AND INFLUENCES BY WHICH INDIVIDUALS AND NATIONS ARE GOVERNED—THE CAUSES AND CHIEF INSTRUMENTS OF DESPOTISM, AND OF FREEDOM AND INDEPENDENCE—THE DIFFERENT FORMS OF GOVERNMENT, THEIR ORIGIN AND EFFECTS—AND THE EFFECTS OF POLITICAL PARTIES, OF OUR MODE OF ELECTIONS, AND OF CERTAIN COMBINATIONS AND ASSOCIATIONS OF MEN.

SEC. 1. *On the mode and influences by which individuals and nations are governed.*

Governments are instituted to protect men's rights; among which are life, liberty, and property. Nations ever have been, and ever must be governed by and through, some of the following means and influences.—First of intellect and intelligence.—Secondly, of association and organization.—Thirdly, of usage, custom, and precedent; which may have been the result of circumstances, but were moulded into form by the first intellects of the country. Fourthly, of opinions and principles, which have been conceived and formed by the leading minds of the nation, though generally suggested by circumstances and self-interest.—Fifthly, by fear, superstition and prejudice. And lastly, by force.

Some suppose that nations are governed by physical force, by standing armies; but what is it that governs the armies, collects the means of their support, and uses them as the means of governing and oppressing the mass of the people? Did the British Queens, Elizabeth and Anne, and the present Queen Victoria, govern the army and navy of Great Britain by force? An army without an intellectual head to govern it, is always powerless, and soon crumbles to pieces.

In the common pursuits of life, the mass of mankind, whose minds are uncultivated, are governed mostly by imitation and habit; but in the more complicated affairs of government and religion, they are governed by custom, usage, public opinion, and the reasoning of the most active, energetic, talented and ambitious men of the state. Public opinion has been the most powerful agent in all ages, and all countries, in exercising dominion over the human mind. And how is public opinion formed? It partly arises from the customs, usages and institutions of the country; but is it not mostly originated by the leading minds and master spirits of the nation, who thus form as well as guide the public mind, and often introduce principles, which enable a class of men to lead and govern the mass of the people for centuries? Look at the principles of Confucius of China, of Zoroaster of Persia, of Aristotle and Lycurgus of Greece, of Mahomet of Arabia, and their effects in forming public opinion, and aiding certain classes in governing and keeping in subjection, the great mass of the people. Look also at the principles of legitimacy, of hereditary political power, which have been the principal agents in governing Europe, and subjecting the mass of the people to arbitrary power, and oppression for more than ten centuries. Look at the fact, that all the nations and people of the earth, until a comparatively recent period, were governed either by kings, military chieftains, priests, or by an aristocracy of some kind. All savage and barbarous tribes have been governed by chiefs or princes, usually elected for life, on account of their talents, or some superiority.

SEC. 2. *On the causes and instruments of despotism—and of liberty and independence.*

It has been often remarked, that the tendency of political power is to escape from the many to the few. This is literally true in all countries where the mass of the people are uneducated, and ignorant. But more properly speaking, power and property also escape from the simple, ignorant and indolent, to the cunning, the intelligent, and the industrious. Hence the ignorant and the indolent are generally poor, and their poverty arises from natural causes. By reason of their ignorance, they cannot make their labor very productive, nor can they make the best use of what they have; and they are often improvident also. They generally consume all their earnings, lay up nothing for the future, and thus accumulate no capital, and therefore necessarily remain poor. While *ecclesiastical governments and superstitions have been the principal instruments of despotism in all ages, ignorance has been the sole condition which has invited and led to it.* Even military despotism has never been very permanent, without the aid and support of an united priesthood.

It is impossible for an ignorant multitude to be guided by the reasoning, and the independent action of their own minds; and they must be, and are excited to action, and guided by leaders of more intelligence, talents and cunning than they themselves possess. Even Athens in the days of her republican glory, was in some measure an aristocracy; the right of suffrage and of citizenship being very limited, nearly all the laboring classes being slaves; a few leaders at all times controlled the republic; and in the days of Pericles, he ruled Athens with more power than half the kings of Europe possess at this day. The plebeians, or popular party of ancient Rome, in the days of the republic, were likewise governed by talented, ambitious, cunning party leaders, such as the Gracchi, Marius, Pompey, and Julius Cæsar, and not by the independent operations of their own minds.

But the adage, that the tendency of power is to escape from the many to the few, does not apply to states and countries where all the people enjoy the advantages of a common school education, and have learned to read and write, and the nature and use of numbers: where knowledge is universally diffused by means of the press, and by popular preaching in their mother tongue; and where the people are free in spirit, as well as in person, and enjoy the means, as well as the liberty, of reading and thinking for themselves. The intellects of such a people are always active; they are generally intelligent, ambitious, industrious, and enterprising; and their minds are filled with schemes and projects to raise themselves to distinction and wealth. Such a people can seldom be influenced by authority, or managed by party leaders, in either temporal or spiritual matters; but each one seems to be governed by the independent operations of his own mind, and relies upon his own judgment; and as he cannot perceive any defects in his own reasoning, he is apt to conceive that he can avoid the errors into which others have fallen, and that his intellect is superior to almost all others, until sad experience often teaches him his mistake, and the folly of his lofty ambition.

There is no danger of such a people being too much under the influence of leaders, but the tendency is to the contrary; they are apt to have too much confidence in themselves; and to pay too little heed to the opinions and experience of others, to the instructions of the aged, and the lessons of history. They are almost all too great to recognize the superiority of others, or to follow them as leaders. The only restraint upon individuals arises from public opinion, associations, and the laws of the country; and public opinion is nothing more than the general sense of the whole community, except so far as it may be perverted by associations, and party combinations. Such a people may therefore be truly said to govern themselves; in as much as each one helps to make the laws, and to form the public opinion, by which they are governed. *The only restraint upon their powers of self-government, arises from party combinations and associations, to form and control public opinion, and the elective franchise;* and such is the vicious organization of our elective system, the majority only of each election district being represented, and the minority entirely disfranchised, that men who spurn the dictation of party leaders, are compelled to submit to the dictation of party combinations, or run the hazard of defeating the objects they are most anxious to promote. In these party combinations, principle is frequently an obstacle to success, everything is controlled by management, bargain, intrigue, false professions, and promises; whereby talent and character are often overlooked, and second, third, and fourth rate men who are active, cunning politicians, elevated to place and power.

SEC. 3. *Democracy defined. It cannot be sustained in its purity, among a very ignorant people.*

A pure democracy in its strict sense, means a government in which all the adult males of the community have equal political rights, and equal political power, and participate equally in the practical business and administration of the government in all its branches, legislative, executive, and judicial. This is the case in the Baptist and Congregational Churches, where each distinct body of worshippers constitute an independent church and government; and being few in numbers, and the subject and proper jurisdiction of ecclesiastical government being very limited, such a system and form of government can be carried into effect; but it is utterly impracticable when applied to a state or a country. But if a representative democracy, instead of a pure democracy, is intended, and every one is to have equal political rights, and equal political power, in order to carry this principle into effect, as each man has the same right as his neighbor to hold office without any regard to character, or qualification, all officers should be elected by lot, as jurors are, and as many officers in Athens were, and not by choice and favoritism; and no man should be elected to, or hold office more than one year, until all his fellow citizens have had their turn, and the circle of rotation is completed. And in legislation, the representative should be bound in all cases by the will of the electors of his representative district, and *all laws should be a compound of the opinions and wills of all the electors of the state or nation; so that the opinions of each and every elector should have precisely the same amount of influence upon the legislation and government of the country.* This is the theory in its exact length and breadth, without detracting from, or adding to it, one jot or tittle.

This is a beautiful theory, and if all men were virtuous, possessed equal talents and equal learning, intelligence, and ability, or were inspired by the Deity with equal wisdom and goodness, it might be equally beautiful in practice as it is in theory. But let us look to such countries as Mexico and the South American Republics, where but a very small proportion, perhaps not a tenth part of the people can either read, write, or have a knowledge of numbers; and a much smaller number still, any accurate knowledge of history, law, or the science of government; and where the mass of the people are under the influence of the clergy, the great land-holders and men of wealth, and the military and civil officers of the government. How can an ignorant multitude who have no definite opinions upon matters of government, have an equal influence in legislation, and administering the government, with the educated and wealthy classes, who think for them, and control them? How can the laws of the country be a compound of the opinions of men who have no opinions on such subjects? If this is impossible, on what is based the democratic doctrine of instruction; of the right of constituents to instruct their representatives? Or is all this difficulty to be avoided by party combinations and party machinery, whereby party leaders in conventions and assemblies of the people, prepare and introduce resolutions, addresses, &c., &c., and have the people without understanding them, adopt them as their own?

These illustrations are sufficient to show, that it is impossible in the nature of things, for the mass of a people who are illiterate and ignorant, to have a real and substantial influence and participation in legislation, and the administration of the government; they may have an apparent and nominal participation, but a nominal one only. They may have a nominal power equal to that of the priesthood and the educated classes who form their opinions, but it cannot be real. How indispensably necessary, therefore, that in a republican form of government, all the people should have at least a common school education; have their minds improved and expanded by reading and general intelligence, so as to be able to think and judge for themselves. *Intellect, talent, cunning, activity and energy, ever have, and ever will govern the world: no matter what the form of government, the result will be the same, if the mass of the people are ignorant.*

Prior to the invention of the art of printing, and to the great protestant reformation, no government ever existed except that of Athens, which had even the forms of democracy; all mankind were subjected to the monarchical and aristocratic forms of government, or to combinations of the two, with some popular elements infused. Sparta had a mixed government, compounded of the elements of a military monarchy, and a military and landed aristocracy, slightly tinctured with democracy. The government of Athens was a compound of aristocracy and democracy, in which the greatest, most talented, and cunning leader or leaders, usually constituted either a dictator or an oligarchy. About four-fifths of the people of Sparta and Athens were slaves, destitute of all power, and divested of all civil rights. In this age of democratic equality and universal suffrage, it sounds very much like aristocracy to vest all the political power of the State in one fifth part of the adult males, as was the case in Athens.

SEC. 4. *Aristocracy defined, and the character and influence of the different classes stated.*

Let us analyze the term aristocracy, and see what are its characteristics. In speaking of the aristocracy, we usually mean a class of persons, possessed of powers, rank, or privileges, not possessed by the mass of the people. Any characteristic or quality, except mere physical strength or activity, which distinguishes an individual from, and by which he greatly excels, the mass of the community in which he resides, and which gives him rank and influence in society, is a mark of aristocracy; and it may be said that the cause of this superiority and influence constitutes the very essence of aristocracy itself. According to this view of the subject, it may be divided into the following classes: first, the aristocracy of official power and station, including military and naval officers; secondly, the great property holders, or heads of families of large possessions, who in ancient days in western Asia were called Patriarchs, at Rome Patricians, and in Europe during the middle ages Barons; those are the aristocracy of wealth: thirdly, the members of the learned professions, engineers, and professional teachers of the higher institutions of learning, constitute the aristocracy of order or profession: fourthly, men of great talents and wisdom, who wield a great influence over the public mind while in private stations, may be called the aristocracy of intellect; fifthly, the aristocracy of birth and hereditary rank: and sixthly, the aristocracy of fashion. Official power and station, talents, wealth, and scientific and professional knowledge, have, in every age and country, conferred on their possessors rank and influence; and elevated them above the body of the people. These several kinds of aristocracy seem to be natural and unavoidable, for they exist in every civilized country, let the form of government be whatever it may. In as much as wealth, by the laws of nature, descends from parents to children, the aristocracy of wealth is in some measure hereditary; but the idea of hereditary power and official station, as well as hereditary rank, seems to an American republican, like an absurdity

There may also be reckoned many subdivisions of aristocracy. *The officers of government may be divided into a civil and military aristocracy; and the possessors of wealth, into a landed or feudal, a commercial, a manufacturing, and a monied aristocracy.* Every species of aristocracy conferred by election or appointment, or acquired by the exertions of the individual, is an evidence of superior ability or acquirements. But persons who are cradled in luxury, bred in indolence, and acquire their rank and station by descent, without any exertion of their own, are generally proud, indolent, and inefficient; and often thoughtless, and devoted to frivolous amusements.

A military spirit, military enterprise, wars and conquests, tend to exercise all the intellectual and physical faculties of man; but unfortunately they foster the animal passions and appetites, and leave the moral faculties to languish and decline; while all his faculties are exerted to consume and destroy the products of industry, instead of increasing them. Wars exhaust a nation, by destroying human life, as well as consuming, dissipating, and destroying the fruits of industry; and thus they have a three fold tendency, to retard the progress of improvement and civilization, and to injure and degrade the human family. The increased wealth of Rome under the republic, during several centuries, arose mostly from conquest and plunder; but when the policy of the government was changed by Augustus Cæsar after the battle of Actium, and the attention of the people was turned from war, conquest and plunder, to the useful arts, and productive industry, the Roman people, during the two succeeding centuries, increased in numbers, comforts, and wealth, under a monarchy nearly absolute, more rapidly than during any former period of their history; though they suffered during several intervals of that period, the severest tyranny. A purely military aristocracy is not therefore favorable to improvement, either in population, productive industry, wealth, or civilization.

It has been shown, on treating of the Priesthood and Ecclesiastical government, that a powerful ecclesiastical aristocracy often restrains the human mind, and holds it in perfect bondage; and thereby paralyzes the energies of the mind, checks and depresses a spirit of inquiry and discovery, and prevents men from making discoveries in natural science and inventions in mechanism, and hence checks them in the progress of improvement, and in civilization. It seems certain to my mind that *the tyranny of the ecclesiastical aristocracy of the church, after it was united with the temporal power of the empire, and the religious persecutions and wars growing out of the schisms in the church during the 4th, 5th, and 6th centuries, had as much influence in depressing the spirit of the Roman people, and causing the decline and fall of the empire, as the tyranny of the emperors, and the power and corruptions of the Pretorian guards and standing armies.*

A landed aristocracy is generally stable, has very little tendency to change or improvement, and is not very favorable to progress in population, wealth, or civilization. Poland affords the best specimen in the annals of history, of the tendency and effects of a landed aristocracy, controlling the destinies of a country; Poland always was poor and weak, as nations exclusively devoted to agriculture must be. Ireland affords an example of a similar character.

The mechanic arts and manufactures are based on the use of the metals; they prepare and fit the raw materials of agriculture, for use and for commerce; *and the chief propulsive energies and progressive tendencies of any and every modern nation, consist in its mechanical, mining and manufacturing industry, and its commerce.* These departments of industry lead to inquiry, mental activity and independence, enterprise, useful inventions, discoveries, and to an increase of productive industry, and of the comforts of life. They increase wealth and capital more rapidly than agriculture, or even success in conquest and military plunder; and hence they soon form a commercial and manufacturing aristocracy, which usually comprises great ability, and is highly favorable to progressive improvement and civilization, and to increase in productive industry, wealth, population, and civil liberty. These great departments of industry are almost inseparably connected, and if we except mining, neither has ever flourished much in any country, without the others; nor have they ever flourished where personal rights were not tolerably well secured; and where they have flourished most, the people have enjoyed the highest degree of civil liberty. In proportion as they have increased in importance in Great Britain, the spirit of liberty and the power of the people have increased.

Though the government of ancient Tyre was nominally a monarchy, *yet the chief power, after all, was wielded by the commercial and manufacturing aristocracy. Carthage, Venice, Genoa, Florence, and Holland, were all governed by commercial and manufacturing aristocracies, with more or less popular elements, for centuries, during the most flourishing periods of their existence.* Though the citizens of Athens disdained manual labor, yet by means mostly of their slaves, they carried on the mechanic arts, manufactures and commerce to a very great extent; which gave tone to the genius and spirit of the people; and is the principal reason of the great development of the Athenian mind in the fine arts and letters, and of the popular character of their government. While Sparta was ruled by the iron hand of the military and landed aristocracy, and made no progress in civilization, or in any thing but the art of war.

During the dark ages, the power of the kings of Europe was almost nominal, and *the people were ruled with a rod of iron, by a triple aristocracy; the ecclesiastical, the military and the landed the two latter species being blended in the feudal aristocracy ; and it is difficult to say, which of the three was the most unfeeling, oppressive, and tyrannical.* This period was marked by scenes almost constant, of wars public and private, waged by kings, barons, popes, bishops, and individual adventurers ; by plunder, pillage, robberies, piracies, confiscations, excommunications, interdicts, and every species of violence, oppression, and human suffering ; while the mechanic arts were at the lowest ebb, and manufactures and commerce scarcely had any existence.

The governments of Mexico, and of all the Spanish American States, have been nominally republican for more than a quarter of a century, and the elective franchise extended to all, or nearly all the adult males ; but as very few can either read or write, or have any intelligence or knowledge of government, *the whole power is substantially exercised by a triple aristocracy ; the popish clergy, the military officers, and the wealthy land-holders.* The mechanic arts, commerce, and agriculture are at a very low ebb, mining has declined, and those countries are very little if any more prosperous than they were while under the government of Viceroys from Spain.

Rome during the republic, nearly five hundred years, was governed mostly by the Senate, which was elected by the censors every five years, and *composed of several grades of aristocracy ; military and official, and the aristocracy of wealth and talent.* The Consuls, Pretors, and some other high officers, who were chosen annually by the people, were thenceforward Senators for life, unless degraded on account of misconduct ; and the remaining part of the Senate was filled up by the Censors, from the most talented, distinguished, and wealthy citizens of Rome. The office of Senator was strictly elective, and not hereditary ; an election to a few of the highest executive and judicial offices by the people, was equivalent to an election to the Senate for life, after the termination of the annual magistracy ; and no one was eligible until he was about thirty years of age. Hence the Senate during many centuries, comprised nearly all the first talents of Rome ; civil as well as military. It possessed great stability, was an exceedingly able body of men, and as the spirit and genius of the age and of the people was military, it is not wonderful that under the guidance and sagacious policy of such a Senate, they should have constantly extended their dominions, and conquered the best portion of the world.

This military aristocracy, and spirit of conquest, was not however adapted to a very high state of civilization, nor to very rapid increase of population or progress in improvement. The opinion is advanced by Gibbon, and such seems to be the general opinion

of historians, that the population of the Roman empire was greater towards the latter end of the second century of the Christian era, than at any former period; and that the decline was rapid during the 4th and 5th centuries. The emperor Augustus changed the whole character and policy of the Roman people; and converted them from a military aristocracy, ambitious of military glory and conquest, into quiet citizens, cultivating and pursuing the arts of peace. He boasted that he found Rome built of wood, and left it built of marble; and there is no reason to doubt that there was much truth in his boast. At his death, the Roman people were rich compared with their condition when the republic was overturned; and much wealthier still at the end of the reign of the Antonines, A. D. 180.

Sec. 5. *On the centralization of power—and the origin and importance of local power.*

The powers of the ancient governments, were all concentrated at the seat of government. The system of centralization prevailed universally, and local power was unknown—except that in some instances where a people were conquered, they were required to pay tribute, and allowed to retain their own local government. In the monarchies of antiquity, all power was vested in the monarch, and all appointments to office emanated from him—or from him and a central council or aristocracy—who appointed all the principal civil and military officers, and the governors of provinces—and they appointed and removed at pleasure their subordinate officers. The Elders of Israel were the principal men of their respective tribes, and derived their powers from local sources. This is the only exception to the general rule of centralization, which occurs to me. In Tyre and Carthage, the whole powers of the nation, were concentrated in the hands of the aristocracy in those cities; and even in republican Rome—though citizens could come from any part of the republic to vote for consuls, pretors, and other officers at the city of Rome; they could not vote in any other place; nor could they send representatives to vote for them.

The senate appointed the governors and other high officers of the provinces, and those officers appointed their own subordinates. The people of the provinces and even of Italy, at a distance from Rome, were not allowed to select any of their local officers, nor to participate in the legislation by which they were governed, unless they went to Rome to do so, which was impossible, except for a very few. They in fact enjoyed none of the privileges of self-government—but were governed by the populace and senate of Rome. Practically, they enjoyed no greater privileges, and their rights were no better protected, under the republic, than under the empire. The people of a nation residing out of the capital, can enjoy the privileges of self-government, only by means of local power, by electing their own local officers, and the principles of representation. All these things were unknown in that age of the world.

The ancients, with the exception of the Israelites before the captivity, seem to have had no conception, that local elections and local power could exist, consistently with the central supreme power of the government. The Romans denominated local power an imperium in imperio, [an empire within an empire,] and were suspicious of it. The principle of local elections by the people, and of local power, seems to have been borrowed by the Church from the ancient Hebrew Government, and transplanted into Europe, among the barbarians who overran the Roman Empire. Charters have been granted to cities and towns, to elect their own officers, and to govern themselves, so far as regards local matters, in nearly all the countries of Europe, since the tenth or eleventh century. These charters were the origin of local power, and the germs of freedom in Europe. Without local power, no such thing as freedom can exist. Local elections and local power, are the main bulwark of political and civil liberty.

Local power is of two kinds: 1st, that which is conferred and regulated by the central power, and dependent upon it.—2d, that which is within certain limits, independent of the central power—and forms of itself a centre, and regulator of other subordinate, local powers. The powers of cities, counties, villages, and towns of Great Britain and Ireland, and also their provincial governments, are all local powers of the first class; which are derived from, and dependent upon, the central government of the kingdom. So also are the powers of the districts, cities, and communes of France—strictly local, and dependent on the great central power of the nation—as well under the republic, as under all the previous monarchies. The governments of the several states of the American Union, constitute local powers of the second class. Within their sphere, they are independent of the national government; and they constitute and regulate the local governments of counties, cities, villages, towns, and corporations; all of which are subordinate to, and dependent upon them.

The Union of Utrecht in 1579, of the seven provinces, afterwards known as the United Provinces, (or Holland) constituted the first Federal Government that ever was formed—leaving the State Governments full power to regulate all their local concerns. This was the first instance of the existence of local power of the second class, and it may be regarded as a great era in the progress of government and civilization. Our Federal Government was formed after that model, to a very great extent. The confederacies of Greece, consisted of two or more independent States, united by treaty, without the formation of a general or Federal Government; each State retaining its own entire sovereignty and independence. Such also was the confederation of the American States before the adoption of the present Federal Constitution. The confederation of the Cantons or States of Switzerland, is of the same character; being peculiarly situated, it has proved partially successful—while all others of that character have finally failed.

The appointing power is exercised by chief magistrates and cabinet officers secretly; no reasons are given publicly, for either removals or appointments; and numerous contracts are made in the same manner. The revenue, disbursing, and accounting departments of the government are very complicated, and embrace an immense number of transactions, which are generally without that kind of publicity, that attends courts of justice, and legislative proceedings. The mode of discharging those executive duties are such, as to leave the executive officers practically irresponsible to the people—though not exempt from selfishness, partiality, and prejudice. The exercise under such circumstances, of extensive powers, affecting great numbers of persons, and very complicated claims and interests, tends to invite and promote favoritism, intrigue, profligacy, and corruption.

Where executive patronage is large, it tends to unite political partisans, to give direction to, and to promote party organization, and to increase party spirit—and has an undue influence over the action of the legislature, and over elections by the people. It has been aptly termed the cohesive power of public plunder. It increases the influence of party leaders, who become organs of the administration; destroys all independence and freedom of action among political partisans; leads to the tyranny of the majority over the minority—and to a disregard of the rights and welfare of the mass of the people. Participation in the appointing power, gives senators an influence over executive officers, which is sometimes pernicious. All these influences are dangerous, in proportion to the extent and magnitude of the patronage, contracts and expenditures of the government, and the claims against it—to be provided for by legislation, passed upon and paid by the executive officers.

The greater the central power, the more difficult to acquaint the people with the details of its proceedings; and it becomes less responsible to the people, less influenced by public opinion, more subject to extravagance, profligacy, intrigue, corruption, and tyranny, in the legislative as well as in the executive departments of the government.

It is impossible for a majority of the members of the legislature of a great nation to become sufficiently acquainted with the wants, resources, and condition of the people of every section and district, to legislate judiciously in relation to all their local affairs and interests. Hence the advantage of confining the legislation and action of the central government, to national and international affairs; and organizing local governments to legislate for, and attend to all the local matters and interests of the people.

Political liberty consists in the exercise by the people, of the powers of self-government—the power of making their own laws, and selecting their own rulers. Intelligence, liberty of speech, freedom of discussion, the freedom of the press, and a spirit of inquiry, are necessary to its full and proper exercise. The organization of local powers, together with the system of local elections, representation in legislative bodies, and trial by jury, constitute the principal means and mode of its exercise.

In a consolidated government like that of France, under the constitution of 1848, with a large standing army—an immense patronage in the hands of the President—the press muzzled by severe libel and sedition laws; and all local powers dependent on the central power; the people out of the capital, have comparatively little influence over the action of the government, and only partially enjoy the privileges of self-government. Their rights and privileges are subject to be trampled upon, and taken from them, by means of intrigues and factions at the seat of government. The power and prize of the Presidency are so great, and the struggle to obtain it so violent, that every Presidential election will endanger the peace of the country, and threaten a revolution.

State governments constituting local powers, independent as to local affairs, and within a certain sphere, are as necessary to the exercise and perpetuation of political liberty in the United States, as Union, and a Federal Government are to peace, national security and prosperity. The perpetuation of all the powers reserved to the several States by the Federal Constitution, is as necessary to the future welfare of the people of this country, as the preservation of the Union itself. If the State governments should ever lose their substantial powers, and sink into mere dependencies on the Federal Government—our country would have substantially a consolidated government like that of France; and would soon become profligate, corrupt, and tyrannical, and every Presidential election would threaten civil war.

Great corporations with extensive powers, special privileges and large capitals, which must necessarily be wielded by a central power, by a comparatively few persons, and their agents, are anti-republican in their tendency. The East India Company is nearly as despotic in its rule in British India, as the Hierarchy of Rome in the states of the Church. The Bank of England exercises such control over the commerce and business of that country, that it is difficult to carry on great commercial operations successfully, without its aid, and occasional indulgence. Such is the influence also of the Bank of France; such was the influence (though to a less extent) of the great national banks incorporated by the United States; and such is the influence of State Banks, which enjoy a monopoly of the business of banking in some of the States. But local banks, organized under general laws, and without any special privileges, by reason of their competition with each other, have a more liberal and republican tendency.

Sec. 6. *Origin of the representative system of legislation, and the importance of two chambers.*

There is no reason to doubt, that the system of councils, and assemblies of deputies or representatives of the free cities, and the freemen of counties and departments, which assembled from time to time in the western nations of Europe, ever since about the tenth or eleventh century, to deliberate on national affairs, and to make laws, was borrowed from the church; and that the church borrowed it from the government of the Israelites, and the organization of the Jewish Sanhedrim, or Council of Elders. Though the Greeks, Romans, and the barbarous nations of all western Europe, and even the native tribes of America, were in the habit of having their assemblies of the people; yet the church set the first example of holding councils of mere deputies, or representatives of the churches of distant provinces and countries, assembled for general purposes of deliberation, and legislation, in matters of church doctrine, discipline, and government. This system of deliberation, and legislation by assemblies, consisting of deputies chosen at stated periods by the people, or particular classes of the people, is the greatest improvement ever made in civil government.

The division of a national assembly into two distinct chambers for deliberation separately, first occurred rather accidentally than otherwise, in England, during the civil wars of the 13th century. It serves not only to check hasty legislation, but to prevent any one individual from acquiring such an influence and ascendency by his talents and eloquence, as to control the whole action of the legislature. It is very difficult for one member to acquire a controlling influence in two separate chambers. If the legislative power is vested in two chambers instead of one, and the acts of neither are of any validity as laws without the other; it is difficult for factious partisans to form combinations, produce a schism, and divide the chamber, each party claiming to be the legally organized assembly; for the reason that neither faction can act as a chamber or branch of the legislature, unless it is recognized as such by the other chamber. If the General Assembly of the Presbyterian Church of the United States, had consisted of two distinct chambers instead of one, it would not have been possible for it to have been divided, in the manner it was divided a few years since; and on the contrary, if the Congress of the United States had consisted of but one chamber, it is hardly probable the government could have survived the violent struggle of the two parties for the ascendency in 1838; when the Seal of New-Jersey, and the certificate of her Secretary of State as to the election of five members, were disregarded in the organization of the House of Representatives. A dissolution of the State government of Ohio must have been the result of the double organization of the House of Representative, and the factious conduct of many of the members in December 1848, if the legislature of the State had consisted of but one body.

The system of dividing a legislative body into two chambers, may be regarded as adding greatly to the stability of a government, and as being one of the greatest improvements made in modern times.

It appears from the facts and authorities collected by Hallam, in his history of the middle ages, that in the 13th and 14th centuries, the system of representative legislative assemblies had made about as much progress in the kingdom of Arragon in Spain, and in France, as in England, except the division of the Parliament of England into two houses.

Sec. 7. *Origin and Progress of the Laws and Government of England.*

Prior to the Norman Conquest, the Anglo-Saxons were inferior to both the French and Spaniards. When the Saxons first came to England in the 5th, 6th, and 7th centuries, they were among the most ignorant and despicable savages in Europe, and often sold their own children as slaves. They had scarcely a single virtue, which was not produced by the cold and severity of the climate in which they lived. They were partially christianized, and civilized during the 7th, 8th, and 9th centuries. In the early part of the 11th century they were conquered by the Angles, now called Danes, then a nation of pirates from the north; and in the year 1066, they were again conquered by a little handful of Normans, despoiled of their property, and reduced to the most abject slavery. The Normans, as well as the Angles, or Danes, had been piratical adventurers, but both were greatly superior to the Saxons, and help to form and improve the English character. These facts may be learned from almost any of the British historians, and they show that we have no great reason to be proud of our early ancestors, or to boast of our Anglo-Saxon blood. Nearly all the laws and institutions of King Alfred, and of the Saxon and Danish kings were overturned; and the feudal system and feudal law, a system and law of absolute power and dominion on the part of the prince and his barons, and of vassalage on the part of the people, were firmly established; and form the basis from whence has arisen the present common law of England.

The government and common law of England was originally established by force and conquest, but usage ripened into law. What was at first acquired by conquest, that is to say, by force and robbery, was confirmed by time, and was finally claimed and regarded as an established, and vested right. During the nearly eight centuries that this vast fabric of law and government has been ripening into its present state and condition, the people of England have made comparatively little change in their laws and government, except what has been the silent effect of time, wrought by usage and precedent; by a system of executive and judicial legislation, heaping precedent upon precedent, and confirming or discarding usages at pleasure; parliament having done very little except to vote taxes on the people, and acquiesce in the precedents, usages, and proceedings of the king, the ministry, and the judiciary.*

From the time of the Norman conquest to the reformation, there was not a very great difference between the government, condition, pursuits and genius of the people of England, France, and Spain; the Belgians and Italians were greatly superior to all of them. All the effects of Magna Charta, and of all the great charters and oaths extorted by the barons from the kings in the 13th century, were apparently extinguished; the form and character of the House of Commons only remained, which grew out of the Leicester civil war in the year 1264.

The Pope then held absolute spiritual dominion over nearly the whole of Europe. Henry VIII. of England, was really one of the most absolute sovereigns, who ever sat upon a throne; after he quarrelled with the Pope, for refusing to divorce him from his

* See the character of the common law, in sec. 6 of Chapter I

queen, he controlled parliaments, courts of justice, prelates and bishops, and established the liturgy, creeds, forms, and laws of the church, as well as of the kingdom. His will seemed to be law on every subject, spiritual and temporal, throughout the kingdom. His quarrel with the Pope, and the establishment of the absolute spiritual power of the king, took place in the year 1533. It may be regarded as an era that prepared the way for the religious and civil liberties of the people, by breaking in upon the spiritual monarchy of the Pope, which was almost universal, showing them that it was not invincible, and teaching them that it was not infallible.

The Court of Star Chamber had been established during the reign of Henry VII., and the Court of High Commission in Ecclesiastical causes, was established during the reign of Queen Elizabeth, A. D. 1558. These two courts were the most summary, and arbitrary tribunals, and the greatest engines of tyranny, in the hands of the monarch, which ever existed in England; and they continued in force until they were repealed by the Long Parliament in 1641.

Scotland having thrown off the papal yoke also, adopted the Protestant religion, and established the Presbyterian form of church government, still retained that form after the union of the crowns of England and Scotland under James I. in the year 1602. Charles I. came to the throne in 1625, and from 1628 to 1640 he called no parliament; attempted to levy taxes, and carry on all the affairs of government by his own prerogatives; claimed absolute power, both temporal and spiritual, over the lives, liberties, consciences, and property of his subjects, and that he was accountable to heaven alone, for the exercise of his power. With the advice of Archbishop Laud, and some of the other English bishops, he attempted to force the people of Scotland to surrender their religious liberties, and to adopt the Episcopal liturgy, and form of church government; and on their resisting, he marched an army into Scotland, to compel them to submission. They raised an army to resist him; he then began to negotiate, and finally called a parliament which met April 13th, 1640, dissolved it May 5th following, and sent a second army of over twenty thousand men to compel them to submit; they raised about 26,000 men, and set him at defiance. He then summoned another Parliament, known as the Long Parliament, which met in November, 1640. This parliament abolished the Star Chamber and High Commission Courts, and all the arbitrary powers and privileges claimed by the king; and finally overturned the throne itself, and taught the nation, that the real sovereignty of the country was vested in parliament, and that the king could not trample on the religious liberties and privileges of the people with impunity. The Habeas Corpus act was passed in 1678.

When James II. attempted, by a similar high handed course, to introduce popery again into England, he was deposed by parliament in 1688, William III. of Orange, and Mary, were elevated to the throne; and the Protestant religion and free toleration were established. The constitution and the constitutional liberties of the people of Great Britain were thus confirmed, and established on a firm basis, as they existed until the passage of the bill to reform the House of Commons in 1833.

It is evident that the people of England only changed masters at the reformation; that they were only liberated from one master to be subjected to another; but the effect was, to weaken the power of papal despotism in Europe, by leading the human mind to inquire into the principles upon which it is based; to give courage to the Protestants; and to encourage in England, freedom of thought, and the free expression of opinion, at least so far as Popery is concerned. Hence arose diverse sects dissenting from Episcopacy, as well as Popery; and in conjunction with the Presbyterians of Scotland, they spread freedom of opinion, independence of mind, and a spirit of inquiry among the people throughout Great Britain, and thereby led to the reform of many abuses by the Long Parliament in 1641; sustained the energies of the people during the usurpations of Cromwell, and the corruptions and trying scenes of Charles II.; and nerved them for the contest with James, which terminaied in the establishment, to a limited extent, of their liberties, both civil and religious, at the revolution of 1688.

The despotism of Charles I. was overthrown by the joint efforts of the Protestant dissenters of England, and the Presbyterians of Scotland. The Episcopal Hierarchy remained nearly passive during the struggle, though many of its members took side with the king. The bigotry and despotism of James II. and his attempt to establish the Roman Catholic Church in England, alarmed the hierarchy so much that many of its members, and many of the aristocracy were induced to join the dissenters and the Presbyterians of Scotland, in the glorious revolution of 1688.

The cause of liberty owes nothing to either feudalism or prelacy. It was the object of the church after its union with the State under Constantine, of the Persian Magi, of Mahometanism, Popery, Prelacy, and the Greek Church, to enforce uniformity of opinion and religious worship, and unity of government, both ecclesiastical and civil. Uniformity of opinion is inconsistent with the freedom of the human mind, and the nature of man. It cannot be produced without absolute despotism on the part of the government and priesthood, and a system of education and discipline which reduces the mind to the most abject slavery.

The common law of England grew out of, and is founded upon, the feudal institutions of the Norman conquerors. The law regulating the descent of personal estate, the principles of equity—jurisprudence and of international law—and the rules for the construction of contracts, were borrowed from the Roman civil law. The maritime law, much of the system of commercial law, and the laws relating to partnerships and associations, were borrowed from the laws of continental Europe. The common law courts have been for centuries, silently borrowing principles of law and justice from courts of equity, and from all those several sources, and engrafting them upon the common law, without giving credit; and the British Parliament has pursued the same policy. Whatever virtues the institutions and laws of Great Britain possess, are mostly owing to those causes and sources, and to the free spirit and influence of the Protestant Dissenters, and of the Presbyterians of Scotland. With the exception of the system of trial by jury, and the emancipation of children at twenty-one years of age from the control of their parents, very little good ever sprung from Norman feudalism, or from the institutions of our Saxon ancestors—and none from the Episcopal Hierarchy.

The civil and political liberty of modern nations, has arisen from the spirit of free inquiry inculcated by the Protestant religion, from inventions and improvements in the mechanic arts, the dissemination of the scriptures, and of science and information by means of the press, and the principles of free toleration on all subjects of government, science, and morals as well as religion, established generally by the Protestants during the 16th and 17th centuries.

The following great and important eras may be marked in British history, whose effects are manifest at this day, and perhaps will be for centuries to come. First, the Norman Conquest in 1066; secondly, the quarrel of Henry VIII. with the Pope in 1533, soon after the commencement of the reformation; thirdly, the meeting of the Long Parliament in 1640, and the reform of abuses by it; fourthly, the deposition of James II. and the elevation to the throne, of William and Mary, in 1688, and immdiately after the revocation of the edict of Nantes; and fifthly, the general introduction of machinery and of the steam engine, about the time of the commencement of the American revolution, in 1775. The first was an era that introduced despotism; the four last have all contributed to advance the cause of civil and religious liberty, the progress of improvement, civilization, wealth and population.

SEC. 8. *Character of the House of Lords.*

The House of Peers of the united kingdoms of Great Britain and Ireland, has been generally treated as an assembly of hereditary nobility; as composed of members who have inherited their rank, station and political power. This is true in part only; more nominally than in substance, for *nearly all the leading, talented, and influential members who prepare the business of that house, direct its proceedings, and control its action, hold their seats by election of some sort, or direct appointment, and not by descent.* The American Almanac for 1834, gives a list of the Peers, their respective births, and the date of the creation of each hereditary Peerage. On comparing their births with the date of the creation of their titles, I conclude that *about* 200 *of them including the bishops, held their seats by election or appointment, and* 227 *by descent. Of the whole number, there was not one who held his title by descent from one of the Norman Barons, or from any Peer created during the* 11*th*, 12*th*, *or first half of the* 13*th century;* but two, from Peers created during the last half of the 13th century; nine held titles created during the 14th and 15th centuries; forty-two held titles created during the 16th and first eighty-eight years of the 17th century; fifty held titles created between the revolution of 1688, and the death of George II. in 1760; and no less than two hundred and forty-six, held titles created between the years 1760 and 1833; making 349 hereditary Peers. There were also four Royal Dukes, 16 representative Peers of Scotland elected for one term of Parliament only, 28 from Ireland elected for life, two Archbishops and twenty-four bishops of England, and four representative bishops of Ireland; making in all 427 members. About half of the 246 created between the years 1760 and 1833, were then living, which added to the 44 elected for Scotland and Ireland, and the 30 Bishops made nearly two hundred. Only a trifle over half of the whole number held their seats and their titles by descent.

The Peerage has long been the great object of ambition of the most talented men of the kingdom; including lawyers, physicians, military and naval officers, authors, commercial men, bankers, and manufacturers, as well as clergymen. *It is regarded as the greatest and highest mark of distinction which they can attain; and very few have attained it, until they have distinguished themselves by valiant deeds in arms, or the exhibition of a superior order of intellect in civil life.* Very few are made Peers until they have attained the age of forty-five or fifty years, and often sixty. Even the Duke of Wellington was not raised to the Peerage until after his splendid victories in Spain, and when he was 45 years old; Lord Lyndhurst was 55 years old; Lord Stowell, 76; Lord Eldon, 62; and Lord Brougham, 51 years old; Lord Nelson, Lord Vincent, and Lord Duncan, were all of plebeian descent, and raised to the Peerage after they had distinguished themselves by the most splendid naval victories of the age. Lord Hood also, and several others were raised to the Peerage on account of their distinguished naval sevices. The greater part of the naval officers of Great Baitain have descended from commoners; a much larger proportion of the military officers, are sons of the nobility, who are generally more desirous of enjoying their ease, and the fruits of luxury, than to acquire military fame and science by toil and labor. This may account for the fact, that much fewer of their military, than of their naval officers, have distinguished themselves; and that their armies in in America, as well as in Europe, except under the Duke of Wellington, and a few others, have not been very efficient or successful.

The chief strength and ability of the House of Peers, like the Senate of ancient Rome, is in those members who have obtained their seats by election, or appointment, on account of their distinguished services, or great talents. Sir Robert Peel who had more influence upon the measures of government, than any other man has had since the death of Mr. Pitt, was a commoner, the son of a distinguished cotton manufacturer. Lords Castlereah, Liverpool, Wellington, Grey, and Messrs. Addington and Canning, and nearly every prime minister of Great Britain during the present century, was by birth a commoner; and during that period, no Peer by descent, and no son of the royal family, has been recognized as a man of the first order of talents.

The stimulus of ambition is equally great in a republican form of government, as in a monarchy or an aristocracy.

It is therefore safe to say, that Great Britain is not indebted to the hereditary Peerage, nor to the landed, clerical, or legal aristocracy, for any part of her present prosperity, wealth and power; but on the contrary, that her prosperity, wealth, and power, are owing to her manufacturing, mining, and commercial industry and enterprise; and to the talents, sagacity, genius, and energy of the aristocracy arising from these classes; and that the nation has arisen to greatness, in spite of the grievous burthens and oppressions imposed on the people by the privileged classes. The relative power in the nation of the manufacturing, commercial, and mining classes, has been increasing for a century past, until they seem to have fairly gained the ascendency, and achieved a victory over the hereditary and landed aristocracy; and the result is the relief of the people from the oppressive influence of the Corn Laws. This will have as great an influence upon the prosperity and progress of the British nation, as upon the comforts of the poor and the laboring classes; and render it more necessary for France and the nations of the continent, as well as the United States, to give adequate, and perhaps additional protection to their domestic industry.

Sec. 9. *On party combinations, and the frauds perpetrated by them.*

I have heretofore alluded to the great and pernicious influences of party combinations in forming and controlling public opinion, and destroying all freedom of mind on the part of individuals. With the exception of the Jacobin Clubs of France during the early period of the revolution, there is perhaps no country where party combinations have been more permanent, and more powerful, than in the United States. Such have been their power and influence that very few men have been long successsul as politicians, unless they were willing to sacrifice their independence of mind, thought, and action, and make all their acts and professions conform to the last published creed of the party to which they are attached, and acknowledge fealty to the party leaders. If any man not at the head of one of the great political parties, manifests the least independence of mind, he is looked upon with suspicion, and is often denounced as a political heretic, by the leaders of the party to which he belongs. *Devotion to the party, is regarded as a substitute for patriotism; the principal object of party leaders seems to be, not to promote the interest and welfare of the nation, but the party; their constant appeals are made to party prejudice, and party creeds, and not to reason or public opinion, and the chief inquiry is, what will be popular and strengthen the party, and not, what will benefit the country.* Such is the tendency of party combinations, and party spirit, that our elections seem to be a mere scramble for office; and very little regard is paid to the character, or qualifications of candidates, provided they are popular, devoted to the party, and have intellectual capacity to subserve its interests.

The principal part of this evil is the natural result of our system of elections; whereby the minority of the people in every election district are entirely disfranchised; and an inducement held out, too great for the virtue of political partisans to withstand, to attempt to defraud their political opponents of their rights of suffrage, by an unfair mode of forming election districts, the system of general ticket, and other devices of like character.

By a fraudulent system of forming election districts in Ohio, the party in the minority, elected one of their partisans to the United States Senate in 1836. Other instances might be enumerated.

Sec. 10. *Evils of the system of elections by general ticket, and a remedy suggested.*

The system adopted in the states of New Hampshire, New Jersey, Georgia, Alabama and Missouri, and persisted in, for several years by some of these states in violation of an express act of Congress, passed in 1842, of electing the whole congressional delegation by general ticket, *is still more iniquitous in its effects, than the most odious gerrymandering ; in as much as it entirely disfranchises, all the voters of the state who belong to the minority party, and gives them no representation whatever in Congress, in either House.* The same evil exists in the election of members to the State Legislature ; the minority of the voters in the several election districts are not represented at all in one branch of the Legislature, and generally not in either branch. Take the city of New York for an example prior to 1846. It was represented in the Assembly of the State for many years, by ten or twelve members, all of whom were usually elected by one of the great political parties, and represented the peculiar opinion, principles, and wishes of the members of that party, but did not represent either the opinions, principles, interests, or wishes of the other party. The city also, with a few small counties, composed a Senatorial district, and the same party which was in the majority in the city, constituted a majority in the Senatorial district, so that the voetrs of the same party who were represented in the Assembly, were represented also in the Senate, while the voters of the minority party were not represented at all, in either branch of the Legislature. This evil was partially corrected in the new constitutisn of 1846, by the formation of single Senatorial and single Assembly districts. Though the whig voters in the State of Michigan, as indicated by the vote of 1842, 1843 and 1844, constituted about 45 per cent. of all the voters, and the democratic voters but little over 50 per cent., yet during those three years, the whigs did not elect a single member of the Senate, were totally unrepresented in that body, and had only from three to ten representatives in the other House. There are several states where the democratic party have been equally unrepresented, or but partially represented in proportion to their numbers.

The principle on which our government is based, is that all the voters shall be equally represented, as far as practicable, in the law making councils ; that the peculiar opinions, wishes, interests and views of public policy of each individual, as well as of every class of individuals, shall be fairly and as near equally represented as possible. This mode of giving a majority the whole representation, and disfranchising the minority, is contrary to the whole theory on which our government is founded. Its tendency is to foster party spirit, faction, bargain, intrigue, and corruption; to encourage political combinations; to give great power and influence to party leaders; and to depress individual talent, individual efforts, and honesty of purpose.

The same evil exists in the organization of all our banking, railroad and other incorporated companies, with the exception of a very few, in which a sovereign state or the nation is a party. In these few excepted cases, such as the two national banks created by Congress, in which the United States held a portion of the stock, the right was reserved to the nation to choose several of the Directors, in proportion to its amount of stock, and the other stockholders chose the remaining directors. In all other cases, the holders of a majority of the stock choose all the directors, and have the whole control and management of all the business of the corporation; and the holders of the minority of the stock, though it may amount to forty-nine per cent. of the whole, have no voice in the matter, and no right even to examine the books, papers, or proceedings of the directors, to learn whether the business is fairly or properly conducted or not. What facilities this power of the majority gives for secresy, favoritism, bargain, intrigue, speculation, corruption, fraud, and knavery! This was proven by the difference between the management of the late United States Bank, while a national institution, and subject to the examination, and participation of the government directors in its management, and the same Bank substantially, after it became a state institution, under the name of the United States Bank of Pennsylvania, and free from the examinations and influence of government directors.

The framers of the Constitution of the United States provided that each elector of President and Vice President should cast his vote for two persons; expecting that three, four or more persons would be voted for, as A. B. and C. or A. B. C. and D.; that some of the same persons who voted for A. as their first choice, would vote for B., and some for C., for their second choice; that some who voted for B., as their first choice, would reciprocate the compliment, and vote for A. as their second choice, and so on; that the person having the greatest number of votes, would be elected President, and the next greatest Vice President. In this mode the majority would elect, and be represented by the President, and the minority would elect, and be represented by the Vice President. But unfortunately in this design, they did not duly weigh the jealousy, cunning, management, and intrigue of political partisans. The error was, in allowing each elector to vote for two persons instead of one At the first and second elections, there was no contest for President, General Washington received a vote from each of the electors in 1788, and from all but three of them in 1792; John Adams received the votes of a majority and was elected Vice President. In 1796, there were 138 electors; 71 votes were cast for Adams, 69 for Thomas Jefferson, 59 for Thomas Pinckney, 30 for Aaron Burr, 48 scattering, for diverse other persons. Mr. Adams was elected President, and Mr. Jefferson Vice President. Before the next election, party combinations were formed, and party lines strictly drawn, so that at the election of 1800, there being 138 electors, 73 of them voted for Jefferson and all the same persons for Burr; and the remaining 65 electors, all voted for Adams, and 64 of them for Charles C. Pinckney. There being a tie between Jefferson and Burr, Jefferson was elected by the House of Representatives, President, and Burr Vice President. In this mode, the 73 electors elected both President and Vice President, and the votes of the 65 were entirely lost. *If each elector could have voted for but one man, instead of two, Jefferson would have been elected President, and Adams Vice President;* and if this policy could have been carried out, and parties had been otherwise the same, Mr. Van Buren would have been elected President in 1836, and Gen. Harrison Vice President; and in 1840, the scale would have been turned, and Gen. Harrison elected President, and Van Buren Vice President; and in such case, we should not have been either Burred or Tylerized.

A policy of a similar character might be carried out in the election of nearly all the officers of government. In the election of members of the House of Representatives of the United States, each state might be divided into districts, so that each district should elect two or three members, generally three. In a district electing three members, let each voter cast his vote for two persons; and in a district electing but two members, let each person vote for but one; and provide that in the first case, the three persons having the highest number of votes, should be elected, and in the second case, the two highest. In this mode, in the treble district, the majority would elect two, and the minority but one. The same rule would apply equally well to the election of Senators, and members of the lower house of the several State Legislatures; Aldermen of cities; trustees, assessors, commissioners of highways, of the poor, &c. of towns; and to commissioners, boards of auditors, &c. of counties, and to many other officers.

This mode of election would secure to the minority a partial representation, a voice, participation, and influence upon all the measures of the government, and give them a check upon the majority, who would still unavoidably have a larger representation than their numbers would justly entitle them to. At the Presidential election of 1836, only about 51 per cent., or two per cent. majority of the popular vote was cast for Mr. Van Buren ; in 1840, Gen. Harrison was thought to have an overwhelming majority, and yet it was but 53 per cent. or 6 per cent. majority of the popular vote ; and in 1844, Mr. Polk was elected President, and Mr. Dallas, Vice President, by a plurality only, and less than a majority of the whole popular vote. What a burlesque upon our representative system of government, that by means of party combinations, and the schism produced by a few fanatics, a minority of the voters should elect both President and Vice President, and the voice and will of the majority should be entirely defeated ! Yet this is the practical result of almost every election under our state governments, from the election of Governor down to township constables. The system itself lies at the foundation of the evil ; and encourages party combinations, party machinery, and often gross frauds. The most active, cunning, bargaining, managing and adroit partisans, who make politics a trade and their principal study, acquire an ascendency in all political parties. Under such a system, party leaders elected to office, have little or no time to study the great principles of government, of morals, political economy, legislation, and general jurisprudence, in order to qualify themselves to discharge properly the duties of important offices, but devote their time for years to party purposes, in order to entitle themselves to a portion of the spoils of political victory, and to the honors, emoluments, and sometimes the speculations of office.

The system of elections here suggested, would have a tendency to weaken party combinations, prevent fraud, and place every candidate before the people upon his own merits, and his own individual popularity ; and make it necessary for every one to qualify himself for any station he may desire, and to study the interests of the whole people, and not the interest of any political clique, faction, or party. It would be likely to secure to the people of every class and pursuit, a representation and an influence, approximating to equality, in the executive, as well as the legislative branches of the government, and in the administration of the laws in counties, cities and townships.

Similar principles might be applied to the election of the

directors of incorporated companies. Let us suppose that a company, having a stock of $1,000,000, is to be managed by ten Directors:—let any of the stockholders who see fit so to do, having $100,000 stock, unite in the election of a director, and so on, until all have united, that can agree to do so; and let the remaining stockholders elect by majorities the balance of the directors to be chosen. In this mode, all or nearly all the stockholders would be fairly represented; no esprit de corps would be likely to exist among the directors; much favoritism and corruption, and many frauds would be prevented by reason of jealousy, and fear of exposure from each other; and the interest of the stockholders protected.

SEC. 11. *Effect of Anti-masonry—Anti-slavery; native Americanism—Catholicism and Mormonism upon our elections.*

Anti-masonry, abolitionism, and native-Americanism, all have too narrow a base, and their ideas and principles are too few, and too contracted, to serve as the foundation of a national political party. I do not intend to speak of the merits of these parties, and of the moral tendency of their principles so long as they act as moral associations, and thereby attempt to influence and give direction to public opinion, but refer simply to the fact, that their separate political organization is not adapted either to the nature or condition of man, and can never have much effect, except to defeat the objects they profess to have in view. The fact that a third political party never did exist for any great length of time, in any age or country, is good evidence, that is not adapted to the condition of man, and never can be maintained.

Political anti-masonry, not only drew the principal part of its members and friends from the then existing National Republican party, but it drove thousands of masons from that party, into the Jackson party, as an asylum, or protection from what they deemed the persecutions of anti-masonry. This not only served to strengthen, but to cement the bond of union, and increase the enthusiasm of that party, and make its power irresistible; and it aided very much to re-elect Gen. Jackson in 1832, to perpetuate the power of the party, and to elect Mr. Van Buren as his successor in 1836.

A strange concurrence of causes and circumstances contributed to secure to Mr. Polk in 1844, a meagre plurality over Mr. Clay of about 1½ per cent. of the popular vote for President. The principal of these causes were abolitionism and nativeism, (which distracted and weakened the whig party); but the desire for an extension of territory, party spirit, party organization, catholicism, and lastly Mormonism, all contributed to increase the confidence and strength of the democratic party. The motives of the Southern people were obvious; they not only desired to increase and perpetuate their political power and control over the national government, by means of the admission of Texas, and their ascendency in the Senate; but they also wished to increase the value of their slave property. Avarice and ambition, two of the strongest passions which can operate upon the human mind, concurred to influence them in their course.

The Catholics of the United States in 1844, according to their own claims, were over twelve hundred thousand, and probably did amount to ten or eleven hundred thousand; about 150,000 of whom voted, at least 96 per cent. or 144,000 for Mr. Polk, and not over 6,000 for Mr. Clay. The great mass of the Catholic population, at least nine tenths of it, have for many years, regularly voted with the democratic party; and thereby they have secured, not only the election to office of great numbers of themselves, and of persons most favorable to them, but have obtained many laws, favorable to the promotion of their peculiar religious opinions and tenets. A few of them, mostly in Maryland and and Louisiana, of English and French descent, who have been bred in the United States, and imbibed from their childhood the free protestant spirit of our political institutions, have kept themselves independent of the political influence of their priesthood, and usually voted with the whig party; but a much less number in 1844, than ever before. The Catholics, by a perfect unanimity of opinion and concurrence of action in political matters, have managed to acquire the balance of power between the two great political parties of the country; and by acting with the democratic party, they gave Mr. Polk the entire vote of the states of Louisiana and Missouri; with the aid of the abolitionists, they gave him the vote of the states of New York, Pennsylvania, Indiana, and Michigan; and with the aid of the abolitionists and the the Mormons, they gave him the vote of Illinois. They also gave him a popular vote of about 10,000 in Ohio, ten or twelve thousand in Maryland, and many thousand in other states. By these means, they not only controlled the election of President, but also caused the election of a majority of the members of Congress, and of several of the state legislatures, and thereby secured to the democratic party, (of which they constitute about one eighth part,) the entire control of all the branches, executive, legislative, and judicial, of the national government. The Mormons by connecting themselves with the democratic party in Illinois, aided that party materially, obtained its support and protection, and a city charter conferring on them extraordinary powers and privileges.

Such are the natural effects of union and combination. What, on the other hand, have the abolitionists and Native Americans effected, by acting on the opposite principles of separation, disunion, and raising their own political standard? What a contrast between the policyof the Catholics, Mormons, and Anti-renters of New York, and that of the Abolitionists and Native Americans.

The government of the Roman Catholic church, is an elective monarchy, nearly absolute; supported by an ecclesiastical aristocracy, in which the people have not the slightest participation. Why is this strong sympathy of feeling between the democratic party in this country, and the Catholics? Is there any similarity between the principles of government of the Pope, and those of the democratic party, with its system of organization, party machinery, and proscriptive policy? These are problems for my readers to solve; I shall not attempt to discuss them.

By the Constitution of the State of Illinois, aliens not naturalized, are allowed all the political as well as the civil privileges of citizens, and are allowed to vote for all officers, national and state; thus abolishing all real distinction between citizens and aliens; and the state was admitted into the Union with this provision in it more than thirty years since. What then could the Native Americans effect, if they should attain their object? A mere nominal change of the naturalization laws. We have an immense unsettled country, and to give foreign emigrants who settle among us, civil privileges, such as the aid and protection of our laws, protection of person and property, and the right to hold and convey property, is right in itself, and cannot harm us. Such rights might safely be extended to them immediately after their arrival in our country; but political rights are of a character very different. Citizenship does not imply the right of voting, for if it did, the citizenship of our females, children, and young men under 21 years old, would confer on them that right.

To vote and participate in electing the rulers of the country, is the exercise of the highest right of citizenship, which man can possess; and it is difficult to perceive, how it can be anything but a violation of the constitution of the United States, to allow aliens to vote. But the tendency of public opinion is towards liberalism—to extend the right of suffrage to all adult male immigrants, who have declared their intention of becoming citizens; and so far as regards township officers in new settlements, where foreign immigrants constitute nearly the whole population, such extension seems necessary.

Similar privileges might with propriety, be extended to Indians occupying reserves in States or Territories. They might have township governments organized, with the privilege of electing their own local officers, subject to the laws and government of the State or Territory. And as to the tribes of Indians who have been removed by the United States west of the Mississippi river, it seems but just as well as expedient, to organize a territorial government for them; to appoint the highest grade of executive and judicial officers; and allow them to elect a legislative assembly, and all local officers, and to legislate for themselves, to the same extent as other territories. Such a government would furnish the most effectual means of weaning them from their roving habits, and of encouraging them to adopt the habits and mode of living of the whites.

Sec. 12. *On the progress of civil liberty, and of reform in matters of government.*

The fundamental principles of the Protestant religion, which distinguish it from Catholicism, are freedom of thought, free inquiry, and the right of private judgment. These are also the fundamental principles of political and civil liberty, of republican, democratic, and all free systems of government. The great reformation commenced by Luther, in the sixteenth century, was the germ of liberty, mental, civil and political, as well as religious. It sowed the seeds, and its principles prepared the way, for all the reforms in matters of government, from that time to the present.

The great eras of reform in government, resulting from that cause, are as follows:—First, the general revolt of the Dutch provinces about the year 1576, which terminated in the establishment of the Republic of the Seven United Provinces, or Holland. Secondly, the edict of Nantes, passed by Henry IV. of France, in 1589, which allowed free toleration in religious matters, to the Protestants of that kingdom. Thirdly, the reforms made by the Long Parliament of England, in 1641 and 1642. Fourthly, the glorious revolution in England of 1688. Fifthly, the great American revolution, which commenced in 1775, and terminated in establishing the independence of the United States, and the American constitutions, which had been adopted. Sixthly, the French revolution of 1789, which overturned popery and feudalism in France. Seventhly, the revolutions of the Spanish American provinces, which commenced in Mexico, Colombia, and Buenos Ayres, in the year 1810. Eighthly, the French revolution of 1830. And ninthly, the revolutions of France, Germany, Prussia, Italy and Austria, in 1848. The cause of liberty and of civilization has been promoted by each and all of these great events.

There is no reason to doubt that human laws and systems of

government, and all human institutions, as well as civilization, are progressive, and capable of a higher degree of perfection than has been yet attained. We do not look to the dark ages for light in matters of science, nor need we look to ancient precedents, much less to the dark ages of feudalism, for a good system of either law or government. The people of the United States changed and improved very much their laws, constitutions and forms of government, when they threw off the yoke of Great Britain, and have been changing them from that time until the present; adapting them to each other, to the condition and customs of the country, to the spirit of the age, and to the laws of nature. The opinion seems to be gaining strength and extending to a larger proportion of the people, and to a greater number of the learned and professional classes, that our system of law and government, and particularly the former, admits at the present time of great improvement. We hear of constitutional conventions and propositions to reform the laws or the constitution, or both, in many of the states. In fact, I may say, the impression is becoming very general, that in the formation of the first American constitutions, statutes and forms of proceedings in the administration of justice, too much was borrowed and retained from the laws and usages of monarchcial and aristocratic England; and hence the anxiety for reform—for constitutional reform, executive reform, legislative reform, judicial reform, and legal reform.

The Institutes, Code and Pandects of Justinian, collected and adopted in the sixth century, constituted the best and most complete system of law, and the greatest achievement in jurisprudence, of ancient times. The patricians as a class, with all their exclusive and aristocratic privileges, had passed away; all the people were equal in view of the law, and enjoyed equal privileges, except that slavery still existed, and the superior officers of the empire, and the governors of provinces, had too great powers. With these exceptions, the laws were founded on the laws of nature and the principles of equality, and equally protected the rights of all.

The common law of England, on the contrary, grew up as a system of usages and rules to secure the exclusive privileges of the Norman barons, and was and is essentially aristocratic in its character—treating the crimes and offences of the commonalty, and their default in the payment of debts, with terrible severity —giving against the peers of the realm, no substantial remedies for the collection of debts, and making the administration of justice so excessively expensive, as to amount to a denial of justice to the poor. The punishment for the inferior grade of crimes, was, until recently, so severe and abhorrent to feelings of humanity, that courts of justice were induced to lean in favor of persons charged with crime, until they built up a system of technical rules, which, when applied in this country, renders it very difficult and almost impossible to convict the guilty.

The judiciary act of the United States of 1789, is a model of excellence in its style, and in many of its provisions. It made some improvements upon the common law modes of proceeding, and contributed greatly as a model to improve the jurisprudence of the several states.

The Napoleon Code is the greatest achievement in jurisprudence in modern times, and has served as a model for the nations of the earth. It was followed by the Revised Statutes of New York of 1830, by those of Massachusetts of 1836, and by improved revisions of statutes in many of the other states. The Napoleon and Louisiana codes of procedure, suggested the new code of practice of New York of 1848; and there seems to be a disposition in many of the states, at the present time, to abolish the old common law system of remedies, pleading, and practice, and much of the law of evidence, and to adopt a system better adapted to the attainment of justice.

The general impression was, until recently, that there are but three departments of government; the legislative, executive, and judicial; and that the appointment of all judicial officers, and of all subordinate executive officers, properly belongs to the chief magistrate as a part of the executive power. This is a monarchical idea, which prevails wherever monarchy exists. It forms a part of the system of the centralization of power. Though it is entirely anti-republican, yet it generally prevailed in the United States, until about the commencement of the present century; and in all the early American constitutions, the power to appoint judicial, and nearly all inferior executive officers, was vested in the Governor, Governor and Senate, or Governor and Council; and in framing the Constitution of the United States, the same policy prevailed. The truth is, the appointing or elective power really constitutes a distinct department or division of power, which, in a republican or democratic system, is, in most cases, properly vested in the people, though it may be vested in the Legislature, or in the Chief Magistrate, either alone or in connection with a Senate or Council.

The public men and educated classes of the United States, seemed at first to distrust the popular branch of the legislative power, and the capacity of the people to select the greatest part of their rulers; and to repose implicit confidence in Chief Magistrates, Cabinet Officers, Senators, and Judges. Hence they gave the President and the Governors of States, a qualified veto upon the proceedings of Congress, and of most of the State Legislations; and took from the people and conferred on them, with the concurrence of the Senate, the appointment of all judicial, and nearly all inferior executive officers, in accordance with the practice of the monarchical governments of Europe. They also in most of the states, as well as in the federal government, provided for the appointment of high judicial officers during life. This is anti-republican. The supposition seemed to be, that the President and Governors are safer depositaries of power, than Congress, the State Legislatures, or the people; that the only danger from the judiciary arises from the dependence of the judges on either the executive, the legislature, or the people; that when they are entirely independent and irresponsible, they are most likely to be pure, capable, and impartial; and therefore they made the judges independent of the people, and of all the other departments of the government. The experience of the country during the last sixty years, has dissipated many of these ideas as delusions. The education of the people has been improved, and their knowledge increased; and as they have gradually acquired more power experience has proven their capacity to use it, as well at least as it has been used by chief magistrates, and cabinet officers.

The principal evils of all governments arise from the passions, ignorance, and selfishness of man. Selfishness prompts public men to use their official power and influence to promote the interest and aggrandizement of themselves and their personal favorites, regardless, in many instances, of the rights of others, and of the general welfare of the community. Four things or conditions are required to check selfishness and prevent corruption in public officers;—first, responsibility made effective by frequent elections or appointments;—second, incapacity to act in any matter in which they are interested; third, publicity of their acts, and reasons in support of them; and lastly, a sound public opinion and perfect freedom in the expression of opinions. Secrecy is inconsistent with responsibility; it prevents the operation of public opinion, and is a shield to all kinds of selfish purposes and schemes—to intrigue, corruption, fraud, and crime. All legislative bodies and courts of justice sit, in this country, with open doors. Their purity can be maintained, tyranny prevented, and individual rights secured, only by means of the publicity of their proceedings, and the salutary influence of public opinion.

Nearly all special legislation is brought forward and supported by legislators, to promote either their own personal interests, or the interests of their friends. It is prompted by personal considerations and favoritism, rather than by a regard for the public good; and hence it is frequently injurious to the public, and generally corrupting in its tendency. No man is allowed to be a judge in his own case, or in cases where his family or near relatives are interested; why should he be allowed to legislate for the special benefit of himself and his friends?

The tendency of the public mind in the United States, is to decentralize and make more popular and local, the powers of government; to prohibit special legislation, and to simplify the laws and the administration of justice, as far as practicable.

Selfishness and the corrupt tendencies of centralization have been checked, and the evils of party spirit diminished, in New York and several other states, by stripping the Governor and Senate of all patronage, making nearly all officers, executive, administrative, and judicial, as well as legislative, elective by the people in their respective counties and districts, providing for the election of legislators by single districts, prohibiting all special legislation, and making all power local, as far as practicable and consistent with general laws.

We have built up in this country, and are still improving, a noble system of constitutional and of federal law, which will be a guide to the nations of the earth, as long as this globe shall be inhabited by man. The boundaries of power are more accurately defined and better understood in the United States, than they were fifty years since; and much better than they are, or ever were, in the old world.

CHAPTER VI.

ON THE NATURE AND CONSTITUENTS OF WEALTH, AND HOW PRODUCED AND ACCUMULATED.—ON VALUE, EXCHANGEABLE VALUE AND PRICE—CAPITAL, AND MATERIALS, AS DISTINGUISHED FROM PRODUCTS FOR CONSUMPTION.—PRODUCTION, THE RESULT OF THE COMBINED ACTION OF LABOR AND CAPITAL, BOTH MATERIAL AND IMMATERIAL, UPON RAW MATERIALS. —WEALTH ACCUMULATED BY INDUSTRY AND FRUGALITY.—PURSUITS PERSONIFIED, THEIR RELATIVE IMPORTANCE.

SEC. 1. *Basis of Values,—Nature and character of our wants.*

What constitutes wealth, and what constitutes value, and the measure of both wealth and value, are questions which meet the learner at the very threshold of his inquiries, on the subject of political economy. These questions should be settled in the beginning, as landmarks by which to verify and correct all his observations and deductions.

It is obvious that both wealth and value are based on the wants of man, and the capacity of things to satisfy those wants, which constitutes their utility. As our wants are partly material and partly immaterial, so values may be divided in like manner, into material and immaterial. Our physical or material wants are founded in, and arise from, the appetites and necessities of our nature. Our immaterial wants comprise those of an intellectual, moral, educational and social character. So far as our wants, both material and immaterial, are of such a character that their satisfaction tends to promote our general welfare and happiness, they may be said to be natural and real—but so far as they depend entirely on opinion, fashion, custom, habit, and ambition, they are factitious. Many of our wants are of a mixed character, being natural and real wants, with factitious refinements and matters of taste and ornament engrafted upon them. Our physical wants are few in number, and depend much on climate, situation, and the season of the year ; but our immaterial, factitious, and mixed wants, multiply themselves to infinity, with the development of our intellectual, social, and moral faculties, and the improvement of our condition.

Those things which are necessary to satisfy our physical wants, are called necessaries ; or the necessaries of life. They comprise such food, drink, clothing, fuel, housing, and lodging of a common quality, as are necessary to sustain life, and promote the health, strength, and activity of persons of ordinary health and constitution, to the highest degree which their nature admits of.

The comforts of life include such things as are necessary to satisfy the most of our mixed wants, so far as material things are concerned. They comprise a finer and better quality of things of the same or a similar character as those denominated necessaries—being such as tend to increase human enjoyment, to promote the health of the young, the feeble, and the delicate, and to increase their longevity.

Luxuries correspond to our factitious, and to some also of our mixed wants. They comprise matters of art, taste, and ornament, beautiful, elegant, and magnificent things that please the eye; delicious food and drink, that gratify the appetite; music that delights the ear; reading, riding, and travel for pleasure, and other intellectual amusements, that excite, occupy, and interest the mind.

SEC. 2. *The utility of luxuries is partly real, but mostly factitious.*

In as much as many luxuries tend to stimulate the mind and ambition of mankind, to cultivate their taste, and to increase their activity and industry, the most of them have a certain degree of utility; that is, whenever they are adapted to the condition and circumstances of the individual—are confined within so narrow limits as not to interfere with his duties, and the full enjoyment of all the comforts as well as the necessaries of life—and do not interfere with his general welfare, and that of the community, they have a certain degree of utility in the strict and philosophical sense of the word. (Vide ante Sec. 5, of Chap. I.,) Utility, like our wants, may be divided into real and factitious—that is, whatever has a capacity to satisfy our real wants, and tends to promote our general welfare and happiness, has a real utility; on the contrary, whatever tends to satisfy only our factitious wants, has only a factitious utility; while those things which satisfy our mixed wants, have a real utility to some extent, depending on their character and adaptation to the condition and circumstances of the person. The wealthy can indulge in luxuries and not affect their ability to enjoy all the necessaries and comforts of life. Luxuries of a rational character may, therefore, aid in developing their intellectual and social faculties—add to their enjoyments in the aggregate—and promote their general welfare. But when the middling classes indulge in expensive luxuries, they do so at the sacrifice of other things, that would be much more valuable to them; and thus they sacrifice a greater, for a less good, and prejudice their general welfare. The utility as well as the value of everything is, therefore, rather relative than positive, and is greater to one person than to another. This view of the subject shows that the real utility and value of many luxuries are much greater to the wealthy, than they are to the middling classes; but to all classes, their utility and value, are more or less factitious.

Every person should supply himself first with necessaries; secondly, with the comforts of life, and with luxuries of an intellectual character; and lastly with such other luxuries to a reasonable and limited extent, as are in accordance with his condition and circumstances in life—but should never indulge in any luxuries unless he can do so, without injury to the general welfare of himself or his family, and without setting a public example of an injurious tendency.

SEC. 3. *On values—their character and basis.*

The character of a thing (as I have said) depends on its utility, or capacity to satisfy our wants. The utility of a thing is not however perceived by instinct; it must be discovered by experience, observation, attention, judgment, and the deductions of reason. Value, therefore, depends first on our wants; secondly on the utility or capacity of a thing to satisfy our wants; thirdly, on the recognition of its utility; and fourthly, on the demand for it, in consequence of its utility, or supposed utility.

As one necessary, and one style or kind of luxury may be substituted for another; and there is a wide field of choice between different articles and modes, and also a great variety of opinions and tastes; it follows that the demand for the necessaries and comforts of life, as well as for luxuries, depends much on the habits of life, education, customs, and opinions of different people and communities, and is liable to fluctuate with the opinions, fashions, and customs of the day; and that their exchangeable value must fluctuate accordingly. Hence all the products of human industry have a value which is more or less increased or diminished by fashion, custom, and public opinion, and is therefore factitious.

When exchanges are introduced, things which can satisfy the wants of man may serve us in two ways, first directly, when we employ them for our own use, and secondly indirectly, when we exchange them for other commodities, or sell them for money. Whatever can be exchanged for something else that is useful, has an exchangeable value. This value depends not on the opinion of the producer, but upon that of the consumer. This value is direct or indirect, depending on the fact whether the purchaser buys for his individual use, or to sell again at a profit. A thing may have a direct value for use by reason of its utility, without an exchangeable value; but it cannot have an indirect value, unless it has a direct one also—and as soon as the consumers of a thing cease to acknowledge its utility, the demand ceases, and with it, its exchangeable value ceases also.

The direct utility of a thing also depends on the want of it, and the demand for it; for however great may be its capacity to satisfy the wants of man, if it is not needed, and there is no present want that can be satisfied by it, its utility is prospective only; and if it perishes rapidly, like vegetables and fruits, and like meats and grain also in hot climates, it often happens that it is of no use whatever to the community. The utility of things as well as their exchangeable value depends, therefore, on the want of them, and the market for them.

The value of a thing depends on the demand for it, but the price depends on the proportion which the supply bears to the demand, and depends as much on the one as the other. When a farmer, mechanic, or producer of any class, produces more of any article than he wants for his own consumption, if he cannot exchange the surplus for something else, it is of no value whatever to him; and if he has only a partial market for his surplus products, just so much of that surplus as exceeds the market, is totally worthless to the community, and if thrown upon a market already surfeited, serves to depress the price of the whole supply in the market, and really reduces, instead of increasing its aggregate market value.

SEC. 4. *On wealth and its basis.*

Wealth consists of values, and may be divided into material and immaterial. Immaterial values and wealth comprise the intellectual, moral, industrial, and social faculties and habits of the people; together with their customs, laws, and institutions. Material wealth comprises all material things which have either a present or prospective exchangeable value. As utilities and values both material and immaterial, are divided into real and factitious, so the wealth which they constitute should be divided in like manner; and as the utility and value of luxuries including expensive and magnificent dwelling-houses, and splendid furniture and equipages, are more or less factitious, so much of the wealth which they comprise, is also factitious. Intoxicating liquors to be used as a beverage have an exchangeable value, and therefore, are reckoned as a part of the wealth of a country; but as their use does not promote, or tend to promote, the general welfare of the consumer, but the contrary, they have no real utility, and their value, and the wealth which they constitute, is entirely factitious, as much so as that of an obscene picture or book. It has been shown that the real utility and value of many luxuries are relative; being much greater to the wealthy who are able to have them, than they are to the middling classes; the wealth which they constitute, is therefore relative, and more or less factitious; depending on the condition and circumstances of the person using them.

SEC. 5. *Definition and uses of capital.*

As the question embraces the subject of capital, we must enquire what is capital? Adam Smith says the general stock of a country is divided into three portions:

1st, That portion which is reserved for consumption and affords no revenue to the country; consisting of food, clothes, household furniture, dwelling houses, horses and carriages used for pleasure, pictures and all such things as contribute directly to human comfort or pleasure, and do not aid in producing or adding to the value of material objects which are desired by man.

2d. That portion generally denominated fixed capital; consisting of material agents, instruments and powers which aid man in producing or adding to the value of such material objects as are desired by mankind. Fixed capital includes, first, lands, and all the stock, improvements and instruments of husbandry, and all the tools, machinery and buildings used in mining, the mechanic arts, manufactures and commerce, navigation and transportation, the fisheries, and the forest. 2d. It includes the acquired and useful abilities of all the community. A useful education costs a real expense, and constitutes a part of the fixed capital of individuals, and also that of the community to which they belong.

3d. That portion usually denominated circulating capital; which comprises materials to be manufactured, the products of agriculture, mining and manufactures, the forest and fisheries, and the money or coin of the country.

Property may be divided into, first,—natural materials and products—and secondly, artificial materials and products. The first include all things in their natural state, and all the natural resources of a country; the second comprise all things produced or converted into a certain form, and fitted for use, by human industry.

Property may also be divided into, first, stock or materials to be manufactured and fitted for use; secondly, products for use and consumption, which do not aid industry, nor yield a revenue to the country; and thirdly, capital which comprises products, materials, and natural agents, converted into instruments and means to aid the industry of man, and thereby produce a revenue.

Though property consists of material things, yet the most of the value of them, which constitutes them property, is added to them, by the industry of man. Wild and unimproved lands in a new country do not constitute capital; but improvements made on them to fit them for production, and to secure the crops, and also the natural properties of the land when improved, do constitute capital. It is so with mines. In their natural state, they are not capital; but when opened, drained, and preparations have been made to extract the ores, they are converted into capital. It is so with water power, and all natural resources. They do not constitute capital, until they have been converted to use by the industry of man.

Capital should be sub-divided into material and immaterial (the former only constituting property). All capital, both material and immaterial, is fixed, that is unchangeable in its character and functions. What Smith and his disciples call circulating capital, consists, 1st, of raw products in the hands of the manufacturer to be worked into something else; 2d, of agricultural products for consumption; 3d, of the finished products of the manufacturer, mostly in the hands of the merchant for sale; and 4thly, money or coin.

All they put down as circulating capital, with the exception of money, consists only of products for consumption or manufacture. It is true that all products in the hands of merchants for sale, perform the functions of capital to them, but not to the community. So dwelling houses, theatres, gambling houses, &c., in the hands of a landlord who lets them for rent, perform the functions of capital to him, but not to the community; because to him they yield a revenue; but they do not add to the aggregate revenue of the community. They merely take from the tenant what is paid to the landlord. So household furniture, and even clothing, may be rented and yield an income to the owner, the same as horses and carriages let for pleasure; and yet those articles must all be ranked as products of consumption, and not capital; because they do not add to the aggregate revenue of the community, nor increase the revenue of the person who hires them, however much they may increase his comforts.

The reader will perceive inconsistency apparent on the face of the positions of Dr. Smith. Provisions he calls alternately articles or stock for consumption, and circulating capital. His arguments are all founded on the assumption, that the capitalist and laborer are necessarily different persons, and that the provisions furnished by the former, are necessary to enable the latter to labor, and therefore constitute a species of capital. In our free States, three-fourths of the laborers furnish their own capital, work for themselves, and unite the characters of capitalist and laborer. Do the provisions this laboring capitalist and his family consume, constitute a circulating capital? If so, then why are not his clothes and furniture also capital, and his grog likewise, if he have any? Stock, or products accumulated for consumption, are here confounded with circulating capital; and this confusion runs through the writings of all the disciples of Smith. Mr. Say has invented the awkward and inconsistent phrases "*productive consumption*," and "*unproductive consumption.*" A grosser misnomer never crept into human language.

The words production and consumption express opposite meanings. One is the Creation, and the other the Destruction of Value.

All the free trade school seem to forget, that food is necessary to support life. Nothing is strictly capital, except what comes within Smith's definition of FIXED CAPITAL; that is, *natural agents, instruments, power and faculties, which aid man in producing or adding to the value of such material objects as are desired by mankind.* All else are products or materials for manufacture or consumption; the latter may contribute to the comforts and enjoyments of man, but do not aid production. Capital must be confined to INSTRUMENTS, agents, powers, and faculties, which aid in production, and does not include the thing produced.

Immaterial capital includes the powers and faculties of the mind, together with the knowledge, science and experience acquired, as a guide to direct the industry of man, and make it productive. It also includes the whole process of an industrial education,* and the skill acquired by practice and experience. Material capital includes what is defined by Smith as fixed capital; it also includes gold and silver coin.

Gold and silver coin is put down by Smith and all his followers as circulating capital, because its use consists in circulating from one individual to another. They have put it in the same category with food and other articles of consumption, and with the merchant's stock on hand for sale; which I have endeavored to show, do not constitute any part of the capital of the community, because they do not add to the aggregate revenue or income of the community. If capital is to be divided into two classes, it should be denominated fixed, and changeable, capital; and not fixed and circulating. The term fixed, does not mean local, and when applied to material capital, it does not mean that its owner-

* See Section 9 of Chapter II.

ship is unchangeable, but that it is fixed and unchangeable in form, function and character.

A stock of materials to be worked up into manufactured products, if capital at all, is not properly circulating capital, *but changeable capital*, as contrasted with fixed capital; that is, it is to be changed by being worked up into something else. If the fact of the frequent transfer of money, merchandize, &c., from one person to another, makes them circulating capital, then the live stock on a man's farm, and even the farm itself, might be called circulating capital.

Sec. 6. *Coin, an Instrument of Commerce.*

In this view of the subject, gold and silver coin should be ranked as FIXED CAPITAL; because, first, its form, function, and character are as fixed and unchangeable as that of a mill, storehouse, factory, or any machinery or instrument of industry; and secondly it is an INSTRUMENT OF COMMERCE, without which an active domestic commerce cannot be carried on.

Gold and silver, on account of their durability, utility and beauty, are objects of desire to the whole human family, and therefore they have come into general use; first, as a measure of value; secondly as an instrument, medium, or means of payment; and like tools and instruments to aid and promote industry, they serve as tools and instruments of commerce, to facilitate exchanges between producers and consumers. They are not, however, necessary to the prosecution of foreign commerce—which is usually carried on, first, by selling one article and buying another in the same market; and secondly by means of bills of exchange drawn by the exporter on the consignee, for the proceeds of the property exported; which bills are sold to persons wishing to pay for other goods purchased in the country where the property is sold. These modes of doing business are, in a national point of view, equivalent to barter; because no money passes either way, from one nation to the other. Money is the *great instrument of domestic commerce*, and necessary to its very existence; without which it would soon grow languid, and industry would languish with it. In this country, it is the policy of the law to secure with peculiar care, the tools and instruments of industry of the laborer, mechanic and farmer; *and the nation should secure from exportation its coin as an instrument of commerce, with equal care.* The mechanic and farmer sell their products, but keep their tools and instruments of industry as capital, in order to continue producing. So with nations which do not produce a surplus of the precious metals. They should not treat gold and silver as products to be exported as merchandize; or suffer them to be exported on the same terms the products of the country are exported; but should treat them as *fixed capital, as tools and instruments of domestic commerce*, and preserve them with great care, as necessary to the healthful industry of the country. The most effectual mode to check the exportation of the precious metals from such countries, is to levy a duty on such export of ten or twelve per cent.; which would tend to encourage the exportation of the domestic products of the country, and increase their value.

SEC. 7. *Production and productive iudustry defined.*

Production does not consist in the creation of matter, but of values, which are more or less durable in their character. It may be divided into material and immaterial; depending on the application of the causes or means of production, so as to give value to matter or to man. Though any and every labor and human effort which tends to promote human happiness and enjoyment, is useful to man, yet those that produce utilities which are consumed with and at the time of production, such as household labor, the labor of domestic servants, and that of all the agents of mere amusement and pleasure, are not reckoned as productive. The distinction between such kinds of labor, and productive industry, is nearly the same as that between products for consumption and capital. Growing crops and animals, and adding value to material things, by means of labor, constitute material production. Communicating useful instruction to man, or promoting the security of his person and his rights, by means of government and the administration of justice, constitutes immaterial production. The former only is classed in common parlance with productive industry; and if material values are produced, no matter whether they consist of the necessaries of life, or the most worthless luxuries, the labor of producing them is reckoned as productive industry.

Political economists usually class merchants, navigators, and transporters of products, not as producers, but as distributors of wealth, though statisticians uniformly reckon their income as part of the productive industry of a country. The transportation of products adds value to them, and is a kind of quasi production of value; though much might be avoided by a more complete division of employments, in accordance with the wants of the people. But as to trade and commerce, including only the business of buying and selling, however necessary it may be and useful to the community, it cannot be properly classed as productive industry; unless every species of useful labor is so classed.

SEC. 8. *Use of Capital—Immaterial and Material Capital.*

Products of all kinds, whether raw materials to be manufactured, food to be consumed, manufactured products for use and consumption, or materials and products to be converted into capital, are produced and preserved by labor, aided by capital, both material and immaterial. Timber is said to be produced by cutting and preparing it for use, and ores, by raising them from the mines.

The following things are necessary to the production of material values.

1st. Materials or lands to work upon.

2d. Instruments, or capital to work with, aided by the laws of nature and natural agents

3d. Skill—and,

4th. Intellectual capacity, science and business talent, to direct the labor. The two last have been classed in section five, as immaterial capital.

Immaterial capital is even more necessary than material capital, to the progress of individuals and communities in productive industry. It is true that a certain amount of material capital is necessary to make labor effective; yet intellectual capital, experience, and skill, are still more indispensably necessary; without which man labors to no purpose. If he live in a country of great natural resources, and have an abundance of immaterial capital, no matter how destitute he may be at first of material capital, in a few years, by means of properly directed industry and frugality, he can accumulate sufficient products for a year's subsistence in advance, and sufficient capital to make his industry effective. This is verified by thousands of examples of the facility with which men of talents, education, industry, and economy, rise from poverty to the station of employers; uniting the character of business men and capitalists; not only in the United States, but also in Great Britain, and many other countries of Europe. On the contrary, if a man have very little intellectual capital, skill, experience and capacity for business or labor, it will require the use of a comparatively large amount of material capital managed by others, to support him and a family comfortably.

The same remarks apply equally well to nations that have great natural resources. Material capital can be accumulated by communities and nations, by means of industry properly directed, together with frugality, much more rapidly than it is possible for them to accumulate immaterial capital. Nations and communities which have a very small amount of immaterial capital, usually produce so little, that all or nearly all their products are consumed as fast as they are produced

Common agricultural labor, and the most common processes of mining and the mechanic arts, are comparatively simple, easily learned by the ignorant, and require only observation, attention, and practice, and very little development of intellect, to perform them tolerably well. But the more complicated branches of mechanism and what may properly be termed machine-factures, or production by means of machinery, are always more or less difficult to learn, require considerable intelligence and practical skill in the workmen, and a high degree of science, and great vigilance, attention, and business talent in the superintendants; which can be acquired only by a mind well disciplined by study and application to practical business.

As a general rule, it requires several years of training and discipline of both body and mind, to fit persons for any nice mechanical or manufacturing employment, and make them skilful workmen. Great difficulty has, therefore, been experienced in every country, in introducing the mechanic arts and any new branch or modes of manufacture, and obtaining skilful workmen to carry them on successfully; and many of the monarchs of Europe during the last five centuries, have made great efforts, and held out strong inducements to encourage skillful workmen from other countries to settle in their dominions, and establish their respective branches of manufacture. The mechanic arts and manufactures have never flourished in any country, without the fostering care of the government. Why did the ancient Spartans remain for centuries a rude, ignorant, uncultivated people, without change or improvement, devoted to agriculture and the arts of war, while their neighbors, the Athenians, were making rapid strides in the mechanic arts, commerce, literature, and refinement? Was it not owing to the difference in the policy of the government as well as in the spirit of the people? to the fact that in Sparta, the mechanic arts, commerce, literature, and everything but agriculture, physical strength, and the arts of war, were discouraged by the laws and the officers of the government, and held in contempt by the people; while in Athens they were encouraged by the laws and government, and held in esteem?

We find that nations increase in productive industry in proportion as they increase in intelligence, in the use of the metals, and a knowledge of mechanism. An industrial education is as necessary, as a literary and scientific one. There is not a sufficient number of men of science and of practical knowledge and experience, in Catholic, Mahomedan, or Pagan countries, to direct the industry of the people; nor is there intelligence, practical knowledge, and skill enough among the mass of the people, to make their industry very productive.

SEC. 9. *Division of Employments, and limits to division.*

Great importance has been generally attached to a division of employments, which has been often miscalled a division of labor. A division of employments beyond a doubt contributes greatly to increase the productive industry of a nation or people; first by saving much time in changing from one employment to another; secondly by dispensing with many tools and much capital which are necessary to pursue several different employments; and lastly, by enabling laborers to acquire more skill, by confining themselves to a more simple process or routine of labor.

A division of employments presupposes an exchange of the surplus products of each producer. A man who devotes himself exclusively to one occupation, produces what is necessary to satisfy but one want, and would have no means of satisfying his other wants, if he could not exchange his surplus products for the products of others. The division of employments is therefore limited by the demand for the products of each laborer respectively; or in the language of science, by the extent of the market; and cannot be carried to any great extent, among the people of a sparsely settled country. The extent of the market depends much on the character of the products; whether they are perishable or not, and whether they are more or less valuable in proportion to their weight and bulk. Markets are extended by increased facilities of transportation.

Nature has fixed limits to the division of employments. As agricultural employments vary with the season of the year, they do not admit of much division. Nor do mining, smelting metals, navigation and transportation, or even commerce, except in cities, admit of a very minute division of employments. In fact, quite too much importance has been generally attached, to a minute subdivision of employments; and too little to invention, to the combination of labor, and to immaterial capital.

SEC. 10. *What constitutes a field of employment—the importance of securing it.*

Before men can labor productively, they must have a field of employment. A field of employment consists, first, of the natural resources of a country; or lands and materials to work upon. Secondly, of the capital employed, or tools and natural agents to work with. And thirdly, of the demand, and market for the products of labor. All these things must concur; and each must be co-extensive with the number of laborers, in order to employ advantageously all the inhabitants of a nation.

Markets for products are nearly as necessary to encourage

industry, as lands and materials to work upon, and tools to work with. When either is wanting, industry will languish. Markets depend much on a proper division of employments, and the distribution of labor and capital among the several employments, in accordance with the natural resources and wants of the country; so that each class of laborers and producers may aid in creating a market for the products of every other class.

Political economists of the free-trade school, have attached too much importance to material capital, a minute subdivision of employments, foreign commerce, and natural facilities for foreign commerce—and quite too little, to immaterial capital, and domestic commerce. They have generally overlooked the importance of a division of employments in accordance with the natural resources of a country, and the wants of the people—and of securing the domestic market, as a field of employment, for the laborers of the country. There is in Great Britain and Holland vastly more property than can be advantageously employed as capital, strictly speaking; and hence the large amount sent abroad for investment, and the immense amount invested in palaces, splendid dwellings, furniture, and objects of taste and pleasure.

The natural resources of a country consist of its territory, soil, climate, fertility, timber, fuel, mines, minerals, quarries, navigable waters, rivers, brooks, water-power and fisheries; and their value depends much on the distribution of them over the country, so as to be convenient of access to all the inhabitants.

Ireland has very few productive mines, but little ore of any kind, and very little fuel. Its natural resources are too limited, to furnish a sufficient field of employment for so large a population. The people, however, might (under other circumstances) manufacture for themselves; but by means of free imports from Great Britain, their markets are substantially taken from them, for the benefit of British manufacturers and laborers, and the manufacturers and laborers of Ireland are deprived of a field of employment, which properly belongs to them. All the provinces, colonies, and dependencies of Great Britain are in a similar condition. Their markets, which should furnish a field of employment for their own laborers, are, to a very great extent, monopolized by the British people; and the industry of the Colonies, is left to wither—and they are kept poor and dependent.

The same evils, (to a limited extent,) have been visited upon these United States—by means of delusions on the subject of free-trade. Our markets have been partially sacrificed for the benefit of British and French manufacturers and laborers, and foreign importers, and much of the field of employment, which justly belongs to our own citizens, has been transferred to foreigners. This has depressed nearly all branches of industry and business, and greatly lessened the aggregate amount and value of the industry of the nation.

SEC. 11. *On the production and accumulation of wealth.*

As production depends on labor, aided by capital, the laws of nature and natural agents, the rapidity of production depends on the effectiveness and productiveness of labor. The effectiveness of labor is determined by the quality and quantity of its products; but its productiveness is determined as well by their exchangeable value, as by their quantity and quality; and their value depends on the demand for them, when compared with the supply in the market. Labor is effective, in proportion as it is aided by skill, good tools, and machinery, and directed by intelligence, science, and business talent. But labor is productive in a national point of view, in proportion to the utility to the community of its products, and whenever any thing of a perishable nature is produced that is not needed, and not wanted, either for use at home, or for exportation, it is useless and valueless in a national point of view, as explained in Section 3. The same is the case when a larger quantity of perishable commodities are produced than are needed; the surplus is wholly useless and valueless to the nation. And when such surplus does not consist of perishable commodities and is of value to the community to retain for future use, it reduces prices so much, that the producers get less for the whole product, than they would if the aggregate quantity was less; and therefore they are injured, instead of being benefited by the surplus. This fact has been well illustrated by Tooke on Prices.

That nations as well as communities are capable of producing, and often do produce, much greater quantities of certain products than they need for their own use, and can sell to advantage, is well known to every intelligent reader. This surplus causes a glut of the market and a depression of prices. People are not willing to labor for nothing, or for a mere trifle, and as the demand for any particular branch of industry falls below the supply, and the price declines, production soon declines also, and industry languishes. The industry of a country can be increased in amount and value, only in proportion as it is diversified, directed into different channels, and employed upon different objects, in accordance with the resources of the country, and with the wants of the people, and of the commercial world. In this mode, all the commodities produced, could be disposed of at fair prices; the farmer, mechanic, miner, and manufacturer, each furnishing a market for the others; the wants of all would be supplied about equally well, and no surplus left, to be wasted.

The material wealth of a country depends more on the aggregate value, than it does on the quantity of property in it. The exchangeable value of the farming and wood lands of Great Britain is about twice as great as that of all the lands of the United States. This is in consequence of the density of the population, and the demand for the products of land to supply their wants. If, however, we regard the future prospects of landed wealth in a nation, more depends on the quantity and quality of its lands, than on their present value; for as the population becomes more dense, the demand for food and for lands will increase; which will necessarily enhance the aggregate value of the landed and other property of the country, even without the aid of any other cause. Population is therefore an element of wealth, as well as of power. Population is an element of wealth, first, by creating a demand and furnishing a market for property and products, and thereby enhancing their value; secondly, by means of such increased demand and market, it promotes the division of employments, facilitates domestic commerce and the mutual interchange of products, and encourages and increases the productive industry of the country, and renders the labor of each man more effective, and more valuable. This view of the subject shows that there are two sources of wealth—first, productive industry, and secondly, population; but they must be aided by economy, and a desire to save, or they will both be of no avail.

The accumulation of wealth depends as much on frugality and economy, as it does on production. The annual production of almost every community, is equal in value to from one fifth to one seventh of the entire amount of their property; and their consumption is usually nearly equal, and in some quite equal, to their production. This being the case, no matter how wealthy a people may be, a few years of indolence and extravagance will reduce them to poverty: on the contrary, a few years of well directed industry and frugality, will raise them to a state of competency.

Frugality and economy being necessary to the accumulation of wealth, let us examine the subject of consumption or expenditure. In this age of science, intelligence, and machinery, it is not difficult, in a country like ours, for every industrious adult of good health to supply himself with the necessaries of life; and nearly all those who are intelligent as well as industrious, can supply themselves also with the comforts of life, and with some luxuries, and yet save some portion of their annual earnings, to be accumulated, either as capital, or as products for future consumption. Our natural wants are easily supplied in this country; but our artificial or factitious wants, comprising the luxuries of life, are unlimited in their character, and may be indulged in by individuals to their total destruction. Luxuries may be divided into two classes; first, those of sensuality, and secondly, those of ostentation. The first are the most limited in their character, but the most dangerous to the health and morals of the individual. The second are founded in a desire to appear rich, and are wholly unlimited in amount, and the range of subjects to which they apply, and when indulged in to excess, generally produce pecuniary embarrassment and bankruptcy.

There is no way for individuals to accumulate property, but to consume annually less than their income, and to save the surplus. The necessaries of life are comparatively cheap, and require but little labor to produce them, in proportion to their capacity to satisfy our natural wants—while luxuries are generally dear, and require much labor to produce them; and yet, the most of them do not even supply the place of necessaries, which are required as much with, as without them. Where a taste for luxuries pervades the middling as well as the wealthy classes of a community or nation, they often consume all their income from year to year, and from century to century, without progress, or increase of either wealth or population.

The accumulation of wealth, therefore, depends,

1st. On production, or productive industry—

2d. On frugality and economy, so as to keep expenditures below income, and leave a surplus—and,

3d. On a proper direction of industry, in accordance with the resources of the country, and with the wants of the people, and of the commercial world; so that all real wants may be supplied, and the surplus left may not comprise articles that are of a perishable character, but may consist of capital, articles which may be converted into capital, and dwelling houses, furniture, clothing, books, and such other articles as are not immediately consumed in their use, including very few luxuries.

The rapidity with which wealth is accumulated, depends—first, on the amount and value produced over and above what is annually consumed—and secondly, on the character of that surplus—whether it consists of perishable articles and frivolous luxuries, or capital, articles that may be converted into capital, and those not immediately consumed in their use, which have a substantial utility.

Perishable articles do not admit of being accumulated to any considerable extent, for future use. It is therefore impossible to increase the wealth of a community or nation in the smallest amount, by increasing the production of perishable products, beyond the wants of the people, and the demands for export, within a comparatively short period. On the contrary, the metals of all kinds are very durable in their character, and are mostly converted into, and used as capital. Products of wood, stone and brick, and improvements on lands, roads, &c., are all comparatively durable, and of substantial utility to man. Books and clothing also, and the raw materials to make into clothing, and even some kinds of provisions, may be preserved by care, for many years, and may be accumulated for future use. The industry of a people should therefore be so distributed among the several employments, that the substantial wants of all may be supplied—that the surplus annually produced, may be of the character described—and that as much of it may consist of capital, as can be useful in promoting industry. Production is, however, very much influenced, and, in many cases absolutely controlled, by foreign commerce.

Liberty and security of person and property, are necessary to the production and accumulation of wealth, to any very considerable extent. There can be no reason to doubt that civil liberty, free domestic competition, and freedom from legal restraint and from monopolies, tend to promote industry and the production of wealth. Every citizen should be free to pursue such employment as he sees fit—provided it is not inconsistent with good morals, and the general welfare. Production should be unrestrained by laws, though legislation may often aid it—by regulating the mode of conducting business by associations—by collecting and disseminating information of the aggregate products and wants of the nation, and of the commercial world—and by encouraging the diversion of industry into new channels, in accordance with the condition and wants of the people. But commerce should often be regulated; in order to check extravagance, and the use of what is pernicious, and to secure the home market to the citizen, as a field of employment which properly belongs to him, and as a means of encouraging domestic production.

SEC. 12. *Markets, the principal stimulants of industry. Colonial policy of Europe.*

Population alone, adds value to lands and property of every kind, and is, therefore, one of the principal sources and causes of wealth. And *why is it so? Simply because it creates a market, by causing a demand for property and products.* It enhances their price and exchangeable value, rewards the producer for his industry, and encourages and increases industry and production. Population thus creates markets, and markets operate to enhance prices, and to increase wealth, industry, and production. *Markets are therefore among the principal causes and sources of value and of wealth, and stimulants of industry.* The farmer, mechanic, miner, and manufacturer, are all beneficial to each other; for the reason that each wants the products of every other, in exchange for his own—and thus each creates a market for the products of all the others, and thereby enhances prices and stimulates their industry. Hence the advantage to the farmer, of increasing mechanical, manufacturing, and mining industry, as far as practicable, in his own country, in order to create a market for his products, and to encourage domestic commerce.

The fact is, that mechanical industry in most countries is about twice as profitable as agricultural industry, and manufacturing with machinery is generally from three to five times as profitable. Every manufacturing nation can produce more manufactured products than are needed at home, and hence the importance of markets to them, and the anxiety with which they seek markets abroad. The fact of markets being among the principal causes and sources of wealth, has led to the colonial system of Europe—and prompted manufacturing nations to plant colonies and extend their foreign dominions, as a means of creating markets for their mechanical and manufacturing industry. And in order to render their colonies as good markets as possible, they endeavor to confine their colonists as far as practicable, to agricultural pursuits; to prevent them from manufacturing even "a hobnail" for themselves. Great Britain not only holds in colonial bondage British India, Canada, and numerous islands and other provinces and possessions, but she holds Ireland also in the same condition, and for the same purpose—to furnish a market for the products of her manufacturing and mining industry at high prices, in payment of agricultural products at comparatively low prices.

Markets being of great value to a nation, it is not only good policy, but a matter of justice to herself and to her own citizens, for every nation to secure her own markets, for the benefit of her own citizens, so far as they are capable of supplying them, and to encourage an increase of any particular branch of industry, which may be adapted to the climate and natural resources of the country. So far as foreign manufactures imported into a country supply the place of those which might be manufactured at home, and thus supplant so much domestic industry, they do not add one dollar to the wealth of the country beyond what they destroy in the shape of its industry; but on the contrary, the country loses every single dollar that is paid for them; unless something is exchanged for them which is not needed, or one luxury is exchanged for another. Such importations also tend to undermine and destroy the manufacturing laborer as well as the capitalist—to check the increase of manufactures, and to disperse the capital and the laborers already employed in the business—and thus they undermine and destroy at the same time, the markets for the farmer, and produce a permanent injury to all classes of the community.

The consumption of many expensive luxuries is prejudicial to the prosperity of a country; but the degree of injury arising from it, depends on the condition of the country, and whether they are produced at home, or imported from abroad; and if the latter, whether they do, or do not, come into competition with domestic industry. When domestic luxuries are consumed, the demand for them stimulates and increases domestic industry; but when foreign luxuries are imported, the possession of them, by supplying or aiding in supplying the market, lessens the demand for domestic products, and thus diminishes the domestic industry of the country—and makes it poor to the full extent of the value to the country, of the money or other commodities given in exchange for them. If on the contrary, foreign luxuries imported do not come in competition with domestic industry, and something is exchanged for them of which the people have a surplus—their importation may not, under such circumstances, be of any injury whatever.

SEC. 13. *The different employments and pursuits personified.*

The sentiment is frequently rung in our ears by partisan politicians and partisan newspapers, that the farmers and agricultural laborers of the United States, are "THE BONE AND SINEW OF THE COUNTRY," as they express it; and nearly the whole newspaper press in the greater part of the slave States, inculcate the idea, that *planters and professional men are the only personages of much importance; that mechanics and commercial men are an inferior order of beings; and that the farming and planting interests only should seriously occupy the attention of Congress.* Let us examine this question, and in order to do so, let us personify civilization and analyze civilized society, and see what its parts are composed of. It is claimed that agriculturists are "the *bone and sinew* of the country," and of the social fabric; very well, admit it.

Iron, copper, gold, silver, tin, and other metals, and the miners and workers in metals who convert them into edge tools, and into various tools, instruments, implements, and machinery, and thereby lay the very corner stone and foundation of all productive industry, agricultural, mechanical, and manufacturing, as well as of navigation and transportation by both land and water, may be said to constitute the HEART OF THE SYSTEM; in as much as they furnish the power which puts in motion, sustains and propels all the productive industry of the civilized world. Civilized man does nothing in any capacity, and can do nothing without the use of the metals; and the quantity of the metals used by any people may be taken as a fair test of the amount of their productive industry, and of the progress they have made in the useful arts, and in the march of civilization. A people without the use of the metals, using stone axes, and stone spades, and other utensils made of baked clay or stone, must be utterly unable to make cloth of any kind, or cultivate the earth, must dwell in caves and miserable huts, live on natural fruits and the spontaneous productions of the earth and the game they can kill, as their only food, and clothe themselves in furs and skins. They are necessarily in the lowest state of savages, like the tribes of North America, north of Mexico, and those of the southern part of the Continent, at the time of its discovery; a grade below the German and Celtic tribes of northern Europe in the time of the Roman empire, who had some knowledge of iron, and other metals, and had a small quantity of iron in use to point their spears, and to make an edge to a few rude tools and instruments of agriculture.

Mechanics and the mechanic arts, with the aid of machinery in modern times, comprise the stomach, the digestive and assimilating organs, and the entire muscular part of the system. By making the tools and implements, they create almost the whole power and means by which even agriculture is or can be pursued. They prepare raw materials for use; make them into cloth, clothing, bedding, furniture, dwellings, workshops, &c., &c., and by fitting raw materials for use and for market, they furnish the principal part in value of the materials of commerce.

Agriculture, and agriculturists, do in fact form the great framework, and constitute the bones and cartilages, or *bone and sinew*, as the democracy express it, the mere skeleton of the system; to which the whole is attached, and on which it all, in some measure, depends. It may be fairly likened to a skeleton in more than one particular; first, it is so entirely dependent, on the mechanic arts, and on commerce, that without them, it is necessarily inactive, and nearly torpid. The agriculture of all savage and barbarous nations where there is very little commerce, and not much is known of the mechanic arts, is mostly confined to the rude culture of a very little grain, and a few vegetables, and to raising cattle, sheep, camels, goats, &c.; hence famines were frequent, in early ages of the world, though they are entirely unknown in modern times, among civilized nations. Secondly, it may be likened to a skeleton, because all nations exclusively, or mostly devoted to agricultural pursuits, are sparsely scattered over a large territory in proportion to their numbers, and are always poor; destitute of many of the comforts of life; and have very little industry or activity, compared with manufacturing and commercial nations. Look abroad among the nations of the earth, both ancient and modern, and see if any people ever became rich and powerful, or enjoyed in abundance the comforts of life, who depended on agriculture alone for a support, and on the people of other nations to furnish them with the products of mechanical industry. If history furnishes such a case, it has escaped my notice. On the contrary, ancient Tyre, Carthage, and Athens, and in more modern times, Venice, Genoa, Holland, and England, are all striking examples, of nations becoming rich and powerful by means of commerce and the mechanic arts, with a very small territory, and little aid comparatively from agriculture.

To carry out the figure, public roads, navigable waters, canals, railroads, and common carriers, constitute the bloodvessels, arteries, veins, glands, and secretory ducts of the system. Commerce and commercial men constitute the lungs and life blood of civilization; without which it never did exist in any age of the world, or any country, and without which it never can exist so long as man is partially a physical material being. The ancient civilization of the world, of Greece and Rome, and the modern cases of China and Japan, show, however, that an extensive domestic commerce only is necessary to support civilization; that though foreign commerce may aid, yet it is not indispensable. And though commerce is as necessary to civilization as the circulation of the blood is to the human system, yet, since the precious metals have become the universal medium of commerce, and standard of commercial exchanges and of contracts, foreign imports may be stimulated to such an unnatural degree of activity, as to resemble the circulation of the blood in the heat and violence of a burning fever, which is soon succeeded by exhaustion and debility. Such was the condition of the foreign commerce of the United States from 1834 to 1842 inclusive, when, by means of the excessive importation of foreign goods, beyond our immediate ability to pay, we got into debt to Europe about two hundred millions of dollars, a drain of the precious metals ensued to pay the interest on our foreign debt and a portion of the principal, and commercial embarrassment, depression of property and business, and severe distress, spread throughout the country, and produced ten times as much suffering as the Asiatic cholera, or any other epidemic or scourge which ever afflicted us as a people. We suffered similar evils from like causes from 1783 to 1789, and from 1815 to 1824.

The public press, printers, and publishers of books and papers, the post-office department and the conductors of it, and the modern system of telegraphic communications, constitute the nervous system; and our scientific and learned men, authors, schools, and seminaries of learning, and the conductors of them, legislators, high executive and judicial officers, members of the learned professions, business men, and editors, constitute the brain and directing mind of the nation. All parts of the social system, and all branches of industry, are dependent upon each other, and are necessary to make the whole complete. Agriculture, of all others, probably, has the least influence upon the wealth and power of a nation. Turkey, Spain, Portugal, all Spanish America, and all the nations of Africa, are striking instances of the indolence, inactivity, poverty, weakness and ignorance of nations devoted almost exclusively to agriculture and war, depending on foreign commerce to supply them with manufactured goods, and enjoying substantially the blessings of free trade.

Sec. 14. *Effect of the mechanic arts and of commerce on the character and enterprise of nations.*

Where men are congregated together by commerce, manufactures, and the mechanic arts, in cities and large towns, they see more objects to stimulate them to activity and enterprise, than those do who are scattered over the country as agriculturists; their intellectual passions are more stimulated, and become stronger; and at the same time, the division of employments being more complete, and their minds more concentrated for years upon one department of industry or business, they are generally enabled to attain a higher degree of science and skill than is attainable under less favorable circumstances. Hence the minds of these classes of persons become more active and acute in their respective employments, more inventive, more inclined to seek after new discoveries and inventions, and new modes of enterprise, than agriculturists; and hence nearly all the discoveries, inventions, and useful improvements, have been made by the mechanical, manufacturing, and commercial classes. Hence their minds are more full of schemes and projects, often ill digested; and they have more enterprise, but less stability of character, as a general rule, than agriculturists. They are more daring and hazardous, but less safe; and their operations frequently partake of the character of gambling speculations. But even their wildest visions, such as the constant search of mechanics after principles upon which to construct a perpetual motion, have often resulted in the discovery of mechanical principles which have been of great value to mankind.

With the exception of William Penn, Lord Baltimore, and their followers, and the Puritans who emigrated to New-England to enjoy freedom of conscience, and freedom of religious opinions, all the colonies on the western continent, north of Mexico, were planted by commercial companies, and for commercial purposes. Such also was the mode and purpose for which the colonies of Holland, Great Britain, France, and Portugal, were planted in the East Indies. The English East India Company, while a mere commercial company, backed up by the manufactures of Great Britain, which furnished its chief materials of export, has waged war on a larger and more magnificent scale than was ever done by any of the modern nations of Europe, prior to the French revolution; and since 1770, has conquered, and subjected to the British dominion, over one hundred millions of inhabitants. Such are the effects of mechanical and manufacturing industry, and commercial enterprise, upon the progress and power of nations. Such employments and pursuits seem to have furnished the propulsive energies which have led to progress in improvement, in wealth, and in civilization, in all ages of the world. This position is verified by the history of Tyre, Carthage, Athens, Venice, Genoa, Belgium and Holland, as well as Great Britain; while the influence of agriculture has been of a conservative character, inclining the people to remain the same, unchangeable, and without innovation, improvement, or progress.

Sec. 15. *Effect of the mechanic arts and manufactures upon markets and agriculture.*

The prosperity of any people, the comforts they enjoy, and their wealth and power, depend on the amount and value of their productive industry. No matter what the soil, climate, or the resources of their country, or their form of government, religion, or social system, without industry, it is impossible for them to procure or enjoy many of the comforts of civilized life. The productiveness of industry depends as much on the price and aggregate value, as it does on the quantity and quality of its products; and as the price of commodities depends on the demand for them, and the extent of the market, the productiveness and profits of industry are dependent upon, and governed by, the market for its products.

It is inconsistent with the very nature of things, and therefore impossible, for agricultural industry to be very productive and profitable, without the aid of the mechanic arts, and the enlivening and fostering influence of an active commerce, steady demand, and regular markets for its products. Nine-tenths of the products of agriculture are so heavy and bulky in proportion to their value, and the cost of transporting them any considerable distance is so great, that if there is not a large mechanical and manufacturing, or commercial population in the vicinity, there can be no demand of any amount for them, no regular market, and not much value. In many of the interior districts of the Western States, Indian corn has been worth but ten or twelve cents a bushel, and frequently could not be sold for cash at even that low price. The principal market for the common kinds of breadstuffs and provisions of all sorts, is necessarily a domestic one in all countries; it is a market created by persons engaged in the mechanic arts, manufactures, commerce, mining, war, or some employment or pursuit other than agriculture. Farmers cannot furnish a market for each other; and cannot live by bartering and exchanging with each other their products.

Agriculture never did flourish in any country, where the mechanic arts were not flourishing; if we except a few islands in hot climates, whose products are in great demand, which procure in exchange for them an abundance of all the products of the mechanic arts, at reasonable prices. Such is the situation of the Island of Cuba, and in fact of all the West India, and many of the East India islands. Cuba, under the dominion of the Spaniards, the Roman Catholic religion, and the enervating influence of slavery and a tropical climate, is much more flourishing than the Province of Upper Canada, under the influence of civil liberty, a mild climate, the Protestant religion, and the boasted energies of the Anglo-Saxon race and character. The contrast between the prosperity of Cuba and that of the old tobacco-growing States, is very great indeed; and it is quite striking also, between Cuba and the southern cotton-growing States. This must be owing to the fact that the demand for coffee and sugar, the staple products of the island, has been rapidly increasing, and has nearly kept pace with the supply; so that the price has declined only 30 or 40 per cent. since the year 1780, not more than the decrease in the expense of cultivation, by reason of the improved mode of culture; and these products are so valuable, in proportion to their weight and bulk, that they will bear transportation to any part of the world. On the contrary, the increase of slaves in our slave States has been great, and the principal part of slave labor devoted to growing cotton, tobacco, and Indian corn, until the supply of those great staples has greatly exceeded the demand, and depressed their prices very low, the greatest part of the time, for many years past.

It has long been the policy of the slaveholding States, to discourage the mechanic arts, as well as the more complicated manufactures with machinery, and to rely upon agriculture. The pernicious consequences of that policy are developing themselves rapidly; there is very little foreign market for corn or provisions of any kind; tobacco has long been much depressed in price; and now the culture of cotton is but little better than that of tobacco. The rule laid down by political economists as general and universal, that the price of an article depends on the proportion between the demand and supply of the market, is fully verified by the constant decline of the price of cotton for the last sixty years. Though the demand has increased more than twenty fold, yet the supply has increased still more, and faster, and thus depressed its price beyond all example.

Corn being worth only from a quarter of a cent to a cent per pound, and the expense of transporting it a single hundred miles, by teams, being nearly half a cent per pound, it is obvious that the principal market for it must be a domestic one, and confined to a small circle; while coffee, sugar, cotton, wool, and all manufactures of cloths and costly goods, will bear transportation thousands of miles, and the markets for them, were it not for commercial duties and restrictions, would be coextensive with the civilized world. The principal market for the agricultural products of all countries above the thirty-fifth degree of latitude, must be a domestic one, even if all the world should adopt the theory and practice of free trade; for the reason that nearly all their products are so bulky and heavy in proportion to their value, that they will not bear transportation very far. The price of the farmer's produce depends upon the demand, compared with the supply; the demand depends upon the number of consumers, and their ability to pay; the consumers of most kinds of produce must reside within a comparatively short distance of the producer; the mechanic arts and manufactures supply the means of subsistence to a dense population, and enable them to pay good prices for all the products of the farmer, and thus create a demand and a market, for the produce of the farmer in his own vicinity, and at the same time furnish the means of payment, and the very kind of payment the farmer needs to supply his wants.

It is therefore obvious, that agriculture is dependent on the mechanic arts and manufactures, not only to supply the necessary tools, instruments, and implements for carrying it on advantageously, but also for a market for its products, without which it cannot be prosperous and flourishing. No exclusively agricultural nation above the thirty-fifth degree of latitude, ever did, or ever can become rich or prosperous. Without the advantages of the mechanic arts, and of manufactures, and a large mechanical and manufacturing population near at hand as consumers, markets are necessarily poor and dull; the demand for provisions and most kinds of agricultural products, small in proportion to the supply, and their prices low and depressed; the country constantly drained of its precious metals to pay for foreign luxuries and manufactured goods, and its commerce thereby embarrassed; industry and improvements of every kind discouraged for want of a proper and certain reward for labor; the mass of the people inactive, indolent, and necessarily poor, for want of sufficient industry; and the whole population in a dull, stagnant, and stationary condition, merely vegetating in times of peace, having little or no activity, enterprise, or energy, except what is excited by war, and a desire for conquest and plunder. Such was the state and condition of ancient Sparta, as contrasted with Athens; such was the condition of all Europe, during the dark and middle ages; and such is now the condition of Turkey and all Mahometan countries, of Spain, Portugal, part of Italy, and nearly the whole of South America and Mexico; and the same anti-manufacturing policy has a powerful and depressing influence also, upon the greater part of the slave States, and upon a large portion of the free States. The free trade between Ireland and the Canadas, and Great Britain, together with the statutes of the British Parliament to discourage manufactures and the mechanic arts in those countries, and keep them dependent on England, has had the same depressing influence, and kept the Canadas, as well as Ireland, poor. Why is China much more prosperous, wealthy, and flourishing than Turkey, Spain, Portugal, and even Mexico? It cannot be owing to the government, for the Emperor of China is equally absolute and unlimited in his power as the Sultan of Turkey. Can any cause be assigned, except the mechanic arts and an extensive domestic commerce?

It is generally, if not universally admitted, that from the 8th to the latter end of the 12th century, the Saracens were more advanced in the mechanic arts, commerce, and all the arts and refinements of civilized life, than the Christian nations of Europe; that the Moors of Spain were in advance of the Spaniards; and that the Christians learned many of the arts, as well as the refinements and luxuries of civilization, from the Saracens, during the crusades of the 11th and 12th centuries, and imported them from thence into Europe. This superiority in civilization and refinement of the Saracens over the Christians, could not have been owing to their religion, nor to their government, nor to the superiority of their social system. It must have been owing partly to the greater mildness of the climate, better adapted to the situation and condition of man in a low state of civilization; but mostly to the more improved and advanced state of the mechanic arts, and the greater amount of their productive industry; though the state of the mechanic arts among them was very low, and the amount of their productive industry small, compared with that of the Romans, during the most flourishing period of the empire, and much more so when compared with many nations at this time.

CHAPTER VII.

ON THE METALS—THEIR USE—THE DISCOVERY AND HISTORY OF WORKING THEM, AND THE PROGRESSIVE PRODUCTION OF THEM.

SEC. 1. *General history and use of the metals.*

Iron is the most abundant, the strongest, hardest, and most useful of all the metals. It is so important, and its uses so numerous and indispensable to the successful pursuit of almost every species of productive industry, that its use has been generally treated as the chief test of civilization. It appears from the 4th chapter of Genesis, that Tubal Cain (the seventh generation from Adam) was an instructor of every artificer in brass and iron. Working in gold, silver, and brass is mentioned in Exodus xxxi: 3, 4, and 5. The use of iron and brass is also referred to in the book of Job xx: 24; xxviii: 2; and xl: 18, supposed to refer to a period more than 1500 years before Christ; also in Leviticus xxvi: 19, and Deut. xxviii: 23, and 48, referring to periods nearly 1500 years, B. C.

Mr. Jacob of England, in his learned Historical Inquiry into the production and consumption of the Precious Metals, makes the following remarks in the introduction: "The general voice of antiquity affirms, that Gold, Silver, and Copper, or Brass, were the first metals discovered; and that they were used partly as ornaments, and partly as instruments of war, or of industry; for though, from their softness, they were not the best calculated for the latter purposes, they were better adapted than those of flint or other hard stones, or hard wood, which had been before used by the most ancient tribes, and which were also found among the savage people inhabiting Australia, when they were discovered in the middle of the last century."

A well known passage of Hesiod affirms, that in remote ages, "The earth was worked with brass, because iron had not then been discovered" and Lucretius bears testimony to the same purpose in Book V: l. 1286. "Et prior æris erat, quam ferri, cognitus usus." [The use of brass was known before that of iron.] This is confirmed by the implements of copper found in the ancient mines, in Siberia, and in Nubia; whose working must have ceased some thousand years ago.

"When Brazil was first discovered by the Portuguese, the rude inhabitants used fish hooks of gold, but had no iron, though their soil abounded in that metal. The people of Hispaniola (now called St. Domingo,) and Mexico, were, in like manner, unacquainted with Iron when first visited by the Spaniards; though they had both ornaments and implements of Gold, and weapons of Copper; which latter, we learn from the analysis of Humboldt, they had acquired the art of hardening by an alloy of tin.

This subject has been illustrated in Denmark by opening many Scandinavian tumuli of very remote ages, from which have been collected specimens of knives, daggers, swords, and implements of industry, which are preserved and arranged in the Museum at Copenhagen. There are tools of various kinds formed of flint or other hard stone, in shapes resembling our wedges, axes, chisels, hammers, and knives, which are presumed to have been those first invented. There are swords, daggers, and knives, the blades of which are of gold, whilst an edge of iron is formed for the purpose of cutting. Some of the tools and weapons are formed principally of copper, with edges of iron; and in many of the implements, the profuse application of copper and of gold, when contrasted with the parsimony evident in the expenditure of iron, seems to prove, that at the unknown period, and among the unknown people who raised the tumuli, which antiquarian research had lately explored, gold as well as copper were much more abundant products than iron."

McCulloch in his Commercial Dictionary, title Iron, makes the following remarks, "Iron, though the most common, is the most difficult of all the metals to obtain in a state fit for use; and the discovery of the method of working it seems to have been posterior to the use of gold, silver and copper. We are wholly ignorant of the steps by which men were led to practise the processes required to fuse it, and render it malleable. It is certain, however, that it was prepared in ancient Egypt, and some other countries, at a very remote epoch, but it was very little used in Greece until after the Trojan war.'

Sec. 2. *Iron in Great Britain.*

At what period the art of smelting ore and making iron was introduced into England is unknown; but Brande says there is authentic evidence to show that iron-works were established by the Romans in the forest of Dean in Gloucestershire and in other parts of the kingdom; and that they were also established at an early period in Kent and Sussex. To make a ton of pig-iron requires nearly four tons of mineral coal, or the charcoal produced by burning seven or eight cords of wood; and to convert it into bar iron or castings, requires about half as much.

In 1619, Lord Dudley invented the process of smelting iron with pit or mineral coal; but his works were soon after destroyed by a mob. In the early part of the eighteenth century, well founded complaints were made of the waste and destruction of wood and timber by the smelting of iron; and the dearth and scarcity of fuel that was thus occasioned, led, about the year 1740, to the general adoption of Lord Dudley's process of using pit coal.

Wood was becoming scarce in Great Britain, and it was found impossible to smelt iron with fossil or mineral coal, with a bellows worked by the hand, or horse power. The manufacture of iron was therefore comparatively small, until after the improvement of the steam engine by Watts, in 1767, its application to mining, to iron works, and to working the bellows in blast furnaces to smelt the iron with mineral coal, and the use of the reverberatory air furnaces invented by Mr. Cort in 1783. As the beds of coal are inexhaustible, the manufacture of iron advanced rapidly from that period. The quantity of pig iron made in England and Wales in 1740 from 59 furnaces was but 17,350 tons; 22,000 tons in 1750, and perhaps not over 30,000 tons in 1770. In 1788 it had increased, by means of the steam engine and the use of fossil coal, to 68,300 tons; in 1796 to 108,793 tons, and including Scotland, to 124,879 tons, having more than doubled in Scotland in eight years. In 1802, the annual product of Great Britain was estimated at 170,000 tons; in 1823 it had increased to 442,066; in 1828 to 703,184 tons, by 278 furnaces in blast; in 1839 to over 1,200,000 tons; and in 1844 it was estimated at 1,500,000 tons; while Spain produces annually but about 8,000 tons. The hot blast for smelting iron was introduced in 1828, which produces more iron from the same quantity of ore, and with much less fuel than the cold blast.

Various improvements were made in the manufacture of BAR IRON, particularly by the substitution of HAMMERING MACHINERY FOR HAND LABOR; by Mr. Cort's invention for puddling, (patented in 1783,) and, also, by that gentleman's invention of MACHINERY FOR ROLLING IRON, (patented in 1784.) These astonishing results in the manufacture of iron were brought about by the steam engine, and its application to mining and the blast furnace, by the invention of machinery for hammering and rolling iron instead of doing it by hand labor, and by the use of pit or mineral coal.

Statement of the production of iron in England and Wales in 1740 and 1750, and in Great Britain at other periods, the number of furnaces in blast, and the average production of each furnace.

Year.	Furnaces.	Tons produced.	By each Furnace.
1740	59	17,350	294
1750	—	22,000	—
1788	85	68,300	804
1806	169	258,206	1,528
1828	278	703,184	2,529
1840	402	1,396,400	3,475
1844		1,500,000	
1848		2,000,000	

The annual production of iron in Great Britain from 1840 to 1846, varied from about 1,200,000 to 1,600,000 tons, according to the demand for railroad iron.*

The above are the quantities of pig iron made at different periods. The quantity of bar iron increased in a corresponding ratio; the usual estimate has been, that seven-tenths of the pig iron is made into bars, bolts, rods, sheets, nails, chains, anchors, &c., &c., by hammering, rolling, slitting and other machinery. It is said that, by the introduction of machinery for rolling iron, instead of hammering it, to convert it into malleable iron bars, bolts, &c., fifteen tons are obtained in twelve hours, while, in the same time, only one ton could be drawn from the hammer.

The quantity and value of iron annually made in Great Britain from 1842 to 1844, are stated in Mr. Watterston's Cyclopedia of Commerce, as follows:

Pig iron, 1,500,000 tons, worth £4 per ton,	£6,000,000
Cost and profits of converting seven-tenths of it into bars, bolts, &c.,	3,000,000
Total value of products of iron,	£9,000,000

exclusive of the additional value produced by converting a part of it into hardware and cutlery.

The quantity of pit coal consumed in 1840 in making 1,396,400 tons of pig iron, was estimated at 4,877,000 tons, and in making bar and other wrought iron, 2,000,000 tons.

About three-quarters of this prodigious quantity of iron appears to be used in Great Britain; the greater part of it being used in making machinery, steam-engines, railroads, carriages, cars, locomotives, steamboats, and other vessels, cannon, and other fire-arms, stoves, and ploughs. McCulloch states the quantities exported as follows; in 1767, at 11,000 tons; and the average

* See Porter's Progress of the Nation and McCulloch's Statistics.

annual export during the three years ending with the year 1806, at but 28,000 tons.

The quantity of foreign iron consumed in Great Britain and the British iron and hardware exported, are stated by Porter as follows

Years.	Foreign Iron used. Tons.	British Iron exported. Tons.	Hardware exported. Tons.
1806	27,411	36,925	4,629
1828	13,984	100,403	12,100
1836	18,920	192,352	21,072
1840	13,263	268,328	14,995
1844	21,599	458,745	22,552

The declared or real value of the British iron and steel hardwares and cutlery exported is stated by Porter in pounds sterling as follows—

Years.	Iron and Steel.	Hardware.	Total.
1828	£ 1,226,617	1,387,204	2,613,821
1836	2,342,674	2,271,313	4,613,987
1840	2,524,859	1,349,137	3,873,996
1844	3,193,368	2,179,087	5,371,455

Sec. 3. *Production, and consumption of iron in France, the United States, and Ireland.*

The learned M. Malte Brun in his Geography estimated the produce of the iron mines of France in 1826 at less than 80,000 tons; and Mr. Murray in his Geography estimated it in 1826, on the authority of M. Dupin of France, at 161,000 tons. About four-fifths of the fuel consumed in making it consists of wood, and as it is comparatively scarce and dear, the price of iron is proportionably high.

The quantity made in France from 1837 to 1841 appears from the official documents to have been as follows, stated in tons; the principal part of the pig iron having been finally converted into the malleable, wrought, or bar iron.

Years.	Pig Iron.	Malleable Iron.
1837,	321,679 tons.	224,618 tons.
1839,	350,177 "	231,761 "
1840,	347,773 "	237,379 "
1841,	377,142 "	263,747 "

The quantity of iron and hardware annually imported into France from 1840 to 1843, was between twenty and thirty thousand tons; the imports from Great Britain in 1842 amounting to 23,428 tons, 16,464 of which was pig iron. The total annual consumption of iron in France, was less than 400,000 tons; and less than the quantity consumed in the United States, by about half as many inhabitants.

Prior to the American Revolution, the British government discouraged and prohibited almost every kind of manufactures in this country except those of a domestic character. Mills for rolling and slitting iron and plating forges were prohibited, and many efforts were made to prevent the colonists from manufacturing any thing for themselves. Very little iron was made in the colonies prior to the Revolution, perhaps not over two or three thousand tons per year.

Mr. Morse, in the fifth edition of his Geography, published in 1805, treating of Pennsylvania, says, " Iron-works are of long standing, and their products increase in quantity, and improve in quality. The furnaces are 16, and the forges 37. The slitting and rolling-mills are said to cut and roll 1500 tons per annum. On the west side of the Allegany mountains are 11 forges, which by estimation make annually about 400 tons of iron. There are about as many furnaces; some of these have failed for want of ore." The quantity of iron then made annually in Pennsylvania was about 2000 tons, and about the same quantity in Massachusetts, according to Mr. Morse's statements.

The quantity of pig-iron made in Pennsylvania in 1839 was over seventy thousand tons.

A committee appointed by a convention of manufacturers of iron, held at Philadelphia in 1830, reported the amount of iron made in the United States, as follows:

	1828.	1830.
Pig iron, tons,	108,564	137,075
Castings from the ore at blast furnaces,	14,840	18,273
Bloomed bar iron made from the ore, equal in pig iron at 28 cwt. pig iron, to a ton of bar iron, at	7,477	8,194
Total iron made, reck'd in pigs and cast'gs,	130,881	163,542

The pig iron was all converted into castings, bar iron, nails and other wrought iron. The quantity of iron made in the United States in 1810, 1830 and 1840, according to official reports and estimates, and in 1844, according to the estimates in the March No., 1845, of Hunt's Magazine, was as follows;

	1810.	1830.	1840.	1844.
Pig iron and castings made from the ore (tons,)	53,908	191,536	286,903*	486,000
Bar and other wrought iron,	24,541	112.866	197,233	291,000
Castings, made from pig iron,	.	.	.	121,500

* Perhaps 40,000 tons of the castings were made from pig-iron, leaving only about 250,000 tons of iron made from ore in 1840.

The production in the United States of iron from the ore may be estimated at 250,000 tons during each of the years 1840, 1841 and 1842. It increased rapidly under the tariff of 1842; amounted to nearly 500,000 tons, in 1844; to about 600,000 tons in 1845, and to about 800,000 tons annually during the years 1847 and 1848. The influence of large importations under the tariff of 1846, checked the further increase and caused a decline in the production to about 650,000 tons during the years 1849, 1850 and 1851.

The value of the unmanufactured iron and steel (that is the bar and pig iron and steel) and the manufactured iron and steel, (that is the hardware, castings, sheet iron, nails, and cutlery) imported into the United States, have been as follows.

	1839.	1844.	1850.
Bar and Pig-iron, etc.,	$6,302,539	$3,313,796	$10,586,795
Hardware,	6,507,510	2,380,027	7,078,603
Total	$12,810,049	$5,693,823	$17,665,398

The quantity of unmanufactured iron and steel imported into the United States in 1839 amounted to over 100,000 tons; in 1844 to 68,924 tons, and in 1850 to over 351,000 tons; the weight of the hardware and other manufactures of iron and steel cannot be ascertained with certainty from the custom-house records, but probably amounted to over 40,000 tons in 1839, to 20,000 tons in 1844, and 50,000 tons in 1850; making the whole imports of iron and manufactures of iron in 1839 about 140,000 tons; in 1844 nearly 90,000 tons, and in 1850 about 400,000 tons.

The annual consumption of iron and hardware in the United States increased from 1840 to 1850 from less than 400,000 to about 1,000,000 tons; and the annual consumption in Great Britain increased from about 1,000,000 to over 1,300,000 tons; while the consumption in Ireland did not probably exceed 50,000 to 75,000 tons.

Iron is found in many parts of Ireland; and the great increase of iron works in the early part of the 17th century is said to have been a principal cause of the destruction of the forests. But these having been exhausted, and coal not having been found of such quality and in such quantity as to supply the deficiency, the Irish iron works have been almost wholly abandoned. The above are the remarks of McCulloch who states the importation of iron and all manufactures of iron and hardware into Ireland during the year 1835, at 49,930 tons.

SEC. 4. *Production of Iron and other metals in the several countries of Europe.*

Estimate made in 1826 by Von Malchus, a statistician of Prussia, of the annual production of Iron, Coal, Copper, Lead and Salt in the different countries of Europe.*

	Iron. *Tons.*	Copper. *Tons.*	Coal. *Tons.*	Lead. *Tons.*	Salt. *Cwts.*
Sweden and Norway,	78.913	1,418	30,650	30	65,000
Russia, - -	106,160	3,684	—	909	1,818,100
Denmark, - -	—	—	—	—	—
Great Britain, -	225,000	6,000	9,000,000	15,000	3,630,000
Holland and Belgium,	18,125	—	2,770,000	—	—
Prussia, - -	117,439	750	230.000	2,961	1,216,090
Saxony, - -	4,000	30	31.000	521	30,000
Hanover, - -	6,091	70	43,492	2,885	293,528
Austria and Hungary,	56,513	2,500	113,000	4,000	5,469,951
Bavaria, - -	15,000	9	6,000	—	555,500
Other German States,	29,805	1.861	16,100	1,055	1,022,785
France, - -	202,750	100	1,025,000	1,250	5.000,000
Spain, - -	8,750	12	—	1,550	5,800,000
Portugal, - -	225	—	400	45	2,650,000
Switzerland, - -	3,750	—	—	—	15,000
Italian States, - -	3,405	14	5,090	132	4,648,000
Turkey, - -	—	—	—	—	3,400,000
Total (Von Malchus,)	875,926	16,448	13,270,732	30,338	35,613,954
Add for Great Britain,	375,000	3,858	6,000,000	5,000	3,218,000
Do for Ireland, -	3,000	500	100,000	—	—
Total, - -	1,253,926	20,806	19,370,732	35,338	38,831,954

The table of Von Malchus seems to have been compiled mostly from official reports, and may be regarded as approximating very nearly to accuracy, except so far as regards Great Britain.

As to Great Britain it gives the quantities of the metals produced about the year 1806; the learned writer perhaps not being aware of so rapid an increase in the production of the mines of that country, there being no official reports of the products of iron from 1806, to about the year 1825. It thus appears that, about the year 1825, the annual product of iron and copper in Great Britain was about as great as it was in all Continental Europe; and that the proportion of coal and lead produced in Great Britain, was still greater. The annual product of British iron was then, very likely, from five to ten, and at present from ten to twenty times as great as the whole quantity produced in the Roman world, during the most flourishing period of the empire.

* See the American Almanac for 1833, page 240.

The quantity of iron annually produced in the United States at this time (1851) is much greater than was produced in all Europe, half a century since. The iron mines of the United States are numerous and extensive, scattered through more than half the States of the Union, and apparently inexhaustible; and instead of importing annually over 100,000 tons of iron, steel and hardware at an expense of from ten to thirteen millons of dollars, we should divert a portion of our farmers from farming to mining; make at home the whole quantity of iron, steel and hardware we need; and thus lessen the quantity of agricultural products annually raised, create a home market for them, and save our country from being drained of specie to pay the balance of trade against us.

The metals, as has been observed, are the principal instruments and agents, and constitute the very main-spring of productive industry, of every kind. There are but few mines, however, in the world, which could be worked with facility, or to much advantage, until after the invention of gunpowder to blast the rocks, and of the steam engine to raise and clear the mines of water, as well as to raise the ore from the bottom of the mines to the surface of the earth, often several hundred and in some instances over two thousand feet. Without the use of gunpowder, it was obviously impossible for the ancients to do much at mining; and without the use of the steam engine, it was equally impossible to work mines very deep below the surface of the earth. Though the power of steam had been previously discovered, and many experiments made with it, yet the first person who constructed a machine in which steam was successfully applied to purposes of usefulness, was Captain Thomas Savary, of England, who obtained a patent for his invention in 1698. He applied his steam engine to pumping water out of the Cornish mines, and to raising the ore from the mines. A material improvement was made in Savary's engine by Thomas Newcomen of Devonshire in 1705; and the movements of the engine were simplified in 1717 by Mr. Beighton, without changing its principle; but after this time, no considerable improvement was made until the great improvements of James Watt about the year 1769. It is therefore safe to say, that mining was never carried on to any great extent in any age or any country, until after the introduction of the steam engine, in the 18th century.

The annual products of the mines of England about the time of the revolution of 1688 are stated in Macaulay's History of England as follows: Iron, 10,000 tons: Copper, 375 tons: Tin, 1,600 tons: Coal consumed in London about 350,000 tons: and in other parts of the kingdom about as much more.

Estimate of the number of tons of iron made annually in Europe at different periods, founded on the researches of Von Malchus, Mc Culloch, and others, and taking into consideration the condition of each country, and calculating probabilities as to the quantities produced prior to Von Malchus' estimates; and in many cases since.

Years.	1500	1700	1750	1800	1840
Great Britain, - -	7,500	14,000	25,000	150,000	1,300,000
Ireland, - - -	2,500	5,000	7,000	4,000	2,000
France, - - -	14,000	22,000	30,000	60,000	350,000
Sweden and Norway, -	4,000	10,000	18,000	40,000	80,000
Russia, - - -	1,000	3,000	18,000	40,000	180,000
Prussia, - -	5,000	10,000	18,000	40,000	130,000
Austria and Hungary, -	8,000	16,000	20,000	40,000	90,000
German States, - -	7,000	10,000	12,000	20,000	65,000
Belgium, - - -	4,000	5,000	8,000	20,000	135,000
Spain and Portugal, -	8,000	8,000	8,000	8,000	9,000
Italian States & Switzerland,	3,000	4,000	4,000	5,000	10,000
Total, - - -	64,000	107,000	168,000	427,000	2,351,000

The quantity of iron made in the United States according to official returns and reports (as heretofore stated) amounted in 1810 to 53,908 tons: in 1830 to 191,536 tons: in 1840 to about 250,000 tons: in 1850 to about 650,000 tons; and probably did not exceed 10,000 tons, in the year 1800; and 1000 or 2000 tons in the year 1750.

As iron is the great handmaid and agent of industry, the quantity of it used by any people, is a test, and evidence of the amount of their productive industry. This test shows the great advancement of the British during the past century; their superiority over every other nation in productive industry; and the great superiority of modern over ancient nations. Next to Great Britain, the United States, Belgium and France have been making the most rapid progress in productive industry, and wealth.

Sec. 5. *Of Copper—its use and production.*

It is remarked by McCulloch, that if we except gold and silver, copper seems to have been more early known than any other metal. In the first ages of the world, before the method of working iron was discovered, copper was the principal ingredient in all domestic utensils, and instruments of war; and even now it is applied to so many purposes, as to rank next to iron in utility.

Alloys of copper are numerous, and of great value. Those of copper and zinc, forming brass and bronze, are the most ancient, and the most common; but those of copper and tin are perhaps the most important. Tin alloyed with copper makes it more fusible, less liable to rust, or to be corroded by the air and other substances, harder, denser and more sonorous. This is the kind of alloy in use among the natives of Mexico, at the time of the discovery of America, and with which they constructed axes other tools, and instruments of industry.

Copper is spoken of in Brande's Encyclopædia of Science and Art, as an abundant metal; and though it is found in many ores, and in many countries, yet it is a very scarce metal, and found in but few places and mines, and in but small quantities, compared with iron. Great Britain has various copper mines, in Cornwall, Devonshire, Wales, &c., but particularly in the first. Though known long before, the Cornish copper mines were not wrought with much spirit until the last century. From 1726 to 1735, the mines of England and Wales produced on an average annually, only about 700 tons of pure copper; during the ten years from 1766 to 1775, they produced on an average 2,650 tons annually; in 1798, the produce exceeded 5,000 tons; and in 1830, McCulloch estimated their produce at 12,000 tons, the produce of the mines of Scotland about 2,000 tons, and the Irish mines 500 tons, making the annual product of all the mines of the United Kingdom at that time 14,500 tons.

McCulloch states that copper ores are abundant in Sweden, Saxony, Russia, Persia, Japan, China, and Chili; that in the province of Dalecarlia in Sweden, there is a celebrated copper mine, supposed to have been worked nearly 1000 years; which, in the forepart of the 17th century, yielded an annual product of nearly 4,000 tons of pure copper; but it has since greatly declined.

He quotes Thomson's travels in Sweden, p. 221. This statement sounds a little fabulous, when we take into consideration the products of the Cornwall mines, and the low state of productive industry, at that period, and also the fact that but about 723 tons of copper were exported from Stockholm, the principal place of export, in the year 1832. The product of the copper mines in the province of Olenetz, in Russia, is estimated at 3,375 English tons a year. The copper mines of Chili are also very rich, and their produce is imported into Calcutta and Canton, direct from Valparaiso. The copper mines of Japan are said to be among the richest in the world; the Dutch annually import about 700 tons of their produce into Batavia, and the Chinese from 800 to 1000 into Canton and other ports. Considerable quantities of copper are exported from the Persian mines, and some from the Russian mines of Georgia into Calcutta.

Dr. Ure states the products of all the Russian copper mines in 1830 at 8,860 tons; in 1831 at 3,904 tons; in 1832 at 3,620 tons; and in 1833 but 3,387 tons.

This and the table of Von Malchus comprise the substance of the meagre accounts I have met with in relation to the quantity of copper produced in the world; from which it would appear, that the products of the mines of Great Britain are greater than the products of the mines of all the rest of Europe, and probably nearly as much as those of the mines of all the rest of the world.

The quantity of copper and manufactures of copper and brass, exported from Great Britain, and their value, have been as follows:

Years.	Copper.	Copper and Brass.	Value.
	Tons.	*Tons.*	
1820	6,098	—	——
1830	9,157	9,479	£867,344
1835	9,111	12,104	1,094,749
1840	5,926	15,557	1,450,464
1844	—	19,444	1,736,545

Brass is an alloy of copper and zinc; the excess of copper and brass over pure copper, shows the quantity of brass exported, and also the rapid increase of the exportation of products of brass.

Very little copper has been heretofore produced in the United States; in 1844, the value of copper imported was $1,370,274, and the quantity retained for consumption no less than $1,268,977; nearly two-thirds of which came from Great Britain, a little from Holland, and nearly all the balance from South America and the West India Islands. The value imported into the United States annually on an average of five years, ending September 30th, 1838, amounted to about $1,300,000; and the quantity annually imported must have been about 2,500 tons.

The recent explorations and mining operations in the upper peninsula of Michigan, Isle Royal, and on the northern shore of Lake Superior, seem to render it probable, that nearly the whole coast of that Lake, and part also of the north eastern coast of Lake Huron, are filled with veins of native copper, and copper ore, which will yield vast quantities of copper and much silver; that the mines and veins are more numerous and extensive than all those which have been hitherto wrought in the world; that the hills are of such moderate height, the climate so favorable to health and physical energy, and the facilities for transporting the ores and copper by navigable waters so great, that they can be worked to better advantage, and cheaper, than almost any other mines on the earth. If our citizens will turn their attention to the business of mining and smelting copper, they can soon supply our country

Sec. 6. *Tin—Its Use and Production.*

McCulloch states in his Com. Dict., title tin, that the ores of this metal are found in comparatively few places; the principal, and perhaps the only ones are Cornwall, Galicia, Erzgeberg in Saxony, Bohemia, the Malay countries, China, and Banca in Asia. They are peculiar to primitive rocks, generally in granite, either in veins or beds, and are often associated with copper and iron pyrites. Brande says it is also found in small quantities in Mexico and Chili.

Tin is principally used as a covering of other metals; to cover iron and prevent it from oxydizing, or rusting, and also to cover copper. Thin plates of iron are dipped into molten tin, which not only covers the iron entirely, but penetrates it, and gives the whole a white color. It is then called sheet tin, and is used for a great variety of kitchen and cooking utensils, and sometimes to cover the roofs of buildings. It is also alloyed with lead, to form pewter; but as tin is used only as an alloy, and as a very thin covering to other metals, the quantity needed is very trifling, when compared with iron, lead, and some other metals, and very small also when compared with copper and silver.

The tin mines of Cornwall have been worked from a very remote era. The voyages of the Phœnicians to the Cassiterides, or tin islands, are mentioned by Herodotus, lib. iii. c. 115. After the destruction of Carthage, the British tin trade, which was always reckoned of peculiar importance, was carried on by the merchants of Marseilles, and subsequently by the Romans. Besides Britain, Spain furnished the ancients with considerable quantities of tin; but we have no precise information as to the purposes to which they applied it, except to cover copper vessels.

Mr. McC. remarks, that Queen Elizabeth brought over to England some German miners, by whom some of the processes were improved. During the civil wars, the mines were much neglected; but at the commencement of the last century, the business of mining was carried on with renewed vigor; and from 1720 to 1740, the annual produce of the British mines was about 2,100 tons. The produce went on gradually increasing, till it amounted, in the ten years from 1790 to 1800, to 3,254 tons a year. During the next fifteen years, it was under 3000 tons per year; since that time it has increased, and in 1827 and 1828 amounted to nearly 5000 tons each year, and in 1837 to 5,130 tons; and he says the average produce of the mines, might then be estimated at 4,500 tons annually, about one-fourth part of which is exported, and three-fourths of it used at home.

He gives a table embracing an estimate of the annual produce of the east coast of the Malay peninsula at 17,000 piculs; of the west coast of that peninsula, including Banca and the neighboring islands, at 53,000 piculs; making in all 70,000 piculs, or little over 4,000 tons, each picul being about 136 pounds. He says the average export from Singapore, during each of the years, 1820 and 1827, amounted to 16,342 piculs, or about 970 tons, and that the great marts for the consumption of tin are China, Hindostan, and the continent of Europe. The annual export of tin from the Island of Java from 1828 to 1837 is stated at 36,000 piculs, or a little over 2,000 tons.

From these facts it would seem that the total annual product of all the tin mines of the world does not exceed 15,000 tons, about one-third part of which is from the single island of Great Britain. The amount specified as exported to the United States in 1833, is about 237½ tons; and the value of tin imported into the United States in 1842, is stated in the report of the Secretary of the Treasury at $28,599, and of glazed or tinned hollow ware at $26,742.

He gives a table showing the quantity of British and of foreign (Banca and Malay) tin exported by the British to different countries of Europe, America, and western Asia, in 1833, specifying the quantities shipped for each, showing an aggregate of about 1,250 tons of British tin, and about 2,000 tons of foreign tin shipped that year.

The value of tin, and of tin and pewter wares exported from Great Britain annually on an average from 1831 to 1835 inclusive, amounted to £284,295; and in 1844 to £506,691.

Sec. 7. *Lead—Its Use and Production.*

Lead is one of the most useful metals. From its great durability it is extensively used in the construction of water pipes and cisterns, and as a covering for flat surfaces or tops of buildings; and when converted into a carbonate of lead, or white lead, it is mixed with oil and serves as the basis of white paint, and also as the principal basis of paints of several other colors. Alloyed with tin, it forms pewter, and with antimony, it forms the alloy with which printing types are made.

The lead mines of Great Britain have been worked from a very remote era; but those of Derbyshire only were explored previous to 1829. Their products cannot be accurately ascertained, but were estimated by McCulloch in 1833 as follows: those of Derbyshire from 5,000 to 6,000 tons annually; those of Cumberland and Northumberland from 11,000 to 12,000 tons, and the Scotch mines at 4,120 tons annually. He estimated their products in his Register in 1839 at from 45,000 to 50,000 tons annually. He states the quantity of lead, and manufactures of lead exported in 1821, at 19,770 tons, and in 1833 at 13,898 tons; in 1844 it amounted to 15,664 tons. He attributes the great fall in price since 1825, principally to the vast supplies of that metal that have been recently furnished by the mines of Adra, in Grenada in Spain; and says the richness of the ore and the facility with which it is obtained enable the Spaniards, who are but indifferently skilled in the arts of mining, to undersell every other people, and to supply most markets to which they have access. So much is this the case, that several of the least productive of the lead mines of Germany, and other countries, have been already abandoned; and it it is even doubtful if the duties on foreign lead will be sufficient to hinder some of the British mines from sharing the same fate.

He says the consumption of lead in France is rapidly increasing; that it is nearly all imported; that the imports averaged annually from 1819 to 1822 inclusive 6,211,500 kilogrammes, and in 1829 and 1830, 15,742,192 kilogrammes annually, and that the imports are almost entirely from Spain; and he attributes the increased consumption in France to the fall of the price. A kilogramme is nearly two and one-fourth pounds avoirdupois weight, and 1,000 kilogrammes about a ton; showing the quantity imported into France in 1830 to have been about 15,740 tons.

He estimated the quantity produced in the United States in ten years, from 1823 to 1832, inclusive, at 55,903,888 pounds; equal to about 25,000 tons, or 2,500 tons annually. The quantity produced from the mines of the United States in 1839, according to the returns with the census of 1840, was equal to nearly 14,000 tons, and the quantity mined is increasing with great rapidity. The quantity of lead exported from the United States, as reported among our domestic exports for the year 1842, was about 6,500 tons, valued at $523,428; and the quantity exported during the year ending June 30th, 1844, amounted to nearly 8,200 tons, valued at $595,238.

The imports into the United States of lead, besides white and red lead, during the eight years, ending Sept. 30th, 1828, amounted to $2,010,981, or an average annually of $251,372; in 1841 they amounted to $3,702, and since that time to only a few hundred dollars annually. The imports of lead into the United States during the year ending September 30, 1835, amounted to over 1,500,000 pounds, valued at $54,112, and the red and white lead imported amounted to 832,215 pounds, valued at $50,225. The value of lead exported the same year amounted to only $17,346, leaving a balance against the United States that year for lead, of nearly $86,991; while the balance in favor of the United States in 1844 for lead exported, over and above the amount imported, was no less than $582,884; showing a difference in favor of the United States, between the years 1835 and 1844, of no less than $629,875. Prior to 1835, the imports of lead into the United States were large; the present balance in their favor is of great consequence; and there is no good reason why the United States should not soon supply themselves with iron and copper, as well as lead, and have a surplus of each to export, instead of importing to the amount of from ten to twelve millions of dollars annually.

The quantity of lead, copper, and manganese produced by the mines of France in 1841, and the quantity imported that year for consumption, is stated as follows:

Lead produced from the mines		638 tons.	Imported	17,375 tons.
Copper	do	do	100 "	do	9,910 "
Manganese	do	do	4,978 "	do	1,341 "

SEC. 8. *On Zinc—its use, and the trade in it.*

Zinc appears to be a rare metal, found in but few countries, and in no very great quantities. McCulloch says it is procured in Flintshire in Wales, and in the Isle of Man; in the province of Yunan in China; and in Gleinitz in Upper Silesia, from which latter place, the foreign zinc brought into England is principally procured. Besides its employment in the manufacture of brass, bell metal, &c., to alloy with copper, zinc has of late years been formed into plates, and applied to many uses for which lead was formerly used, such as the roofing of buildings, the manufacture of water spouts, dairy pans, &c.

I have not met with any statement of the amount produced in Great Britain, or in any other country. The imports into Great Britain in 1831 were 3,820 tons, and the exports 3,134 tons, and in 1832 the imports amounted to 3,438 tons, and the exports to 2,487 tons.

The value of the zinc imported into the United States in 1842 was $105,984, and in 1844 it amounted to $113,099, only $1,139 of which was re-exported. From these statements, it is evident that the quantity produced in the world is comparatively small, and that it is a metal of no very great importance, as it is principally used as a substitute for tin, lead, and pewter, on account of being cheaper than those metals. McCulloch remarks that the word zinc occurs for the first time in the writings of Paracelsus, who died in 1541; but the method of extracting it from its ores was not known until the early part of the last century.

Sec. 9. *Coal—its use and production.*

Fuel is as necessary to the existence and comfort of man in cold climates, as either bread, meat, or clothing. Though coal is of very little use to a people in a new country, while wood for fuel is abundant; yet a dense population cannot exist in a cold climate without great difficulty and suffering, unless they have a good supply of pit or mineral coal for fuel to warm their dwellings and work-shops, as well as to propel machinery. The peat of Ireland serves as a partial but poor substitute for coal.

There are no means of ascertaining with accuracy the quantity of coal raised from the mines of Great Britain; the quantity shipped coastwise from one port to another, and to Ireland in 1841 was 7,649,899 tons; 1,848,294 tons were exported the same year to British colonies and foreign countries; the consumption of the British iron works annually was estimated at 6,877,000 tons, and the quantity consumed in the manufacture of glass, cotton, wool, flax, silk, copper, tin, and in the potteries, about as much more, or nearly 7,000,000 tons; nearly all of which was used on the spot, and not included in any accounts of shipments. Beside this, large quantities are used for fuel near the mines, not included in the shipments, and the total quantity produced by the mines were estimated at over 30,000,000 tons annually. McCulloch in his Register estimated it in 1839 at 31,024,417 tons; which serves as a substitute for about 40,000,000 cords of wood.

The production of coal in Great Britain has increased with the increase of the mining and manufacturing industry, and the number of the inhabitants.

The number of coal fields opened in France in 1836 was forty-six, and in 1841 they numbered sixty-two, comprising 256 mines, situated in forty-one of the sixty-eight departments; of which number, nine furnished anthracite coal only, fourteen lignite only, and the remaining thirty-nine furnished bituminous coal, five of them yielding anthracite coal also.

The following statement shows, in round numbers, the number of tons of coal raised from the French coal mines at four different periods, and the quantity in tons of foreign coal consumed in France during the same years:

	1814.	1826.	1836.	1841.
Tons raised,	665,610	1,301,045	2,544,835	3,410,200
Foreign coal consumed,	165,345	505,180	999,452	1,619,160
Total consumed in France,	820,000	1,800,000	3,517,000	4,980,000

the exports of coal being small. Of the imports of coal in 1841, it is stated that 992,226 tons were from Belgium; 196,502 tons from the Rhenish provinces of Prussia and Bavaria; 429,950 tons from Great Britain, and only 482 tons from all other countries. The number of workmen employed in raising the various kinds of coal in France in 1841, was 29,320, of whom 22,595 worked in the mines.

The production of pit or mineral coal in the United States in 1839, was about 1,800,000 tons.

SEC. 10. *Salt—the production and consumption.*

All the salt made in the United States, is made by either boiling or solar evaporation of salt water, and is strictly a manufactured and not a mineral product; but the principal part produced in Europe is taken from mines in a crystallized state (See the table from Von Malchus ante, section 4.)

Porter states the production and exportation of salt from Great Britain and Ireland as follows:

Years.	Production. Cwts.	Exportation. Bushels.
1827	6,347,280	7,475,025
1830	8,666,440	10,499,778
1835	7,200,080	8,317,029
1840	11,063,280	12,847,663
1844	11,062,240	13,476,884

The whole of this large quantity of salt was produced in England, and no part of it in Ireland; and in addition to the exportation to the colonies and foreign countries above stated, large quantities are exported to Ireland for the supply of that country, which amounted during the year 1835, to 1,646,614 bushels.

Though we produced in the United States in 1839—6,179,174 bushels, and the production has been annually increasing since that time, yet there were imported into the United States in 1850—11,224,185 bushels, at an expense of $1,237,186; the exports are but a trifle. Macaulay says the first bed of rock salt discovered in Great Britain, was found in Cheshire in the reign of Charles II, but it does not appear to have been worked during that age.

SEC. 11. *General reflections.*

Iron, the most useful of all the metals, is diffused throughout the earth, and is found in greater or less quantities in almost every country, but is much the most abundant in high northern latitudes. Comparatively little iron ore is found in any of the countries bordering on the Mediterranean sea, and it would seem from ancient profane history, as well as from the scriptures, that copper and its alloy, brass, and even silver, and in western Europe, tin also, were about as abundant, and used in nearly as

8

large quantities as iron. The quantity of copper produced in Europe and western Asia at this time, from the best information I have been able to collect, does not exceed 25,000 tons annually; and including all Asia, America, and the West Indies, not over 31,000 tons; and it is not probable, in the comparativly low state of the natural sciences, and of mining and other productive industry among the Roman people, that the annual product of copper could have been more than 10,000 tons, and of iron more than from 20,000 to 30,000 tons, or 50,000 tons annually at the most, during the most flourishing period of the Roman Empire. It is only during the last century, that much attention has been given to statistics, and all the estimates prior to that time, are founded on the state of science, industry, and condition of the people; but those of a recent period are mostly of an official character, and generally collected with care.

It appears that at this time, Great Britain produces about half of all the iron made in the world; nearly half the copper; and nearly one-third part the tin; beside a pretty large supply for home consumption of lead, and some for export; and also a considerable supply of zinc, and several other metals of minor importance; but if we look back no further than the revolution of 1688, prior to the invention of the Steam Engine by Capt. Savary, to a period before that revolution and the revocation of the edict of Nantes had produced much effect upon the relative condition and enterprise of Great Britain and France, we shall find that the products of British industry, and of British mines, did not exceed those of many other countries of Europe in proportion to the number of inhabitants.

Only a century and a half since, the commerce of Holland was more extensive than that of Great Britain; and the productive industry and wealth of England and Wales scarcely exceeded that of Holland and Belgium, with less than half as much territory. Holland then had extensive possessions in the East Indies, and Great Britain nothing but a few trading factories; whereas she now holds dominion over a hundred millions of people, who have been conquered by a company of British merchants. A century since, (in 1750) Great Britain did not hold a foot of territory on the continent of America, which she now holds; all her western possessions consisted of a few small Islands in the West Indies, the original thirteen states of this Union, and the unsettled territories attached to them, comprising about one million and a half of inhabitants.

Prior to the accession of Henry VII. to the throne in 1485, England was mostly a grazing country; poor when compared with the Italian States, Spain, France, Burgundy, (now Holland and

Belgium,) and even Portugal; and though her herds of cattle and sheep were numerous, which constituted her chief wealth, and her population was less than one-fith part as great as it is now, yet it would appear from the frequent dearths and famines, that the quantity of grain raised, was much less, and probably not half as great, in proportion to the population, as it is now. The tin and lead mines were then considerably worked, (as they were the most productive of any in Europe,) and tin, lead, wool, and a few coarse, unfinished woollen cloths, which were sent to Burgundy or Flanders to be dyed, dressed, and finished, were the principal exports. Jacob says, in his historical enquiry in relation to the precious metals, Chap. xii: p. 183, that "By comparing the price of wool as given in the reign of Edward the Third, with the exchequer records of the year 1354, we find that the quantity of wool exported amounted to full 12,715,200 pounds weight. Besides the wool, there were in the same year coarse cloths exported, whose value amounted to £16,266 in the money of that time, or to $41,490, in our present money.

Wool then, and up to the latter part of the sixteenth century, constituted the principal part in value, of the exports of the kingdom. During the 13th and 14th centuries the average annual exports were only between two and three hundred thousand pounds sterling—during the 16th century they amounted to from £1,000,000 to £1,500,000 annually; during the first half of the 17th century, to from £2,000,000 to £2,500,000; and during the reign of Charles Second, to about £3,000,000 per annum.

The average exports of Great Britain during the three years ending with 1701, amounted to £6,449,594;—during six years ending with 1755, they amounted to £12,220,974—and during eight years ending with 1792, to £18,621,942.

The official value of the exports of the products of Great Britain and Ireland in 1835 amounted to £77,932,616; and in 1844 to £131,564,503. The standard prices of official valuations have not been changed since 1696; and they therefore show the relative quantities of goods exported at different periods. But a mere trifle is exported from Ireland.

Nearly half the exports during the 17th century consisted of woollen goods; at present about half their exports consist of manufactures of cotton, and cotton yarn. The manufacture and trade in cotton has grown up since the year 1780, and the commerce with Great Britain has been doubled by that means. The reason why the commerce of Great Britain was so small up to the revolution of 1688, and even up to the American revolution, was this-they had very little to export which any nation wanted

Henry VII and his successors encouraged domestic manufactures and commerce; and as soon as these branches of industry, together with mining, began to improve and flourish, agriculture improved with them, until England became an agricultural as well as a manufacturing country. Mining and manufactures not only supply the tools, and instruments of agriculture, but they create a market for, and raise the prices of agricultural products; and thus stimulate agricultural industry.

The quantity of wheat raised annually in Great Britain is now eight or ten times as great as it was three centuries since—and that of other grains and vegetables about three or four times as much. These are singular facts, and show the close dependence of agriculture on commerce, and on mining, mechanical and manufacturing industry.

The amount of iron now used in Great Britain in the shape of tools and instruments for agricultural purposes, is probably ten times as great as it was two centuries since. Ploughs were then rude things made of wood, with only a point of iron; now all that part running in the ground is made of iron. Then the farmer could only scratch the surface of the earth a very little—but now he can plough as deep as he pleases. The agricultural tools of the present day render labour two or three times as effective as it was then, enable the farmer to plough his lands deeper, better, and easier, to cultivate them more thoroughly and subdue them more perfectly; and therefore they produce more abundantly.

To make the machinery of Great Britain and her railroads required an immense amount of iron, and a large quantity is required annually for new mills, factories, machinery, railroads, &c, &c., as well as to repair the old, and supply such as has been worn out.

Nearly all her machinery is moved by the Steam Engine, by means of coal. Her manufactures are thus dependent on the products of her mines. The manufactures and domestic products exported from Great Britain have increased with, and nearly as fast as the aggregate products of her mines of iron, copper, tin, lead and zinc, which have caused, as well as furnished the instruments of her increased productive industry.

While England remained a grazing country, up to the end of the 17th century, and her principal exports were wool, coarse, unfinished, not dyed woollen cloths, a small quantity of tin, copper and hardware, and a few horses and cattle, the people were comparatively poor, and the nation feeble, and the population doubled only once in three or four centuries. During the first half of the eighteenth century, when the people turned their attention more to mining and manufactures, agriculture finding better markets, improved more rapidly than it had ever done before; the people were much better supplied than at any previous period, with grain as well as vegetables, and for the first time in her history, Great Britain exported large quantities of grain, and her population increased about 24 per cent. in fifty years. After the British people had made great progress in inventions, and in mining and manufacturing industry, and about one-third part only of the adult male population were engaged in agriculture, the population has increased nearly four times as fast, during the present century, as it did during the first half of the last century; and agriculture is so much improved, that if they did not import a bushel of grain, the whole people, though nearly six times as numerous as they were three centuries and a half since, would not only be much better housed, and supplied with better clothing, lodging, fuel and other necessaries, but better supplied with bread, vegetables, and every kind of food except meat, at the present time, than they were then. Her manufacturing power and industry is based on the production of her mines; her mining and manufacturing industry furnishes nearly all the materials of her immense commerce, and is the source of her great wealth and power; and by means of the improvements in tools and implements furnished by the mechanic arts, and the valuable markets furnished by her millions engaged in mining, manufactures and commerce, her agriculture has been improved to a degree unequalled in any country, in any age of the world.

We have in the United States supplies of ores of iron, copper, and lead, in all probability, more abundant than Great Britain, and much more easily obtained, than they can be in that country at this day. We have also large and numerous coal fields, an unlimited amount of water power, extensive forests and an abundant supply of timber, and the means of furnishing ourselves with a domestic supply of wool, flax, hemp, and silk, as well as cotton for manufacturing, four or five, if not ten times as great, as can be supplied by the British Isles. The natural advantages of the United States would seem to be much greater than those of Great Britain; and we are nearly as much advanced in wealth, and much more so in mining and manufacturing industry, than she was half a century since. What then is our correct policy? Is it to confine our industry mostly to agriculture as England did prior to the year 1688, to discourage mining and manufactures by means of free trade, and try to feed the British and French, and let them clothe us, and furnish us with the metals we need? Shall we follow the example of England of the 16th and 17th centuries, which kept her poor and feeble? Or shall we follow her example of the 18th and 19th centuries which has made her rich and powerful? *Shall we remain tributary to England, as we were while colonies, and keep ourselves poor as agriculturists, to foster and enrich her manufacturers and miners, or shall we make ourselves independent, and improve our condition, by furnishing the metals and manufactures for ourselves?*

Gold and silver will be treated of in another chapter

CHAPTER VIII.

ON THE ORIGIN AND PROGRESS OF AGRICULTURE AND THE MECHANIC ARTS, AND THEIR EFFECTS UPON THE HEALTH, CONDITION, AND INCREASE OF MAN.

SEC. 1. *Origin and condition of the useful arts, and of agriculture among ancient nations.*

THE native Mexicans were unacquainted with the use of iron at the time of the discovery of America, but had learned the art of mining and forging copper, and hardening it, with which they made a rough species of edge tools to work in wood, as well as implements of a rude character for digging up and cultivating the earth. It seems, however, that they had no domestic animals which they used as beasts of burden, no knowledge of the use of animals for ploughing or drawing wheeled carriages, and that they had no such thing as a plough or wheeled carriage, wagon, or vehicle of any kind. When the nations about the eastern part of the Mediterranean sea first learned the use of wheeled carriages and ploughs, is unknown, as that time was prior to the period of authentic profane history, and the sacred Scriptures are silent on the subject. At the time of the Trojan war, nearly twelve hundred years before Christ, wheeled carriages seem to have been common among the Greeks. In 1 Kings xix. 19, which was nearly nine hundred years before the birth of Christ, we read of Elisha's ploughing with twelve yoke of oxen. The Indians north of Mexico, at the time of the discovery of America, had some rude axes and other instruments and implements made of stone, with which they could dig up and cultivate the earth by manual labor; but it must have been a very laborious and slow process; and it was utterly impossible to do much in cultivating the earth, in such a mode, and with such implements. Agriculture must necessarily have been confined to the raising of a few vegetables and the cultivation of a mere trifle of grain. Such was the condition of the Canaanites and of all the nations of Western Asia, at the time the Israelites went down to Egypt to buy corn; hence famines were common in those days.

The art of masonry, making mortar, making and burning brick, and the use of brick, stone, and mortar in building dwelling houses and constructing temples, walls for the defence of cities, &c., was also learned at a very early period of the world. This we know from the accounts in the Scriptures of the building of the cities of Babylon and Nineveh, and the accounts of profane history of the building of the city of Thebes, in Upper Egypt.

The ruins of Thebes exhibit columns, statues, and fabrics of stone, curiously wrought with the chisel, and many of them cut out of a single solid stone of such an immense size, that it required a great number of men, and the most powerful machinery and complicated mechanism to move them from the beds where they were quarried, and elevate them to their proper positions; where they have remained for thousands of years, no human being can determine how long, monuments of the mechanical power, skill, and industry of the Thebans.

The Thebans must have been acquainted with iron, making and using edge tools, and working in wood, otherwise it would have been impossible for them to make wheeled-carriages, build scaffolds, and construct machinery of sufficient power to move many miles, and elevate to their respective places, such immense columns and stones of various shapes and sizes. Those cities were built and all these things were done when agriculture, strictly speaking (that is, cultivating the earth by ploughing or otherwise digging it up, and sowing grain,) was in its infancy and scarcely known. The Egyptians seem to have been the first nation that made any considerable proficiency in the mechanic arts, and particularly in the arts of building and sculpture, as well as in agriculture, about or nearly 2,000 years before the Christian era, as is supposed; and these arts spread from there to Western Asia, and to Greece, and from there to Rome, and the nations of Europe. *The mechanic arts in Egypt were in advance of agriculture, which followed, and could neither precede them, nor advance any faster than they did; and such would appear to be the condition of all countries, if we except, perhaps, colonies; agriculture is dependent upon the mechanic arts, and upon commerce, and cannot advance any faster than they advance.*

The Israelites were at first a pastoral, and eventually became an agricultural people; the Tyrians, as well as the Egyptians, Assyrians, and many other nations, were greatly in advance of them in the mechanic arts. When King Solomon formed the design of building a great and magnificent temple at Jerusalem, he sent to Hiram, King of Tyre, for carpenters and laborers to get out the timber and do the wood-work, assigning as a reason, that the Tyrians were more skilful mechanics and workers in wood than the Israelites. These Tyrian carpenters and laborers were paid by Solomon, with provisions and other agricultural products. See 1 Kings, Chap. v., 6–9.

SEC. 2. *Improvements in agricultural implements in modern times.*

The tools and implements of husbandry of the first necessity, consist of the plough, spade, or pick-axe, hoe, pruning-hook, wagon, and axe. The ploughs in use among the Egyptians, Hebrews, Greeks, and Romans, were of various shapes and rude form, some of them having a little iron share, and a piece of wood very ill constructed, intended as a mould-board to turn over the ground, but the majority of ploughs had nothing of the kind. In more modern times, some ploughs were made with wheels, and the mould-board was improved in shape, and became better adapted to use; but the plough was still a large, ill-shapen, rough wooden instrument, until after the invention of iron mould-boards, and iron landsides fitted to shares, constituting all that part of a plough which runs in the ground. The first iron plough was made of wrought iron in Scotland, towards the close of the eighteenth century. Cast-iron ploughs were invented soon afterwards, and were introduced into general use in Great Britain and many parts of the United States in the first part of the nineteenth century. As all that part of the plough which runs in the ground is now made of iron, it soon wears perfectly smooth, runs much easier, cuts a more uniform furrow, and turns it over smoother, and more perfectly, than a wooden plough possibly can. It does its work much better and faster than a wooden plough, and requires not over half as much animal power to draw it through the ground. It is one of the greatest and most important improvements in agricultural implements which has ever been made.

During the present century, carriages and wagons have been greatly improved, and made to run much easier, by the introduction of iron axle-trees, the use of more iron in their construction, and making the woodwork lighter. All the implements of agriculture have been greatly improved during the present century, and many new ones have been invented, such as machines and instruments for threshing, planting, hoeing, raking hay, &c. Very little improvement seems to have been made in agricultural implements for thousands of years, until after the middle of the eighteenth century; in fact, *the whole history of the world shows, that agriculture is the last department of industry in which improvements have usually been made; and when made, that they have been, in most cases, only new applications of some mechanical power or instrument previously used.*

SEC. 3. *Civilization—its origin in warm climates.*

The art of building with brick and stone was brought to a tolerable state of perfection, first in Upper Egypt at Thebes, and afterwards at Babylon, Tyre, Sidon, Lower Egypt, Asia Minor, and Greece, whilst most of the other mechanic arts and agriculture were in a comparative state of infancy. This may have been owing to the following causes; in the warm climates of Egypt, south-western Asia, and in the valleys of the rivers Tigris and Euphrates, the earth produced enough spontaneously, and with very little attention from man, to supply him with food; the warmth and even temperature of the climate seemed not to require much clothing; *and the scorching sun in the heat of the day, rendered a dwelling to shelter him from its rays, an object of greater necessity, than any thing else which nature did not furnish him. Hence a dwelling was the first, and greatest object of necessity which man was required to furnish for himself, by his own art and industry;* and hence large and magnificent dwellings, palaces, castles, and temples, became objects of pride, ambition, and rivalship, among the wealthy and powerful, which stimulated kings and princes to tax their subjects to labor for years, for the erection of vast fabrics, for the gratification of their vanity, pride and ambition. The inventive genius of man being exercised for centuries in making the necessary edge tools to work in wood; in constructing wheeled-carriages, and machinery for moving the materials, and raising them; and in devising and inventing all the tools, implements and mechanical powers, which constituted the great chain of means proper and necessary to be used in constructing and erecting those vast monuments; these means, implements, and tools suggested to his mind the mode of gratifying other wants, and providing himself with other comforts, and were converted to other uses; and thus led the way to other and more extensive inventions and improvements in the mechanic arts, and to the application of many of them to agricultural purposes.

Architecture seems to have been among the first of the mechanic arts, which occupied the attention of man, and led the way to the introduction of other arts, and to the civilization of mankind. *The germ of civilization thus put forth, and bore its first fruits in warm climates, and was transplanted from age to age, by colonists, travellers, merchants, and warriors, to more northern countries.* In the cold and severe climates of the north, the earth produced spontaneously very few fruits, scarcely any grains, and very little vegetable food of any kind wholesome for man; he found it necessary to live mostly on animal food, and was overwhelmed with wants. The severity of the climate in winter, rendered not only a warm hut or cabin, but a goodly quantity of warm clothing absolutely necessary to his existence ; and the only practicable mode of living, was by hunting, as he could live on the flesh, and clothe himself with the skins of his game ; and if he had any surplus skins, he could use them in covering his cabin, and making it more comfortable.

Not only the sciences, but nearly all the mechanic arts, the civilization of the world, and the improvements, inventions and productive industry of man in agriculture, as well as in the mechanic arts and in commerce, and the principal part of the human family, were confined to warm and dry climates, to the warm countries bordering on the Mediterranean sea, and the southern parts of Asia. In fact, in those periods of the world, when the mechanic arts were comparatively in their infancy, man enjoyed so few comforts of life, and was subject to so many privations and sufferings from the severity of the weather, cold and dampness of the atmosphere in high latitudes, as to produce very great mortality, particularly among children—and render it impossible for the inhabitants to increase. Though Italy is not larger than the island of Great Britain, and now contains but few more inhabitants, and in a few years will contain less ; yet the population of Italy was probably seven or eight times as great as that of Great Britain, during the second and third centuries after the Christian era.

The early civilization of the old world was entirely confined to countries lying below the 35th degree of latitude ; from thence it spread to Asia Minor, the isles of the Mediterranean Sea, and to Greece, and extended to the 40th degree of latitude, where it remained until the Roman power extended it a few degrees farther north. In those early ages, all the inhabitants living above the 50th degree of latitude, subsisted by hunting and fishing ; and those living between the 40th and 50 degrees of latitude subsisted mostly in the same manner, though some of them were wandering shepherds, and subsisted upon the flesh of their flocks and herds, and made clothing and tents of their skins. These were the only modes of existence in countries where the winters were cold and severe, before any considerable progress had been made in the mechanic arts. To cultivate the earth without tools and implements of husbandry, was impossible ; and such tools and implements cannot be made, until a people have made some progress in the useful arts. For want of fixed habitations, and of scythes and instruments to cut and secure hay for their flocks, they were under the necessity in many countries, of going south in winter, and returning again to the north in summer.

M. Compte, a learned French philosopher, in a very able work, entitled "Traité de Legislation," shows that in the early ages of the world, and until within a comparatively few centuries, the natives of all the isles of the ocean, as well as the inhabitants of continents, in cold climates, were generally more rude and savage, and had made less progress in civilization and productive industry, than those of warm climates. This is the case with our North American Indians even at this day; those of the south have made more progress in civilization, are generally more intelligent, have more industry, and are more inclined than those of the north, to abandon the chase, and live like the whites, by agriculture and the mechanic arts. A hunting people live very much isolated and scattered, have but few bonds of union, very little society, and scarcely any government except a chieftain to lead them to battle in time of war. Each one is exerting himself in solitude to procure food for himself, or his children, and they rarely act in concert, except in matters of war. In warm climates, subsistence is much more abundant, population more dense, the bond of union which holds society together, the natural sympathy of man for man appears much stronger, society is generally more firmly knit together under a strong monarchical government, in most cases absolute; and the mass of the people are more or less subject to the control and direction of the monarch and his principal officers; and hence the practicability of effecting great objects, building cities, magnificent palaces, temples, &c., by concert of action; and hence the rise and progress of the art of building and of the mechanic arts.

Sec. 4. *Glass-windows, Chimneys, Stoves, the Steam Engine, Fuel, Cold and Heat, and their influence on the comforts and industry of man.*

It is somewhat uncertain when and by whom the art of making glass was discovered; but it is supposed to have been discovered in Syria, three or four centuries before the Christian era; it was not much used or known at Rome until the time of Augustus Cæsar, and totally unknown to the Egyptians, Greeks, and all the nations of antiquity. Its principal use among the Romans seems to have been to make bottles, drinking vessels and matters of ornament; it does not appear to have been much used, if at all, for windows. It was occasionally used in churches, palaces and castles, in some parts of Europe, as early as the seventh century, though very expensive and rarely used, until after the 12th century; and it was not introduced even into the better sort of farm houses in England, until the commencement of the seventeenth century. Prior to the use of glass, windows were made sometimes of white linen cloth, but most generally of lattice work, and must have let in more wind and cold than light.

Originally houses were built with an aperture in the roof, (like an Indian wigwam or cabin,) for the smoke to escape; but the Greeks and Romans generally warmed their houses by portable stoves, pans or brasiers, without any pipe, in which they used charcoal and charred wood, and threw perfumes on it to prevent unpleasant effluvia. Seneca says that flues were introduced at Rome when Nero was Emperor; but other authors make no mention of chimneys, elevated funnels or flues for carrying off smoke, nor were any to be found in the houses discovered at Pompeii and Herculaneum; they are therefore supposed to be a modern invention, and to have been first erected in Italy in the eleventh century, under the name of camini. They were introduced into England and France in the 12th or 13th century, but did not come into general use among the middling classes of people, until the reign of Queen Elizabeth, in the 16th century. See the History of the Middle Ages, Chap. IX. part 2d, by the learned Henry Hallam, who states substantially the same facts in relation to the origin and introduction of glass-windows and chimneys.

Stoves with pipes or flues, were invented according to Mr. White, in 1680, by one Delaslme, and were wholly unknown to the Greeks, Romans, and all other nations of antiquity, whose stoves were but open pans, in which fires were made, mostly of charcoal and charred wood. Stoves were at first made of bricks, somewhat similar to an oven; sometimes they were also made of earthen, and were not often, if at all, made of iron, until near the commencement of the present century.

Though the power of steam was previously known, and some attempts had been made to construct engines to convert it to the use of man, yet the first steam engine of any practical utility, was constructed by Thomas Savary, to whom a patent was granted in 1698. The steam engine was, however, so imperfect in its construction, and so expensive to keep in operation, in proportion to its power, that it was of comparatively little use, until it was improved by James Watt, a Scotchman, about the year 1767; soon after that time, it was rapidly brought into use, and has been for over half a century extensively used in working pumps for draining mines, and in raising coal, iron ore, and other ore from the mines, as well as for working machinery for mechanical and manufacturing purposes. Some of the coal mines of England have been worked to the depth of nearly 1000 feet, and the coal all raised to the surface of the ground by the steam engine.

Great Britain had in 1841, over eighteen and a half millions of inhabitants, and the consumption of coal in 1839, for domestic purposes alone, was about fourteen million tons, or over three-fourths of a ton for each person. This enormous quantity of fuel contributed immensely in that high latitude, and comparatively cold and damp climate, to aid in keeping up an uniform temperature of atmosphere in their houses and work-shops, to keep them dry, and promote the health of the people.

After acknowledging the kind agency of Providence in supplying the coal beds, they were still almost useless to man, without the aid of the steam engine to raise the coal out of the mines. Prior to the year 1740, the quantity of iron made annually in Great Britain, was only about 20,000 tons: at present it amounts to about 2,000,000 tons annually, and about 7,000,000 tons of coal are consumed annually in making it. *Without the steam engine, coal could not be raised in very great quantities; without vast quantities of coal, such an immense quantity of iron could not be made; nor could such an enormous quantity of machinery as is used in the cotton, woollen, silk and other manufactories be kept in motion; without a vast quantity of iron, railroads could not be made throughout all parts of the kingdom, nor could such an immense quantity of machinery be constructed; without all these railroads, and all this machinery, a population of about twenty millions, could not be supplied with such an enormous quantity of coal for fuel, nor could they be furnished with employment, whereby they might obtain a subsistence upon so small an island.* The subsistence of millions of people may be said to depend on the steam engine.

McCulloch, in his Gazetteer, remarks as follows: coal stands at the head of the mineral products of England; and we are probably more indebted to our inexhaustible supplies of this valuable mineral, than to any thing else, for the extraordinary progress we have made in manufacturing industry. The coal mines are all in the north and west parts of the Kingdom, and these consequently are the great seats of our manufactures.

He estimated the production and consumption of coal in Great Britain in 1839, as follows:

	Tons.
Domestic consumption and smaller manufactures,	18,000,000
In the production of pig and bar iron, -	6,000,000
For Cotton manufactures, - -	800,000
" Woollen, linen, and silk do. -	800,000
" Copper smelting, brass manufactures, &c.	925,000
" Salt works, - - -	350,000
" Lime works, - - -	500,000
" Railway carriages, steam boats, &c. -	1,200,000
Total consumption in England in 1839,	28,575,000
Exported to Ireland, do. -	1,000,000
Do. to colonies and foreign parts do. -	1,449,417
Total, - -	31,024,417

During the same year, the imports of coals into London amounted to 2,638,256 tons.

Let us pause and contemplate these facts for a moment. Great Britain in the year 1839 consumed over twenty-eight and a half million tons of mineral coal, raised from her mines, generally severally hundred feet in depth, by the aid and power of the steam-engine. This enormous quantity of fuel is equal to about 36,000,000 cords of wood of average quality; and would be about as much as could be procured from 500,000 acres of wood-land, of average quantity of wood. There are about fifty-six million acres of land in the Island of Great Britain, and it would require one-third of the whole, or more, to supply such a quantity of fuel annually for a single century. Let it be borne in mind, also, that about two-thirds of this vast quantity of fuel, is consumed in cooking and warming dwelling-houses, work-shops, stores, manufacturing establishments, &c. &c., the principal part of which is required in consequence of the severity and dampness of the climate. Not over one-third part as much fuel is needed for warming dwellings, work-shops, stores, &c. in Italy, Greece, or Spain, as in Great Britain.

Even in Greece, sunny Greece, the warm climate of Greece, while that country was in the height of her glory, in the days of Aristotle, the comforts of life produced by mechanical power were so few, and the power of the people to protect themselves from the cold during the mild winters of that sunny climate, was so small and limited, that cold was regarded as the greatest evil man had to contend with; greater than even hunger itself. (See Aristotle's Politics, Book 2d, chap. iv., sections 7 and 8.) In this age of the world, mechanical power is increased to such an extent, that man can provide himself with a plenty of clothing, warm, dry, and comfortable dwellings, and an abundance of fuel, and can protect himself perfectly against the cold, in as high a latitude as will furnish sufficient vegetation for food. Heat is now the great enemy of the human family; it relaxes and enfeebles the system, so that man will scarcely do more than half as much labor annually at the 30th, as he can from the 40th to the 50th degree of latitude; it operates upon and excites the nervous system, and the action of the brain; increases the circulation of the blood, and the secretion of bile, and produces fevers and diseases of various kinds, often so sudden and powerful in their effects, as to baffle the science of medicine. Greece is in nearly the same latitude, and it is quite as warm as the States of North Carolina and Tennessee, and probably warmer, and yet the mortality of those States is nearly twice as great as the mortality of the States north of the 41st degree of latitude.

Even in the city of Philadelphia, as far north as the 40th degree of latitude, Dr. Emerson, a learned physician, in commenting upon the bills of mortality of that city, puts down heat, the excessive heat of summer, as the most powerful cause of the great mortality of the citizens. Examine the bills of mortality of the city of New York, and it will be found that the deaths from cholera infantum during the month of August, run from 30 to 70 weekly; during the month of July, from 20 to 50 weekly; and during the winter months not over 2 or 3 weekly. What but the excessive heat of summer could produce such effects? Cold was once, and until a comparatively recent period, the greatest enemy of man; but he has now almost entirely overcome it by means of mechanical power, new inventions and discoveries in mechanical science, and the consequent accumulation of the comforts of life. Heat is now his greatest enemy, against which, as yet, he has found no effectual protection, though the modern improvements in building, in the medical sciences, and the general increase of the comforts of life, have diminished the ratio of mortality considerably among the middle and higher classes of people even in hot climates, though probably not one-fourth part as much there, as in cold climates.

My readers will readily perceive the impossibility of mechanics and manufacturers working in cold climates, except in summer, in houses and workshops constructed, warmed and lighted, as they were in ancient times. In order to perform much labor of a mechanical or manufacturing character in cold and damp climates, good, dry, and comfortable, well-lighted, and well-warmed workshops are absolutely necessary; otherwise the labor of the workmen must be mostly confined to a few months of the warm season, and they must lie almost idle during more than half the year. Not so in warm and dry climates, where the atmosphere is so warm and dry during the most of the year, that all the mechanic needs is a shelter or covering sufficient to protect him from the heat of the sun, to enable him to continue his labor, with but little interruption, during the whole year. It is not, therefore, surprising that the inhabitants of France and England, as well as of all Central and Northern Europe, remained in a rude and barbarous condition, living either in the pastoral or hunting state, ignorant of the mechanic arts, and destitute of what even the poor now esteem the ordinary necessaries and comforts of life, for centuries after the inhabitants of Egypt, Southern Asia, Greece, Italy, Spain, and Northern Africa had made considerable progress in the mechanic arts, commerce, and civilization.

SEC. 5. *Invention of Saw-Mills—mode of building, and condition of dwellings before that time.*

When the first mill was erected for sawing lumber by mechanical power is not known; it is certain, however, that saw-mills were not in use among the Greeks, Romans, Egyptians, or any of the ancient nations. The first saw-mill, of which we have any record, was erected on the Island of Madeira in 1420; and the first one in Norway, in 1530. Saw-mills were not introduced into England until the seventeenth century, and for a long time occasioned alarm, commotion and excitement among the sawyers, for fear they might be thrown out of employment. The first one was erected in London in 1633, but it was demolished soon afterwards, for fear it might be the means of depriving the poor of employment, and the means of subsistence. Saw-mills were introduced into the colony of Massachusetts about the same time. *Prior to the invention and use of saw-mills, boards and plank were sawed by hand, which rendered sawed lumber very scarce and excessively dear. It must have cost as much as eight, or ten times, and perhaps twenty times as much labor to make it, as it does now.*

The Greeks, Romans, Egyptians, and other ancient nations, understood sawing stone and marble much better than wood, and could probably do it nearly as cheap. Hence all the ancient nations built their houses, and other edifices, of brick, stone, or marble, and used wood only for doors, casings, and perhaps upper floors, and roofs in some cases, and a few other purposes. When they had any lower floor, it was stone or brick laid on the ground; but the great mass of the people had no floors at all, and cooked, eat, and lived on the bare ground; in fact, such appears to have been the case among the wealthier class of Romans, while Rome was in the height of her power and glory.

Jacob, in his "Historical Inquiry into the Precious Metals," Chap. xxi. p. 277, says that "When Erasmus visited England in the former century, (the 16th,) the houses were built of mud and wood, were *thatched with straw, and instead of* FLOORS THE BARE EARTH WAS COVERED WITH RUSHES OR STRAW; but in the latter end of the 17th century, the dwellings in towns were chiefly constructed of stone or brick, were covered with slate or tiles, and FLOORED WITH TIMBER."

Let us take a retrospective view, and see what was the kind, condition, and comforts of the dwellings and work-shops of the ancient nations, as well as those of the people of Europe, up to the 12th century, and even of the great mass of the people up to the latter part of the 17th century. Their buildings were made of brick, mud, wood, and stone, without chimneys or flues to carry off the smoke, and without stoves having pipes; being warmed by means of a fire built on the ground, in the middle of a room, or by coals or charred wood in a brasier or open pan, without a pipe, the smoke rising into the room and passing off through an aperture in the roof, in many respects like an Indian wigwam or cabin. Secondly, Their buildings were without glass windows, and lighted from the aperture in the roof, and by means of windows sometimes made of white cloth, but more generally of wooden lattice work, which in cold weather let in more wind and cold than light. Thirdly, the labor and expense of sawing lumber was so great, that their buildings were generally without floors of any kind, there being nothing but the naked ground to stand, work, and put their furniture and work upon, or brick or stone floors, lying upon the ground, and generally equally damp, cold, and unhealthy, as the ground itself. In foggy, cloudy, rainy or snowy weather in winter, in England, the north of France, or any of the central and northern parts of Europe, such dwellings would necessarily be cold, damp, smoky, dark, gloomy, and unhealthy. Such buildings were totally unfit for work-shops during more than half the year; hence the utter impossibility, in cold and damp climates, of prosecuting the mechanic arts to any great extent in such buildings, and for want of the mechanic arts agriculture was in a very backward, rude, and infant state; husbandry being mostly of a pastoral character, and the principal business of the farmer, the raising of cattle.

SEC. 6. *More people suffer for want of comfortable dwellings, clothing, and fuel, than for want of food.*

Though food is the first want of man, and while in a savage and barbarous state, undoubtedly millions have perished for want of a regular and sufficient supply of nourishment; yet where man has acquired the art of making iron, and instruments and utensils of husbandry, the mechanic arts and commerce have sprung up, and a division of employments has taken place, the earth in all warm and temperate, as well as hot climates, and generally up to nearly the 60th degree of latitude, seems to bring forth abundantly, and to increase her productions in proportion to the progress the people have made in the mechanic arts, and in commerce; famines become unknown, a general failure of all the different crops of a country never occurs, and the people seldom perish, nor are their days shortened for want of food. Though the island of Great Britain has about eight times as many inhabitants as it had seven or eight centuries since, yet the whole population would be better supplied now, without importing a pound of breadstuffs, than they were then. In fact, it may be said with truth, that famines, dearths, and scarcities of provisions, and suffering for want of food, have always occurred among savages, barbarians, hunters, shepherds, and agricultural nations; but have rarely been very destructive to human life in any age of the world, among any people who had made much proficiency in the mechanic arts.

As a general rule, man, in all civilized countries not even excepting Great Britain, can supply himself with a sufficiency of food to promote health and longevity, much easier than he can procure a comfortable dwelling suitable to promote health, and a sufficient supply of comfortable clothing, bedding, and fuel. M. Quetelet, a learned Belgian writer, in his Essais sur L'Homme, shows that the mortality annually in the poorest district of Paris, is nearly twice as great as in the wealthiest district; that the mortality increases regularly, from the wealthiest to the poorest district; and that it is very little affected by any cause, except the degree of comfort, and the wealth and ease or poverty of the inhabitants. The lives of the poor are not shortened in Paris by want of food, as much as those of the rich are by high living, over-eating, and want of exercise, which often bring on the gout, dyspepsia, and a long train of other diseases. The cause of the great mortality of the poor in Paris, and in all civilized countries, is not a want of food, but a want of warm, dry, airy and comfortable dwellings, and a want of sufficient good bedding, clothing, and fuel, to keep up as near as practicable, an uniform temperature of the human system day and night, during the year.

In this age of the world, when food and clothing seem to be generally abundant in every civilized country, the greatest enemies to human life, and the most active causes which produce disease and death, are heat, cold, and dampness in excess. Though the laboring classes are more exposed to these elements and causes of disease than the wealthy, yet moderate and regular exercise daily, contributes to health, and they are not subject to the endless train of diseases brought on by luxury, excessive indulgence, and indolence; and, upon the whole, the laboring classes in the United States who have comfortable dwellings, live quite as long if not longer than the wealthy and luxurious. Such is not the case however, among those who are engaged on our public works, canals, and railroads, who live in temporary shanties, so open that rain drives in at every storm or shower, and destitute of any floor except a few loose boards laid on the ground. Such dwellings are always wet in wet weather, and the floors are kept damp and cold during the principal part of the year, by the ground on which they lie. They are soon heated through by the sun in summer, and are penetrated with the cold and the winds very quickly on a change of the weather; in fact, they afford to their inmates very little protection from the weather, and leave them almost as much exposed to heat and cold, wind, rain, and dampness, as if they were under the shelter of nothing better than a forest tree. Such dwellings, together with an insufficient quantity of bedding, are the fruitful source of disease and death; and accordingly we find the mortality of persons in such circumstances is immensely great, generally two or three times as great as it is among persons in the middle ranks of life. The same difficulty and danger attend persons who are poor, on settling in a new country; they live in miserable dwellings, or huts, with floors as just described, of loose boards either lying on the ground, or within a few inches of it; they are hot during the day in summer, and damp and cold at night, and damp during the greater part of the year. Such is the case also, to a considerable extent, in large cities, where thousands of persons live in cellars, and miserable shells of houses, on low wet ground by the side of water courses, where the air at night is generally damp, and often foggy; and in addition to all this, *great numbers are crowded together in small apartments, and lodgings poorly ventilated, where they necessarily suffer from each other's breath and the exhalations from the human system. Wherever such diseases as the plague, yellow fever, Asiatic cholera, dysentery, &c. have appeared in cities, they have uniformly made their appearance among the poor in such dwellings, along the water courses; and there also they have continued the greatest length of time, and been the most destructive to human life.*

Such also was the condition of the dwellings to a very great extent of all the people, both rich and poor, throughout the world, prior to the invention of saw mills, glass windows and chimneys. Even the rich had no floors except brick or stone, laid upon the ground, and as damp and cold as the ground itself; and the poor generally had no floors but the naked ground. They had no glass windows by which they could admit the light, exclude the cold and dampness of the atmosphere, and shut out the damp atmosphere at night; nor had they any chimneys or stoves by which they could warm their houses and dry them when necessary, and at the same time carry off the smoke, without letting in the cold.

Great care is now taken, by persons who are able, to have either cellars under their houses, or to raise them up some feet from the ground, so that the dampness of the earth may not affect their floors, and thus penetrate into their rooms; and in building brick houses, many persons put studs upon the inside of the brick wall, and lath and plaster upon them, in order to keep the dampness of the walls from penetrating through into the rooms. All these improvements of modern times, have contributed to increase the comforts, promote the health, lessen the sickness and mortality, and lengthen the life of man.

SEC. 7. *The Mariner's Compass, and its influence on Navigation.*

Prior to the invention of the Mariner's Compass, it was impossible to navigate the ocean with safety, or even at all, except along its coasts; and hence navigation and transportation by water was pretty much confined to the Mediterranean, Black, and Red Seas, and the coasts of the Atlantic and Indian Oceans. This invention is claimed by the Neapolitans to have been made by one of their citizens about the year 1302 ; while the Venetians state that they introduced it from China about the year 1260. This valuable invention extended, and changed the character of navigation, led to the discovery of the New World, by Columbus in 1492; and stimulated man, by opening to his view, the broadest field of commercial enterprise which he had ever witnessed.

SEC. 8. *Progress of improvement in the mechanic arts, and manufactures; and their effects upon man.*

The increase of population, of power, and of wealth, has progressed step by step, in all civilized countries, with the inventions and improvements in the mechanic arts, the increase of productive industry, and the extension of commerce; and accordingly we find that for centuries prior to the Christian era, as well as long afterwards, the nations about the Mediterranean sea and southern Asia, had from five to ten times as much population, in proportion to their territory capable of cultivation, as the nations of central and northern Europe; though the latter are now much more densely populated, and in most instances, have two or three times as dense a population as the former.

Though the art of spinning and weaving wool and flax into cloth was introduced by the Romans into Gaul, now France, and into Great Britain, before the Christian era, or about that time, yet the manufacture of cloth in these countries was extremely limited, until within the last two or three centuries. Flanders or Burgundy, now Belgium, was the first country in a high latitude and cold climate where the manufacture of cloth of any kind was ever carried on to such an extent as to make it an article of foreign commerce and exportation. Though the Flemish seem to have been in advance, in the manufacture of cloth, of the

English, French, Spaniards, and all the nations of central, western, and northern Europe during the time of the crusades, and for some centuries previous; yet they were behind the Venetians, *and did not make very rapid progress in manufactures until the latter part of the thirteenth century, after the introduction of chimneys with flues, and glass windows in their houses and workshops.* Flanders flourished and increased in population, wealth and power during the whole of the fourteenth and fifteenth centuries, and until the commencement of the religious persecutions and wars of Philip II. of Spain, and the Duke of Alva, about the year 1567, with greater rapidity than any other part of Europe, except Venice. Venice prospered by means of manufacturing industry and commercial enterprise combined; but the chief source of the prosperity and increase of population and wealth in Flanders, was their extensive manufactures of wool, linen, laces, &c. Vast quantities of wool were sent annually from Spain, England and France to Flanders, to be manufactured into cloth, and the cloth, when manufactured, transported back to the countries which furnished the wool. This course of business made all those countries, in some measure, tributary to, and contributors to the prosperity and wealth of the little Dukedom of Burgundy. During the fourteenth and fifteenth centuries, Bruges, and afterwards Antwerp and Amsterdam, were more wealthy and prosperous; and Bruges, in the height of her prosperity, was also more populous than either London or Paris. The revenues of the Duke of Burgundy were then estimated as greater than those of England or France. (See Hallam's Middle Ages, Harper's edition, 192, note.)

The first impulse to the manufacture of wool in England was given in the 14th century, by Edward III., who invited, and gave great encouragement to Flemish manufacturers to remove to England and establish themselves there, in the woollen manufacture; and during the religious persecutions and civil wars in the Netherlands, the latter part of the 16th century, the greater part of the Protestant refugees fled to England, and sought the protection of Queen Elizabeth, where they contributed to increase and extend the manufacturing skill, science, industry, and prosperity of the British nation. Louis XIV. of France, revoked the edict of Nantes in 1685, and commenced the violent persecution of the Protestants of his dominions; and it has been generally estimated, that half a million or more escaped from the country; and that an hundred thousand of them went to England, the most of whom were mechanics and manufacturers. These several emigrations of mechanics and manufacturers to England, may be regarded as the principal causes of the growth of manufactures in that country, prior to the general introduction of machinery and of the Steam Engine, about the year 1775.

To enable the reader to judge of the changes in the condition of the people of England, made since the beginning of the Reformation, I have collected the following statements from the history of England by Sir James McIntosh, and from Henry Hallam's history of the middle ages. Referring to the 14th century, Sir James writes as follows: "The frequency of famines, and the excessive fluctuation of the prices of the necessaries of life, were among the most wide-wasting evils which afflicted the middle age. In a period without commerce, the scarcity of one district could not be relieved by the redundant produce of another." "*The pestilential fevers which raged with such malignity may in part be ascribed to want of food, fuel, air, and clothing; to towns crowded and filthy, as well as to the low state of medical knowledge.*" Mr. Hallam, in his ninth chapter, *shows the style of building during the middle ages; the miserable and comfortless condition of the dwellings, even of the wealthy; the character of their clothing, made mostly of leather, furs, and skins; the scantiness of their furniture, having but a few beds, chairs, or benches, tables, and kitchen furniture, mostly of a very coarse kind, with very little bedding; and their want of a great proportion of the comforts of life, now enjoyed by mechanical and manufacturing laborers.* They had a little plate, a few ornaments, very few looking glasses, or even glass windows, which were then regarded as moveable property and rather rare; and the servants of even the wealthy slept on mattresses of straw. The industrious, temperate, and provident portions of the manufacturing classes of England, at this time, have better clothing, lodging, and furniture, than the nobility had in the 15th century.

SEC. 9. *On Paper—its uses and manufacture.*

Paper is manufactured of vegetable mater reduced to a pulp by means of water and grinding. For the chief purpose to which it is applied in modern times, the ancients had recourse to a variety of materials; such as stone—tablets of wood, plates of lead, skins, parchment, linen, and above all, the papyrus. Of all these articles, papyrus was found the most useful for ordinary purposes as a subsitute for paper. The art of making papyrus into paper was invented in Egypt several centuries before the Christian era. The art of making paper of cotton cloth or rags is suppposed to have been borrowed from the Chinese or Persians, and introduced into Europe in the eleventh century by the Saracens; the practice of making linen into paper commenced in the 12th or 13th century, and in France and England early in the 14th century.

The application of paper to purposes of writing and printing, and the fact of its being indispensable for such uses, render its manufacture of the highest utility and importance. France, Holland, and Genoa, had for a long period a decided superiority over England, in the manufacture of paper. The first paper mill erected in England was built during the reign of Queen Elizabeth; but even during the 17th century, the greatest part of the paper used in England was imported from the continent, and much of it from France. The manufacture is said to have been considerably improved by the French refugees, who fled to Great Britain in 1685; the manufacture of white paper was commenced in England in 1690. The quantity annually manufactured in Great Britain was estimated about the year 1721 at 300,000 reams; which was about two thirds the whole consumption of that country. In 1783 the value of the paper annually manufactured in Great Britain was estimated at £780,000. Dr. Brande estimated it in 1840, at from £1,200,000 to £1,300,000, and McCulloch, at £1,500,000. The former says there were then about 700 paper mills in England, from 70 to 80 in Scotland, and very few in Ireland. (See Brande's Encyclopædia of Science and Art.)

Porter states the licenses granted for the manufacture of paper, and the quantity charged with excise duty in 1841 as follows. Licenses granted in England 370, Scotland 49, and Ireland 48, total 467; and the quantity made at 97,103,548 pounds. Ireland is partially supplied with paper from England.

The value of the paper, pasteboard, cards, &c., manufactured in the United States in 1810, according to the census of that year, amounted to $1,939,285; and in 1840 to $6,153,092; the paper mills at the latter period numbered 426. The imports of paper of all kinds into the United States in 1842, were valued at $92,771. The value of paper, paper hangings, and all manufactures of paper made annually in France, is estimated at 43,000,000 francs or about $8,184,000

Sec. 10. *On the production, manufacture, and trade in Wool and Woollen goods.*

We read that Abel was a keeper of sheep, (Gen. iv: 2 and 4,) and in the same chap. v. 19, that Jabal was the father of those that dwelt in tents and of such as have cattle; that Noah dwelt in a tent, and his sons covered his nakedness with a garment, (Gen. ix: 21, and 23.) Whether the tents and garments spoken of in 4th and 9th Gen. were made of skins, or wool spun and wove into cloth, is perhaps uncertain; but we read in Leviticus xiii. 47, and 59, that the Israelites after they left Egypt had garments made of both wool and flax. Woollen and linen cloths, together with leather and skins, constituted almost the entire clothing of the ancient Egyptians, Israelites, Phœnicians, Greeks, and Romans, and of all the nations of Europe, except the Saracens and Turks, until the introduction of the cotton manufacture at a comparatively recent period. In temperate as well as in cold climates, sheep, next to cattle, are the most useful to man, of all the animal creation. They afford a large supply of food and the principal material of clothing, and can be reared in situations and soils unfit for agriculture, and do well, where other animals would scarcely live. England, as shown in Chap. VII., was mostly a grazing country, until the 17th century, and up to that time the principal exports of the English consisted of wool, coarse unfinished woollen cloths, a small quantity of tin, copper, and hardware, and a few horses and cattle ; and up to the end of the15th century, the exports were but trifling in amount, consisting of wool, cattle, horses, and tin.

The total number of sheep and lambs in England and Wales in 1800, including the number slaughtered and lost that year, was estimated at 26,148,463 ; and their product of wool at 384,000 packs of 240 lbs. each ; equal in the aggregate to 92,160,000 pounds. The number of sheep in Scotland was estimated in 1814 at 2,850,000, and in 1837 at 3,500,000 ; in Ireland at 2,000,000 ; and in England and Wales at 26,500,000 ; making in all in the United Kingdom 32,000,000. Dr. Campbell, in his "Political Survey of Great Britain," published in 1774,observes : —"Many computations have been made upon this important subject. According to the best information that can be obtained, there may be from 10,000,000 to 12,000,000 sheep in England, some think more. The value of their wool may, one year with another, amount to £3,000,000 ; the expense of manufacturing it may probably be £9,000,000, and the total value £12,000,000. We may export annually to the value of £3,000,000, though one year we exported more than £4,000,000."

About the year 1696, Gregory King and Mr. Davenant estimated the value of the wool shorn in England and Wales at £2,000,000 per annum ; and they supposed the value of the wool, including that imported, was about quadrupled in the manufacture, making the annual value of the manufactures of wool £8,000,000.

The quantity of wool imported into Great Britain, the quantity retained for home consumption, and the official as well as the real or market value of woollen manufactures exported from the United Kingdom of Great Britain and Ireland at different periods, were as follows.

	1810.	1820.	1830.	1838.
Wool imported, lbs.	10,914,187	9,789,020	82,318,059	88,076,413
do. retained for consumption..		7,691,778	81,522,859	89,066,620

Woollen Manufactures exported.

	1820.	1830.	1835.	1840.
Official value,	———	£5,558,709	£ 7,406 909	———
Declared value,	£5,586,188	4,850,884	6,840,511	5,827,853

The declared value of the exports of woollen manufactures and yarn in 1844, amounted to £8,204,836, and the quantity of wool imported amounted to 65,079,524 pounds. McCulloch states that in 1700 and 1701, the official value of the woollen goods exported, amounted to about £3,000,000 a year; and that the average official value of the exports for the six years ending with 1789, was £3,544,160 per annum. Since the introduction of machinery and the prodigious increase of the cotton manufacture, cotton fabrics have for many uses supplied the places of woollen, as well as of linen cloths, and the woollen manufacture has increased very slowly in Great Britain during the last century and a half. McCulloch estimates in his Gazetteer, the value of the fabrics of wool annually manufactured in Great Britain at that time (1840,) at £22,000,000, and those of cotton at £35,000,000; and if the estimate of Dr. Campbell, of the value of woollen manufactures in 1774, at from ten to twelve millions of pounds sterling, was very near correct, the manufacture of wool has not increased since that time, as fast as the population.

McCulloch states that the total annual product of wool in England and Wales was then (1840,) estimated at 470,000 packs of 240 lbs. each; amounting in the aggregate to 112,800,000 lbs. He states the number of sheep in France at 39,000,000, and the wool annually produced by them on an average from 1830 to 1840, on the authority of Berghaus, at 42,000,000 kilogrammes; about 93,000,000 lbs.

Let us compare the number of sheep in those countries, and the quantity of wool annually produced, with the number of sheep in the U. States, and the production of wool in 1840, according to the census.

	No. of sheep.	Pounds of wool.	Pounds to each sheep.
In England & Wales,	26,500,000	112,800,000	over 4.25
" Scotland, about	3,500,000		
" France,	39,000,000	93,000,000	2.4
" our Free States,	12,144,468	27,488,407	2.25
" " Slave States,	7,166,906	8,313,707	1,16
United States,	19,311,374	35,802,114	1.85

These facts indicate the character of the husbandry of those countries, and show very clearly, that the same truth holds good in relation to growing wool, as well as to other branches of agriculture; that wherever manufactures are flourishing, there is an active demand for raw produce at good prices, and agriculture is generally flourishing, and conducted with science and skill; and that wherever there are no manufactures, there is but little demand for raw produce, and agriculture is generally in a very sluggish and low state, and wages and lands, as well as produce, very low.

Sheep do well on rough, rocky, hilly and mountainous lands, which are totally unfit for cultivation; they also do well on the dry and rolling prairies, as well as on the dry opening lands of the North-western States. The Alpaca or Peruvian sheep has been introduced into England, and naturalized in that country within the last fifteen years. It is a large, hardy sheep, accustomed to climbing and living on short fare among the lofty Andes of Peru; has done well in England, and is said to yield an average of ten pounds of fine wool, worth from 1s. 8d. to 2s. 6d. sterling per pound. There are great quantities of rough, and mountainous lands, in the States of Pennsylvania, Maryland, Virginia, and Tennessee, and some in the Carolinas, Georgia, Kentucky, and many other states, of but little value for anything but grazing, on which many millions of Alpacas and other sheep might be kept; and instead of producing about one-third part as much wool in the United States as is produced on the island of Great Britain, our present States and Territories are capable of producing ten times as much.

We not only import large amounts of woollen manufactures, but large quantities of wool also. Our imports of wool in 1842 and 1845 were as follows: in 1842 wool costing less than eight cents per pound, 10,637,251 pounds, value $685,649; over eight cents per pound, 783,701 pounds, value $111,733; and in 1845, wool not exceeding seven cents per pound, 23,382,097 pounds, value $1,593,789; and over seven cents, 450,943 pounds, valued at $136,005.

The value of manufactures of wool imported into the United States, were, in 1825, $11,392,264; in 1830, $5,766,396; in 1835, $17,834,424; in 1840, $9,071,184; in 1845, $10,666,176; and in 1850, $17,151,500.

The value of the woollen fabrics manufactured in the United States in 1840 according to the returns of the census, amounted to $20,696,999, besides mixed goods, and about $25,000,000 worth of woollen cloths made in families.

The woollen fabrics made annually in France, have been estimated by Berghaus at about $50,000,000, and by other persons much higher. Their exports of manufactures of wool from 1831 to 1837, averaged annually, nearly $8,000,000 ; from 1838 to 1842, nearly $12,000,000 annually; and in 1843 they amounted to $14,835,000. While France as well as Great Britain export a large amount of manufactures of wool, both Ireland and the United States import a large proportion of the woollen goods consumed by their inhabitants—and import wool also.

Sec. 11. *The production, manufacture, and trade in the manufactures of Flax and Hemp.*

Flax is a native plant of Egypt, and of almost every country of Europe, and has been used for cloth from the earliest periods of profane as well as sacred history; but its use at present is almost superseded by cotton, which is generally supposed to promote health much more, and to be better for clothing on that account than linen.

Flax was carded, spun, and woven by hand all over the world, until about the year 1810, when machinery was first applied to its manufacture. The imports of flax into Dundee in Scotland, increased from 74 tons in 1745, to 2,444 tons in 1791; and from about 3000 tons, in 1814, to 15,000 tons in 1830. The imports amounted during the year ending May 31st, 1833, to 18,777 tons of flax, and 3,380 tons of hemp: the whole quantity imported into Great Britain and Ireland in 1834 was 40,586 tons; in 1840, 62,662 tons; in 1845, 70,931 tons; and in 1849, 90,339 tons.

The low wages of spinners in Ireland hindered the application of machinery to the spinning of flax many years after it had been extensively introduced into England and Scotland. But the rapid progress of the manufacture in Great Britain, made it evident that unless similar machinery were set in motion in Ireland, the linen manufacture of that country would be entirely annihilated. There were in 1834, 152 flax factories in England, 170 in Scotland, and but 25 in Ireland; the spinning of flax in Ireland, being at that time mostly done by hand. McCulloch estimated the annual value of the manufacture of linen, in Great Britain and Ireland, from 1834 to 1838, at £8,000,000, as follows.

Value of raw material one third, . .	£2,666,666
Wages of laborers, ...	3,333,334
Profits, use, wear and tear of capital, wages of superintendants, &c., 25 per cent, .	2,000,000
	£8,000,000

The value exported from the United Kingdom in 1830 amounted to £2,066,424, in 1835 to £3,208,778, and in 1844 to £4,075,476. The exports from Ireland to Great Britain, except yarn, are nearly as much annually, as the exports from Great Britain to foreign countries, so that the manufactures of linen in Great Britain, except yarn, are about equal to, or very little more than the consumption. Since the application of machinery to spinning linen, the weight of the linen yarn exported has increased from 2,611,215 lbs. in 1835, to 17,733,575 lbs. in 1840, and to 25,970,569 lbs. in 1844; valued in 1844 at £1,050,676 sterling; all of which was spun in Great Britain. Such is the effect of machinery.

The manufactures of flax and hemp in France consisting of linen, thread, lace, &c., are still more valuable than those of Great Britain and Ireland; they were estimated in 1839, at 260,000,000 francs, equal to $48,880,000; the average annual exports of which, including linen clothing from 1836 to 1840, amounted to over $8,000,000.

The value of the manufactures of flax (exclusive of mixed and family made goods) in the United States in 1840 was only $322,205. The value of the manufactures of flax and hemp imported into the United States, has been as follows.

	Of Flax.	Of Hemp.
1825,	$3,887,787	$2,134,384
1830,	3,011,280	1,333,478
1835,	6,472,021	2,555,847
1839,	7,703,065	2,096,716
1842,	3,659,184	1,273,534
1845,	4,923,109	897,345
1850,	8,134,674	588,446

The United States produced in 1839, according to the returns of the census, 95,251* tons of flax and hemp (mostly hemp,) and we might produce sufficient of each, to supply the wants of the country, and furnish the value (when manufactured), of many millions of dollars for exportation annually.

SEC. 12. *The production, manufacture and trade in Silk and Silk Goods.*

Though silk was made into cloth at a very early period in China, India, Persia, and some other countries of Asia, and its use became known to the Romans before the Christian era, yet the rearing of silkworms and the silk manufacture were not introduced into Europe until the time of the emperor Justinian, about the year 530. But after the introduction of these arts at Constantinople, Thebes, Corinth, and Argos, Greece continued to be the only European country in which they were practised until about the middle of the twelfth century, when they were

* About 11,674 tons should be deducted for error in Virginia.

introduced into the island of Sicily. From this island they spread into Italy; and Venice, Milan, Florence, and Lucca, were soon after distinguished for their success in raising silk-worms, and for the extent and beauty of their manufactures of silk.

The silk manufacture was introduced into Tours in France, by some workmen from Italy, on the invitation of Louis XI., about the year 1480, and at Lyons in 1520; and into England about the same time, though it did not make much progress in England until the age of Queen Elizabeth.

England is situated in too high a latitude to rear the silk-worm, and produce raw silk to advantage; the quantity of raw silk produced in that country is small. The quantity of silk manufactured in Great Britain is indicated by the quantity of raw, waste and thrown silk imported at different periods. It was very trifling until the civil wars in Flanders drove many of the Flemish manufacturers and artisans to England during the reign of Queen Elizabeth; and the revocation of the edict of Nantes in 1685, which drove great numbers also from France; many of whom fled to England. But the manufacture progressed very slowly, until after the introduction and use of machinery.

The average annual importation of raw, waste, and thrown silk into Great Britain at different periods, was as follows, stated in pounds.

	Raw and Waste.	*Thrown.*
1765 to 1767	352,000 lbs.	363,000 lbs.
1785 to 1787	544,000 "	337,000 "
1801 to 1812	760,000 "	350,000 "
1821 to 1823	2,044,000 "	355,000 "
1830	4,256,982 "	436,535 "
1840	4,531,115 "	288,147 "
1849	5,004,232 "	614,689 "

There has been scarcely any increase in the quantity of thrown or spun silk annually imported (into Great Britain since the year 1765); but the importation of raw silk has kept pace with the invention, improvement, and use of machinery. There were in 1834, no less than two hundred and fifty-six silk factories in England, six in Scotland, and but one in Ireland; employing in England 29,947 persons, in Scotland 686 persons, and in Ireland but 48. In 1839, the number of silk factories in England had increased to 286, employing 33,470 persons, while there was no increase in Scotland and Ireland.

The value of silk goods of all kinds manufactured annually in Great Britain and France about the year 1840, was estimated by

McCulloch as follows: in Great Britain, £10,000,000 sterling, and in France 300,000,000 francs, equal to about £12,000,000.

The average annual value of silk and silk goods exported from France from 1836 to 1841 was about 137,000,000 francs, equal to about 45 per cent. of the whole value produced; while the declared value of British silks exported from Great Britain and Ireland from 1841 to 1844, averaged annually only £695,872 sterling; or less than eight per cent. of the value manufactured.

The value of silk goods imported into the United States, during the undermentioned fiscal years, was as follows:

1825	$10,299,743
1830	5,932,212
1835	16,677,547
1839	21,742,369
1840	9,835,757
1845	9,928,411
1850	*19,692,818

SEC. 13. *The production, manufacture, and trade in Cotton and Cotton Goods—the prices of cotton, &c.*

Though cotton is a native plant of India, the interior of Africa, and Mexico, and perhaps of some other warm countries, and it has been spun into cloth, and furnished the principal clothing of the Hindoos from time immemorial, and of the natives of Mexico at the time of the discovery of America; yet its manufacture seems to have been unknown to the ancient Egyptians, Greeks, and Romans, and to have been first brought into Europe by the Moors, who introduced it into Spain in the ninth or tenth century. It was first introduced into Italy in the thirteenth or fourteenth century, and into Flanders and France at a still later period; and was not introduced into England until the sixteenth century. The fibres of cotton being shorter than those of flax, and more difficult to spin and weave by hand, the quantity manufactured in Europe was very small, until after the invention and general use of machinery for spinning and weaving it; and the Europeans were principally supplied with cotton cloths from India, and some from China, during the whole of the last century, and to a considerable extent, down to the close of the wars growing out of the French revolution in 1815.

* This is the amount according to the valuations, including silk and worsted goods, valued at $1,653,809. There is no reason to doubt that they were undervalued from fifteen to twenty per cent. on an average, and that their real value for the fiscal year, ending June 30th, 1850, was as much as twenty-three millions of dollars.

Mr. Baine, in his "History of the Cotton Manufacture," expresses the opinion, that the cotton manufacture was first introduced into England by the Protestant refugees who fled from Flanders, during the religious persecutions, the latter part of the sixteenth century. He shows that the average importation of cotton into England from 1701 to 1705 was only 1,170,881 pounds; in 1730, only 1,545,472 pounds; in 1751 it amounted to 2,976,610 pounds; the average quantity imported from 1771 to 1775, was only 4,764,589 pounds; and the average from 1776 to 1780, but 6,766,613 pounds. These facts show how small and trifling the quantity of cotton manufactured in England until after the invention of the spinning jenny by Hargreaves in 1767. Though the culture of cotton had been introduced into these United States, (then colonies,) prior to the revolutionary war, and small quantities were made into cloth by females by hand for domestic uses, yet no cotton was exported by them until about the year 1784, and very little until after the invention of the cotton-gin by Mr. Whitney in 1793. The quantity exported in 1791 was but 189,316 pounds; and in 1792 but 138,328 pounds; in 1794 it increased to 1,601,700 pounds.

The following tables show the cultivation, manufacture, and foreign trade in cotton at different periods:

I. Statement showing the millions of pounds of Cotton exported from the United States during the undermentioned years and periods—the average price per pound, and the aggregate value in millions of dollars, according to the custom-house valuations. Also the quantities manufactured in Great Britain, France, and the United States.

Average of years.	Millions of pounds exported.	Value in milions of dollars exported.	Average price per lb. Cents.	Quantity manufactured, stated in millions of pounds, by		
				G. Britain.	France.	U. States.
1700 to1750	None		30 to 75	1.9		a trifle.
1751	do		do	2.97		do
1764	do		do	3.87		do
1771—1780	do		do	5.75		do
1781—1790	do		do	18		.5
1791—1800	5.53		33.8	30.5	10	6
1801—1810	43		22	67.2	18	12
1811—1820	69.67		20.5	104.8	30	25
1821—1830	203.4		13.2	180.3	69.6	50
1831—1840	431.73		12.24	340.9	102	80
1841—1850	699.35		8.29	560	170	175
1820—1821	124.89	20.1	16	114	47	40
1821—1822	144.67	24	16.6	120.5	61	
1822—1823	173.72	20.4	11.6	177	50.5	
1823—1824	142.37	21.9	15	131	75	
1824—1825	176.45	36.8	21	206	60	
1825—1826	204.53	25	12.2	150.25	96	
1826—1827	294.31	29.3	9.9	250.5	87	
1827—1828	210.59	22.5	10.2	208.25	61	50
1828—1829	264.84	26.5	10	190.75	71.5	
1829—1830	298.46	29.6	10	255	87.3	
1830—1831	277	25.3	9.1	257	65.5	
1831—1832	322.21	31.7	9.5	268.8	78	75
1832—1833	324.7	36.2	11.1	286.3	87	
1833—1834	384.71	49.4	12.9	302.4	80	80
1834—1835	387·36	64.9	16.6	330.9		
1835—1836	423.63	71.2	16.7	375.2	112	90
1836—1837	444.2	63.2	14.2	368.5	120	
1837—1838	595.95	61.5	10.3	455	137	
1838—1839	413.62	61.2	14.8	365	114	110
1839—1840	743.94	63.8	8.5	500	160	124
1840—1841	530.2	54.3	10.2	450	158	125
1841—1842	584.71	47.5	8.1	475	159	114
1842—1843	792.3	49.1	6.2	560	160	137
1843—1844	663.63	54	8.1	580	160	150
1844—1845	872.9	51.7	6	600	165	170
1845—1846	547.5	42.7	7.8	500	170	190
1846—1847	527.2	53.4	11	480		200
1847—1848	813.6	62	7.6	620		230
1848—1849	1,026.1	66.4	6.6	750		240
1849—1850	635.4	72	11.3			230
1850—1851	927.2	112.3	12.1			190

II. Summary statement of the production and export of cotton by all the principal cotton-growing countries of the world at different periods, stated in millions of pounds.

Years,	1791.	1801.	1811.	1821.	1834
In the U. States,					
Millions of pounds produced,	2	30	80	180	460
exported,	¼	20⅞	62¼	124⅞	384
Brazil produced,	22	36	35	32	30
exported,	20	24	31	28	30
West Indies produced,	12	10	12	10	8
exported,	12	17	7	9	8
Egypt produced,			⅛	6	25⅓
exported,				5	23
The rest of Africa produced,	46	45	44	40	34
exported,					
India produced,	130	160	170	175	185
exported,		30	41	50	80
The rest of Asia produced,	190	160	146	135	110
exported,	5	7	6		
Mexico and S. America, except Brazil, produced,	68	56	57	44	35
exported,		22½			
All other countries produced,		15	11	8	13
exported,					
Total produced in the world,	490	530	555	630	900

Mr. Woodbury estimated in millions of pounds the quantity manufactured in different countries as follows:

	1791.	1801.	1811.	1821.	1834.
China and India,	285	280	270	260	242
Mexico and S. America,	50	45	48	42	35
Germany,	15	22	25	30	36
Spain,	2	3	5	8	10
Prussia,	2	5	6	7	20
Turkey and Africa,	52	50	48	45	42
Other countries except those stated in table No. 1,	60	50	50	45	40

Prior to the year 1820, no country of Europe except Great Britain, manufactured any cotton cloths for exportation. Mr. Woodbury states the value of the exports of cotton manufactures from India in 1802 at $20,000,000, and in 1813 at $18,000,000;

the exports of cotton goods from China in 1806 at $4,000,000; in 1820 at $3,000,000, and in 1826 at but $1,750,000. Under the withering influence of free trade with England, the manufacture of cotton has declined in India, China, Turkey and South America, as above stated, and their markets filled with British goods, and many of the manufacturers ruined.

The quantity of cotton spun in the United Kingdom in 1838, as stated in Brande's Encyclopædia, was as follows.

In Great Britain,	426,090,116 lbs.
and in Ireland only	4,412,860 "
Total,	430,502,976

These tables show the wonderfully great and rapid increase in the manufacture of cotton during the present century, in a few countries only, and particularly in Great Britain, while the manufacture in India, China, Turkey, South America, and Africa has declined. Though there has been very little increase in the cultivation of cotton in any country except the United States, the increase here has been so immensely great, as to exceed the demand, and leave large stocks on hand at the close of almost every year.

They also show that the price of cotton is governed entirely by the relative proportion between the supply and demand in the market, and that there is no truth in the assumption of some of the free trade politicians, that our tariff of duties on foreign goods, and particularly on fabrics of cotton, tends to depress the price of cotton. We had a tariff passed in 1824, which took effect in 1825; another passed in 1828; and it is just as reasonable to assume that the tariff act of 1824 raised the price of cotton in 1825, from fifteen to twenty-one cents per pound, as shown in Table No. 1, as it is to argue that the tariff of 1842 depressed the price in 1843 and 1845. What depressed the price in 1848—and again in 1849?

We see that the tariff of 1828 produced no sensible effect on its price, for it remained about the same after as before the tariff, being about ten cents per pound in each of the years 1827, 1828, 1829 and 1830. What but the excessively great crop of 1839, depressed the price in 1840, from nearly fifteen to eight and a half cents per pound? What but the smaller crop of 1840 again raised the price in 1841 to ten and a fifth cents per pound? What but the medium crops of 1841, and 1843, kept the average price at over eight cents, while the excessively great crops of 1842, and 1844, depressed the price to about six cents per pound? It is easy to see that the high prices of 1834, 1835, and 1836, were caused by our bloated paper currency, and speculating mania; and that the high prices in 1837, 1838, and 1839, were caused by the operations of Mr. Biddle and other bankers, speculating in cotton, and making heavy loans to cotton speculators.

The extraordinary fact is shown, that the middling crops raised in 1838, 1840, and 1841, of from 1,360,000 to 1,684,000 bales, were worth nearly as much in the market, as the heavy crops raised in 1839, 1842, and 1844, of from 2,177,835 to 2,394,503 bales; and the amounts produced by the crops raised from 1842 to 1850 prove conclusively, that a crop of two million bales is worth more in the market than one of two and a half million bales.

These tables show the causes which govern prices, in the clearest and most conclusive manner, and prove that the prices of commodities are not directly affected by their utility, nor by the amount of labor required to produce them, but solely by the demand compared with the supply; their utility, and cost of production, having only an indirect effect, by increasing or diminishing either the supply or the demand. The tariff acts of the United States, by increasing the manufacture and the demand for raw cotton, and the supply of cotton goods, have a strong tendency to raise the price of cotton, and lower the price of cotton goods; because they increase the demand for the former, and the supply of the latter.

Cotton will grow on almost any land adapted to Indian corn, or any other grain, from the equator to about the thirty-eighth degree of latitude, though it flourishes most, and is mostly confined in the United States to those states lying below the thirty-fifth degree of latitude. As it will grow in about half of North America, two-thirds of South America, the whole of the arable part of Africa, in Spain, Portugal, Greece, Turkey, all southern Asia, New Holland, and all the islands in the torrid zone, and is so valuable in proportion to its weight, that it will bear transportation thousands of miles, the production can be increased to any amount, which the wants of the commercial world require; it is impossible to monopolize it.

The cotton crop of the United States in 1839, according to the returns with the census of 1840, amounted to 790,479,275 pounds, only about 84,000,000 pounds of which were raised in the States north of the thirty-fifth degree of latitude, including North Carolina, Tennessee, and all the states north of them.

Power Looms.—The power loom was invented in 1787; but it was at first so imperfect, that it was not applied to any practical use until 1801; and so great was the prejudice of hand-loom weavers against it, that it was introduced very slowly. The estimated number of power looms in use in Great Britain in 1813, was but 2400, and in 1820 only 14,150. In 1834 the number in the United Kingdom had increased to 116,891.

III. Statement of the number of Power Looms in use in Great Britain and Ireland in 1834, according to the Report of the Factory Inspectors, employed in Weaving:

In	Cotton.	Wool.	Worsted.	Silk.	Linen.	Total.
England and Wales,	90,525	2,136	3,123	1,714	41	97,539
Scotland,	17,531	22	——	——	168	17,721
Ireland,	1,416	——	——	——	190	1,606
	109,472	2,158	3,123	1,714	399	116,866
For mixed materials in England, -	-	-	-	-	-	25
		Total in the United Kingdom,				116,891

Notwithstanding this great increase in the number of power looms, and the fact that the same number of persons can weave about eight times as much per week with power looms, as they can with hand-looms, yet the number of hand-loom weavers in Great Britain in 1833, was estimated at from 200,000 to 250,000.

IV. Statement of the number of Cotton, Woollen, Linen and Silk Factories at work, the number not in use, and the number of adults and children employed in them respectively, in England, Wales, Scotland, and Ireland, in 1834, according to the official returns. See McCulloch's Statistics, title Cotton.

1834. *Cotton.*	Factories. at work.	Empty.	No. of Persons employed in them Under 18.	Over 18 years old. Males.	Females.	Total Persons.
England,	1,070	42	78,007	50,675	53,410	182,092
Wales,	5	—	443	250	458	1,151
Scotland,	159	—	14,424	6,168	12,403	32,995
Ireland,	28	—	1,283	960	1,553	3,796
Total,	1,262	42	94,157	58,053	67,824	230,034
Woollen.						
England,	1,102	9	31,807	18,613	15,041	65,461
Wales,	85	—	521	190	66	777
Scotland,	90	—	1,736	1,083	686	3,505
Ireland,	36	—	508	674	341	1,523
Total,	1,313	9	34,572	20,560	16,134	71,266

1834. *Silk in*	Factories. at work.	Empty.	No. of Persons employed in them Under 18.	Over 18 years old. Males.	Females.	Total Persons.
England,	231	25	18,083	4,009	7,855	29,947
Wales,	—	—	—	—	—	—
Scotland,	6	—	415	103	168	686
Ireland,	1		27	2	20	49
Total,	238	25	18,525	4,114	8,043	30,682
Flax.						
England,	152	—	9,263	2,551	4,379	16,193
Wales,	—	—	—	—	—	—
Scotland,	170	—	5,999	1,550	5,860	13,409
Ireland,	25	—	2,047	463	1,171	3,681
Total,	347	—	17,309	4,564	11,410	33,283
Grand Total,	3,160	76	164,563	87,291	103,411	355,265

V. The number of spindles in use in cotton factories at different periods, is estimated in McCulloch's Statistics as follows:

In 1819 in Great Britain,			7,000,000
1832 do. do.			9,000,000
1845	*Mule Spindles.*	*Throstle Spindles.*	
In England & Wales,	11,364,584	4,190,035	15,554,619
Scotland,	1,476,083	253,795	1,729,878
Ireland,	159,333	56,170	215,503
	13,000,000	4,500,000	17,500,000

In the German Customs Union,	815,000
Austria and Italy,	1,500,000
France,	3,500,000
Belgium,	420,000
Other countries of Europe,	1,350,000
Total on the Continent of Europe,	7,585,000

Statement of the number of cotton and woollen factories in the United States, the spindles in use, persons employed, and capital invested in 1840, according to the census of that year.

	Cotton.	*Woollen.*
Number of factories,	1,240	1,420
" spindles,	2,284,631	—
" persons employed,	72,119	21,342
Capital invested,	$51,102,359	$15,765,124

The number of spindles in use in cotton factories in the United States in 1845, was over three millions, or about the same as in France.

Table IV. shows that in 1834, there was a large number of cotton factories in Great Britain not in use; and the fact is, that factories and machinery for manufacturing cotton might be multiplied still more rapidly in that country than they have been, if they could command the markets of the world, and the demand for their products were unlimited. Nothing but a limited market for their products, checks their increase. The supply is now greater than the demand three quarters of the time; and the manufacturers by arrangements among themselves, in order to prevent an excessive glut of the markets, and to keep up prices, stop some of their factories, and work short time in others, whenever the markets are over-stocked, prices low and dull. At the end of May 1847, there were in Lancashire (England) 12,107 factory hands out of employment, and 6,628 working short time; and such is often the case. Great Britain has the capacity to increase her manufactures of cotton and iron, to such an extent, as to supply all the nations of the earth; and if she could command their markets by means of unlimited Free Trade, the manufactures of every other country would wither, and gradually sink into insignificance, like those of Ireland. Look at Tables III. IV. and V.; contemplate the relative condition and manufacturing industry of Great Britain and Ireland, and the effect on the latter of free trade with the former, and you have a sample of what would be the depressing and blighting effects on almost every country of Europe and America. This subject is farther illustrated by the following tables in relation to the trade in the manufactures of cotton.

VI. Statement of the value of manufactures of cotton of all kinds, including twist and yarn, exported from Great Britain at different periods.

Years.	*Official value.*	*Declared, or real value.*
1697	£5,915	
1720	16,200	
1751	45,986	
1764	200,354	
1780	355,060	
1790	1,662,369	
1800	5,854,057	
1810	18,951,994	
1815	22,289,645	£20,620,956
1830	41,050,969	19,428,664

Years.	*Official value.*	*Declared, or real value.*
1840	73,152,251	24,668,618
1844	91,039,574	25,805,348
1849	*	26,890,794

In addition to the above exports,. Great Britain exported annually a large quantity of cotton goods to Ireland. The quantity of cotton cloth and calico exported to Ireland in 1835 amounted to 14,170,000 yards.

VII. Statement in millions, of the quantity and declared value of the cotton goods and yarn—and also the value of the hosiery, lace, and small wares, exported, and the estimated value of the manufactures of cotton retained for home consumption in Great Britain and Ireland, during the undermentioned years.

Years.	Cotton Cloth. Yards.	Manufactures. Value. £.	Cotton-yarn, and Twist, lbs.	Value. £.
1830	444,5	14,1	64,6	4,1
1835	557,5	15,1	83,2	5,7
1840	790,6	16,3	118,4	7,1
1842	734,0	12,8	137,4	7,7
1844	1,046,6	17,6	138,5	6,9

Years.	Hosiery, Lace, &c. Value exported.	Total value exported.	Value retained for home consumption	Total value produced.
1830	£1,2	£19,4	£11,6	£31,0
1835	1,2	22,1	13,9	36,0
1840	1,2	24,6	13,1	37,9
1842	1,0	21,6	11,9	33,5
1844	1,2	25,8	12,7	38,5

By comparing tables I. and VII., the reader can see how the proceeds of the manufacture of cotton are divided between the planter and the British manufacturer. Take for example the years 1840 and 1845. In 1840 there was manufactured in Great Britain about 500,000,000 lbs. of cotton, for which the manufacturer paid 5½d sterling per pound, or £10,500,000—8½ cents, or 4¼d of which went to the planter, and 2½cts or 1¼d to pay for transportation, commissions, insurance and mercantile profits. The whole proceeds amounted to nearly £38,000,000, about £8,000,000 of which went to the planter, about £5,000,000 to the commercial classes, including commissions on sales of the goods in Great Britain, and £25,000,000 for the cost and profits of manufacturing the cotton. In 1845 the planter received still less for his crop, not realizing much over five cents per pound for

* See on this subject, Section 29 of Chapter XII.

his cotton, while the profits to the British manufacturer were as great as they were in 1840.

The value of cotton goods of American manufacture exported annually from the United States from 1847 to 1850, was less than five millions of dollars. On the contrary, the manufactures of cotton imported into the United States in 1836

were valued at - - -	$17,876,087
in 1845, at - - -	13,863,282
and in 1850 they were valued at - -	*19,685,936

Account of the cotton manufacture in the United States, during the years ending May 31st, 1840, and 1850.

	1840	1850
Capital invested,	$51,102,000	$74,500,000
Value of Manufactures,	46,350,000	61,869,000
Value of raw materials used,	not stated,	34,835,000
Males employed,	72,119	33,150
Females employed,		59,136

The increase of the cotton manufacture has been checked, and during the last two years (1850 and 1851) it has declined, under the tariff of 1846. The effects of that tariff on manufactures of cotton, wool, and iron, have been very nearly the same.†

Sec. 14. *Leather, and manufactures of Leather.*

The art of curing the skins of animals to fit them for clothing, was one of the first learned and practised by man. Skins cured with the fur or hair on them, constituted the entire clothing of savages, and nearly the whole of that of the pastoral nations of antiquity. The art of tanning hides and converting them into leather was learned at a later date, and has been much improved even during the present century.

The leather manufacture of almost every civilized country is of very great importance; that of the United States and France, being inferior in value and importance, only to that of cotton; and that of Great Britain being inferior in value only to cotton, wool and iron. If we examine the instruments of husbandry, the harness on our horses, the implements used in most of the mechanic arts, and in the structure of a great number of engines and machines; or if we contemplate the necessary parts of our clothing, shoes, boots, slippers and gloves, and also our trunks, valises, books, carriages and many other things, we shall at once realize the great importance of leather—and its adaptation, in a great

* The imports under the tariff of 1846, have been undervalued at least 20 per cent., and amounted in 1850 to about $23,500,000.

† See on this subject, ante pages 158 and 201; also Hunt's Magazine for October, 1851, pages 461 and 484; do. for November, 1851, pages 576 to 581.

variety of circumstances, to aid the industry, and supply the wants of man, in every state and condition of life. Without it, or even without it in great quantities, to what difficulties should we be exposed?

Prior to 1812, the excise duty on leather tanned in Great Britain was 1½d sterling per lb., when it was raised to 3d per lb.; no duties have been levied since 1832. The average quantity of leather made in England and Wales annually from 1824 to 1830 was about 50,000,000 lbs., and in Scotland about 6,000,000.

The value of the leather made annually about the year 1830 was estimated by McCulloch at £4,000,000, and the entire annual value of the manufactures of leather at £12,500,000. The quantity of leather made annually in Great Britain about the year 1840 has been estimated at 65,000,000 lbs.—and the entire value of the manufactures of leather at £13,500,000 sterling.

The value of the leather wrought and unwrought, saddlery and harness exported from Great Britain amounted in 1830 to £335,451, in 1840 to 417,074, and in 1844 to £465,042.

The value of the manufactures of leather in the United States in 1840, according to the census, amounted to $33,134,403. The value of the hides, of leather and manufacturers of leather imported into the United States have been as follows in

	1840.	1848.
Raw Hides, . . .	$2,756,214	$4,262,069
Leather and manufactures of leather,	542,498	1,346,492
Exports of do do	233,917	330,000

The value of the manufactures of leather in France in 1839 was estimated by Berghaus at 163,000,000 francs, or about $30,644,000. This was less than that of the United States. The value of the manufactures of leather exported from France, and the value of raw hides imported into that country stated in millions of francs have been as follows:—

	1836.	1836 to 1840.	1841.
Exports of manufactures of leather,	28	25,6	29,5
Imports of hides,	19,6	18,9	27,1

Prior to the sixteenth century, a very large proportion of the clothing (including breeches, frocks, gowns or loose coats) of the common classes of people of central and northern Europe, were made of leather. Leather, in those days, had a much greater relative importance than it has at present. This change has been effected by the improvements made in the art of spinning, weaving, coloring and dressing cloths; and by the introduction of machinery and the cotton manufacture, during the last hundred years.

CHAPTER IX.

ON THE PRINCIPAL PRODUCTS OF AGRICULTURE.

SEC. 1. *On the Cereal Grains, or Bread Corns.*

THE seeds of certain plants have been used by man from time immemorial for making bread. The principal bread corns are wheat, rye, oats, barley, buckwheat, maize or Indian corn, rice and millet. These grains grow spontaneously in some climates and countries, and the most of them are native plants of many countries; but all the grains, vegetables, plants, fruits, grasses, which man has cultivated with labor and attention for ages, and transferred from one climate and country to another, have gradually improved in quality, and become more productive.

Wheat, barley, and rye, have been cultivated in Egypt from time immemorial, and constituted the principal bread corn of that country, as appears from the Scriptures. See Exodus, ix. 31. Wheat and barley appear to have been the principal bread stuffs of the Israelites. See Genesis, xxx. 14. Deut. viii. 8.

SEC. 2. *The production and consumption of Wheat.*

Wheat is the most valuable to man of any species of grain; but unfortunately it is the most tender, and easily affected by the weather, wind, soil, climate, heat, dampness, insects of various kinds, and frosts, of any of the grains; and requires greater care and attention in preparing and cleaning the ground, securing it against water, and getting good seed, free from foul stuff, than any other crop which the farmer cultivates. Though it grows over a large part of the globe from the 30th to above the 60th degree of latitude; from Italy and the shores of the Mediterranean Sea, to, and including the southern parts of Sweden and Norway, yet it requires a fine, rich, loamy limestone, or gravel and clay soil; neither very wet nor very dry, and a favorable season to bring forward as well as to ripen and harvest the crop. When sown on very rich interval or bottom lands, the straw often grows so rank and large that it is tender, falls down, and the wheat blasts; when sown on light and poor sandy soils, it will often scarcely produce as much as the seed; when sown on wet ground, and the water stands on it during the winter, it seems to turn to chess or cheat; when sown on stiff clay soil, and the early part of the spring is unfavorable, and the top of the ground thaws during the day, and freezes at night for many days in succession, the ground often heaves, breaks the roots, and kills the wheat; and when the wheat gets large in the fall, it is sometimes smothered and killed by deep snows. When the soil, climate, season, aud mode of cultivation are all favorable, it yields an abundant and rich harvest, and is in some countries, the most profitable crop a farmer can raise, but in most soils, it is the most unproductive and hazardous.

Mr. Hallam makes the following remarks, in the ninth chapter of his Middle Ages. "The culture of arable land was very imperfect. Fleta remarks, in the reign of Edward I. or II. that unless an acre of land produced more than six bushels of corn, the farmer would be a loser, and the land yield no rent. And Sir John Collum, from very minute accounts, has calculated that nine or ten bushels were a full average crop, on an acre of wheat. An amazing excess of tillage accompanied, and partly, I suppose, *produced this imperfect cultivation.*" These remarks refer to England, but would apply to the United States at the present time; the crops of wheat per acre, even in wheat-growing districts, do not average over twelve or fifteen bushels;* and taking the whole United States, will not average over ten or eleven bushels per acre; while the average crop for the whole of England was estimated by McCulloch some years since, at twenty-six bushels per acre, and it has been estimated by some authors as high as twenty-eight to thirty bushels per acre. The annual crop of wheat in England and Wales is over 100,000,000 of bushels: it is estimated in Brande's Encyclopædia of Science and Art, at 120,000,000 bushels. The wheat crop of the United States, in 1839, amounted to but 84,823,272 bushels; and the great crop of 1845, did not exceed 110,000,000 bushels.

As wheat is much superior for bread to any other grain, and the quantity which can be raised more limited than that of the coarser grains, the surplus wheat beyond the wants of the country, is never very great in the United States. There is scarcely any wheat cultivated in the States of Massachusetts, Rhode Island, Connecticut, Louisiana, Mississippi, Arkansas, and Florida, and in many large districts of country in most of the other States; and the supply for the whole population of the Union, is less in

* The wheat crop of New York of 1844 averaged only about 13 bushels per acre, as appears by the census of 1845.

proportion to the inhabitants than the quantity raised in Great Britain is for the inhabitants of that island.

During the reign of Henry VIII., England produced very little wheat;* the wealthy only lived on wheat bread; the mass of the people lived on rye, barley and oats; and at the revolution of 1688, the annual wheat crop of England and Wales was estimated at but 1,750,000 quarters, or fourteen million bushels, over and above the seeds; or about one-sixth part as much as it was in 1840.

Even as late as the year 1765, the annual wheat crop was estimated at less than thirty-five million bushels. Up to the year 1828, the production of wheat in Great Britain increased faster than the population, and was greater then, in proportion, to the population, than it was one, two, three, or even five centuries since.

Mr. Jacob says, "In ancient times in England, wheat could not be considered as the chief food of the inhabitants; very little of it was used by the agricultural population, which then composed nine-tenths of the inhabitants; and among the people in the towns, it was by no means the universal, or principal food. Rye and barley were the chief articles of consumption."

The inhabitants of Great Britain, as a whole, eat more wheat annually, in proportion to their numbers, than the people of the United States; and whatever want and suffering there may be in Great Britain among the poor, is owing entirely to an unequal and unjust distribution of the products of labor, and not to any general want, nor to any deficiency in the aggregate amount of the comforts of life.

Sec. 3. *Production and use of Rye.*

Rye grows and flourishes in all countries and climates, and on all soils where wheat will grow; but being coarser, and less palatable for bread, it is much less esteemed, though it contains very nearly the same amount of nourishment. It has been cultivated from time immemorial, and is supposed to be a native of the Island of Crete. The berry is much less plump than wheat, and on that account wheat, on first rate soils, and good seasons, will produce the greatest number of bushels; but it is very little affected with the many casualties, which often occur to ruin wheat; and will grow and fill well, on any soil and any land, rich or poor, high or low, wet or dry, which is fit for either wheat, barley, oats, corn, or most other grain. It is one of the least hazardous crops which can be cultivated, and together with Indian corn, is the principal grain used for bread, by nearly half of the agricultural population of the United States of America. The quantity of rye raised in the United States in 1839, was

* See the Com. Dict. title bread.

18,645,567 bushels. Mr. Ellsworth, in his report as Commissioner of the Patent Office, estimated the crop of 1842 at 22,762,952 bushels, and that of 1844 at 26,450,000 bushels. Much of it has been heretofore distilled into whiskey. It constitutes the principal bread corn of Germany and Russia. The cultivation of rye in the United States may be increased to almost any extent which the market may demand.

Sec. 4. *Production and use of Oats.*

Oats grow in any climate and country where wheat and rye do. They were cultivated by the ancient Romans, and are now extensively used for bread in Ireland, the highlands of Scotland, and some in England, and various countries on the continent. The quantity raised in the United States in 1839, was 123,071,341 bushels. They are almost all used for horsefeed, and none, or scarcely any is made into bread. They make bread greatly inferior to that of either rye, or Indian corn, and are not esteemed of very great value in the United States, as their place can be supplied by other grains, which are more nutritious. We have reason to believe, that they were much used among the Romans, as frequent mention is made of them in the works of Roman authors. They are much more easily cultivated than wheat, in a low state of agriculture.

Sec. 5. *Production and use of Barley.*

Barley has been cultivated about the shores of the Mediterranean Sea, from time immemorial; its native country is unknown, some ascribing it to Tartary, others to Siberia, and a few to Scotland; and like many other plants and grains, it is most likely that it is a native of many countries. It grows and flourishes in the same climates as wheat, rye, and oats, including all temperate and cold climates and countries. In Spain and Sicily, it is said to produce two crops a year. It was extensively cultivated in Palestine, and used for bread, as appears by the scriptures of the Old and New Testament. It is used for bread at this day in many countries of Europe, and some in Great Britain; though its principal use in Great Britain, and its only use in the United States, is to malt, and make into beer.

*Statement in millions of bushels of the quantity of malt consumed in the United Kingdom.**

	England and Wales.	Scotland.	Ireland.
In 1801,	18 millions,	6 millions,	1 million,
1821,	26 "	1.3 "	2 "
1831,	33 "	4.1 "	2.1 "
1841,	31 "	4. "	1.1 "

The average consumption to each individual in England and Wales during the present century, has been about two bushels. A century since, it was over four bushels to each person.

The quantity of barley cultivated in the United States is small, and considering the use to which it is applied, it is fortunate for the country that it is so; and the quantity, according to Mr. Ellsworth's estimates, is declining. It amounted in 1839, to 4,161,504, and in 1844, to but 3,627,000 bushels; more than half of the whole is raised in the single State of New York, where the temperance reformation has taken deep root, which has occasioned a decline in its cultivation.

SEC. 6. *Production and use of Buckwheat and Millet.*

Buckwheat is supposed to be a native plant of Asia, and to have been introduced into Europe but a few centuries since. It has been cultivated in Great Britain since the latter part of the sixteenth century, though not to any great extent. It is considerably used for bread in the United States, France, and some other countries of Europe, but is not much used in Great Britain. The quantity raised in the United States in 1839, was 7,291,743 bushels; in 1842, it was estimated at 9,483,400, and in 1844, at 9,071,000 bushels.

Millet is a coarse grain, used mostly for poultry, but little cultivated, and of but little value comparatively to the human family.

SEC. 7. *Production and use of Rice.*

Rice has been cultivated from time immemorial, and furnished much of the bread stuff of the inhabitants of India, and of the greater part of southern Asia, and the neighboring islands. It requires wet, flat and marshy lands, and does the best on lands covered with water a part of the year, by the overflow of rivers, marshes or artificial irrigation. It grows only in hot and warm climates, and requires such peculiarities as to soil and irrigation, that its culture can never be very extensive; and in the United States, it is mostly confined to the states of North and South Carolina, Georgia, and Louisiana. The total amount cultivated in

* Five bushels of barley will make about six bushels of malt.

the United States in 1839, was only 80,841,422 pounds, equal to nearly 1,350,000 bushels of wheat for food. The quantity raised in 1842, was estimated by Mr. Ellsworth, at 94,007,000 pounds; and in 1844, at 111,759,000 pounds. As the quantity of land adapted to it, and on which it can be cultivated advantageously, is quite limited, the increased demand keeps pace with the supply, and keeps it up to a fair price; and it is almost the only article cultivated in warm climates, by the labor of African slaves, which has not fallen rapidly in price, during the last half century.

SEC. 8. *Production and use of Maize, or Indian Corn.*

The discovery of America led to the introduction to the civilized world, of the knowledge, use and cultivation of maize, or Indian corn, and potatoes, which are native plants of the western continent, and have done more to benefit mankind, than all its mines of gold and silver. Indian corn is a native plant of a warm climate, but by planting it farther north, and replanting the seed thus grown from year to year, the climate has had an effect to lessen the blade and stalk, as well as the ear and kernel, and so far changed its character, as to adapt it to the climate; so that corn which has been planted in Canada for a series of years, being small, grows quick and generally ripens as far north as the 46th or 47th degree of latitude. It grows, and can be cultivated to advantage from the equator to about the 46th degree of latitude, though wheat, rye, barley, oats, and buckwheat cannot be cultivated much below the 30th degree, except on lands several thousand feet above the ocean. McCulloch remarks that, "It was introduced into the Continent of Europe, about the beginning, and into England a little while after the middle of the sixteenth century. Its culture has spread with astonishing rapidity; being now extensively grown in most Asiatic countries, and in all the southern parts of Europe. It has the widest geographical range of all the cerealia, growing luxuriantly at the equator, and as far as the 50th degree of north, and the 40th of south latitude. It has been raised in England in nursery gardens near the metropolis, for more than a century."

It will also grow on any soil, rich or poor, high or low, wet or dry, clay, loam, sand, gravel, or any mixture of them, on which any grain whatever will grow; except that it will not grow like rice, on lands covered with water a great portion of the time. It may be cultivated to advantage on the arable lands, of more than three quarters, if not seven eighths of the whole inhabited part of the globe, though it grows the most luxuriantly, and yields the most, in a warm climate, and rich loamy or alluvial soil, neither very wet nor very dry, and in a country where showers are frequent during the summer. Below the 40th degree of latitude, it yields from two to three times as much as wheat, rye or barley, on the same land; and from the 40th to the 44th degree of latitude, it generally yields much more, and often twice as much as either of those grains, and frequently yields abundantly even above the 44th parallel of latitude. It is about as nutritious as rye or barley, nearly as much so as wheat, and about twice as much so as oats. It now constitutes the principal part of the bread corn of a large proportion of the human family; and wherever it has been introduced and long cultivated, it has entirely superseded the use of barley and oats as bread corn, and rendered them useless to man; except that the latter is useful as food for animals, and the former is distilled and used as a powerful agent to intoxicate and brutalize mankind.

As Indian corn flourishes in warm climates, on high and dry land, where rice will not grow, it will enable Hindostan, and all the countries of southern Asia, including Turkey, and the isles of the ocean, to maintain at some future period a population twice as numerous as they could without it; and as it is a very certain and safe crop, it will relieve those countries from the severe famines with which they have often been afflicted, and thus contribute immensely to the comforts, and welfare of the human family. The quantity cultivated in the United States is immensely great, more than all other grains added together. Nearly every region of the United States can, and almost every county not containing a city actually does, raise sufficient for the wants of the people. The western and south-western states produce so large a surplus of corn annually, beyond the wants of the country, that in all the interior districts of those states, remote from large towns and navigable waters, it is a drug in the market, will often scarcely sell for money at any price, and much of it is destroyed by wild animals, and otherwise wasted. It formerly sold in remote districts, where the quantity raised is great and the population sparse, at from ten to twelve cents per bushel, and frequently would not sell in any considerable quantities, at even eight cents in money.

SEC. 9. *Production and use of Potatoes.*

The potatoe, next to Indian corn, is the most important plant for food, which is a native of the Western Continent. It was introduced into western Europe during the 16th century, and into Ireland in 1610; but was cultivated in England in gardens only, and in small quantities, as a great luxury, until the year 1684, when it was raised for the first time, in the open fields of the county of Lancashire. In Scotland, potatoes were raised in gardens only, until the year 1728.

It was estimated by McCulloch, some years since, that about 5,000,000 of the population of Ireland, subsisted mostly on potatoes; that 1,200,000 acres of land in England and Wales, were annually appropriated to the cultivation of potatoes and turnips, and 130,000 acres in Scotland to potatoes only. The crop of potatoes in France, in 1818 was 29,231,807 hectolitres, about 82,500,000 bushels, and it amounted in 1835 to about 204,000,000 bushels. If we suppose 500,000 acres of land in England and Wales, and the 130,000 in Scotland, to be appropriated to potatoes, and to produce on an average two hundred bushels per acre, the whole potatoe crop of Great Britain would amount to no less than 126,000,000 bushels annually. The potatoe crop of the United States in 1839 amounted to 108,298,000 bushels. Some authors estimate that one bushel of wheat contains as much nourishment for man as four bushels of potatoes, others estimate three bushels of potatoes as equal to one of wheat. Perhaps it would be safe to say, that four bushels of potatoes are equal to one of wheat, and that three and a half are equal to one of rye or Indian corn. In the greater part of the free states, from eight to ten times as many bushels of potatoes as wheat can be raised on the same ground, as potatoes usually yield from 100 to 150 bushels per acre, and sometimes more. They will yield four or five times as much as corn. These facts show the great importance of the potatoe to the human family. The principal drawback to the utility and value of potatoes, and in fact to all vegetables, is their perishable nature, and their being so bulky and heavy in proportion to their value, that they will not bear transportation to any great distance. In the neighborhood of a commercial or manufacturing city, which furnishes a market for large quantities, an acre of good land planted to potatoes, will yield two or three times as much value as the same land sown to wheat; but like all other vegetables, coarse grains, poultry, &c., they will bear transportation by land but few miles.

The disease of the potatoe, that causes it to rot, commenced in 1846, and has greatly lessened the value of it; but the probability is, that that scourge will not be permanent.

Sec. 10. *Production of grain in the United States, Great Britain, Ireland and France.*

Summary statement in millions of bushels of the products of the undermentioned crops in the United States in 1839 according to the census—in Great Britain annually from 1835 to 1840, according to the estimates of McCulloch,—and in Ireland in 1847, according to the British Almanac for 1849.

	Free States.	Slave States.	Great Britain.	Ireland
Wheat,	54¾	30.	104	23⅓
Rye,	14¼	4⅓ }	36½	11
Barley,	4	⅙ }		
Indian Corn and Millet,	125	252		
Buckwheat,	7	⅓		
Oats,	80	43	150	92.
Pease and beans,			6	
Other small grain,				2
Total grain,	285	330	296	130
Potatoes & turn'ps,	93	20	336	234

Summary statement in millions of hectolitres of the quantity of GRAIN RAISED IN FRANCE ANNUALLY, ON AN AVERAGE, FROM 1801 TO 1812, both inclusive, according to the statement of Chaptal; also the QUANTITIES IN 1818, 1835, and 1841, ACCORDING TO OFFICIAL RETURNS OR ESTIMATES. A hectolitre contains about 2.84 Winchester bushels:

	Aver. ann'lly. 1801 to 1812.	1818.	1835.	1841.
Wheat,	51,5	52,6	71,6	69,5
Rye,	30,2	24,7	32,9	27,8
Maize,	6,3	6,1	6,9	7,6
Barley,	12,5	13,1	18	16,6
Buckwheat,	8,4	3,3	5	8,4
Oats,	32	29,7	49,4	48,8
Mixed and other grain,	12	13,6	19,6	11,9
	153	143,5	204	190,6
Equal in bush. to	434,5	407,5	579,8	542,2
Potatoes, bush.	56,2	83,0	204,4	222,7

The 204,165,194 hectolitres of grain raised in France in 1835 were equal to about 580,000,000 bushels; of which it was estimated that 107,277,801 hectolitres were consumed by man; 42,185,005 by horses, cattle, &c.; 29,734,371 required for seed, and 2,833,575 distilled and brewed; leaving a surplus of 24,053,205 not needed for use, a part of which was exported. The population of France was 33,540,000, the quantity consumed by man was about nine bushels for each person; and by animals, for horse feed, and to fatten hogs, cattle, &c. for food, was equal to about three and a half bushels for each person, beside potatoes and other vegetables.

These and other well established facts show, that the United States produce less wheat in proportion to their population, than either Great Britain or France. The quantity of agricultural products of France, and particularly of wheat and rye, have been increasing with greater rapidity than the population, since the peace of 1815, and the attention of the people has been directed to mining and manufacturing industry, and to public improvements.

SEC. 11. *Production of grain in Russia, the empire of Austria, Spain, and other countries of Europe.*

Account from the official returns or estimates of the produce of grain in Russia in Europe, exclusive of Poland and Finland, during the undermentioned years.*

	Autumn sown Wheat & Rye, Chetwerts.	Spring sown Barley, Oats, &c Chetwerts	Total in millions of Chetwerts,	Total in bushels.
1835,	92½ mill's.	121½ mill's	214 mill's,	1,198 mill's
1836,	101½ ”	136½ ”	238 ”	1,336 ”
1837,	73 ”	123 ”	196 ”	1,098 ”
1839,	52 ”	83 ”	135 ”	750 ”
1840	54½ ”	128½ ”	183 ”	1,025 ”
Av. an'ly,	75 ”	118 ”	193 ”	1,081 ”

Average annual production of grain in the Austrian Empire, including Hungary, Lombardy and Venice, from 1835 to 1838.†

Wheat, in English imperial bushels,		49,830,000
Maize and Rye,	"	166,840,000
Barley,	"	69,696,000
Oats,	"	132,446,000
Total,	"	418,812,000

The population was then about thirty-five millions—and the production of grain equal to about twelve bushels to each person, and yet there was a surplus to export.

* See McGregor's Com. Statistics vol. ii. p. 736.

† This is taken from a table made by McGregor from facts and official returns and estimates collected by him.—See McGregor's Com. Stat. I. p. 10 and 14.

Quantity of grain produced in Spain in 1803, according to the official returns, as stated by McGregor.*

Wheat,	46,915,000 bushels
Barley,	22,883,000 "
Rye,	15,471,000 "
Oats, Maize, Rice, &c.,	9,946,000 "
Total,	95,215,000 "

This was less than ten bushels to each person, the population being then about ten millions.

According to the statistics of Von Malchus, published in Prussia in 1826, the average annual production of grain of all kinds at that time in the undermentioned countries, was as follows, stated in English bushels;

	Bushels.	Bushels to each person.
Sweden and Norway,	34 millions.	about 10
Prussia,	230 "	" 16 or 17
Russia,	875 "	" 22
Austrian Empire,	580 "	" 17
Holland and Belgium,	78 "	" 12
Italian States,	184 "	" 11
Spain,	108 "	" 10
Portugal,	34 "	" 10

The most of these are derived from official estimates, and may be regarded as approximations to accuracy.

Sec. 12. *Trade in grain and flour, at different periods.*

There was comparatively little international commerce in grain and flour, previous to the beginning of the 18th century. The excess of exports of flour and wheat from England, over the imports in four years, from 1697 to 1700 inclusive, was only 69,433 quarters, or 555,464 bushels. A small quantity of wheat and flour was exported from Great Britain during the first half, and central part of the 18th century, and until the year 1767, when her imports first exceeded her exports. The excess of exports over imports, from 1700 to 1725, amounted to 3,057,515 imperial quarters, or 24,460,120 bushels in 25 years; from 1755 to 1765 both inclusive, the excess of exports over imports was 19,570,824 bushels in the 11 years; from 1766 to 1780, the excess of imports over exports was equal to 6,773,264 bushels in the 15 years; from 1781 to 1800, it was equal to 5,512,487 quarters, or 44,099,896 bushels.

The excess of wheat and wheat flour imported into Great Britain over and above the exports, from 1801 to 1820 both inclusive, was 11,962,296 quarters—equal to 4,784,912 bushels

* See McGregor's Statistics, ii. p. 1013.

annually ; and from 1821 to 1840, the excess of imports amounted to 24,256,897 quarts—equal to 9,707,758 bushels annually, during the twenty years. A very large proportion of these imports were from Ireland, as will be seen by the following table.

I. Average quantities of all sorts of grain, and the average quantities of wheat, rye, barley, oats, peas and beans respectively, annually imported into Great Britain from each country during twenty-five years, from 1801 to 1825 inclusive, stated in Winchester quarters, of eight bushels each :

From	Wheat Qrs.	Rye Qrs.	Barley Qrs.	Oats. Qrs.	Peas and Beans. Qrs	All grains Qrs.
Ireland,........................	187,438	253	33,331	639,857	4,922	865,968
Russia, ...	53,377	9,968	7,112	46,652	785	117,902
Sweden and Norway,..........	9,576	960	987	2,446	428	14,397
Denmark, ...	16,324	1,123	18,808	30,672	823	67,847
Prussia,........................	157,359	5,689	18,718	39,209	7,609	228,584
Germany, ...	58,103	5,189	24,839	75,828	7,144	171,103
Holland and Belgium,..........	56,817	1,690	9,500	84,269	5,802	158,078
France and South of Europe, ...	24,649	293	1,097	1,953	9,124	37,932
United States, ...	74,024	2,341	31	3	201	*80,712
British Am. Col., ...	24,863	——	51	1	697	25,627
Other Foreign Nations, ...	4,836	1,438	2,194	1,703	151	10,363
Total,..................	667,366	28,944	116,668	922,608	37,686	1,778,518

II. Quantities of wheat and flour, given in quarters of wheat, imported into Great Britain from each country except Ireland† in the years 1847, 1848 and 1849—and the average quantity annually imported, during a period of 22 years, ending with 1849.

	1847. Quarters.	1848. Quarters.	1849. Quarters.	Average of 22 years. Quarters.
Russia, .	850,587	523,138	599,556	209,237
Sweden and Norway, .	8,647	5,346	6,494	2,566
Denmark, . .	73,568	191,787	243,213	91,797
Prussia, . .	492,928	528,156	618,690	435,791
Germany, . .	154,839	532,591	498,984	232,034
Holland, . .	11,800	163,978	308,482	88,704
Belgium, . .	27,469	178,398	366 099	
France, . .	179,259	320,010	742,023	124,102
Spain, . .	24,700	917	498	29,408
Italy, . .	64,850	83 170	281,530	108,137
Malta, . .	46,251	8,576	9,049	12,219
Greece, . .		4,129	61,136	3,733
Turkey, Syria, and Egypt,	266,779	40.340	295,542	38,490
British North America,	398,793	186,254	142,295	128,543
United States,	1,834,142	296,102	617,131	242,094
Other countries, .	30,145	19,339	44,558	24,212
Total, .	4,464,757	3,082,231	4,835,280	1,771,067

*The aggregate includes 5,163 quarters of Indian corn, of which 4,022 were from the United States.

† There were exported from Ireland to Great Britain in 1849—249,489 quarters, equal to 2,035,912 bushels of wheat—1,076,364 quarters of oats, and 201 811 cattle, beside calves, sheep and pigs.

In addition to the wheat and wheat flour imported into Great Britain, and what came from Ireland, there was imported in 1849, 1,389,858 quarters of barley and barley meal—1,307,904 quarters of oats, and oatmeal—246,843 of rye and rye meal—2,277,224 of Indian corn, and meal—236,525 of pease and pea meal—and 458,651 quarters of beans.

SEC. 13. *General reflections on the agricultural products of Europe, and their increase.*

Though all the countries in the northern and central portions of Europe have increased in population, and many of them very greatly, during the last century and a half, yet their agricultural products have increased more than the population. The people are at this time (1851) better supplied with vegetable food and with all the comforts of life, except animal food and fuel, than they were fifty or an hundred years since, or at any former period. This seems almost incredible, when we consider the age of the nations of Europe, and their increase in population.

We have reason to believe that the population of Europe did not much, if any, exceed an hundred millions, at the time of the discovery of America, near the close of the fifteenth century. In the year 1700, I suppose it was about one hundred and thirty-five millions—in 1800, it amounted to about one hundred and eighty millions—in 1840, to about two hundred and forty millions—and in 1850 it was about two hundred and fifty-five millions. The increase of population has been sustained and caused, by an increase of agricultural products, and of the comforts of life, by reason of an increase of science, and of mechanical and mining industry.

Nearly all the countries of Europe have ordinarily for many years past, produced a surplus of grain to export. This is shown by the tables in the last section. The history of the world until a recent period, is filled with dearths, and great scarcities of provisions, amounting almost to famines; which carried great distress, suffering, and sickness among the people, and swept off thousands, and sometimes millions, by means of the debility and diseases consequent upon a want of sufficient food, and other necessaries to make them comfortable. Such scenes of suffering, sickness, and mortality as existed in Ireland in 1847, were common in every country of Europe, during the thirteenth, fourteenth, fifteenth and sixteenth centuries, and still more common during earlier periods of the world. Agriculture was then in a very low condition, the amount of grain cultivated comparatively small, and crops very precarious and generally light. This was owing to a variety of causes, among which may be noticed, the low state of physical science and of the mechanic arts, the total ignorance of agricultural chemistry and science—a want of proper tools and instruments to plough and subdue the earth properly—and a want of extensive markets, and of facilities to transport their products to market, which operate as stimulants to industry. It was impossible for population to increase very much, in such a condition of things, and the fact of a great increase of population during the last seventy-five years (since the year 1775) is of itself, evidence, that food and other comforts of life are more abundant among all classes of people, and scarcities less frequent, than they were two, three, or five centuries since.

The increase of physical and mechanical science, of productive industry, agricultural products, and population, all go hand in hand, and neither can advance very much without the others; the increase of agricultural products and of population being natural consequents of the others, operating as causes. Agricultural chemistry, has grown up during the present century. Plants, soils and manures have been analyzed, their constituent elements ascertained, the deficiencies of any soil to produce a particular crop, and the mode of supplying the deficiencies by manures of various kinds, lime and gypsum, bone dust and guano, has been learned, the utility of a rotation of crops, and the use of the grasses, clover and other green crops, have been suggested and tested by experiments. Many of these things have been suggested ex priori, by physical science and agricultural chemistry, and all of them have been tested, and their real utility ascertained, by the observation and experience of great numbers of persons, in different countries, and the results published to the world

The quality and productiveness of grains, grasses, plants, fruits and animals, have been improved by cultivation; and by transferring them from one country, and one climate to another, sowing and planting only the best grains and seeds, and breeding from the best animals, all these things have been improved in quality, as well as in productiveness, in all the well cultivated countries of the earth. Great advantages have been derived also from iron ploughs, and other instruments, to aid in turning up, at a considerable depth, subduing and cultivating the earth, and in sowing the seeds, gathering, securing and cleaning the crops, and fitting them for use.

Nearly all these improvements have been effected during the last hundred years, since the year 1750, and the result has been a great increase in agricultural products, in nearly all the countries of Europe. The average product of wheat per acre in England and Wales, is about four times as great at present, as it was four centuries since—being now about 27 or 28 bushels per acre—it was then only about seven bushels. The average annual crop of wheat in England and Wales at, and immediately previous to, the revolution of 1688, was from sixteen to seventeen million bushels; as late as from 1770 to 1775, it was only about thirty-five million bushels; but since 1835 it has been generally supposed to average nearly one hundred million bushels.

The average crops of grain of all kinds in France in 1784 were but little over nine bushels per acre—they are now about fifteen bushels per acre. The crop of wheat in France in 1784 was only about one hundred and thirteen million bushels; it now amounts to about two hundred million bushels per annum. The production of all kinds of grain in 1760 amounted to about 450 litres, or $12\frac{3}{4}$ bushels to each inhabitant; the average production for some years past, has been estimated at 541 litres, or $15\frac{1}{3}$ bushels to each person, notwithstanding an increase of population of twelve and a half millions, or over fifty per cent. The population of France in 1760 was about twenty-three millions—production of grain at $12\frac{3}{4}$ bushels each 290,000,000 bushels. Population in 1846 about 35,400,000, annual production of grain about 543,000,000 bushels.*

The progress and improvements in agriculture have been much greater in Great Britain and Belgium, than in France—they have been very great also in all the central and northern countries of Europe. The crops generally are more certain, as well as more abundant, and better secured, than they were a century since, and the science of agriculture is still advancing. If all Europe were as well cultivated as Great Britain and Belgium now are, there is no reason to doubt, that it might produce sufficient food and wool for five or six hundred millions of inhabitants. Considering the advance in the sciences and the increase in the crops of some countries during the last hundred years, by reason of the advance in physical, agricultural, and mechanical science, we can scarcely assign any limits to the quantity of food which may be produced. There is at this day, and will be for all future time, more suffering in nearly every country of Europe, for want of sufficient fuel, clothing, and comfortable dwellings, than for want of food.

These facts and considerations should make the free trade advocates, statesmen and agriculturists of America, pause and reflect, what dependence they can reasonably put on Great Britain as a market for our grain and provisions? Whether we are not giving too much attention to the production of food, and too little to the production of other comforts, and of the instruments of

* See L'Annuaire de L'Economie Politique et de la Statistique of France for 1850, p. 370 to 375.

industry? Whether by striving and expecting to feed the Europeans and furnish them with raw materials, and to be clothed by them and furnished with manufactured products, they are not nourishing a false hope, which will produce disappointment, debt, embarrassment, the depression of many important branches of industry, panic, revulsion, and a general depression of property and business? Nothing but the mines of California has prevented the heavy balance of trade against the United States from producing a severe shock and revulsion, before this time. The exports of coin during the first six months, from January to June inclusive, of the present year (1851) amounted to over twenty-five millions of dollars. Such an immense drain of specie could not have been sustained at any former period in our history, without producing a panic, and wide spread bankruptcy.

SEC. 14. *The introduction, production, and consumption of Sugar.*

A century since, sugar was regarded as a great luxury, to be used only by the wealthy; now it is looked upon by all classes in this country as a necessary, which cannot be dispensed with. The Greeks and Romans had very little knowledge of sugar; the Saracens introduced the culture of the sugar cane, and the manufacture of sugar into the islands of Cyprus, Crete, Sicily and Rhodes, and also into Spain, in the ninth century; and the Spaniards introduced the manufacture of sugar into the West India islands. The art of refining sugar, and making what is called loaf sugar, is a modern European invention, the discovery of a Venetian about the end of the 15th or beginning of the 16th century.

Mr. McCulloch remarks, that even in the early part of the 17th century, the quantity of sugar imported into Great Britain was very inconsiderable; and that it was used only in the houses of the rich and great. It was not until the latter part of the century, when coffee and tea were introduced, that sugar came into general use.

Mr. McCulloch's statement of the quantity of sugar consumed in Great Britain, at different periods:

In	1700	10,000 tons.	1786 to 1790,	average	81,000 tons.
"	1710	14,000 "	1801 to 1810,	"	123,265 "
"	1734	42,000 "	1811 to 1820,	"	118,147 "
"	1754	53,270 "	1821 to 1830,	"	149,600 "
1770 to	1775	72,500 "			

During the whole of the present century, the inhabitants of Great Britain have, on an average, consumed more than twenty pounds of sugar annually; during the 18th century, the consumption by them increased, as their productive industry and the means of paying for it increased. Owing to the poverty of the great mass of the Irish people, they consume very little sugar; McCulloch states that the whole quantity retained for consumption in Ireland, in 1825, was about 12,600 tons, and in 1835, only about 9,300 tons.

The quantity consumed in Great Britain and Ireland from 1831 to 1840 inclusive, averaged annually 187,298 tons. This prodigious quantity was consumed, notwithstanding it was loaded down with so heavy duties, that the nett revenue amounted annually on an average, during the ten years, to £4,532,214 sterling, or about $21,700,000.

Statement and calculation of Porter,* of the quantity of sugar consumed in Great Britain and Ireland respectively, the average consumption of each person, and the rate of duty.

In Great Britain in,	1801.	1811.	1821.
Tons consumed,	149,542.	164,616.	123,587.
Consumption of each person,	30½ lbs.	29¼ lbs.	19¼ lbs.
Rate of duty per Cwt,	20 s.	27 s.	27 s.

In Ireland in,	1800.	1810.	1821.
Tons consumed,	14,903.	21,004.	19,030.
Consumption of each person.	6⅕ lbs.	8 lbs.	6¼ lbs.

Statement taken from the British Almanac for 1851 of the quantity of Sugar entered for consumption in Great Britain and Ireland respectively, in 1849, and a calculation of the average amount to each person:

	In Great Britain.	In Ireland.
Tons of sugar consumed,	276,587.	23,290.
Average consumption of each person,	29 lbs.	about 8 lbs.

Mr. McCulloch states the consumption of foreign and colonial sugar in France as follows:

		Consumed by each person
In 1788,	at about 21,300 tons,	about 2 pounds.
" 1801,	" 25,200 "	" 2 "
" 1812,	" 16,000 "	
1816 to 1819,	36,000 "	nearly 3 "
1822 to 1824,	47,250 "	" 3½ "
1826 to 1827,	62,500 "	" 4½ "
in 1830,	67,250 "	" 5 "

He estimated the quantity consumed in France in 1832, including beet root as well as foreign sugar, at 88,000,000 kilogrammes, about 88,000 tons, or 195,000,000 pounds; being

* See Porter's Progress of the Nation, title Sugar.

about six pounds for each person, and less than one-third part as much as is consumed by each inhabitant of Great Britain. The foreign and colonial sugar entered for consumption in France in 1841 was about 84,000 tons.

Mr. McCulloch states the average quantities exported from the principal producing countries during each of the three years ending with 1833 as follows:

	Tons.
British West Indies, Demerara and Berbice,	90,000
Mauritius,	30,000
Bengal, Isle of Bourbon, Java, Siam, Philippines, &c.,	60,000
Cuba and Porto Rico,	110,000
French, Dutch and Danish West Indies,	95,000
Brazil,	75,000
Total,	560,000

The United States then produced about 50,000 tons, and in 1844 about 100,000 tons, including maple sugar.

About one-fourth part of the whole quantity of sugar made in the world, appears to be consumed by the inhabitants of the island of Great Britain. Why is it, that they can pay for, and afford to enjoy so many more luxuries than their neighbors?

Statement in millions of pounds of the quantities of sugar imported into the United States during the undermentioned years, its aggregate value and value per pound each year.

			Value.	Value per lb.
In 1790,	22¾	millions.		
" 1800,	50½	"		
" 1810,	29⅓	"		
" 1821,	59½	"	$3,553,582	nearly 6 cents.
" 1830,	86½	"	4,630,342	about 5⅓ "
" 1835,	126	"	6,860,174	nearly 5½ "
" 1840,	121	"	5,580,950	nearly 4⅔ "
" 1845,	115½	"	4,780,555	about 4⅛ "
" 1850,	218	"	7,504,424	" 3⅔ "

Estimate by Edmund G. Forstall of New Orleans of the crops of sugar raised in Louisiana, during several years, in hogsheads of 1000 pounds each, and the prices or value on the plantations of the sugar per pound, and molasses per gallon, during the month of March each year; which is the usual time of selling.

Years.	Crop in hhds.	Price of Sugar.	Price of Molasses
1832–1833	70,000	5½ to 5¾ cts.	10 cts.
1834–1835	110,000	5¾ to 6 "	18 to 19 cts.
1835–1836	36,000	10 to 11 "	33 to 34 "
1839–1840	119,947	3¾ to 4 "	15 to 16 "
1841–1842	125,000	3½ to 4½ "	13 to 13½ "
1842–1843	140,316	3¾ to 4 "	11 to 12½ "
1843–1844	100,346	5½ to 6½ "	20
1844–1845	204,913	3⅞ to 4⅓ "	14 to 15½ "

The production of Sugar in the United States is now so great as to affect materially its price throughout the world. A large crop depresses prices, and a short one causes prices to advance.

A very considerable proportion of the sugar imported into the United States is re-exported; the quantity exported in 1842, amounted to over 15,000,000 pounds, leaving about 157,000,000 pounds of foreign sugar for home consumption, beside domestic sugar. In 1840, the quantity of maple sugar made in the United States, was about 35,000,000 pounds; call it the same in 1842, the crop of Louisiana in 1841 was about 125,000,000 pounds, making the whole supply and consumption of the United States for 1842, about 317,000,000 of pounds, for a population of 16,000,000 of persons, exclusive of field slaves, less than twenty pounds for each person. It appears that the free population of the United States consume less sugar on an average than the inhabitants of Great Britain; though the latter pay duties on all they consume about five times as high as the former, amounting in the aggregate to more pounds sterling, than we pay dollars.

SEC. 15. *The production and consumption of Coffee.*

The coffee plant is a native of that part of Arabia called Yeman; but it is now very extensively cultivated in the Southern part of India, in Java, the West Indies and Brazil. McCulloch says it is supposed that coffee was not roasted and the decoction used as a drink earlier than the 15th century; and that it was introduced into England and France between the years 1640 and 1660. From 1660 to 1808 the duty on coffee in Great Britain was from 1s. 6d. to 2s. sterling per pound, which prevented it from being consumed in very great quantities. The quantity consumed in Great Britain did not amount to a million pounds annually, prior to the year 1804, except during the years 1791, 1793 and 1795.

Statement of the quantity of Coffee consumed in the United States, Great Britain and Ireland respectively during the under-mentioned years:

	United States. lbs.	Great Britain. lbs.	Ireland. lbs.
1810,	5,852,082	5,308,096	
1821,	11,886,063	7,327,283	265,718
1830,	38,363,657	21,840,520	851,000
1840,	86,209,761	27,298,322*	
1849,	150,963,000	33,417,675	1,013,399

The average custom-house valuations of coffee imported into the U. States have been as follows—in 1821—twenty-one cents

* Consumption in Great Britain in 1841.

per pound—in 1830 eight cents—in 1840 nine cents—and in 1849, five and a half cents.

The duties on coffee imported into Great Britain were reduced in 1808 to 7d. sterling per pound, raised in 1819 to 1s., and reduced in 1824 to 6d. In the United States, the duties from 1794 to 1812 were five cents; from 1812 to 1816 ten cents; from 1816 to 1830 five cents; since 1832, coffee has been imported free of duty.

Estimated production of coffee in the world in Hunt's Magazine for Sept. 1845.

	Pounds.
Brazil,	170,000,000
Cuba,	45,000,000
St. Domingo,	38,000,000
Porto Rico and Laguayra,	36,000,000
British West Indies,	10,000,000
Dutch West Indies,	3,000,000
Ceylon,	7,000,000
Sumatra and Java,	140,000,000
East Indies and Mocha,	6,000,000
French Colonies,	4,000,000
Total pounds,	459,000,000

Mr. McCulloch states the product of Mocha and the other Arabian ports at that time (1836) at 10,000 tons, and the total product of the world at 147,000 tons; equal to 329,280,000 pounds.

Nearly two-thirds of all the coffee now produced in the world, is from the western hemisphere; Mr. Hunt states the production and increase in Brazil as follows: in 1820 at 95,700 bags; in 1830 at 391,785; and 1840 at 1,063,805 bags. In 1752 the export of coffee from Jamaica amounted to only 60,000 pounds; in 1775 to 440,000 pounds; in 1797 to 7,931,621 pounds; and in 1832 the exports amounted to 19,811,000 pounds. These results show how active the slave trade has been, and how actively it is still prosecuted by the Brazilians.

The coffee imported into France for three years from 1830 to 1832 inclusive, was less than 35,000 tons, or nearly 27,000,000 pounds annually; while the amount retained for home consumption in the United States during the same three years was 68,990 tons, or nearly 23,000 tons annually; and nearly twice as much as the consumption of France, though the population of the latter was then about three times as great as the free population of the former. The quantity entered for home consumption in

France in 1821 was 12,954,116 kilogrammes, or about 12,900 tons, according to the official reports.

The coffee tree will grow on almost any soil, high or low, rich or poor, in the torrid zone. Though it grows most luxuriantly and produces the most abundantly on rich loamy and alluvial soils, yet it does well, and produces better flavored coffee on high, dry and sandy soils, on the sides of hills and even mountains, and there is scarcely any limit to the quantity which may be produced. The increased production has exceeded the demand for it, and hence the fall in price.

SEC. 16. *The introduction and consumption of Tea.*

Brande remarks, in his Encyclopædia, that "tea was wholly unknown to the Greeks and Romans, and even to our ancestors, previously to the end of the sixteenth or the beginning of the seventeenth century. It seems to have been originally imported in small quantities by the Dutch, but was hardly known in this country (England) till after 1650. In 1664 the East India Company bought two pounds and two ounces of tea as a present to his majesty. In 1667 they issued the first order to import tea, directed to their agent at Bantam, to the effect that he should send home one hundred pounds of the best tea he could get."

McCulloch says "the tea shrub may be described as a very hardy evergreen, growing readily in the open air, from the equator to the 45th degree of latitude. For the last sixty years it has been reared in this country (England) without difficulty in green-houses; and thriving plants of it are to be seen in the gardens of Java, Singapore, Malacca and Penang; all within six degrees of the equator. The climate most congenial to it, however, seems to be that between the 25th and 33d degrees of latitude, judging from the success of its cultivation in China." "Its growth is chiefly confined to hilly tracts, not suited to the growth of corn." There is no good reason to doubt that a sufficient quantity of tea for the consumption of the country might be cultivated in the United States, if the same efforts were made to introduce it as were made to introduce the cultivation of rice and cotton.

Statements extracted from the Commercial Dictionary, showing the progress of the consumption of tea in Great Britain from 1711 to 1780.

1711	141,995 pounds.	1750	2,114,922 pounds.
1720	237,904 "	1760	2,293,613 "
1730	537,016 "	1770	7,723,538 "
1740	1,302,549 "	1780	5,588,315 "

Account of the quantities of tea entered for home consumption in each of the kingdoms of Great Britain and Ireland, and the aggregate amount of nett duties paid thereon each year:

Years.	Great Britain.	Ireland.	Duties collected.
1790	14,639,299 lbs.	1,736,796 lbs.	£580,362
1800	20,358,702	2,926,166	1,222,086
1810	19,093,244	2,923,369	3,647,737
1820	22,452,050	3,150,344	3,527,192
1825	24,830,015	3,889,658	4,030,019
1830	30,047,079 *		3,387,097
1841	36,675,667 *		3,978,198
1849	43,641,372	6,383,316	† 5,471,641

Statement of the quantity of tea imported into the United States, during the undermentioned fiscal years.

Years.	Quantity in pounds.	Years.	Quantity in pounds.
1790,	3,047,242	1835,	14,415,572
1800,	3,797,634	1840,	20,006,595
1810,	6,647,726	1842,	15,692,094
1820,	4,891,447	1845,	19,812,500
1830,	8,609,415	1850,	29,872,654

The quantity of tea exported from the United States in 1830 amounted to 1,536,314 pounds; in 1840 to 3,123,496 pounds; in 1842 to 2,290,786; in 1845 to 2,483,308 pounds; and in 1850 to 1,673,063. By deducting the quantity exported from the imports, the reader will have the quantity consumed.

Statement of the quantity of tea, the quantity of coffee, and the aggregate quantity of tea and coffee, reckoned as coffee (calling one pound of tea equal to five pounds of coffee) consumed in the United States and in Great Britain respectively, in 1830—1842—and in 1850—and the amount to each person.

United States.	1830.	1842.	1850.
	lbs.	lbs.	lbs.
Tea consumed,	7,173,091	13,401,308	28,199,541
Tea equal to coffee,	35,865,455	67,006,540	140,997,705
Coffee,	38,363,689	107,383,577	129,791,466
Tea and coffee equal to coffee,	74,229,142	174,390,117	270,789,171
Average for each person,	5¾	9¾	about 11¾

* The quantities given for 1830 and 1841 include the consumption in both Great Britain and Ireland.

† Gross duties—See the British Almanac for 1851, page 145.

Great Britain,	1830. lbs.	1842. lbs.	1849. lbs.
Tea consumed,	30,047,079	32,500,000	43,641,372
Tea equal to coffee,	150,235,395	162,500,000	218,206,000
Coffee,	21,840,520	24,300,000	33,417,675
Tea & coffee equal to coffee,	172,075,915	186,800,000	251,623,675
Average for each person,	10½	10	12¼

The duties paid on tea imported into the United States in 1830 were from 6 to 40 cents per pound, and on coffee, 2 cents per pound. Since 1833, tea and coffee have been imported, free of duty; which has tended to increase their consumption very much; and yet the consumption of these articles, in Great Britain, where they are loaded down with enormous duties, is greater in proportion to the population, than it is in the United States, and about three times as great in proportion to the population, as it is in Ireland.

It has been shown in section fourteen, that more sugar is consumed in Great Britain, in proportion to the population, than in the United States; here it appears, that more tea and coffee in the aggregate are also consumed. The amount of duties collected in Great Britain on tea, coffee and sugar exceeds the whole amount of duties collected on all the imports of the United States. High duties seem to have but little effect, to check the consumption of luxuries among a people who have the means of paying for them. The people of Great Britain, being extensively engaged in mechanical, manufacturing, and mining industry, which is much more profitable than agricultural industry, are able to pay high prices for, and to consume more of these luxuries, than the people of the United States can pay for at low prices. The agricultural population of Ireland cannot pay for, and therefore cannot consume more than about one third part as much in proportion to their numbers, as the manufacturing population of England, who are often sneered at in this country as paupers.

The consumption of tea on the continent of Europe is small. It is stated in the Commercial Dictionary that in 1832 the quantity of tea imported into Russia amounted to 6,461,064 pounds; that the quantity consumed in Holland annually was about 2,800,000 pounds; that the consumption of France was not supposed to exceed 230,000 pounds a year; that the importations into Hamburg vary from 1,500,000 to 2,000,000 pounds annually, the greater part of which is forwarded into the interior of Germany; and that the imports into Venice and Trieste do not exceed a few hundred pounds a year. I find no account of the quantity of tea consumed by the other countries of Europe and America. According to official reports, the quantity of tea entered for home consumption in France in 1841, amounted to 154,100 kil.; about 346,000 pounds.

Sec. 17. *Physical and Moral Effects of Tea and Coffee.*

"The introduction of tea and coffee, it has been well remarked, has led to the most wonderful change that ever took place in the diet of modern civilized nations; a change highly important both in a moral and physical point of view. These beverages have the admirable advantage of affording stimulus without producing intoxication, or any of its evil consequences. Lovers of tea or coffee are, in fact, rarely drinkers (that is of alcohol) and hence the use of these beverages has benefited both manners and morals. Raynal observes that the use of tea has contributed more to the sobriety of the Chinese than the severest laws, the most eloquent discourses, or the best treatises on morality." (Scotsman, 17th Oct. 1827.)

Dr. Ure in the supplement to his Dictionary of the Arts, article tea, quotes the following remarks from Professor Liebig. "Recent researches have shown in such a manner as to exclude all doubt, that thein and caffein (the peculiar properties of tea and coffee) are in all respects identical," and he adds, "*we may consider these vegetable compounds so remarkable for their action on the brain, and the substance of the organs of motion,* AS ELEMENTS OF FOOD FOR ORGANS *as yet unknown, which are destined to convert the blood into* NERVOUS SUBSTANCE, AND THUS RECRUIT THE ENERGY OF THE MOVING AND THINKING FACULTIES." "At a meeting of the Academy of Sciences of Paris, lately held, M. Peligot read a paper on the chemical combinations of tea. He stated that tea contains essential principles of nutrition, far exceeding in importance its stimulating properties; and showed that tea is, in every respect, one of the most desirable articles of general use."

In this view of the subject, it would seem that tea and coffee are likely to assume a physiological importance not realized or thought of until recently. They both contain a large per centage of tannin, and some other astringent substances, and act directly upon the nervous cords, more as tonics than as stimulants; and tea particularly seems to act upon the brain and nervous cords, rather as a sedative and tonic than as a stimulant.

The nervous substance or fluid, and the nervous cords and filaments of the brain, are very different things, the latter being but the tubes in which the former is contained; and if, as suggested by Prof. Liebig, any considerable portion of tea and coffee, when taken into the system and assimilated, is secreted by the blood, and forms nervous fluid, these drinks are of essential importance in supplying the substance on which all our mental and muscular action depends. And though they may in some sense be called stimulants, yet *they act as natural stimulants, by increasing the quantity of the nervous substance or fluid*,(which is the natural stimulant of the brain and nerves,) *and not by changing its character, substance or action*. They may thus act as stimulants to the brain and nerves, by increasing the quantity of the nervous substance, in the same manner as nutritious food acts as a stimulant to the whole system, by supplying the materials which constitute the blood, and thereby increasing its quantity; but inasmuch as persons may injure themselves by consuming too much nutritious food, more than is requisite to supply a sufficiency of blood; so persons of sensitive and excitable nerves may, in like manner, by using too much tea or coffee, and supplying too much nervous fluid, produce too much mental and muscular activity, and thereby injure their health and constitutions. Alcohol, on the contrary, is an unnatural stimulant; inasmuch as the direct effect of the extra quantity of hydrogen which it contains, is to stimulate the system, and increase the action of the blood to an unnatural degree, without furnishing much nourishment; and exhaustion is the necessary consequence.

SEC. 18. *The Production and Consumption of Wine*

The vine has been cultivated and wines made, from the earliest periods of history. The limits within which it is cultivated in the northern hemisphere of the Old World, vary from about 15 to 48 and 52 degrees. The vine grows in every sort of soil; but that which is light and gravelly produces the best quality of wines; though rich soils produce the largest crops. Wines are made in more than half of Europe, and may be made in abundance in nearly half of the inhabitable portions of the earth. The production greatly exceeds the demand. France alone might supply all the northern countries of Europe and of America, with all the wine and brandy needed by them.

The average annual production of wine in the Empire of Austria exclusive of Hungary, exceeds one hundred and fifty million imperial gallons. The general estimate from the official reports of the average quantity of wine made in France annually, for more than twenty years past, is about thirty-seven millions hectolitres—equal to about 976,000,000 wine gallons, or 814,000,000 English imperial gallons. In 1820 M. Chaptal estimated the vine culture in France at 1,613,930 hectares,*

*A hectare is about 2 acres 1 rood and 35 square rods of ground. And a hectolitre about 22 English imperial gallons, or wine gallons.

producing about 35,358,890 hectolitres* of wine. In 1824 the Department of Finance reported the produce of wines at 35,000,000 hectolitres; and M. Covolean estimated the vineyards of France in 1827 at 1,736,056 hectares, and the average quantity of wine produced annually, at 36,945,820 hectolitres.

Statement of the quantity and value of the wines and brandies of France exported during the undermentioned years.

Average of years.	Wines in millions of Litres.	Wines in millions of Francs.	Brandies in millions of Litres.	Brandies in millions of Francs.
1815 to 1817	103,9	38,6	11,7	9,4
1821 to 1823	109,	42,7	22,8	18,2
1827 to 1829	114,9	49,1	33,2	27,
in 1840	135,3	49,3	19,2	16,2
1843 to 1847		50,9		12,3
in 1847		55,4		16,7
in 1848	153,4	54,5	official value	20,7
in 1848	real value	43,1	real value	24,1

The standard of official values was adopted in 1826 and has been continued ever since. The official and real values were both taken in 1848, when it was found that prices had fallen more than twenty per cent. The 1,534,000 hectolitres exported in 1848 was really worth but a trifle more than the 1,090,000 hectolitres exported annually from 1821 to 1823. The export, until recently, has been less than one thirtieth part of the quantity produced.

A commission instituted a few years since to inquire into the excise on wine, and the evasion of the excise, estimated the annual production of wine in France, and the disposition of it, as follows:

Consumed by the proprietors, not being subject to duty.	9	millions.
Made into Brandy,	6.4	"
Loss and waste among the growers,	4.1	"
do. in conveyance and among the dealers,	2.	"
Exported,	1.2	"
Made into vinegar,	.5	"
Duty paid on consumption,	14.	"
Fraudulently consumed without paying duty,	4.8	"
Total produced.	42.0	"

Supposing the annual production to be but 37 million hectolitres, the estimate of waste and loss, and the quantity fraudulently consumed without paying duty are probably five millions too high, and the other items of the estimate nearly correct. According to these estimates, the average annual consumption of wine in France by each person, is equal to about 18 imperial

*One hundred litres make one hectolitre.

gallons, or 22 wine gallons; and the consumers pay duties on it, amounting to from twelve to fourteen millions of dollars.

There is consumed annually in Great Britain and Ireland, about six million gallons of wine, about 330,000 gallons of which is from France.

The quantity of foreign wines consumed in the United States in 1839 and some previous years, amounted to over six million gallons; but the quantity consumed in 1840, the quantity consumed in 1850, and the average quantity consumed annually during the intervening years, was less than six million gallons.

France being the best wine growing country in the world, the free-trade writers of Great Britain have been for half a century or more, trying to satisfy the French that it was folly for them to endeavor to build up the mining and manufacturing industry of the kingdom by duties on foreign products imported, and that they might better turn their attention more to the production of wine, and the culture of silk, (in which they have natural advantages over all the northern nations of Europe,) abandon the mining, iron, and manufacturing interests to their fate, and buy their iron, hardware, cotton-yarn,coarse cottons, and coarse woollen goods of the British, and trust to the exportation of their wines, brandies, and silks, for the means of payment. This free-trade system operates well for Great Britain, but what would be its effects on France! The most that France has ever been able to export, is about one twenty-fourth part of her wine crop, and they generally export less than one thirtieth part; and yet the exports are so large that, coming in competition with the wines of other countries, they have greatly reduced prices. The question is not, how much wine France can produce, but how much can she sell to advantage; her annual exports of wine are worth at the place of export only a little over $8,000,000, and the brandy less than $5,000,000, making in all about $13,000,000. The whole quantity of wine (about 6,000,000 gallons) consumed annually in Great Britain and Ireland, cost at the place of export about $1,500,000; less than one fifteenth part of which comes from France. The average quantity of brandy consumed in Great Britain for several years past has been about 1,675,000 imperial gallons per annum, worth at the place of export about $1,400,000. If France should open her ports and admit all British products at a nominal or very small duty and thereby sacrifice her mining interests, and her manufactures of iron, hardware, cotton-yarn, coarse cotton and woollen goods, to the amount of fifteen or twenty million dollars per annum, she might thereby increase her sales of wine and brandy to Great Britain, perhaps, to the amount of a million of dollars per year. And even that small increase of exports of French wines and brandy, would be at the expense of their neighbors of Spain, Portugal, Italy, and Germany, whose exports of those articles must decrease to the same or nearly the same extent. These illustrations show the selfishness of the gratuitous advice of the free-trade economists of Great Britain to other nations, and the sophistry of their leading arguments.

SEC. 19. *The Production and Consumption of Tobacco.*

Tobacco is a plant indigenous to America. It was first intro duced into Europe the fore part of the 16th century, but it has long been extensively used throughout Europe as well as America. When tobacco leaves are distilled they yield an essential oil, which is a virulent poison. It is a remarkable fact, that this weed, of which man uses so much, is avoided by animals ; that it will destroy animal life, and is frequently used to destroy vermin ; that it is nauseating to the stomach ; that it cannot be taken into the system in even as large quantities as arsenic, laudanum or other poisons, without dangerous consequences ; and that it is taken into the mouth and nose merely to stimulate the surface of the skin and some of the glands, and its contents, together with all the saliva raised by and mixed with it, carefully spit out. It may be useful to some persons of a very full and plethoric habit, but it is generally supposed to be very deleterious to the human system.

Statement of the quantities of tobacco retained for home consumption in Great Britain and Ireland, and the amount of duties and excise collected thereon during the years therein stated.*

	Great Britain.		Ireland.	
	Pounds used.	Amount of duty.	Pounds used.	Amount of duty.
1790	8,960,224	£512,383	2,900,437	£133,195
1801	10,514,998	923,855	6,389,754	285,482
1821	12,983,198	2,600,415	2,614,954	528,168
1831	15,350,018	2,338,107	4,183,823	626,485
1841	16,830,593	2,716,217	5,478,767	863,946

Statement of the quantity in hogsheads, the value of the leaf tobacco, and the value also of the manufactured tobacco, exported from the United States, during the undermentioned fiscal years.

	Leaf Tobacco.		
	hhds.	value.	Manufact'd Tobacco & Snuff.
1821	66,858	$5,648,962	$140,083
1830	83,810	5,586,365	346,747
1840	119,484	9,883,957	813,671
1845	147,168	7,469,819	538,498
1850	145,729	9,951,023	648,832

* The duties in Great Britain varied from 1s 7d to 4s Sterling per pound, and in Ireland from 1s to 3s per pound.

The tobacco crop of the United States of 1839, (as reported in the census of 1840,) was 219,163,319 pounds. A hogshead of tobacco is about 1,400 pounds, which makes the export of leaf tobacco in 1840, about 167,000,000 pounds. The manufactured tobacco and snuff exported that year amounted to 6,824,297 pounds—making in all, nearly 174,000,000 pounds exported, and leaving over forty-five million pounds for home consumption.

The planters of Virginia, before the Revolutionary war, paid their principal attention to the culture of tobacco, and used to export generally about 55,000 hogsheads a year. Maryland and the Carolinas also exported large quantities of tobacco, and the whole annual export from the colonies has been estimated as high as 100,000 hogsheads. The hogshead in those days contained only from 600 to 700 pounds each. Though considerable quantities are cultivated in France, and other countries of southern Europe, yet the tobacco of America is preferred; and such is the universal custom and fashion of using it, that the demand seems to be increasing of late, in proportion to the ability of the people to pay for it.

The duties levied on tobacco in Great Britain have been for some years, four shillings sterling per pound, or from 600 to 1200 per cent., and all the countries of Europe have imposed enormously heavy duties on it, yet the people will have it; and the amount we export, shows that it is not materially diminished by either European or American tariffs, so long as it is not so high as to be beyond the ability of the mass of the laboring classes to pay for it. The fluctuations in the prices of tobacco have been less than in any other staple product of the United States. The demand has been steady and increasing with great uniformity, and the production generally greater than the demand; which has kept prices the most of the time, at the lowest point that would compensate the planter.

CHAPTER X.

THE PRECIOUS METALS, COIN, AND BANK NOTES.

SEC. 1. *The utility of Gold and Silver; and the properties which fit them for measures of value, and for currency.*

GOLD and silver have been extensively used in the arts, for domestic utensils, ornaments, objects of luxury, and numerous other purposes, from the earliest times. Their great utility and intrinsic value, together with their beauty, durability, and the facility of converting them from one form into another without much loss, have made them general objects of desire by the whole human family, and the universal currency of civilized nations, from the earliest periods of history.

As a currency, or money, they have been used as measures of value, and also as instruments or means of payment. (Vide ante sec. 6 of Chapter VI.) On account of their durability, convertibility, and great intrinsic value, in proportion to their weight and bulk, they constitute the best and safest currency which the world can furnish; though a currency composed mostly of paper, based on the precious metals, is much cheaper, and more convenient. Gold and silver have an intrinsic value in the public estimation, to the amount at which they pass as money; while bank notes, and other paper money, are but the representatives of value; and they are often only the evidence of an obligation to pay what it is not in the power of the obligor to pay, according to the terms of the obligation.

Even the precious metals do not constitute an invariable standard or measure of value; for their value, like that of everything else, depends upon the relative proportion between the supply and the demand; and when we compare their value in the market at periods distant from each other of a century or more, we find their fluctuation in value greater than that of breadstuffs; but as they are comparatively rare metals; as great labor is generally required to produce them; as the production of the mines is not affected by frosts, droughts, rains, and other changes of the seasons, and the quantity in use can never be suddenly increased nor diminished, if you take periods of time of from one to ten years, they are subject to very little fluctuation, and furnish a standard of value almost perfect.

Nature has not determined the relative value of the two metals. That depends partly on the uses to which they may be applied, and the consequent demand for them, and partly on the production of the mines, and the average amount of each, produced by the employment of a given amount of labor and capital. Prior to the discovery of America, an ounce of gold was equal in value in Europe to about ten ounces of silver. The American mines have produced in quantity about forty times as much silver as gold, which caused a gradual rise in Europe of the relative value of gold, when compared with silver, until the former became in different countries, from fourteen to fifteen and a half times as valuable as the latter; it was made fifteen times as valuable in the United States by the act of Congress of April, 1792, and sixteen times as valuable by the act of June, 1834. If the Russian mines should continue to furnish large supplies of gold, and the present anticipation should be realized of an immense and inexhaustible supply of gold from California, the relative value of gold must decline; and the time is not far distant, when it will not be worth more than ten or twelve times as much per ounce as silver. But no fears need be apprehended that the aggregate amount of the precious metals will increase faster than the population, and the wants of commerce, and of the world of fashion. The probability is, that they will not increase as fast, and that if the price of gold should fall, the price of silver will increase more and faster than gold falls. It may be important for Congress to act on this question very soon, to reduce the relative price of gold to the former standard, of fifteen times the value of silver, and to increase the quantity of gold to be coined into a dollar; or else silver coin, being relatively more valuable to export than to use in this country, will be rapidly exported.

British gold coin is made of eleven parts pure gold and one of alloy; every pound troy, or 12 oz. of standard silver, is composed of 11 oz. 2 dwts. of pure metal, and 18 dwts. of alloy. From the Norman conquest, in 1066, to the year 1300, a pound of standard silver, (that is 11 oz. 2 dwts. pure silver, and 18 dwts. alloy) was coined into 20 shillings, or one pound, sterling money. The number of shillings into which the same quantity of silver was coined was increased from time to time, until in 1527 it was coined into 40 shillings, or two pounds, and soon after into 45 shillings; in 1560, and from that time until 1600, it was coined into 60 shillings; from 1600 to 1816 into 62 shillings;

and since 1816 into 66 shillings. From 1543 to 1553, the coin was much more debased.

The number of grains of pure silver, and of pure gold, contained in one pound, or twenty shillings, sterling money, at different periods, has been as follows :—

Years.	Silver. Grains.	Gold. Grains.	Proportion of Gold to Silver.
1560 to 1600	1,776	160	1 to 11. 1
1600 to 1604	1,718.7	157.6	1 to 10. 9
1604 to 1626	1,718.7	141.9 to 128.8	
1666 to 1717	1,718.7	118.6 to 113	
1717 to 1816	1,718.7	113	1 to 15. 2
Since 1816	1,654.5	113	1 to 14. 23

Gold only is a legal tender in Great Britain for any sum above two pounds sterling.

The acts of Congress prescribe that all coins of the United States shall be nine parts pure silver or gold, and one part alloy. By the act of April 12th, 1792, a dollar is required to contain 371¼ grains pure silver, and the same by the act of June,1834; gold being declared fifteen times as valuable as silver by the former act, and sixteen times as valuable by the latter act.

The number of grains of pure silver, and pure gold, contained in five dollars under each act, has been as follows :—

Years.	Silver. Grains.	Gold. Grains.	Proportion of Gold to Silver.
1792 to 1834	1,856¼	123¾	1 to 15
Since 1834	1,856¼	116	1 to 16

Sec. 2. *Quantity of pure silver and gold in the coin of Great Britain and the United States, at different periods.*

The British gold sovereign is nearly equal in value to $4 87, American gold coin, though it is declared by the act of 1834 worth only $4 84. Calling a dollar 4s. 6d. sterling, the par exchange on England, payable in gold, is over 9½ per cent, payable in silver it is nearly 2 per cent in our favor; but as more than nine-tenths of the circulating coin of England is gold, and silver is sold in quantities at less than its legal value, as compared with gold, and the tenth part of an American eagle is worth only 4s. 1⅛d. sterling, in British gold, we may fairly reckon a dollar at 4s. 2d. sterling, and the real par exchange at 9 per cent nominal value.

Sec. 3. *Mr. Jacob's estimates of the amount of coin in the Roman Empire, and in ancient Europe.*

The learned historical inquiry into the production and consumption of the precious metals made by William Jacob, Esq., of England, was published in 1831. Mr. Jacob says it has been estimated by several diligent enquirers, that the whole annual revenues of the Roman empire, in the time of Augustus, amounted to a sum equivalent to forty millions sterling of English money, of its present standard of fineness and weight. This seems not improbable, as the population of the empire has been generally estimated at over one hundred millions, during the first and second centuries of the Christian era. He estimates the amount of the precious metals of gold and silver in the empire, at the death of Augustus, A. D. 14, as equal to the enormous sum of £358,000,000 sterling of English money; which seems to me incredible, considering that the knowledge of mining, and of the mechanical powers necessary to carry it on advantageously were then comparatively in their infancy, and that the mines of Europe, Asia, and Africa, have yielded very little since that time. He states that the mines were all nearly exhausted, and that the precious metals decreased from that period by friction and actual loss, at the rate of 10 per cent every 36 years, leaving in the year A. D. 410 but £107,435,924; and in the year A. D. 806 but £33,674,256. The quantity named at the latter period seems more probable than the former.

All these estimates are vague conjectures, without any accurate and reliable evidence to support them. The amount of coin in Europe, at the discovery of America, is estimated by him at about £34,000,000 sterling, or $163,000,000, which does not differ much from the estimates of other authors, and is probably not far from correct.

SEC. 4. *Production of Gold and Silver from* 1492 *to* 1850.

All the record evidence, and the estimates of authors, merchants, and public officers, of the production of the American mines from the discovery of America to the year 1803, were investigated with so much care and science by the learned M. Humboldt, that his estimates have been generally adopted as approximating as near to accuracy as is practicable. One thing, however, is very certain. He has greatly over-estimated the amount of gold and silver smuggled out of the colonies both of Spain and Portugal, without paying duty, and without being registered, or else their loss, and the amount used in the arts, and converted into plate and other utensils and ornaments, has been much greater than has been generally estimated. The amount in circulation, as coin, has been overrated by almost every writer of the present century, except Storch; and yet, it is difficult to account for the consumption of the precious metals, unless the amount produced by the mines has been greatly overrated.

Baron Humboldt estimated the quantity smuggled, in order to avoid the payment of duties, and unregistered, as equal to one-fourth the amount registered in the Portuguese colonies, and to over one-fifth the amount registered in the Spanish colonies. This is all conjecture, and, so far as Mexico, Peru, and Chili are concerned, which have very few ports from which it could be smuggled, it strikes me that the estimate is too great, by more than half, to be probable.

I. Statement of M. Humboldt of the value of gold and silver extracted from the mines of America from 1492 to 1803, as registered.

From the Spanish colonies	$4,035,156,000
" Portuguese colonies	684,544,000
Total registered	$4,719,700,000
Estimated amount smuggled and not registered from Spanish colonies	816,000,000
From the Portuguese colonies	171,000,000
Amount of contraband, as estimated by him	$987,000,000
Total production of the mines	5,706,700,000

II. The amount of precious metals registered, and estimated by M. Humboldt as smuggled, produced in the countries of America respectively, from the year 1492 to 1803, as follows:

	Registered.	Not Registered.	Total.
Mexico, or New Spain	$1,768 millions.	$260 millions.	$2,028 millions.
Peru and Buenos Ayres	1,936 "	474 "	2,410 "
Chili and New Granada	331 "	82 "	413 "
Portuguese Colonies	684 "	171 "	855 "
Total	$4,719 "	$987 "	$5,706 "

III. The average annual products of the gold and silver mines of Europe, Northern Asia and America, at the beginning of the present century, were estimated by M. Humboldt in millions of francs and millions of dollars, as follows:—

	Gold in francs.	Silver in francs.	Total in francs.	Total in dol's.
Europe	4,4 millions.	11,7 millions.	16,1 millions.	3, millions.
North Asia	1,8 "	4,8 "	6,6 "	1,2 "
America	59,5 "	176,8 "	236,3 "	44,3 "
Total	65,7 "	193,3 "	259, "	48,5 "

IV. Estimate of M. Humboldt of the average amounts of gold and silver exported annually from America to Europe, and also the aggregate amounts exported during the under-mentioned periods, stated in millions of dollars; to which I have added a column of deductions of one-twelfth part the aggregate amount for supposed over-estimates, and the amount exported, by my estimate, on making such deductions:—

Periods.	Exported per year.	Humboldt's aggregate.	One-twelfth part deducted.	My estimate of exports to Europe.
1492 to 1500....	$0.25 millions.	$2 millions.	$0.2 millions.	$1.8 millions.
1501 to 1545 ...	3 "	135 "	11.25 "	123.75 "
1546 to 1600....	11 "	605 "	50.4 "	554.6 "
1601 to 1700....	16 "	1,600 "	133.33 "	1,466.67 "
1701 to 1750....	22.5 "	1,125 "	93.75 "	1,031.25 "
1751 to 1800....	35.3 "	1,765 "	147 "	1,618 "
1801 to 1810....	43.5 "	435 "	36.25 "	398.75 "
Total		$5,667 "		$5,194.82 "
Exported from the western coast of America to Asia, per Humboldt,		133 "		133.00 "
Remaining in America in coin, plate, &c.....................		153 "		140.18 "
Total produced up to 1810....		$5,953 "		$5,468.00 "
Produced up to 1804		5,706 "		

In 1696, Gregory King made an estimate of the gold and silver produced by the mines of Europe; the amount imported and exported from the discovery of America to that time, and the amount in Europe in coin, plate, &c., at different periods. This estimate is contained in a manuscript now in the British Museum, (see Took on Prices, appendix, page 2, to part 1.) Mr. King's opinions and estimates on such subjects are entitled to as much, and, perhaps, to more weight, than those of any other man of the age in which he lived.

V. Estimates of Mr. King.

Stock of gold and silver in Europe in 1516, in coin, bullion, plate, gilding, watches, jewelry, and all other forms	£45 millions.	$216 millions.
Produced in Europe from 1516 to 1696	8 "	38.4 "
Imported from Asia in manufactures	2 "	9.6 "
" Africa in gold dust................	15 "	72 "
" America in coin..................	520 "	2,496 "
Produced and imported prior to 1596	205 "	984 "
Consumed and exported to Asia..................	150 "	720 "
Estimated stock in Europe in 1596	100 "	480 "
Produced and imported from 1596 to 1696........	340 "	1,670 "
Exported to Asia from 1596 to 1696.............	119 "	571 "
Consumed from 1596 to 1696	96 "	460 "
Increase during the 100 years..................	125 "	600 "
Estimated stock in Europe in 1696	225 "	1,080 "

VI. The stock of gold and silver in Europe in 1696 was estimated by Mr King as follows, in millions of pounds sterling :—

	In England.	France.	Holland.	Other nations of Europe.	Total in Europe.
Silver coin	£8.5	£18	£7	£76.5	£110
Gold coin	3	5	2	18	28
Bullion	1	1.5	1.5	4	8
Plate of laymen	4	9	1.5	31.5	46
" churches	.2	3	.1	16.7	20
Medals and rarities	.2	.9	.3	3.6	5
Gold and silver thread, wire, &c.	.4	1.4	.1	4.1	6
Do. in stock for trade	.2	.6	.3	.9	2
Total	£17.5	£39.4	£12.8	£155.3	£225

Though these are but estimates founded on very imperfect evidence, yet they were made by one of the best informed and most competent men of the age to judge with accuracy, and constitute the best evidence on the subject that is attainable. Being made by an Englishman, we have reason to believe that the estimates are sufficiently favorable to England; and yet they show England inferior in wealth to both Holland and France. What a picture they exhibit of the amount of the precious metals engrossed by the church in Catholic countries!

VII. Statement of the coinage of several countries of America during the undermentioned periods.

	1801 to 1810.		1811 to 1820.		1821 to 1830.		Annual average. 1831 to 1840.	
Mexico......	$227.24	millions.	$112.16	millions.	$99.76	millions.	$12.	millions.
Peru........	45.7	"	60.25	"	16.73	"	2.25	"
Bolivia.....	35.87	"	20.66	"	15.7	"	.7	"
Chili.......	.....	"	9.7	"	2.	"	.4	"

The foregoing table shows the rapid decline of the produce of the mines of the principal mining countries of America, during the period of their revolutionary struggle to throw off the yoke of Spain.

VIII. Statements and estimates of the amount of gold and silver produced in Europe and the principal mining countries of America, during the undermentioned periods.

	1801 to 1810.		1811 to 1830.		1831 to 1840	
Mexico..................	$227.2	millions.	$211.92	millions.	$121.7	millions.
Peru....................	45.7	"	76.98	"	22.3	"
Bolivia.................	35.8	"	36.36	"	7.	"
Chili...................	h20.	"	11.7	"	4.	"
Buenos Ayres............	h48.5	"	j30.	"	}	
Guatemala...............	....		2.89	"	} 35.	"
Brazil, estimated.......	20.	"	j20.	"	}	
Total of America....	$397.2	"	$389.85	"	$190.	"
Total of European and Russian mines & gold dust imported from Africa.	h42.8	"	h110.15	"	75.	"
Total............	$440.	"	$500.	"	$265.	"

The numbers marked *h* are stated on the authority of Baron Humboldt, and those marked *j* on the authority of Mr. Jacob.

IX. Statement of the amount of gold from the mines of California, and from all the other mines of the United States, deposited for coinage at the mints of the United States, during the undermentioned periods.

	California.	Other mines.	Total.
1824 to 1830....................	....	$715,000	$715,000
1831 to 1840....................	....	5,658,025	5,658,025
1841 to 1848....................	$44,177	7,223,856	7,268,033
1849....................	6,151,360	927,784	7,079,144
1850....................	36,273,097	665,217	36,938,314
1851 to June 30th,..............	25,748,684	309,606	26,058,290
" July 1, to Sept 30,......	11,945,613	121,251	12,066,864
Total..............	$80,162,931	$15,620,739	$95,783,670

The quantity of silver from the mines of the United States deposited for coinage in 1848 was only $6,191; in 1849, it was $39,112; and for the first four months of 1850 it amounted to $51,197; which was mostly parted from California gold.

X. There has been a great increase since 1820 in the production of gold in Asiatic Russia. The amount produced has been as follows, stated in sterling money:—

In 1819 and 1820	£175,337	In 1841 to 1845	£11,298,993
1821 to 1830	4,734,641	1846	3,527,000
1831 to 1840	9,180,891	1847	3,738,000

SEC. 5. *Consumption of Gold and Silver—Coin exported to Asia, and the amount in Europe and America, from* 1500 *to* 1840.

The wear and loss of coin has been variously estimated at from one-fourth to one-half of 1 per cent. annually. Mr. Jacob estimated it at 10 per cent in thirty-six years. My estimate is one-third of 1 per cent per annum, which is equal to about 3 per cent in ten years; 13 per cent in fifty years; and 25 per cent in one hundred years.*

I. The amount of gold and silver used in the arts for plate, gilding, watches, jewelry, and other utensils and ornaments, the amount exported to Asia, and the amount of coin remaining in Europe at different periods, were estimated by Mr. Jacob as follows:—stated in millions of pounds.

	Used in the arts.	Exported to Asia.	Coin in Europe.
In 1492	....	....	£34 millions.
1492 to 1600	£28. millions.	£14 millions.	130 "
1600 to 1700	60.2 "	33.2 "	297 "
1700 to 1810	352 "	852 "	380 "
1810 to 1830	112.2 "	40 "	312 "

The reader will see that these estimates are very different from those of Gregory King, stated in tables No. V. and VI. of the last section. On comparing the two together, and with the condition and commerce of the several countries of Europe, it appears to me that Mr. King's estimates are the best evidence we have on the subject, and are entitled to our confidence.

Mr. Jacob estimated the amount used in the arts, in Europe and America, annually, from 1810 to 1830, over and above the amount of old plate, &c., melted, equal in value to £5,612,611. Humboldt estimated it in 1804 at but 87,182,800 francs, equal to £3,459,000. McCulloch estimated the whole amount annually in 1833 as follows:—

* The loss from fire is probably nearly one-tenth of 1 per cent annually; from burying and transportation by land and water, about as much more; and from friction, more than one-tenth of 1 per cent annually.

In Great Britain and Ireland	£1,842,916
France	866,190
Switzerland	350,000
All the remainder of Europe	1,204,118
America	300,000
Total annual consumption in the arts	£4,563,224
One-fifth part derived from the fusion of old plate	912,644
New gold and silver annually used in the arts	£3,650,580

It appears to me, also, that the estimates of Mr. Jacob of the amount of coin in Europe at each period are entirely too high; and that the estimates of the quantity of gold and silver used in the arts prior to the year 1700, are too low by about half; during the eighteenth century, too high by nearly half; and too high, also, for the period from the year 1810 to 1830; and that the estimates of Humboldt and McCulloch are too low.

Humboldt estimated the coin in France in 1803 at 1,850 millions livres, or francs, equal to nearly $347,000,000, for a population which he estimated at 26,363,000; that is, seventy francs, or about $13 each. Europe then contained, according to Hassel, 182,600,000 inhabitants; of which Russia, Sweden, Norway, Denmark, and the Sclavonian and Sarmatian nations constituted more than 62,000,000. "Allowing (said he) for Great Britain and for the west and south of Europe 55 livres per individual, (or about $10⅓ each,) and for other countries less advanced in civilization 30 livres (or about $5⅔ each,) we shall find the total specie of Europe cannot exceed 8,603 million livres." Carry out the principles of his calculation, and the result is as follows:—

	Population.	Livres.	Livres.
France	26.4	at 70 each	1,850 millions.
Russia and other eastern nations	62 millions.	30 "	1,860 "
Other nations of Europe	94 "	55 "	5,170 "
Total for Europe	182,400,000		8,880 "
Equal to about			$1,665 "

II. The coin and bullion of several countries of Europe have been variously estimated at different periods, as follows:—

Great Britain by Davenant	1600	£4,000,000 sterling.
Gregory King	1696	8,500,000 "
Anderson	1762	16,000,000 "
Dr. Price	1777	15,000,000 "
Lord North	1778	18 to 19,000,000 "
Adam Smith	1786	18,000,000 "
Rose	1802	44,000,000 "
Chancellor of the Exchequer	1830	38,000,000 "
France by Law in	1716	1,200 million livres or $225 mill'ns.
Neckar	1784	2,200 " 414 "
Arnould	1791	2,000 " 376 "
Humboldt	1804	1,850 " 347 "
Spain by Musquiz	1782	80 "
Austrian Empire by Hassel	1807	80 mil'ion florins or 39 "
Prussia by Mr Krug	1804	56 " roubles or 42 "

III. Mr. Storch, (in his political economy, published in 1814,) after carefully collecting and commenting on the estimates of different authors, of the specie in the different countries of Europe, estimated the amount as follows:—

Great Britain	$90 millions.
France	420 "
Spain	80 "
Austria, exclusive of about $13,000,000 copper coin	26 "
Prussia, in 1805	42 "
Russia, exclusive of $18,000,000 copper coin	84 "
Other countries of Europe	528 "
Total of Europe	$1,220 "

We have now much more accurate statistics and ample materials for estimating the amount of specie exported to Asia during the last two centuries, and the amount in the several countries of Europe and America at different periods, than were possessed by any of the authors named. As the banks in the United States are numerous, the greater part of the specie is kept in their vaults, and the government has kept a record of the exports and imports of specie since the 30th of September, 1820, we have the means of estimating the amount of specie in the United States with greater accuracy than it can be estimated in any other country. And as the amount of circulating money needed in every country depends on the amount and value of its productive industry and commerce, the relative amount of money in circulation in different countries can be determined with a reasonable degree of accuracy.

The following table of estimates is formed partly from official estimates, and the estimates of numerous writers, and partly by comparing the condition and the amount and value of the productive industry and commerce of all the nations of Europe and America with each other, and calculating the relative amount of circulating money which each probably employs, as indicated by its condition.

IV. Estimates of the population and circulating money, including specie, bank-notes, and paper money of all kinds (over and above the depreciation of the paper money) in America and each country of Europe, and the amount to each person at the end of the year 1800.

	Millions of Inhabitants.	Millions of Circulating Money.	Am't to each person.
Great Britain	10.4 millions.	$156 millions.	$15
Ireland	4.8 "	38.4 "	8
France	27.3 "	327.6 "	12
Holland and Belgium	5.0 "	65 "	13
Spain and Portugal	13.5 "	100 "	7½
Italy	20 "	160 "	8
German Austria	13 "	78	6
German States	12 "	84 "	7
Prussia	10 "	66 "	6
Denmark, Sweden, and Norway	4.5 "	22 "	5
Russia, Hungary, Turkey, and other eastern nations of Europe	60 "	210 "	3½
Total of Europe	180.5 millions.	$1,307 millions.	..
America and West Indies	24 "	108 "	4½
Total	204 millions.	$1,415 millions.	$7

Mr. Jacob estimated the coin in Europe at the discovery of America at £34,000,000 sterling; and Mr. King estimated the whole amount of gold and silver in Europe in 1516 at £45,000,000 sterling, over two thirds of which, perhaps, was coin. (See tables V. and VI. of section 4.)

V. Estimates of the produce of the mines of Europe and America, the amount used in the arts and exported to Asia, and the amount made into and remaining in coin and bullion at different periods. (See ante, table IV. of section 4.)

Amount of coin in Europe in the year 1500	$150	millions.
Produce of the mines of America during the 16th century	680	"
Produce of the mines of Europe and imported from Africa	40	"
Total	870	"
Wear and loss of old coin, one fourth part	38	"
Exported to India, China, and other parts of Asia	200	"
Used in the arts to make into plate, watches, jewelry, gilding, images, etc., in churches, and other utensils and ornaments	240	"
Made into coin, $280,000,000—wear and loss of new coin 1-10th part	28	"
Amount to be deducted	$506	"
Specie and bullion in use in Europe and America, Dec. 31st, 1600	364	"
Produce of the American mines during the 17th century	1,466	"
Produce of the mines of Europe, and gold dust imported from Africa	70	"
Total	1,900	"
Wear and loss of the old gold, one-fourth part	91	"
Exported to Asia over £1,000,000 per annum	500	"
Used in the arts	600	"
Made into coin, $436,000,000—wear and loss of new coin, 1-10th part	43	"
Amount to be deducted	1,234	"
Specie in use, December 31, 1700	666	"
Produce of the mines of America during the 18th century	2,650	"
Produce of the mines of Europe, and gold dust from Africa, according to Jacob, less one-eighth part	366	"
Total	3,682	"
Wear and loss of old coin, one-fourth part	166	"
Exported to Asia, £2,000,000 per year	960	"
Used in the arts, over £2,500,000 per year	1,260	"
Made into coin, $796,000,000—wear and loss of new coin, 1-10th part	80	"
Amount to be deducted	2,466	"
Specie in use December 31, 1800	1,216	"
Produce of the mines of America to December, 1810, about	400	"
Produce of the mines of Europe, Siberia, and gold dust from Africa, per Humboldt and Jacob	42	"
Total	1,658	"
Wear and loss of old coin at 3 per cent	86	"
Exported to Asia, £2,500,000 per annum	120	"
Used in the arts, £3,500,000 per annum	167	"
Made into coin and bullion, 152,000,000	....	
Amount to be deducted	828	".
Specie in use December 31, 1810	1,335	"
Produce of mines of America to December, 1830	890	"
Produce of Europe, Russia, etc	110	"
Total	1,885	"

Wear and loss of old coin, 5½ per cent	73 millions.
Used in the arts, £4,000,000 per year	384 "
Exported to Asia, £2,000,000 per year	192 "
Amount to be deducted	$649 "
Specie in use, December 31, 1830	$1,186 "
Produce of mines of America to December, 1840	190 "
Produce of mines of Europe, Russia, etc	75 "
Total	1,451 "
Wear and loss of coin, 3 per cent	35 "
Used in the arts, £4,500,00 per year	216 "
None exported to Asia	
Amount to be deducted	$251 "
Specie in use, December 31, 1840	$1,200 "

All the accounts and estimates seem to agree, that most of the American mines were growing less and less productive, and the total supply of the precious metals much less annually from 1820 to 1840, than it was half a century since, while the population of Europe and America, and the wants of the commercial world, as well as the world of fashion, were rapidly increasing.

Since 1840 there has been a great increase in the production of the gold mines of Russia; which, together with the amount of gold procured during the years 1848, 1849 and 1850, from the mines and sands of California, and the prospect of an immense increase from the latter source, renders it probable that the production of the precious metals may, for some years to come, equal, and perhaps exceed, the consumption and the increase of population in the civilized world.

It should be remarked, that prior to the nineteenth century, and, to some extent, also, as late as 1816, large quantities of cotton and silk goods were imported from India into Europe and America, and large sums of coin exported to India in payment, as well as to China and the East India islands, to pay for tea, spices, &c. M. Humboldt estimated that at the commencement of the present century, more than half the product of the American mines, (over twenty-five millions of dollars annually of gold and silver) were exported to Asia. Since the machinery of Great Britain, and the prodigious increase in the manufactures of that country, have driven the cotton goods of India not only out of the markets of Europe and America, but to a considerable extent out of their own markets, and pretty much ruined and broken them down; and the British have also battered down the barrier which excluded the products of Europe and America (except specie) from the markets of China, the drain of the precious metals to China, India, and all Asia, has ceased, or nearly so. It appears from the reports of the Secretary of the Treasury of the United States, that the balance of gold and silver exported to China and other parts of Asia, over and above the amount imported from them, have been as follows:—During the year ending Sept. 30, 1835, it amounted to $1,995,140; in 1842 it amounted to $837,094; in 1844, to $574,000; and in 1845 to only $239,874. The exports of the manufactures of Great Britain to China, as well as India and Turkey, have been so great since 1830, that very little specie has been exported from Europe to Asia; and for ever hereafter we may expect the balance to be the other way, and that specie will be exported from China and other parts of Asia to Europe.

Let us compare the population of Europe and America at several different periods with the estimated amount of coin at those periods, in order to see how their increase compares with each other; this will enable us to judge of the probable effect of the increase or decrease of coin upon the prices of commodities in the commercial world.

Estimates of the population of Europe and America (exclusive of wandering Indians) at different periods; also the amount of coin and bullion in use, and the amount to each person.

Years.	Population of Europe.	Population of America.	Total population.	Total specie.	Am't to each person.
1500........	100 millions.	....	100 millions.	$150 millions.	$1 50
1600........	114 "	6 millions.	120 "	364 "	3 00
1700........	134 "	12 "	146 "	666 "	4 50
1800........	180 "	24 "	204 "	1,216 "	6 00
1810........	195 "	28 "	223 "	1,335 "	6 00
1830........	224 "	39 "	263 "	1,186 "	4 50
1840........	240 "	46 "	286 "	1,200 "	4 20

SEC. 6. *Origin and progress of banking, and the amount of paper money in Europe and America, at different periods.*

The Bank of Venice was the first banking establishment in Europe. It was founded in 1171, and subsisted till the subversion of the republic in 1797. It was a deposit bank only, and issued no notes.

The bank of Amsterdam was established in the year 1609, and that of Hamburg in 1619; they were deposit banks only, and issued no notes.

The Bank of England was incorporated in the year 1694, and was the first bank which ever issued notes, or bills to circulate as money, in the ordinary transactions of trade and commerce. The Bank of Scotland was established in 1695, with a capital of but £100,000, which was raised to £200,000 sterling in the year 1744, and in 1804 to £1,500,000. The original capital of the Bank of England was but £1,200,000 sterling, consisting of a loan of that amount to the government. These two were the only banks (if we except some private companies and bankers in London) that ever issued notes for a circulating medium, or money, and as a substitute for coin, prior to the eighteenth century; and the credit of the notes of the Bank of England was at first so poor, that the bank became involved in difficulties in 1696, and was compelled to suspend payment of its notes in coin, and the notes fell in value, and passed at a heavy discount. The amount in circulation February 28th, 1700, was but £938,240, and in August of the same year only £781,430.

The circulating medium of the commercial world was scarcely increased at all by bank notes, or paper money in any shape, in the year 1700, at the commencement of the eighteenth century, and the whole amount of coin and bullion then in use in Europe and America was probably less than $700,000,000.

The eighteenth and the nineteenth centuries have been *fruitful in all sorts of schemes and projects of a financial character, to make credit, and too often the credit of bankrupts, spendthrifts, knaves, and visionary speculators, a substitute for coin.* One of the first, greatest, and most ruinous, was the great Mississippi scheme, got up at Paris, by John Law, the forepart of the eighteenth century. After this great bubble burst, France confined herself to a specie currency until after the issue of the government assignats, during the French revolution, and no bank for issuing notes was established in France, until the bank of France, in 1803; to which was granted the exclusive privilege of issuing notes for a period of forty years. Mr. Jacob estimated the circulation of the Bank of France in 1810 at but two millions sterling; and in 1830 at nine million pounds sterling. This bank was slow in acquiring the public confidence, so as to get much circulation for its own notes.

The Netherlands had no money but coin until the establishment of the Bank of the Netherlands in the year 1814, with a capital of 5,000,000 florins, and the exclusive privilege of issuing notes for twenty-five years. Mr. Jacob says its circulating notes then, (1830,) were not supposed to exceed one million sterling.

Banks have also been established at St. Petersburg, Vienna, Berlin, and Copenhagen, besides numerous other banks in the British dominions, and in the United States of America.

Mr. Jacob remarks that Russia was then (1830) the only country of Europe which had not returned to specie payments. When bank notes were first issued, and the quantity small, the rouble was worth about three shillings and four pence sterling, or seventy-five cents, and was of the same value as the Russian silver coin of that name. The increased quantity gradually depreciated the metallic value of the paper, till one silver rouble was worth four of paper. It had nearly attained this low value in 1810, when the paper roubles amounted to 577,000,000. It was nearly the same, but of somewhat greater value in 1830, though the amount had increased to 639,000,000 roubles. He estimates their exchangeable value, in 1810, as equal to 23,000,000 pounds sterling, and in 1830 to £25,250,000.

The first issue of paper-money in Russia consisted of 40,000,000 roubles of assignats in 1769 ; the second consisted of 60,000,000 roubles in 1787. The silver rouble is equal to about seventy-five cents.

I. The amount of assignats in circulation in Russia, and the per cent of depreciation at different periods, is stated by Storch as follows :—

Years.	Circulation.	Per cent discount.	Years.	Circulation.	Per cent discount.
1790........	111 million roubles.	13	1805........	292 million roubles.	23
1795........	150 " "	31⅓	1810........	577 " "	66⅔
1800........	212 " "	35	1814........	577 " "	75

Mr. Jacob states that the paper-money of Austria had increased, prior to 1810, to 1,060,000,000 of florins, and had at one time so depreciated, that a silver florin would purchase ten or twelve paper florins, and that they were worth in 1810 only about one-fifth part of their nominal value. Calling their nominal value about two shillings sterling, and their real exchangeable value in 1810 one-fifth part as much, he estimated their total exchangeable value in 1810 at 21,000,000 pounds sterling. About the year 1825 they were redeemed at two-fifths their nominal value, and specie payments resumed, and he estimated the amount of paper in circulation in 1830 at 100,000,000 florins, equal to £10,000,000 sterling.

He says the notes of the Bank of England in circulation in 1810 amounted to about £24,000,000 sterling, and estimated the notes of the private and joint stock banks, and the other banks of Great Britain and Ireland at the same amount—that is, at £48,000,000 in all. The tables in Brande's Encyclopædia of Science and Art, title bank, show that the circulating notes of the bank of England in 1810 amounted to £21,019,600, and the coin and bullion in the bank £3,501,410 ; excess of circulation over coin and bullion, £17,518,190 ; and that in 1830 the circulation was £20,050,730, the coin and bullion £9,171,000, and the excess of notes in circulation but £11,559,730.

The country bank-notes of England and Wales in circulation in 1810 are estimated in the Commercial Dictionary at £23,893,868 ; in 1833 they were reduced to £10,152,104. The notes of the Bank of Ireland in circulation in 1810 are stated at $3,170,064, and in 1832 at £3,975,322.

After the suspension of specie payments by the Bank of England in 1797, the excessive issue of bank-notes occasioned their decline in value ; and their depreciation in 1810 was nearly 13 per cent, and in 1814 over 25 per cent. The basis of the private and joint stock banks relied upon to redeem their notes, was not specie nor bullion, but notes of the Bank of England; so that nearly the whole amount of their circulation was an addition of so much to the money or circulating medium of the country.

As the Bank of Russia, and also that of Austria, were both in a state of suspension in 1810, and the former also in 1830, they probably had very little specie or bullion to redeem with, and I shall estimate the same at but ten per cent. M. Jacob remarks that in the smaller states of Germany, in Italy, (except that part of it which is under the dominion of Austria,) and in Spain, and Switzerland, the currency has been invariably metallic; and in Denmark, Norway, and Sweden, a paper currency existed in 1810, and still circulated; but the whole amount, as well as the variations in those countries, has been so small, that they affect, in a very trifling degree, the view here taken.

There was no bank in the United States until the Bank of North America was established in Philadelphia in 1781. The first banking association formed in the State of New York was a joint stock company organized in the year 1784, under articles of association, under which it did business as a bank nearly seven years, when it was incorporated in March, 1791, by the name of the Bank of New York. In 1792 the Bank of Albany was chartered, and in 1793 the Bank of Columbia. No other banks were chartered by the State of New York until the year 1800, when the Manhattan Company was incorporated. The first United States Bank was established in 1791; after the year 1800, banks began to increase in all parts of the United States; and we have pretty accurate information of the amount of banking capital and of bank notes in circulation at different periods, from December, 1810, to the present time.

There is much less positive evidence of the amount of paper-money in circulation in Europe and America in the year 1800, than in the year 1810, and since that time. The circulation of the Bank of England in August, 1800, was less than £15,000,000 sterling, but was nearly £24,500,000 in August, 1810. Though the United States were flooded with what was called continental money during our Revolutionary War, and some of the New England colonies issued great quantities of paper-money before the war, yet from the close of the war until after the year 1800, we had comparatively little paper-money in our country. Paper-money was increased immensely in many countries of Europe between the years 1800 and 1810, and there was probably nearly twice as much in circulation at the latter, as at the former period.

II. Estimates in millions of pounds sterling, (taken mostly from Jacob's inquiry,) of the exchangeable value of the paper circulation of Europe and America in 1810 and 1830, the depreciation, (from which the nominal amount may be calculated,) the amount of specie and bullion in the vaults of the banks, and the increase of the circulating medium by the means of bank notes:—

		Depreciation, per cent.	Exchangeable value of bank-notes in circulation.	Bullion and specie in the banks.	Excess of bank notes over specie and bullion.
Bank of England....	1810	14	18	3.5	14.5
" ...	1830	par	20	9.17	10.9
Private and joint st'ck banks in..........	1810	14	20	1.5	18.5
Do	1833	par	10	2 15	8
Banks of Ireland....	1810	14	2.7	.5	2.2
do	1830	par	5	2.	3
Banks of Scotland....	1810	14	3	.6	2.4
do	1830	par	3 5	1.4	2.1
Bank of France......	1810	par	2	.8	1.2
do	1830	par	9	3.5	5.5
Bank of Russia......	1810	72	23	2.3	20 7
do	1830	75	25.2	2.5	22.7
Bank of Austria.....	1810	80	21	2	19
do	1830	par	10	3.5	6.5
Holland in	1810	..	..	..	..
do	1830	par	1	.4	.6
Portugal	1810	30	1.4	.2	1.2
do	1830	..	2	.5	1 5
Prussia..............	1810	..	..	..	..
do	1830	par	2	.7	1 3
United States........	1810	par	5.8	3 2	2,6
do	1829	par	12.8	4.6	8.2
Total........	1810		£97	£14.6	£82.4
"	1830		100.5	30.3	70 2
"	1800			estimated at £46	

III. Statement of the circulation of bank notes in the United Kingdom of Great Britain and Ireland at different periods, in millions of pounds sterling.

	December. 1842.	December. 1845.	December. 1848.	December 1849.
Bank of England.....	£19.5 millions.	£20.2 millions.	£16.9 millions.	£17 9 millions.
Private banks, Engl'nd	5.0 "	4.5 "	3.5 "	3.5 "
Joint-stock banks...	3.0 "	3.1 "	2 5 "	2.6 "
Banks in Scotland....	3.0 "	3.3 "	3 3 "	3.2 "
Banks in Ireland.....	5 2 "	7.4 "	4.8 "	4.7 "
Tot., United Kingdom	£35.7 "	£38.5 "	£31.0 "	£31 9 "

Mr. McCulloch estimated the amount of coin in circulation in the United Kingdom of Great Britain and Ireland in 1833 at £30,000,000 sterling; but when we reflect that they have a large bank-note circulation, and that nearly all the merchants keep their deposits in, and do their their business through banks, I doubt if the average circulation of coin during the last twenty years has exceeded £20,000,000, and have estimated it at that sum. The notes of the Bank of England constitute the principal means of all the other banks and bankers of the kingdom, with which to redeem their notes; and hence they are used as a substitute for coin to the amount of perhaps £6,000,000, which should not be treated as any portion of the circulation of the country. This amount should therefore be deducted from the gross circulation of England, and the deduction is made in the following table. The average circulation of bank-notes in the United Kingdom from 1833 to 1840 was about the same as from 1841 to 1849.

IV. Statement of the average circulation of coin and bank-notes among the people, from 1841 to 1849, and the amount to each person, after deducting £6,000,000 sterling, Bank of England notes supposed to be held by other banks.

	Bank notes.	Coin.	Total.	Each person
England and Wales.......	£21 millions.	£14 millions.	£35 millions.	$$10\frac{1}{4}$
Scotland....	$3\frac{1}{8}$ "	$2\frac{1}{4}$ "	$5\frac{3}{8}$ "	$9\frac{1}{2}$
Ireland	$5\frac{1}{2}$ "	$3\frac{3}{4}$ "	$9\frac{1}{4}$ "	5

The circulation of the Bank of France ordinarily fluctuates from 210 to 240,000,000 francs :—

Its circulation in July, 1830, was about..................................	$43,200,000
In October, 1839, it was..	39,937,000
" 1845, it was..	48,589,000

It is most probable that the amount of paper-money in Europe and America was very nearly the same in 1840, and but little more in 1845 than it was in 1830.

Sec. 7. *Banking capital, coin, and paper money in the U. States from* 1810 *to* 1849—*Exports and imports of coin.*

I. Estimate of Mr. Gallatin of the capital, notes in circulation, and specie in the banks of the United States at the end of the year 1829.

	Capital.	Notes.	Specie.
281 banks, ascertained........	$95 millions.	$39.2 millions.	$12 millions.
48 banks, estimated.........	15.2 "	9.1 "	2.9 "
United States Bank..........	35 "	13.0 "	7.2 "
Total.................	$145.2 "	$61.3 "	$22.1 "

It is obvious that if the capital of the forty-eight banks is properly estimated, the notes in circulation are estimated too high, by more than $2,000,000, and the specie in them too high by about $1,000,000, to correspond with the 281 banks, whose condition was ascertained. I shall, therefore, reduce the estimate, to make all the parts correspond, and shall call the circulation but $59,000,000, and the specie $21,000,000.

Mr. Gallatin estimated the amount of specie in the banks of the United States at the end of each year as follows: of 1810 at $15,400,000; of 1814, at $17,000,000; of 1815 at $19,000,000; and of 1819, at $19,800,000.

The commercial records of the exports and imports of the precious metals, show that the amount in the country, from 1824 to 1828, must have been about $9,000,000 less than it was in 1820; and about $5,000,000 less in January, 1830, than it was in 1820. We cannot reasonably assume that the amount of coin in circulation in January, 1830, was less than $4,000,000, which, taking the exports and imports of specie into consideration, and Mr. Gallatin's estimate of the amount in the banks, would make the amount in circulation in 1820 over $10,000,000, and may be illustrated as follows, (the amount brought in by immigrants, not entered at the custom-house, being estimated at from $10 to $20 each, on an average:—)

Estimated amount of coin and bullion in the United States, October 1, 1820		$30 millions
Imported in four years to September 30, 1824		24.9 "
Estimated amount brought in by immigrants		2 "
Total imports and supply		$56.9 "
Exported during the same four years	$34.67 millions.	
Estimated amount used in the arts and made into plate, utensils, jewelry, and other ornaments, over and above old metal used and the produce of our own mines.	1.23 "	
Total export and consumption		35.9 "
Leaving in the United States but		$21 "
October 1st, 1824, when the tariff of 1824 took effect:—		
Imported in four years, to September 30th, 1828		$28.67 "
Estimated amount brought in by immigrants		2 "
Total imports and supply		$51.67 "
Exported during the same four years	$29.4 millions.	
Estimated amount used in the arts	1.27 "	
Total export and consumption		30.67 "
Leaving in the United States only		$21 "
October 1st, 1828, when the tariff of 1828 went into operation:—		
Imported in six years, to September 30th, 1834		$53.75 "
Amount brought in by immigrants, estimated at		4 "
Total imports and supply		$78.75 "
Exported during the same six years	$26.46 millions.	
Used in the arts	2.29 "	
		28.75 "
Leaving in the United States		$50 "
October 1st, 1834, soon after the free trade compromise act of March, 1833, made the first reduction of duties on foreign manufactures:—		
Imported in three years, to September 30th, 1837		$87 "
Estimated amount brought in by immigrants		2 "
Total imports and supply		$89 "
Exported during the same three years	$16.78 millions.	
Amount used in the arts, over and above product of our mines during this extravagant period of speculation	9.22 "	
		26 "
Leaving in the United States		$63 "

October 1st, 1837, when nearly all the banks in the nation were in a state of suspension.

As the imaginary wealth of the people of the United States was greatly increased during the speculative period from 1834 to 1837, by the multiplication and expansion of the banks, the increase of paper-money, and the increase of prices, which was the necessary consequence; the extravagance of the people, and the increase of gold and silver made into plate, watches, chains, and other ornaments and utensils, was also immensely increased.

The value of the products of the precious metals manufactured in the United States in 1839, according to the returns of the census, amounted to $4,734,960; which must have consumed an amount of gold and silver exceeding $3,000,000.

The products of our gold mines in 1839 amounted to only $529,605; and the amount of silver was so small that it was not returned separately from other metals. The amount used in the arts for ten years, from 1837 to 1847, over and above the products of our mines, and the old gold and silver worked over, probably amounted to over $2,000,000 per annum.

Estimated amount of specie and bullion in the United States, October 1, 1837, brought forward		$63	millions
Imported in one year, to September 30, 1838		17.75	"
Amount brought in by immigrants, estimated at		.50	"
Total supply,		$81.25	"
Exported during the year	3.5 millions.		
Used in the arts	1.75 "	5.25	"
Leaving in the United States, October 1st, 1838		$76.	"
Imported in four years, to September 30, 1842		23.55	"
Amount brought in by immigrants, estimated at		2.45	"
Total supply,		$102	"
Exported during the same four years	$32.3 millions.		
Used in the arts, estimated at	7.7 "	40	"
Leaving in the United States		$62	"
October 1, 1842, when the tariff of 1842 went into operation.			
Specie imported in three and three-quarter years to June 30, 1846, under the tariff of 1842		$36	"
Estimated amount brought in by immigrants		5	"
Total supply,		$103	"
Specie exported during the same period	$10.5 millions.		
Used in the arts and loss by friction, etc., estimated at	8.5 "	28	
Leaving in the United States, June 30, 1847		$75	"
Specie imported during the year ending June 30th, 1847, in consequence of the short crops in Europe and the great demand for our flour and grain		24.1	"
Amount brought in by immigrants, estimated at		1.4	"
Total supply,		$100.5	"

Brought forward,		$100.5 millions.
Specie exported during the same year............	$2.5 millions.	
Specie expended abroad by the navy, and by the army in Mexico, estimated at..................	4 "	
Used in the arts and lost by friction, etc...........	3 "	9 5
Leaving in the United States, June 30, 1847, and over $80 millions on the 1st of December, 1846, when the tariff of 1846 took effect.		$91.0
Specie imported in four years to June 30, 1851........................		$22.6 "
Amount brought to our mints from California.........................		68.2
Estimated amount brought by immigrants............................		7.2 "
Total supply, - - - - - - - - - - - - - -		$189.0 "
Specie exported during the same period...........	$58 millions.	
Used in the arts, and lost..........................	14 "	
Expended abroad by the army and navy..........	3 "	
		75 "
Leaving in the United States on the 30 June, 1851 - -		$114 "

The greatest part of the specie imported into the United States, comes from Mexico and South America—while that exported, mostly goes to the Old World. The reader will see from a comparison of the exports with the imports of specie, that the principal part of the produce of the mines of California goes to Europe.

There is much reason to believe that there never was more specie in the United States, in proportion to the population, than there was during the general suspension of specie payments by the banks, from May, 1837, to May, 1838; and consequently the suspension could not have been caused by the small amount of specie, but by the excessive amount of paper money, the wild and extravagant spirit of speculation, the excessive imports of foreign goods, (which served to paralyze the industry of the country) and the rapid accumulation of a foreign debt; all of which causes contributed to alarm capitalists, bankers, and business men; to destroy confidence and credit; to depress property, and to derange business.

While the several States were making loans, and selling their bonds in Europe, and to the agents of European capitalists in America, from 1833 to 1838, in order to establish banks, make canals, railroads, and other improvements, and were increasing their debts in Europe about $100,000,000, the specie of the United States was increased, by means of importations, about $26,000,000, and the balance of the loans was imported in the shape of European manufactures. After our debts became so large that European capitalists became alarmed, and would not loan us any more money, nor buy our State stocks and bonds at scarcely any price less than a discount of from 20 to 80 per cent., the merchants and foreign manufacturers still continued to glut our markets with foreign goods; and during four years, under the operations of the free trade compromise act of 1833, they drained the United States of specie, and reduced the quantity in the country from $76,000,000, October 1st, 1838, to $62,000,000, October 1st, 1842. From October 9th, 1839, when the most of our banks suspended specie payments the second time, to the passage of the tariff act in August, 1842, was one of the most gloomy periods in the history of our country; about as gloomy as the six years next prior to the passage of the tariff act of 1824, immediately after the heavy importations of 1815, 1816 and 1817, and exceeded only by the general embarrassment, depression, prostration, and suffering of the country, during the period from 1784 to 1789, after the heavy importations of foreign goods at the close of our Revolutionary War, when the country enjoyed, to the fullest extent, that *glorious system of free-trade* which the *nullifiers* have long been sighing after.

While the tariff act of 1842 was in operation, (from October 1st, 1842, to November 30th, 1846,) it operated to check and lessen the importation of foreign goods, to secure the home-market, to a considerable degree, to the laborers and producers of our own country, and to increase the industry of the nation. The balance of trade was in our favor, a part of which was applied to the payment of the interest and principal of our large foreign debt, and a part paid to us in specie; the specie of the country increased about $18,000,000; and, at the end of that period, our commerce, finances, banks, mining, manufacturing, and agricultural industry, were in a very flourishing condition.

II. Statement in millions of dollars, of the capital and gross circulation of the banks of the United States, and the specie in them, at the time of their reports, the nearest to the 31st of December of each of the undermentioned years; also, estimates, in accordance with the bank reports and the foregoing calculation, of the coin in circulation, the whole circulation of coin and bank-notes, the population, and the average circulation to each person at each period.*

	1810.	1814.	1815.	1819.	1824.	1829.
Capital, in millions....	$52.6	$82.5	$89.8	$137	..	$145.2
Bank-notes issued ....*	28.1	45.5	68	44.8	..	59
Specie in banks ......*	15.4	17	19	19.8	$18	21
" circulation..	15	11	8	10.2	3	4
Total circulation......	43.1	56.5	76	55	50	63
Population, (millions).	7 3	8.3	8.4	9.6	11	12.6
Dollars to each person.	6	6¼	9	5¼	4½	5
	1833.	**1836.**	**1842.**	**1845.**	**1846.**	**1849.**
Capital in millions....	$200	$290¼	$234	$202	2207	$218
Bank-notes issued....	94.8	149.1	66	108½	112	132
Specie in bank.......	..	37.9	35.4	43	38	45.4
" circulation.	15	22	26.6	32	42	34
Total circulation.....	110	171	92.6	142½	154	166
Population (millions).	14	15¼	18.3	20	20¼	22½
Dollars to each person.	7¾	11	5	7⅛	7⅔	7⅓

* A portion of the amount of bank-notes in circulation, and specie in the banks at the end of the years 1810, 1814, 1815, 1819, and 1829, are estimates of Mr. Gallatin, which have been generally adopted and contained in our official reports since 1831. The whole column for 1824 are estimates of mine.

Our foreign commerce has not only affected the specie in our country, but it has had a general influence also upon the circulation of our banks. Prior to the acquisition of California in 1848, the production of gold and silver annually by our mines, was but little over half a million of dollars. About $2,000,000 more than the products of our mines were needed annually to satisfy the pride of the people, and supply them with utensils and ornaments; and to keep pace with the increase of our population, requires an increase of coin of $2,500,000 annually; so that we needed about $5,000,000 annually to supply the wants of the country, and have a sufficient specie basis to sustain our banks, and maintain the credit of our paper currency. The amount of specie in the United States is so exceedingly small, in proportion to the population and commercial wants of the country, that large importations of foreign goods, and an exportation of specie to the amount of $4,000,000 or $5,000,000 a year, for two or three years in succession, will inevitably weaken the banks very much, produce a panic, and a run upon many of them, and cause many failures, if not a general suspension of specie payments. This is verified by the commercial revulsion from 1837 to 1842. In May, 1837, nearly all the banks in the United States suspended specie payments; during the year ending September 30th, 1838, our imports amounted to but $108,486,616, including $17,747,116 specie, and but little over $90,000,000 in merchandise and foreign products; our exports the same year amounted to $113,717,404, including but $3,508,046 in specie—that is, we exported exclusive of specie, over $110,000,000 in amount, and imported but little over $90,000,000; paid off several millions of debts, and got a balance of over $14,000,000 specie to sustain our banks. This enabled nearly all the banks in the old States, and many in the new ones, to resume specie payments during the spring and summer of the year 1838, and to go on for some time prosperously; but the free-trade compromise act again invited large importations of foreign goods, amounting during the year ending September 30th, 1839, to $162,092,132, including only $5,595,176 in specie; while our exports were but $112,251,673, exclusive of specie to the amount of $8,776,743; showing a nominal balance of trade against us that year of about $44,000,000; a drain of over $3,000,000 of specie from the country, and a large increase of our foreign debt.

This large balance of trade against us and drain of specie, occasioned a second suspension of specie payments on the 9th of October, 1839, by Mr. Biddle's United States Bank of Pennsylvania, which was soon after followed by nearly all the banks south and west of the State of New York. No other country ever felt so quickly and sensibly, and suffered so severely, the disastrous effects of excessive importations of foreign goods, and an unfavorable balance of trade; for no other country ever had so small an amount of specie in proportion to the extent of their commerce; and in no other country was the credit system ever carried to so great an extent, upon a foundation so slight and frail.

The amount of specie in the United States, October 1st, 1839, being about $73,000,000, and October 1st, 1842, but $62,000,000, in round numbers; the quantity in the banks $45,000,000, in 1839, and but $33,545,000, December, 1842, averaging about $39,000,000, left in circulation, including what was hoarded up and withdrawn from use, from $28,000,000 to $29,000,000.

When specie is exported, it is withdrawn entirely from the vaults of the banks in the commercial cities, and they draw the specie from the banks of the country and the interior cities, and the amount in circulation is scarcely affected at all. Export two years in succession to pay for foreign goods, $5,000,000 each year more specie than is imported, accompanied by a great increase of debt by means of heavy importations, these $10,000,000 being withdrawn from the banks, reduces their specie to about $30,000,000, and this, of itself, will often produce a panic and a run upon the banks, and cause a draw upon them of $5,000,000 or $10,000,000 more, and thereby occasion a failure of many of them, and perhaps a general suspension of specie payments. The suspension of October, 1839, was occasioned by the exportation of specie, and the heavy importations of goods the previous year, though the balance of specie exported was but little over $3,000,000; and the suspension of May, 1837, was in consequence of the immense importation of foreign goods; the rapid accumulation of a heavy foreign debt, and the anticipation of large exportations of specie to pay it; the great expansion of the banks, and their heavy loans to speculators who could not pay. All these things contributed to create a panic, and induce a withdrawal of deposits, and a run upon the banks, and soon led to a general suspension of specie payments in self defence, and before the anticipated exportation of specie to pay our foreign debt had commenced.*

SEC. 8. *Money to each person in the United States, and in each country of Europe.*

I. Statement of the amount of bank-notes issued to each inhabitant, and the estimated amount of coin and bank-notes in circula-

* As long as the free trade tariff of 1846 continues in force, nearly all the products of our mines of California (like those of Mexico and South America,) will be exported to Great Britain and France; and those nations will derive the principal benefit of them.

tion, in each of the following divisions of the United States, at the date of their reports nearest to the last day of December of each of the undermentioned years.

	1836. Bank notes.	1842. B'k-n'ts.	1842. Coin and B'k-n'ts.	1845. B'k-n'ts.	1845. Coin and B'k-n'ts	1849. B'k-n'ts.
Maine, New Hampshire, and Vermont,	\$5½	\$2⅔	\$4	\$4	\$5½	\$5
Massachusetts, Rhode Island, and Connecticut	15⅔	9⅝	11	18	19½	16
New York, New Jersey, and Pennsylvania	12	4⅛	5⅝	6¾	8½	7
Ohio, and other North-Western States, including Iowa	5⅜	1⅞	3¼	2	3½	2⅞
Delaware, Maryland, Dist. of Columbia Virginia, and North Carolina	6⅞	3⅜	4⅞	5⅜	7	6
Kentucky, Tennessee, and Missouri	4⅜	2⅓	4	5	6¼	5
Slave States south of 35° of latitude	14¾	4⅙	5½	4	6¾	5¼
United States	9½	3⅝	5	5⅜	7⅛	5⅞

For some months, annually, after harvest, including the fall and forepart of the winter, the bank-notes of the commercial and manufacturing States are sent into the agricultural States to pay for agricultural products; and during that portion of the year, the circulating money of the agricultural States is greater than is indicated in the above table; but the merchants soon collect the greater portion of it and send it to the commercial cities to pay for goods; so that during half or more of the year, it is much less, and perhaps did not average more than is above stated, during the years referred to.

Bank paper being a cheaper currency than coin, its natural tendency is to displace coin, and induce its exportation and consumption in the arts. The balance of trade being generally in favor of manufacturing and commercial, and against agricultural States, the tendencies of trade are to drain the latter of their coin, and to transfer it to the former. The products of manufacturing labor, when sold in the markets of the commercial world, amount to about twice as much as those of agricultural labor employed in either cold or temperate climates; but not so when the latter is employed in the culture of cotton, sugar, coffee, and other tropical products, in a soil and climate adapted to them. Labor employed in mining and manufacturing in Great Britain, or in the United States, is more than twice as productive as agricultural labor can be made in Ohio and the North-western States. In fact, the average income of the people of the manufacturing States of Massachusetts and Rhode Island, and of Great Britain, is more than twice as great as that of the agricultural State of Ohio, and nearly twice as great as that of the agricultural State of Vermont.

A majority of mankind are inclined to spend all they can earn, and all they can get credit for, and as the wants of agricultural communities are generally greater than their incomes, they often buy more than they can pay for with their crops within the year; and hence agricultural countries are usually involved in debt; the balance of trade is almost universally against them; and this drains them of the precious metals, and tends to depress their industry and the price of their products still more. Poverty, and nothing but poverty, a want of ability to pay promptly, and a loss or diminution of credit, tends to check importations, and to restore the balance of trade, by lessening the demand for, and the price of goods, and the inducement to import them.

As long as the balance of trade is against a country, it must either export its specie to pay such balance, or buy on credit, accumulate a debt, and eventually be drained of its specie to pay interest, as well as the principal of the debt. Bank-notes may, for a time, supply the place of coin, and thus afford a temporary remedy; but in the end, they aggravate the evil. By inflating the currency in some instances, and in others keeping it full, they keep up, and often raise the price of both domestic and foreign products, and thereby tend to prevent the exportation of domestic products; to encourage importations; to increase both the quantity and value of goods imported, and exports of specie to pay for them; and to diminish the industry of the country by depriving its own citizens of the benefit of its markets for their products. The necessary consequence is, a run upon the banks for coin, a great diminution in their circulation, many failures of banks, and numerous bankruptcies among the people, attended with a depression of property and industry, and wide-spread embarrassment throughout the country. Such a revulsion necessarily checks importations for a time, and as exportation goes on as usual, the balance of trade is eventually turned in its favor; specie again flows in, and the country partially recovers from its embarrassments.

Any measures which tend to increase the productive industry of a country, by securing its markets to its own laborers and producers, tend also to increase its wealth and domestic commerce; to lessen its imports of such articles as are, or may be produced at home; to turn the balance of trade in its favor; and to attract to it, and retain, a large amount of the precious metals as a necessary means of carrying on its domestic commerce. Hence every country, taking a long series of years together, attracts and retains an amount of the precious metals, and maintains an amount of money in circulation, just in proportion to its condition, and the value of its productive industry and commerce; and hence you can readily deduce the amount of its productive industry and commerce from the average amount of its circulating money: and *vice versa*. Compare the average circulation of Massachusetts, Rhode Island, and Connecticut, from 1836 to 1850, with that of Ohio and the other North-western States, or even with that of Maine, New Hampshire, and Vermont, and the reader will have a complete illustration of this truth.

This is the principle upon which Gregory King in 1696, and Humboldt in 1804, estimated the amount of money in circulation in each of the countries of Europe; and this is the principle upon which many of the estimates in the following table are formed. As nations are now accustomed to keep records of their foreign commerce, and as the record evidence of the circulation of paper-money in the United States, Great Britain, Ireland, and other countries, is nearly perfect, these records furnish data for an estimate approximating to accuracy, of the amount of circulating money in every country of Europe, such as was not possessed by Humboldt when he wrote, nor by any author before his time.

II. Estimates founded partly on official estimates and records, of the population and circulating money, including coin and bank notes, in each country of Europe and America, and the amount to each person, at the end of the year 1840.

	Population.	Circulating money.	Amount to each person.
Great Britain	18.2 millions.	$192 millions.	$10½
Ireland	8.2 "	44 "	5½
France	34 "	272 "	8
Holland and Belgium	7.5 "	67.5 "	9
Spain and Portugal	15.8 "	79 "	5
Italy (including Lombardy)	22.5 "	123.5 "	5½
German Austria	15 "	60 "	4
German States	15 "	75 "	5
Switzerland	2.2 "	11 "	5
Prussia	14.6 "	65 "	4½
Denmark, Sweden, and Norway	6.1 "	24 "	4
Turkey and Greece	10 5 "	22 "	2⅛
Russia, Hungary, and other Eastern Nations of Europe	70.4 "	211 "	3
Total of Europe	240.0 "	$1,246 "	..
United States	17.3 "	138 "	8
West India Islands	3.0 "	30 "	10
British N. American Provinces	2.0 "	8 "	4
Brazil	6.4 "	38 "	6
Mexico, and all Spanish American nations	17.3 "	53 "	3
Total of Europe & America	286 "	$1,513 "	$5½

III. Statement of the result of the foregoing facts and estimates of the amount of coin and paper-money in circulation in Europe and America, and the average amount to each person at different periods from A. D. 1500 to 1840.

Years.	Coin.	Paper-money.*	Total.	Amount to each person.
1500............	$150 millions.	——	$150 millions.	$1 50
1600............	364 "	——	364 "	3.00
1700............	666 "	$5 millions.	671 "	4.50
1800............	1,216 "	220 "	1,436 "	7.00
1810............	1,335 "	395 "	1,730 "	7.75
1830............	1,186 "	336 "	1,522 "	5 85
1840............	1,200 "	313 "	1,513 "	5.30

As there was a vast amount of paper-money in circulation from 1805 to 1815 in several countries of continental Europe, as well as in Great Britain and the United States, which was really depreciated from 10 to 50 per cent. below specie, and yet passed nominally at par in the purchase of merchandise and other property, we may treat the circulation of paper-money in 1810 as equal, in the common transactions of trade, to $450,000,000, and the whole circulation as equal, nominally, to $8 to each person. Here we can see a good cause for a great decline of the prices of manufactured goods since 1810, independent of the less amount of labor required to produce them.

The largest amount of money, including bank-notes and coin, in proportion to the population, which ever existed in the civilized world, or probably ever will exist, was during the existence of the bloated paper currency in Great Britain, Russia, and Austria, from 1805 to 1815; when half of Europe seemed deluded with the idea that mere promises to pay were as good as payment itself; and they sought to aid themselves with their miserable paper currency to conquer Napoleon. The paper, however, rapidly depreciated from 10 to 80 per cent., in proportion to the excess put in circulation beyond the commercial wants of those countries respectively, and their ability to redeem it in coin; and their golden and delusive dreams were soon dissipated. Nothing less than the frosts of a Russian winter gave the first check to the increasing and colossal power of Napoleon.

SEC. 9. *Depreciation of Paper Money, Failures of Banks, losses and evils resulting, and remedies suggested.*

The invention of paper-money seems to have been made by the English, the latter part of the seventeenth century, and first carried into effect by means of the Bank of England. It gained but little credit for many years; but such has been the mistaken confidence and delusion of the public in many countries on this

* That is, the excess of paper money over and above the amount of coin and bullion in the banks.

subject, at several periods, that it has served to stimulate a wild spirit of gambling speculation, and has probably done more to foster reckless extravagance, fraud, and knavery, and to promote dishonesty and corruption in business, during the past century, than all other causes combined. Nearly $2,000,000,000 must have been lost by the holders of paper-money during the last century and a half.

A great Real Estate Bank was got up at Paris by John Law, in 1719, usually known as the Mississippi scheme; the stock of which was puffed into consequence, and rose several hundred per cent. in its exchangeable value; all Paris, and a large portion of the capitalists and business men of France, became excited on the subject, speculated largely in its stock, and fancied that they had made themselves rich; but in a few months the bubble burst, the bank exploded, and the circulation of the notes of the bank, (which was extensive,) as well as its stock, became worthless, and embarrassment, ruin, and bankruptcy, was suddenly spread and extended throughout the nation. This disastrous experiment entirely cured the French people of their mania for paper-money, and they confined themselves to a specie currency for more than two-thirds of a century; until the madness of the democratic party, during the French revolution, the latter part of the eighteenth century, induced the government to issue many millions of paper-money, called assignats, which were payable in the confiscated lands of the clergy and nobles. This experiment failed also, and was very disastrous in its consequences, though not equally so as the great scheme of Law.

During the American revolution, our forefathers resorted to the experiment, which had become very prevalent in Europe, of issuing government notes, called continental money, to aid them in their emergency. From 1776 to 1781, $359,547,027 were issued by order of the American Congress, and it depreciated so rapidly that in 1780 it was not worth more than two and a half cents on the dollar, and in 1782 less than one cent on the dollar. The result was most distressing to the army, and very disastrous and ruinous to a large portion of the whole nation. It was funded in 1790 at only one cent on the dollar.

As heretofore shown in table number II. of section 6, the paper-money of Russia, Austria, and Portugal, as well as that of England, France, and the United States, has been greatly depreciated, and great losses have consequently been sustained by the holders of it, in each and all of those countries.

It is stated in Brande's Encyclopædia that no fewer than two hundred and forty of the country banks failed in England and Wales during the years 1814, 1815, and 1816, occasioning nearly as much distress, loss, bankruptcy, and suffering, as the great Mississippi scheme of France in 1719. During the years 1816 and 1817, a great number of banks failed in the United States; many failed in 1825 also; and the failures in the United States during the revulsion from 1837 to 1842 amounted to over one hundred and sixty, with a nominal and pretended capital of over $132,000,000, and a circulation of over $43,000,000.

A paper currency, which the maker is not able and legally bound to redeem in coin at the will of the holder, whether issued by the government, by incorporated or joint stock banks, or by individual bankers, is one of the greatest evils which can afflict any country. But notwithstanding the numerous frauds, losses, and evils, resulting from paper-money, the conveniences and advantages arising from well managed banks are very great; and banking is so interwoven with our system of doing business, that it is difficult, and perhaps not advisable to attempt to dispense with bank-notes, as a part of the circulating medium of the country. Something, however, should be done to secure the public, and to prevent, as well as to punish fraud. The individual liability of bankers, without more speedy and efficient remedies to enforce such liabilities than the common law affords, and different judges from some we have in the United States, proves to be almost worthless. I entertain no doubt, however, that remedies may be devised, which would make the individual liability of bankers available to promote the security of the public.

The public mind seems to be tending towards the following points, as necessary safeguards in our system of banking:—First, that government stocks in good credit should be deposited with some government officer, in pledge to redeem their outstanding notes; secondly, that such officer should keep the bank-plates, have all the notes struck off, countersigned and registered in his office, and delivered to the bankers, and that uniformity, as far as practicable, should be preserved in the plates of all the notes of the same denomination in the State; thirdly, that every bank should keep on hand in specie, and in specie funds subject to draft at sight, an amount equal to from 30 to 50 per cent. of all their liabilities to the public, to enable them to pay their debts in coin, or its equivalent, whenever called on; fourthly, that none but those who have capital to lend, and do not wish to borrow money, should become bankers, and to secure this object, that no bank should be allowed to make loans to its directors, officers, or stockholders, either directly or indirectly; fifthly, that the directors and other managing officers should be personally liable for all the debts of the institution, and that the private property of the stockholders should also be holden to an amount equal to their stock; sixthly, that the power to alter and amend the charter, in order to correct abuses, should be reserved; and seventhly, that all violations of law by the stockholders, as well as the officers, should be declared and punished as crimes; and that neither the bank, nor any stockholder, director, nor other officer thereof, should be allowed to set up any violation of law, as a defence to a suit on any contract of such bank, bank officer, or stockholder.

The first point stated is substantially the basis on which the Bank of England (the first bank which ever issued notes) has always done business, and the same principle of banking is now in operation in the States of New York and Ohio. The second point is important to secure the stockholders of banks, as well as the public, against fraudulent and excessive issues; and also to guard against counterfeits. This provision also is in operation in New York and Ohio, under their general banking laws. The third point seems absolutely necessary to secure at all times the redemption of bank-notes in gold and silver; and notwithstanding the opposition of bankers, it appears to be increasing in importance in the public mind. As to the fourth point, the case of the late United States Bank of Pennsylvania, as well as of numerous others, has created a very general impression in this country, that the payment of the capital stock of a bank in coin, to any amount whatever, affords but little security to the public, if the directors or officers of the bank can take it half or all out again, in the shape of loans to themselves; that when the directors, managing stockholders, and officers, have thus loaned to themselves perhaps two or three times as much as the amount of their stock, it is often for their interest to have the bank fail, and its notes depreciated, to enable them to buy them up at half price, or less, and apply them in payment of their own obligations; their indirect gains by such failure being much greater than the loss of their stock. To allow speculators, as well as business men who want money, to manufacture paper-money at pleasure, and loan it to themselves, presents too many, and too great temptations for over-issues, and improper loans, to be consistent with a sound currency, and the security and safety of the public. The fifth and seventh are also important, to deter selfish and cunning men from attempting to make bank-paper an instrument to defraud the public; and also to prevent them from setting up their own violations of law, to defeat the honest claims of their innocent, confiding, and deluded creditors. But what appears to me equally as important, and perhaps more so, than any of the points above named, is a radical change in the mode of electing directors, so as to give all the stockholders a fair voice in the election of directors, and the management of the bank, and not allow a few, who own a majority of the stock, to combine together and control the whole, for their own private advantage, regardless of the safety of the public, and of the rights of the other stockholders.*

It is very difficult to sustain banks in agricultural States, against which there is a constant balance of trade; but very easy to sustain them, with ordinary prudence and good management, in manufacturing States, in whose favor there are generally heavy debts, as well as a balance of trade. Hence the necessity of greater checks, and greater prudence, in the former than in the latter.

* See chapter V. section 9, where this subject of elections is discussed.

CHAPTER XI.

ON THE INCREASED POWERS OF PRODUCTION OF THE PRESENT AGE —THE CONSUMPTION BY THE PEOPLE OF THE UNITED STATES, OF THE PRINCIPAL NECESSARIES OF LIFE, AND THE PROPORTION OF THEIR SEVERAL WANTS—THE PROPORTION OF ADULT MALES EMPLOYED IN AGRICULTURE, AND IN OTHER EMPLOYMENTS, IN THE UNITED STATES AND IN GREAT BRITAIN AND IRELAND—AND THE IMPORTANCE OF ADAPTING THE DIVISION OF EMPLOYMENTS, AND THE INDUSTRY OF THE PEOPLE OF A NATION, TO THEIR WANTS, CONDITION, RESOURCES, AND THE WANTS OF THE COMMERCIAL WORLD.

SEC. 1. *On the increased production of the present age—and the capacity of Great Britain and the U. States to produce.*

The increase of knowledge in the natural sciences has been so great, and their application to agriculture so extensive since the middle of the last century, that, by the aid of more efficient tools, crops of all kinds have been doubled in quantity, in every well cultivated country; and they are now three times as great per acre on an average, in Great Britain and Belgium, as they were three centuries since. The inventions made during the last hundred years (since the year 1750) have had an effect upon mining, mechanical and manufacturing industry still greater, and more surprising. The productiveness of industry has been increased by machinery employed in spinning, about thirty fold—employed in weaving, about eight or ten fold—employed in rolling iron, perhaps five fold—in the navigation of rivers, transportation on Canals and Railroads, and in all other mechanical, manufacturing, and mining operations, from two to five fold. The increased supply of products has kept pace in Great Britain, the United States, and some other countries, with the increased power and efficiency of human industry. This has been shown in chapters VII, VIII and IX.

The physical wants of man are limited, by his constitution and nature; and though his artificial and factitious wants are unlimited, yet the demand for articles of luxury and fancy to supply them, is limited in most cases, by his ability to pay for them.* The fact is well known to every intelligent merchant and manufacturer, that the ordinary supply of products, both natural and manufactured, greatly exceeds the demand. This is true of almost every thing but the precious metals. The question is no longer, what a nation is capable of producing, but how much the people can consume, and sell to advantage. The facts exhibited in chapters VII and VIII, show that Great Britain alone could soon manufacture cotton and woollen goods, iron and hardware, for the whole of Europe and America; if she could command their markets for the sale of her products. She has laborers enough, and water power, fuel and capital sufficient, to increase her machinery and manufacturing power to an almost unlimited extent; and she would do so, if the markets, and the demand for her products at good prices, were equally extensive.

The natural resources and capacities of the United States for mining and manufacturing, are more extensive then those of Great Britain. The United States have also the capacity of producing Indian corn, vegetables, fruits, provisions of most kinds, and all the materials for clothing, sufficient for five hundred millions of inhabitants. But it would be the height of folly and madness to develope their agricultural resources any faster than an increase of the population of the earth, shall have caused a demand for their products. The quantity of each and all of our products should be adapted to our wants, and the extent of our markets. Whatever a nation produces which it does not want and cannot sell to advantage, is not only worthless, but is often worse than worthless. The excess tends to depress the price and market value of all its products for which there is a demand, and thus tends to lessen the value of its exports.

SEC. 2. *The division of employments, and the industry of a nation, should be adapted to the wants of the people.*

Foreign as well as domestic markets being limited, and the capacity of most nations to pay for foreign products being also limited; the division of employments, and the industry of a nation, should be adapted to, and in accordance with, the wants of the people and of the commercial world—and with the natural resources and condition of the country. It should be the business of legislators and governments, as well as producers, to learn the wants of the people and of foreign commerce, as well as the quantity of the products of each class of producers, and the natu-

* See sections 1 and 10 of chapter VI.

ral resources of the country, and to endeavor to give such direction to industry as to adapt it to such wants and resources. This leads to the inquiry, what are the wants of the people? and what is the extent of each of their wants?

SEC. 3. *How much of each class of provisions, breadstuffs, and vegetables, do our people need?*

How much in quantity, on an average, do a people need of breadstuffs, meats, and vegetables? The evidence and estimates which I have met with generally tend to show, that the inhabitants of most countries of Europe consume more breadstuffs and much less meat and vegetables, on an average, than the people of the United States. In Great Britain, the people consume much more meat than they do on the continent, though much less than in the United States. The consumption of grain in Great Britain is about eight bushels, and in France it has been generally estimated at from nine to ten bushels per annum, for each person.

In the United States, the allowance to adult field slaves is usually one peck each per week, or thirteen bushels per year; but the consumption of the free population and the house servants, does not exceed seven and a half bushels of grain for each person. From the best evidence I can collect, I estimate the average quantity of meats of all kinds consumed annually by each free person in the United States, at one hundred and fifty pounds; consisting of one hundred pounds of pork, ham, and bacon, fresh and salt, and fifty pounds of beef, mutton, and veal. The inhabitants of Great Britain are supposed to consume a little over one hundred pounds per annum each, on an average, while the French consume less than fifty pounds, and the people of Ireland, and some other nations, not over thirty pounds each.

The census of 1840 shows that the white and free colored population of the United States, and the house servants, amounted to about fifteen millions, and the field slaves and their children, to about two millions.

The disposition of the wheat crop of 1839–40, was about as follows:—

	Million bushels.
Consumed by the fifteen millions free persons and house servants 4 bushels each, - - - -	60
Exported in 1840 in flour and wheat, about - -	10.2
Required for seed one eighth part, - - -	10.5
Used for starch, soured, and wasted, - - - -	4.1
Total crop harvested in 1839, - - - - -	84.8

	Million bushels.
Rye consumed one bushel each, - - - - -	15.
Exported in grain and meal about, - - - -	.3
Used for seed about one eighth of crop, - -	2.3
The remainder distilled, - - - - - -	1.
Total crop harvested in 1839, - - - - -	18.6

The quantity of buckwheat raised was reported at 7,291,743 bushels; which would afford nearly half a bushel for each inhabitant. The crop of oats was returned at 123,071,341 bushels, and was equal for food, to nearly half as many bushels of corn.

The quantity of potatoes raised was reported at 108,298,060 bushels. A bushel of wheat furnishes an amount of nourishment equal to about 4½ bushels of potatoes; and a bushel of rye or Indian corn is equal to about 4 bushels of potatoes. The potatoe crop was equal to about twenty-six million bushels of grain.

Reckoning oats equal to half as many bushels of other grain, and potatoes and turnips according to their equivalent in grain, the quantity of grain and its equivalent in potatoes and turnips used annually for each free person, on an average, in the United States and in France, may be estimated as follows:—

	United States.	France.
Eaten by man, - - - -	8¼ bushels.	10 bushels.
Distilled and brewed, -	1	¼
Used for seed, - - - -	2½	2½
Fed to animals to convert into meat & for horse feed,	11¼	2¼
Total, - - -	23*	15

* This estimate is much less than the supply for the year 1839–40 according to the census. The returns of the census of the crop of wheat, rye, barley, and buckwheat, may be relied on, as they were generally harvested with care, and measured. But very little of the crop of Indian corn in the states south of the Potomac, and west of Pennsylvania having been measured, the returns were mere guess-work of the farmers and planters, and (as I think) at least 25 per cent. too high. It amounted to over 330 million bushels in those states, and less than 47 million bushels in the six eastern and five middle states. My estimate of the consumption of the corn crop of that year is as follows:—

Required to raise the swine about 2 bushels, and to fatten them, about 5 bushels of corn, or its equivalent in other grain and potatoes, over and above milk, grass, and meat, for each 100 pounds of pork.

	Bushels.
To make 1,900,000,000 pounds, the estimated amount that year,	133,000,000
Consumed by two million field slaves, - - - - - -	24,000,000
Consumed by fifteen million other persons, - - - -	30,000,000
Distilled into whiskey, - - - - - - - - -	12,000,000
Used for seed, - - - - - - - - - - -	6,000,000
Exported in corn and corn meal, - - - - - - -	1,500,000

The proportion of each kind of grain and vegetables eaten by the free population and house servants of the United States, was nearly as follows, viz., four bushels of wheat, one of rye, two bushels of Indian corn, half a bushel of buckwheat, and potatoes and other vegetables equal to three fourths of a bushel of grain. The quantity consumed annually, on an average, by the inhabitants of Great Britain, Prussia, and Russia, for breadstuffs, and to convert into meat, may be about eighteen bushels, while the consumption of the countries of Southern Europe does not exceed about twelve bushels to each person. Eighteen bushels would be sufficient in this country, if none of it were wasted, and no more meats and distilled liquors were used, than the health of the people require.

The crop of grain including half the bushels of oats and the equivalent in grain of the crop of potatoes, raised in each division of the United States in 1839, according to the census, would afford to each person for food, horse feed, and to convert into meat, the number of bushels following.

	Grain.	Potatoes equal to grain.	Total bushels.
New England States,	7½ bush.	3½ bush.	11
Five Middle States, including Delaware, Maryland, and Dis. Col.	22	2	24
Virginia, N. and S. Carolina, Georgia, and Florida,	36	¾	36¾
Other Slave States,	50½	½	51
Western Free States,	44	1	45

The population of the six New England States in 1840, was 2,234,822. The crops of those states in 1839 being sufficient to supply the inhabitants what was equivalent to only eleven bushels each, when their consumption was about twice as much, the deficiency was equal to over twenty-four million bushels of grain, which was supplied by the western and southern states in the shape of grain, flour, meal, pork, hams, beef and lard. The

Fed to cattle, sheep, and poultry, one tenth part as much as to hogs, - - - - - - - - - - - -	13,000,000
Fed to horses perhaps, - - - - - - - - - -	6,000,000
Deduct one fifth of the 330 million bushels returned for the southern and western states as an over estimate,	66,000,000
And it still leaves a large quantity wasted for want of care, by reason of want of markets, and depressed prices, amounting to about, - - - - - - - - - - -	86,031,000
Total crop according to the census, - - - - -	377,531,000

population of the five middle states and the District of Columbia was then 5,118,076, and though they contain the great commercial cities of New York, Philadelphia, and Baltimore, yet their crops were sufficient to supply all their wants, and leave a surplus.

The farmer can see from this illustration, the advantage to him, of the manufactures of New England, and the importance of increasing the manufacturing and mining industry of all the States, in order to create markets for his products. Were it not for manufactures, the people employed in them in New England and the Middle States, would have been dispersed in the Western World, mostly engaged in agriculture, increasing the supply and depressing instead of raising the price of breadstuffs and provisions. The farmer should also take into consideration, that a very large proportion of the people of New York and Philadelphia are employed in the mechanic arts and manufactures; that it requires but a very small proportion of the population of any country to be engaged in commerce, navigation, and retail trade; that a comparatively few thousand men are required to attend to the commerce, navigation, and retail trade of a great nation; that commercial men, therefore, furnish but a very trifling market to the farmer in any country, and that the principal markets he enjoys, are furnished by persons employed in the mechanic arts, manufactures, and mining.

The farmers of New England can furnish a supply of breadstuffs and provisions equal in quantity to what is consumed by themselves, and by all the persons, with their families, who are employed in navigation and commercial pursuits. So that the entire market in New England for the farmers of other States, may be said to be created by manufactures. The mining, mechanical, and manufacturing population of the Middle States, was much greater in 1840 than that of the New England States, and consumed and furnished a market for the farmer for a quantity of his products, exclusive of hay, products of the dairy, poultry, eggs, fruit, vegetables, wood, and many other things, including only half the oats—equal to about sixty million bushels of grain. How insignificant are commercial pursuits when compared with the mechanic arts, manufactures, and mining industry, in supplying markets for the farmer!

Estimate of the quantity of pork, ham, bacon, and lard—fresh and salt, made in the United States in the year 1839; consumed by fifteen million free persons, and house servants.

100 pounds each on an average, -	1,500	million.
Consumed by over two million field slaves, at 185 lbs. each, - - -	375	"
Exported, about, - - -	25	"
Total consumed and exported, - -	1,900	"

The quantity of beef, mutton, and veal consumed during the year 1840, may be estimated at fifty pounds for each of the fifteen million free persons and domestic servants, equal to

750 million pounds.

Beef exported during the year, 19,681 bbls. which is less than - - 4 " "

The consumption in 1840 of bread-stuffs and provisions, by the white and free colored population of the United States, including house servants (fifteen million) may be estimated as follows—the prices being taken as average prices in all parts of the country at the places of production, during six years, from 1840 to 1845, inclusive :—

Pork, ham, &c., 100 lbs. each at $4 00, -	$60,000,000
Beef, mutton, and veal, 50 lbs. each, -	30,000,000
Wheat and flour, 4 bushels each, at 80 cts.,	48,000,000
Rye, corn, and buckwheat, 3½ bushels each, at 45 cts., - - -	23,625,000
Total value of the grain and meats consumed,	$161,625,000
Products of the dairy consumed about -	$33,000,000
Milk and cream not reported in census, one third as much, - - -	11,000,000
Products of the orchard, valued at -	7,256,000
Products of market gardens, -	2,601,000
Products of gardens for domestic use, estimated at	10,000,000
Poultry of all kinds, whole value returned -	9,344,000
Eggs, two thirds as much as poultry -	6,230,000
Potatoes and turnips, 3 bushels for each, at 20 cts.	9,000,000
Total - - -	$250,056,000

The consumption is equal to $16⅔ for each person. The inhabitants of cities and villages paid on an average 50 per cent. above these prices, on account of the expense of transportation, traders' profits, &c.

Add for consumption of two million of field slaves

24 million bushels of corn at 33⅓ cts.	$8,000,000
4 million bushels of potatoes at 20 cts. -	800,000
Products of gardens, - -	1,000,000
Pork and beef, 190 lbs. each, at $4 per 100 lbs.	15,200,000
Total for slaves, - -	$25,000,000
And making a total of - -	$275,056,000

value of breadstuffs and provisions produced by the farmer and consumed in our own country.

The whole amount exported during the fiscal year 1840 was valued at about sixteen millions of dollars.

Here we see that the quantity of each class of provisions, breadstuffs, vegetables, fruits, &c. necessary to satisfy the wants of our people, is very limited, compared with the capacity of the country to supply them; so limited that our markets have been generally glutted, and prices very much depressed; and the foreign demand has generally been very trifling. The short crops in Europe in 1845 and in 1846, and the consequent foreign demand for our products, raised prices in 1846 and 1847; and the partial failure of the potato crops in Europe since, has tended to increase the demand for our products, and to keep up prices. It may, however, be safely affirmed that, for four years out of every five, (from 1820 to 1845) our crops were so much beyond the wants of our country, and the foreign demand for them, that no increase of quantity could have increased their aggregate value in the least. On the contrary, an increase of one fourth part, or even less, in quantity, would have diminished their aggregate value very considerably; and a large diminution in quantity would have increased their aggregate value. Such being the case, any increase of industry employed in agriculture at the present time, though it might benefit the persons employed, could not benefit the country in the least; and in a national point of view, the labor would be useless and entirely lost. On the contrary, if such labor could be employed in producing such mineral, mechanical, and manufactured products, and erecting such buildings as are wanted by our people, it would be productive in a national, as well as in an individual point of view.

SEC. 4. *How much salt, fish, tea, coffee, spices, sugars, &c. do our people need, and consume annually?*

Let us now inquire, in the progress of the examination, what quantities of salt, fish, tea, coffee, spices, and sugars, dried fruits, and rice, the people of the United States consume annually.

The reports on commerce and other evidence show that the average annual consumption of such articles for the years 1839, 1840, and 1841, and the prices paid by the consumer, were nearly as follows:—

	Millions.
Six million bushels domestic salt, and the same quantity of imported salt, cost the consumer about	$4.
Fish cost the consumer - -	6
About 12 million lbs. of tea cost in China about 30 cts., but cost the consumer on an average 70 cts. per lb. - -	8 .4

	Millions.
100 million lbs. coffee cost abroad about 9 cts., but cost the consumer about 13½ cts.	13.5
300 million lbs. sugar cost consumer about 9 cts.	27.
25 million gallons of molasses at 40 cts.	10.
Spices cost abroad about $400,000, and cost the consumer three times as much	1.2
Dried fruits and almonds cost abroad about $1,200-000, and cost the consumer about	2.4
30 million lbs. of rice at 5 cts.	1.5
Total cost to the consumers	$74.

of these articles not produced by the farmers of cold and temperate climates, but mostly products of warm countries; equal to nearly $5 for each person.

SEC. 5. *What clothing do the people need annually?*

Estimate of the value of the various kinds of clothing consumed by the people of the United States annually, during the years 1839–40 and 41.

	Millions.
Manufactures of cotton, according to the returns of the census of 1840, retained for home consumption	$42.8
Manufactures of wool retained	20.6
" silk	119
" flax	.322
" mixed materials	6.545
Cloths made in families of wool, flax, and cotton	29.023
Hats and caps	8.600
Straw bonnets and hats	1.476
Manufactures of leather, valued at $33,134,403, of which the boots and shoes were about	30.
Total of the above materials for clothing produced at home	$139.485
Cost abroad of the same articles imported and consumed on an average, each of these years	$44.
Duties paid on them, about	11.
Freight, cost and profits of importing, 15 per cent.	6.6
Jobbers' profits on about 120 million dollars of the foreign and domestic goods for clothing at 12½ per cent.	15.
Expenses, freight, and profits, of the retail merchant on 150 million dollars sold at 25 per cent.	37.5
Over 200 million dollars of these articles consist of cloths and trimmings, including home-made cloths, to be made into clothing, the cost of making being one third as much as the materials	67.

	Millions.
Total for the annual cost of clothing, including bedding, carpeting, and other furniture, made of fabrics that are woven.	$320.585
Perhaps the clothing and bedding for the two million field slaves cost about half as much as that of the free persons or $10 each. - -	20.
This leaves for the free persons, and domestic servants—equal to twenty dollars to each person. -	$300.585

SEC. 6. *What fuel, lights, soap, and furniture, do the people need?*

The fuel, lights, furniture, and soap, consumed in 1840, may be estimated as follows. Wood for domestic use equal to one cord and a half for each free person and domestic servant, worth when cut and sawed for use, on an average throughout the United States, about $2.50 per cord, and one sixth part as much for workshops, stores, etc.,or its equivalent in coal, exclusive of what is used for steam engines, and in furnaces; $4,37½ for each of

15 million persons. - -	$71.250
Sperm and wax candles, 2,900,000 lbs. at 40cts.	1.160
Tallow candles made by chandlers, as returned, about 17 million lbs., at 11 cts. - -	1.870
*Tallow candles made in families, estimated at -	5.
Oil and gas consumed for lights, estimated at	6.
Soap consumed, as returned by the census, about 47 million lbs., at 4¾ cts. - -	2 220
†Soft soap made in families, estimated at -	6.
The value of furniture made in 1839, was returned at $7,555,405. This does not include beds, crockery, glass and stone ware—stoves, hollow-ware, hardware, brass, silver, copper and tin ware, clocks, etc. Taking all these things into consideration, the amount annually expended for the whole, exclusive of carpeting and bedding, may be estimated at - -	15.
Total - - -	$108.5

Equal to more than $7 for each person, for fuel, lights, soap, and furniture for the year.

*The tallow candles consumed in Great Britain as stated by Porter, amounted to 66,402,684 lbs. in 1801, to 93,816,346 lbs. in 1821, and to 155,586,192 lbs., in 1830.

†The soap consumed in Great Britain, is stated by Porter as follows—about 53 million lbs., in 1801—nearly 93 million lbs., in 1821—and over 170 million lbs., in 1841.

SEC. 7. *What kind and value of dwelling houses, out-houses, grounds, shade trees, etc., are needed?*

It is difficult to determine what kind and value of dwelling houses, improvements about them, and out-houses, a people need, to promote their comforts, and secure the greatest degree of health that is practicable. One thing is very certain, that nearly all the diseases and weaknesses to which man is subject, are aggravated by cold, heat, and dampness in excess, by great changes in temperature from day to night—and many of them are produced by the same causes. All of which can in a great measure be guarded against, by good dwellings, beds and bedding, yards, shade trees, and attention to drainage and cleanliness.

The dwelling houses built in the United States in 1839 are valued in the census at over 41 million of dollars, and this sum does not include the repairs and improvements of old houses, nor the erection of fences, out-houses, and other improvements. The value of all the dwelling houses in the United States in 1840—and the improvements around them, including yards, fences, out-houses and trees, may be estimated at over a thousand million dollars; and the annual wear and destruction of them, and of keeping them in repair exclusive of rents, may be estimated as high as thirty millions of dollars, and the cost of building for the increasing population, thirty millions; making in all sixty millions of dollars, equal to four dollars for each free person. This sum seems very large, and yet there is a large proportion of our people very badly housed. I have no doubt that the health, as well as the comforts of a large majority of them, might be promoted by expenditures for such purposes judiciously made, at least two or three times as great as have been heretofore incurred.

SEC. 8. *Expenditures for books, information, education, pleasure-horses and carriages.*

	Millions.
The expenditures for books, pamphlets, newspapers, and other periodicals, as indicated by the census, amounted to about - -	$5.
Expenses annually of keeping horses and carriages for pleasure, estimated at -	20.
The expenditures for education, exclusive of books, board, and the personal expenses of scholars and students in New England and New York, was equal to about fifty cents to each inhabitant, and perhaps half as much for each free person in the other states. - - -	5.
Total - -	$30.

Equal to two dollars to each free person.

SEC. 9. *Cost of tobacco and intoxicating drinks consumed annually.*

	Millions.
The tobacco manufactured during the year preceding the census of 1840, exceeded the amount exported over five millions of dollars, and the value of tobacco, snuff, and cigars consumed,* must have cost the consumers at least - -	$7.5
The quantity of spirits, wine, and strong beer consumed during the year, was equal in intoxicating properties, to nearly fifty million gallons of distilled spirit; perhaps seven eighths of it was used for drink, and cost the consumers not less than	30.
Total cost of stimulants, - -	$37.5
Equal to $2,50 to each free person. -	

SEC. 10. *Recapitulation of the consumption of the people and reflections on the imperfect division of employments, in the United States.*

Recapitulation of the annual consumption of the people, and the average amount to each person, except the field slaves.

		To each person
Amount stated in Sec. 3, exclusive of consumption by field slaves -	$250million.	$16⅔
Amount stated in Sec. 4 -	74 "	5
Amount stated in Sec. 5 exclusive of consumption by field slaves -	300 "	20
Amount stated in Sec. 6 -	108.5 "	7
" " 7 - -	60 "	4
" " 8 -	30 "	2
" " 9 - -	37.5 "	2½
	$860 "	$57⅙
Amount stated in Sec. 3 for field slaves	25 "	
" " 5 " "	20 "	
Total - - -	$905 "	
All of which were consumed, worn out, wasted, and destroyed, except the following, which were accumulated, to wit, furniture to the amount and value of - - - -	8 millions.	
An increase of dwelling houses valued at	30 "	
Books, pleasure carriages and horses	2 "	
Total value included, that were accumulated - - - -	40 millions.	$2⅔
Total amount actually consumed.	$865 "	$53½

* See chapter IX section 19.

These estimates are intended to comprise the value of all the material products of industry, annually consumed by the people of the United States, during the years 1839-40 and 41—together with the amount paid for teachers' wages, which are not usually included with productive industry. Almost all industry is in some sense productive; but none is generally ranked by political economists as productive, however useful it may be, except such as produces material products, or adds value to them by transportation, and sale, which is a sort of *quasi* productive industry. Hence we exclude from the rank of productive industry, housekeeping, the labor of domestic servants, all professional business, teaching of all kinds, all matters of pleasure and amusement, official labor, military services, and the administration of justice.

The aggregate amount of these several kinds of employment and business, not ranked as productive industry, may be estimated at from $150 to 200 million per annum; and the values reckoned as productive, produced by industry and capital during each of those years, may be estimated at about one thousand million of dollars.

The amount accumulated during each of those years is estimated as follows.—

	Million dollars.
In houses, furniture, &c., as heretofore estimated,	40
Clearing and fencing about two million acres of new lands - - - -	24
Draining & other improvem'ts made on other lands,	6
Increase in amount and value of agricultural tools, implements, teams, and stock, about 3 per cent., or	12
Increase of manufacturing, milling, mechanical, and mining capital, about 5 per cent., or nearly	16
Increase in capital employed in commerce, retail trade, navigation, transportation, and the fisheries, about 3 per cent., - - -	15
Expenditures in building railroads, canals, and water works, over and above the accumulation of foreign debts for them,	12
Increase in other public property, such as roads, bridges, churches, national, state, and county buildings, forts, harbors, &c., - -	10
Total accumulated, - - -	135
Amount consumed, brought forward, - -	865
Total produced, - - -	1000
Estimated amount produced in 1850, -	1400

It thus appears that the quantities of our products respectively, are not adapted to our wants, and the wants of the commercial world. Of some articles we produce a great surplus, much of which is wasted, and the labor employed in producing them totally lost, while of others we produce much less than we really need, to supply our wants and promote our comforts.

The capital employed in the United States in 1840 in producing the following articles, the gross value produced, and the average value imported annually, in 1839, 1840, and 1841, was nearly as follows, stated in millions of dollars.

	Capital.	Produced.	Imported.
Cotton goods,	\$51 mil.	\$46 mil.	\$11 mil.
Woollen goods,	15½	20½	13
Mix'd goods, cotton & wool,	4½	6½	
Home made goods,		29	
Bar, pig iron, & castings,	20½	17½	5
Machinery,	8	10½	4½ (Machinery and Hardware together)
Hardware, cutlery, &c.,	5½	6½	
Total, - -	\$105 mil.	\$136½	\$33½*

The labor employed in producing the Indian corn, pork, and other grain, provisions, and vegetables, not wanted, but actually wasted for want of sufficient markets, if properly trained, would have been amply sufficient to produce twice as much clothing, iron, and hardware as we imported—and an additional capital of about sixty millions of dollars invested in such employments, would have been sufficient to produce them. The amount annually accumulated in the shape of agricultural improvements and capital, at the same time, (as I have endeavored to show,) was equal to over forty millions of dollars, so that all that was necessary to furnish capital sufficient for these objects, was to divert from agriculture, the increased amount invested in it, during a single year and an half; three fourths of which, in the form of investments in agriculture, have no present value whatever, in a national point of view. By these means, we should not only increase the quantity and value of our mining and manufacturing industry, and save over thirty millions of dollars then annually paid for those classes of foreign products, and also save the cost of importing them; but we should increase the quantity and value

* Comparatively few of these goods were re-exported, except manufactures of cotton to the amount of about one million, and woollen goods valued at less than half a million dollars, leaving for consumption here what cost abroad about thirty-two millions of dollars, and were worth in this country, after the duties were paid, about \$44,000,000.

of our capital invested in these great departments of industry—and all this would be effected, without diminishing the exchangeable value of our agricultural products, or the present value of our agricultural capital, a single dollar. The reader will perceive the truth of the latter portion of the proposition (relative to agricultural products and capital) when he reflects, that the prices of all kinds of commodities and property are regulated by the proportion between the demand and the supply in the market, and that a large crop, furnishing a surplus beyond the wants of the market, is generally worth less in the aggregate, than a deficient crop.

The people of the United States have a great surplus beyond their wants, and what they can sell, of food of all kinds, which the climate can produce, and of tobacco, and intoxicating drinks, and cannot possibly improve their condition, by an increased production of such things—but their comforts, and enjoyments may be increased by a greater amount of most of the things specified in sections four, five, six, seven and eight, comprising, sugar, tea, coffee, many tropical fruits, clothing, bedding, furniture, lights and fuel; and their condition and well being would be greatly improved, by an increase of capital invested in manufacturing and mining industry, and by an expenditure three or four times as great, judiciously made, for books, education, dwelling houses, out-houses, yards, shade and fruit trees, and drainage about their premises. These remarks are intended to be general, and apply only to the average expenditure for such purposes. There are numerous cases in the cities and large villages, of individuals expending from two to five times as much for dwelling houses, furniture and many other things, as is consistent with the general welfare of themselves and their families.

SEC. 11. *What proportion of the adult males should be employed in agriculture, in different climates.*

When we take into consideration the whole industry of our country, and the wants of the people, and see that less than one third part in value of its products are consumed by our people for food—and that the foreign demand for food is generally comparatively trifling—and compare the prosperity and wealth of manufacturing nations and states with those devoted mostly to agriculture; we may safely conclude, that in temperate climates (like all that portion of the United States lying above the 35th parallel of latitude) in order to produce the highest degree of prosperity, only from thirty to forty, or at most fifty per cent. of the adult male population, should be employed in agriculture. In lower latitudes, the people need much less clothing—the earth is more productive, many of its products less perishable, more available in proportion to their weight and bulk, and may be taken to more distant markets; and hence the profits of agricultural pursuits are much greater than they are in high latitudes, and the inducements to, and advantages of manufacturing much less. The following tables have been formed to illustrate the subject.

Estimates deduced from official returns, reports, and the best authors and authorities, of the values* produced annually, from 1838 to 1844 from labor and capital employed in agriculture, and in all other pursuits, together with the population, and the amount produced to each person.

In the	Values produced annually. By agriculture.	Other pursuits.	Total.
United States,	$550 millions.	$450 millions,	$1000 millions.
Great Britain,	£135 "	£195 "	£ 330 "
Ireland,	£40 "	£25 "	£65 "

	Population.	Amount produced to each person.	
United States,	17 millions		$59
Great Britain,	18.5 "	£17 16, or	85
Ireland,	8.1 "	£ 8	38

Statement of the whole number of males over 20 years old employed in agriculture in Great Britain and Ireland, at the undermentioned periods, according to the returns; and the number so employed in the United States in 1840, estimated from the returns of the census.

	In 1831.	In 1841.
In England and Wales,	1,075,912	1,041,980
Scotland,	167,145	166,009
Great Britain,	1,243,057	1,207,989
Ireland,	1,167,054	

The number of males over 15 years old employed in agriculture in Ireland in 1841 was, -	1,594,682
the number over 20 years old is estimated at -	1,250,000
The number over 20 years so employed in the United States in 1840, is estimated at - -	3,000,000
the whole number returned as employed in agriculture in the United States, without limitation as to age being, - - - - -	3,719,951

Great Britain contains nearly twice as many square miles as Ireland, and about twice and a half as much arable land; and yet there was in 1841 a greater number of persons employed in

* I have included in the aggregate values produced, all agricultural and other improvements public and private, roads, railroads, public buildings, and everything usually classed by political economists with productive industry,

agriculture and grazing in the latter country, than in the former. Great Britain is one of the best cultivated countries in the world, and the fact that the number of persons employed in agriculture did not increase from 1831 to 1841, is proof that no greater number was needed; the remainder of the people were more profitably employed in other pursuits. Nearly the whole increase of the population of Ireland was either employed in agriculture, or remained idle; for the reason that there was very little increase of other pursuits to employ them. The agricultural laborers of Great Britain accomplished about twice and a half as much as the same number in Ireland, which affords conclusive evidence that the latter must have been idle much of the time, perhaps half of the time on an average, and many of them work to bad advantage, when they do labor. By reason of large markets in the immediate vicinity of the farmers of Great Britain, furnished mostly by the manufacturing and mining population, they realize much higher prices also for their products, than the farmers of Ireland, and the aggregate annual value of their products is about three and a half times as much as it is in Ireland.

The number of persons employed in the cotton, woollen, worsted, silk, lace, hose, flax, and linen factories, in the United Kingdom, was as follows:—

	In 1839.	In 1847.
In England and Wales,	349,294	455,042
Scotland,	59,314	67,243
Great Britain,	408,608	522,285
Ireland,	14,863	22,591

In addition to these, there were great numbers employed in hand loom weaving, and in household manufactures.

The number of persons employed in mining in 1841, was as follows:—

	Males over 20 years old.	Males under 20 and females.
In England and Wales,	125,059	48,209
Scotland,	14,179	6,378
Ireland, males over 15,	3,016	
Ireland, males under 15 & females,		80

Statement of the proportion in a hundred, of the adult male population in different parts of the United States, and in England and Wales, Scotland, and Ireland, employed in agriculture and grazing, and the per cent. employed in all other pursuits; including in the latter division all idle, infirm, and unemployed persons, at the undermentioned periods; also the estimated amount annually produced to each of the whole population from 1339 to 1841.

In 1840, in	In Agriculture. per cent.	All others. per cent.	Amt. produced to each person.
Maine, New Hampshire, and Vermont, -	73.5	26.5	$56.
Massachusetts and Rhode Island, -	38.7	61.3	100.
Connecticut, -	58.	42.	86.
New York, New Jersey, and Pennsylvania, -	61,7	38.3	72.
North Western Free States,	79.	21.	44.
Northern Slave States lying above the 35th degree of latitude, -	83.4	16.6	45.*
Southern Slave States,	91.	9.	60.*
In the year 1831.			
England and Wales,	31.7	68.3	
Scotland, - -	30.4	69.6	
Ireland, - -	64.6	35.4	
In the year 1841.			
England and Wales,	25.	75.	85. (England and Wales and Scotland)
Scotland, - -	27.	73.	
Ireland, - -	66.	34.	38.

The reader will see from the foregoing tables, that the annual earnings and incomes of communities in temperate as well as in cold climates, are generally in proportion to the number of the people employed in pursuits other than agriculture; and that free labor employed in our North Western States in the culture of wheat, Indian corn, and other products, is less productive than slave labor employed in the Southern Slave States in the culture of cotton, sugar, and rice, and less productive also, than slave labor employed in Kentucky and Missouri, in the cultivation of tobacco and hemp.

* In these calculations, slaves are treated as persons who produce, and the profits to the owners of raising slaves in the Northern Slave States are not taken into the account.

Statement in English quarters of the average quantity of wheat, and wheat flour, and of all other grain and meal, including peas and beans, exported annually from Ireland to Great Britain during the undermentioned years:—

	Wheat and wheat flour.	All other grains & meal
1801 to 1810,	70,833 qrs.	387,125 qrs.
1821 to 1830,	460,709 "	1,451,154 "
1831 to 1840,	540,415 "	2,175,461 "
1841 to 1845,	410,687 "	2,519,980 "
1846,	393,462 "	1,431,932 "

The numbers of cattle, sheep, and swine, exported to Great Britain were as follows:—

	In 1835.	1846.	1847.	1848.
Oxen, cows, steers, &c.	98,150	186,483	189,960	196,042
Calves, -		6,363	9,992	7,086
Sheep and lambs,	125,452	259,257	324,179	255,682
Swine,	376,191	480,827	106,407	110,787

Mr. McCulloch estimated the exports of Ireland in 1835 at £17,394,813, of which £445,900 in value were sent to British colonies and foreign countries, and the remainder (amounting to nearly £17,000,000) to Great Britain. Mr. Spackman estimated the value of the grain, flour, meal and animals, exported from Ireland to Great Britain in 1845 at over nine millions sterling—the exports in 1846, (the first year of the dearth,) were nearly as great, and the exports of animals during the famine year (1847) continued about the same. With the exception of potatoes and a few other crops, not far from one fourth part of all the agricultural products of Ireland were exported to Great Britain, from 1820 to 1846 inclusive—the quantity exported being sufficient to supply nearly two millions of inhabitants—and yet it may be safely affirmed, that the agricultural products of Great Britain, during that period, were greater in proportion to the population, than those of Ireland.

The potato crop failed in Ireland in 1846 and in 1847, and has partially failed several years since. The failure caused a scarcity of provisions, and great distress, during each of those years, amounting in 1847 among the poor peasants to a famine, which swept off many thousands of the inhabitants by starvation, and by diseases caused by a want of food, clothing, fuel, shelter and bedding, sufficient to make them comfortable. During the years 1847 and 1848 considerable quantities of grain, flour, and meal were imported into Ireland from Great Britain and from foreign countries; and the government made large expenditures on public works in that country, in order to employ the laboring poor, supply them with the means of making purchases, and save them from perishing.

Why were those exports of agricultural products from half fed Ireland to pampered Britain? Can the advocates of free trade account for the anomaly, consistently with their principles and theories? My explanation is this. The exportation was the result of necessity produced by their condition; by the want of a proper division of employments, and the employment of a sufficient number of persons in mining and manufactures, to supply their necessities; by free trade with Great Britain, which supplied and glutted their markets, and prevented the growth of manufactures; and by absentee landlordism. These causes compelled them to export to Great Britain agricultural products of the value of about £3,500,000 annually, to pay their rents to absentee proprietors; and about eight or nine millions sterling to pay British manufacturers and miners for the products of their industry, which should have been produced at home, by Irish labor. How could Ireland and the Irish people be otherwise than poor and depressed, under such a state of things? They have more than twice as many agricultural laborers as are necessary to cultivate their little island, and they must necessarily be poor, until the surplus population is employed in manufactures, and the breadstuffs and provisions retained at home to feed them, instead of being sent abroad, to pay for products of British labor. Spackman* says, "The state of Ireland at the present time bears a strong analogy to that of England in the reigns of Henry VIII. and Elizabeth, when the land was overrun with beggars, and the most cruel punishments could not suppress the crime of mendicancy."

The present system is depopulating Ireland, by reducing the people to poverty, distress, and starvation—and driving great numbers out of the island. The population decreased from 8,175,124 in 1841, to 6,515,784 in 1851.

Sec. 12. *General reflections on the effects of an improper division of employments.*

No people can produce very much, or be very flourishing in their condition, and be idle from one third to half the year; and without a proper division of employments, and a large proportion of the population employed in mechanical, manufacturing, mining, and other pursuits, it is impossible to furnish labor for them all, and to avoid great numbers being idle much of the time for want of employment. In view of these facts, can any one wonder at the extreme poverty and distress of the Irish, and the great wealth and power of the British people? Would an Irish Par-

* See Spackman's Analysis of the occupation of the people of Great Britain and Ireland—published in 1847, page 50.

liament be of any use to the people ? Could it increase the productiveness or value of their industry ? Do not their sufferings and distress arise from an improper division of employments, and the idleness resulting from it ? from a want of mechanical, manufacturing, and mining industry, to enable the people to provide themselves with comforts other than breadstuffs and provisions ? Do they not need better and more houses, more clothing, more tools and implements to work with, more tea, coffee, sugar, spices, &c. &c. ? and more employment to enable them to earn the means of paying for such comforts ? The same causes operate upon and depress British India, and all the British Provinces in America.

These considerations apply with nearly the same force to our Free States, and to the Northern Slave States, as they do to Ireland. We can never clothe ourselves, and obtain all the comforts we need by raising breadstuffs and provisions, part of which are sold at extremely low prices, and a part actually lost for want of a market. The Irish enjoy free trade with England, and the benefits of the English markets for their agricultural products, which are of great consequence to them, and which we do not and never can enjoy ; and yet they are miserably poor ; and we should be equally poor, were it not for the more equal distribution of wealth and the products of labor, and the fact that our agricultural population being generally educated, and not subject to the paralyzing and depressing influence of Catholicism, are more industrious and ingenious in making domestic cloths, tools, and implements, and erecting and fitting up houses, workshops, and other buildings, for their own use and comfort. In consequence of the division of employments being more in accordance with their wants, the value of the productive industry of the people of Massachusetts and Rhode Island is much greater in proportion to their numbers, than that of the inhabitants of any other State in the Union.

Vegetables and fruits nearly all perish within a short time after they ripen ; flour and most kinds of grain cannot be kept more than a year or two without great difficulty, except in very high latitudes and a dry atmosphere ; and the same difficulty attends the keeping of almost every kind of meat. It is impossible for a people to accumulate the products of their industry of this kind for a series of years, and to keep them on hand waiting for a demand, and a market for them ; but they are obliged to dispose of them soon after they are raised, to save them from spoiling ; and whatever they produce more than they need for consumption, and more than they can find an immediate market for, is in most cases an entire loss. Whenever, therefore, in any country, more persons are employed in raising perishable products, than can be consumed at home, or sold to advantage, the labor of the extra number so unnecessarily employed, is not only an entire loss to the community, but the clothing they wear, and the other comforts they consume or enjoy, all constitute a draw-back from the earnings of their fellow citizens.

The evil does not stop even here; it has been shown in reference to cotton, Indian corn, and some other articles, that the price of commodities is regulated by the relative proportion between the demand, and the supply in the market; by an over-production of perishable commodities, not only the surplus not needed is lost, but that surplus serves to depress the market price of what is actually sold, so that a surplus is actually worse to the producers in the aggregate, than a deficient crop. How important it is then, that the division of employments among every people should be nicely and accurately adapted to their own wants, and to the wants of the commercial world! that they should produce as far as practicable whatever they need for their own consumption and comfort; and that they should produce nothing in any greater quantities than they need, unless it is wanted by the commercial world, and will sell at good prices.

It is therefore impossible for a people to improve their condition by the production and accumulation of breadstuffs and provisions, beyond what are needed for immediate use. Wool, cotton, flax, hemp, silk, tea, coffee, sugar, spices, and some other articles produced in warm climates, may be accumulated for future consumption; but they are dead property while lying and waiting for a market. The metals, and almost all manufactured products can, on the contrary, be accumulated to any extent, and be preserved and kept in use for a series of years, either administering directly to the comforts and enjoyments of man, or serving as useful agents in facilitating his labors, and increasing the products of his industry and the comforts of life. None of the metals have ever been produced and accumulated beyond the wants of man; and with the exception of the inhabitants of Great Britain, no people have ever produced or obtained in any mode whatever, a sufficient supply of tools, instruments, machinery, and utensils of industry, to increase to the greatest extent practicable, the products of their industry. Buildings of wood, well built, with proper repairs, will last and administer to the wants and comforts of man for half a century or more; those well built of brick or stone will sometimes last for centuries; agricultural improvements, such as buildings, fences, fruit-trees, drains, and under drains, with proper care, attention and repairs, last a great length of time; and canals, rail-roads, and most other public improvements, with proper attention and repairs, will last as long as man will have occasion for them. Nearly all these things serve as active capital, are in their nature productive, and serve as agents to aid man in producing and distributing the comforts of life. They are not like the necessaries and luxuries we eat and drink, which are immediately consumed in their use, and useless until needed for consumption. They constitute the principal elements of wealth, and the instruments with which it is produced and distributed. Though the people of nearly all the nations of the civilized world, with the exception of occasional years of poor crops, can procure a supply of food sufficient to secure the greatest degree of health, strength, and longevity which is consistent with the climate in which they live; yet no people, as a whole, not excepting even the inhabitants of Massachusetts and Great Britain, ever were provided with dwellings in such numbers, and of such kind and construction, as would tend to secure the greatest degree of health, strengtn, and longevity, which might be attained in the country where they resided.

Those things, therefore, which are productive in their nature, together with good dwelling houses, clothing, beds, bedding, furniture, books, and other things, not perishable, nor immediately consumed in their use, are what we should strive to produce and to accumulate in this country. We should also strive to acquire and disseminate among the people useful knowledge and skill; which constitute the most effective and valuable capital that man can possess. But the public mind in the United States has attached too much importance to agriculture, to the production of food and raw materials, and too little to the production of clothing, shelter and lodging; too much importance to commerce, railroads, canals, and other instruments for distributing wealth, and quite too little consequence to the agents and instruments necessary to produce it; too much importance to internal improvements and the agents and instruments of transportation, and too little to mining, mechanical and manufacturing industry, which are necessary to produce the greater portion of the comforts of life, and the materials of commerce. Great Britain, Massachusetts, and other manufacturing and mining states, are deriving great advantages from their railroads in the transportation of raw materials to be manufactured, and in the distribution of the products of their manufactures and mines; but the great state of New York has at present (1851) comparatively few manufactures and mineral products of her own to transport. How much benefit is that state (with the exception of the cities of New York and Buffalo) now deriving from her splendid canals and numerous railroads; compared with what might have been derived, if the manufacturing policy had been pursued by the people? With the exception of the people of those cities, have not the British derived greater advantages from those works, in the increased facilities of introducing their manufactures into the interior of the United States, than the citizens of the state of New York have? These queries are suggested for the consideration of the reader.

Nearly all the cloth made in every country, and every age of the world, prior to the year 1767, was spun on a one thread wheel, and woven in a hand loom. Spinning, weaving, and making cloth in this mode, constituted a large proportion of the employment of females in every civilized country. It was common in ancient times for ladies of the first rank, and even princesses, to engage in such pursuits, and it was deemed honorable. In this mode, females were employed, and in this mode the people were furnished with clothing, until a comparatively recent period; but the custom seems to have been mostly superseded by the use of machinery at the present time; and Great Britain has been long striving to clothe the world. Where machinery for carding, spinning, weaving, and other processes in making cloth, are introduced, women and children can do a large proportion of the work; their labor is rendered from ten to thirty times as productive as by the ancient processes; the division of employments is not deranged; and no portion of the community need be without employment, where such manufactures are carried on extensively.

But where the practice of manufacturing in families is abandoned, and the people are clothed with the manufactures of other countries, there is scarcely any employment for children, and comparatively little for females. Where manufacturing cloth in families is abandoned, as it is mostly in this country, not over two fifths of the male population should be engaged in agriculture, and the remaining three fifths in mechanical, manufacturing, mining, commercial, and other pursuits. If, instead of having the male portion of over three fourths of our population engaged in agriculture, not more than one half were so engaged, and the remaining half were employed in other pursuits, the markets would be well supplied, but not so much surfeited with agricultural products; such products would rise in price; the earnings of the half engaged in agriculture would exceed in value the earnings of the three fourths at the present time; the country might be well supplied with cloths of every kind, and with iron, steel, copper, lead, hardware, and all manufactures of the metals made at home; we should have no occasion to import metals of any kind except silver, tin, and zinc; and our imports like those of Great Britain and France, would consist mostly of raw materials to be manufactured, and of the products of tropical and warm climates, which do not come in competition with the industry of our own citizens. In such case, the division of employments would be in accordance with the wants of the people; we should produce everything we need, which our country is capable of producing; and instead of selling raw materials at extremely low prices to pay for manufactured goods at high prices, we should export manufactured goods to pay for raw materials which we could not produce, or not in sufficient quantities for the consumption of the country. Instead of producing twice as much Indian corn and some other articles as the country needs, and half or two thirds as much iron, hardware, cotton, woollen, silk, and linen goods, we should produce about as much of the former as the country might require, and a surplus of the latter to pay for our tea, coffee, sugar, spices, and other products of warm and tropical climates; and the balance of trade would soon be in our favor.

Under the compromise act prior to the tariff of 1842, our country was filled with the products of foreign industry, which displaced so much of the products of the industry of our own citizens, who were consequently idle for want of employment; many of them were obliged to live very poor, and were finally driven to agricultural pursuits for a support. The country became involved in debt for foreign goods, and eventually drained of its specie to pay for them; agricultural products being still more increased beyond the demand for them, fell more and more in price; and thus, by the system of free trade, the proper division of employments was disturbed, the productive industry of the country was lessened, and instead of producing what we wanted, we produced a great surplus of what we did not want, and ran into debt for what we did want. The tariff of 1846 is producing similar effects.

It makes no difference what a people pay for any kind of necessaries or comforts, provided they pay for them in the products of their own industry at corresponding prices. The price of the one equalizes that of the other, and the tendency is to stimulate the industry and increase the production of both parties; but when one party refuses to take the products of the other in payment, and requires money, the tendency is to paralyze the industry of the latter, in as much as it exhausts his means and furnishes him no market for the products of his labor, and no facilities for extending his business and increasing his industry.

SEC. 13. *Utility of competition—Injurious effects of excessive competition.*

In as much as the price of a commodity depends not only on the amount of labor, skill, and capital required to produce it, but also on the proportion between the demand and the supply in the market, an increased production tends to lower prices, and diminished production tends to raise them. The public are therefore interested in having the supply of every commodity equal to the demand, in order to keep down prices to the general level of other products, which cost the same amount of labor and skill. A sufficient amount of competition to produce this result is useful to the community. When, however, the production of any thing exceeds the demand and consumption of the country, and the wants of commerce, the competition among sellers in the market is so great, that the producers are not only injured by the consequent depression of the price, but the labor bestowed upon the production of the excess not needed, is in many cases a total and in others nearly a total loss to the community.

Though some individuals may derive benefit from the reduction of prices produced by excessive competition, yet they never derive as much benefit as the competitors suffer loss—for the reason just given; that the labor bestowed, and the expense incurred in the production of the excess, is generally a total loss to the community. It is therefore a national loss. This rule applies to all employments, professions and pursuits. In the United States. we have many more lawyers and physicians than can live by their professions, and more than the wants and good of the public require. By excessive competition, they injure each other, without materially benefiting the public; for the time of the supernumeraries is spent without advantage to the public. Such is sometimes the case with steamboat owners, stage proprietors, and other common carriers. So also with merchants, the great number in this country often produces so excessive competition and great anxiety to sell, as to induce them to urge upon the people on credit, or at low prices, more goods than they really need, or are able to pay for; and the result is, much extravagance—many bankruptcies and failures to pay,—great losses by merchants, and serious injuries to the community.

An arrangement among the owners of coal mines in the north of England, to regulate the price of coal, by limiting the production and sale of it, has existed with some partial interruptions ever since the year 1771.*

This is effected by means of a committee appointed by them; who sit regularly in the town of Newcastle; to ascertain the con-

*See Porter's "Progress of the Nation," title Coal.

sumption of coal, and the supply in the market—*fix the prices at which the various qualities may be sold, and the quantity which may from time to time be shipped from each Colliery to supply the demand;* the quantity assigned to each, depending on the number and size of the pits opened, the number of mines, and the amount of capital invested.

The Coal mines of Great Britain are so numerous and extensive, that were it not for some such arrangement, the production of coal might at times greatly exceed the demand; and thereby depress prices to so low rates, as to be ruinous to the trade; and reduce to bankruptcy and distress, great numbers of persons employed in it, and in the mines. By regulating and limiting the production of the principal mines in the kingdom, from whence coals are transported to London and other large cities, and adapting it, (in conjunction with the supply from the other mines) to the public wants, prices have been kept steady, sufficiently high to remunerate persons employed in the mines, and in the trade, and the business rendered safe; and yet the competition from the smaller mines in the kingdom has kept down prices to a reasonable standard.

The Iron Masters of Great Britain have had frequent meetings and conventions for years past, to make reports, collect information of the production, consumption at home, and exportation of iron, the supply in the market, and the probable future demand for it—in order to increase or limit the production according to circumstances—adapt it as near as practicable, to the demand, and establish prices, by conventional arrangements among themselves.

A similar course (though to a much less extent) has been pursued by the cotton manufacturers of Great Britain. They have held frequent conventions, in order to confer together, and when the markets are glutted, the most of the cotton mills work short time; so as to sustain the operatives by partial employment, and at the same time, to lessen the production, adapt it to the wants of the public, and keep up prices.

The producers of cotton in the Southern states having learned a lesson of wisdom from these examples, have held conventions, collected information on the subject, and come to the conclusion, that the depression of the price of cotton from 1840 to 1849, was caused by over production, beyond the immediate wants of the world, and by checking the increase of the production, they have succeeded in raising prices.

Lawyers and physicians in all parts of our country, have been in the habit of holding meetings, conferring together, and regulating the prices of professional services, as far as practicable, in order to keep them up to a proper standard. Were it not for such conventional arrangements, and the sentiment of honor among professional men to maintain them, the spirit of competition would soon depress the prices of professional services so low, as to discourage high professional attainments, degrade the character of the professions, and destroy their usefulness.

It was common in England from the 12th to the 17th century, to fix the price of labor by act of Parliament. This system was arbitrary, productive of much injustice and oppression, and with the aid of monopolies then common, it tended to destroy competition, and discourage and depress industry. It can never be expedient to fix prices by statute, except for official labor—not to grant monopolies, except for short periods of time, to encourage invention, and to establish new branches of industry. But much good may be done by the government, and by associations, meetings, conventions, committees, authors, reports, books, newspapers, and other periodicals; by collecting and disseminating information of the quantity of the products of each branch of industry, and of the consumption and wants of the public; to divert industry from employments in which it is not needed, to others in which it is needed; and to adapt the industry and productions of a country, to its conditions, the wants of the people, and the foreign demand. These are the principal uses of our annual reports on commerce, and of the statistics collected by our national and state governments. Such information is not only useful, but indispensably necessary to the legislator, to enable him to legislate in such a manner, as to promote the general welfare of the nation; for though the industry of a country cannot be regulated with safety, by positive rules, yet much may be done by a system of patents, premiums and bounties, and by regulating commerce, to encourage the increase of such branches of industry, as may be needed most.

CHAPTER XII.

ON PRICES; THE LAWS WHICH REGULATE AND GOVERN THEM, THE CAUSES OF THEIR FLUCTUATION FROM AGE TO AGE, IN DIFFERENT COUNTRIES.

SEC. 1. *Necessity of a standard, or measure of value—use of gold and silver as the standard.*

IN making exchanges or sales of property, a common standard or measure of value is necessary, by which the commodities exchanged or sold may be compared, and their relative values determined. The precious metals, on account of their utility, intrinsic value, beauty and durability, and the general desire for them, have been made the common measure of value, and universal currency, of civilized nations, from the earliest eras of history. In order to facilitate the use of gold and silver in making exchanges, governments have made them into coin—that is, they have assayed them and weighed and divided them into pieces convenient for use, and stamped them with a government stamp, as an evidence of the weight of pure metal contained in each piece, as fixed by law. Coin is called money, because its weight and quality has been ascertained and stamped upon it, according to law. Coining adds a little, and but a little, to the value of the metal, by ascertaining its true value, and thereby increasing the facility of effecting exchanges with it; but the substantial value of coin, consists in the intrinsic value of the metal, for other uses.

SEC. 2. *Causes of the Changes in Value of Gold and Silver.*

The precious metals do not furnish an invariable standard and measure of value. It seems to be generally admitted by statesmen, and by writers on political economy, that the exchangeable value of gold and silver is affected, like all other commodities, by the amount in circulation, in proportion to the demand for them; and that their fluctuations of value are often local as well as temporary, depending on the relative amount in circulation.

The demand for the precious metals in every country is in proportion to the number and wealth of the inhabitants, and the value of their productive industry. When gold and silver are abundant, their relative value declines, and the prices of all other things rise; and when they are scarce, their relative value is increased, and other things fall in price. Hence the importance of giving the reader a statement of the amount of coin and paper-money in circulation in the commercial world, at different periods, and the amount to each person—to enable him to understand the causes of the constant depreciation in the value of coin, and the rise of commodities—from the year 1500 to the year 1810—to compare present prices of labor and products, with prices at any past period—and to understand one of the principal causes of their fluctuations. (See Sections 6 and 8 of Chap. X.)

The value of all goods and products in England in 1696 was then adopted as the standard by which to estimate the value of all exports from and imports into the kingdom. That standard has been retained from that time until the present, and the commercial records of England show the fluctuations in the nominal prices of goods, from year to year, for more than a century and a half. By means of these records and other records of the prices of grain and some other articles for several centuries together with the facts collected and condensed in Section 8 of chapter X, of the amount of money in circulation at different periods, it becomes practicable to determine with reasonable accuracy, how much of the nominal fluctuations in prices have been produced by differences in the amount of circulating money, and how much by other causes. The amount of circulating money to each person I have estimated in that section as follows,—in the year 1500 at but $1,50—in 1700 at $4,50—in 1810 at about $8; in 1840 at $5,30. It was about the same in 1850 as in 1840—Call the amount in 1696, $4,40, and we have an efficient cause (other things being the same) why products should be about eighty per cent. higher in 1810, and twenty per cent. higher from 1840 to 1850, than they were in 1696.

SEC. 3. *On the Price, or Market Value of Products.*

The only fair criterion or measure of value of an article, is the quantity of other commodities, or money, which can be readily obtained for it in exchange, whenever the owner wishes to part with it. This, in all commercial dealings, and in all money valuations, is called the current price.

The price, market value, current or exchangeable value, of all commodities and species of property, depends on the proportion between the demand and the prospective as well as the actual supply in the market, and on the amount of money in circulation in proportion to the population, and industry. The demand*

* See on this subject of demand and value, section 3, of chap. VI.

depends first, on the utility of the thing, and its capacity or supposed capacity to promote the comfort, convenience, and enjoyment of man, to increase his wealth, or to gratify his pride, vanity, or ambition; secondly, on the number of persons in the circle or district where it may be used, who may desire it; thirdly, on the number of persons in that district who are able and willing to pay the current price for the thing desired.

As manufactures are generally very valuable in proportion to their weight and bulk, most of them will bear transportation thousands of miles, in wagons, on camels' backs, packhorses or mules; and hence the market for such products, and the district in which the demand for them exists, is co-extensive with the commercial world. But food of most kinds is very bulky and heavy in proportion to its value, and liable to perish in a comparatively short period; and hence the extent of the market for flour, grain, and meat, is necessarily limited by the nature of things, to a narrow circuit, which it cannot pass; except at periods of short duration, when crops are deficient in other countries, and prices extraordinarily high. In ordinary seasons the prices of rye, Indian corn, oats, and all other coarse grains are so low, that they will not bear transportation more than from fifty to one hundred miles by teams, before the cost of transportation will exceed the value of the article after it is transported. The intensity of the demand for food in any country, must therefore depend on the density of the population; for the coarse grains, vegetables, fruits, and most of the flour and meat, must be consumed in the immediate vicinity where they are produced.

The supply of agricultural products depends, first, on the climate, soil, and season; secondly, on the advancement made by the people in the natural sciences, and in the mechanic arts; thirdly, on the number and proportion of the population devoted to agriculture, in the district of country which supplies the market, and the amount of capital accumulated and appropriated to agricultural purposes; and, fourthly, on the prices of products, which generally affect very materially both the present and prospective supply of them. The supply of the products of mining, mechanical, and manufacturing industry, depends mostly on the same causes; first, on climate, which determines the wants of the people and acts as a stimulant or otherwise to industry; secondly, on their advances in the natural sciences and the mechanic arts; thirdly, on the number and proportion of the people so employed, and the skill acquired, and capital accumulated and employed by them; and fourthly, on the price of their products in the market. This fourth condition has much more influence upon the production and the supply of manufactured, than of agricultural products; first, because manufactures are conducted by a much less number of persons, who are mostly capitalists and men of intelligence, who have their correspondence with each other, in relation to the markets, hold conventions, and to some extent regulate prices, by withholding a portion of their products from the market when the supply is too large, and prices depressed, by working short time, and lessening the production, until the supply and demand are equalized. On the contrary, agricultural products depend much on the season; their quantity cannot be increased or diminished at will, by working twelve, eight or six hours per day; they are perishable in their nature, and cannot be kept very long on hand, but however much the market may be glutted and prices depressed, they must be thrown upon it before they perish, though the necessary effect must be to depress prices still more.

SEC. 4. *Natural limit to the demand for Food; no limit but Poverty, to the demand for objects of Ornament and Fashion.*

There is a natural limit to the demand for food. Every person needs to sustain life and promote health, a certain quantity in the aggregate of bread, and of animal, vegetable, and other food. He may vary the quantity of the different kinds, but cannot materially increase the aggregate quantity, without making a glutton of himself. Here is an impassable barrier to the increase of demand beyond a certain quantity, though the demand often falls short of this barrier, by reason of the poverty of a people, and their inability to pay for as much as they really need. That was the case in 1847 with the people of Ireland, the highlands of Scotland, and some parts of France, but it was mostly confined to the agricultural population. On the contrary, to the demand for, and consumption of, fine and costly silks, satins, laces, muslins, worsteds, broadcloths, watches, jewelry, and other personal ornaments, silver plate, furniture, carriages, horses, books, pictures, fine houses, pleasure grounds and gardens, objects of taste, fashion, and amusement, there is scarcely any barrier or limit, except the want of ability of persons to pay for them; and the passion for such things is so strong, that multitudes are ruined by indulging it beyond their means. Such things, not being perishable in their nature, or not rapidly perishable, may be accumulated to any extent consistent with the ability of the people; and they may be kept on hand by the producer, until they are wanted, and may be accumulated by the consumer for future use. The manufacturer, therefore, has the advantage over the farmer, in the comparatively unlimited demand for his products, in their imperishable nature, and the small expense, compared with their value, of transporting them to any market, however distant.

SEC. 5. *Effect of Demand and Supply on each other, and on prices.*

The production of articles, (the demand for which is limited by the laws of nature,) should be confined to that limit, and all the population not needed to produce so much as may be needed of such articles, should be employed in other pursuits. Supply and demand mutually act and react upon each other; and where there is a proper division of employments, supply may be increased ten fold, and the demand still keep pace with it, and prevent prices from falling, if the supply consists of all the different articles, and in the proportions needed by the community. For in such case, one class of producers would exchange through the medium of commerce, their products which they do not want for their own use, with other producers, for other products which they do need; and thus the products of every man's industry would become available to procure for him their full value in such articles as he or his family need; there would be no surplus products thrown upon the market without buyers; the market would never be glutted, and prices never depressed. In this way, the splendid conception of Dr. Smith, stated in the Wealth of Nations, might be realised; production might go on *ad infinitum*, and the production and bringing to market a commodity wanted, would, through the operations of commerce and the stimulus exerted on the mind of man by the commodity itself, call into existence equivalent commodities to be exchanged for it at fair prices.

A large surplus greatly depresses prices, and a deficit raises them. If the division of employments of a nation could be in perfect accordance with the wants of the people, and their markets properly secured from over imports of foreign products, their products would be in accordance with their wants, and the wants of the commercial world; the interchange would be made without difficulty; all but the idle, dissolute, and infirm, would be well supplied; there would seldom be any deficit, and never a large surplus to depress prices, embarrass and ruin producers.

SEC. 6. *The Prices of Labor are governed by Natural Laws.*

The prices of labor are governed by the same natural laws that regulate the prices of the products of industry.

The prices of the same kinds of labor, both in Europe and America, are usually about fifty per cent. higher in cities than in the country. Manufactures are mostly situated in cities and large towns; and the average wages of good journeymen mechanics and skilful adult male manufacturing laborers, are generally about twice as high as those of agricultural laborers in the same country.

Estimates of the average* wages of agricultural laborers, and of good journeymen mechanics and manufacturing laborers, in the United States, from 1840 to 1850—and in the undermentioned countries of the Old World from 1830 to 1850, per week, without board, from which one third should be deducted in case board and lodging are furnished by the employer.

	Agricultural laborers.			Mechanics and manufacturers.
United States,	†15s.	sterling or	$3.60	$7.20
Great Britain,	10s.	"	2.40	4.80
Ireland, -	5s.	"	1.20	—
Holland and Belgium,	7s.	"	1.68	3.36
France, -	6½s.	"	1.56	3.12
Prussia and north part of Germany,	6s.	"	1.44	2.88
Austria, interior of Germany, and Italy,	5s.	"	1.20	2.40
Spain and Portugal,			1.00	2.00

The real value of labor depends on the value of its products; but its price depends on supply and demand and the amount of money in circulation, and is determined by the proportion which the number of competent laborers bears to the demand for labor.

In as much as mechanical and manufacturing employments require much more experience, skill, and science, than agriculture does, the number of persons who have attained the experience and skill required for the former, is small, when compared with the number of agricultural laborers; hence the wages of agricultural laborers are low, in consequence of a great surplus of numbers; and the wages of mechanics and manufacturing laborers are much higher, by reason of their numbers being less, in proportion to the demand for their labor.

The demand for labor depends much on its productiveness; that is, on the quantity of commodities it will produce in a given time, and the price they will sell for. A people who have made great advances in the natural and mechanical sciences, and have accumulated a large amount of machinery, tools, and instruments, can make their industry much more productive than a rude and

* These are intended as average wages for men throughout each country. Very skilful mechanics and manufacturing laborers will sometimes earn two or three times as much as here estimated.

† The shillings in the first column are sterling money, for agricultural labor.

ignorant people, but little acquainted with the mechanic arts, and destitute of machinery. Hence wages among the former are generally much higher than among the latter people; hence wages are at present nearly twice as high in England as they were a century since—fifty per cent. higher than they are in France—about twice as high as in Austria, the interior of Germany, and many other countries of Europe; and agricultural labor is nearly twice as high in England as in Ireland.

The high prices of labor in the United States are maintained, partly by the skill, activity, science, and general intelligence of the people, which contribute to make their industry effective; partly by the spirit of freedom which inspires them with the ambition to labor for themselves, and not to sell their services to others, unless they can get more for them than they are really worth; and partly by the prospective value of lands in the new States. Agricultural labor in the North Western States is mostly paid for in barter, at prices nominally from twenty-five to fifty per cent. higher than its products would sell for in money.

If manufacturing laborers in Great Britain and the United States were equally skilful and efficient, the real value of their labor would be the same in both countries, if the prices of manufactured products were the same. It costs the British manufacturer but a trifle more to send his products to the New York market, than it does the manufacturer of Massachusetts or of the interior of our country. If by means of under valuations, the imported products are subject to a duty of only twenty per cent. on their real value, the American manufacturer would have an advantage over the foreign manufacturer of only from twenty to twenty-five per cent. if the price of labor were the same in both countries—and consequently, the real value of manufacturing labor is only about twenty-five per cent. greater here than it is in England—though the price paid for labor here is fifty per cent. greater than it is in England, and more than twice as much as it is in France. The raw materials of fine cotton goods comprise only about one-fourth part of their value; and the raw materials of iron and hardware are dug out of the earth, and cost not much but labor. Hence the foreign manufacturer has an advantage over the manufacturers of the United States under the tariff of 1846, and the system of valuations in use, of from fifteen to twenty-five per cent., and hence the former can undersell the latter in our own markets, and at the same time sell at such prices as to make large profits on their business, whereby they can and have supplied our markets with the greater part of the finest quality of goods, and nearly all the hardware and rail-road iron used here—supplanted and ruined great numbers of our manufacturers—thrown thousands of our laborers out of employment—and greatly lessened the aggregate industry of our country.

Though the price of labor in this country has been generally above its real value, the superabundance of laborers in Europe has depressed it below its real value—and the consequence has been, that while capitalists there have oppressed the laborer by an unjust division of the products of labor—by retaining too large a share for the profits of capital and superintendence, and allowing the laborer too small a share ; in this country, the high price of labor has often injured, and sometimes ruined, the employer. If the tariff of 1846 is to be continued, labor must come down to the standard of its true value, as measured by the commercial value of its products, which is but little above its real value in Great Britain.

Sec. 7. *On the Prices of Lands.*

The prices of lands, like all other property, are governed by the relative demand for them, and the supply in the market. But as unimproved lands are generally unproductive, and can be made productive only by means of improvements made by the labor of man, the demand for lands depends; 1st, on their productive qualities; 2nd, on the amount of labor judiciously expended on them ; 3rd, on the demand for agricultural produce, and the price it commands in the vicinity; and the demand for, and the price of produce, depend on the density of the population of the country. Two elements, therefore, in addition to its intrinsic qualities, enter into the price of land, which create the demand for it and give it value ; 1st, population in the vicinity of it ; 2d, labor expended in improving it, and in making roads, building bridges, mills, towns, villages, &c., in the vicinity of it. Lands in the interior of New Holland, Van Diemen's-land, Oregon, California, Missouri Territory, Texas, and many other countries, would have no value whatever, were it not that the increase of the human family renders it probable that at some future period, there will be a demand for them for occupation and use. There is, therefore, a prospective demand, which gives them some value.

Population is an element of price and value ; whatever value lands may have in addition to the improvements made by human labor, must depend on population ; and is in proportion to the density of the population, which creates the demand for food, and therefore creates the demand for land which produces food. Perhaps it would not be far from the truth to estimate the average quality of lands fit for cultivation, or good for grazing, as worth over and above the improvements judiciously made on them, about 10 cents per acre for every inhabitant to the square mile in the vicinity; making lands worth over and above improvements, in counties of 10 inhabitants to the square mile, $1 per acre; in counties of 20 to the square mile, $2 per acre; of 40 to the square mile, $4 per acre; and of 60 to the square mile, $6 per acre; and when you get above that number, the increase in price and value is much more rapid than the increase in population.

From seventy-five to eighty per cent. of all the private property in Great Britain consists of real estate, and the buildings, and other improvements upon it—all the personal estate not much exceeding twenty per cent. Real estate bears quite as high a proportion to personal estate in this country and generally higher in the agricultural states, than it does in Great Britain. Only about three-fifths of the whole value of the real estate in Great Britain, and about the same proportion in this country, was produced by human labor, on the land itself, by buildings and other improvements, and two-fifths or more, comprising at least thirty per cent. in value, of all the property in every well settled country, may be said to be added to the land by population; which creates a demand and markets for its products—and by public roads and other public expenditures and improvements.

Estimate of the *value added by population alone* to the real estate of Great Britain, and to the real estate of the States of Massachusetts, New York, and Ohio in 1840, and *the amount added by each one of the population*—calling such addition of value equal to twenty-five per cent. of the whole amount of private property.

	Value added.	Amount by each.
In Great Britain	£760,000,000	
equal to .	$3,648,000,000	$200
Massachusetts	$82,000,000	$112
New York	$242,000,000	$100
Ohio	$86,000,000	$56

These estimates may not be entirely correct, they are probably too low, but it is sufficiently correct for the purpose of illustration—to show the reader how rapidly an increase of population adds to the value of property—and that the same number adds three or four times as much to its value, in a densely populated country, as they do in one very new, and sparsely inhabited.

The prices of improved lands depend on the rents they will command; and the amount of rent depends on the surplus value of the produce, over and above the price of the labor and the costs of cultivation. The amount of rent and the price of land, therefore, depend much on the price of labor. Where the population is dense, and there is a super-abundance of laborers, as in many countries of Europe, labor is usually very cheap, and produce, rents, and the prices of land are necessarily high. Where there is a super-abundance of land, and a deficiency of laborers, if labor is productive, as in the United States, it is usually high, and produce, rents, and the prices of land, are necessarily low. So far from the aggregate value of the property of the people of the United States being increased by an increase of territory, by the acquisition of Texas, New Mexico, California, and Oregon, and scattering the population over those vast countries, it has been, and will be for many years to come, diminished by these causes. The prospective value of the lands of those distant regions is so remote, that they are not worth three cents per acre, in the aggregate, exclusive of the precious metals contained in them. So far as population gives value to land, a given number of inhabitants densely peopling a small territory, increases the aggregate value of the land much more than the same number scattered over a territory five or ten times as large So far as value is produced by human labor, combined labor is the most productive, and there is a great loss in scattering the population over a large surfrce, and thereby increasing the expenses of making roads and other internal improvements, and of transporting products from the producer to the consumer in distant regions.

From these facts and illustrations, the reader may learn why the value of real estate depends so much on the density of population; and why farming lands, of an average quality, are worth, over and above the improvements on them, in England, 40 to 50 pounds sterling per acre; within a few miles of the cities of Boston, New York, and Philadelphia, $40 to $50 per acre; in the centre of the grand prairie of Illinois, remote from population, timber, fuel, and water, and in the very new counties of Michigan, Wisconsin, Iowa, and Missouri, not over forty or fifty cents per acre; and in the interior districts of Texas, Missouri Territory, Oregon, California, and New Mexico, not more than as many mills per acre.

The only way to keep up the price of wild lands, and render the public lands of much value, is to adhere rigidly to the minimum price of one dollar and a quarter per acre; to give none away to individuals, and whenever grants are made to States, to prohibit their sales for less than that price. This system kept up prices nearly sixty years, until the large amount of bounty lands given to the soldiers and volunteers of the Mexican war were thrown into the market, without limitation as to price; which depressed prices nearly one half. The large quantities which will be thrown into market by means of the bounty land bill, (of 1850) may depress prices much more.

It is now proposed to give the lands away, in limited quantities, to actual settlers. Such a policy would draw from the Treasury of the United States, the cost of extinguishing the Indian titles, of making surveys, and other expenses incident to the land system, and render valueless the whole public domain, all the school lands of the Western States, and all the lands granted to the States for making internal improvements, and for other public purposes. But inasmuch as the principal part of the value of wild lands in a new country, is created by population,—by improvements made in the vicinity—and by the prospect of an increase of population—it seems just and reasonable, that a portion of the value thus created by the early settlers, should enure to their benefit. In my opinion, twelve or fifteen sections in each surveyed township, of six miles square, should be appropriated for schools, roads, county, and state purposes. For example; about three or four sections instead of one, should be appropriated for the support of common schools; three or four for making township roads, and bridges, when the country is new; three or four for making county roads, and bridges, building court house, jail, and poor house—and as many more for making canals, state roads, and other internal improvements.

All such expenditures would enhance the value of the remaining lands retained by the general government, and at the same time increase the advantages of the settlers and relieve them of some of the burthens of taxation, which are often very oppressive in a new country. Such a policy would give them, in the shape of public schools and improvements, a portion of the value, which they themselves create, and thereby put them in possession of a portion of the advantages enjoyed by the inhabitants of the old States, which were produced and made by their common ancestors.

SEC. 8. *On Rents, and what regulates their Value.*

The prices of rents are governed by the same laws that regulate the prices of products, labor and lands. The great regulator is the proportion between the demand for, and the supply of, improved lands. The intensity of the demand depends, first, on the density of the population, which affects the prices of products. Second, on the state of improvement and the productiveness of the land itself; and lastly, on the price of labor. Rent is the value of the residue of the crops after paying for the labor of cultivating the land and selling the crops, and for the use of the capital employed. Hence the amount of rent depends mostly on the value of the crops that may be raised, and the value of the crops depends on the number and density of the population that want them ; but the rent also depends some on the price of labor.

In all new countries, where wild lands are abundant and cheap, where any man can procure lands sufficient to improve and cultivate for a trifle, there are very few who wish to rent other men's lands for cultivation. Improved lands in new countries will seldom rent for sufficient to pay the taxes annually levied on them, and the interest on the cost of the improvements; and it sometimes happens that the owner can scarcely get rent enough from good lands to pay taxes, the cost of superintendence, and the expenses of keeping the fences, buildings, and other improvements in as good condition as when they were rented. On the contrary, the annual rent of good lands, within a few miles of large cities in Great Britain, is generally from five to eight pounds sterling ($24 to $38) per acre. Hence we may deduce the conclusion, that the amount of rent which good improved lands will command, depends almost entirely on the number of inhabitants in the vicinity to consume their products. Hence the value of lands and the price of rents increase, with the increase of population.

The modern Malthusian theory of rent teaches that it is the difference between the productiveness of first rate lands, and the inferior qualities of land, which are successively brought into cultivation. This theory and all its assumptions are fanciful and fallacious; and all the reasoning in support of it is sophistical. The rich river bottoms in the new states, generally command as little rent as the poor hills above them, back from the rivers, for the reason that the latter are more healthy than the former, and as the prices of agricultural products are extremely low, the greater productiveness of the rich lands rarely compensates for their greater insalubrity.

Sec. 9. *Interest on Money, and Profit on Capital.*

The rate of interest on money loaned, depends much on the proportion between the demand and the supply in the market; though the interest on the great mass of loans is regulated by law. The natural rate of interest, is the average profits which can be made by the use of property, which the money will pay for, after paying all expenses attending its use, and a reasonable compensation for superintendence.

The profits on capital depend on circumstances. The profits on land may be regarded as synonymous with rents. They depend mostly on population, which causes a demand for its products, but partly on productiveness, and some on the price of labor, as shown in the last section. The average profits of improved farms in Ohio and all the North-western States, do not exceed, if they equal, three per cent. per annum, over and above taxes. One of the principal sources of profit from holding lands, consists in their average annual rise in value of three or four per cent., caused by an increase of population.

The profits on capital invested in manufacturing, mining, or any other pursuit, consist of the residue of nett income after paying the wages of labor employed, the cost of superintendence keeping the capital good, and incidental expenses. Hence the profits depend on the field of employment, on the extent of the market and the prices of products, and on the prices of labor. The profits of the manufacture of cotton goods, iron and hardware in Great Britain, during the high prices from 1800 to 1815, must have been generally as high as from twenty to thirty per cent. annually; and they have sometimes, for short periods, ranged as high as from ten to fifteen per cent. in the United States. At many other periods, the manufacturers in this country have run their factories for very trifling profits, and sometimes at a loss, owing to the markets being glutted with foreign imports, the depression of prices, and the fact that laborers demanded more for their labor, than its products in the shape of manufactured goods, would sell for in the market.

Though the wages of labor have been increased in Great Britain by mining and manufactures, and the condition of the laboring population greatly improved since 1780, yet labor having been very abundant, and labor of most kinds superabundant, the greater part of the time, capitalists have derived the principal and most extensive benefits from the introduction of machinery and the wonderful increase of the manufacturing and mining industry of the kingdom. In the United States, the wages of labor having been about fifty per cent. higher than in Great Britain, the result has been different. As mining and manufacturing create a market for labor, and also for agricultural products, they have benefited the laborer and farmer in this country, much more than they have the capitalist. Those branches of industry tend to build up cities and villages, and to increase the value of real estate both in cities and in the country. They have raised the value of all the farms, as well as other real estate in the vicinity where either of them is carried on; and as the manufacturing capitalists of the United States are generally large owners of real estate, I presume that their manufacturing enterprises and business have benefited them indirectly, (by increasing the value of the real estate owned by them) to an amount nearly equal to the nett profits realized by them from the business of manufacturing.

The profits of manufacturing being the residue after paying wages and all expenses, wages have been so much higher in this country than in Great Britain, that the profits of the capitalists have been much less, and perhaps on an average, not more than half as great as in Great Britain. This is shown by the vast accumulation of wealth in that country, and the prodigious number of princely castles, and magnificent dwellings, erected during the present century by the manufacturing and commercial classes. Though the great mass of the people live in miserable cottages, yet the aggregate value of all the dwelling houses, out-houses, and pleasure grounds around them, in Great Britain, were worth in 1842 (according to the income tax) nearly three times as much as the same kind of property in the United States.

The average profits of capital are now much greater, and perhaps twice as great in nearly all northern Europe, as they were a century since. This is owing to the greater productiveness of industry, more extensive markets for its products, and greater facilities for commerce. In the great chain of causes and effects, these things were caused by machinery, by new and improved tools and implements, by greater knowledge of the physical sciences, and by canals, steamboats and railroads, which in their turn have contributed to increase population and to enlarge the field of employment for both capital and labor. All those things mutually act and react upon each other.

Profits having been high in Great Britain, capital has rapidly accumulated, become superabundant, and greater than the field of profitable employment. This has coöperated with the statute, to make interest low. The low rate of interest at home has encouraged capitalists to invest their capital in foreign loans and enterprises, and in manufacturing, mining, railroads, and splendid buildings, rather than to loan it at home at low rates; and by these means, the increase of the wealth of the kingdom has been accelerated with still greater rapidity, than it otherwise could have been.

The high rate of interest in the State of New York has had the contrary effect, and has greatly retarded manufacturing industry in that State. It has encouraged men to employ their capital as money lenders, rather than to invest it in manufacturing and other pursuits on their own account, and at their own risk —and I have no doubt that there is more money lent in that State, in proportion to the population, than in any other State or country in the world. The lender takes all the securities he can procure from the borrower, watches over him constantly for the purpose of increasing his own security, and often to take advantage of the embarrassments of the borrower, to compel him to pay extra interest or to sell his property at less than its value. All these things tend to create an antagonistical interest between the lender and the borrower, to embarrass and injure the borrower, and to discourage and destroy enterprise. On the other hand, in States where interest is low, capitalists are inclined to form limited and other copartnerships, to invest their money on their own account, and to superintend its employment themselves, rather than to loan it. It appears to me that this is one of the principal causes, coöperating with the system of manufacturing corporations, which has caused manufacturing industry to increase with so much greater rapidity (during the last thirty years) in Massachusetts and Rhode Island than it has in New York.

Sec. 10. *Free Trade theory of Cost and Price.*

Dr. Wayland says, in the introductory chapter of his work on political economy: "The AMOUNT OF LABOR expended in the creation of a value, is commonly denominated its COST. This is always the STANDARD by which, for long periods, the degree of EXCHANGEABLE VALUE may be ESTIMATED. When, however, we here speak of labor, we speak of it as simple labor; that is, without taking into consideration the DEGREE OF SKILL which may be combined with it, or the other circumstances which may conspire to create variation in its value. We suppose, in the remarks above, in all cases labor of the same kind is to be compared together. I have said above, that cost forms the standard by which the degree of exchangeable value for long periods is to be estimated. Temporary circumstances may create a variation from this standard; and may for a short time elevate this value above or depress it below the cost.—These, however, can continue to operate but for a short period; the TENDENCY OF EXCHANGEABLE VALUE IS ALWAYS TO GRAVITATE TOWARDS COST."

He says, in Book II. Chap. III. Sec. 6, "Although free competition is necessary to reduce PRICES to their NATURAL RATE; yet beyond this, COMPETITION, within long periods, can have NO EFFECT WHATEVER. The PRICE OF EVERY ARTICLE IS DETERMINED BY THE COST of its production; that is, by the LABOR and CAPITAL necessary to produce it."

Sec. 11. *Free Trade theory of the effect of competition.*

He says in Book II. Chap. 1. Sec. 2, "that the general rate at which every thing is exchanged, is the amount of labor which it costs to produce it." The producer can never for a long period, charge more than a fair remuneration for his labor and capital; because, then it would be *cheaper for the other party to produce it for himself*. He cannot, for a long period, charge less; because in this case, he will be ruined, and must leave the employment; and thus the number of producers will be diminished, and the value of the product will rise to the average rate of profit. Nevertheless, *for short periods*, the exchangeable value of any product may be raised above the reasonable rate of profit. If the demand exceed the supply, there will be a competition among the buyers; the more wealthy will overbid the less wealthy, and the price will rise. This rise of price will induce others to devote themselves to supplying the demand, and thus the price will fall. If the supply be greater than the demand, there will arise a competition among the sellers, and the price will fall, and will remain depressed, until either the demand increases, or until so many leave the employment, as shall reduce the supply to the average demand."

Again, he says in his introductory chapter, p. 22: "The moment the price of an article falls below its cost, it ceases to be produced, until the price rises. As soon as it rises above ordinary profit, capital and labor are directed to it, and it is produced in sufficient quantity to meet the usual demand. When the price of any article is low, men leave off this kind of production in too great numbers, and hence follows a comparative scarcity of the product which they furnish. When the price is high, men rush, in too great numbers, into this sort of production, and hence arises a temporary glut, and a depreciation of its exchangeable value."

Dr. Wayland comes to the following general conclusions;

"1. COST, that is, *labor bestowed*, is the foundation of exchangeable *value, and from which, it can never, for long periods, materially vary;* that is, an *article can always be had for what it costs to produce it;* including in this, the ordinary profit of the producer. Notwithstanding this, there will, however, arise various fluctuations, depending upon the following circumstances.

Other things being equal,

2. The greater the supply, the less the exchangeable value.

3. The less the supply, the greater the exchangeable value.

4. The greater the demand, the greater the exchangeable value.

5. The less the demand, the less the exchangeable value.

6. And in general, cost being fixed, exchangeable value is inversely as the supply, and directly as the demand.

7. Or still more generally, at any particular time, exchangeable VALUE WILL BE AS THE COST, plus the effect produced by the variation in supply and demand."

The foregoing principles of cost and value, together with the assumed causes and facilities of the increase and diminution of the supply of commodities, constitute the foundation and chief corner-stone of the doctrines and principles of the Free Trade Party. They originated substantially with the distinguished author of the Wealth of Nations; but were much more fully developed by Mr. Ricardo, and more explicitly stated by Dr. Wayland, than by Dr. Smith. They were but partially adopted by M. Say, and entirely discarded by Dr. Chalmers of Edinburgh, in his Political Economy.

Sec. 12. *False assumption involved in the Free Trade theory of Price.*

This whole theory is based on the assumption that common labor, unaccompanied with extraordinary skill or science, is a certain rule or measure of value, which determines the cost, and thereby regulates the price of every commodity produced by it. That is, if one article cost two days' labor, and another but one, the former cost precisely twice as much as the latter, and its exchangeable value must necessarily be just twice as much, plus or minus the effect produced by the variation in supply and demand which (the theory assumes,) does not regulate, but tends to disturb the natural price. Both of these assumptions are untrue; so far from labor being either a *rule or measure of value*, by which *to determine the cost, price, or value of its own products*, its value is equally fluctuating as the value of its products; its value in fact depends mostly on the price or value of its products; like everything else, its price is regulated by the principles of supply and demand, and the proportions between them; and an increased demand for, and an increased price for its products, produces an increased demand for labor, and raises its price also. Both are mutually dependent on each other; both are equally fluctuating and uncertain in value, and neither can be a rule or measure by which to determine the price or value of the other; the prices of both are raised, depressed, fixed, regulated, and adjusted by the competition between buyers and sellers in the market; the laborer being a seller of his labor, and the hirer being the purchaser. The proportion between supply and demand, that is, the competition between buyers and sellers, fixes and regulates the price and the exchangeable value of everything; while the amount of labor required to produce an article, has only an indirect and incidental effect on its price, by increasing or diminishing the facility of producing it, and thereby affecting the supply. The proportion between supply and demand is the PRINCIPAL AND EFFICIENT CAUSE, which DETERMINES AND REGULATES THE PRICE of an article, and the amount of labor required to produce it, is but an INCIDENTAL CAUSE, which AFFECTS the PRICE INDIRECTLY, by increasing or diminishing the supply of the article. The *free trade economists have elevated the incident to the rank of the principal, and degraded the principal to the station properly belonging to the incident.*

SEC. 13. *False Assumption of the facility of Labor and Capital, changing from one employment to another.*

The theory of Free Trade, as above quoted from Dr. Wayland, also involves the farther assumption, that laborers can change, and capital be changed, from one employment to another with as much facility as water runs down hill; that by a sort of instinct, natural or gravitating tendency, the moment the price of an article falls below its cost, both laborers and capital leave the employment by which it is produced, and it ceases to be produced until the price rises; and that these shifting laborers, and this floating capital, are moved on by some irresistible natural impulse and rush into that species of employment, whose products are above the assumed standard of cost. In this manner they assume that by means of the impulses of nature, prices, trade, and all human employment, if unrestricted by human laws, will regulate themselves with unerring certainty, in accordance with the laws of nature and the wants of man, the same as water tends, by an inherent impulse or gravitating principle, to find its own level.

This assumption I have drawn out in my own language, but it is substantially the same as that above quoted from Dr. Wayland; and it is not peculiar to him; it runs through the writings of Dr. Adam Smith, Conde Raguet late of Philadelphia, and of nearly all the free trade writers of the age. It contains about an ounce of truth, to a pound of error. There is a slight tendency of the character assumed, but it is very slight indeed. It is much stronger among an educated, than it is among an illiterate people; or rather it does not exist at all among the latter; and the assumption in its full length and breath as maintained by the free trade writers, is contrary to the experience of all ages and countries, since the commencement of the era of authentic history. The wages of agricultural labor have long been about twice as high in Great Britain as in Ireland. If the theory were true, this could not have been the case; on the contrary, the average wages for labor would have been very nearly the same in all countries, men and capital would frequently change from one employment to another, and the division of employments, and the productions of every country, would be adapted to its condition, and the wants of the people.

Until a very recent period, such a thing as a change of the

laboring classes from one employment to another, was almost unknown; and to this day, not only the laboring classes of Asia, but almost all those of the Continent of Europe, are nearly as much fixed and confined through life, by the stern laws of necessity, to the employment in which they were educated, as the everlasting hills and mountains are immoveably fixed in their respective localities. They have and understand but one employment, by means of which they can procure subsistence, and they are compelled to work at that through life; and when sick or infirm to live on either public or private charity, or starve. Even among the people of our own free states, (the best educated of any people in the world as a whole), perhaps not over one in twenty ever attempt to change the employment to which they were bred; and many who do change are injured by it. A child may be educated to one employment as well as another, but after pursuing any one for a period of fifteen or twenty years, the mental and physical habits become so adapted to it, that both mind and body in ninety-nine cases in an hundred, are unfitted for any other employment. All the way in which the proportion between the number of persons in any country engaged in the different employments can be changed, is by the education of the youth; it is next to impossible to change the employment of laboring adults.

It is so also, with most kinds of capital. Direction may be given to it before it is invested, but when once invested in agriculture, real estate of any kind, mills, factories, tools or machinery, it is invested forever, and can never be recalled. Though the owner of it may exchange it for other property, *yet it remains the same; and it is the owner only that is changed, and not the capital. The truth is, only the rising generation and newly created capital, can be turned into new channels, and established in new employments.* And this can be effected only during the progress of a long series of years, by means of a system of training and education, both physical and mental. It cannot be the result of the self-regulating operations of nature, for nature does not teach man mechanism, nor does it teach him the laws of trade, nor any of the physical sciences, either by instinct, intuition, or otherwise.

SEC. 14. *Errors of the Free Trade theory, arising from false assumptions.*

These positions will be illustrated by reference to statistics, in the progress of the work. The greater proportion of the errors and heresies of the free trade economists or advocates, result directly and indirectly, from their two leading principles above stated; both of which are assumptions compounded of truth and falsehood, in which the latter greatly predominates. These principles, or assumed principles, are nothing more nor less than the old doctrines of fatalism and necessitarianism, slightly modified, and engrafted upon the principles of political economy. Fatalism and necessitarianism both teach that man is so utterly helpless, as to be incapable of either conception or action which does not originate either in the impulses of nature, or with the special operation of the Spirit of God. They deny man all freedom of action, all freedom of will, and all power of originating action of any kind. The advocates of free trade are a little more liberal to him. While they insist that the prices of commodities and all the laws of trade are governed by the fixed and immutable physical laws of the Universe, that men will buy where they can buy nominally the cheapest, and that man should allow himself to float down the current of time in accordance with these physical laws; exposed to the violence of all the elements of the material world, without ever making a struggle to resist or evade their destructive influences upon him, they admit his power to resist these laws to a very limited extent, but insist that his struggles are necessarily unavailing to do any good, and only contribute to make his condition still worse.

Fatalism and necessitarianism deny that man has any power to originate any action whatsoever, whereby his condition may be changed, or affected, either for the better or the worse. The doctrines of free trade, following closely in their footsteps, deny that he has any power to improve his condition. They admit that he has the power to alter his condition and to change his fate; but only to make it worse, and never to make it better. They inculcate the principle that man should always conform to the physical laws of Nature; while true policy, in my view, requires that he should act in accordance with the moral laws of nature, as explained in the first chapter of these essays. Dr. Chalmers in his political economy, labors to show the importance of communities and nations as well as individuals, conforming to the moral law in all cases, in order to promote their highest earthly good and prosperity.

SEC. 15. *Tables showing the prices of Wheat in England from 1120 to 1557.*

Statement of the prices in England of wheat per quarter of eight Winchester bushels, at various periods from the 12th to the 16th century, in sterling money of those several periods; and the prices also in the money of the present time. To which I have added a calculation of the price or value, on comparing the amount of the money then in circulation for each person in

Europe, with the amount in circulation in 1840, calling the amount for each person in Europe and America at the latter period, equal to $5⅓ and at all the former periods up to the year 1500, only $1.50; in 1600, $3 and in the year 1700, $4.50 as stated in Section 8 of Chapter X.

In the year	Price in money of that time. s.	d.	Price in money of the present time. s.	d.	Comparative price per quarter. s.	d.
1120,	2		6		21	
1197,	18	8	56		196	
1223,	12		36		126	
1237,	3	4	10		35	
1243 and 1244,	6		18		63	
1257,	24		72		252	
1258, a great famine,	40		120		420	
*1270, a famine,	96		288		1008	
1286, early part of,	2	8	8		28	
1286, after h'vy storm,	16		48		168	
1290 and 1294,	16		48		168	
1299,	1	8	5		17	6
1317, before harvest,	44		132		462	
1317, after harvest,	14		42		147	
1324 to 1329, Ox. av.	4	7	13	9	48	
1349, 1361 and 1387,	2		5	3	18	10
1359,	26	8	67	4	239	
1423, 1447 and 1451,	8		16		56	
1434, before harvest,	26	8	53	4	212	
1434, after harvest,	5	4	10	8	37	
1449 and 1459,	5		10		35	
1486,	24	8	32	10	115	
1494 and 1496,	4		5	4	17	8
1497 and 1521,	20		26	8	93	
1553 to 1556,	8		8		28	
1557, before harvest,	53	4	53	4	186	
1557, after harvest,	5		5		17	6

SEC. 16. *Average and comparative Prices of Wheat from 1583 to 1800.*

Summary statement of the average prices of wheat per quarter of eight Winchester bushels, at Oxford, England, during the undermentioned periods; also the highest average and lowest average for a year during each period; being formed from an

* There was in 1270 a famine in England, so severe that, according to Peckham, as quoted by Fleetwood, "provisions were so scarce that parents did eat their own children."

average of the highest and lowest prices of each year, taken at Lady-day (25th March) and Michaelmas (29th September). To which I have added an estimate of the comparative prices on taking into consideration the amount of money in circulation at each period, and comparing it with the amount in circulation from 1840 to 1850.

Years.	Sterling money. s.	d.	Comparative price.
1583 to 1590 average,	21	10½	42s.
1586 highest "	36	2	70s.
1588 lowest "	14	5½	28s.
1601 to 1610 average,	29	6½	54s.
1608 highest "	44	6	81s.
1604 lowest "	24	4	44s.
1641 to 1650 average,	46	7	73s.
1649 highest "	62	6	98s.
1642 lowest "	32	9	51s.
1651 to 1660 average,	38	5½	58s.
1659 highest "	53	1	79s.
1654 lowest "	19	10	30s.
1691 to 1700 average,	47	0	60s.
1698 highest "	58	1	73s.
1691 lowest "	29	11	38s.
1701 to 1710 average,	29	3¼	36s.
1710 highest "	61	10	75s.
1702 lowest "	24	6	30s.
1741 to 1750 average,	28	5¼	30s.
1741 highest "	43	3	45s.
1743 lowest "	21	1	22s.
1751 to 1760 average,	37	7	38s.
1757 highest "	60	5	60s.
1760 lowest "	26	2	26s.
1771 to 1780 average,	49	2½	46s.
1774 highest "	62	2	57s.
1779 lowest "	34	8	32s.
1791 to 1800 average,	63	11	52s.
1799 highest "	88	11	70s.
1794 lowest "	49	5	40s.

SEC. 17. *Average Prices of Wheat from* 1801 *to* 1850.

Summary statement of the average prices of wheat throughout England and Wales, per quarter of eight imperial bushels, during each decennial period from 1801 to 1850; also the highest and lowest averages during any year of each period, as ascertained by the receivers of corn returns.*

Years.		Money. s.	d.	Comparative price.		
1801 to 1810 average,		83	11	60s.		
1801 highest	"	119	6	90s.		
1803 lowest	"	58	10	44s.		
1811 to 1820 average,		87	6	66s.		
1812 highest	"	126	6	95s.		
1815 lowest	"	65	7	49s.		
1821 to 1830 average,		59	5	52s.		
1825 highest	"	68	6	60s.		
1822 lowest	"	44	7	39s.		
1831 to 1840 average,		56	11	56s.		
1839 highest	"	70	8	70s.		
1835 lowest	"	39	4	39s.		
1841	"	64	4	Year.	s.	d.
1842	"	57	3	1847	69	9
1843	"	50	1	1848	50	6
1844	"	51	3	1849	44	4
1845	"	50	10	1850	40	3
1846	"	54	8	1851 about	39	0

The average prices of wheat in Great Britain, per quarter, in 1845, 1846, and 1847, were as follows:

	1845. s.	d.	1846. s.	d.	1847. s.	d.
January, -	45	7½	56	1	68	4
February, -	45	4	54	7½	73	3½
March, -	45	4	55	4	75	4
April, -	46	1½	55	6	75	4¼
May, -	45	10	56	4	91	1
June, -	47	5	52	5	92	10
July, -	49	3	51	7	78	10
August, -	55	7	45	11	70	6
September, -	54	5	50	1	54	3
October, -	57	10	May 29, -		102	5
November, -	58	10	August 21, -		62	6
December, -	57	10	" 28, -		60	4

Grain was higher in England after harvest in 1845, than it was before harvest; higher in October and November, than it was the following winter and spring. There was an alarm in the fall of 1845 of a short crop which was not justified by the result; the crop was better than was supposed, and prices consequently declined in the winter and spring following.

* The Imperial bushel contains nearly 3¼ per cent. more than the Winchester bushel.

The potato crop of 1846, failed both in Ireland and Great Britain; the grain crop also was short, which produced a famine in Ireland and much alarm in England, and prices went up constantly from September 1846 until the last of May, 1847, when they attained their maximum of nearly 103s. per quarter, or $3 per bushel. The high prices, together with the opening of the ports, and allowing free trade in grain and flour, invited large importations, and caused great speculations in those articles. The importations into the United Kingdom during the year 1847, consisted of over twenty-one million bushels of wheat, nearly fifty million bushels of other grain, and over three million and six hundred thousand barrels of flour, besides considerable quantities of meal. The markets became overstocked and glutted, prices began to fall early in June, and fell constantly, until the end of the year, and much of the wheat which was purchased in May at over 100s. per quarter, was sold the last of August and in September at from 50s. to 62s.

The result of so large importations was, that the balance of trade was turned against Great Britain, large amounts of specie were exported to pay that balance, a panic was produced, several banks failed, and about two hundred and fifty mercantile firms failed, whose liabilities amounted to over one hundred millions of dollars.

SEC. 18. *Comparison of the population with the products of Wheat, and prices at different periods; showing the poverty of the People.*

The facts stated in the foregoing three sections are of a very curious and interesting character, when we take into consideration the increase of the population of the island of Great Britain, from about 2,300,000 in the year 1200, to 18,527,439, beside the army and navy, by the census of 1841. It amounted in the year 1500 to about 3,800,000; in 1600, to about 5,000,000, and in 1750, to only about 7,800,000. In selecting the examples, I have endeavored to take the highest, the lowest, and the medium prices, in order to present to the reader a fair view of the prodigious fluctuations in the price of wheat in the English market. On looking at the comparative prices (which are the real standard, on taking into consideration the amount of money in circulation at different periods), the reader will see that they were the lowest during the first half of the eighteenth century, that they ever were. In all the numerous examples I have found for the period from the twelfth to the end of the sixteenth century, there are very few where the comparative price was less than 20s. per quarter, many more where the comparative prices were each over 100s. per quarter; and the famine prices were from 200s. to 1008s. per quarter.

The returns were made annually, without any omissions, and may be depended upon from the year 1583 ; and from that year to the year 1680, the average comparative price of each decennial period, was over 40s. per quarter, and the average of the whole ninety-seven years over 56s. per quarter ; while the average comparative price of each decennial period from 1700 to 1760, was less than 43s. per quarter ; and the average of the whole sixty years but 37s. per quarter. The comparative prices of wheat were more than fifty per cent. higher on an average during the former than they were during the latter of those periods, though the population was about thirty per cent. greater during the latter period than the former.

Prior to the accession of Henry VII. to the throne, in 1485, England was mostly a grazing country; famines and famine prices were frequent, as shown by the foregoing tables ; and the prices would indicate and confirm the history of the country, that the people often suffered severely, and died by thousands and tens of thousands for want of food. The population was sparse, the people poor, and the exports of the country mostly confined to wool, a few coarse unfinished woollen cloths, tin and lead. Some wheat was exported between the years 1696 and 1767, but very little at any other period. Agriculture was at a very low ebb until after the revolution of 1688, when the annual crop of wheat of England and Wales was estimated at only 16,500,000 bushels ; which is less than the present annual crop of the State of Ohio, and only one seventh part the present annual crop of England and Wales. But the prices would indicate that the annual crop was then (about the year 1688) not only much more certain and regular, but generally two or three times as large as it was ordinarily during the 13th, 14th, and 15th centuries.

It appears from the authorities collected by McCulloch, in his Com. Dict., title Bread, that during the sixteenth and seventeenth centuries, only the wealthy of England lived on wheat bread ; that their servants and the great mass of the people lived on rye, barley, and oat bread, and were so poor they could not afford to live on wheat; and even as late as 1758, it was estimated, that but little, if any more than half of the people lived on wheat. The consumption of wheat during the last forty years, has been as large in Great Britain in proportion to the population as in any of our free States, and nearly fifty per cent. more than our free States will average. Rye and Indian corn, which are extensively used in our free States, are thought by the manufacturing laborers of Great Britain (who get good wages), quite too coarse fare for their delicate palates. What has produced this change? Should it not be mostly attributed to the prodigious increase in the value of their mining and manufacturing industry?

McCulloch says in his statistics, title Vital Statistics, "If any proof were wanted of the inadequate supply of food and the unhealthy dwellings of the English people down to the 17th century, it would be found in the famines and plagues which still prevailed with little mitigation. They occurred in 1407, 1440, 1477, 1485, 1493, 1500, 1506, 1510, 1517, 1528, 1545, 1551, 1557, 1558, 1563, 1569, 1585, 1592, 1593, 1606, 1625, 1636, and 1665. In 1407 it was computed that 30,000 persons died within a short time in London, while the mortality was still higher in the country towns." He shows that the plague and other diseases swept off in 1593, about 31,891 of the population of London, comprising 24 per cent. of the whole, and that the mortality in 1625 was 31 per cent.; in 1636, 13 per cent., and in 1665, no less than 43 per cent., amounting to 56,558.

No wonder need be excited, that plague, dysentery, fevers and a numerous train of other diseases were often brought on by want of food, comfortable dwellings, lodging and clothing, and swept off thousands and tens of thousands of the inhabitants. The difference in the productive industry and condition of the country, and the comforts enjoyed by the people, is sufficient to account for the fact, that the ratio of mortality has declined nearly one half in Great Britain during the last two centuries; and that the increase of the population prior to the revolution of 1688, was usually only from 20 to 30 per cent. in a century, although it was nearly 15 per cent. every ten years, during the bloody wars of that nation with Napoleon.

SEC. 19. *Rent of land, wheat produced per acre, and prices of labor in the twelfth and thirteenth centuries.*

It is said in the Pictorial History of England, Chap. IV., that "Sir T. Collum supposes 4d. per acre to have been about the average rate at which land was let, towards the close of the 13th century; and that the average price of wheat per quarter was 4s. 6d., and the average produce about twelve bushels per acre. A century earlier, according to the law book entitled Fleta, land often yielded only three times the quantity sown. At a later period, sixty-one acres in the manor of Hawsted produced seventy quarters of wheat annually, on an average of three years." "There are items in the Hawsted accounts, showing that sixty persons were paid for one day 2d. each to weed the corn." This was the latter part of the 14th century.

The four pence rent per acre above referred to, was equal in the weight of coin, to 12d. of the money of the present time; and when the amount of money in circulation for each person at that time is compared with the amount at this time (1850,) the rent was equal to 3s. 6d. sterling, or about eighty-four cents per acre. The two pence per day for labor in the 14th century, was equal in weight of coin to about 5½d. of sterling money at present, and equal in comparative value to about 1s. 7d., or thirty-eight cents of the money of the present time.

It is stated in the Chronicum, that workmen took their wages in 1351 in wheat at the price of 16d. per bushel; the nominal price being as stated in the following table; to which I have added the amount in money of the present time, and the comparative value.

	Nominal price.	Price in money of present time.	Compar. price.
Weeders and haymakers per day,	2½d.	6¼d.	$0 46
Reapers, "	4d. to 6	12½	92
Masons and tilers, "	6½	16½	1 20
Other laborers, "	1¼	3¼	23
Farm servants per year,			
Bailiff or overseer, "	31s.	77s.	$68
A first hind, "	21 3d.	53	45
Carter and shepherd, "	21 3	53	45
Cowherd and swineherd,	14 4	36	31
A woman servant,	12 8	31 6d.	27

These yearly wages are the prices fixed by the statute of 12 Richard II., Chap. 2 (about the year 1400;) and it is presumed they are beside food and lodging, though that does not appear by the act.

Sec. 20. *Value of Ships, Iron, Wool and Wines in Flanders, in* 1470.

In 1470, seven Spanish ships loaded with iron, wine, fruits and wool, on their voyage to Flanders, were captured by some English vessels, and brought to England. The owners applied to the King, Henry VI., for redress, and exhibited on oath an account of the burden and value of the ships, and prices at which the merchandize would have sold in Flanders. The tonnage of the seven ships was as follows: one of 40 tons; one of 70 tons; one of 100 tons; two of 110 tons each; and two of 120 tons each. Their nominal value per ton, as sworn to, and the value of the merchandize, is stated in the following table; to which I have added their value in weight of coin of the present time, and the comparative value when taking the amount of circulating money into consideration.

	Value sworn to.	Value in money of the present time.	Comparative value.
Ships per ton,	£ 1.4s.	£2.00s.	£ 7¼
Bordeaux wine pr. pipe,	6	9.15	35
Bastard wines per pipe,	5	8.2	29
Iron per ton,	11	17.12	63
Wool pr. sack of 196 lbs.	5	8.2	29

The nominal value of the wool as claimed, is a little over 6d. sterling per pound; and its comparative value about 34d. or 68 cents per pound of our money; and the comparative value of the iron about $300 per ton. Iron must have been extremely scarce at that period, otherwise it could not have been so very valuable, when the price of labor was so low.

Sec. 21. *Exports of England in* 1354, *and condition of the laboring classes.*

This view of the value and scarcity of iron, and the value of wool, is confirmed by the following statements, extracted from Chap. IV. of the Pictorial History of England. "The most ancient record which presents a general view of the foreign trade of England, is an account preserved in the Exchequer of the exports and imports of England, and the amount of customs paid on them for the year 1354. The exports here mentioned are about 31,651½ sacks of wool at £6 per sack; 3036 cwts. of wool at 40s. per cwt.; 65 woolfels, (sheep and lamb skins with the wool on,) valued at 21s. 8d.; hides to the value of £89 5s; 4,774½ pieces of cloth at 40s. each; and 8,061½ pieces of worsted stuff at 16s. 8d. each. Total value of exports £212,338 5s. paying customs to the amount of £81,846 12s. 2d. Wool would therefore appear by this account to have constituted about thirteen fourteenths of the whole exports of the Kingdom." From other accounts, it appears that iron, tin, and lead were also sometimes exported, which are omitted in the above account. The author remarks, "It may be presumed also, that IRON was occasionally exported during this period, from the statute 28 Edward III., ch. 5, (passed in 1354,) which enacts that NO IRON, whether made in England or imported, shall be carried out of the country."

The nominal value of the exports of England in 1354, above referred to, their value in weight of coin of the present time, and their comparative value, taking the amount of money in circulation into consideration, and estimating the sack of wool the same as the present English sack or pack, 240 lbs., and the pieces of cloth and worsted stuff at 30 yards each piece, would be as follows:

	Export value stated.	Value in money of present time.	Comparative value.
7,596.370 lbs. wool in sacks at	6d. pr. lb.	1s. 4d.	$1 17
340,032 lbs wool in cwts. at	4¼ pr. lb.	11	84
65 woolfels at	4 each.	11	80
143,235 yds. cloth at 1s.	4 per yd.	3 6½	3 10
241,845 yds. wors'd st'ffs, at	6⅜ per yd.	1 6	1 32

The cloth exported was mostly of a coarse quality in an unfinished condition, and was sent to Flanders to be colored and finished. The condition of the laboring peasantry of England must have been deplorable indeed in the 12th, 13th, 14th and 15th centuries; when the comparative value of their wages was only from 23 to 40 cents per day, and about $31 per annum, with board and lodging; the comparative price of common woollen cloth from $2 to $3 per yard; fine wool from 84 cents to $1 per pound, and coarse wool perhaps half as high; and the comparative prices of grain and provisions on the average much higher than they are now, and often from two to five times as high. The sufferings of the laboring classes, and particularly of agricultural laborers, must have been constantly great for want of comfortable clothing and dwellings; and when the crops were short and provisions scarce and dear, their sufferings must have often been intense for want of food. These are the principal causes of the mortality of children under five years old, having been nearly three times as great as it is at present; and the mortality of adults, taking the years of plague and other pestilences into consideration, nearly twice as great as at the present time.

SEC. 22. *Prices of rents, wages, provisions, &c., in the thirteenth and fourteenth centuries.*

Mr. Hallam estimated the average price of rents of arable lands, the latter part of the 13th century, at 6d. per acre; the average prices of wheat 4s. per quarter of 8 bushels, and barley and oats in proportion; sheep at about, or a little less than 1s. each; oxen at 10s. to 12s. each; and butchers' meat, in the time of Henry VI., (1425 to 1464,) at 1½ farthings per lb. The statute of laborers, in 1350, fixed the wages of reapers during the harvest at 3½d. per day, they finding themselves; that the statute of 1444 fixed the reapers' wages at 5d., and those of common workmen in building at 3½d., and established the yearly wages of a chief hind, or shepherd, at £1 4s., with food; and those of a common servant in husbandry, at but 18s. 4d., with meat and drink. These prices were established by law as the maximum prices which could be demanded by laborers, and Hallam thinks them above the average rate of wages paid at those periods. In a note it is said, "In the Archæologia, vol. xviii., p. 281, we have a bailiff's account of expenses in 1387, where it appears that a ploughman had 6d. per week, and 5s. a year in addition, with an allowance of diet, which seems to have been only pottage.

Taking these prices, stating their amount in money of the present time, and their comparative amount, taking the amount of circulating money into consideration, and the result is as follows:

	Price stated. s. d.	Price in money of the present time. s. d.	Comparative price.
Rent of land per acre,	0 6	1 3	$1 10
Wheat per quarter,	4 0	10 0	9 00
Sheep,	1 0	2 6	2 20
An ox,	11 0	27 6	25 00
Meat per lb.,	1½ far.	¾	5½
Reapers per day in 1350, without board,	3½	9	66
By statute in 1444,			
Reapers per day without board,	5	10	73
Laborers in building per day,	3½	7	50
Shepherds per year,	£1 4 0	48 0	42
Farm laborers per year,	18 4	36 8	32 00
Ploughman per week, in 1387,	7½	1 3	1 10

SEC. 23. *Comparative condition of the laboring classes in the fourteenth and nineteenth centuries.*

These facts show that the comparative prices of the rent of land and the wages of labor were much lower than the products of labor, when we compare them with present prices. This can only be accounted for by supposing, that at that early age, the physical sciences, mechanic arts, and the standard of agriculture, were in so low and rude a condition, and agricultural implements of so rude a character, that labor was not very productive; and that it then required about three times as much labor to cultivate agricultural products, and even to raise animals in that cold climate, as is now required. Even the poor of Great Britain of the present day, need not envy the lot and condition of their ancestors, at any time prior to the 18th century. The comparative price of common agricultural labor per annum, was then about $30 to $40; now it is from three to four times as much. Then they lived on bread made of rye, barley, and oats, with pottage, and a little coarse meat, barley broth, and water gruel; now they live mostly, and the manufacturing laborers entirely, on wheat bread ; the latter have an abundance of meat, good clothing and comfortable dwellings ; and their earnings are generally so great as to furnish the means to gratify, and in their present ignorant state, tempt them to indulge in frequent dissipation. These facts and results are confirmed not only by the writings of Mr. Jacob and Mr. McCulloch, but by numerous other British authors.

SEC. 24. *Table of Prices in the sixteenth century.*

Many facts in relation to prices in England during the 16th century, taken from Sir Frederic Eden's tables, are published in Chap. VII. of Book VI. of the Pictorial History of England, from which the following are extracted and the price in money of the present time, and also the comparative price added.

	Year.	Price stated. *s.*	*d.*	Price in money of present time. *s.*	*d.*	Com. price.
Mason's wages per day,	1500	0	4	0	6⅔	$0 50
do. allowed for diet,	"		2		3⅓	24
do. wages per day,	1775	1	0	1	½	50
House-painters do.	"	1	0	1	½	50
Common laborers per day,			8		8¼	33
Ditchers and hedgers do.	1590		4		4⅛	16
Gardener do.	"		6		6¼	25
Pigeons per dozen,	1500		4		6⅔	50
Eggs per hundred,	"		6*a*7		11	80
Chickens,	"		1		1⅔	12
A goose,	"		3*a*4		5¾	42
A lamb,	"		6		10	73
An ox,	"	11	8	19	5	17 00
A heifer,	"	9	0	15	0	13 00
A fat cow,	1589	60	0	62	0	28 00
A milch cow,	"	33	4	34	5	15 00
A fat goose,	"	1	to 14d.	1	2	54
A turkey,	"	1	4	1	4½	63
Pigeons per dozen,	1590	1	0	1	½	50
Butter per lb.,	"		4		4⅛	16
Beef per stone of 14 lbs.,	1597	1	11to26d.	2	1	90
Cheese per lb.,	"		3		3⅛	11
Sugar per lb.,	"	1	4	1	4½	56
Stockings per pair,	1525	2	4	3	11	2 80
Shoes per pair,	"	1	4	2	7	1 86
Stockings per pair	1590	2	8	2	9	1 31
Men's shoes,	"	1	6	1	6½	75
Paper per quire,	1570		3		3⅓	15

	Price stated.			Price in money of present time.		Com. price.
	Year.	s.	d.	s.	d.	
Candles per lb.,	1578		3½		3⅔	16
A shirt,	1589	1	8	1	8⅔	85
Soap per lb.,	"		8		8¼	33
Coals per cauldron,	1590	9	0	9	3½	4 40
Master mason per day,	1601	1	2	1	2	52
Common laborer do.	"		10		10	37

It appears that the comparative price of labor was as low in the 16th century as it was during the 13th, 14th, and 15th centuries; while the comparative prices of food and clothing were quite as high, if not higher. In fact, labor was not very productive, and there was no great demand for it, until the improvement of the steam-engine and the invention and introduction of the spinning-jenny and other machinery, the latter part of the 18th century; and as population increased, the demand for provisions and all the comforts of life increased also, and the condition of the laboring classes seemed to be more and more depressed. Such is the history of the retrograde condition of the laboring classes in all agricultural countries, which have but little manufacturing industry. England in the 16th century, and Ireland at the present time, are not solitary instances. Were it not for the warmth of the climate, the suffering among the laboring classes would be nearly as great in Italy as it is in Ireland.

SEC. 25. *Contract Prices of provisions and labor at the Royal Hospital at Greenwich, from* 1730 *to* 1835.

YEARS.	Flesh per lb.	Butter per lb.	Salt per bus.	Carpenters per day.	Masons per day.	Shoes per pair.	Coals per chaldron.
	d.	s. d.	s. d.	s. d.	s. d.	s. d.	£ s. d.
1730, . .	2¾	5	5 0	2 6	2 6	4 0	1 4 0
1735, . .	1⅞	3⅝	4 0	2 6	2 6	4 0	1 5 0
1740, . .	3	5	4 0	2 6	2 8	3 10	1 9 0
1750, . .	2⅞	5⅛	4 0	2 6	2 8	3 9	1 7 7½
1760, . .	3⅗	5½	4 0	2 6	2 8	4 0	1 12 8
1770, . .	3	6½	4 8	2 6	2 8	4 0	1 9 1½
1780, . .	3½	6½	4 8	2 6	2 10	3 11½	1 17 3¼
1790, . .	3⅞	6½	4 8	2 6	2 10	3 11½	1 14 4¼
1800, . .	6⅞	11½	14 0	2 10	2 10	5 8	2 11 7
1805, . .	6⅗	11¾	16 10½	4 6	5 0	5 9	2 11 8¾
1810, . .	7⅝	1 1⅜	19 9	5 8	5 3	5 6	3 0 8
1815, . .	7½	1 2	19 9	5 6	5 9	4 7	2 15 6¾
1820, . .	7½	9½	19 9	5 3	5 8	4 4½	2 5 9
1825, . .	6⅗	10½	2 10	5 0	5 0	4 6	2 8 2
1830, . .	4⅗	6½	1 8	5 6	5 5	3 6	1 12 11
1835, . .	4⅗	7½	1 3	5 5	5 3	3 8¼	16 8. per ton.
1831 to '35 average.	4¼	8½	1 6¼	5 5	5 3	3 6½	

The number of inmates of the hospital in 1830 is stated to have been 2,710. The quantities of provisions consumed must have been large, and the prices wholesale, not retail; but as it is located only five miles from London where provisions and labor are the highest of any place in the kingdom, the prices may be regarded as about equal to the average of retail prices throughout the island of Great Britain. A chaldron of coals, (36 bushels,) generally weighs about 3,000 lbs. or nearly 27 cwt. gross; and is equal to nearly two cords of hard wood of average quality.

The population of the island of Great Britain in 1730 was about 7,200,000, and in 1830 about 16,200,000; so that during the century the demand for provisions more than doubled, and the supply of laborers more than doubled; and though the comparative prices of provisions kept pace with the increase of population, and nearly doubled also; yet the demand for labor increased more rapidly than the laborers, and the comparative wages of carpenters and masons more than doubled during the century. It should be remarked, also, that most kinds of clothing, coal for fuel, and salt, declined in price during this period, so that, on the whole, the wages of labor would command nearly twice as many of the comforts of life in the aggregate in 1830, as they would in 1730.

Sec. 26. *Exports from London to France, and Prices of the same in 1751; and the official value of goods.*

An account of the export of certain articles from the port of London to France, during the year 1751, and the Custom-House value of the same, which was the official value fixed in the year 1696. See Lex Mercatoria, 515 to 520.

	Quantity.	Price.		
Brass, wrought, cwt., -	550	£8	0	0
Copper, do -	50	5	0	0
Iron, tons, -	25	12	10	0 to 17½*l.*
Cast-iron do. -	74½	12	10	0
Iron do. -	2	14	0	0 to 18*l.*
Iron, wrought, lbs. -	6,134	2	0	0 pr.cwt.
Lead, cwt. - -	1,832	0	12	0½
Shot, do. - -	605	0	14	0
Tin, do. - -	606	3	15	0
Gunpowder, lbs. -	800	0	0	7 to 7½ *d.*
Coals, chaldrons, -	42	1	5	0
Earthenware, pieces, -	17,800	0	0	1
Glass, do. -	7,200	0	0	8
Stoneware, do. -	200	0	0	2
Butter, firkins, -	530	1	0	0
Cheese, cwts., -	32	1	5	0

	Quantity.	Price.
Coffee, lbs., - -	14,896	£0 1 8½
Rice, lbs., - -	632,464	0 0 2 to 2⅛
Pepper, lbs., - -	219,699	0 0 11
Pimento, lbs., - -	56,459	0 1 0
Raisins, lbs., - -	1,200 nearly,	0 0 3¾
Tobacco, lbs., - -	3,270,688	0 0 3
Beans, qrs., - -	1,765	1 1 0
Wheat, qrs., - -	57,380	1 4 to 34s.
Wheat meal, qrs., -	1,582	1 16 to 51s.
Barley, qrs., - -	410	0 15 0
Rye, qrs., - -	5,200	0 13 to 15s.
Oats, qrs., - -	200	0 10 to 15s.
Cloths, long, - -	556	10 0 0
Do. short, -	81	8 0 0
Frieze, yards, - -	250	0 3 0
Flannel, do. - -	1,730	0 1 0
Linen, do. - -	3,000	0 1 4
Do. ells, - -	19,100	0 1 8
Diaper, yards, -	210	0 1 4
Wool, sheep's, lbs., -	26,988	0 2 0
Do. lamb's, lbs., -	250	0 1 6
Shoes, doz. pairs, -	280	0 10 0
Hats, doz. - -	10	2 10 0
Cordage, tons, - -	130	1 5 0
Hemp, cwt., - -	758	0 17 to 22½s.
Total value, - -		£272,199 16 10

Among the imports from France into London the same year, 1751, are stated the following articles :

			Price. £	s.	d.
Cambrics, sup. half pieces, -	20,506	at	1	0	0
Cotton yarn, lbs., - -	896	"	0	1	6
Thread, lbs., - - -	3,621	"	0	15	0
Twist, doz., - - -	252	"	0	10	0
Linen, ells, - - -	6,581	"	0	1	8
Iron, tons, - - -	11	"	12	10	0
Indigo, lbs., - - -	657,441	"	0	2	6
Eggs, - - -	6,000	"	0	2	per 100

From the account, I infer that the official value of cast-iron is £12 10s. per ton; of bar-iron, £12 10s. per ton; of bolt and rod-iron, £17 10s.; and of wrought iron made into chain cables, anchors, &c. £40 per ton. The prices of all the articles stated in the foregoing table may be regarded as their official value at the present time, and as their average market value in Great Britain in 1696, (when the standard of official values was adopted,) and during several preceding years. In this view, it is exceedingly important in aiding the inquirer to institute a comparison between the prices of articles at the present time, and their prices in 1696.

Mr. Baine, in his History of the Cotton Manufacture, p. 351, gives the official valuation of cotton goods, and their average declared or market value in 1829, as follows:

	Official Value.				Average rates of market val.		
	Value in English money.			In dollars and cents.			
	£	s.	d.		£	s.	d.
Calicoes, white or plain, per yard,	0	1	3	$0 30	0	0	6
Do. printed or checked do.	0	1	6	36	0	0	8¾
Muslins, white or plain, do.	0	1	8	40	0	0	7¾
Do. printed or checked do.	0	1	10	44	0	0	9¾
Cot. and linen cloth, mixed do.	0	1	3	30	0	0	8¾
Fustians, velvets, &c., do.	0	2	6	60	0	0	10½
Lace and patent net, do.	0	0	8	16	0	0	3
Counterpanes each, do.	0	10	0	2 40	0	3	2½
Stockings per pair, do.	0	2	6	60	0	0	11½
Cotton sewing thread per lb.	0	4	0	96	0	3	3¼
Cotton twist and yarn per 112 lbs.	10	0	0	48 00	7	5	0

The £10 per 112 lbs. for twist and yarn is equivalent to nearly 1s. 9½d. or 43 cents per lb. These are the only data I have met with of the standard adopted in 1696 fixing the official value of goods. They show the value of cotton and linen cloths about the same—that is, linen 1s. 4d. per yard, plain cotton calicoes, muslins, shirtings, sheetings, &c., 1s. 3d ; printed, dyed, or colored, 1s. 6d., and flannel made of wool only 1s. per yard. They show also the effect of supply and demand on prices. The prices of cotton yarn per lb. indicate that raw cotton must have been much cheaper at that time, (1696,) when the demand for it in Europe was very trifling, than it was in 1780, when the demand was about five times as great as at the former period. The cotton is said to waste in cleaning, picking, carding, roving, and spinning about 1½ oz. in a pound, and that 100 lbs. of cotton will make only about 90 lbs. of yarn; and in Massachusetts, on coarse cotton, the waste is estimated at 11 lbs. in 100. If the yarn was worth only 1s. 9½d. per lb. the yarn spun out of a pound of cotton was worth less than 1s. 7½d. Both the cotton and the cotton yarn were mostly imported from India, where the yarn was spun by females, whose labor was only 2d., or 4 cents per day. Perhaps the value of the cotton might have been estimated higher than the labor of spinning it even on a one-thread wheel. Call the cotton 10d. per lb., and it would leave but 9½d. for spinning; and even this price is less than half the average price of cotton in England in 1780, which is stated by

Mr. Baine at about 32d. per lb. The probability is, that none but a very inferior quality of cotton was spun as early as 1696, for sale in yarn, as the official value of cotton sewing thread is stated at 4s. per lb., or more than twice as much as cotton yarn.

Sec. 27. *Official and declared values of the leading articles exported from Great Britain in* 1832 *and* 1834.

Account of the official and also the declared or market value of the British and Irish products and manufactures exported from the United Kingdom during the years 1832 and 1834, to which I have added the per cent. which the declared values bear to the official values. See 1st Murray's Encyclopædia of Geography.

	In 1832.			In 1834.		
	£ Official value.	£ Declared value.	per cent	£ Official value.	£ Declared value.	per cent
Cotton manufactures,	37,206,480	12,675,622	34	44,266,903	15,302,571	34
Cotton yarn,	6,726,563	4,722,759	70	6,802,238	5,211,015	76
Linen manufactures,	2,785,549	1,774,726	64	3,850,764	2,443,345	63
Linen yarn,	5,898	8,705	147	82,169	136,312	166
Silk manufactures,	475,166	529,990	111	533,683	637,198	125
Wool, sheep's,	149,991	219,650	146	81,383	192,176	236
Woollen manufactures,	6,556,294	5,244,558	80	6,514,703	5,736,870	88
Woollen and worsted yarn,	122,125	235,307	192	99,933	238,544	239
Brass and copper manufactures,	1,126,247	916,563	81	1,086,594	961,823	89
Hardware and cutlery,	878,362	1,434,431	163	947,477	1,485,233	157
Iron & steel, wrought & unwrought,	2,408,184	1,190,748	49	2,621,672	1,406,872	53
Tin, wrought and unwrought,	858,259	855,056	99	370,116	370,382	100
Soap and candles,	348,286	315,645	90	382,198	263,972	69
Salt,	353,825	149,678	42	371,470	152,127	41
Sugar, refined,	1,292,489	1,038,790	80	1,141,566	916,391	80
All other articles,	4,232,981	5,532,293	126	4,678,680	6.194,358	182
Total,	£65,026,699	36,344,521	56	73,831,549	41,649,189	56½
Whereof from Great Britain,	£64,582,034	35,946,024		73,495,534	41,286,592	
From Ireland,	444,665	398,497		336,015	362,597	

By comparing the articles in the foregoing table and the per cent. which their declared or market value bears to the official value of the same articles as stated in section 26, the reader can calculate not only the variations in price, the rise in many cases, as well as the fall in others, but he can also calculate the average Custom House price per yard, pound, ton, &c., of many of the articles. It shows many curious facts. Hardware and cutlery advanced in price about 60 per cent., while iron, which constitutes the principal material of which they are made, fell 50 per cent. See Sec. 31, of this chapter. The price of cotton yarn was, comparatively, little lower in 1832 than in 1696; though the price of cotton as I have estimated it was 10d. per lb. in 1696 and only about 6½d. duty paid, in 1832; and the process of picking, carding, roving and spinning by machinery, enabled a given number of persons to produce at least 30 times as many pounds of yarn at the latter, as they could at the former period.

Similar remarks may be applied to woollen and linen yarn, both of which are spun and mostly woven also by machinery. One person can tend two or three power looms, and weave ten or twelve times as much as in the old-fashioned hand looms, before the introduction of the fly-shuttle, which was as late as 1738. These facts show that there is no comparison between the decline in the prices of cotton, woollen, linen and silk goods, and also in hardware and cutlery and the metals generally, and the diminution of labor required to produce them, by means of the invention, introduction and improvement in machinery during the last century; and that though wages have increased, yet the profits of manufacturers in England must have increased also, most enormously.

The labor saved in cleaning, picking, carding, roving, and spinning cotton into yarn by means of machinery, must be at least 96 per cent., while the saving in weaving is only from 80 to 90 per cent.; and yet the decline in the price of woven fabrics up to 1832 was about twice as great as on cotton yarn. This shows the effect of American competition in woven fabrics. While the British manufacturers must compete with the Americans in the sale of cotton cloths, they supply the markets of the world with cotton yarn without a competitor; and as Germany, Russia, and all the nations of Northern Europe, are but little advanced in manufacturing, have but few manufacturers, few skilful workmen, and very little machinery, or capital invested in spinning cotton, and manufactures are mostly of a domestic character, families find it cheaper to buy cotton yarn at high prices, and to weave it themselves, than to buy the cloth already woven.

The British exports in 1845 of plain or white calicoes, shirting and sheetings, which come into competition with American goods, amounted to 613,138,645 yards, at the declared value of £8,302,919. The weight of cotton yarn reported as exported in those goods amounted to 146,897,796 pounds, at an average value of only 1s. 1½d. The same year, the cotton yarn exported, exclusive of thread, amounted to 131,937,935 pounds, valued at £6,596,897 sterling, equal to 1s. per pound of yarn. On comparing the number of yards exported with the pounds of yarn contained in them, it appears that each pound of yarn was made into nearly 4¼ yards of cloth; and this 4¼ yards of cloth is sold, in consequence of American competition, at only 1½d. or three cents more than a pound of yarn; so that the only compensation the manufacturer got for weaving it, (if the yarn was sold at fair prices,) was 1½d. for 4¼ yards, or a little over ¼d. sterling, or ½ a cent per yard. If the cloth was sold at a fair profit, the profits on the yarn must have been very great.

SEC. 28. *Official and declared Values of British Exports annually from* 1798 *to* 1845 *; and the Amount to the U. States since* 1821.

Account of the OFFICIAL AND DECLARED OR REAL VALUE in millions of pounds sterling, of British and Irish products and manufactures exported during the following years ; together with the proportion per cent. that the declared or real value bears to the official value ; and the per cent. of money in circulation to each person, compared with the amount in 1696.

Years.	Official value.	Declar'd value.	pr ct. dec'd val.	Declar'd value of British and Irish products exported to the U. States by the British reports.	Per Cent. of money.
1696,					100
1798,	£ 18.5	£ 31.2	168.4		150
1800,	22.8	36.9	162.8		155
1801,	24.5	39.7	162.3		157
1802,	25.1	45.1	179.3		160
1803,	20.0	36.1	180		162
1804,	22.1	37.1	167.7		164
1805,	22.9	37.2	162.5		166
1810,	33.2	47	141.1		177
1814,	32.2	43.4	135		168
1815,	41.7	49.6	119		166
1819,	32.9	34.2	104		146
1820,	37.8	35.5	94		144
1824,	48	37.6	78.3		138
1825,	46.4	38	81.9		137
1826,	40.3	30.8	76.4		136
1830,	60.4	37.6	62.3	£6.1	132
1831,	60	36.6	61	9	131
1832,	64.5	36	55.8	5.4	130
1833,	69.6	39.3	56.4	7.5	129
1834,	73.4	41.2	56.4	6.8	128
1835,	77.9	46.9	60.2	10.5	127
1836,	84.8	53.	62.4	12.4	126
1837,	72.3	41.9	57.9	4.6	125
1838,	92.4	50	54.1	7.5	124
1839,	97.4	53.2	54.6	8.8	123
1840,	102.7	51.4	50	5.2	122
1841,	102.1	51.6	50.4	7	121
1842,	100.2	47.3	47.3	3.5	120
1843,	117.8	52.2	44.4	5	120
1844,	131.5	58.5	44.5	7.9	120
1845,	134.5	60.1	44.7		
1849,	164.5	63.5	38.7	11.9	120

For an estimate of the amount of money in circulation at each period See Chapter X, section 8.

The per cent. of money in circulation at each period compared with the amount in 1696, shows the proportion which the declared or real value of goods would have borne to the official value, if prices had been affected by no causes, except the increase and decrease of money in circulation. The difference between the per cent. of the declared value of goods, and the per cent. of money in circulation at each period, is the true test of variation of prices by reason of new inventions, improvements in machinery, variations of supply and demand, and all other causes, except an increase or decrease of circulating money in proportion to the population.

As remarked in Section 27 the decline of prices bears no proportion to the saving of labor by means of machinery; labor not only advanced in price, but the main cause of its advance was its greater productiveness, and the larger profits realized by the manufacturer, which induced greater numbers to engage in mining and manufacturing industry, and by their competition for laborers, raised the price of labor. All the most important inventions for carding and spinning by machinery were invented between the years 1767 and 1785, and were generally in use in Great Britain before the year 1790. The power loom was invented by Dr. Cartwright, in 1785, but was of comparatively little value until it was improved by Horrock and Radcliffe in 1803 and 1804, when it soon came into general use in Great Britain; though it was not introduced into the United States until 1815, and on the continent of Europe at a still later period. Nearly all the improvements in mining, smelting the metals, working in them, and manufacturing hardware, were also invented before the year 1790, and were in general use in Great Britain before the year 1800.

Notwithstanding the immense saving of labor by means of all the inventions and improvements made in manufacturing during the 18th century, and though most of them had been in general use in Great Britain from ten to fifty years prior to the peace of 1815, yet manufactures of all kinds (as shown by the foregoing tables) continued higher down to 1804, and many articles were higher in 1834 (as shown in Section 27) than they were before the invention of this labor-saving machinery. In fact, prices did not give way at all, until after the establishment of Napoleon's continental system, and the American embargo and non-intercourse acts; which, in a measure, shut out British goods from the United States and from the most of the continent of Europe, and thereby made the demand for them much less than it otherwise would have been, whereby the supply increased faster than the demand, and prices declined a trifle from 1806 to 1814. It was not until after the general peace, that the British manufacturers put down the prices of their products in order to *undersell the manufacturers of the United States, and the continent of Europe, and to break them down, drive them out of their own markets, and thus be enabled to monopolize the markets of the world without a competitor.*

How could Mr. Ricardo or Dr. Wayland explain these facts and make them consistent with their theory of prices; which assumes that the cost and the average price of every commodity, (taking a series of years into consideration,) is in proportion to the amount of labor required to produce and bring it to market?

The British manufacturers, by associations, conventions and conventional arrangements of prices among themselves, kept up prices until foreign competition forced them to come down; and then they, from necessity, reduced the prices of their products, in order to continue to undersell their neighbors, and thereby maintain their ascendency in foreign markets. In truth, though prices were affected some by the tariff of the United States of 1824, yet they declined very moderately, until the adoption of the tariff of 1828, and the still more stringent tariffs in France, Russia, Prussia, and nearly all the Northern nations of Europe just before that time, which placed their manufactures on a firm basis, and enabled their manufacturers to compete successfully in their own domestic markets, with British goods. When competition was thus raised up on every side of Great Britain, their fabrics, except cotton yarn, were almost driven out of the North of Europe, and the consumption of them much checked in the United States by means of the increase of our own production under the fostering influence of the tariff of 1828; the supply of British manufactures increased more rapidly than the demand for them; and the necessary consequence was, that prices sank rapidly from 1828 till 1833.

The compromise act of 1833, increased the imports and depressed the industry of our country; which together with the enormous increase of banks and paper money, the mania for speculation thereby produced, and fostered by means of the government funds being loaned freely to speculators as well as to business men, caused not only the prices of products of lands but of labor also to advance rapidly, until the panic, and suspension of the banks in May, 1837.

Public records show that there was no increase of paper money in Great Britain from 1830 to 1836 inclusive; and yet British manufacturers took advantage of these local causes in our country and the increased demand for their products consequent upon them, to increase the price of all their exports, and to sell them

in the aggregate at nearly one-eighth higher in 1836, than they did in 1832. Here is clear evidence that mere local causes affected materially the markets of the whole commercial world. It shows how sensitive the markets are, and how quickly affected and prices raised by a comparatively slight increase in the demand for goods. That the rise of prices in 1835 and 1836 of all British products was caused by the increased demand for them in the United States, is made perfectly clear by the foregoing table, taken in connection with the fact that there was no more than the ordinary quantity of British goods exported to other countries during those years.

On comparing the total declared value of British exports from year to year from 1827 to 1845, with the amount exported to the United States during the same years, the reader will perceive that the exports to all countries except the United States increased with great regularity about a million annually, with but very little fluctuation in amount; and that nearly all the fluctuations in the whole exports to all the world, from a regular annual increase, arose from the great difference in the amount exported to the United States. The average amount exported annually to the United States during five years from 1830 to 1834 inclusive, was only £7,015,788; while the amount in 1835 was increased to over ten and a half million pounds sterling, and in 1836 to £12,425,605. This enormously increased demand for British goods, equal in amount to nearly five million pounds, over one eighth part the usual amount of goods annually exported, was sufficient to raise the price of goods one-eighth part, as shown by the table. These heavy imports of British goods into the United States in 1835 and 1836, involved the country in debt, caused the alarm, and suspension of specie payments in the spring of 1837, and sunk the exports of British goods to the United States in 1837 to £4,695,225, and depressed the price of goods in 1838 below the price of 1833. The comparatively small imports again in 1840 and 1842, during the embarrassed condition of the United States, and in 1843, under our new tariff, again depressed prices very sensibly. It is a little remarkable that the small increase of exports to the United States in 1839, and again in 1841, enabled the manufacturers to rally prices, and raise them very considerably each of those years.

Similar remarks may be made in relation to the rise in the price of British exports in 1825. I am unable to state the amount of British goods exported to the United States in 1825, but the gross amount of imports from Great Britain, and all her colonies and dependencies, was nearly ten million dollars more than it was either in 1824 or 1826, and over eight million dollars more than

in 1823. This enormous increase in 1825, consisted mostly of products of cotton, wool, silk, and iron, caused great speculations in Great Britain, in those commodities, and a very great rise in their price ; much greater than is indicated by the Custom House Reports, which give the average through the year, and not the temporary speculative fluctuations.

These facts ought to be sufficient to satisfy the most strenuous advocates of free trade, of the great influence which an increased or diminished demand in the United States for British and French goods has upon the prices of such goods ; and to show them how an American tariff, by increasing the supply of domestic goods, and thereby lessening the demand for foreign goods, must necessarily, and by the ordinary operations of the laws of trade, tend to reduce the price of goods throughout the commercial world.

SEC. 29. *Official and declared value of manufactures of wool, cotton, linen, silk, and other articles of British produce, exported annually from* 1814 *to* 1837.

Statement of the average prices of upland cotton and of the official and declared values* of manufactures of cotton, cotton yarn and twist, and of woollen manufactures, exported from Great Britain during the under mentioned years, and the per cent. which the real value bears to the official value.

	MANUFACTURES OF COTTON.			COTTON YARN AND TWIST.				MANUF'S OF WOOL.		
Years.	Official value.	Real value.	Per cent.	Prs. Cot. in Eng.	Official value.	Real value.	Per cent.	Official value.	Real value.	Per cent.
1814,	£ 16.5	£17.2	104.3	*d.* 28	£ 1.1	£ 2.7	249	£	£	
1815,	21 4	18.9	88.1	20½	S	1.6	207			
1816,	16.1	12.9	80.0	18½	1.3	2.6	190	5.5	7.8	140.4
1820,	20.5	13.6	68.4	11½	2.0	2.8	139	4.3	5.5	128.0
1824,	27.1	15.2	56 1	8½	2.9	3.1	105	6.1	6	97.9
1825,	26.5	15.	56,6	11½	2.8	3.2	110	5.9	6.2	104.4
1826,	21.4	10.5	49.7	6¾	3.7	3.4	93	5	4.9	99.6
1830,	35.3	15.2	42.9	6⅞	5.6	4.1	73	5.5	4.8	87.3
1832,	37	12.6	34.0	6⅚	6.7	4 7	70	6.6	5.4	82.1
1834,	44.2	15.3	34.6	8¾	6.8	5.2	76	6.5	5.7	88.0
1835,	44.8	16.3	36.5	10¼	7.4	5.7	77	7.4	6.8	92.0
1836,	50.6	18.4	36.5	10¼	7.8	6.1	78	7.5	7.6	103.3
1837,	41.9	13.6	32.5	9¼	9.2	6.9	75	4.6	4.6	99.4

The average annual official value of manufactures of cotton exported from Great Britain during several previous years, was as follows :

Average of 3 years, from 1764 to 1766 inclusive,	£ 223,153
" 1 year, 1780,	355,060
" 5 years, from 1786 to 1790 inclusive,	1,232,529
" 5 " 1791 to 1795 "	2,088,525

For the prices of cotton at different periods, see Chapter VIII. Section 13.

* The values are stated in millions of pounds sterling, and fractions.

British exports of linen and silk manufactures.

Years.	Manufactures of Linen. Official value.	Declared value.	Per cent.	Manufactures of Silk. Official value.	* Declared value.	Per cent.
1816,	£1.5	£1.4	93	£161,874	£480,522	296
1820,	1.9	1.6	85	118,370	374,114	316
1824,	3.2	2.4	74	159,648	442,582	277
1825,	2.7	2.1	78	150,815	296,677	197
1826,	2.	1.4	74	106,738	168,453	157
1830,	3.1	1.9	62	435,045	519,919	119
1832,	2.6	1.6	62	476,509	529,808	111

Exports of all other articles of British produce.

	Official Value.	Declared Value.	Per cent.
1816,	£9.5	£14.8	155
1820,	8.6	11.2	130
1824,	8.2	10.3	124
1825,	8.1	11.2	137
1826,	7.9	10.1	128
1830,	10.3	11.	107
1832,	11.	11.	100

The foregoing tables illustrate more in detail, the conclusions and truths deduced from that in Sec. 28, and the most of the remarks in that section and in Sec. 27, apply equally well to the tables in this.

It may be remarked that while cotton yarn advanced in price in 1825 five per cent., equal to about half the advance on cotton, the rise in cotton cloths was less than one per cent.; and that though the declared value of cotton yarn was then ten per cent. above its official value, yet the declared value of cotton cloths of all kinds was over 43 per cent. below their official value. These are remarkable facts; they show the effects of American competition, and the American tariff of 1824, in reducing the price of cotton cloths, in contrast with the high price of yarn, in the production of which for market, the American manufacturers did not come in competition with the British. The same may be remarked of the rise in the price of cotton goods in 1836. The compromise act of 1833 effectually checked the further increase of American manufactures, so that American competition was not sufficiently strong to prevent the rise in cotton cloths in 1835 and 1836, and the per cent. of the advance of their declared value, was from 34 to 36½; while the advance in the declared value of

* The whole values of the exports of silk are given; all other exports are stated in millions.

cotton yarn, (where the British had no American competition to contend with,) was from 70 to 78 per cent.

The only way in which our tariff could operate to reduce prices has been, by increasing our manufactures and domestic products, and thereby lessening the demand for British goods; and whenever the prices of cotton have been high as in 1825, 1835 and 1836, and we have had a bloated paper currency, both of which have stimulated a spirit of speculation, the uniform tendency has been to stimulate foreign commerce, increase our imports, and raise the prices of imported goods. In connection with our gross imports from Great Britain, let the reader give attention to our imports of cotton, woollen and other goods, in different years; and he will find the amount of our imports apparently had a very important influence upon prices; that when our imports were very large, causing a heavy demand in the foreign market, prices advanced; and when our imports were comparatively small, prices generally fell off.

The effect of our tariff acts of 1824 and 1828, in diminishing the importation of both cotton and woollen goods, and reducing prices from 1824 to 1833, is very obvious; and the contrary effect of the compromise act of 1833, and the subsequent bloated paper currency, in swelling our importations, and enhancing prices in 1835 and 1836, and again in 1839, is equally obvious. The effect was more striking on woollen than on cotton goods; and the cause of this is shown more clearly, by comparing the total exports of woollen goods from Great Britain, with their exports of like goods to the United States. There was a remarkable degree of uniformity from year to year, in the exports of Great Britain to all other countries than the United States, of woollen and silk goods. Nearly all the fluctuations from year to year in the quantity of such goods exported, was in the exports to the United States; and inasmuch as the quantities exported in different years generally indicate the intensity of the demand, which regulates the price, all, or nearly all the fluctuations in prices, arose from the greater or less demand for the American market. The embarrassed condition of the people of the United States, and our comparatively small importations in 1837, 1838, 1840 and 1842, in consequence of our embarrassments, contributed to reduce the price of goods throughout the commercial world, by lessening the demand for them.

The great and striking contrast between the official and the declared value of linen and silk goods from 1816 to 1824, affords the clearest evidence I have met with, of the entire falsity of the leading doctrine of prices of Mr. Ricardo and Dr. Wayland, that the prices of commodities are determined by the amount of labor

required to produce, and bring them to market; and it affords equally clear evidence of the great truth, that the prices of articles are governed by the relative demand and supply in the market, without any reference whatever to the labor required to produce them, except the indirect effect which that may have on the supply. Machinery was applied to the manufacture of silk, much earlier than to the manufacture of flax; the first mill for throwing silk having been erected in England as early as 1719, after the model of the silk mills then in use in Italy. Spinning linen by machinery commenced in Scotland in the early part of this century, though in Dundee, the great seat of the linen manufacture, there were in 1811 but four flax mills, which were increased in 1831 to thirty-one, employing 2,065 spinners and 405 flax dressers. Flax mills were introduced into Ireland at a much later date; until since 1825, nearly all the Irish linen was both spun and woven by hand; and much of it was spun by hand (according to Mr. McCulloch.) as late as 1838. Though there were in Scotland in 1834, (according to the official returns) 170 flax mills in operation, employing 13,409 hands, there were only 25 in Ireland, employing 3,681 hands.

Notwithstanding nearly all the silk was thrown or spun with machinery, and the linen by hand, prior to 1825, yet the prices of silk from 1816 to 1824, appear from official accounts of exports, to have been nearly three times as great as they were in 1696; though the prices of linen were considerably lower during the same period, than they were in 1696. This looks like a strange anomaly; while manufactures of cotton, wool, silk and iron (all of which had received important aids from the use of machinery), had all advanced in price; linen goods, which were mostly spun on a one thread wheel, and woven in hand looms, had actually declined in price, and were lower than they were 120 years previously. This can be explained only by the fact, that cotton had in some measure superseded the use of linen, and lessened the demand for it; and as the demand decreased, the price fell. On the contrary, as the people of Great Britain, Northern and Western Europe and the United States grew more wealthy, and greater numbers of them became able to wear silk, the demand for silk goods increased much faster than the supply; and the prices were raised by this increased demand, to about three times the standard established as their official value in 1696.

SEC. 30. *Importation into the U. States, Production and Prices of Iron; and Improvements in the Manufacture.*

The prices of English pig and bar iron at Birmingham, and of Swedes bar iron in London, exclusive of duty of £4 to £6 10s.

per ton, are stated by Mr. Babbage on the Economy of Manufactures, sec. 149, as follows:

	1818.	1824.	1828.	1830.	1832.
Pig iron per ton,	£6 7½	£6 10	£5 10	£4 10	£
Bar iron per ton,	10 10	9 10	7 15	6	5
Swedes iron per ton,	17 10	14	14 10	13 15	13 2

The wholesale selling prices at Liverpool of merchants' bar iron per ton from 1806 to 1820, were as follows:

Years.	£.	s.		£.	s.	Years.	£.	s.		£.	s.
1806,	16	0	to	17	10	1814,	13	0	to	14	0
1807,	15	0	to	17	0	1815,	11	0	to	13	10
1809,	14	5	to	16	0	1816,	8	15	to	11	0
1810,	14	0	to	15	0	1817,	8	10	to	13	0
1811,	14	0	to	14	10	1818,	10	0	to	12	15
1812,	12	15	to	13	13	1819,	11	0	to	12	0
1813,	12	0	to	13	0	1820,	9	10	to	10	10

The prices at Liverpool are necessarily higher, as a general rule, than they are at the forges, and the reader should bear in mind that in England a ton is 2,240 pounds, though in many of our states 2,000 pounds is called a ton.

It is stated in Hunt's Magazine, for March, 1845, that pig iron which sold in England and Wales from 1803 to 1815, for £6 to £7 10s. per ton, was reduced in 1844 to £3; and that some contracts were made in Scotland as low as £2; that bar iron which sold during the same period, at £12 to £16 per ton, was reduced in 1844 to £4 15s.

ACCOUNT OF THE BAR IRON made by rolling, imported into the United States from 1821 to 1850 inclusive; the custom house valuation thereof, and duties upon the same, and the value of rolled bar iron in England during the same years.

Years.	Tons.	Value in dollars.	Value per ton.	Duty per ton.	Value in Great Britain per ton.
1821,	2,189	$117,947	$54 00	$30 00	$8½ to 9½
1822,	5,066	253,335	50 00	"	8 to 8½
1823,	5,346	245,950	46 00	"	8 to 8½
1824,	5,790			"	9 to 12
1825,	4,250	224,497	52 80	"	10 to 14
1826,	4,437	223,259	50 35	"	8⅓ to 11
1827,	8,102	347,792	42 90	"	8 to 9¼
1828,	10,294	441,000	42 83	"	7½ to 9
1829,	3,320	119,326	35 94	37 00	5½ to 7⅛
1830,	6,949	226,336	32 65	"	5¼ to 6¾
1831,	15,245	544,664	35 70	"	5¼ to 6⅛
1832,	21,387	701,549	32 60	"	5 to 6¼
1833,	28,028	1,002,750	35 80	30 00	5½ to 7½
1834,	28,896	1,187,236	41 00	27 80	6 to 7½
1835,	28,410	1,050,152	37 33	27 60	5½ to 8¼
1836,	46,675	2,131,828	45 60	25 75	9 to 11½
1837,	47,839	2,573,367	53 80	26 00	7 to 10¼
1838,	36,174	1,825,121	50 40	24 00	8 to 10
1839,	60,282	3,181,180	52 70	24 25	8½ to 10¼
1840,	32,828	1,707,649	52 33	22 00	7 to 9
1841,	63,055	2,172,278	34 40	20 75	6 to 7
1842,	61,599	2,053,453	33 33	14 00	5¼ to 6½
1843,	15,757	511,282	32 46	25 00	4⅓ to 5½
1844,	37,891	1,065,582	28 12	"	4¾ to 6¼
1845,	51,188	1,691.748	33 00	"	6 to 10
1846,	24,108	1,127,418	46 75	"	8½ to 9¼
1847,	40,183	2,129,489	53 00	30 pr ct.	7¾ to 9½
1848,	81,589	3,679,598	45 00	"	5½ to 7½
1849,	173,457	6,060,068	35 00	"	5¼ to 6⅝
1850,	247,951	7,397,166	30 00	"	

The prices above stated of iron in Great Britain, are for merchants' bar iron; the prices of railroad iron being about one and a half pounds sterling per ton higher. The lowest prices stated, are for the lowest prices during the year at the forges; the highest are for the highest prices at Liverpool, where iron is usually from 15 to 30s. per ton higher than it is at Cardiff.

The rolled bar iron imported into the United States is nearly all from Great Britain, and is made by machinery, in rolling mills; the bar iron made by hammering, is nearly all from Sweden and Norway, and is better to make into steel and for edge tools than the iron made by rolling. The expense of making pig iron into bar iron by rolling, perhaps does not require one-tenth part as much labor as to make it by hammering; and hence English rolled iron is gradually superseding the use of hammered iron, for all common purposes to which it can be applied.

These tables of the prices of iron imported into the United States, and of the prices in England, are sufficient to show the prices during the whole of the present century. The tables in Section 26 show the prices in 1696, established as the official valuations in England for iron exported and imported. The improvements in the manufacture of both pig and bar iron in Great Britain, and the enormous increase in the production of each furnace, as well as of the aggregate productions, indicate, that at least three times as much pig or bar iron could be made in 1806, and five or six times as much in 1845, with the same labor, as could have been made a century since. And yet we see, (that notwithstanding this immense saving of labor,) the prices of iron were kept up, until after our tariff of 1818, to nearly the old standard of 1696; and had receded comparatively little, even as late as the year 1824. It is easy to see, from the foregoing table of imports and prices, the effect of our increased tariffs of 1828 and 1842, in reducing the prices of iron from 1829 to 1832, and in 1843 and 1844; and, also, the effect of the compromise act of 1833, in raising them from 1833 to 1840. The effect of these acts was much greater on the prices of rolled bar iron, (which was imported from Great Britain,) than it was on hammered bar iron imported from Sweden; and shows the determination of the English iron masters, to maintain their ascendency in the American markets, however much it might be necessary to reduce prices. The railroad excitement which commenced in Europe in 1845, and raged during the years 1845 and 1846, increased the demand for iron so much in Europe, that the iron masters raised the prices in 1846 to nearly double what they were in 1843, notwithstanding the comparatively light importation into the United States.

The prices of iron in 1846 were about as high as in 1818, and nearly twice as great as they were in 1831, 1832, 1843 and 1844; and yet the low prices during those years did not prevent a constant increase in its production. If the making of iron was profitable during those years of low prices, how immensely profitable it must have been in 1846, and previous to the year 1828? If making iron prior to 1740 would fairly pay for the labor and use of capital, then making it in 1832. 1843 and 1844 at only about $37\frac{1}{2}$ per cent. of the ordinary price from 1696 to 1750, but with only one-fifth part of the amount of labor formerly required, would pay nearly twice as large a compensation for both labor and capital; and making it from 1810 to 1820, and in 1846 and 1847, would afford compensation for labor and capital about four times as great as it did a century since. These immense profits and high wages paid to laborers have caused a very great increase in the number of laborers and the amount of capital employed in the manufacture of iron in Great Britain; and increased its production beyond all parallel in the history of the world, with the single exception of the manufacture of cotton.

In 1835 about one third part, and in 1836 nearly half the British exports of iron were to the United States; and during the whole period of the compromise act, (from 1833 to 1842 inclusive,) we used more than one fourth part of the whole quantity exported by Great Britain. What an immense influence this large American demand for British iron has had on the market, in keeping up prices! The official statements of the quantity of iron made in the United States, show that the increase was comparatively small from 1830 to 1840; it is well known that the duties were so light under the compromise act in 1841 and 1842, that many furnaces and forges stopped, and the manufacture declined; and there was very little increase in the production between the years 1835 and 1840. The increase was also very slow until after our tariff act of 1828. On the contrary, the production increased with astonishing rapidity, in 1843 and 1844, to 1846, under our tariff of 1842.

The table of imports shows that our tariff of 1828 not only reduced the imports of rolled bar iron in 1829 and 1830, but checked their increase very much some years afterwards: and if it could have been maintained, there can be no reasonable doubt that the domestic manufacture would have increased as rapidly from 1834 to 1842, as it did the previous years, and did also under the tariff of 1842; and if so, the demand for British iron must have been much less, and its price would necessarily have fallen much lower than it did in 1843 and 1844. The reader can see how sensitive the market is! how it was raised in 1845 and 1846 about 80 per cent., by the railway speculations in Europe, and the increased demand for railroad iron. What if we had remained under the compromise act, and the production of iron in the United States had been about 250,000 tons in 1846, as it would have been instead of 500,000 tons, as it was under the tariff act of 1842, and we had imported from Great Britain 200,000 or 250,000 to make up the deficiency, instead of importing from them but 24,108 tons; what effect would this immensely increased demand have had on the market and the prices of iron? Would not the prices of British iron have advanced to £12 or £15 per ton?

All these illustrations tend to show the effect of demand and supply on prices; and to show how an American tariff, by increasing the manufacture of products in this country, and thus increasing the supply, and also lessening the amount we have occasion to import, and thereby diminishing the demand for foreign products, must necessarily tend to reduce prices. The facts show that we cannot trust much either to the tender mercies of British manufacturers, or to their competition among themselves to reduce the prices of iron, or of manufactures of any kind; nor can we trust to the free trade theory, that improvements in manufactures will necessarily reduce prices.

Sec. 31. *Prices of Copper, Tin, and Lead, at different periods.*

The average prices of copper per ton in Great Britain are stated in the Commercial Dictionary as follows:

		l.	s.	d.			l.	s.
Average in	1800	133	3	6	highest in	1808,	100	7
"	1801 to 1810,	129	5	3	"	1805,	169	16
"	1811 to 1820,	117	17	0	"	1818,	134	15
"	1821 to 1830,	110	17	2	"	1825,	124	4
"	1831,	100	0	0	"	1821,	103	0

Mr. McCulloch, in 1838, estimated the average price from year to year, at from £90 to £100 per ton. The prices of copper in the London market from May to October, 1846, were from £88 to £96, averaging about £93 per ton; which is about 20 cents per pound.

The average prices of tin exported from Great Britain are stated in the Commercial Dictionary as follows, per cwt. of 112 pounds;

		l.	s.	d.		l.	s.	d.
Average in	1820	3	13	6	highest in 1823,	5	5	6
"	1821 to 1830,	4	1	8	lowest in 1830,	3	10	0
"	1832,	3	13	0	tin in bars in 1834,	3	17	6

Mr. McCulloch says the total quantity of tin produced in Devon and Cornwall in 1837–38, amounted to 5,130 tons of the average value of £82, making its total value £420,660. The average price of British tin from 1811 to 1815 inclusive, was about £7 per cwt., or £140 per ton.

The average prices of tin in bars in the London market during the summer of 1846 were about £4 12s 10d. per cwt., or £92 16s. 8d. per ton.

The prices of lead in Great Britain per ton are stated in the Commercial Dictionary, as follows:

		l.	s.	d.			l.	s.	d.
Average in	1800,	19	16	0	highest in	1801,	22	8	6
"	1801 to 1810,	28	12	6	"	1806,	35	12	6
"	1811 to 1820,	22	13	9	"	1818,	27	5	
"	1821 to 1830,	19	12	0	"	1825,	25	6	
"	1830,	14	00	0	in	1832,	13	10	6

The average prices of common pig lead in the London market

during the summer of 1846, were about £19 per ton, and for refined lead £21 per ton. The Custom House price of the 18,420,407 pounds of lead exported from the United States during the year ending June 30th, 1844, was $595,238; or about 3¼ cents per lb., equal to £15 3s. per ton. The quantity exported from the United States during the years 1845–46 amounted to 16,823,766 pounds, valued at $614,518, or nearly 3⅔ cents per pound; equal to £17 per ton.

By referring back to the prices of copper, tin, and lead, in 1751, in Section 26, the reader will see that the prices of copper were a trifle, and but a trifle less in England in 1846 than in 1751; that tin has been about 25 per cent., and lead about 40 per cent., higher for a few years past, than they were a century since. Though the fluctuations in prices have been very great in these articles, they have not been as great as in the prices of iron.

SEC. 32. *Prices of Hardware at different periods.*

Prices of the following articles of hardware at Birmingham in the undermentioned years, as stated by Mr. Babbage on the Economy of Manufactures, Section 148.

	1818.		1824.		1828.		1832.	
	s.	*d.*	*s.*	*d.*	*s.*	*d.*	*s.*	*d.*
Anvil, per cwt.,	25	0	20	0	16	0	14	0
Bolts for doors, 6 in. per doz.,	6	0	5	0	2	3	1	6†
Braces and 12 bits for carpt. set,	9	0	4	0	4	2	3	5†
Buttons for coats, gross,	4	6	6	3	3	0	2	2†
Brass candlesticks 6 in. pair,	2	11	2	0	1	7	1	2†
Gun locks, single roller each,	6	0	5	2	1	10	1	11
Brass knobs, 2 in. doz.,	4	0	3	6	1	6	1	2†
Locks for doors, 6 in. iron rims doz.,	38	0	32	0	15	0	13	6†
Stirrups, plated, pair,	4	6	3	9	1	6	1	1†
Stirrups, com. tin'd, 2 bar, doz.,	†7						2	9
Shoe hammers, doz.,	6	9	3	9	3	0	2	9†
Trace chains, cwt.,	28	0	25	0	19	6	15	0
Vices for blacksmiths, cwt.,	30	0	28	0	22	0	19	6†

Here the reader will see that the fall in prices of hardware from 1818 to 1832 varies from about 35 to 75 per cent., averaging about 50 per cent. Tables like this are spread before the world by English authors, to show the effect of improvements in manufacture, and of the competition of British manufacturers among themselves, in reducing prices. By referring back to Section 27, the reader will see that the declared value or market

* All these marked with the dagger for 1832, are prices for the year 1830 instead of 1832.

† Price in 1812.

price of British hardware and cutlery in 1832 was 63 per cent. higher than the official value; though the prices of iron and steel which constitute the principal materials of which such articles are made, were less than half as high at the later as they were at the earlier date. As prices in 1818 were about twice as high as in 1832, when we compare prices in 1696 with those of 1818, we find those of hardware were about three times as high at the latter as they were at the former period. If the introduction of machinery, and improvements in the manufacture between the years 1696 and 1832, have enabled the same number of laborers to produce twice as much at the latter as they could at the former period, (which cannot be reasonably doubted,) then the earnings of labor and capital employed in the manufacture of hardware and cutlery at the current prices, (taking the amount of circulating money and cost of materials into consideration,) would be about four times as much in 1832, and five times as much in 1818 as in 1696. Let the reader bear in mind that these conclusions are not vague conjectures, founded on hypothesis and assumed facts, (like many of those of the free trade economists;) but they are *arithmetical deductions from facts furnished by British records, and collected by British authors.*

The Com. Dict., title Hardware, states, "the total exports of hardware and cutlery from Great Britain in 1831 at £1,622,429, of which the United States took no less than £998,469, and the British possessions in North America and the West Indies nearly £190,000." The United States, it seems, took more than 60 per cent. of the whole.

The whole amount of the declared value of the exports of hardware from Great Britain, the amount exported to the United States, and the amount exported to all other countries were as follows:

	1834.	1836.	1837.	1839.
Total amount,	£1,485,233	£2,271,313	£1,460,807	£1,828.521
Amount to the United States,	647,216	1,318,412	574,876	849,640
do to all other countries,	833,017	952,901	885,931	978,882

Here the American demand for hardware, as in the case of iron and cotton, woollen, silk and linen goods, was exceedingly great but very fluctuating, which materially affected prices; while the demand of all other countries was comparatively regular. The aggregate quantities of British hardwares exported to all countries other than the United States were very little greater in 1835 and 1836, than they were in 1834 and 1837, yet, in consequence of the increased American demand the purchasers were compelled to pay for them from 10 to 20 per cent. higher prices. This heavy American demand had an immense effect in keeping up prices. If we could have had a tariff ever since 1812 sufficient not only to protect our manufacturers of such products, but to encourage others to embark in the manufacture, so as to nearly supply the country, and had thereby lessened this demand for British hardware £500,000 per annum, the necessary effect must have been, to reduce prices very much, as well as to increase the productive industry of our country. The reduction of prices which did take place from 1818 to 1832, was submitted to by the British manufacturers, on account of the growing competition in the United States and the North of Europe, in order to undersell their competitors, and maintain their ascendency in foreign markets. In fact, such is the cunning and management of British manufacturers, by means of conventions and extensive correspondence among each other to regulate prices, that we have very little evidence that their competition with each other ever subtantially and permanently reduced the prices of any thing; on contrary, we have abundance of evidence, that the reduction in prices has generally arisen from the competition of other European nations, and the United States, and the necessity thus forced upon British manufacturers of reducing prices in order to undersell their competitors.

SEC. 33. *The Western Produce Market, giving prices, at different places and periods.*

I. Statement of the number of hogs packed annually at the city of Cincinnati, during the four years, ending with the seasons of 1838–39, and for each subsequent year to 1845–46; and also the price per 100 lbs. at which the market opened each year; taken from the report of the Commissioner of Patents, of December, 1845, p. 1,029.

	Number of Hogs.	Prices.
1835–36 to 1838–39, average.	151,750	$4 00 to $5 81
1839–40,	95,000	3 00 to 3 50
1840–41,	160,000	3 50 to 3 75
1841–42,	220,000	2 00 to 2 50
1842–43,	250,000	1 62 to 2 00
1843–44,	240,000	2 25 to 2 65
1844–45,	213,000	2 50 to 2 70
1845–46,	287,000	4 00 to

The number of hogs slaughtered in fifty-three of the principal cities and towns in Ohio, Indiana, Illinois, Kentucky and Missouri, are estimated in Hunt's Merchants' Magazine, for April, 1846, as follows:—In the season of 1843 and '44, at 856,000; in 1844 and '45, at 593,500; in 1845 and 46, at 758,100. The average weight may be estimated at 225 pounds, equal, after taking out the heads, feet, &c., to about a barrel of pork each on an average. This and the foregoing table will give the reader some idea of the extent of the Western pork market, the extremely low prices of pork, and the effect of the enormous quantity in proportion to the demand for it, in depressing prices. The reader should bear in mind, that to make every 100 lbs. of pork, requires about two bushels of corn to raise the hogs, over and above grass, slops, &c., and five bushels of corn to fatten them; so that every 100 lbs. of pork represents about seven bushels of corn, or its equivalent in other grain, beside grass, slops, the labor of feeding, taking care of the hogs, and taking it to market.

II. Statement of the average prices of wheat per bushel and flour per barrel in the city of Cincinnati during the month of July of each year from 1841 to 1845, compiled by the editor of the Cincinnati Gazette, from the commercial reports of that paper, published in Hunt's Magazine for September, 1845; to which I have added the prices of flour in the city of New York during the same months.

	Average of wheat and flour in Cincinnati. Flour per bbl.	Wheat per bush.	Flour in N. Y
July, 1841,	\$4 06¼	\$72¾	\$5 37½
do 1842,	3 49¾	49½	5 93
do 1843,	3 73	70	5 62½
do 1844,	3 29	59	4 31¼
do 1845,	3 26½	64¼	4 62½

Mr. C. C. Whittlesey, of Missouri, in giving the resources of that state, published in Hunt's Magazine, for June, 1843, based on the returns of the census of 1840, estimated their wheat crop at only 30 cents per bushel; oats, rye and buckwheat at 20 cents per bushel; Indian corn and potatoes at 15 cents per bushel; barley at 50 cents per bushel; and tobacco at 3 cents a pound.

III. Prices of flour and grain at St. Louis and Cincinnati in March, 1843,

	Cincinnati.	St. Louis.
Flour per bbl. March, 1843,	\$2 50 to \$2 56	\$2 50 to \$2 75
Wheat per bushel,	45 to 50	35 to 37
Corn per bushel,	16 to 20	14 to 15

The price of flour in the city of New York at the same time was \$5,75.

IV. Prices of the leading articles of agricultural products in July, 1842, as stated in Hunt's Merchants' Magazine for August, 1842.

	New York.	Boston.	N. Orleans.	Cincinnati.
Flour bbl.	\$5 94 to 6 00	6 00 to 6 12	4 75 to 5 00	3 75 to 4 00
Wheat bu.	1 25 to 1 28		94 to 95	50 to 60
Corn bu.	55 to 57	60 to 61	32 to 33	20 to 25
Beef m's bbl.	7 00 to 7 75	9 00 to 9 25	8 50 to 9 00	6 00 to 7 00
Pork m's bbl.	7 50 to 9 50	7 00 to 8 00	6 50 to 7 00	5 00 to 5 50½
Hams lb.	6 to 7½	5 to 6	4 to 5	3 to 5 00
Sugar N. O. lb.	3 to 5	3½ to 5	2 to 5¼	4 to 6
Wool Am lb.	35 to 45	40 to 42	8 to 12	20 to 30
Lead pig lb.	3½	3½ to 3¾	3 to	3 to 4

These tables and estimates show a very great difference between eastern and western markets for produceand, the importance to the farmer of a market for his produce, and particularly for coarse grains, in his immediate vicinity. While Indian corn was worth 60 cents per bushel in Boston, in consequence of the demand created by the manufacturing population in the vicinity, it was worth but 32 cents in New Orleans, 20 to 25 in Cincinnati, and 20 in St. Louis, and not over 10 cents in many remote interior places in Illinois, Indiana, Tennessee, Kentucky and Missouri. But look at the depressed prices of mess pork at Cincinnati; only about $5 25 on an average per barrel, and the salt, barrel and packing, and other expenses, would be about $1 37½, leaving only $3 88 for about 225 lbs. of pork, including the waist of heads, feet, &c., being about $1 75 per 100 lbs. of pork; or 25 cents per bushel for the corn and the labor of feeding it out, taking care of the hogs, and carrying the pork to market.

When the reader reflects that much of the farming country in the Western States lies from 50 to 100 miles from navigable waters or canals; that it costs about ten cents per bushel to transport grain by wagons 30 to 33½ miles, and that the cost of hiring it transported 60 or 70 miles would generally be greater than the value of corn in the western cities, he need not wonder that the whole crop of corn in Missouri should be estimated at 15 cents per bushel as stated at the bottom of Table II.; nor need he wonder that there is often no money market for it at any price, in the interior districts remote from navigable waters, and that it usually sells in barter in such districts, at from ten to fifteen cents per bushel.

The reader will see from these examples, the effect of a large supply in proportion to the demand, in depressing prices; and on comparing these prices with prices in Boston and New York, as stated in Table IV., and with the prices in Great Britain, as stated in sections 16, 17, and 25, he may learn how prices are raised by an increased demand, by means of the competition among buyers, that the demand for food is in proportion to the density of the population; and he may thus realize the importance to the farmer, of manufacturing towns in his vicinity to create a demand and furnish a market for products, which will not bear transportation to distant markets. In this way he may realize how much more it promotes the agricultural industry and prosperity of any people, to encourage agricultural industry among themselves, and thus effect the double purpose of increasing their national industry, and creating a market for their agricultural products, than it does to consume the manufactured products of other countries, and thereby patronize and encourage the industry of foreign nations, and contribute to support foreign laborers, and to create a market for the farmers of foreign countries.

SEC. 34. *Exports and Imports of the United States; monthly prices of flour in New York; export and import prices from* 1828 *to* 1846 *of Flour, Wheat, Corn and Butter.*

I. Statement of the quantities of flour and wheat exported from the United States annually for the years 1828 to 1842, ending September 30th, for 9 months, ending June 30th, 1843, and for the years ending June 30th, 1844, to 1851; together with the average Custom House prices or valuations per barrel and per bushel of the same; and the average prices of flour in New York City during the same years.

		Flour Exported.		Wheat Exported.	
Years.	Prices of flour in New York.	Quantity in bbls.	Prices.	Quantity in bushels.	Prices.
1828	$5 02	860,809	$4 90	8,906	$ 75
1829	6 96	837,385	6 92	4,007	1 50
1830	5 40	1,227,434	4 96	45,289	1 02
1831	5 71	1.806,529	5 50	408,910	1 28
1832	5 80	864,919	5 55	88,304	1 06
1833	5 78	955,768	5 87	32,221	90
1834	5 19	835,352	5 40	36,948	1 06
1835	5 62½	779,396	5 60	47,762	1 07
1836	7 00	505,400	7 13	2,062	1 00
1837	9 87½	318,719	9 37	17,303	1 56
1838	7 92	448,161	8 04	6,291	1 30
1839	7 92	923,151	7 50	96,325	1 48
1840	5 61	1,897,501	5 34	1,720,860	96
1841	5 13	1,515,817	5 15	868,585	94
1842	5 83	1,283,602	5 68	817,958	1 12
1843	4 73	841,474	4 46	311,685	87
1844	4 91	1,438,574	4 70	558,917	89
1845	4 75	1,195,230	4 45	389,716	86
1846	5 34	2,289,476	5 95	1,613,795	1 04
1847	6 08	4,382,496	5 97	4,399,951	1 37½
1848		2,119,393	6 22	2,034,704	1 31
1849		2,108,013	5 35	1,527,534	1 15
1850		1,385,448	5 12	608,661	1 06
1851		2,202,335	4 77	1,026,735	1 00

The wholesale prices of superfine flour in the city of New York, from the first of June to the last of October of the year 1851, varied from $3 50 to about $4 25; averaging less than

$4 per barrel. The flour and breadstuffs exported to Europe were trifling in amount, and the European market for them of very little value to the American farmer.

The quantities of Indian corn exported from the United States annually, and the average export prices have been as follows:

Average per year.	Bushels.	Prices.
1831 to 1840,	365,391	$0.76¼
1841 to 1846,	838,710	.55½
1847,	13,326,050	.88
1848 to 1850, average	8,556,678 annually,	.61
1851,	3,426,811	.51½

II. Statement showing the average value of Genesee flour per barrel in the city of New York during each month of the undermentioned periods:

	1823 to 1830.	1831 to 1840.	1841 to 1847.	September 1846 to August 1847.
September,	$5 36	$6 46	$5 01	$4 18¾
October,	5 59	6 45	5 27	5 62½
November,	5 79	6 71	5 52	6 00
December,	5 79	6 88	5 56	5 31¼
January,	5 90	6 96	5 28	5 75
February,	5 97	7 10	5 41	6 87½
March,	5 88	6 98	5 57	7 12½
April,	5 86	6 88	5 65	7 68¾
May,	5 53	6 36	5 41	7 25
June,	5 52	6 38	5 50	8 87½
July,	5 38	6 35	5 16	6 50
August,	5 27	6 33	5 02	5 62
General average,	$5 65	$6 65	$5 36	$6 40

Though wheat is harvested in most countries in the month of July, it does not usually begin to come to market until September, so that the grain and flour year for each crop commences in September and ends the following August. With the exception of the year 1847, flour fell constantly nearly every year from February or March until the end of August—showing clearly that the supply was greater than the wants of the country, and the demand for exportation. In 1847, prices were raised by the speculative demand in Great Britain, and kept advancing until July, when they fell suddenly, having fallen early in June in Great Britain. That the demand in Great Britain was mostly speculative, and the imports greatly in excess and beyond the wants of that country, is shown by its sudden fall in June, and the disastrous results as shown in Sec. 17.

III. Statement of imports into the United States of wheat flour, wheat, potatoes, and butter, over and above what was re-exported during the years ending Sept. 30, 1836, 1837, and 1838; and the quantities of domestic produce exported the same years, to the whole of the Old World and the British North American Colonies included; and, also, the amount exported to the remaining part of the New World.

	Flour, bbls.	Wheat, bush.	Potatoes, bush.	Butter, lbs.
Imported in 1836,				
From the Old World,	5,000	323,571	58,514	70,270
From Brit. N. Amer'n Colonies.	11,500	260,327	21,720	91,984
Exported to Old World,	50,634	2,062	835	11,793
Exported to New World,	454,766		90,746	349,602
Imported in 1837,				
From the Old World,	7,289	3,577,289	34,212	72,936
From Brit. N. Amer'n Colonies,	10,184	317,170	12,455	3,491
Exported to Old World,	24,366	17,303	3,531	23,538
Exported to New World,	294,353		97,172	258,401
Imported in 1838.				
From the Old World,	10,568	866,000	50,017	10,718
From Brit. N. Amer'n Colonies,	10,878	14,163	4,201	2,682
Exported to Old World,	32,256	6,241	1,562	21,831
Exported to New World,	415,905	48	117,065	473,277

There was more than twice as much cheese as butter imported from Europe, during those years.

The average import prices, according to the Custom House Reports, were as follows.

	1836.	1837.	1838.
Wheat, per bushel,	$0,85	$1,06	$1,02
Potatoes, per bushel,	39½	44	37½
Butter, per pound,	12⅓	15½	12½
Cheese, per pound,	12⅓	11¾	11½

These Tables, (I, II and III,) should be examined together and carefully compared, in order to understand the causes of the fluctuations in the price of flour; which, being exported in larger quantities than wheat, affords a much more certain test of its market value. The small quantity of wheat exported in 1836, appears quite too low to correspond with the price of flour. The reader will see from Table I, that the prices of flour during the four successive years, 1836 to 1839 inclusive, ranged very high. By looking at Table III, he will observe the extraordinary fact, that during each of the three years in succession, 1836 to 1838 inclusive, the United States not only imported considerable quantities of wheat and flour from Canada and the other British Colonies north of the United States, but they actually imported more from Europe than they exported to the whole of the Old World and those Colonies together; and by examining the reports of the Secretary of the Treasury he will see, that wheat was imported into the United States during those years from Great Britain, France, Holland, the Hanse Towns, Italy, Austria, and from almost all the maritime countries of Europe.

Table I, also shows, that in 13 years out of 18, the average price of flour through the year was greater in the city of New York, our principal exporting city, than the average export price. It must be obvious to every one, that it cannot be exported when the domestic demand is such as to raise the price above what buyers can afford to pay for it, to export. We can export only when we can sell as low as our neighbors. Though flour was exported during each of these 13 years, when the average price in New York was above the average export price, yet it was exported from New York only during intervals when the price was below the average price. The reader can see how little effect the foreign market has had on the prices of wheat and flour in this country; that our prices have been so high the principal part of the time, as to prevent exportation; that our market is mostly a domestic one; that in nine years in ten, the European market is utterly valueless to us, almost all our exports being to the West Indies and the continent of America; and that high prices tend to lessen, and when they get to a certain point, actually preclude exportation, and invite importation, and thus tend to depress and destroy the industry of the country.

The consumers of produce must always pay much higher for it, than the producers can sell it for; they must pay the expenses of transportation, and the profits of the intermediate dealers or merchants. When we were the consumers of European wheat, we had to pay the cost of its transportation across the Atlantic, which raised the price of flour made of both foreign and domestic wheat, to from $7 to about $11 per barrel some portion of the time. This was a memorable era of FREE TRADE AND PAPER MONEY! *of speculation in Bank and Railroad stocks, wild lands and paper cities! when men were getting rich beyond the dreams of avarice, by their wits instead of industry; by importing their clothing and a portion of their food, instead of producing them by their own labor; and busying themselves in contracting debts, making state and corporate stocks, paper money, paper cities, and paper railroads also*, to a very great extent.

The gross circulation of bank notes in the United States, according to reports made the nearest to January 1, 1830, was $61,323,898; the nearest to January 1, 1834, $94,839,570; the nearest to January 1, 1837, was $149,185,890; the nearest to January 1, 1840, was $116,572,790; and to January 1, 1843, it had sunk to $58,563,688. Since that time it has increased as is shown in Chapter X. The States contracted debts and issued bonds, in three years, from 1836 to 1838 inclusive, amounting to about $100,000,000—the most of which were sold in Europe, and the proceeds applied to pay for goods. When our people were afflicted with such delusive dreams of wealth, they were unfitted for the sober pursuits of industry; and as the bloated paper money raised the prices of labor, as well as of produce and property, our markets furnished a rich and tempting reward to the industry of other countries, and we vainly thought we could supply our wants, by importing the products of foreign industry, cheaper than by our own labor. Paper money, therefore, by raising prices in this country much higher than they were in Europe, tended to diminish exportations, as well as to encourage and increase importations, and thereby to undermine and depress the industry of the country, and involve us in foreign debts. The evils of free trade were thus aggravated and increased, by an excessive amount of paper money.

The exports and prices of Indian corn, show also the effect, to some extent, of paper money on both prices and exports. Prices were generally high, when our paper money was excessive in amount; when prices ranged above seventy cents per bushel, our exports were but a mere trifle; and they have always been trifling in amount, compared to our enormous crops, of over three hundred million bushels annually. It may also be remarked, that nearly all our exports of corn, up to 1846, were to the West Indies and the Continent of America; and that the European market for our corn was entirely worthless. The effective European demand for it commenced in 1846—prior to that time, with the exception of the years of excessive paper currency, from 1835 to 1840, the average prices of corn in New England and the city of New York, were above the export prices stated in the table. The reader will, therefore, see that the prices of corn generally depend entirely on the domestic market, and are scarcely affected at all by the foreign markets. Is it, or is it not, of consequence to the farmer, to divert a large portion of our population from agriculture to manufactures, that they may become consumers, and not producers, in order to increase the American market for corn, pork, lard, &c., and to lessen the supply of those articles? In Massachusetts, Connecticut and Rhode Island, the average price of corn is from 60 to 75 cents per bushel, while it is only from 12 to 20 cents in many of the western and south-western states, as shown in Section 33.

Though it is advantageous to a nation to sell their products at as high prices as practicable, yet they cannot sell, unless they sell them as low or lower than their neighbors; and it is impossible to export them to any extent, unless the prices of their products at home are considerably less than they will sell for abroad. The tendency of goods and of products of all kinds is towards the best markets, where prices are highest; the exportation of products must always be from districts and countries where they are comparatively cheap, to other countries or districts where they are enough higher to pay the cost of transportation, and reasonable profits. No country can export products to another, unless the former can produce them cheaper than the latter, and as cheap as they can be procured from any other nation. The laws of trade when undisturbed by restrictions and tariffs, are in accordance with, and governed by the physical laws of nature; and the tendency of products to seek the highest prices, is as regular, certain, constant, and strong, as the tendency of water is, to run down hill, and to seek the lowest level. High prices, therefore, tend to stimulate industry, if they are raised and kept up by a foreign demand, which stimulates exportation and domestic industry; but the moment prices are raised by the home demand, paper money, and high wages, or other causes, above the prices of other countries, they preclude exportation and invite importation, and thereby tend to supplant, discourage, depress, and diminish domestic industry.

Great Britain, by means of her inexhaustible beds of coal for fuel, her productive mines of iron and other metals, her extensive internal improvements and water power, her insular situation, fine harbors, bays, and rivers, her bracing and healthy climate, her immense amount of machinery, great numbers of skilful artisans and workmen, great power and capital, and extensive commerce, is capable of producing almost every thing manufactured, cheaper than any other nation. These advantages give the English a sort of monopoly that may properly be termed the UNDERSELLING MONOPOLY; *which enables them to reduce prices just low enough to undersell, and eventually to supplant their rivals, and, at the same time, to keep them up to the highest point consistent with the full enjoyment of the markets of other nations.*

SEC. 35. *Prices of Wheat in France from* 1829 *to* 1850.

Summary statement of the average prices of wheat in France during the undermentioned years and periods according to the report of the Minister on Agriculture—stated in English sterling money, per quarter of eight bushels—also the price per bushel.

Years.	s.	d.	Prices per bush.
1829	52	5	$1 57
1830	51	11	1 55
1831 to 1840, average	39	0	1 17
1839, highest	51	4	1 54
1834, lowest	35	4	1 06
1841 to 1849, average	47	3	1 42
1847, highest	67	4	2 02
1849, lowest	36	6	1 10
1848	38	7	1 16
First 6 months of 1850	33	0	99

Prices were raised by the high prices in Great Britain during the year 1847, and the demand to export to that country; with the exception of that year, the average prices in France were but a trifle higher from 1841 to 1850 than they were from 1829 to 1840.

The Government of France published an account of the crop of agricultural produce of that kingdom, for the year 1841, with an estimate of the gross value of each article, from which I have deduced the average price or value per bushel, in our currency, as follows: Wheat $1,05, rye 66 cents, barley 55 cents, oats 40 cents, Indian corn 62 cents, buck-wheat 48 cents, mixed and other grains 80 cents, and potatoes 14 cents per bushel. These prices are below the average prices of grain in our manufacturing States on the seaboard; and show that we cannot export either grain or flour to France, when their products are so abundant as to keep prices so low; which is the case during about four years in every five. The reader should bear in mind, also, that these are official accounts, collected by the government, and not mere individual estimates, founded on speculation and conjecture, without data.

SEC. 36. *Prices of Freights and cost of Transportation.*

The freight on flour per barrel from New York to Liverpool, in November 1841, and April 1842, was only 1s. 6d. sterling, or 36 cents; in January 1844, January 1845, and January 1846, it was 3 shillings, or 72 cents; in August 1845, and August 1846, only 2s., and in January 1847, it rose to 5s. or $1.20. Freights were the lowest they have ever been in the years 1841 and 1842, but were generally higher in 1840 and previous, than they were in 1845 and 1846, until the great rise in the fall of 1846. The freight from New York to Liverpool, from 1840 to 1847, on cotton, varied from ¼d. to ⅞d. sterling, per lb.; on goods, per ton, from 20s., or $5, to 85s., or $20.40; on grain per bushel in August, 1846, but 8d., and in January 1847, 18d. to 19d., and some vessels to Ireland obtained 20 to 21d. On beef per bbl. in August 1845, 2s, and in January, 1847, as high as 6 shillings.

Freights from New York to Havre, (France,) were the lowest in 1841–2, and highest in 1847—on ashes per ton, varying from $6 to $12, generally from $8 to 10; on measurement goods, from $8 to $12, generally $10. The freights on flour per barrel, from Detroit, Sandusky, and other ports near the west end of lake Erie, to Buffalo, varied during the seven years, (1841 to 1847,) from 10 to 50 cents. per barrel, the ordinary price being from 15 to 20 cents; but such was the anxiety to get flour to market before the close of navigation in the fall of 1846, that some parcels were sent down in November at 53 to 55 cents per barrel, and the rise of canal freights was almost equally great.

The reader will see how the prices of freights, like the prices of products, are affected and governed by the principles of supply and demand; that the freight market is quite as sensitive as the market for perishable products; and that an increased amount of freight and demand for vessels, causes a rapid increase in the rate of freights.

Statement of the proceeds and expenses of sending 13,489 barrels of flour from St. Joseph County, (Michigan,) down the St. Joseph river to Lake Michigan in boats, shipping it from there to Buffalo, during the season of navigation of 1846, and from there to Boston, part of it being transported from Buffalo to Albany and thence to Boston by railroad, and part of it all the way to Boston by canals and vessels.

Gross proceeds of the 13,489 bbls.	$69,657.21
Equal per barrel to	5.16
Freights, charges, commissions for selling, insurance and other expenses per barrel,	2.30
Net proceeds per barrel,	$2.86

realised in the summer and fall of 1846, and winter of 1847, for a crop of wheat raised in 1845.

The tariff of freight established by the Michigan Central Railroad Company in August 1848, on flour, wheat, and merchandize, was as follows, between

Detroit and	Dexter 49 miles.	Kalamazoo 146 miles.
On 10 bbls of flour (nearly a ton,)	$2.30	$ 6.00
On 1 ton of wheat, (2,240 lbs.)	2.24	6.04
On 1 ton of merchandize,	5.37	11.64

Though these prices seem high, yet they were much higher, during the previous years. The ordinary freights on 10 barrels of flour on the Erie Canal from Buffalo to Albany (363 miles,) have been from June to October from $5 to $6.25; and in April, May, and November, from $6 to $11. The cost and charges for transporting dry goods, and most kinds of merchandize on canals and railroads, as well as on our lakes, are usually about twice as much per ton, as for transporting flour and other heavy agricultural products and iron, varying between New York and Cleveland or Detroit, from $12 to $30 per ton on merchandize, and from $8 to $15 per ton on flour, pork, potash, &c.

The average freights across the Atlantic during the last ten years, may be estimated as follows:

On dry goods, &c., between New York and Liverpool,			$10
On flour, iron, &c.,	"	"	6
On dry goods, &c.,	"	Havre,	11
On ashes & other heavy g'ds,	"	"	7

McCulloch states the prices of waggoning goods in England, at from 6d. to 12d. sterling per ton per mile, averaging 9d., or 18 cents, and about half as much on the Liverpool and Manchester Railroad, or $2.79 per ton for 32 miles. The average price for transporting by teams in this country a bushel of wheat or corn, or 50 pounds of merchandize, 50 miles, has been about 20 cents, and 40 cents for 100 miles, equal to about 15 cents per ton per mile for grain, or $15 per 100 miles, and 18 cents per mile, or $18 per 100 miles, for the transporting of a ton of merchandize.

Canals and railroads have reduced the cost of transporting heavy goods, and coarse agricultural products, on an average nearly three fourths, and merchandize about one half. Steam navigation has cheapened transportation on rivers above tide water about as much. The Erie Canal, (of New York,) has reduced prices much more than this estimate. And yet the cost of transportation on Railroads is generally nearly as much for 150 miles, as it is across the Atlantic, between New York and Liverpool, or Havre; that is, it is nearly twenty times as much in proportion to the distance on Railroads, as on the ocean.

The cost of transporting produce on the Mississippi and its tributaries is stated in Hunt's Magazine, for June 1847, by a very intelligent writer, as follows: Indian corn to New Orleans, from the vicinity of St. Louis, in arks and steamboats in a good stage of water, 12½ cents per bushel; corn from the Wabash, Illinois, and other small rivers of the Western States which float only boats and arks of light draft, nearly twice as much, or from 20 to 25 cents per bushel; and it sells in New Orleans at from 30 to 50 cents per bushel, averaging not far from 35 or 40 cents. He says, "The New Orleans corn is put into sacks, which cost from five to six cents per bushel; the warehouse charges, commissions, &c., are very heavy; it shrinks about 4 per cent. in shipping to an Eastern port, and the risk of its injuring is equal to about 10 per cent. more." He says Boston imported during the year 1841, 2,045,000 bushels of Indian corn; 36,700 of which were from New Orleans, and the balance from the Chesapeake and Delaware; and that "large quantities of corn were sold in Boston, during the summer of 1846, from the valley of the Mississippi, which did not pay freight and expenses; and the shipper fell in debt to the consignee."

These examples show the importance of canals, railroads, navigable waters, and steam vessels, in facilitating transportation, cheapening freights, and raising the price of wheat and flour in the Western country; but they have comparatively little effect upon the price of corn, rye, and other coarse grains, the value of which is so small that they will bear transportation but a short distance, before the cost is equal to the value of the whole product transported. A very trifling amount of Indian corn, rye, and other coarse grains ever reaches Albany and New Orleans; and of the small amount arriving at Albany, not one tenth part is from the Western States.

Though canals, railroads, and steamboats, have improved very greatly the markets of the Western States, yet the increase of mining and manufacturing industry, would create a demand at home for their products, and particularly for such things as will not bear transportation very far, and would improve their markets much more.

Sec. 37. *Average prices of Wheat, Indian Corn, Oats, and Potatoes, in each of the United States, from* 1840 *to* 1846 *inclusive.*

When the reader takes into consideration the great cost of transporting produce, and the incidental expenses of storage, forwarding, insurance, wharfage and commissions on selling, risk of spoiling, &c., he need not wonder at the great difference in the prices of produce in different parts of the United States, as shown in Section 33. It was estimated by a distinguished British writer, that a deficiency in the wheat crop of Great Britain of one-tenth, would raise the price of the whole crop three tenths, and a surplus of one tenth would depress the price of the whole crop three tenths, and so on in like proportion; so that a deficient crop would actually sell for considerably more money than an abundant one, yielding a large surplus. This is most clearly illustrated in Chapter VIII. in the case of cotton exported from the United States; 663,630,000 pounds of the crop of 1843 was sold in 1844 for nearly $5,000,000 more than 792,300,000 pounds brought the previous year; and over two million dollars more than 863,500,000 pounds brought the year following.

In estimating the causes of the great disparity in the prices of products in different countries, we must look first to the fact whether the country produces a surplus, or produces less than the inhabitants need; if the former, to what market it can be sent, at what expense, and at what prices it can be sold; and if the latter, from whence it can derive supplies, and at what cost of transportation. For instance, Vermont, though an agricultural State, produces for each of its inhabitants, according to the returns with the census of 1840, less than two bushels of wheat, less than one of rye, and less than three of corn, and must, therefore, import flour or grain; while Ohio produced for its inhabitants that year over ten bushels of wheat, over half a bushel of rye, and about twenty-two bushels of Indian corn, and had therefore a large surplus to export. Ohio sent her products mostly to the New York market, via the Erie Canal and Albany; and the producer got the New York prices, say $5 per barrel for flour, less about $2 25 for the cost and expenses and profits of sending it to market and selling it; while the people of Vermont were obliged to send to Albany for a portion of their flour, pay about $5 per barrel for it, beside about 75 cents for the cost and expenses of getting it, and the profits of the produce merchant; and this raised the price of all the flour made in the State to the same standard; so that the Vermont farmer got more than twice as much for his wheat, and three times as much for his corn, as the Ohio farmer. All these facts are taken into consideration in estimating the average prices of products in the several States. They serve to show the effect on the prices of produce, and the advantages to the farmer, of a mining, manufacturing, or commercial population in his vicinity, to create an increased demand for his products.

The average prices of grain in the several townships of Massachusetts, according to the returns of the town assessors in April, 1845, for the crop of 1844, were as follows: wheat $1.14, per bushel, barley 60 cents, rye 74 cents, corn 68 cents, buckwheat 47 cents, oats 32 cents, potatoes 27½ cents, and other vegetables 32 cents. In forming the following table of prices, I have examined carefully the estimates of Prof. Tucker, compared them with the information I have collected from prices current and other sources, and with the quantities raised in each state, and in a majority of cases, have adopted his estimates as correct, but in many cases differ widely from him.

An estimate of the average market prices of wheat, Indian corn, oats, and potatoes per bushel, from 1840 to 1846 inclusive, in each of the United States, at the nearest market towns to the places of production, to which the same may be taken without any expense to the producer, except his own labor and the use of his teams

	Wheat.	Corn.	Oats.	Potatoes.
Maine,	$1.12½	$0.66⅔	$0.33⅓	$0.20
New Hampshire,	1.12½	62½	33⅓	20
Vermont,	1.12½	62½	30	20
Massachusetts,	1.12½	66⅔	33⅓	25
Rhode Island,	1.12½	62½	33⅓	25
Connecticut,	1.12½	62½	33⅓	25
New York, South. District,	1.12½	62½	33⅓	25
New York, Northern "	87½	45	30	20
New Jersey,	1.12½	62½	33⅓	25
Pennsylvania, East. District,	1.12½	62½	33⅓	25
Pennsylvania, Western "	87½	40	25	20
Ohio,	60	20	15	15
Indiana,	50	15	15	15
Illinois,	50	15	15	15
Michigan,	60	25	20	15
Wisconsin,	50	20	15	15
Iowa,	50	15	15	15
Delaware,	1.00	60	33⅓	25
Maryland,	1.00	50	33⅓	25
Virginia, Eastern District,	1.00	50	33⅓	25
Virginia, Western "	50	20	15	20
North Carolina,	1.00	40	30	20
Tennessee,	50	15	15	20
Kentucky,	50	15	15	20
Missouri,	50	15	15	20
South Carolina,	1.00	40	30	20
Georgia,	1.00	33⅓	30	25
Alabama,	1.00	30	30	25
Mississippi,	1.12½	30	30	25
Louisiana,	1.12½	40	33⅓	40
Arkansas,	1.00	25	30	25
Florida,	1.12½	30	30	30

CHAPTER XIII

On Commerce.

Sec. 1. *The nature, object, and legitimate sphere of foreign and domestic Commerce.*

If the pursuits and products of all mankind were the same, there would be no occasion for commerce. Commerce depends upon a diversity of products; first, upon the difference in the character of natural products, arising in a great measure from the difference in the climate, soil, and physical condition of a country; and secondly, upon the mechanical labor bestowed upon natural products to fit them for different uses and purposes—and this depends mostly on the division of employments, and the progress made in the mechanic arts, and the natural sciences.

The earth is so constituted, that there are different soils, and different climates, which are capable of producing different kinds of vegetables, fruits, grains, timber, and animals, and contain beneath their surface, metals and minerals of various kinds. If the world had been so constituted as to give each country the same length of day and night, the same degree of heat and cold, the same kind of soil, the same degree of moisture, and the same minerals; and all countries were fitted for the same vegetable and animal productions, there would have been no occasion for international or foreign commerce. In such case, each country would possess in itself, every kind of raw commodity and material that the world could produce. No country could receive any natural product which it did not previously enjoy—nor could it give in exchange any such product, not already in the possession of every other nation. The only commerce which could be necessary or useful under such circumstances, would be internal or domestic commerce between citizens of the same nation, pursuing different employments.*

If the people of all nations were equally advanced in the natural sciences, in mining, the mechanic arts, and skill in manufacturing,

* See Section 6 of Chapter III, and Sections 6–12–13–14 of Chapter VI, which treat on Commerce.

there would be no occasion or utility in international commerce, except in natural products, or what are called raw materials for use, or to be manufactured. So far as international commerce consists of the mutual interchange between nations, of natural products, or raw materials, it depends on the nature and constitution of things, is in accordance with the laws of nature, and is necessary to the highest degree of civilization, comfort, and enjoyment, of the people; but so far as it seeks to import into any country manufactured fabrics of any kind, which might be produced at home, in case the people would learn to do so, it is entirely artificial, not required by the constitution of things or the laws of nature; and when tolerated except under heavy duties, the necessary effect is to undermine and lessen the domestic industry of every new country, and of every nation not as far advanced in mechanical and manufacturing industry, as its neighbors. The natural, legitimate and useful sphere of international commerce, is therefore much narrower than that of internal or domestic commerce; for while the former is confined to natural products or raw materials—the latter extends to and includes both natural and manufactured products of all kinds fit for the use, or of being fitted for the use of man.

Sec. 2. *The result of all proper commercial transactions, is to effect an exchange of commodities.*

Commerce in its primitive character consists in an exchange of commodities. In an advanced state of society, domestic commerce very generally consists in an exchange or sale of commodities, for money—which is at the same time a measure to determine their value, and a means of payment—the money being used by the seller, as a means of paying for other commodities which he may wish to purchase. The final result of all commerce, which is in accordance with the constitution of things and the laws of nature, and equally advantageous to both parties, is but an exchange of commodities, the production of which cost an equal amount of labor, skill, and capital. When one party continues to pay out more money or value in commodities than he receives, he becomes exhausted and impoverished, and often ruined—and if he lives beyond his means and buys on credit for consumption, he soon exhausts his credit, and ruin is the necessary consequence.* It may therefore be laid down as a general rule, (which is subject to very few exceptions) that all purchases for consumption, beyond the income of the purchaser, and all purchases for consumption made on credit and beyond the means of immediate payment, are disadvantageous to the purchaser; and if so, they are not within the proper and natural sphere of commerce.

* See Section 12, of this chapter.

What is true of individuals, is true when applied to communities and nations. International commerce should be an exchange of products of equal commercial value, the production of which cost in the aggregate, an equal amount of labor and skill. It should not be accompanied by the payment on either side of any money, or the accumulation of debt to be paid in future, and in the mean time to depress and weigh down the debtor community, like the chains of despotism. It should exhibit an exact equilibrium in its operations and in its effects, and produce no balance to be paid either in money, obligations, or stocks; or accumulated in the shape of a mercantile debt.

Some portion of this rule does not apply in all its force to countries like Mexico, and many of the South American States, which produce large quantities of the precious metals more than they need, and as a commodity for exportation.

SEC. 3. *On what is termed balance of trade—and the principal causes which produce it*

When commerce between nations is equally poised and confined to its natural sphere (as shown in the last section), it consists of a mere exchange of commodities of equal commercial value, costing an equal amount of labor and skill, leaving no balance to be paid in specie by either party, and no debt to be settled in future. When commerce, either between nations, states, provinces, or communities, is not thus balanced—when one party purchases from another, a greater aggregate value of products than it exports in payment, it must either pay the balance in specie, or accumulate in some form a debt, to be paid with interest, in future. This balance, whether paid down in specie or accumulated in the form of a debt, is termed the balance of trade.

The invention and application of machinery to many branches of mechanism, and to almost every department of manufacturing industry, as well as to mining, smelting, and working in metals, have increased the power and productiveness of the industry of man, from two to thirty fold. It must therefore be evident to every reflecting mind, that the industry of nations and communities must be effective in proportion to the amount of machinery they employ; hence manufacturing nations which employ a large amount of machinery, have the advantage in many particulars over agricultural nations, living in high latitudes.

First, because the latter must do their labor mostly by hand, and animal power, with few and very simple tools.

Secondly, the products of the latter are mostly of a perishable character, and must be disposed of soon after they are raised, whether they are wanted or not, and let prices be as low as they may—while the products of the former can be kept for years, and until there is a demand for them.

Thirdly, the products of the latter are mostly so bulky in proportion to their value, that they must be consumed in the vicinity where they are produced, and will not bear transportation to distant markets ; while the greater part of the products of the former will bear transportation to any part of the world, where there may be a demand for them—and,

Lastly, the laborers employed in mechanical, manufacturing, and mineral industry, necessarily consume mostly the breadstuffs, provisions, etc., of the farmers in the vicinity, and thus create a market for them ; while the farmers of agricultural nations and communities have no market whatever for the greater part of their products, except what is furnished by the few mechanics, merchants, and professional men among them ; and the prices of their products are therefore very low.

The effect of these causes is, that the value of the productive industry of manufacturing nations is more than twice as much as that of agricultural nations, in proportion to the number of inhabitants—and while the average value produced by the former, amounts to from $60 to $100 annually, that of the latter amounts only from $20 to $50. If they were to exchange the products of an equal amount of labor, those of the former would amount in value to more than twice as much as those of the latter. And hence we find, that the balance of trade is generally greatly in favor of manufacturing nations and communities, and against those which are mostly devoted to agriculture; and that the latter are usually involved in debt to the former, constantly embarrassed and drained of their specie, to pay the balance of trade against them.

Sec. 4. *Domestic commerce depends on a division of employments.*

Commerce depends on production, and the wants of the people, and yet production depends on commerce, to dispose of its products, and furnish an inducement to industry. Commerce when unregulated, is governed by the physical laws of nature, together with the whims, passions and artificial appetites of the people. Domestic commerce arises from division of employments—and the amount of it depends on the variety of employments pursued in a country, the extent of its industry, and the facilities for internal transportation. It is the greatest in amount, when the greatest amount of machinery and skill is employed, and the division of employments is in accordance with the wants of the nation—so that there may be products of every variety sufficient to satisfy all the natural and rational wants of the people, and no surplus of articles not needed for exportation.

Every class of producers want more or less of the products of every other class; and so far as regards articles of fancy, taste, and all intellectual wants, the disposition as well as the capacity to enjoy, is generally limited only by the ability to pay for—that is, by the income of the individual—his income is limited not only by his power to produce, but by the demand for, and the value of the products of his industry. On the contrary, if the division of employments and industry of the people were more perfectly adapted to their wants, and all persons not needed to supply their natural wants, were employed in producing intellectual and immaterial values, and articles of taste and luxury suited to their condition—there might be employment for all, and the ability of each to purchase and enjoy the products of others, would be limited only by his power to produce.

As all the people of a country of every class and pursuit, consume more or less of the products of almost every other class, and thus create a demand, and furnish a market for their products—all are dependent on each other, and have in some measure a community of interest—whatever increases the aggregate industry of the whole, tends also to promote the individual interest of each member of the community. The advocates of free trade admit this principle, and say it extends to, and includes the whole civilised world, as one community, bound together by the ties of commerce. This is untrue, in the extended sense in which they apply the principle. It is true, there may be some commerce between the people of each and every nation of the earth, and those of every other nation—but there is no necessity and no occasion for much commerce, between distant communities enjoying snbstantially the same climate, and possessing similar natural resources—their commerce must, from the nature of things, be very limited. The greatest part of the products of the northern farmer, will bear transportation to market but a comparatively short distance. Hence his market for the sale of the most of his products, is confined to the mechanics, manufacturers, merchants, miners and other classes, not employed in agriculture, within a few hundred miles of him; and for many things, his market is confined to those residing within a few miles. Though he may send his flour, pork and beef to Great Britain for a market perhaps one year in five, he can very seldom send to advantage, to so distant a market, coarse grains, vegetables, fresh butter, meats and fruits, hay and many other products of his farm. On the other hand, the British miners and manufacturers, and all their laborers, and their families, consume almost exclusively, the agricultural products of the British farmers in their vicinity, and those agricultural products of the British Isles, may be said to be converted into the iron, hardware, cotton, woollen, linen and silk goods, made by the consumers of them, and to comprise a part of the value of such manufactured products. Hence there is an intimate community of interests, and a strong bond of union, between the British farmers and the British miners and manufacturers; and a like community of interest between the farmers of every part of the United States, and the mechanics, manufacturers and miners of our own country, who consume their products. But there is scarcely any community of interest, between the British manufacturers and miners, and any portion of the agricultural population of the United States, except the cotton planters.

Every man is more or less dependent on his fellow citizens for protection of person and property; for a market for the products of his industry; for aid in distress, and in case of helpless old age; for social enjoyments; and even for his education, the development of his intellect, and the formation of his opinions. This dependence, and the community of interest existing between all the citizens of a country, arise from the constitution of things, from the constitution and condition of man; and from the moral laws of nature. It is the duty of man to act in obedience to the moral laws of nature, which were established by the Deity and adapted to his welfare. Those laws impose on him a moral obligation to reciprocate the aid he derives from his fellow citizens, arising from the operation of those laws, and from his condition as a citizen, and as a producer, laborer, man of business, or capitalist. Charity begins at home. We may therefore regard it, as not only the interest, but also the moral duty, of every man to aid his fellow citizens, and to consume the products of their industry, in preference to the products of foreigners.

This reasoning, and this view of the subject, is entitled to the careful examination and deliberate consideration of the reader and of the public. If it is correct, whoever consumes British iron or wears British or French cloths, not only contributes to furnish a market for, aid and patronage to, the foreign manufacturer, but to the British and French farmers also; to the injury of the farmers and manufacturers of his own country—of his own fellow citizens and neighbors. The farmers of our country who consume foreign, in preference to domestic products, are guilty of a suicidal policy; which is injurious to themselves, and unjust to their fellow citizens.

SEC. 5. *The natural tendency of commerce is to conform to the physical laws of nature.*

The natural tendency of foreign as well as domestic commerce, is to conform to the physical laws of nature; but as these laws are numerous, and depend on various causes, their operations depend on the relative condition and circumstances of the different nations between which it is carried on. The character and amount of both the exports and imports of every country, are influenced, and in some measure controlled, by the relative natural resources, industry, condition, and wants of itself, and of those nations with which it has commercial intercourse. Foreign commerce is, however, very much influenced by duties, bounties, drawbacks, and legal regulations; which should be established in accordance with the moral laws of nature, with a view of promoting the industry, and general welfare of the people.

The wants of the people are constant and regular—and domestic industry, and internal commerce, and the prices of products are generally very uniform and regular, when not disturbed by foreign influences. But foreign commerce, when unrestricted or badly regulated, is so extremely variable as to baffle all foresight and rational calculation. It makes prices excessively changeable, and business (to a very great extent) a mere game of chance, and often spreads terror and ruin among the merchants, as well as among the manufacturers and laborers of our country.

SEC. 6. *On protective duties, and their effects.*

When foreign commerce was free, and governed only by the natural tendency of things (as it formerly was), the greatest part of the commerce of the world was monopolized by one or two nations or states, by means of their superiority in productive industry, navigation, and maritime power. Thus Tyre, the cities of Greece, Carthage, Venice, Genoa, Holland, and the Hanse-Towns, successively engrossed the greatest part of the commerce of the world, until the policy of protection to domestic industry was introduced by Great Britain, about the middle of the seventeenth century. This policy was soon adopted by other nations, and has wrought a complete change in the industry, as well as the commerce of the world. The war of tariffs and navigation laws gave the first powerful stimulus to industry in Europe. By securing the home markets to the domestic producer, it encouraged new branches of industry, varied employments, increased the markets, the productive industry, and the consumption and comforts—secured the industrial independence, and promoted the social well-being of the people of nearly all the nations of Europe.

During more than a century, the practice has been very general among the nations of Europe of imposing duties on articles imported from other countries which come in competition with domestic products, for the double purpose, of raising revenue, and securing the domestic market for the benefit of the domestic laborer and producer. Whenever heavier duties have been imposed on one class of imports than on another for the latter purpose, they have been denominated protecting or discriminating duties. Since Great Britain has acquired an ascendency over all the nations of the earth in mining and manufacturing industry, by reason of her superior natural resources, a greater amount of machinery, cheap labor, and a greater number of skilful laborers and artisans—she can produce cheaper than any other nation—the cheapness of her products secures her own markets from the intrusion of foreigners—and enables her to supply other nations at prices nominally lower than their own manufacturers can. The manufacturers of Great Britain have found, that so far as free trade can be established, they can monopolize the markets of all such nations as establish it; and hence, nearly all the politicians and public writers of Great Britain have been endeavoring to spread the doctrines of free trade for half a century past, and the practice of the government on that subject, has recently undergone an entire change

The immediate effect of imposing duties on articles which come in competition either with those of the same kind, or with those so similar in their purpose, that one may be substituted for the other, is to raise their cost to the consumer and lessen their consumption. The consumption of foreign products and the demand for them being lessened, if the production continues the same, the price will necessarily fall. Hence the duty at first operates as a tax, partly on the consumer, and partly on the producer; but as in the succession of events, every effect produced gives effect to a cause, in such a manner as to seem to operate as a cause in and of itself, so the duty seems to produce a succession of effects in regular order. The first effect is, to lessen the importation of the articles charged with duty; that of itself will increase the market and the demand for domestic products to supply their place and raise their price a little, so as to make them equal to the imported article, with the duty paid; the increased price and demand for domestic products, stimulate and increase production in countries and among a people adapted to it; and this increased production and supply react upon the market, and reduce the prices of both the domestic and the imported article; so that, in the end, the price of the domestic article is often reduced below the price of the imported one before the duty was imposed. The foreign producer must either abandon the market, or submit at each step in the process to such a reduction of prices, as to sell, after the duties are paid, as low as the domestic producer; and thus the whole amount of the duties is eventually thrown as a tax on the foreign producer and the importer.*

The ultimate effect of all duties imposed on articles imported, which come in competition with domestic products, is to aid in securing the domestic markets for the benefit of the domestic laborer and producer; to encourage and build up new branches of industry, and to diversify employments. They tend to secure to the citizens and laborers of every country, a field of employment which properly belongs to them.† By multiplying employments, increasing the mechanical, manufacturing, and mining industry of the country—they create a demand for labor —increase the number of persons employed in such pursuits, create markets for agricultural products in the immediate vicinity of the farmer, raise the price of those products, and thus increase the industry, and the aggregate amount as well as value of every department of industry.

Sec. 7. *On Free Trade and its effects.*

Many of the politicians, statesmen, and writers of this country, and on the continent of Europe as well as in Great Britain, having adopted the doctrines of free trade—it becomes important to examine those doctrines, and the principles involved in them. Their advocates are divided into two classes, or sects. The most strict sect insist that no duties should be levied on either exports or imports—that no taxes should be levied on consumption or industry, or even on the industry of foreign nations—that every government should be supported by direct taxation of the property of its own citizens—that international as well as domestic commerce should be entirely unrestrained, custom-houses abolished —and the people of all nations allowed to trade with each other freely, as if they were a band of brothers, and citizens of the same community. They claim that every man has a natural and inherent right, to sell or exchange his own property, with whomsoever and for such other property as suits his pleasure; and to import, use, and sell the same, without tax or restriction.

Another class or sect, a little less radical and perhaps the most numerous of the two, are advocates of a modified system of free trade. They admit the right and expediency of taxing imports

* See on this subject of prices, Sections 26 to 30 of Chap. xii.

† See ante Sec. 10, of Chap. VI.

for the purpose of raising revenues to support the government—but insist, that duties should be imposed on imports with reference to revenue only—and that the true rule is, to levy duties in such a manner, as to encourage as large importations as are practicable, under a rate of duties so high, as to raise the greatest amount of revenue. Like the stricter sect, they insist that every man has an inherent right to buy where he pleases—that it is for his interest to buy where he can buy cheapest—that he is under no obligation to patronize his fellow citizens, and to consume their products, in preference to those of foreigners—that duties levied on imports, not only raise their price to the full amount of the duty, but raise in a corresponding manner, the price of all domestic products with which they come in competition—that while the duty thus operates as a tax on the consumer for the support of government, the enhanced price of the domestic products amounts to a tax on the consumer, without any equivalent, and for the sole benefit of the producer; whereby one class is unjustly taxed for the benefit of another. They therefore deny the propriety of discriminating between such imports as compete with the domestic industry of the country, and such as do not, for the purpose of lessening that class of imports, and promoting domestic industry. They insist, that it is the duty of the government to avoid raising the prices of domestic manufactures, and to encourage foreign competition, and the importation of foreign manufactures in their finished state, rather than raw materials to be manufactured, for the double purpose, of reducing the cost to the consumer of domestic goods, and increasing the aggregate value of the imports—and the amount of duties, when levied on the ad valorem principle. In order to effect these objects, higher duties were in many instances imposed by the tariff of 1846 on raw materials to be manufactured, and on products which do not come in competition with domestic industry, than on manufactured products, which do come in competition with domestic products.

This system of policy is directly opposed to the protective system, and instead of discriminating in favor of the industry of the country, it actually discriminates in favor of the industry of foreign nations—and against our own citizens.

If free trade in its strict sense were adopted by all the nations of the earth, the natural tendency and necessary effect would be this—in the universal competition among nations, that nation which, by means of greater natural advantages, cheaper labor, greater skill, industry and capital, can manufacture an article cheaper than any other nation, can undersell all others—command the markets of the world for that article, and supplant all their competitors. These are the necessary effects produced under such circumstances, by the *physical laws of nature*—and hence it is important, that every nation should regulate its foreign commerce in accordance with the *moral laws of nature*, so as to secure its own markets and a proper field of employment, for its own people, and avoid such evils.* No general rule of policy for regulating foreign commerce, can be adapted to the condition of all nations. Every country should adapt its commercial policy to its own peculiar circumstances, natural resources, condition and industry, in such a manner as to promote the industry and welfare of its citizens.

It has been shown that Great Britain has the natural resources and capacity to expand her manufactures of iron, hardware, cotton, and woollen goods, so as to supply the whole civilized world with manufactures of that kind. All that is wanted, is *free trade* to enable the British manufacturers to accomplish that object, so far as concerns manufacturing by machinery. Such manufactures in the United States as well as in nearly every country on the continent of Europe, would be ruined, the industry of the country depressed, laborers thrown out of employment, the prices of labor reduced, the people involved in debt, and kept in debt as much as the British manufacturers would dare to trust them, and the people impoverished, until they were compelled to resort to the old system of manufacturing in families, by spinning on the one thread wheel, and weaving with the hand loom.

The manufactures of iron in the United States have been almost entirely prostrated already, by the operations of the tariff act of 1846, and many of the cotton and woollen factories have stopped running. It is said, that more than half of the blast furnaces for making pig iron, and nearly half of the rolling mills for making bar iron in Pennsylvania are now (1851) doing nothing; and that a very large proportion of them have been sold by the sheriff under execution.

Such have been the effects already in the short space of about five years, under the tariff of 1846; which imposes a nominal duty of thirty per cent. on iron and manufactures of cotton, which are partially evaded by under valuations. The effects were about the same (from 1816 to 1824) under our tariff act of 1816, which imposed duties on those articles amounting to from 20 to 30 per cent. They were also about equally depressing to the industry and destructive to the interests of our country during the operation of the compromise act, from 1834 to 1842. Though the duties under those acts were imposed mostly for purposes of

* See Sections 2, 3, and 4 of Chapter I. and Section 10 of Chapter VI.

revenue only, yet they afforded very great incidental aid and protection to American industry. How much more our own industry would be supplanted and depressed under a system of strict free trade, the reader can well imagine. Our imports of foreign manufactures would be increased immensely for a few years. American industry would be supplanted, our country drained of specie, loaded down with debt, incumbered with thousands of British mortgages, the most of the bonds issued by our states, cities, and incorporated companies, together with the stocks of our banking institutions, railroad companies, and much of the most valuable real estate in the nation, would pass into the hands of British capitalists, and we should be reduced to a condition of dependence, very similar to that of Ireland, Canada, and other provinces of Great Britain. Labor, agricultural products, and real estate, would be reduced to less than half their present prices, and after nearly all our manufacturers had been ruined and driven out of the business, and the British and French had got the complete control of our markets; the prices of manufactures would be likely to be raised, and alternately raised and lowered as their interests might dictate, so as to destroy competition, command our markets, and keep us in a state of dependence. To be an agent for British capitalists, or an attorney for British creditors, would then be (in this country) as it has long been in Canada and other British provinces, the most profitable business that could be pursued.

This is no fancy picture. We have evidence enough of its truth, in the effect of a partial system of free trade at different periods; and we have before us the example of Ireland and the British provinces, which have long enjoyed the advantages (if any) of free trade with Great Britain. We have also our own colonial experience on the same subject.

SEC. 8. *The exports of a country depend on the character, variety, amount, and prices of the products of its industry.*

The extent and value of the exports of a people, depend on the amount and character of their productive industry; on the adaptation of their products to the wants of the people of other nations; and the facilities for exporting them. The greatest proportion of agricultural products of countries lying in cold and temperate climates, are so bulky and cheap, that they will not bear transportation to distant markets; and hence agricultural countries of high latitudes, have but a small amount of exports.

The quantity and value of the exports of all great commercial nations depend, first, on the extent, variety, and skill of their mechanical, manufacturing, and mining industry, and the adaptation of their industry and their products to the wants and tastes of the people of other nations. Secondly, on the effective demand of foreign nations and colonies for their products. And, lastly, on their capacity to sell as cheap, or cheaper, than their rivals, and to compete successfully with them in foreign markets.

These causes and conditions depend on others, as antecedents; on the natural resources, climate, and condition of a country; on the advancement made by the people in the sciences and useful arts; on their skill, habits of industry, genius, and enterprise; on their imports, and the adaptation of their laws to develope their natural resources and promote their industry; and on the capital accumulated, and the machinery employed by them. Secondly, on the numbers, wants, tastes, customs, industry, resources, and condition of their customers in foreign countries and colonies; and lastly, on the geographical position of a country, in reference to other countries; upon its navigable rivers, harbors, bays, canals, and other facilities for internal and external communications; on the commercial genius and spirit of the people, and the adaptation of their laws and institutions to the purposes and pursuits of commerce.

SEC. 9. *On what the imports of a country depend.*

The imports of a country depend,

1st. On the wants, tastes, habits, customs, and spirit of the people.

2d. On the resources of the country, the industry and condition of the people, and their capacity to supply a greater or less number of their own wants.

3d. On the productive industry of other nations with which they have commerce, and the prices at which those nations respectively sell their products.

4th. The quantity imported of any particular article which comes in competition with domestic products, depends much on the amount of duties levied on it, and the encouragement thereby given to domestic industry, to produce a similar article to supply the market.

5th. The aggregate amount and commercial value of the imports of a country, may be lessened for a few years, by high duties levied on articles which come in competition with the products of its own people; but such aggregate value cannot be lessened during a period of ten years or more. The amount must finally depend on the value of its exports, and its ability to pay for a greater or less amount of imported articles. Exports, imports, and domestic production, are all, in some measure, mutually dependent on each other. Production, and the wants of other nations determine the amount of exports; and the commercial value of the exports of a country, taking long periods into consideration, determines the aggregate amount and commercial value of its imports. Though duties lessen the importation of some articles, yet their indirect effect is, to increase the importation of others, or of specie.

6. Duties on imports, which tend to lessen the importation of such articles as come in competition with domestic products; to secure the domestic market to our citizens; and to diversify as well as to increase the industry of the nation; tend also to prevent the accumulation of a foreign debt, to increase the wealth of the people, to increase the products of the country for exportation, to increase its exports, to increase its ability to pay for imports, and finally, to increase the aggregate amount and value of its imports. The duties effect some change in the character of its imports, and for a few years lessen their amount, but they finally (taking a long series of years into consideration,) increase their aggregate amount and value. These truths are illustrated by the commerce of Great Britain, France, and Belgium, in Sections 14, 15, and 16. The commerce and the productive industry of all those countries, have grown up under the protecting system.

SEC. 10. *Influence of paper money, and the credit system, on exports and imports, and on domestic commerce.*

Commerce both foreign and domestic, is very much influenced by paper money, and the credit system. The notes issued by banks, are loaned to individuals, who use them to buy property, pay laborers, debts, &c. They are put in circulation as money, and increase the circulating medium of the country, and so far as they exceed the coin deposited in the vaults of the banks to redeem with, they are based on credit. The banks depend on loaning their notes as a means of profit; and half the business men of this country depend more or less on bank loans, as a means of carrying on their business. Paper money, and the credit system, thus mutually depend upon, and act and react upon each other.

Paper money, by increasing the circulating medium of a country, and the facilities for obtaining loans, tends to increase the prices of goods, and all kinds of property—to increase the number of merchants, business men, and speculators of all classes—to increase competition in all mercantile and speculative operations—and to increase the anxiety of the dealers to sell, and to sell on credit, in order to make large sales, hoping and expecting to realize a large income. Large sales on credit increase the con sumption of goods, and tend to increase the demand for them, and to enhance prices still more.

An increase of the prices of goods and products, when they get above the prices in other countries, tends to encourage and increase the importation of the products of foreign countries—to diminish the exports of domestic products—to produce a balance of trade against the country—to involve it in debt—to raise foreign exchanges—to cause an exportation of the precious metals—and to drain the banks of their specie—until they are compelled to redeem their notes and lessen their circulation. The evils produced by an excessive issue of paper money, do eventually tend to check themselves, but they do not restore to the country the losses they have occasioned. Their mischievous effects upon a new country like ours, are very similar in their character, though much less in amount, than those of free trade; and hence many of the party politicians of our country, have attributed all its commercial embarrassments to an excess of paper money, while others have charged them all to free trade.

The tendency of an excessive amount of paper money, is to increase loans and credits of every kind, retail as well as wholesale—to increase credits for luxuries and goods to be consumed, as well as for goods to sell again, and for capital to do business with. Many are inclined to take advantage of the ease with which credits can be obtained, to buy luxuries which they would not otherwise have thought of, and to engage in more hazardous enterprises on other men's capital, than they would on their own—thinking that they have nothing to lose—that if they are unfortunate, the loss falls on their creditors, and not on themselves—and that, if they venture nothing, they cannot hope to make much gains. Credit being stimulated to the utmost, business is overdone; and goods are urged upon every class of persons who are supposed to be able to pay. In such a state of things, the laborer often consumes his earnings, before he does the work—and laborers, and mechanics, as well as farmers, merchants, and professional men, all anticipate their income by means of credits, consume it before it comes in, and eventually involve themselves in debt. Habits of living are contracted above their means, their expenditures continue to be quite equal to or greater than their incomes, and interest accumulates on their debts, until they become so large, as to embarrass them through their whole lives, and sometimes involve them in hopeless bankruptcy. The consumer becomes indebted to the retail trader—the retailer to the jobbing or wholesale merchant, the wholesaler to the importer, the importer to the foreign manufacturer; and the importers, wholesale and retail merchants, are all involved in debt to the banks, and the banks to the bill holders. There is a perfect net-work of credits, all more or less dependent on each other—and all more or less affected by an exportation of specie to pay the foreign debt and the balance of trade against the country—and often shocked and almost paralyzed for a time, by the panic caused by the exportation of specie, and sometimes by an anticipation only, or fear of such exportation.

SEC. 11. *Depressing effects of debts, upon individuals and communities. Different effects of foreign and domestic debts.*

Debt operates upon individuals and communities like a heavy burthen, which bears them down, and impedes their progress. Persons deeply involved in debt are more or less slaves to their creditors, the degree of servitude depending on the severity of the laws. Imprisonment for debt was abolished in Athens by Solon, to relieve the poor from the oppressions of the rich. The debts contracted by the plebeians to the Patricians of ancient Rome, eventually reduced thousands of them to slavery. Those who had been condemned for default of payment, had a delay of thirty days to liberate themselves by making payment; at the end of that time, the creditor could put them in irons and confine them for two months, and if the debt was not then paid he could expose them to sale as slaves. Even distinguished citizens were not exempt from this deplorable lot.* The peon slavery of Mexico originates in debt, is only a means of securing the creditor, and is very similar in its character, to the debtor slavery among the Romans. The condition of debtors among the Israelites was very similar, and the institution of the Jubilee was established as a remedy, as recorded in the 25th chapter of Leviticus.

The people of Ireland exhibit the most striking example on record, of the deplorable condition of a nation of debtors and tenants. Free trade with Great Britain, and the ignorance of the people, have prevented the growth of manufactures, and together with absentee Landlordism, so drained the country of its products to pay creditors, landlords and manufacturers in England, that the mass of the people are reduced to the most abject poverty, and the whole nation is impoverished. It has been impossible for the greatest portion of the tenants to pay their rents, much of the time, during the last thirty years; and much more difficult than formerly, since the depression of the prices of agricultural products, consequent upon the establishment of the principle of free trade in grain, in 1846. Many of the tenants in default, have been driven from their possessions; others have been

*See Statistique des peuples de l'antiquité, par Moreau de Jonnes, vol. 2, p 407, and authorities there cited.

selling out their leases for more than twenty years past, and emigrating to America. The Irish landlords having lost a large proportion of their rents, have become impoverished and involved in debt; their estates are generally mortgaged, and British creditors are rapidly buying up their estates, and also the leases of the tenants, and letting the lands to English and Scotch farmers; and the time is not far distant, when very little of the real estate of Ireland, will be either owned or occupied by the descendants of the Celtic population of the 16th century.

The influence of debt was severely felt in almost all the States of the Union from 1837 to 1843; and particularly in the new States. In many counties of from twenty to forty thousand inhabitants, there were from five hundred to fifteen hundred suits commenced annually in courts of record, for several years; besides great numbers of suits in Justices' courts, which in most of the western States, have jurisdiction for all debts not exceeding $100 in amount. The business of lawyers, sheriffs, marshals and clerks, was the most prosperous and profitable of any, and the energies of the country seemed to be paralyzed. Though the bankrupt act passed by Congress in 1841 was in force less than two years, yet the number of applicants for the benefit of it, was no less than 33,739, and the aggregate amount of debts and liabilities stated by them in their schedules, exceeded $440,000,000; the amount of property turned over by them, amounted to less than $44,000,000. It would be a moderate estimate to put down the number of individuals who compromised their debts during that eventful period, at 50,000, and the amount of their debts at two hundred and fifty millions of dollars.

The foreign debt of the country was then about two hundred millions of dollars, making a perfect chain of debt, from the consumer to the country and village merchant, from him to the wholesale merchants, who were involved in debts to the banks and the importers, and the importers to the banks and the foreign manufacturer. I have seen fifteen columns of a country newspaper in Ohio filled with notices of sheriffs' sales. The appraisement laws prevented an immense amount of real estate from being sacrificed in many of the new States. If buildings, timber and all personal chattels in the United States could be removed without expense, and made available, immense quantities of them would have been purchased by importers and British creditors. If such had been the case, and the soil of the lands could be removed in like manner, the credit of the country would have been sustained until the people (like the Celts of Ireland) had worn out and consumed, the value of the greatest part of the property in the nation, and the same had been transferred to

British creditors and capitalists. Nothing but the laws of God, established in the nature of things, prevented the utter ruin of the country. Foreign creditors do not buy farms, dwelling-houses, stores, mills, and other immoveable and bulky property in the United States, because such property would be nearly worthless to them; and rather than make such purchases, they prefer to suspend farther credits. But Ireland is so near, and under the same government, that the lands are desirable, and British creditors and capitalists are rapidly buying them up, and will soon own nearly the whole island; and the poor Celt is obliged to emigrate in search of employment, and the means of living.

The large debts contracted by many of the States for Canals and Railroads have rendered it necessary to levy high taxes to pay the interest, which has made the burthens of taxation in some instances excessively onerous. Though the direct taxes levied on property by the several states, countries, cities, towns and villages—are much less in amount than the indirect taxes levied by the federal government on foreign products imported, yet the former are felt with ten times as much severity, and particularly in the new states, as the latter. The duties on imports are mostly levied on articles which come into competition with domestic industry, and are so levied that they not only encourage and promote domestic industry, but the domestic competition throws about three quarters, and in some instances, the whole duty as a tax on the foreign producer.*

Loans made and debts contracted, to procure materials and capital to promote industry or do business with, are often advantageous to the debtor; but when contracted for goods and products of any kind for consumption, they are generally the inceptive steps to his ruin. Debt operates upon individuals and communities like an incubus, which bears heavily upon them, and when they have little or nothing but the products of their industry to pay with, it holds them in a sort of semi-servitude. When a manufacturer or mechanic buys materials to work up for sale, or a merchant buys goods to sell again at a profit, the credit he procures adds to his capital, and enables him to increase his industry or his business. Wholesale credits and credits of that character, when discreetly contracted, are advantageous; but retail credits made to the consumer, are generally destructive to the best interests of the country, and should be discouraged. The bankrupt laws of England make a broad distinction between merchants and traders, to whom wholesale credits are necessary, and the mass of the people, who are only consumers and buy at

* See on this point Sec. 6 of this Chapter.

retail; and in order to encourage wholesale credits, and those only, they give more summary and efficient remedies against the former, than they do against the latter. This important distinction has been overlooked in this country, and the consequences have been very injurious. If goods were sold at retail for ready pay only, wholesale credits would be much less hazardous. This is a matter which can be remedied by state legislation.

A domestic debt is much less burthensome to a community than a foreign debt. The interest on the former being expended in the vicinity of the debtor, serves to create a market for him, and to encourage his industry; while the interest which is paid to foreign creditors is sent abroad, and serves to drain the country of its money, and what is most desirable abroad, without any corresponding advantages to the debtor. It operates on the debtor, and on the country, as absentee landlordism operates on Ireland. A railroad or any public improvement, or investment, is much more advantageous to the country or state where it is made, when made with the capital of its own citizens, than it can be, when made with capital from abroad. In the former case the profits or dividends will be expended or invested at home, to encourage the industry of the country; in the latter they must be sent abroad.

Our imports have exceeded our exports during the last four years (1848 to 1851) under the free trade tariff of 1846. Our foreign mercantile debt has increased rapidly, and a prodigious amount of the stocks and bonds of the United States, of the several states, and of our own commercial cities and incorporated companies, have been sent abroad and the proceeds used for the payment of foreign goods; a substitute for which we might, and ought to have produced at home. All these facts and tendencies should be taken into consideration, in order to regulate properly, our foreign commerce.

Sec. 12. *How, and for what purposes and ends, commerce should be regulated.*

The heat of tropical countries, and of those bordering on the torrid zone, enervates the human system, conduces to lassitude and indolence, and renders human life so short that the population seldom increases much, except by means of foreign immigration. Hence the increase of the free population in tropical countries has been slow, during the last two centuries, compared with what it has been in the cold and temperate countries of Europe, and of the northern parts of North America. Notwithstanding the activity of the slave trade, the products of tropical countries have increased very little faster than the demand for them, so that the decline in prices has been comparatively slow. Coffee, sugar, spices, and most other products of hot and warm countries as well as cotton, are not perishable, can be kept until there is a demand for them, and are so valuable that they will bear transportation to any part of the world, and will generally command a market at fair prices. It is not generally for the interest of the people of such countries, to attempt to manufacture much for themselves, their time can be more profitably employed in agriculture; and they can supply themselves with manufactured goods to better advantage, by attending to agriculture and exchanging their products with manufacturing nations. This is not the case with agricultural nations in cold and temperate climates. Their products are mostly perishable, heavy, and bulky, in proportion to their value; they have but little to export which is wanted and which will bear exportation, their wants are numerous and their means of payment small. Tropical products they must import or go without, and it is impossible for them to pay for such articles, and to pay also for many foreign manufactures, and hence they must from necessity manufacture for themselves, or remain destitute of many of the necessaries, and ordinary comforts of life.

One of the primary objects of regulating commerce, is to tax, or impose du ies on the subject matter of it, for the purposes of revenue; another object is, to give such direction to it, and to the industry of the people, as to increase the value of their industry, and promote their general welfare. Taxing imports which come in competition with domestic industry, or induce luxury or immorality, serve the double purpose of raising revenue and promoting the welfare of the people, by increasing their industry, checking luxury, or immorality. As taxes on imports may, in most cases, be so levied as to promote two objects at the same time, this mode of taxation and raising revenue is the least burthensome, and the most advantageous to the people, of any which has ever been devised.

The commerce of every country should be so regulated as to aid in securing and supplying markets for its citizens, and a demand for their labor and products, or in other words, to aid in furnishing a field of employment for them, adapted to the climate, natural resources, and condition of the country.* No system of commercial regulations, or general rules for imposing duties on the subject matter of commerce and navigation, can be devised adapted to the condition of all nations. The policy of every nation, in regulating its foreign commerce, and encouraging par-

* See on this subject Sections 10, 11, 12, and 15 of Chapter VI.

ticular branches of industry, should be adapted to its natural resources, wants, climate, condition, and the competition its citizens must meet in its own markets, as well as in the markets of the commercial world.

The natural field of foreign commerce is between countries of different natural resources, climates, and natural products. The greater part of the commerce between Great Britain and the nations of Europe, is unnatural and disadvantageous to the latter. The principal part of the imports from Great Britain into our northern, middle, and western states, are of the same character, and destructive to the interests of our country. On the contrary, our commerce with the West India Islands, Mexico, and the South American States, has been advantageous to us as a nation. With the exception of Holland and Belgium, there is no country, either on the continent of Europe or in North America, in which there is not a sufficient number of persons constantly out of employment, to supply the country with manufactures, if they only possessed a sufficient amount of skill, experience, and intellectual capacity, to do so, the foreign commerce of the country had been properly regulated, and manufacturing industry properly encouraged.

No branch of mining or manufacturing industry not well established in this country, and very few under any circumstances, can compete successfully with the machinery, skill, cheap labor, low rate of interest, and large capital in Great Britain, without legislative protection. In fact, experience shows that these causes are so great in favor of British, and in some instances of French manufacturers, as to enable them to supply our markets for all the finer and more expensive qualities of goods, and to displace and supplant the product of American manufacture, which would otherwise supply the market. By this means the manufacturing and mining industry of our country is depressed and lessened in amount, and a larger portion of our capital and labor forced into agriculture. Ever since the general peace of 1815, our agricultural products, (except for the article of wheat and a few others in unfavorable seasons,) have been greatly beyond the wants of the country. They have been so super-abundant, and the foreign demand for them generally so small, that no increase of quantity could increase their aggregate value, or benefit the country in the least. In fact, for at least four years in five since 1815, an increase in quantity, has actually diminished their aggregate value.

When foreign imports lessen the products of any particular branch of domestic industry, by partially displacing them and supplying the market, it rarely happens that they increase the aggregate value of any other branch of industry. The wealth of the nation is therefore diminished to the full value of whatever is paid for those that might be produced at home, unless something is exchanged for them which we do not need, and could not otherwise sell.

Many nations are well adapted by nature for a particular branch of industry, but do not produce all the necessary raw materials. When such a nation imports the manufactured article, instead of importing the raw material and employing its citizens in manufacturing it, the loss to the nation is generally equal to the difference between the cost of the former, and that of the latter.

In as much as the use of intoxicating drinks as a beverage, tends to injure the consumer, and to promote immorality, indolence, vice, and crime, their value for such purposes, is wholly factitious (as heretofore shown.)* Whatever is given in exchange for them, for such uses, and for some other articles, is a total loss to the community.

The value of luxuries is also more or less factitious (as heretofore shown).† Whenever luxuries are imported into a country for consumption, the national wealth is diminished to the full extent of the difference between the value of the money or commodities given in exchange for them, and their utility to the consumer; and it may be diminished to the full extent of their cost, when the importation tends to supplant and diminish domestic industry.

Foreign commerce should be regulated by means of duties with a view to the following objects:

First, The promotion and increase of domestic industry.

Secondly, The collection of revenue, for the support of the government—and,

Lastly, to check luxury, the use of intoxicating drinks, and other things, which may contribute to vice, immorality, indolence, and extravagance; and to make those who will indulge in such things, pay a tax to the government, as a partial compensation for the injury they do the country.

For the purpose of promoting domestic industry, it is the true policy of a country like the United States: First, to encourage new branches of industry; to increase and diversify the employments of the people, as much as is consistent with their condition and the natural resources of the country; and to adapt the division of employments to the wants of the nation, that the people of each employment may create a market for those of every other employment.

* Vide ante, Sec. 4, of Chapter VI. † Vide Sec. 2 of Chapter VI.

Secondly, to cultivate commercial intercourse with the inhabitants of warmer climates, who may want their products, and can furnish such products as they need, and cannot produce for themselves.

Thirdly, to encourage the importation of articles to be used as capital, and raw materials to be manufactured, in preference to manufactured products for consumption—and

Lastly, to prevent a balance of trade against the country, the exportation of coin, and the accumulation of a foreign debt.

SEC. 13. *On the foreign Commerce of the United States, the balance of trade against the country, and the foreign debt, at different periods.*

Statement in millions of dollars, of the exports from the United States, of the value of cotton, leaf tobacco, and rice, respectively—of all other domestic products, and of the aggregate amount of all domestic products except coin, during the undermentioned fiscal years.

Years.	Cotton.	Tobacco.	Rice.	Other Products.	Total of domestic products.
1790	.04	4.35	1.75	13.52	19.66
1800	5.				31.84
1805	9.44	6.34	1.7	24.9	42.38
1810	15.1	5.	2.6	19.96	42.36
1820	22.3	7.96	1.7	19.72	51.68
1830	29.67	5.58	1.98	20.97	58.52
1840	63.87	9.88	1.94	35.97	111.66
1842	47.59	9.54	1.9	32.80	91.8
1845	51.74	7.47	2.16	37.18	98.45
1847	53.41	7.24	3.6	86.32	150.57
1849	66.39	5.8	2.57	56.94	131.7
1850	71.98	9.95	2.63	50.34	134.9

This table shows the very limited foreign demand for our agricultural products, and how slowly it increases. Our agricultural resources are developed to a very small extent, and yet we have not a foreign market (more than one year in five) for one-fourth part of the surplus of many of our products. During the wars of Napoleon, Europe furnished an extensive market for the bread stuffs and provisions of the United States; but since 1815, with the exception of the year 1847, a very trifling amount of such products have been exported from the United States to Europe—

the greater part of our exports of that character, having been made to the West Indies and South America. During the fiscal year ending June 30, 1850, the whole value of flour exported from the United States to the Old World and its islands amounted to only $1,923,931—while the amount exported to all the countries, provinces, and islands, of the New World, amounted to $5,174,639. The failure of the potato crops in 1846 and 1847 in Great Britain and Ireland, and the repeal of the corn laws, were the cause of the introduction of Indian corn and meal into those countries for the use of the poorer classes, and the demand for corn and corn meal in Ireland, bids fair to be permanent—but for flour, wheat, and other agricultural products of the free states, there is no prospect that the European market will be any better during the next ten or twenty years, than it has been during the last ten.* As to tobacco, the value exported is very little greater than it was thirty years since.

Statement in millions of dollars, of the value of the produce of the Southern slave States (those below the 35th degree of latitude) and the value of the produce of the free States and of the Northern slave States, exported annually on an average from the United States, during the undermentioned years,† and the amount to each person.

	Southern Slave States.		Free States & N. Slave States.	
1800 to 1807	$9 millions.	$16 to each.	$30 millions.	$6 to each.
1820 to 1824	23½ "	19 "	23½ "	2¾ "
1830 to 1833	33 "	17 "	30½ "	2¾ "
1835 to 1840	66 "	26 "	36 "	2⅜ "
1841 to 1842	53 "	19 "	45 "	3 "
1844 to 1846	51½ "	17 "	48½ "	3 "
1849 to 1850	71¾ "	18 "	61½ "	3¼ "

What a flattering prospect for the future, the foregoing tables present to the producers of flour, wheat, Indian corn, tobacco, lumber, pork, beef, butter, cheese, and other provisions, in case they depend upon foreign markets for the sale of their products, to enable them to pay for, and clothe themselves with, British and French goods. It should be borne in mind also, that more than half of the exports of the free States, are to the West Indies, Brazil and other parts of South America, to pay for sugar, coffee, spices, tropical fruits and hides. The West Indies and Brazil, furnish a constant and regular demand and steady markets for the products of the free and northern slave states, while the

* See on this subject, Sec. 34, of Chap. XII.

† All the cotton and rice are estimated as coming from the Southern Slave States, and all the other products, from the other States; which is very nearly correct.

markets of Europe are very uncertain, and not to be depended upon. The whole commerce of the United States with the West India Islands, and with the American continent and all its islands, is advantageous, the balance of trade being slightly in favor of our country, which is paid in coin, amounting on an average to four or five millions a year, the greater part of which is exported to the old world, to pay the balance of trade against us.

The products of the free and northern Slave States exported to the West Indies, and to the American Continent and its islands, amounted in 1844 to over twenty-three millions of dollars, and in 1850 to about twenty-eight millions of dollars; in payment for which we received some coin, and many articles of prime necessity, some of which cannot be produced in the United States, and others cannot be produced in sufficient quantities, for the consumption of the country.

The imports into the United States from the old world, which were retained for consumption (consisting mostly of manufactured products) cost in 1844, about seventy millions of dollars, and in 1850 about one hundred and thirty millions, about five sixths of which were consumed in the free and the northern slave states, while the domestic products of those states, taken by the old world in payment, amounted to only about twenty-eight millions of dollars in 1844, and thirty millions in 1850. It is easy to see that such a commerce is very disadvantageous to the northern states, as it makes them not only dependent upon, and tributary to the manufacturing nations of Europe, and involves them in debt, but it also makes them dependent upon, and tributary to the cotton planting states of the south, for cotton as an article of export, to pay their debts to foreign manufacturers.

A very large proportion of the commerce of the United States with the old world, is advantageous only to the cotton planting states, and injurious to all the other states, and it may be said with truth, that the prevalent delusions of the theories of free trade, have induced an unnecessary sacrifice of the markets of the free and northern slave states to the manufacturers of Europe, to obtain markets for cotton. I say the sacrifice has been unnecessary, for if the American markets had been properly secured to the domestic laborer and producer, the domestic market for cotton would have been much more extensive; and the manufacturers of Great Britain and the continent of Europe, would have been compelled to buy our cotton in nearly the same quantities, to avoid being supplanted in foreign markets, by their American competitors.

The improvements in agriculture have been so great in nearly all the countries of Europe since the peace of 1815, that the quantity of breadstuffs seems to have increased more rapidly than their population; and it is still continuing to increase, so that we cannot depend upon a European market for provisions, perhaps for half a century to come. Great Britain and France both produce more wheat in proportion to their population than the United States; and as we produce in the free states, very little that they want in payment for their cloths, silks, satins, wines, iron, hardware, &c., &c., our means of payment for such articles are very limited, and must continue to be so; and the result will be, we shall be compelled to manufacture for ourselves, for our credit was very nearly exhausted during the three years of free trade from 1840 to 1842, as it has been from 1848 to the present time; (1851.)

Some of the WRITERS AND ADVOCATES OF FREE TRADE expressed much sympathy for the British in 1845 and 1846, on account of the operation of the tariff of 1842. It was said that they could not afford to consume the breadstuffs and provisions raised in the free states, because we encouraged manufactures at home, and refused to clothe ourselves with the products of their factories; and it was pretended that the necessary tendency of our tariff was to lessen the consumption of our agricultural products in Great Britain, and to diminish the amount of our domestic exports. The foregoing tables show the fallacy of such a pretence. The nations of Europe purchase our breadstuffs and provisions when they need them, and because they need them; and not because we purchase more or less of their products. They do not purchase our products to accommodate us, but themselves; they buy what they want and no more. Those tender-hearted advocates of free trade may better reserve their sympathies for our own laborers.

It must be evident to any one who will take the trouble to reflect on the subject, that whenever the cost of our imports as a nation, exceeds our exports, the freight earned by American vessels, and the profits of that part of our exports made by American merchants, the excess or balance must exist as a debt against us; that whenever the balance of trade is against us, our foreign debt is accumulating to the precise amount of such balance, and the interest on our former debt added to it; that our exports, freights, profits, and foreign debt, must be precisely equal to our imports, and the interest on our foreign debt, and that the two must balance each other, like a banker's account.

Let us now compare our exports and imports, in order to learn the amount of our foreign debt, the balance of trade, and situation of the country at different periods; and to ascertain the effect of our several tariff acts, upon the prosperity of the country.

Owing to the embargo which was passed by Congress, December 22d, 1807, the various non-importation and non-intercourse acts which followed in quick succession, and the war from June, 1812, to January, 1815, our imports were not very large, and the foreign debt of our merchants could not have been very heavy at the close of the war. Though our national debt at the close of the war was over an hundred and twenty millions of dollars, yet it was mostly owing to our own citizens and to our banking institutions; and the whole amount of debt due from our citizens and our government to Europeans, did not perhaps exceed thirty millions of dollars. But our duties on imports were so low, that immediately after the war, and during the years 1815, 1816, and 1817, our country was literally flooded with British, French, and other foreign manufactures, including cotton and woollen cloths, silks, linens, hats, boots, shoes, iron, and hardware, &c., &c., amounting in all during those three years, (as estimated in the Commercial Dictionary,) to the sum of $359,394,274; while our exports during the same period amounted to only $222,149,774. If we add 25 per cent. to our exports for freight and profits of American merchants and ship owners, they would amount to about $278,000,000, and leave a balance of trade against us during those three years, amounting to the enormous sum of $81,000,000. Our exports in 1818, 1819, and 1820, amounted to $232,115,323; our imports during that period are estimated at $283,325,000; and if we add 20 per cent. to our exports for freight and profits, and call our foreign debt at the close of the war $30,000,000, calculating interest upon it, our aggregate foreign debt, including American stocks held by Europeans, would amount on the 30th day of September, 1820, to about $126,000,000; perhaps sixteen millions of it was lost by the failure and bankruptcy of American merchants and importers; leaving $110,000,000, which has been paid.

All the money and products sent abroad to pay the interest on our foreign debt, and the dividends on our stocks held abroad, appear as part of our exports; and the proceeds of all loans, and moneys and effects sent here to be invested in our stocks, appear in and as a part of our imports. Foreign debt, including the amount of our stocks held by Europeans on the first day of October, 1820, exclusive of sixteen million dollars due from bankrupts, estimated at $110,000,000.

Statement in millions of dollars, of the value of imports into the United States during the undermentioned fiscal years of coin and bullion, other free goods, dutiable goods, and the amount of duties collected during each period.

Years.	Coin and bullion. Millions.	Free Goods. Millions.	Dutiable Goods.	Total imported.	Duties collected. Millions.
1821 to 1824,	$24.9	13	$265	$303.9	$ 90.4
1825 to 1828,	28.7	19.1	301.5	349.3	115
1829 to 1832,	23.7	23.5	297.4	349.6	124
1833 to 1834,	25	75.8	133.8	234.6	43.1
1835 to 1837,	37	202.3	241.6	480.9	74.8
1838,	17.7	43.1	52.9	113.7	19.7
1839,	5.6	70.8	85.6	162	25.5
1840 to 1842,	17.9	135.9	181.4	335.2	51.6
1843 to 1846,	36	71.2	304.8	412	97.1
1847,	24.1	17.6	105.5	147.2	23.7
1848 to 1850,	17.6	50.2	413.2	481	99.8

The tariff act of 1832 exempted from duty all teas imported in American vessels from China and other places beyond the Cape of Good Hope, coffee, spices, fruits, nuts, gums, dyewoods, and nearly all other raw products of the torrid zone, except sugar, and reduced the duties on manufactures of silk, to a rate of from five to ten per cent.

The compromise act of 1833 provided for a prospective periodical reduction of duties until they should be reduced after the 30th of June, 1842, to 20 per cent., added greatly to the free list, and exempted from duty nearly all the manufactures of silk, worsted, silk and worsted, linen, and laces imported from Europe after the year 1833.

Under these acts the value of the goods imported free of duty, increased immensely, as shown by the foregoing table. The manufactures of silk worsted, silk and worsted, linen, laces, and sheeting, imported free of duty in 1839, were valued at over thirty-six million dollars. These heavy imports of articles of luxury contributed to increase the balance of trade against the country, and to involve it in debt.

The imports into the United States in 1841 exclusive of specie were valued at $122,957,544; in 1842 they amounted to only $96,075,071. Perhaps nothing but embarrassments, inability to pay promptly our foreign debts, and the interest upon them, and the low state of American credit abroad, prevented the imports in 1842 from amounting to as much as they did in 1839 and 1841. About two thirds in value of the imports then consisted, and now consist, of manufactured products and metals, the greatest part of which might and ought to be produced in the United States. The effect of the tariff of 1842 was to lessen, by means of increased duties, the importation of articles of luxury, such as silks, satins, laces, wines, and distilled spirits, as well as iron, hardware, and manufactures of cotton, wool, worsted, and linen. It contributed to promote the interest of the country in several modes. 1st. By increasing domestic industry. 2d. By turning the balance of trade in favor of the country and contributing to relieve it from foreign debts and embarrassments. 3d. By increasing the revenue, and 4th by checking luxury. The compromise act of 1833 produced opposite effects in the long run, in all these particulars, and contributed to paralyze the industry of the country, and to impoverish it. Such are the effects also of the tariff of 1846, and the longer it is continued in force the more plainly they will be developed.

	Millions.
Estimated amount of foreign debt, Oct. 1st, 1820	$110
Some of which being a recent mercantile debt bore no interest, but the most of it drew interest at 5 and 6 per cent., averaging perhaps on the whole debt, 5 per cent. for 4 years, to Oct. 1st, 1824,	22
Imports during the 4 years including $24,912,467 coin and bullion,	304
Debt contracted for purchase of Florida,	5
Total imports and debt,	$441
Exports during the same 4 years, including $34,675,778 coin and bullion,	287.8
Freights earned by American vessels, and profits of American merchants, equal to 15 per cent. on exports,	43.2
Total exports, freights, and profits,	$331
Amount of debt against the country Oct. 1st, 1824, immediately after the tariff act of 1824 took effect, though the exports of specie during the four years had exceeded the imports, over nine and a half million dollars,	110
Interest four years to Oct. 1st, 1828,	22
Import including $28,672,610 specie,	349.3
Total imports and debt,	$481.3

	Millions.
Exports, including $29,759,944 specie,	331.7
Freights and profits at 15 per cent.,	49.8
Total exports, freights, and profits,	$381.5
Amount of debt against the country Oct. 1st, 1828, immediately after the tariff of 1828 took effect, the debt having been reduced about ten millions during the previous four years, though the exports of specie had exceeded the imports only a little over one million dollars.	99.8
Interest 6 years to Oct. 1st, 1834,	30
Imports, including $53,755,025 specie,	584.2
Total imports and debt,	$714
Exports, including $26,462,523 specie,	509.2
Freights and profits at 15 per cent.,	76.4
Total exports, freights, and profits,	$585.6
Amount of debt against the country, Oct. 1st, 1834, after the first reduction of debt under the compromise act of 1833, the imports of specie having exceeded the exports during the previous 6 years, (under the tariff of 1828 and 1832,) over twenty-seven million dollars; showing that the balance of trade was in favor of our country, to an amount about equal to the interest on the foreign debt.	$128.4
Interest 3 years to Oct. 1st, 1837,	19.2
Imports, including $37,000,000 specie,	481
Total imports and foreign debts,	$628.6
Received from France, under treaty for spoliations,	5
Exports, including $16.8 millions specie,	367.8
Freights and profits at 15 per cent.,	55.2
Total exports, &c.,	$428.0

	Millions.
Amount of foreign debt, Oct. 1st, 1837,	$200.6
Interest 1 year to Oct. 1st, 1838,	10
Imports, including $17¾ millions specie,	113.7
Total imports and foreign debt,	$324.3
Exports, including $3½ millions specie,	108.5
Freights and profits at 15 per cent.,	16.2
Total exports, &c ,	124.7
Amount of foreign debt, Oct. 1st, 1838, immediately after the general resumption of specie payments.	$199.6
Interest 1 year, to Oct 1st, 1839,	9.4
Imports, including $5.6 millions specie,	162.0
Total imports and debt	371
Exports, including $8¾ millions specie,	121
Freights and profits at 15 per cent.,	18
Total exports, freights, &c.,	139
Amount of foreign debt, on the 1st day of October, 1839, 8 days before the second suspension of specie by nearly all the banks south and west of the State of New York.	$232
Interest 3 years to Oct. 1st, 1842,	34.8
Imports, including nearly $18 millions specie,	335.2
Total imports and debt,	$602
Exports, including $23¼ millions specie,	358.6
Freights and profits had fallen very much, and are estimated at 12½ per cent. on the exports other than specie,	41.8
Total exports, freights, &c.,	400.4
Amount of foreign debt, Oct. 1st, 1842, being about the same as it was, Oct. 1st, 1838, though the exports of specie had exceeded the imports, nearly $8½ million dollars, showing that it required about three years to pay the increased amount	$201.6

	Millions.
of debt accumulated by the heavy importations of the year 1839.	
Estimated losses of European creditors and bondholders by the failure of American merchants, bankers, corporations, and some of the States to make payment during the revulsion from 1837 to 1842, and during the previous sixteen years,	21.6
Leaving, Oct 1st, 1842, a foreign debt of to be provided for and paid, including bonds and stocks of all kinds held abroad, when the tariff of 1842 took effect.	$180
Interest $3\frac{3}{4}$ years to June 30th, 1846,	33.7
Imports, including $36 millions specie,	412
Total imports, and foreign debt,	$625.7
Exports, including $$19\frac{1}{2}$ millions specie,	423.6
Freight and profits on exports other than specie, at 10 per cent.,	40.1
Total exports, freight, &c.,	$463.7
Amount of foreign debt, on the 30th of June, 1846, five months before the tariff of 1846 took effect. The foreign debt was reduced during $3\frac{3}{4}$ years, under the operation of the tariff of 1842, about eighteen millions of dollars, and during the same period, the imports of specie exceeded the exports about sixteen and a half millions of dollars.	$162
Interest 1 year to June 30th, 1847,	8
Imports, including $$24\frac{1}{3}$ millions specie,	147
Total imports and foreign debt,	$317
Exports, including nearly $2 millions specie,	150.5
Freights were high, and together with profits, amounted to 12 or 15 per cent.; but the imports were undervalued, and much of the grain and flour shipped on American account, fell before it was sold; to balance these drawbacks and undervaluations, call the freights, &c., 10 per cent.,	15
Total exports, freights, &c.,	$165.5

		Millions.
Amount of foreign debt, June 30th, 1847,		$151.5
Interest 4 years to June 30th, 1851,		30.3
Imports, including $22.6 millions specie,		696.7
Undervaluations of $560,000,000 of dutiable imports from 5 to 80 per cent., including profits made by foreigners on goods sent here for sale, estimated on an average at 15 per cent.,		84
Total imports and foreign debt,		$962.5
Exports, including $58,000,000 specie,	669	
less fall on cotton shipped by American merchants before it was sold by them, estimated in 1851 at	15	
		654
Freights have been falling many years, estimated on exports other than specie, at 8 per cent.,		48
Am't realized from exports and freights &c estimated at		$702
Showing a foreign debt of about against our country on the 30th of June, 1851.		$260

It is not pretended that these estimates and calculations are entirely accurate; though they are deduced from such a mass of evidence, and the results at the end of each period correspond so well with each other, and with collateral evidence, that I think they cannot be very far from the truth. They are sufficiently accurate to illustrate fairly the relative effects of the several tariff acts, from 1816 to 1846, upon the commerce of the country, upon the amount of its foreign debts, and upon the exports and imports of specie.*

The national debt of the United States on the first day of January of each of the undermentioned years was as follows:

In 1791,	$ 75,169,974.	In 1821,	$89,987,427.
1801,	82,000,167.	1825,	83,788,432.
1812,	45,035,123.	1830,	48,565,405.
1816,	123,016,375.		

The debt was increased $15,000,000 by the purchase of Louisiana in 1803, and $5,000,000 by the purchase of Florida in 1822, and was all paid off prior to January 1st, 1834. The new debt of the United States created since the suspension of specie payments in 1837, amounted on the first of December 1843, to $26,742,949.

* For estimates of the amount of coin brought into the United States by immigrants, see Section 7 of Chapter X.

The Erie Canal of New York was commenced in 1817, and completed in 1825. The work proved so valuable and apparently advantageous to the State, that a large proportion of the people of the United States were suddenly seized with a mania for internal improvements; and after the destruction of the tariff and national bank, about the year 1834, they were taken with a monomania for paper money, and paper cities, accompanied by a high fever for railroads. Almost every man that had sufficient facilities, credit and financiering talent to get into debt enough to ruin him eventually, thought he was on the high road to fortune; and many of the State Legislatures seemed to be governed by very little more wisdom. Some of the states commenced contracting debts for canals, railroads, and other improvements as early as 1820, but from 1834 to 1838 inclusive, the most visionary schemes were devised, and the largest debts contracted, including loans for the establishment of banks, to the amount of over $50,000,000.

Because the Erie Canal, and several canals in Great Britain and Holland, and also many railroads had proved eminently successful, many persons seemed to suppose that canals and railroads would almost instantly make business, and be as useful in a wilderness, as in a densely populated country.

The several States contracted loans, and issued bonds, or stocks, for making internal improvements, and establishing banks, from the years 1820 to 1830, to an amount exceeding twenty-six million of dollars; from 1831 to 1835 to an amount exceeding forty millions of dollars; and from 1836 to 1838, both inclusive, to an amount exceeding one hundred millions of dollars. The debts of the several states, from December 1842, to the present time (1851) have constantly exceeded two hundred millions of dollars. The debt of the United States on the 30th of November, 1850, amounted to $64,228,238. The debt of the City of New York exceeds ten millions of dollars; the debts of other cities of the Union, amount to about twenty millions of dollars—and large amounts of loans have been contracted by Railroad and Canal Companies—so that our National, State, City, and Corporation debts, consisting mostly of bonds, greatly exceed three hundred millions of dollars.

About half of these debts over and above the foreign debts of American merchants, are supposed by well informed dealers in stocks, to be owned abroad. American bonds and stocks were very much depressed in price in 1841 and 1842; and as soon as the country began to revive, under the operation of the tariff of 1842, they began to return to the United States, and were purchased by American capitalists. They continued to rise in price here, and to return to this country in large amounts, up to December, 1846; but during the years 1849 and 1850, and up to the present time, it is very well known that large amounts have been sold in Europe, and the proceeds applied to pay for railroad iron, and other foreign goods. These facts serve to confirm the general accuracy of my estimates, and the correctness of the results.

Though our National, State, Corporate, City and foreign debts, are not one-sixth part as large in proportion to our population as the national debt of Great Britain, yet theirs is almost all owing to their own citizens, and nothing is taken out of the country to pay the interest; whereas, about half of ours is due to citizens of Great Britain, France and Holland; nations which generally take but few of our products, except cotton and tobacco; nations which generally have as large a balance of trade against us for goods and luxuries, as the credit of our merchants and people will permit, and they drain us of our specie to pay such balances, and the interest on the debts we owe them. The debt of Great Britain being due to her own citizens, does not lessen the aggregate wealth of the nation in the least; and if it could be struck out of existence at once, *the people in the aggregate would not be any wealthier than they are now. The debt is equivalent to a mortgage on the part of the creditors of the government, upon the productive industry and the earnings of the people, and thus it tends to oppress one class, for the benefit of another; but the nation as a whole is none the poorer on account of it. The effect is the same upon the nation, as debts due from one citizen to another.* Our case is different. Our debts being due to citizens of Great Britain, in order to estimate our wealth as a people, we should deduct from our aggregate means the whole amount of our foreign debt individually and collectively, including the amount of our stocks held by Europeans.

The calculations show that the balance of trade was against the United States from the close of the war, in 1815 to 1824, also under the compromise act from 1835 to 1839 inclusive—and under the tariff of 1846, from July 1st, 1847, to June 30th, 1851—and that the balance of trade was in favor of the United States, under the tariff acts of 1824, 1828 and 1832—from 1825 to 1834 inclusive—also during the last three years of the compromise act, from 1840 to 1842, inclusive, after the credit of the country had received such a shock as to diminish greatly our imports—also during the operation of the tariff of 1842, from October 1842, to Nov. 30th 1846, and during the first seven months of the tariff of 1846, up to June 30th, 1847, when there was an extensive demand for our flour and grain in Great Britain and Ireland.

A low tariff has always invited large importations of foreign goods, produced a balance of trade against the country—increased the foreign debt—undermined and supplanted to a greater or less extent, the domestic producer and manufacturer—and tended to paralyze the business, to diminish the industry of the nation—and to depress the value of nearly all the property in the United States. And the lower the tariff, and the more it has approximated to free trade, the greater have been it sparalyzing and depressing effects upon industry. Industry and property were both excessively depressed from 1784 to 1790; again from 1818 to 1824, under the low tariff then in operation—also from 1837 to the end of the year 1842, under the free-trade compromise act of 1833—and the manufacture of iron, cotton and wool, and some other branches of industry, have been much depressed during the last three years (1849, 1850 and 1851), under the free-trade tariff of 1846. This has had a depressing influence upon almost every pursuit in the nation. On the contrary, the industry and energies of the country revived, as if by magic, from 1825 to 1834, under the tariff acts of 1824 and 1828—and also from 1843 to the end of the year 1846, under the tariff of 1842.

It strikes me that the imposition of a duty of 10 or 15 per cent. on the exportation of silver from the United States, and five per cent. on the exportation of gold, would have a most salutary influence on the prosperity of the country. It would tend to increase the value of cotton and the exportation of domestic products to pay foreign debts; to check the importation of more foreign goods than we can pay for in domestic products; to lessen the exportation of specie, and thereby prevent runs upon the banks, panics, commercial embarrassments, derangements of the business of the country, and a general depression of the value of property.

Nations like Mexico and the countries of South America, which produce gold and silver as commodities for exportation, have no occasion to pursue the same policy which is necessary for nations, which produce none, or very little. It is not for their interest to check the exportation of the precious metals, and to encourage their importation, which has long been the policy of the most commercial nations of Europe and of China, and ought to be the policy of the United States.

The tonnage of the United States increased as follows:

Registered, enrolled and licensed tonnage of vessels in

1815,	1,368,127 tons.
1820,	1,280,166 "
1830,	1,191,776 "
1840,	2,180,764 "
1850,	3,535,454 "

SEC. 14. *On the Commerce and Commercial Policy of Great Britain.*

The foreign trade of England was very trifling in amount, prior to the time of Cromwell. The total value of exports from England and Wales in the year 1354 were valued at £212,338 5s. (See ante, Chap. XII. Sec. 21.)

The exports from England and Wales for the year ending Michaelmas, 1663, amounted to £2,022,812, and for the year ending Michaelmas, 1669, to £2,063,294.

Statement of the official value, (as fixed in 1696) of all the exports of Great Britain, of foreign and colonial as well as of domestic products, to all parts of the World, including Ireland, and her own colonies, during the undermentioned periods.*

1698 to 1701	average	annually	£6,449,594
1749 to 1755	do.	do.	12,220,974
1784 to 1792	do.	do.	18,621,942
in 1802	do.	do.	46,411,966
1816 to 1822	do.	do.	53,126,195

Statement of the official and declared or real value of British and Irish products and manufactures exported from the United Kingdom during the undermentioned years.

Years.	Official Value.	Declared Value.
1800	£22,831,936	£36,929,007
1802	25,193,389	45,102,230
1810	33,299,408	47,000,926
1820	37,820,293	35,569,077
1830	60,492,637	37,691,302
1840	102,705,372	51,406,430
1845	134,599,116	60,111,081
1849	164,539,504	63,596,025
1850	175,416,000	71,367,885

Real value in 1850, equal to $342,560,000.

* See the Commercial Dictionary—title Imports. The coin and bullion exported and imported, are not included.

The foregoing tables show the great, and almost incredible increase of the domestic exports of Great Britain within a period of one hundred and fifty years, consequent upon the invention of the steam-engine, of machinery for spinning and weaving, rolling iron, &c., and caused by the wonderful increase in the mining and manufacturing industry of that island.

The official values exhibit the relative quantities of goods exported during each period, (as the standard of official values has not been changed since 1696.) Less than one per cent. of these exports since the year 1800 was from Ireland. The value of the domestic exports, of Great Britain alone, was, in 1845, nearly three times as great as those of the United States.

NUMBER AND TONNAGE OF VESSELS, AND THE NUMBER OF SAILORS EMPLOYED AT DIFFERENT PERIODS.

	Vessels.	Tonnage.	No. of Men.
1702 in England and Wales,	3,281	261,222	27,196
1760 " "	6,105	433,922	———
" Scotland,	976	52,818	———
1800, England and Wales,	12,198	1,466,632	105,037
" Scotland,	2,155	161,511	13,883
" Ireland,	1,030	54,262	5,057
1835, England and Wales,	14,825	1,853,112	105,945
" Scotland,	3,287	335,820	23,924
" Ireland,	1,627	131,735	9,282
" Islands and Colonies,	5,774	463,094	31,869
1835, total British Empire,	25,513	2,783,761	171,030
1843, " "	30,983	3,588,387	213,977
" steamers,	942	121,455	———

The cost of building and fitting out new vessels, McCulloch estimated at from £10 to £12 per ton.

Almost all the foreign commerce and navigation of Great Britain has grown up since the revolution of 1688; and mostly since the rapid increase of their mining and manufacturing industry after the year 1770. Mining and manufacturing industry supply almost all the materials of the immense commerce of that great empire. Ireland has no foreign commerce of any account, because she has very little mining and manufacturing industry, and nothing to export but breadstuffs, provisions, and linen goods.

Statement in pounds sterling of the declared or market value of the exports, of the growth, produce, and manufacture of the United Kingdom of Great Britain and Ireland, during the under-mentioned years.

	1830.	1840.	1849.
Brass and Cop'r man'res,	£ 867,344	£ 1,450,464	£ 1,863,287
Coals and Culm,	184,464	576,519	1,088,148
Cotton Manufactures,	15,294,923	17,567,310	20,188,874
Cotton Yarn and Twist,	4,133,741	7,101,308	6,701,920
Earthenware,	442,193	573,184	807,466
Glass and Glassware,	401,543	417,178	254,175
Hardware and Cutlery,	1,412,107	1,349,137	2,198,597
Iron and Steel,	1,078,523	2,524,859	4,967,643
Lead and Shot,	106,789	237,312	287,339
Leather & Man'res of do.,	335,451	417,074	498,567
Linen Manufactures,	2,066,424	3,306,088	3,365,813
Linen Yarn,		822,876	737,650
Machinery and millwork,	208,767	593,064	709,071
Salt,	183,604	213,479	254,126
Silk Manufactures,	521,010	792,648	1,000,357
Soap and Candles,	246,592	450,640	240,713
Tin and tinware,	249,657	499,603	853,226
Woollen Manufactures,	4,851,097	5,327,853	7,330,475
Woollen Yarn,	———	452,957	1,087,867
Value of above articles,	£32,584,229	£44,673,553	£54,437,314
Value art'les not enum'd,	5,687,368	6,732,877	9,158,711
Total domestic exports,	£38,271,597	£51,406,430	£63,596,025

The navigation laws passed in the time of Cromwell (1651), were substantially the beginning of the protecting system in Great Britain, which continued from that time until the year 1846. During all that period it was the constant study of the British government to discriminate between their own industry, and that of foreign nations, by duties, taxes, drawbacks, and bounties, to encourage the importation of raw materials to be manufactured, by low duties or no duties at all; while they imposed heavy duties on all products for consumption, to secure their domestic and colonial markets to their own citizens, by imposing duties on foreign manufactures (amounting in many cases to prohibition) and to extend their foreign markets as much as possible. All this was done with a view to encourage and increase the productive industry of Great Britain, and to undermine and supplant the manufacturing industry of all other nations. Parliament, the Administration, the foreign ministers, the board of trade, and the public press, as well as the merchants and manufacturers, were constantly on the alert, to effect those objects, by any means in their power. During the last fifty years of that period, their authors, editors, chambers of commerce, merchants and manufacturers, were striving to inculcate and spread among the people of other nations, the doctrines of free trade, and great efforts were made by them, to subsidize the public press in the commercial cities of the United States, and to manufacture free trade opinions for the American people, while the British government and people were studying and practising upon the most effective system of protection.

The duties on iron imported into Great Britain and Ireland were changed about a dozen times, between the years 1780 and 1819, when they were finally raised at the latter period to £6½ (or about $31) per ton, when imported in British vessels—and £7 18½s. when imported in foreign vessels. The duties were specific, and always raised at each change, and never reduced, until the year 1832. They never reduced their duties on any thing until it became their interest to do so—until their mining and manufacturing industry was so far advanced, that duties were unnecessary to protect the home market, and it became important to set an example of *free trade*, to gull their less cunning neighbors. On many things, their duties are now (1851) as high as ever.

Having been so fortunate as to originate in Great Britain nearly all the important inventions to promote mining and manufacturing industry of the eighteenth century, they borrowed, and adhered to, (until 1846) the policy adopted by the Venetians many centuries since, and prohibited under severe penalties, the exportation of all tools, instruments, and machines, used in the manufacture of cotton, woollen, linen, and silk goods; or used in making iron, cutlery, glass, and various other manufactures. They enjoyed to a considerable extent, the advantages of a monopoly of the manufacture of the greater part of these commodities for over half a century, supplied half of the commercial world with them at high prices, and thereby engrossed an immense commerce, accumulated great wealth, involved half of the civilized world in debt to them to pay for their manufactures, and were determined to retain this monopoly as long as possible, by withholding from other nations the means of acquiring the necessary tools, instruments, and machinery, and of learning to manufacture for themselves.

Until the year 1819, Great Britain had statutes in force to prevent the exportation of gold and silver; since that time, her manufacturing industry has been so immensely great, and the exportation of her manufactured fabrics so heavy, that there is a balance of trade in favor of the British, and against almost every state, nation, and people, with whom they have any commercial intercourse; and there is a flow of the precious metals almost constantly into Great Britain to pay these balances of trade. Under such circumstances, they get an abundant supply of these metals by the ordinary operation of the laws of trade, and have no occasion for the restrictive policy which they previously, and during the whole of the eighteenth and part of the nineteenth century, found expedient; and they now seek to set an example of liberality, to the other nations of the earth.

The aggregate importation of silver, gold, and gold dust, into Southampton (England) for the year 1849, amounted to £6,788,655 sterling (or over $32,500,000) and in 1850 to £5,703,216 (or over $27,000,000) while the whole exports of the precious metals from Great Britain in 1850 were only £1,565,000 sterling.

Such has been the British policy for two centuries; and its results are exhibited in the foregoing tables.

The repeal of the corn laws took effect in the spring of the year 1847, and that was the first year of free importation of grain into Great Britain.

The potatoe crop of Great Britain and Ireland failed in 1845, and again in 1846—the grain crops were short also, during the latter year—and the trade in grain being free, the speculators imagining the deficiency much greater than it really was, offered high prices for grain and flour, and raised wheat the last of May 1847 to 102 shillings sterling, per quarter—from which time it fell constantly, until the latter part of September, when it was but little over 50s. per quarter—and only 60s. at the end of August. Twice as much was imported as was necessary—the balance of trade was turned against Great Britain—large amounts of coin were exported to pay it—the produce dealers were nearly all ruined by the fall of prices—the adverse balance of trade, the exportation of specie, the extensive speculations in railroad stocks, and the numerous failures of the produce dealers, produced a severe pressure, a general prostration of credit—and one of the greatest panics ever known—and the result was, the greatest number of failures, and the most extensive bankruptcies, which ever occurred in that country. The liabilities of the firms which failed in the summer and fall of 1847 in the city of London, were stated at £10,000,000 sterling—in Liverpool at £3,000,000; in Manchester £2,250,000; in Glasgow, £3,000,000; and in Leeds, Newcastle, Bristol, Dublin, and other cities in the

United Kingdom at £5,000,000; making in all, over twenty-three millions sterling. This was the first bitter fruits of excessive imports—of an adverse balance of trade—and large exports of specie. The British people then drank to the dregs, from the same bitter cup, which they had so long commended to their own colonists, to the Americans, and to the people of other nations.

Statement of the public income of Great Britain and Ireland, specifying the most of its sources, during the years 1838 and 1840.

Customs and Excise.	1838.	1840.
Spirits, Foreign,	£1,389,371	£1,290,581
Spirits, Rum,	1,411,067	1,155,613
Spirits, British,	5,467,201	5,201,664
Malt and Hops,	5,234,986	5,325,042
Wine,	1,846,057	1,791,646
Sugar and Molasses,	4,893,684	4,650,017
Tea,	3,362,035	3,472,864
Coffee,	684,979	921,552
Tobacco and Snuff,	3,561,812	3,588,192
Butter, Cheese, Currants, and Raisins,	666,400	715,136
Grain and Flour,	186,760	1,156,640
Cotton, and Sheep's Wool, imported,	725,445	785,491
Paper, Soap, Candles, and Tallow,	1,536,260	1,578,466
Glass, Bricks, Tiles, and Slate,	1,107,192	1,261,933
Timber,	1,572,618	1,730,551
Excise Licenses,	1,023,202	1,054,115
On all other articles,	2,446,792	2,447,905
Total Customs, and Excise,	£37,115,861	£38,127,408
Stamp Duties,	7,212,487	7,287,823
Land Taxes,	1,184,830	1,181,283
Windows,	1,262,561	1,404,642
Servants, Horses, Carriages, and Dogs,	1,177,452	1,285,443
Other assessed taxes,	278,242	280,919
Post Office receipts,	2,346,272	1,342,604
Crown Lands,	388,642	482,429
Other ordinary revenues and resources,	312,575	300,966
Total income,	£51,278,928	£51,693,510
Total income for the year 1839,		£52,058,349
Revenue from Customs in 1840 in		
Great Britain,		£21,209,082
Ireland,		2,132,731
Total,		£23,341,813

Statement of the net public income (after deducting the expenses of collection) of Great Britain and Ireland during the year 1849.

	Great Britain.	Ireland.
Customs,	£18,695,799	£1,941,122
Excise,	12,753,816	1,231,548
Stamps,	6,365,475	502,073
Property tax,	5,408,160	none.
Post Office,	806,000	26,000
Taxes, (Land and Assessed)	4,303,849	631,717
Miscellaneous,	286,190	
Total,	£48,619,289	£4,332,460
		48,619,289
Total of Great Britain and Ireland,		£52,951,749
Net receipts from Customs,		20,636,921
Cost of collecting the Customs,		1,557,679

The duties have been taken off from grain, flour, and cotton, since 1840—and reduced on a few other articles, but on many things they are now (1851) nearly as high as they were in 1840, amounting on an average to about fifty per cent. on all imports except cotton and bread stuffs. The duties, taxes, exports, and imports of Great Britain, show the protecting policy of the government and its effects, as well as the condition of the people. They show first, that by reason of high duties, so laid as to encourage home industry, as well as to collect revenue, nothing of any account is imported which can be produced in sufficient quantities at home; secondly, that the duties are so heavy as to amount to prohibition on nearly all manufactured articles, and that nearly all the imports consist of raw materials to be manufactured, and of provisions; thirdly, that their exports consist almost entirely of manufactures, the principal value of which arises from the labor and skill bestowed on the raw materials; and lastly, that their exports are increasing, as rapidly as foreign markets, and the demand for their products will permit. The recent census, and the condition of Ireland, and of many of the agricultural districts in Great Britain, show the depressing effects of a free importation of bread stuffs upon the agriculture, and the agricultural population of the kingdom.

SEC. 15. *On the commerce and commercial policy of France.*

I. Statement of the average annual value of the imports and exports of France at the undermentioned periods, in millions of francs and millions of dollars.*

Years.	IMPORTS. Millions of Francs.	IMPORTS. Millions of Dollars.	EXPORTS. Millions of Francs.	EXPORTS. Millions of Dollars.
1716 to 1720,	65	12	106.	20
1721 to 1732,	80.2	15	116.7	22
1740 to 1748,	102.8	19	192.3	36
1787 to 1789,	281.9	53	452.4	84
1819 to 1821,	428	80	487.9	91
1827,	556	104	602.2	112½
1827 to 1831,	588.2	110	602.2	112½
1837 to 1841,	973	182	958.8	179½
1843 to 1847,	1,243 8	233	1,155.4	216½
1847,	1,342.8	251½	1,270.7	238

The gold and silver coin and bullion exported and imported, are not included in the above amounts of exports and imports. The balance of trade was greatly in favor of France, and the excess of imports over the exports of coin and bullion generally very large.

II. Statement of the average annual official value* of the exports, the growth, produce, and manufacture of France, during the undermentioned periods and years, in millions of francs.

	1827.	1827 to 1831.	1843 to 1847.	1847.
Natural products,	348.2	143.3	190.9	191.7
Manufactured products,	185.6	342.8	622.9	699.4
Total domestic products,	506.8	486.1	813.8	899.1

* The values since 1826 are according to the standard of official values adopted that year—but prior to 1826 they are according to the market values at their respective periods.

III. Statement of the average annual official value* of the imports into France for home consumption and manufacture, during the undermentioned periods and years, in millions of francs.

	1827.	1827 to 1831.	1843 to 1847.	1847.
Materials to be manuf'tured,	276.3	279.2	590.5	547.5
Raw materials for cons'ption,	99.6	130	248.1	379.1
Manufactured products,	38.2	33.6	54.4	49.3
Total,	414.1	442.8	893	975.9

IV. Statement in millions of francs, of the official value of the principal articles of export, of the growth, produce, and manufacture of France during the years 1827 and 1847, the average of ten years from 1827 to 1836, and the average of five years from 1843 to 1847 inclusive.

	1827. Millions.	1827 to 1836. Millions.	1843 to 1847. Millions.	1847. Millions.
Manuf'ures of Silk,	115.3	121.4	145.3	165.5
" Cotton,	46	54.3	122.6	154.9
" Wool,	26.9	33.9	99.5	100.5
" Flax & Hemp,	44	32.7	25.5	26.1
" Leather,	12.8	15.4	25.5	28
Paper and books, &c.,	9.9	10.8	21.2	22.3
Pottery and glass ware,	10.8	12.7	20.5	21.9
Linen and Linen clothing,	6.4	7.5	16.4	17.7
Watch and clock work,	4.2	5.8	2.5	2.9
Manufactures of metals,	3.5	3.4	11	12.1
Modes,†	2.2	3.1	3.7	5
Articles of Parisian industry,	5.6	6.7	4.8	3.6
Wines,	47.3	46.8	50.9	55.4
Brandy,	22.3	19.3	12.3	16.7
Flour and grain of all kinds,	8.6	5.4	7.3	4.5
Salted meats,	1.4	1.4	2.3	1.9
Madder,	7.4	8.6	12	10.7
Fruits of table,	4.2	3.4	5.2	5
Butter,	2.0	1.6	3.2	3.3
Raw Silk,			7.1	5.9
Articles not enumerated,	126.0	127.3	215.0	227.2
Total domestic exports,	506.8	521.5	813.8	891.1

* The official value of both exports and imports, is in accordance with the standard of value adopted in 1826, which was then their supposed average market value. The amounts, therefore, show the relative quantity of exports and imports at different periods, but not their market value. Coin and bullion are not included.

† Artificial flowers are included with modes in 1847 and 1843 to 1847.

V. Statement in millions of francs, of the official value of the imports into France, for manufacture and consumption.

	1827. Millions.	1827 to 1836. average in Millions.	1843 to 1847. average in Millions.	1847. Millions.
Cotton,	51.9	58.9	103	80.7
Silk, (raw)	32.3	40	67.9	76.5
Wool,	11.1	16.2	40.8	30.4
Indigo,	14 8	18	20.7	20.6
Hemp,	4.2	3.6	4.2	3.5
Raw Hides,	8.6	14	28.3	25.7
Iron,	4.7	4.7	4.4	4.1
Copper and brass,	9.5	11.4	26.9	31
Lead,	6.2	6.8	9.4	9.1
Sugar,	37.5	45.4	58.9	60.1
Coffee,	10.9	10.1	14.5	15
Tea,	1.	.7	.9	.8
Grain and flour,	.9	23	83.5	209
Cheese,	3.1	2.9	3.8	3.3
Butter,	1.7	1.5	2.2	2.2
Linen and Hemp Cloths,	18.1	16.1	17.1	13.8
Linen and hemp yarn,	7.9	8.9	23.1	7.8
Leaf Tobacco,	7.6	5.9	27.5	22.4
Olive, and other oils,	32.7	39.4	52.4	56
Wood and lumber,	20.4	23.2	43.9	43.1
Flax,			9.9	13.9
Articles not enumerated,	129	129.6	249.7	246.9
Total,	414.1	480.3	893	975.9

The official value of domestic exports in 1848 amounted to 833,700,000 francs; their real or market value amounted to 690,000,000 francs. The official value of imports for consumption in 1848 amounted to 556,600,000 francs, their real value amounted to but 474,300,000. This shows that the average prices of their exports had declined about 17½ per cent. and the average prices of their imports nearly 15 per cent.; 1848 being a year of revolution, their imports fell off more than forty per cent.

The foreign commerce of France, like that of Great Britain, was very small indeed prior to the beginning of the 18th century, and in fact up to the year 1750, compared with what it is now. It expanded very rapidly from 1750 to the breaking out of the Revolution in 1789, but increased very little from that time, until the close of the wars of Napoleon in 1815. Since 1820 it has increased more rapidly than that of the United States, and now greatly exceeds it. Being dependent on domestic production, it was small prior to 1750, because the manufacturing industry of the country was small; but it has expanded with the mechanical and manufacturing industry of the nation, with wonderful rapidity, during the last thirty years (1820 to 1851) until it has become immensely great.

Tables II. and IV. of this section show that nearly all the increase of exports from France consists of manufactured products; Tables III. and V. show that nearly all the increase of imports consists of raw materials to be manufactured, and raw materials for consumption, which are the products of warm countries, and do not come in competition with the industry of France. The whole of their foreign commerce, both imports and exports, comes in aid of, and fosters domestic industry; the home manufacturer commands the home market; and whatever imports come in competition with his industry, are taxed with heavy duties. Under this protecting policy of the government, France has made more progress in productive industry, wealth, and commerce, and nearly as much in population, during the last twenty-five years, as she ever made before in a century. Her progress has not been confined to manufactures and commerce, but her manufacturing industry has been the means of improving her agriculture also.

During the period of twenty-two years from 1827 to 1848, there have been seven years (including the years 1827, 1833, 1834, 1835, 1836, 1837, 1838, and 1841,) when the exports of grain and flour exceeded the imports. The territory of France is but a little more than two thirds as large as the Slave States above the 35th degree of latitude, and yet it has nearly supplied with grain, vegetables, and provisions of all kinds, a population of about 35,000,000. No instance can be found on record, of the growth of manufactures in a country, without a corresponding improvement in agriculture, and increase of wealth, population and commerce.

Since the peace of 1815, France has been pursuing the same policy in relation to manufactures, which Great Britain has pursued for about two centuries; and similar results have followed. British writers and free trade economists have been long harping upon the advantages of France as a wine-growing country; and trying to convince the French people that it was their true policy to produce wines as their chief business, admit British goods free of duty, and pay for them in wine.* Let the reader examine Table IV., and he will see how utterly insignificant the value of wine exported, when compared with silk and cotton goods, and the aggregate of other manufactured products exported. While

* See on this point Sec. 18 of Chapter IX.

the exports of wine increased only seventeen per cent. in twenty years, and the exports of brandy decreased, the other domestic exports of France increased over eighty per cent. What would have been the condition of France at this day, if the government had pursued the very wise and disinterested advice of their *peculiar friends, the free trade* writers and political *economists of Great Britain?*

Sec. 16. *On the commerce and commercial policy of Holland and Belgium.*

It is not in my power to give a reliable statement of the exports and imports of Holland; but quote the following remarks from the works of Sir. Wm. Temple, as expressive of the commercial policy of that country. "The vulgar mistake that importation of foreign wares, if purchased with native commodities and not with money, does not make a nation poorer, is what every man that gives himself leisure to think, must immediately rectify, by finding out that upon the end of an account between a nation and all they deal with abroad, whatever the exportation wants in value to balance that of the importation, must of necessity be made up with ready money.

"By this we find out the foundation of the riches of Holland and of their trade by the circumstances already stated; for never any country traded so much and consumed so little; they buy infinitely, but it is to sell again, either upon an improvement of the commodity or at a better market. They are the great masters of the Indian spices and of the Persian silks; but wear plain woollen, and feed upon their own fish and roots. Yea, they sell the finest of their own cloth to France, and buy coarse out of England for their own wear. They send abroad the best of their own butter into all parts, and buy the cheapest out of Ireland and the north of England for their own use. In fine, they furnish infinite luxury which they never practise, and traffic in pleasures they never taste."

The above extract discloses the policy of the Hollanders and the principal cause of their great wealth and power during the 17th and 18th centuries. The secret of their wealth was productive industry and economy. No matter how many luxuries a people buy, if they buy them to sell again and make a profit on them; but if they buy them to consume in large quantities, unless their wealth and productive industry are very great, they will soon squander their substance, and involve themselves in debt.

Statement in millions of francs, of the average annual value of the exports of the growth, produce, and manufacture of Belgium, during the undermentioned periods and years.*

	1835. Mil. of frs.	1835 to 1839. Mil. of fr'cs.	1843 to 1847. Mil. of fra's.	1847. Mil. of frs.
Raw materials to be used or manufactured,	43.4	45.3	82.2	99.5
Provisions,†	22.4	24.3	19.3	23.7
Manufactured products,	72.2	71.8	79.5	82.5
Total,	138	141.4	181	205.7
Total in millions of dollars,	\$26	\$26½	\$34	\$38½

Statement in millions of francs, of the average annual value of imports into Belgium for home consumption and manufacture during the undermentioned periods and years.*

	1835.	1835 to 1839.	1843 to 1847.	1847.
Raw materials to be used or manufactured,	63.3	67.5	82	84.7
Provisions,	62.4	67.3	98.5	113.6
Manufactured products,	46.9	53.2	37.5	34
Total,	172.6	188	218	232.3
Total in millions of dollars,	\$32⅓	\$35⅓	\$41	\$43½

Belgium has but a few miles of sea-coast, no seaport town of much consequence, very little shipping, more than one third of her imports, and over two thirds of her exports, are by land and by internal navigation, and more than two thirds of her exports and imports by sea, are made in foreign vessels.

Though the Belgians have but a mere trifle of shipping and navigation, yet their foreign commerce has increased with great rapidity. Their domestic exports now amount to nearly nine dollars to each person; while those of the United States amount to only about six dollars to each person. Their commerce aids their industry; while they have greatly increased their imports of provisions and raw materials to be manufactured, their imports of manufactures (which could come in competition with domestic industry) have decreased. These facts show that a nation may

* The values of both exports and imports are stated in accordance with the standard of official valuations adopted in 1833, and do not include gold and silver coin and bullion.

† Sugar, tea, coffee, spice, fruits, and all products to eat and drink, except distilled liquors are classed with provisions.

have an extensive foreign commerce, without much shipping or navigation, and verify the general principle heretofore stated, that commerce, both foreign and domestic, depends on productive industry, on the production of things that are wanted by the commercial world.

SEC. 17. *On the commerce of Austria, Russia, and Cuba.*

McGregor states the exports in 1840 of the Austrian Empire, including Hungary, Lombardy, and Venice, at but £10,383,800 sterling, and their imports at £10,576,600.

The population was then about thirty-six millions and the exports $49,843,000, or about $1\frac{3}{8}$ dollars to each person.

Statement extracted from McGregor's statistics of the value of the imports and exports of the Russian Empire, and the value of the exports to each person at different periods.

Years.	Imports in Millions of Roubles.	Imports in Millions of Dollars.	Exports in Millions of Roubles.	Exports in Millions of Dollars.	Amount to each person.
1742,	3.5	2.6	4.6	3.4	$ .16
1750,	6	4.5	7.1	5.3	.21
1760,	7.3	5.4	9.8	7.3	.30
1770,	11.4	8.5	15	11.2	.40
1780,	15.4	11.5	19.6	14.7	.50
1790,	31.1	23.3	32.7	24.5	.75
1797,	34.9	26	56.7	42.5	1.25*
1830,	56.3	42.2	76.8	57.6	.95
1836,	67.8	50.8	81	60.7	1.05
1841,	79.4	59.5	86.4	64.8	1.10

The examples given illustrate fairly the commerce of Europe. The foreign commerce of Spain, Portugal, and the states of Italy, is less in proportion to the population than that of Austria; and the commerce of Turkey is much less in proportion to the population, than that of Russia.

The domestic exports of the Island of Cuba, exclusive of gold and silver coin, and bullion, have been as follows:

In 1840.	In 1842.
$21,537,181,	$23,447,610.

The population of Cuba was about one million.

* The principal reason of the exports amounting to more to each person in 1797 than in 1830 was the high prices.

SEC. 18. *Value of the exports of the United States, compared with those of Great Britain, France, and other countries.*

Estimate of the average value of domestic products exported annually for some years prior to 1850, and the value to each person from the following countries.

	Millions of dollars.	Amount to each person.
United States,	130	$ 6.00
Free states, and northern slave states,	60	3.25
Southern Slave States,	70	18
Great Britain,	310	15
Ireland,	2	* 25
France,	180	5
Belgium,	36	8
Austrian Empire,	50	1.37
Russian Empire,	65	1.10
Cuba,	22	22.00

* If the exports of Ireland to Great Britain were included with the exports to foreign countries, they would amount to about eight dollars to each person.

CHAPTER XIV.

On the condition, productive industry, and value of property of Great Britain, France, and other countries of western Europe, at different periods; of Mexico and the South American States the first part of the nineteenth century; and of the United States, and the several States in 1840 and 1850.

Sec. 1. *Tables showing the income, value of the real and personal estate, agricultural products, and coin in England, in 1688.*

The means of collecting information in relation to the wealth and productive industry of any country prior to the nineteenth century, are very limited; the estimates made are necessarily more or less uncertain; and yet estimates made by intelligent officers of the government, and by careful practical men, often approximate very nearly to the truth, and may be very useful in aiding us to estimate the progress of nations in productive industry and wealth. The essays of Mr. Davenant published between the years 1688 and 1712, and those of Gregory King, published about the same period, furnish the most reliable evidence that can be obtained of the resources and condition of England and Wales during the 17th and early part of the 18th century. Mr. Davenant stated the rent or income value of all the property of England and Wales in 1688 as valued by the government in assessing the income tax of 4s. on the pound, and gave his own estimate of the same as follows:

Table A.

In 1688 from	Income as rated by the government.	Mr. Davenant's estimates of same.
Lands,	£6,500,000	£10,000,000
Houses and other buildings,	1,500,000	2,000,000
Mines and other real estate,	500,000	1,000,000
Total real estate,	£8,500,000	£13,000,000
Personal estate,	500,000	1,000,000
Total for the Kingdom,	£9,000,000	£14,000,000

Mr. Davenant says, there are undeniable reasons which may be given, that the general rental or income from property of the whole Kingdom in the year 1600, did not exceed £6,000,000; but through the help of that wealth which flowed into the Kingdom from foreign trade, it advanced from six to eight, from eight to ten, and from ten to fourteen millions sterling per annum. His estimate for the year 1600 includes personal as well as real estate, and leaves not over £5,400,000 as the annual rent or income from real estate of all kinds.

He supposed that wealth decreased during the war from 1688 to 1697, and was about the same in 1705, as it was in 1688.

TABLE B.

ANNUAL AGRICULTURAL PRODUCTS OF ENGLAND AND WALES at the average of years and prices, about the year 1688, as estimated by Gregory King, after deducting the quantity used for seed.

	Bushels.			Value.
Wheat,	14,000,000	3s.	6d.	£2,450,000
Rye,	10,000,000	2	6	1,250,000
Barley,	27,000,000	2	0	2,700,000
Oats,	16,000,000	1	6	1,200,000
Peas,	7,000,000	2	6	875,000
Beans,	4,000,000	2	6	500,000
Vetches,	1,000,000	2	0	100,000
	79,000,000	2	$3\frac{5}{8}$	£9,075,000
Seed, about	11,000,000			1,263,000
Total,	90,000,000			£10,338,000

The seed in some cases was estimated one-fifth, and in others one-eighth the whole produce, and was reckoned at 11,000,000 bushels in all, as above stated. Call the seed of wheat on an average equal to two-thirteenths of the crop, it would amount to about 2,500,000 bushels, and make the whole wheat crop 16,500,000 bushels.

Mr. King estimated the rent of the grain land at	£2,200,000
over and above the tithes, amounting to about	700,000
leaving for products of labor and profits,	£6,175,000

Mr. Davenant estimated the rent in 1688, of pasture and meadow lands,	12,000,000 acres at 8s. 8d.,	£5,200,000
Arable lands,	9,000,000 acres at 5s. 6d.,	2,480,000

Other lands, heaths, moors, gardens, woodlands, and parks,	2,320,000
Dwelling houses, yards, and buildings,	2,000,000
Total of the above,	£12,000,000

He estimated the number and value of the LIVE STOCK OF ENGLAND AND WALES IN 1688, as follows:

TABLE C.

	Number.	Value of each.			Total Value.
Neat cattle, including calves,	4,500,000	£2	0s.	0d	£9,000,000
Sheep and lambs,	12,000,000	0	7	4	4,440,000
Swine and pigs,	2,000,000		16	0	1,600,000
Deer and fawns,	100,000	2	0	0	200,000
Goats and kids,	50,000		10	0	25,000
Hares and leverets,	24,000		1	6	1,800
Rabits and conies,	1,000,000			5	20,833
Horses,	1,200,000	2	10	0	3,000,000
Fowls, geese, turkeys, &c.,					472,000
Total					£18,759,633

Mr. Davenant estimated the ANNUAL VALUE about the year 1688, OF ANIMAL PRODUCTS, including the products of the forest and all agricultural products, except grain, as follows:

TABLE D.

Butter, cheese, and milk,	£2,500,000
Wool yearly shorn,	2,000,000
Horses yearly bred,	250,000
Flesh annually used as food,	3,350,000
Tallow and hides,	600,000
Hay consumed by horses,	1,300,000
Hay consumed by cattle and sheep,	1,000,000
Add for fowls, geese, turkeys, and their eggs,	500,000
	£11,500,000
Deduct hay for farm horses, cattle and sheep,	2,000,000
	£9,500,000
Add value of grain over seed, as estimated by Mr. King,	9,075,000
Total net products of agriculture,	£18,575,000
Timber cut for building, &c.,	500,000
Wood for fuel, &c.,	500,000
	£19,575,000

SEC. 2. *Comparative incomes and population of England, France and Holland, in* 1697.

Mr. Davenant estimated the ANNUAL INCOME FROM CAPITAL AND LABOR (over and above the use of dwelling houses,) upon which the people lived, and out of which all taxes, assessments and tithes were paid, immediately after the war ending in 1696, as follows:

TABLE A.

England and Wales, at	£43,000,000
France, at	81,000,000
Holland, at	18,250,000

No details are given of the incomes of the people of France; none of the people of England except those of agriculture and the forest, heretofore stated. He estimated the annual rental or income from lands, houses, and other real estate in Holland, at

at	£ 4,000,000
Income from commerce, navigation, and business,	13,750,000
This estimate includes nothing for the income from agricultural labor and stock, which may be estimated at	3,250,000
Total,	£21,000,000

TABLE B.

The population of England and Wales in the year 1700, was about 5,500,000; of France, about 19,669,000; and of Holland, about 2,000,000.

	Population.	Annual Income.	Amt. to each Person.
England and Wales,	5,500,000	£43,000,000	£ 7 16s., or $37 50
Holland,	2,000,000	21,000,000	10 10½s. or 50 00
France,	19,669,000	81,000,000	4 2½s. or 19 82

Mr. Davenant was engaged in the treasury department of the government, and was well acquainted with the commerce and resources of England; but his information in relation to Holland and France must have been much less complete. We have reason to believe that the incomes of Holland, considering their immense commerce, must have been greater in proportion to the population, than those of England; and if so, the amount I have added is not too much. His estimate so far as regards England and Wales, was based on their official valuations, and income tax, and is entitled to credit; but so far as regards France, it was a mere conjecture, without much official evidence, and quite too low to be probable. We have no reason to believe that the productive industry of France, and the incomes of the people, materially increased from the time of the revocation of the edict of Nantes in 1685, to the revolution of 1789. See tables A. and D. of Sec. 9.

TABLE C.

Estimate of the net ANNUAL INCOME from MINING, THE MECHANIC ARTS, MANUFACTURES AND COMMERCE IN ENGLAND AND WALES about the year 1700; from the best information I have been able to collect of the prices and quantity of products.

Manufactures of wool, £2,000,000 deducted for materials,	£4,000,000
Manufactures of leather, less £500,000 for hides,	3,500,000
Manufacturing 1,170,000 lbs. of cotton, at 2s. 6d. per lb.	146,000
Manufactures of silk,	500,000
Manufactures of linen in 1800 estimated at £2,000,000, perhaps in 1700 about one-third part as much, less the flax,	500,000
Hats and caps, value, less the materials used,	300,000
Making about 13,000 tons of castings, bar and pig iron, at £20 per ton,	260,000
Making two-thirds of it into cutlery, hardware, chains, and blacksmith work, adding £20 value per ton,	170,000
Mining and smelting 700 tons copper, worth £100 per ton,	70,000
Mining and smelting about 1500 tons of tin, worth £75 per ton,	112,000
Mining and smelting, perhaps, 3000 tons of lead and zinc, worth £112,	360,000
Value added by manufacturing copper, tin, lead, and zinc,	542,000
Manufacturing precious metals and jewelry, value added,	100,000
Manufacturing bricks, lime, and lumber, quarrying stone, erecting houses and other buildings, perhaps,	2,000,000
Manufacturing glass and earthen ware,	200,000
Manufacturing paper,	100,000
Mining and transporting about 500,000 chaldrons of coal,	500,000
Grinding grain and making flour, value added,	500,000

Making wagons, carriages, furniture, farming utensils, and ship building, about	1,000,000
All other manufactures and mechanism,	2,000,000
	£16,860,000
Income from foreign and domestic commerce, navigation and transportation, about	6,140,000
Value of grain and vegetables over and above seed, brought forward,	9,000,000
Income from animals, brought forward,	9,500,000
Income from the forest for timber and fuel,	1,000,000
Income from the fisheries, about	500,000
Total amount, as estimated in gross by Davenant,	£43,000,000

SEC. 3. *Acres of land, and rental of Great Britain and Ireland at different periods, from* 1770 *to* 1843.

Summary statement of the number of ACRES OF LAND, AND THE RENTAL of, or income from, the same in GREAT BRITAIN in 1810–11, and in 1814–15, according to the returns of the income tax, and an estimate of the same for Ireland in 1832, compiled from official documents by a parliamentary committee; excluding from each the rental of houses, mines, factories, stores, fisheries, and all real estate in cities and villages. The rental of farm houses is included with lands.

	Acres of land.	Rent in 1810–11. Gross am't.	Per acre.	Rent in 1814–15.
England,	32,243,200	£27,880,085	17s. 3½d.	£32,502,824
Wales,	4,752,000	1,622,985	6 10	1,827,638
England and Wales,	36,995,200	£29,503,070	15 11¼	£34,330,462
Scotland,	18,021,760	4,816,577	5 4½	5,075,242
Great Britain,	55,016,960	£34,319,647		39,405,704
Ireland in 1832,	19,944,209	12,715,478	12 9	

McCulloch says the rental of lands only in England and Wales was estimated by Arthur Young in 1771 at £16,000,000; by Dr. Beeke in 1800 at £20,000,000; that the entire rental of Scotland in 1770, was estimated at only from £1,000,000 to £1,200,000, and in 1795 at a little over £2,000,000; that Brown computed the gross rental of Ireland, including houses, quit rents, tithes, etc., in 1737, at £2,824,000; and that Young estimated it in 1778 at £6,000,000. In addition to the rents, the tenants paid all taxes, and also the tithes, the latter amounting in 1814 for England and Wales to £2,732,690.

The rental of lands only, (including farming lands, pastures, commons, heaths, woodlands, gardens, and farm houses,) according to the returns of the income tax for the year 1843, was as follows:

Great Britain,	£45,753,615
Ireland,	13,000,000
Great Britain and Ireland,	£58,753,615

SEC. 4. *Tables showing the rental and valuation of the different kinds of real property in Great Britain in* 1815 *and* 1843.

TABLE A.

Summary statement of the RENTAL OR ANNUAL INCOME OF REAL ESTATE OF ALL KINDS IN ENGLAND, WALES AND SCOTLAND, according to the returns of the income tax in 1815, as stated by McCulloch; and the rental in 1843, according to the returns of the income tax.

	Rental in 1815.	Rental in 1843.
England,	£49,744,621	£80,519,084
Wales,	3,750,747	5,283,600
Scotland,	6,642,955	9,481,762
Great Britain,	£60,138,323	£95,284,446

TABLE B.

Summary statement of the AMOUNT AND PER CENT. OF THE ANNUAL INCOME OF EACH KIND OF REAL ESTATE IN GREAT BRITAIN IN 1814–15, AND 1843, according to the returns of the income tax of those years. Mills, factories, stores, and warehouses are included with dwelling houses, in the returns of 1814–15, but by the aid of the per centage of each, stated in the Westminster Review, I have been able to separate them with tolerable accuracy.

	Rental of 1814–15.	Per ct.	Rental of 1843.	Per ct.
Lands,	£39,405,704	65.56	£45,753,616	48.0
Dwelling houses,	15,035,000	25.00	38,475,738	40.4
Tithes,	2,732,899	4.52	1,960,330	2.0
Mines, }	678,785	1.13	2,081,337	2.1
Railroads, }			2,598,943	2.7
Canals, }	1,927,342	3.20	1,307,093	1.4
Mills, fact's, wareh's, &c. }			2,394,646	2.5
Manors, fines and quarries,	358,593	0.59	712,742	.9
Total,	£60,138,323	100.00	£95,284,445	100.0

TABLE C.

Summary statement of the AMOUNT OF MONEYS LEVIED BY ASSESSMENT FOR POOR RATES AND COUNTY RATES in England and Wales for the year 1832, as collected and published by the Board of Trade. See McCulloch's statistics, II, p. 421.

	Amount levied on.	Per cent.
Farming lands, gardens, woodlands, &c.,	£5,434,890	63.17
Dwelling houses,	2,635,257	30.61
Mills, factories, forges, mines, &c.,	352,479	4.09
Manorial profits, navigation, warehouses, &c.,	183,874	2.13
Total amount levied,	£8,606,500	100.00

The ninth report of the poor law commissioners is referred to in the Westminster Review for January, 1848, in corroboration of the general correctness of the valuations under the income tax. In that report (p. 8,) it is shown that the proportions of the several kinds of real property charged to the poor rates in England and Wales, were as follows:

Lands,	52	per cent.
Dwelling houses,	37	do.
All other property,	11	do.
	100	

The reviewer remarks, "The one return (the income tax,) embracing all Great Britain, the other (for the poor rates, &c.,) England and Wales only, and being founded on distinct data, we consider the near approximation, speaks strongly for the general accuracy of both."

TABLE D

Summary statement of the VALUE IN MILLIONS OF POUNDS STERLING, OF ALL THE REAL ESTATE IN GREAT BRITAIN IN 1815 AND IN 1843, deduced from the foregoing table B, estimating the value of dwelling houses, other buildings and railroads as equal to twenty-years' rent, and lands, canals, mines, etc., equal to twenty-seven years' rent in 1815, and to twenty-eight years rent in 1843.

	Years' rent.	Value in 1815. Millions.	Yrs' rent.	Value in 1843, Millions.
Lands,	27	£1.064	28	£1.281
Dwelling houses,	20	300	20	769
Tithes,	27	73	28	55
Mines,	27 }	18	28	58
Railroads,	20 }		20	*52
Canals,	27 }	38½.	28	*37
Mills, factories, etc.,	20 }		20	48
Manors, fines and quarries,	27	9½	28	20
Total,		£1.503		£2.320

Increase in the value of dwelling houses and palaces, exclusive of farm houses in twenty-eight years, from 1815 to 1843, £469,000,000. Such an increase is more wonderful than the increase of even the cotton manufacture. All the dwelling houses in the United States in 1843, were not worth perhaps over $1,350,000,000, and excluding farm houses not over $830,000,000; while the magnificent palaces of the nobles and wealthy commoners, and the dwellings of the merchants, manufacturers, mechanics, and other inhabitants of cities and villages in Great Britain, were worth, as above shown, about $3,685,329,000, or nearly three times as much as those of the same classes in our country.

* These railroads cost about £60,000,000, and the canals about £30,000,000.

SEC. 5. *Several estimates of the productive industry of Great Britain.*

TABLE A.

Estimate made by McCulloch in 1838, of the PRINCIPAL ANNUAL CROPS OF ENGLAND AND WALES, THEIR PRICE, TOTAL VALUE, and the number of acres cultivated.

	Acres cultivated.	Bushels per acre.	Total produce in bushels.	Price per 8 bush.	Value in millions.
Wheat,	3,800,000	26	98,800,000	50s.	£30.875
Barley and Rye,	900,000	32	28,800,000	30s.	5.4
Oats and Beans,	3,000,000	36	108,000,000		17.5
Turnips and potatoes,	1,200,000		at £5¼ per acre,		6.3
Gardens & hop-yards,	150,000		at £15 per acre,		2.25
					£62.325
Deduct one-eleventh for seed,					5.665
Leaves for net produce of above crops,					£56.66

He estimated the annual value of the various products derived from pasture and meadow lands at an average of about £3 10s. per acre; being equivalent on 17,000,000 acres to £59,500,000, which he distributed as follows:

TABLE B.

	Millions.
Cattle for beef, 1,100,000, at £13 each,	£14.3
Calves killed, 200,000, at £3 each,	.6
Sheep and lambs killed, 6,800,000, at £1 10s. each,	10.2
Wool, 338,000 packs of 240 lbs. each, worth £12 per pack or 1s. per lb.,	4.056
Hogs and pigs, 555,000, at £1 16s. each,	1.
Horses, 200,000 full grown, produced annually, worth £15 each,	3.
Poultry, eggs, rabbits, and deer,	1.344
Dairy produce of milk, butter, and cheese,	12.
Meadow and grass for work and pleasure horses,	13.
Total,	£59.5

The horses used for farming purposes, are mere instruments for cultivating the ground and raising the grain; the value of those raised for such purposes, more than half of the whole, and also the

hay and pasture consumed by them, amounting to about	8.
should be deducted, in order to ascertain the net products of agriculture, which leaves	51.5
Add for timber and wood cut annually, according to McCulloch,	2.
Total net produce of agriculture and the forest,	£110.16

His estimate for Scotland was as follows:

Value of crops cultivated,	£13,355,000	
Products of meadow and pasture lands,	5,000,000	
Products of uncultivated and wood-lands for timber,	2,000,000	
	£20,355,000	
Deduct for seed, one-eleventh of the crops,	1,251,000	
Total for Scotland,	£19,140,000	£19.14
		£129.3

McCulloch supposed that one-half of the value of farming lands consists of the buildings, fences, drains, and other improvements on them. I presume such improvements do constitute about forty per cent. of their value, or about £500,000,000; more than half of which, or £250,000,000, has been made during the last fifty years; add, therefore, for agricultural labor invested annually in fencing, draining, and improving lands,	£5.
Making the total value produced annually in Great Britain about the year 1839, by lands, agricultural capital and labor,	£134.3

The under estimates in the prices of produce, and the articles omitted, will exceed the wear and tear of tools and agricultural implements.

Compare the foregoing estimate of the agricultural products of England and Wales with the estimates by King and Davenant in Sec. 1, and the increase will appear truly wonderful, when we consider that the country had been settled perhaps more than 2,000 years at the former period.

	Million bushels.
McCulloch says the annual wheat crop of England and Wales was estimated in 1773 at	32
In 1796, by Lord Hawkesbury, afterwards Lord Liverpool, at less than	48
In 1688, by King, as stated in Sec. 1, at about	16.5
In 1838, by McCulloch, as above stated, at	98.8
In 1842, by Brande in his Encyc. of Science and Art, at	120

McCulloch says the Commissioners of the Poor Inquiry in Ireland, estimated the total annual value of its land produce at only £36,000,000; but he thought the estimate quite too low,

and he estimated it at	£44,500,000
From which he deducted for seed, and sums necessary to replace horses, &c.,	6,000,000
Leaving but	£38,500,000
Call the amount of the net product of agriculture in Ireland;	£40,000,000
out of which he estimates	3,500,000
must be sent out of the country to pay rents due to absentee proprietors; leaving but	£36,500,000
to be enjoyed by the people of Ireland.	

These estimates are above those in a very able article in the Westminster Review for January, 1848, which are as follows;

Value produced annually by lands, capital, and labor, employed in agriculture in Great Britain,	£126,899,111
do. do. in Ireland,	27,683,603

In the same article the average wages of labor employed in agriculture, are estimated as follows:

	Per week.		Per week.
Male adults in Great Britain,	10s.	In Ireland,	5s. 0d.
Males under twenty years of age,	5	do.	2 6
Female adults,	5	do.	2 6
do under twenty years old,	2 6	do.	1 3

McCulloch in 1838 estimated the whole value produced annually by capital and labor in Great Britain, at £297,000,000; population at 18,000,000, equal to £16 10s, or $79,22 to each person; while he estimated the value produced to be enjoyed by the Irish people, as less than £6 for each person, or about $28.80,

Table C.

The value produced annually in Great Britain by capital and labor employed in mining, manufactures, the mechanic arts, trade and commerce, navigation and transportation, is estimated in the Westminster Review as follows;

Wages of	1,857,447	adult males at 17s. 6d. per week,	£84,518,388
do.	571,705	do. do. at 15s. do.	22,296,495
do.	448,419	do. do. at 10s. do.	11,658,894
do.	72,395	males under 20 years old at 7s. 6d. per week,	1,411,701
do.	498,508	adult females at 6s. per week,	7,776,724
do.	203,353	females under 20 yrs. old at 4s pr. wk	2,114,870
Total,	3,651,827		£129,777,072
		Deduct for agricultural tools for Ireland,	2,500,000
			£127,277,072
Rental and profits of mines, quarries, ironworks, warehouses, mills, railroads and canals, &c.,			20,000,000
Profits of capital employed in manufactures, and in the distribution of the same, including navigation, the salaries of assistants in retail business, &c.; 25 per cent. on £114,777,072, the wages of labor above stated, except £15,000,000 worth of farming utensils,			28,694,267
Profits of distributing agricultural produce, 20 per cent.			2,879,822
Total for mining, manufactures and commerce,			£203,851,161
Amount for agriculture brought forward,			126,899,111
Total annual value produced in Great Britain,			£330,750,272

This sum for 18,800,000 inhabitants amounts to £17 10s., or about $84 to each.

Estimate of the products of capital and labor in Ireland, over and above the amount paid to non-resident proprietors,

Income from agriculture as above estimated,	£36,500,000
Income from mining, manufactures and mechanic arts,	12,500,000
Income from commerce and navigation, about	12,500,000
Total annually, about	£61,500,000

Equal to about £7 10s., or $36, to each person.

TABLE D.

Summary statement of the NUMBER AND VALUE OF LIVE STOCK IN GREAT BRITAIN IN 1839, according to the estimate of McCulloch and the authorities cited by him in his statistics :

	England and Wales.			Scotland.		
	Number.	Price.	Value in Millions.	Number.	Price.	Value in Millions.
Cattle,	4,120,000	£10	£41.2	1,100,000	£10	£11.
Sheep,	26,148,000	1¼	32.685	3,500,000	1¼	4.375.
Horses,	1,250,000	14	17.500	250,000	14	3.5
Swine and poultry,			2.500			5
Total			£93.885			£19.375.

By referring to table C. of Sec. 1, the reader will see that the number of cattle has decreased since the year 1688, though their aggregate value is nearly five times as great now as it was then. This great increase of price has taken place during a period when the money in circulation in Europe in proportion to the population, has increased only about twenty-five per cent. The price of beef is not over two and a half times as high per pound as it was in 1688, and we may fairly conclude from this, that the improvements in agriculture have been such, during the last century and a half, as to double the average weight of cattle, and thereby increase their value five fold. The number of horses has also remained about the same, though their value has increased nearly six fold. As to sheep, their number has more than doubled, and yet their average value has increased about thirty-five per cent. These are curious facts, illustrating the effect of supply and demand on price. When the population was small in proportion to the stock of horses and cattle in 1688, the prices of such animals were very low, but since the population has become large, the demand large and the supply the same, prices have advanced in a most astonishing manner. Cattle in our western and southern States are worth nominally less now than they were in England in 1688; in the northern district of New York and western district of Pennsylvania, perhaps about the same as in England in 1688 ; but near the large cities, and in or near the populous manufacturing districts of New England, prices are much higher.

In 1771, the capital, other than real estate, employed in agriculture in England and Wales, was estimated by Arthur Young at about £4 per acre, or about £124,000,000 ; in 1839 McCulloch estimated it at from £6 to £7 per acre, or about

£200,000,000; and £30,000,000 in Scotland. This includes the live stock as above stated, wagons, harness, ploughs, and other farming utensils, the seed and labor invested in the growing crops, and the stock of provisions, fuel, &c. on hand, to enable the farmer to carry on his business.

SEC. 6. *Products of the manufacturing and mining industry of Great Britain, and the capital invested; also the foreign investments.*

Summary statement in millions sterling, of the ANNUAL VALUE OF THE PRODUCTS of GREAT BRITAIN; and of the NET VALUE PRODUCED BY CAPITAL AND LABOR deducting materials, mostly according to the estimates made by McCulloch in 1839; to which I have added an estimate of the AMOUNT OF CAPITAL EMPLOYED, supposing the capital to bear the same proportion to the value of products that it did in the United States, according to the census of 1840. I have estimated the aggregate value of houses, vessels, furniture, carriages, wagons, agricultural implements and all articles produced which are not enumerated, except the products of flouring, grist, saw and oil mills, at forty per cent. greater than it was in the United States in 1840; the income of mills the same as in the United States, and the capital in mills only half as much as in the United States:

	Gross Products. Millions.	Net value produced. Millions.	Capital. Millions.
Manufactures of Cotton,	£35.	£26.6	*£34
do Wool,	22.	14.	17
do Linen,	8.	6.	6
do Silk,	10.	7.5	7.5
Hardware, Cutlery, Castings, &c.	9.5	6.333	8.92
Watches, Jewelry, &c.,	3.	1.5	2.5
Leather, Shoes, &c.,	13.5	10.125	5.3
Glass and Earthenware,	4.25	3.188	3.2
Paper,	1.5	.9	1.2
Hats,	2.4	1.44	1.2
	£109.15	£77.586	£86.82

	Gross Products.	Net Value.	Capital.
Iron, 1,150,000 tons,	7.5	5.0	*7.0
Coal, 30,000,000 tons,	15.	14.0	5.0
Copper, 13,000 tons,	1.3	1.1	*2.44
Tin 5,500 tons.	55	5	
Lead, 46,000 tons,	95	8	8
Silver, 10,000 lbs. Troy,	03	025	025
Salt, Alum, and other mineral products,	1.0	7	7
Total of mining, &c.	£26.33	£22.125	£15.965
Houses, ships, and other manufactures,		29,224	20,364
Flouring, grist, saw and oil mills		4,913	6,860
Total of Mining, Manufactures and Mechanic arts,		£133,848	£130,009
Add 10 per cent. for undervaluation, of capital,			13,000
Total			£143,000

I have not the means of stating the tonnage of England, Wales and Scotland at the time of taking the census in 1841, but from the great increase of the tonnage of the British empire from 1835 to 1843, we may conclude the shipping of Great Britain alone amounted in 1841 to about 2,600,000, which at £10 per ton would amount to £26,000,000.

Taking the returns of the United States census of 1840, of the amount of capital employed in commerce, and comparing the amount of the commerce of Great Britain with that of the United States, the capital employed in the former country, including about thirty millions sterling of coin, must amount over and above the shipping to about £126,000,000, making in all about £150,000,000 employed in commerce, navigation, and transportation in Great Britain in 1841, over and above £2,000,000, worth of shipping employed in the fisheries. Taking the returns of the income tax as a guide, which amounted in 1843, to between forty and fifty millions sterling, exclusive of the salaries of clerks, and the earnings of carmen, sailors, and all common laborers, we cannot estimate the earnings of commerce, navigation, and transportation, banking and insurances, which are branches of commerce, including the tolls of railroads

* These are the estimates of McCulloch; and the value of the mines is not included in any of these estimates.

and canals in Great Britain in 1841, at less than £60,000,000 sterling.

McCulloch estimated the income from the fisheries of Great Britain at £3,000,000, and we may estimate the capital employed in the fisheries nearly as much as in the United States, or about £3,000,000. Perhaps it would not be extravagant to estimate the value of furniture, pleasure carriages, plate, jewelry, books, pictures, and ornaments at one fifth part as much as the dwelling houses, which would amount, as shown in table D, of Section 4, to about £153,000,000 over and above what is possessed by farmers and farm laborers, amounting in all to not less than £180,000,000 sterling.

In 1847 Lord George Bentinck presented to the House of Commons of England, a petition in behalf of the British holders of Spanish bonds, in which they prayed for redress against Spain, and for the assistance of that House—stating that the debt of Spain to her foreign creditors amounted to £78,000,000, that for several years past interest had been paid on only £7,105,000, leaving a balance of £70,895,000 on which interest had not been paid. He estimated the amount due from the Government of Spain to British subjects at about £46,000,000; and it was to recover that money, that he presented the petition. Lord Palmerston remarked, "that the time may come when the British Nation may no longer see with the same tranquillity £150,000,000 due to English subjects, the interest and the principal of which are alike unpaid; and that if more proper efforts to fulfil engagements adequately are not made, the government of this country may be compelled by public opinion, aye, and by the votes of Parliament, to deviate from the hitherto established practice, and to insist upon the payment of those debts. Sir, that we have the means to do so, I do not for one moment dispute."

Lord Palmerston must have included in the £150,000,000, on which the interest was unpaid, the amount due from some of the States of this Union, as well as that due from Spain, Mexico, and the South American Republics. And if his estimate is not grossly exaggerated, the whole foreign debt, exclusive of what is due from the colonies to the inhabitants of Great Britain, including the value of all foreign stocks held by them, must exceed £300,000,000. The debts and stocks on which interest and dividends are paid must exceed the amount on which there is a default to pay interest. The amount of state, railroad, canal, and bank stocks of the United States, including city bonds, held in Great Britain, exceeded $100,000,000, or £20,000,000, and our mercantile debt to the British merchants, manufacturers, and miners, was probably about half as much, or £10,000,000. The debt of Mexico and the Mexicans to Great Britain, including British capital invested in mining in Mexico, has been generally estimated at over £20,000,000.

The estimate of Lord Palmerston appears extravagant, and yet I cannot doubt that the whole amount invested by resident citizens of Great Britain in the stocks and property of other coun-

tries, including the whole mercantile debt due them, exceeded in 1841, over and above bad debts,	£200,000,000
The debts of the East India Company in April, 1834, amounted to	35,463,483
and those debts were nearly all due to citizens of Great Britain. The stock of the company is nearly all held by citizens of Great Britain and amounts to	6,000,000
Amount invested by citizens of Great Britain in property and debts, in Canada and the other British colonies, perhaps three fourths as much as in India, or	30,000,000
McCulloch estimates the rents in Ireland due to absentee proprietors, (citizens of Great Britain,) at £3,500,000, which would represent a capital of about	100,000,000
Total amount,	£371,000 000
invested by the resident citizens of Great Britain in their colonies and other countries. With the exception of the investment in Ireland, it yields an income of about six per cent. per annum, amounting in all, to about	£19,000,000

Sec. 7. *Income from, and capital invested in the several departments of industry in Great Britain in* 1841 ; *rental and value of property at different periods.*

Table A.

Summary statement or estimate of the TOTAL AMOUNT OF PRIVATE PROPERTY, and THE INCOME in 1841, from property, labor, and business of all the inhabitants of the Island of Great Britain, in millions of pounds sterling.

	Property.	Income.
Lands as stated in table D. Sec. 4,	£1,281	
Other real estate, "	1,039	

	Property.	Income.
Farming capital over and above lands as stated in Section 5,	£230	£134
Manufactures and mining (£106,-000,000 capital reckoned in, with real estate deducted),	54	133
Commerce, navigation, and transportation,	150	60
Fisheries,	3	3
Furniture, pleasure carriages, plate, books, jewelry, &c.,	180	
Total in Great Britain,	£2,937	£330
Inhabitants in 1841, about 18,500,000, including the army and navy; am't to each,	£159	*£17 16s.
Equal in federal money to each person,	$763	$85.50
Am'nt invested in foreign stocks and in debts, and property in the colonies, and in foreign countries,	£371	£19
Grand total in millions,	£3,308	£349
Amounting for each person to	179	*18 17s.
Equal in federal money to	$859 00	$90.

TABLE B.

Summary recapitulation of THE VALUE of the PROPERTY of Great Britain in the year 1833, extracted from Table XVI., general estimate of the public and private property in England and Wales, Scotland and Ireland; by Pebrer, on the taxation, debt, capital, resources, &c., of the whole British Empire; a work of high authority, published in London in 1833.

	Millions.	Millions.
England and Wales,		
Productive private property,	£2,054.6	£2,428.9
Unproductive, "	374.3	
Scotland,		
Productive private property,	318.3	369.4
Unproductive, "	51.1	
Great Britain TOTAL PRIVATE PROPERTY in 1833,		£2,798.3

* The use or rents of dwelling houses is not included in either of these estimates. See Table B, of Section 4.

Population in 1833, including army and navy, about 17,000,000, equal to £164 12s. or $790 to each person, being equal to $802 to each person in England and Wales, and $721 in Scotland.

	Millions.	
In Ireland,		
Productive private property,	£622.1	£738,500,000
Unproductive "	116.4	

Equal to £92 19s., or about $451 to each person.

Public property in England and Wales,	£42	£103,800,000
" Scotland,	3.9	
" Ireland,	11.9	
" common to Great Britain and Ireland, as the navy, military and ordnance stores,	46	

These estimates of Pebrer include only the property in Great Britain, and not the stocks, property, and debts in the British colonies and foreign countries, and in Ireland, belonging to citizens of Great Britain. The reader will see that the private property, according to his estimate, amounted to a little more to each individual in 1833, than it did in 1841, according to my estimate. As to the amount of private property in Ireland, it appears to me that Pebrer has greatly over estimated it. Taking the value of the products of Ireland as a guide, I cannot estimate the whole amount of private property at more than £550,000,000, about £100,000,000 of which belongs to non-resident proprietors, citizens of Great Britain. There is very little capital in Ireland invested in either mining, manufactures, or foreign commerce, and it seems to me impossible that the amount of property should be so great as estimated by Pebrer, when the business and products are comparatively so small.

TABLE C.

Summary statement of the ANNUAL INCOME OR RENTAL OF REAL ESTATE OF ALL KINDS IN ENGLAND AND WALES at the under-mentioned years, as stated *ante* sections 1, 3, and 4; the real value of the same, and the number of years rent of such value. The estimated rent of houses in 1770 and 1800, is added to the estimated rental of the lands, as stated in section 3:

In year.	Rental of real estate.	Value of real estate. Millions.	Years rent.
1600	£ 5,400,000	£ 75½	14
1688 and 1705,	13,000,000	208	16
1770	20,000,000	400	20
1800	32,000,000	700	22
1815	53,495,368	1,284	24
1843	85,802,684	2,060	24

TABLE D.

Estimated VALUE OF THE PERSONAL ESTATE IN ENGLAND AND WALES during the undermentioned years, the proportion or per cent. which the personal bears to the real estate, and the AGGREGATE VALUE OF THE PERSONAL AND REAL ESTATE. The proportion between the personal and real estate in 1815 and 1843, is nearly the same as stated in Table A, of this section.

In Year.	Per Cent.	Personal Estate. Millions.	Personal & Real Estate. Millions.
1600, nearly	14	£ 10½	£ 86
1688 and 1705,	16⅔	35	243
1770,	20	80	480
1800,	24	168	868
1815,	28	360	1,644
1843,	30	618	2,678

The above is the supposed nominal value, without taking into consideration the amount of money in proportion to the population at each period. When this is taken into consideration, and the comparative value ascertained, by taking the amount of money at the present time as the standard, and adding to the nominal valuation at periods when the amount of money was less, and deducting from it when the amount of money was greater, the difference appears much less.

TABLE E.

Summary statement or estimate of the POPULATION of England and Wales, at the undermentioned periods; the COMPARATIVE VALUE, (taking the amount of money in circulation into consideration,) of the PRIVATE PROPERTY IN THE KINGDOM; the per cent. which is added to or deducted from the nominal value of property to ascertain the comparative value, and the AMOUNT AND ANNUAL INCOME FROM PROPERTY AND LABOR to each person. Also, the amount in 1843, including foreign debts, stocks, and property in Ireland, the colonies, and other countries. The annual income from property and labor, and also the value of property in the years 1200 and 1500, are estimated from the amount in the years 1600 and 1700, and the subsequent years, and from the comparative condition and commerce of the country at those several periods, taking into consideration the present condition and productive industry of Mexico and the South American States, as stated in Section 10 of this chapter.

Years.	Population. Millions.	Per Cent. add.	Per Cent. deduct.	Comparative value of private property. Millions.	Am't to each person. Property.	Am't to each person. Income.
1200,	1.9			£ 40	$100	$24
1500,	3.1			85	130	28
1600,	4.4	75		150	165	32
1700,	5.5	12		270	235	40
1770,	7.1		6	450	300	50
1800,	8.8		19	700	380	75
1815,	11.0		33⅓	1,096	480	90
1843,	16.0			2,678	800	85
1843, foreign debts, &c. included,				3,050	900	90

The reader should bear in mind, that these are not vague estimates of individuals made in gross, without a knowledge of details; but so far as regards the rental of the years 1688, 1811, 1815 and 1843, they are official valuations made by government officers in detail, in the several counties, cities, towns, boroughs, and districts of the Kingdom, for the purposes of taxation; and they may be relied upon as approximating very nearly to accuracy; as near as it was possible to make them. All the calculations of the value of property are based upon those official valuations, reference being had to the increase of population, commerce and productive industry, from one period to another; and the estimates of the incomes, or value produced by capital and labor at different periods, were mostly made by men of the highest intelligence, possessing the most ample means of acquiring information, and are partially founded on the official records of the Kingdom. Wherever I have differed from them, or made estimates of my own, it will appear from a careful examination of the work. Many of the estimates of personal estate are my own, drawn from a comparison between the proportions which personal estate bears to real estate in the United States. As a country grows older and wealthier, personal property increases more rapidly than the enhancement in value of real estate.

The increase of wealth in Great Britain during the present century, is without example in the history of the old world. Previous to the year 1790, the steam engine, and the machinery of England for the manufacture of cotton, wool, silk, and iron, had been brought to a high degree of improvement and efficiency, and before the year 1800, a very large amount of capital was invested in machinery, in mining and manufacturing industry, which was equal to the labor of six or eight million persons in enhancing the productive industry of the Kingdom. See Section 14 of the first chapter of these essays. During this period also, the demand for British manufactures was fully equal to the supply, and at most extravagant prices. Though recently invented machinery had increased the productive powers of the manufacturers from ten to twenty fold, yet prices were actually higher than they were the latter part of the 17th century, and the fore part of the 18th, when everything was manufactured by hand. See Chap. XII., sections 26 to 32 inclusive. The great increase in the amount and value of productive industry, and all the materials and elements of wealth, as well as in the population, during this period, increased the demand for real estate so rapidly, that we may fairly attribute half of the increased value of private property in the Kingdom, as estimated in Table E, to the enhanced value of lands, city, town, and village lots alone, independent of the increased amount and value of the improvements made on them. For an illustration of the causes of this rise of real estate, see Chap. XII., Sec. 7. The increase of wealth in Great Britain, and particularly in Scotland, was very slow prior to the year 1770; and if the reader inquire into the cause of its unparalleled increase since that time, he will find that the primary cause was neither agriculture nor commerce; but the increase in manufacturing and mining industry; which furnished the materials, and formed the basis of commerce, and caused its rapid increase, as well as the increased demand for, and enhanced prices of, agricultural products, farming lands, and other real estate. This truth will be further illustrated by reference to the increased wealth in the manufacturing states of this Union.

SEC. 8. *Productive industry of Holland and Belgium.*

The means of estimating the value of the private property and the income of the people of France, Holland, and Belgium at different periods, are not so complete as they are in relation to Great Britain. All the statistics collected by the government of those countries, which have come within my notice, are more or less partial and incomplete; and none of them cover the whole ground, like the census of the United States of 1840, and the income taxes of Great Britain.

Murray, in his Encyclopædia of Geography, which was written about the year 1834, says, "Careful inquiries carried on by the government of the Netherlands, (including Holland and Belgium,) are considered as having proved that the agricultural capital of the whole country amounted to 10,395,000,000 francs; equal to about $1,950,000,000. He says the following estimate was made of the LANDS CULTIVATED and the ANNUAL VALUE of the AGRICULTURAL PRODUCTS OF THE COUNTRY; which is stated in hectares and francs, and I have reduced them to acres and federal money.

	Acres cultivated.	Value.
Wheat,	864,000	$28,875,000
Rye,	1,728,000	31,500,000
Buckwheat,	500,000	6,000,000
Barley,	710,000	15,750,000
Oats,	740,000	15,750,000
Potatoes,	323,000	7,687,500
Peas and Beans,	271,000	9,000,000
Vegetables,	227,000	10,312,500
Orchards,	133,000	562,500
Hemp and flax,	520,000	23,625,000
Madder,	74 000	3,937,500
Cattle and other animals,		28,125,000
	6,090,000	$181,125,000
Value produced annually by mining and manufacturing industry, estimated from the materials collected by Murray and others at		144,000,000
The income from commerce, navigation, and transportation in Great Britain and the United States, is estimated as equal to more than one fifth part as much as from all other employments and business, call it one fifth,		65,000,000
Total,		$390,125,000

for the whole income from labor, business and capital of the people of Holland and Belgium per year, at that time, equal to sixty dollars to each inhabitant.

There can be no reasonable doubt that from the tenth to the middle of the eighteenth century, the Netherlands were greatly in advance of both England and France in productive industry, commerce, and wealth, in proportion to the population. From the time of the crusades to the year 1567, when the Duke of Alva was sent by the King of Spain to crush the rising spirit of Protestantism in the Low Countries, Flanders (now Belgium,) was much in advance of the country, afterwards known as the Seven United Provinces, or Holland. Flanders was ravaged by the Duke of Alva, with the sword and pillage ; great numbers of the people were destroyed, and thousands fled the country, and from that period Holland made the most rapid strides in productive industry, commerce, and wealth, of any country in Europe, and continued the wealthiest kingdom in the world in proportion to the population, down to the commencement of the French revolution of 1789. In 1690 Sir Wm. Petty estimated the shipping of the Hollanders at 900,000 tons, and that of all the other countries of Europe at only 1,100,000 tons; and McCulloch expresses the opinion that this estimate was rather within than beyond the mark.

The foreign commerce of Holland was ruined by the wars growing out of the French revolution, and by the continental system of Napoleon; and from 1790 to 1814, that country made no advancement; but since the close of the war in 1815, both Holland and Belgium, and more particularly the latter, have been making rapid advances in productive industry, wealth, and population. McCulloch says that Holland, notwithstanding the depression of her commerce, was the richest country in Europe at the close of the war in 1815.

The agricultural capital of the United States is estimated as equal to about three fifths of all the private property, exclusive of slaves. The proportion of personal estate is greater in Holland and Belgium, than in the United States.

	Millions.
Agricultural capital of Holland and Belgium in 1833, as estimated by the government,	$1,950
All other private property 45 per cent.,	1,595
Total,	$3,545

equal to nearly $550 to each inhabitant.

SEC. 9. *Property and productive industry of France, and the amount to each person at different periods, compared with Great Britain.*

TABLE A.

The INCOME OF ALL THE INHABITANTS OF FRANCE arising from AGRICULTURE, MANUFACTURES, MINING, COMMERCE, and RETAIL TRADE, CAPITAL, AND PRODUCTIVE INDUSTRY OF ALL KINDS, at different periods, was estimated some years since by M. Dupin, in francs, as stated in the following table; to which I have added the population at the respective periods, and the amount of income to each person in dollars and cents:

Years.	Income in millions of francs.	Population in millions.	Am't to each person
1780,	4,011	24.5	$30 90
1790,	4,655	25.3	34 50
1800,	5,402	27.2	37 12
1810,	6,270	29.5	39 75
1820,	7,362	30.4	45 37
1830,	8,800	32.5	48 88

The value of the products of agriculture and the entire industry of France was estimated in "Le Bulletin de la Societé de Geographie," Nov. 1829, at only 6,396,019,000 francs; being only about $37 to each person.

TABLE B.

The quantities in hectolitres, and the value of the various agricultural products of France in 1841, were ascertained or estimated by the government, from which, and the estimates of various products of France collected by McCulloch in his Geographical Dictionary, and by Murray in his Encyclopædia of Geography, I have compiled the following TABLE OF THE ANNUAL INCOME OF THE INHABITANTS OF FRANCE. In some cases where the estimates were vague or entirely wanting, I have added my own, by comparison with the productive industry of the United States in the same branches.

		Millions.
Grain of all kinds, 190,986,636 hectolitres, or about 542,210,000 bushels, valued at	$396,910,000	$357.22
Deduct for seed, one tenth part,	39,690,000	
Vegetable products of all kinds, including wine, brandy, cider, and beer, valued at		155.5
Wool, 42,000,000 kilo., about 94,000,000 pounds,		24
Butter, cheese, milk, eggs, and the flesh of animals consumed annually, including their skins, my estimate,		250
Fuel and timber cut annually,		28
Manufactures of cloths of all kinds, leather, the metals, &c., Berghaus' estimate (less one third for materials),		268.43
Add for undervaluation and omissions by Mr. Berghaus,		31.57
Net products of flouring, saw, and oil mills, less four fifths for materials, my estimate,		30
Produced by mining and smelting metals, quarrying stone, &c., partly my estimate,		40
Erecting houses and other buildings, building vessels, making cabinet-ware, wagons, carriages, agricultural tools, and other minor manufactures, and the products of mechanical labor, my estimate about the same as in Great Britain, *ante*, section 7,		140
Products of fisheries, my estimate,		7
Income from commerce, retail trade, navigation and transportation, one fifth part as much as from all other employments and business,		266.3
Total,		$1,598.02

The population in 1840 was about 34,000,000, and the average income to each person by this calculation, about $47. The total value of the products of the mines and manufactures of France was estimated about the year 1830, by Murray, at 2,000,000,000 francs—from which deduct the value of the raw materials, and the amount will fall greatly below my estimate for 1840.

There was a very great increase, amounting to about thirty per cent. in value, and to over forty per cent. in the aggregate quantity of grain and potatoes, produced annually, between the years 1801 and 1841. This increase is evidence of itself of great improvements in agriculture. The foreign commerce of France more than doubled between 1780 and 1840. The mining industry increased eight or ten fold, and the manufacturing industry increased two or three fold also. We have, therefore, good reasons to believe that the annual income from capital and labor of the people of France doubled between the years 1780 and 1840; and though M. Dupin's estimate of the income in 1830 may be too high, and the amount for 1780 too low, yet none of them are probably very far from the truth. I see no reason to suppose that there was much improvement between the years 1780 and 1790, or even between the time of the revocation of the Edict of Nantes in 1685, and the revolution in 1789.

Mr. Murray says, the entire agricultural capital of France, including lands, live stock, farming utensils, &c., was estimated by M. Chaptal at 37,500,000,000 francs, equal to $7,031,350,000. No date is given, but this estimate must have been previous to the year 1820. By reference to Table A, in section 7, the reader will see that the agricultural capital, including lands, live stock, &c., of Great Britain, constitutes at this time about one-half of all the property of that wealthy kingdom, and in 1688 the agricultural capital as shown in section one, comprised about two-thirds of all the property of England. About fifty-seven per cent. of all the property in our free States is vested in agricultural capital, including lands, live stock, farming implements, &c., and but forty-three per cent. in every other species of property, as is hereinafter shown. The proportion of mining, manufacturing and commercial capital in France, when compared with the whole property of the kingdom, is less than it is in our free States, and perhaps not much more than it is in the United States, as a whole. We may safely estimate the agricultural capital of France, including lands, &c., as comprising in 1780 about 65 per cent., in 1815 about 62½ per cent., and in 1840 about 59 or 60 per cent. of all the property of the kingdom.

	Millions.
Agricultural capital of France at the close of the war in 1815, per Chaptal,	$7,031,35
Other private property equal to three-eighths or 37½ per cent. of the whole,	4,218,65
Total for about 30,000,000 of inhabitants, equal to $375 to each person.	$11,250
My estimate of agricultural capital in 1840,	$8,000
Other private property equal to forty per cent.	5,333
Total for about thirty-four million inhabitants in 1840, equal to $392 to each person.	$13,333

TABLE C.

On comparing the condition of the people of France and of the Netherlands, and the resources of those countries at different periods with those of Great Britain and the United States, I have deduced the following estimate of the AMOUNT OF PRIVATE PROPERTY, and the ANNUAL INCOME TO EACH PERSON OF FRANCE AND THE NETHERLANDS at the under mentioned years; to which I have brought forward the AMOUNT OF PROPERTY AND ANNUAL INCOMES OF ENGLAND AND WALES, as stated *ante* Table E, of Sec. 7. Also the amount in 1843, including debts, stocks and property in the colonies and foreign countries. The amounts stated are the comparative values on taking into consideration the estimated amount of money at different periods, and comparing it with the amount in 1845, and making additions and deductions, as stated in Table E, Sec. 7.

	France.		Netherlands.		England and Wales.	
Years.	Amt. to each person. Property.	Income.	Amt. to each person. Property.	Income.	Amt. to each person. Property.	Income.
1200	$100	$24	$120	$26	$100	$24
1500	130	28	160	32	130	28
1600	160	30	200	40	165	32
1700	225	34	300	50	235	40
1780	250	36	420	55	300	50
1800	280	38	450	45	380	75
1815	300	40	450	55	480	90
1843	400	50	550	65	800	85
1843	inc. for'n debts &c	50	600	68	900	90

Nothing is put down on account of debts due the people of

France, stocks and property in the colonies and foreign countries; for the amount so due them is so small as not to be worth noticing; while the amount due the people of England is immensely great.

The manufacture of silk was commenced at Lyons in France during the reign of Francis I., the fore part of the 16th century; under Henry IV., several other manufactures were introduced, and many existing ones improved. France, Germany, Switzerland, the Netherlands, and all the kingdoms of Northern Europe except Russia, were agitated with civil wars between the Protestants and Catholics, and with religious persecutions growing out of the Reformation, during the greater part of the sixteenth century. Soon after the commencement of the Reformation, Henry VIII. of England quarrelled with the Pope, threw off the incubus of Popery and Catholicism, and established the Episcopal Church. He thereby secured the internal peace and tranquillity of England for more than a century; and postponed the civil wars until about the year 1640. During all this period England became the asylum of the oppressed and persecuted Protestants from various countries of Europe, who brought with them and established in England, various mechanic arts and manufactures; which have contributed much to the rapid improvement of that kingdom.

In 1579, the Protestants of the Netherlands threw off the yoke of Philip II. of Spain, and established the Republic of the Seven United Provinces, known as Holland, which then became an asylum also for the persecuted Protestants of other countries. Soon after Henry IV., a Protestant prince, ascended the throne of France, he passed the famous Edict of Nantes in 1598; whereby the Protestants were tolerated, and secured in the exercise of their religious privileges, and all their rights as citizens. This edict continued in force eighty-seven years, until the year 1685, when it was revoked by Louis XIV.; the flood-gates of religious persecution again opened, and from five to six hundred thousand Protestants massacred and driven from the kingdom, who comprised many of the best mechanics, artizans, and manufacturers of France.

During the half century previous to passing that edict, when the Protestants were persecuted in France, and fleeing to England for protection, there can be no doubt that England was improving in manufactures, and increasing in productive industry and wealth more rapidly than France; but during the half century next previous to the revocation of that edict, the Protestants enjoyed security in France, and the people enjoyed tranquillity, while England was agitated much of the time with civil wars and internal discord. The grand impulse to manufactures and commerce in France was given during the latter period by Colbert, the minister of finance under Louis XIV. That great minister had the sagacity to see the importance of increasing the manufacturing industry of the kingdom; and in order to do so, he not only adopted a system for the PROTECTION OF DOMESTIC INDUSTRY, BUT INVITED NUMEROUS FOREIGN ARTIZANS TO SETTLE IN FRANCE. The splendid success of this minister, the apparent great improvement in the productive industry of France during his administration, as well as the great power and successes of Louis XIV., leave no room to doubt that in the year 1685 the wealth and productive industry of France in proportion to the population, was fully equal to that of England, and I have so estimated it in Table C. At this period Protestant Holland was greatly in advance of both France and England.

The bloody religious persecutions in France, consequent upon the revocation of the Edict of Nantes, shocked the Protestant mind of England; set in motion the revolutionary spirit which drove James II., a Catholic sovereign, from the country; placed on the throne William of Orange, a Protestant prince, and established permanently the Protestant religion in England. From this period the progress of the two nations was entirely different. The French mind, under the despotic and depressing influences of the clergy and the Catholic religion, seemed to be active only in matters of form, fashion and amusement, and totally incapable of original thought or hardy enterprise. The result was, that the progress of France, during the next century, and up to the time of the revolution in 1789, was at a snail's pace; and less than it was during the seventeenth century. So torpid was the French intellect, that scarcely a single invention or improvement originated in France during this whole period, which has had any material influence upon the welfare and progress of the human family. On the contrary, during the whole of the eighteenth century, the British mind seemed to be active, and produced a constant succession of valuable inventions, and improvements in the steam engine, in mechanics and machinery, and in the mining, smelting, and working of metals, numbering many thousand; which have contributed immensely to increase the productive industry of that nation, and to elevate it to its present condition of wealth and power. What a contrast between the present productive industry and wealth of Great Britain and France as estimated in Table C! and yet, so far as regards the present time, nearly the whole statement is based on record evidence. Since the nation was released from feudalism and the feudal aristocracy, and the French mind from the dominion of the Catholic clergy, by the revolution of 1789, France has made rapid progress in productive industry and wealth.

SEC. 10. *Productive industry and condition of Mexico, and the South American States.*

There is very little information to be obtained from books, of the productive industry and wealth of Mexico, and the South American States. Baron Humboldt spent nearly two years in Mexico, in 1803 and 1804, and his Essays on Nouvelle Espagne furnish the most reliable and accurate information which I have met with on the subject. The following information is derived from his essays: Mexico suffers for want of water and navigable rivers. Except the Rio Grande Del Norte, and the Rio Colorado, all the rivers of Mexico are mere mountain torrents. "A great part of the table land of Anahuac, (Central Mexico,) is destitute of vegetation, and its arid aspect in some places brings to mind the plains of the two Castiles. Several causes concur to produce this effect. The evaporation which takes place in great plains is sensibly increased by the great elevation of the Mexican Cordillera." "The aridity of the central plain, and the scarcity of trees, obstruct very much the working of the mines." "The extreme droughts to which Mexico is exposed compel the inhabitants in a great part of this vast country, to have recourse to artificial irrigation." "In places which are not artificially watered, the Mexican soil yields pasturage only to the months of March and April." The cultivator frequently loses his harvest from the effects of frost. "Maize (or Indian corn,) is the principal food of the inhabitants and also of the most part of domestic animals. When the harvest is poor, either from want of rain or premature frost, the famine is general, and produces the most fatal consequences." "The frightful dearth of 1784 was the consequence of a heavy frost on the 28th of August, at the inconsiderable height of 1,800 metres." (5,900 feet.)

The reader can judge from these extracts, of the natural resources of Mexico. The country seems almost destitute of every natural facility for commerce and manufactures; and is frequently visited with early frosts, and afflicted with annual droughts, which render artificial irrigation necessary to success in agriculture.

Baron Humboldt estimated the average annual crop of wheat in Mexico at that time (1803,) at 5,000,000 bushels, (or less than one bushel to each inhabitant;) and the average price at from 65 to 80 cents per bushel, throughout the country, and $1,50 in the city of Mexico. The annual crop of Indian corn he estimated at 30,000,000 bushels, and its price from 25 cents to $2,50 per bushel, depending on the season and the place.

The population of the Intendancy of Guadalaxara in 1803, was estimated at 630,500, on a territory of 86,508 square miles, lying just south of the tropic, on the western declivity of the Cordillera, along both banks of the Rio Santiago, to the Pacific Ocean. This Intendancy then comprised about one-ninth part of all the inhabitants of Mexico. M. Humboldt says its PRODUCTS WERE ESTIMATED BY THE INTENDANT for the year 1802, as follows:

Indian corn, 1,657,000 fanegas or about	3,000,000 bush.
Wheat, 43,000 cargas, about	240,000 bush.
Cotton, 17,000 tercios, worth $5 the tercio,	$85,000
Cochineal, 20,000 lbs., at three francs per lb.,	11,250
The value of all the agricultural products was estimated at $2,599,000, and the products of manufacturing and mechanical industry at $3,302,200. Total,	$5,901,000
Equal to about $9 35 to each inhabitant.	
3,000,000 bushels of corn at fifty cents would amount to	$1,500,000
240,000, bushels of wheat, at 75 cents,	180,000
Cotton and cochineal, about	100,000
Leaving for other grains and vegetables, fruits, butter, cheese, with wool and all other animal products, but	819,000

It strikes me that this last item is too low, when we take into consideration the value of the other products of agriculture, and the products of mechanical and manufacturing industry.

M. Humboldt estimated for the whole of Mexico:

Indian corn, 30,000,000 bushels at 50 cents,	$15,000,000
Wheat, 5,000,000 at 80 cents,	4,000,000
Cotton and cochineal, nine times as much as in Guadalaxara,	866,000
All other vegetable products, and all animal products, perhaps were twelve times as much as estimated in said Intendancy,	10,000,000
Products of mechanical and manufacturing industry, nine times as much as in said Intendancy,	29,720,000
Products of the mines of gold and silver at that time, about	20,000,000
Income from commerce equal to 12½ per cent. of all the above products,	11,369,000
Total,	$90,955,000

for a population of about 5,600,000, equal to sixteen dollars to each person.

From 1820 to 1845, the mines were less productive, and averaged annually less than $12,000,000. How insignificant the product of the Mexican mines when compared with the mining industry or the cotton manufacture of Great Britain, or even with the cotton manufacture of the United States!

A correspondent of the New York Tribune, writing from New Granada in December, 1847, says, the people of this commonwealth live in about 300,000 houses, seven-eighths of which are not worth one hundred dollars apiece; and lands have very little value: proprietors of 20,000 or 30,000 acres near rivers, not deriving from them $500 rent per annum.

These facts present a tolerably accurate view, not only of Mexico, but of all South and Central America. All those countries are rather pastoral than agricultural, and the utmost value of their productive industry does not exceed fifteen or twenty dollars per annum to each person, or about one fifth part as much as that of France, and but little over one sixth part as much as that of Great Britain; and the comparative value of property in Mexico and the South American States, is equally small. Agriculture is always at a low ebb, lands and the products of flocks of but little value, and the people generally poor, in all countries, where there is but little manufacturing industry, and the population is sparse.

Sec. 11. *Productive industry and condition of Spain and Portugal at different periods, compared with England, France, Italy, &c.*

Spain and Portugal both retrograded in productive industry and declined in population under the despotism of Popery and the Inquisition, during the 17th and 18th centuries, and the latter part of the 16th; and their condition at the present time (1851,) is not very different from what it was three hundred years since. So far as we can infer the relative condition of the several countries of Europe from the facts of history, we have reason to believe that from the year 1200 up to 1550, there was no great difference in the productive industry, wealth, and condition of the people of England, France, Spain, and Portugal; and that the people of Italy and the Netherlands were far in advance of all the other nations of Europe.

The reader has only to look back to the estimates of the productive industry of England and France, to enable him to make a tolerably correct estimate in relation to Spain and Portugal; and he can then understand the causes and appreciate fully the fact of the poverty and weakness of the latter kingdoms, and the great power and wealth of Great Britain, and the increasing wealth of France since the revolution of 1789. The great mass of the people of Mexico and South America, being of Indian descent, enervated by the heat of the climate, sunk in ignorance, and depressed by ecclesiastical and military despotism, must be in a worse condition, and have less productive industry and wealth than the people of western Europe had at the end of the 12th century; and yet it is not probable that the difference can be very great. The facts which are collected by Baron Humboldt of the condition and productive industry of Mexico, furnish, perhaps, the best evidence we have of the relative amount of the productive industry of the nations of western Europe prior to the Crusades.

Taking the climate into consideration, $16 per year for each person in Mexico and South America, is as good as $20 in Spain and Italy, or $24 in England.

SEC. 12. *Mode of estimating the annual income from Agriculture in the United States.*

In estimating the aggregate value of the productive industry, and the amount of the income of a country, great care is necessary to avoid estimating many things twice; once in their original condition as raw materials, and again when converted into something else. Professor Tucker estimates the annual product of live stock, that is, the increase of horses, mules, cattle, sheep, and hogs, and the product of those killed annually, at one-fourth part, or twenty-five per cent. of their gross value at the time of taking the census in 1840. Hay and some grain also, as well as grass, sustain the cattle and sheep, and produce the wool and the products of the dairy; we estimate the hay and pasture in the wool, butter, cheese, milk, and the animal products, and it is just as reasonable to estimate the pasture separately, as the hay. The horses are mere instruments in producing the grain and other products; and the value of the hay grass and grain consumed by them are included in the products of their labor, and should not be put down separately. They are used to raise oats, corn, etc., but they eat the oats and much of the corn, together with large quantities of hay and pasture, and it would be a gross error to estimate all these as net products of agriculture.

The flesh of horses is valueless, and their annual increase in the United States is less than three per cent.; but inasmuch as great numbers of horses raised in the western States, north of the 35th degree of latitude, mostly on grass and hay, are annually sold to the southern cotton planters, and many are used for purposes of pleasure, commerce, manufactures, etc., I have estimated their annual net products, over and above the grain consumed by them in those States at 12½ per cent. of the value of the whole stock; in the other States north of the 35th degree of latitude, I have estimated the net income at five per cent.; but in the States south of that line there is no net income from their increase.

The greater part of the Indian corn is fed to cattle and hogs, and converted into beef and pork, and the beef and pork is estimated in the shape of corn. Some of the corn is fed also to sheep. The beef made on grass, and the veal, mutton, the lambs killed, and the pork made with grass and the slops of the dairy, over and above the value of the grain fed to cattle, sheep and hogs, may be equal annually, including the increase, to one-fourth part the whole value of these animals in the summer, before fattening, as estimated by Professor Tucker.

These are the principles on which my estimates of animal products are based. As the census gives the number only, and not the value of animals, their valuation in the several States is but an estimate of my own, though it does not generally differ materially from that of Professor Tucker. The same may be said of grain and some other products; the census gives the quantities only, and not their value.

In estimating the annual value of products, my aim has been to estimate their average value during the last seven or eight years at the places of production, or where they are sold by the producer. The prices of grain are estimated, as stated in Chap XII. sec. 37.

The value of hay as well as pasture consumed by farm-horses and other stock, should not be reckoned separately; but in the commercial cities and large towns, considerable quantities of hay are consumed by horses used for pleasure, commerce and other purposes not agricultural, which are sold by the farmer, and should be estimated as part of the income from agriculture. I have therefore estimated with the products of agriculture one-third of the hay in New Hampshire, and half the hay in the other States on the seaboard, from Maine to Maryland, excepting the northern district of New York and the western district of Pennsylvania; the value of the hay in all the remaining portions of the United States is supposed to be included with animal products.

One half of the value of goods or cloths made in families, is deducted for materials, dyeing and dressing, and the remaining half is included with the products of agriculture.

The census of the United States of 1850 shows an average of nearly five acres of improved lands in each of the States to each inhabitant; and the censuses taken by the State of New York in

1825, 1835, and 1845, show about the same result. On that basis I have estimated the quantity of land cleared and fenced in the United States, (mostly in the Western and South-Western States,) during the year 1839 at 2,200,000 acres; at a cost of $12 per acre, equal to $26,400,000. This amount is apportioned among the several States according to the supposed amount of their agricultural improvements, and is added to the products of agricultural industry. I have also added $6,000,000 for draining and other improvements made on agricultural lands in the United States during the year.

SEC. 13. *Agricultural products of the United States in* 1839.

Summary statement of the agricultural products of the United States, according to the census of 1840; and an estimate of the value produced by agriculture and agricultural laborers during the previous year:

			Millions.
Wheat,	*84,207,272	bush., less one-ninth for seed, at 77 cents,	$57.6
Barley,	4,161,504	bush., less one-ninth for seed, at 50 cents,	1.84
Oats,	123,071,341	bush., less 1-12 at 27 cts.,	30.46
Rye,	18,645,567	bush., less 1-9, at 50 cts.,	8.28
Buckwheat,	7,291,743	bush., less 1-12, at 50 cts.,	3.34
Indian corn,	377,531,875	bush., at 28 cts.,	105.7
Potatoes,	108,298,060	bush., less 1-12, at 20 cts.,	19.85
Wool,	35,802,114	lbs., at 30 cts.,	10.74
Hops,	1,238,502	lbs., at 10 cts.,	.12
Wax,	628,303	lbs., at 25 cts.,	.15
Hemp and flax,	†83,577	tons, at $110,	9.19
Tobacco,	219,163,319	lbs., at 4 5-8 cts.,	10.14
Rice,	80,841,422	lbs., at 2½ cts.,	2.02
Cotton,	790,479,275	lbs., at 7¼ cts.,	57.30
Silk cocoons,	61,552½	lbs., at $2,	.12
Sugar, La.,	119,947,720	lbs., at 4 cts.,	4.79
Sugar, in other States,	35,163,089	lbs., at 8 cts.,	2.81
Products of dairy, valued at			33.78
Products of orchards, valued at			7.25
Wine made, 124,734 gallons, at $1,			.12
Home made or family goods, less one-half for materials, carding, dressing, etc., valued at			14.51

* 616,000 bushels deducted for error in Carroll county, Tennessee.
† 11,674 tons deducted for error in Virginia.

Products of market gardeners, sold,	2.06
Products of nurseries and florists,	.59
Clearing and fencing 2,200,000 acres of land at $12 per acre,	26.40
Draining and other agricultural improvements,	6.00
Hay, one-third part in New Hampshire and half of crop in Maine, Massachusetts, Rhode Island, Connecticut, south district New York, New Jersey, east district Pennsylvania, Delaware, and Maryland, from $9 to $12 per ton, about	19.00
Horses and mules in the western States, north of the 35th degree of latitude, 1,850,765, at $40 each, $74,030,600; income from increase and sale for pleasure, manufactures and commerce, at 12½ per ct.,	9.25
Horses and mules in all the other States north of the 35th degree of latitude, and in Arkansas, 1,833,138, at $50 each, $91,656,900; income from increase, etc., at 5 per ct.,	4.58
Neat cattle in the free States, 7,567,020, at an average value of nearly $12 each, $90,800,000; net income from flesh and increase, at 25 per cent.,	22.7
Cattle in the slave States, 7,404,556, at $8 each, $59,236,528; net income from flesh and increase, at 25 per cent.,	14.8
Sheep in the free States, 12,144,468, at $1 62½ each, $19,734,760; net income from flesh and increase, at 25 per cent.,	4.9
Sheep in the slave States, 7,166,906, at $1 37½ each, $9,854,495; net income at 25 per cent.,	2.43
Swine in the free States, 10,090,954, at $2 50 each, $25,228,955; net income from flesh and increase, at 25 per cent.,	6.3
Swine in the slave States, 16,210,336, at $2 each, $32,420,672; at 25 per cent.,	8.1
Poultry, as valued by the census,	9.34
Eggs and poultry, over and above poultry and the grain consumed by them,	3.
Milk and cream consumed by farmers, not returned with the census, estimated at	11.
Products of domestic gardens not returned, estimated at	10.
Total,	$539.9

This table includes for wool, the products of dairy, the flesh and skins of cattle, sheep, and swine slaughtered, the increase of horses, cattle, sheep, and swine, and the products of poultry over and above the grain consumed by animals, the aggregate sum of $130,000,000. This amount, the reader should remember, was produced by pasturage, hay, and other fodder, and the labor of taking care of the stock ; and in addition to this, the hay sold is estimated at $19,000,000, and the hay and pasturage consumed by farm horses would amount to at least $30,000,000, making the whole value of hay and pasturage, when converted into animal products, equal to about $179,000,000 ; when the whole value of the crop of grain, over and above seed, amounted to only about $207,200,000.

Great delusion has existed in the public mind in relation to the value of the annual crop of Indian corn in the United States.*

SEC. 14. *Manufactures and the mechanic arts—their net products, capital, and number of persons employed.*

Statement of the capital and number of persons employed in manufactures and the mechanic arts in the United States according to the census of 1840, and the net value produced by capital and labor, after deducting from the gross value returned the estimated per centage thereof for the value of the materials used : also, statement of the amount of capital to each person employed, and the average net value produced by capital and labor to each person.

PRODUCTS.	Per cent. deducted for materials.	Net value produced in millions.	Capital in millions.	Persons employed.	Capital to each person.	Value to each person.
Machinery, - - -	33⅓	$7.32		13,001		$563
Hardware, cutlery, &c., -	45	3.55		5,492		646
Cannon 274, small-arms 88,073—value estimated, - - -		.75		1,744		430
Precious metals, - -	75	1.18	$20.62	1,556	$381	760
Various metals, - -	60	3.91		6,677		587
Granite, marble, &c., - -	20	1.95		3,734		525
Bricks and lime, - -	20	7.79		22,807		341
		$26.45	$20.62	55,011		
Woollen goods, - -	55	$9.3	$15.76	21,342	$738	$437
Cotton, - - -	40	27.81	51.1	72,119	708	386
Silk, - - -	25	.09	.27	767	357	117
Linen, - - -	25	.24	.2	1,628		148
Mixed goods, - -	40	3.93	4.37	†13,405	326	292
Hats and caps, - -	40	5.22	4.48	20,176	223	332
Straw bonnets, - -	10	1.43				
Leather, boots, shoes, and saddlery—less for hides, - -	25	24.85	28.53	a92,000	310	270
Soap at 5 cents per lb. -	10	2.24				
Tallow candles at 11 cents -	70	.59	2.76	5,641	488	549
Sperm and wax candles at 30 cents,	70	.26				
Distilled liquors at 25 cents, -	60	4.14	9.15	12,223	746	465
Beer at 16⅔ cents per gallon, -	60	1.55				

* (See on this point, and the quantity of the crop, section 3 of chapter xi. and sections 33 and 37 of chapter xii.)

† Deducted 2,500 for obvious error in Kentucky.

Products.	Per cent. deducted for materials.	Net value produced in millions.	Capital in millions.	Persons employed.	Capital to each person.	Value to each person.
Tobacco, - - -	40	$3.49	$3.43	8,384	$410	$416
Gunpowder at 12½ cents, -	50	56	.87	496	1,755	1,130
Drugs, medicines, paints, &c., -	66⅔	1.38	4.5	1,848	2,439	867
Turpentine and varnish, -	66⅔	22				
Glass, - - -	33⅓	1.92	2.08	3,236	644	595
Earthenware, - -	10	.99	.55	1,612	344	616
Sugar refined, - -	80	.65				
Chocolate, - - -	75	.02	1.77	1,355	1,306	915
Confectionery, - -	50	.57				
Paper, - - -	50	3.07	4.74	4,726	1,004	650
Printing and binding, -						
Books, newspapers, &c. estimated, .		5.0	5.87	11,523	510	433
Cordage, - - -	60	1.63	2.46	4,464	552	366
Musical instruments, - -	30	64	.73	908	809	700
Waggons and carriages, -	30	7.63	5.55	21,994	252	346
Ship building, - -	50	3.5	n't stat'd	8,000 *b*		
Furniture, - - -	30	5.3	6.99	18,003	387	293
Houses built, - -	45	*22.42	not stated	85,501		332
Add for repairs, &c., - -	40	6.				
Products of flouring, saw, and oil mills, - - -	75	†23.58	65.86	60,788	1,084	388
All other manufactures, -	33⅓	23.59	21.06	60,000 *c*	350	389
Total net value produced, -		$220.26	$263.7	587,150	$449	$375
Net products except mills, -		196.68	197.84	526,362	375	375
Gross products except mills, -		323.5				
Materials used equal to 39 per cent.		126.8				

* There has been deducted from the gross value of houses erected in Licking County, Ohio, $600,000; and in Pulaski County, Arkansas, $780,000, as stated in Section 19.

† On account of the numerous omissions in the returns of the products of mills in the State of New York, and to make them agree with the returns of the State census of 1835 and 1845, I have added to and raised their net products $2,000,000. I have also raised them $1,000,000 in Pennsylvania, $250,000 in the New England States, and $1,200,000 in the slave States. The census reports the whole products of mills at only $76,545,256, when it is evident that the products of the wheat alone, when ground must have amounted to about as much in value as that sum.

a, *b*, *c*, my estimates of persons employed.

SEC. 15. *Mining, fisheries, and the forest; products of, in* 1840.

Summary statement of the capital, persons employed, and the value produced, over and above materials used, by mining, smelting, and forcing metals, making salt, &c., and in the fisheries and forest in the United States in 1840.

MINING, &c.	Value added.	Value produced. *Millions.*	Capital employed. *Millions.*	Men employed.
About 250,000 tons pig-iron, made,	$30 pr ton.	$7.5		
Bar-iron, 197,233 tons,	40 "	7.88	$20.43	30,497
About 50,000 tons of castings,	40 "	2.		
Lead, 31,239,453 lbs.	2⅛ cts.	.78	*.74	1,017
Gold valued in	census.	.53	.23	1,046
Other metals,	do.	.37	.24	728
Anthracite coal, 863,489 tons,	$1½ pr ton.	1.29	4.35	3,043
Bituminous coal, 27,608,191 bushels,	at 5 cts.	1.38	1.86	3,768
Salt made, 6,179,174 bushels,	at 20 cts.	1.23	†1.95	2,365
Granite, marble, and stone,		3.69	2.54	7,859
Total,		$26.65	32.34	50,323

FISHERIES.	Price.	Value produced. *Millions.*	Capital. *Millions.*	Men.
Dried fish, 773.497 quintals,	at $3	$2.32		
Pickled fish, 472,359 bbls.	at $6	2.83		
Sperm oil, 4,764,708 gallons,	at 90 c.	4.28	$16.43	30,644‡
Whale and fish oil, 7,536,778 gallons,	at 30 c.	2.26		
Whale-bone and other products,		1.15		
		$12.84		
Deduct for wear and tear of vessels, &c. 20 per cent.		2.54		
Total net product of fisheries,		$10.3		

FOREST.	Value produced. *Millions.*	Capital. *Millions.*	Men.
Lumber,	$12.94	Not returned, perhaps $2,400,000 for teams, &c. exclusive of land and mills.	22,042
Tar, pitch, and turpentine, 619,106 bbls. at 16s.	1.23		
Pot and pearl ashes, 15,935½ tons at $100,	1.59		
Skins and furs, census valuation,	1.06		
Ginseng and other products except fuel,	.52		
	$17.34		
Deduct for wear and tear of teams and utensils, and grain eaten by teams, 20 per cent. of lumber,	2.58		
Leaving,	$14.76		
5,088,891 cords of wood sold, estimated at	10.17		
Wood consumed by farmers for fuel, estimated at 20,000,000 cords,	30.		
Total,	$54.93		

* $599,000 deducted for errors in New York.

† $5,040,000 deducted for error in capital at Salina, New York.

‡ 5,940 men deducted for error in the return from Baltimore.

SEC. 16. *Estimates of the income from Commerce, Navigation, and Transportation, in* 1840.

The average annual income of the people of the United States from 1837 to 1842 arising from the distribution and exchange of products (that is, from commerce, retail trade, navigation and transportation), may be estimated as follows. The exports and imports of that period, exclusive of specie, amounted annually on average, to about $220,000,000.

	Millions.
Income, or profits and earnings of American seamen, ship owners, importers, exporting merchants, and insurers, on exports and imports about	$20.
Profits of selling at wholesale $120,000,000 worth of foreign goods at an average of 12½ per cent.,	15
As to the domestic goods, the cottons, woollens, linen silk, and mixed goods, one-third part of the boots, shoes, and saddlery, and perhaps half the distilled liquors, drugs, medicines, paints, oil, glass and earthenware, amounting to about $92,000,000 by the census, they are sold either by the jobbers or wholesale commission merchants, together with the Louisiana sugar, flour and provisions to the amount perhaps of $108,000,000, at an average profit of six per cent.	12.
Selling at retail foreign goods costing $135,000,000, domestic goods bought at wholesale for $100,000,000, books and other articles bought by the retailer of the manufacturer, 15,000,000, at an average profit over transportation of 25 per cent.,	62.5
Selling at retail, sugar, flour and provisions, bought at wholesale for $112,000,000; sugar, flour and provisions, bought of the producer, amounting with iron, to $100,000,000, at an average profit of ten per cent.	21.2
Selling at retail by merchants and grocers, butter, cheese, fruits, vegetables, poultry, eggs, and grain, worth perhaps $80,000,000 at 12½ per cent.	10
Profits of lumber yards and trade, perhaps	5.
Income of butchers and packers,	2.
Income from storage, forwarding, and transporting persons and property, including the coasting business, wharfage, drayage, and tolls on canals and railroads,	36.
Total,	$183.7

Deduct for wear and tear of shipping, stores and warehouses, waggons, horses, &c. used in transportation, and the grain and hay consumed by the horses,	14.7
Leaving for the value produced by commerce, navigation, &c.,	$169.

If we estimate the earnings of the different classes of persons employed, and the income from capital, the result will be as follows—estimating the income from the capital invested at 12½ per cent. per annum.

	Millions.
There were in the United States in 1840, according to the reports of the census, 1,408 commercial houses employed in foreign commerce, and 2,881 commission houses, employing a capital, including navigation, of	$119.29
Also 57,565 retail, dry goods, grocery, and other stores,	250.3
1,793 lumber yards, employing	9.85
Employed in internal transportation, and by butchers and packers,	11.52
	$390.96
Add 10 per cent. for omissions,	39.04
Total capital employed in commerce,	$430.00

Annual profits of the capital at 12½ per cent.,			$53.75
Earnings of 31,515 persons employed in commerce in the cities of New York, Boston, Philadelphia, Baltimore, and New Orleans, at $1,000 each,			31.5
Earnings of 86,092 other persons employed in commerce in the United States, at $600 each,			51.65
Employed in navigating the ocean, exclusive of fishing, about	33,000	65,976, at $350 each,	23.
Employed in navigating rivers, lakes, and canals,	32,976		
Earnings of 4,408 butchers and packers, at $333½ each,			1.6
Income or tolls on railroads and canals in 1840, about			7.5
Amounting in all to the sum of			$169.

for the income from capital and labor employed in commerce, navigation, storage, forwarding, and the transportation of persons and property, including the rent of stores and warehouses, drayage, &c.

SEC. 17. *Mining, manufacturing, fisheries, forest, agriculture, and commerce; their net products, capital, and persons employed.*

Capital invested, with 10 per cent. added for omissions and undervaluations, number of persons employed, and the net value produced by capital and labor in the United States, according to the census of 1840; also the average amount of capital invested and the average amount of income from capital and labor for each person employed, in each of the great departments of industry. No addition is made to the capital invested in fishing, as reported in the census—the capital employed in agriculture and the forest is estimated.

	Net value produced. *Millions.*	Capital employed. *Millions.*	Persons employed.	Capital to each.	Inc. each.
Mining, making iron, castings, salt, &c.	$26.65	$85.6	50,323	$706	$530
Manufactures and the mechanic arts,	196.68	217.69	526,862	412	375
Flouring and grist mills, saw mills, and oil mills, . .	23.58	72.44	60,788	1,084	388
In the fisheries, . .	10.3	16.43	30,644	536	336
In the forest, (except fuel,) .	14.76	2.4	22,042	110	670
	$271.97	344.56	690,159	500	394
Wood cut for fuel, . .	40.17				
Agriculture in Free States, .	278.2	1,387.	1,898,272		144
Do. in N. Slave States, .	145.05	695.*	1,194,900		122
Do. in S. Slave States, .	121.65	375.*	816,315		149
Commerce and navigation, .	161.5	430.	188,000	2,287	
Canals and Railroads, . .	7.5	205.			

* The slaves are reckoned as persons, and their value is not included as a part of the agricultural capital of the Slave States, which, at $350 each, would amount to about $870,000,000.

SEC. 18. *Values produced in each State, and the amount to each person.*

Values produced by labor and capital in each of the States in 1840, according to the census of the United States, in part estimated on the principles heretofore stated.

STATES.	Agriculture. *Millions.*	Manufactures, &c. *Millions.*	Mining, &c. *Millions.*	Commerce. *Millions.*	Fisheries. *Millions.*
Maine	$12.4	$5.66	$0.3	$5.4	$0.96
New Hampshire	8.8	5.37	.07	1.45	.09
Vermont	10.96	3.03	.36	1.24	
Massachusetts	14.6	38.9	1.48	15.75	5.3
Rhode Island	2.	7.9	.14	1.7	.56
Connecticut	9.9	11.55	.7	3.1	.75
New York, S. District	19.6	20.80	1.06	27.20	.86
New York, N. District	53.8	25.55	4.16	16.7	.11
New Jersey	14.6	9.89	.73	3.8	.090
Pennsylvania	53.4	30.8	9.41	20.7	.02
Ohio	37.2	13.37	1.8	12.2	.02
Indiana	16.8	3.56	.07	3.22	.001
Illinois	12.3	2.95	.32	2.54	
Michigan	5.28	1.32	.02	.95	.09
Wisconsin	.72	.3	.37	.55	.045
Iowa	.84	.17	.01	.3	
Free States	$273.20	$181.12	$21.0	$116.8	$8.896
Delaware	$2.95	$1.5	$0.03	$0 58	$ .21
Maryland	14.55	5.9	.74	5.5	.36
District of Columbia	.19	87		.69	.13
Virginia	41.20	7.97	1.83	7.9	.15
North Carolina	24.70	2.45	.32	2.	.38
Tennessee	23.4	2.65	.9	2.7	
Kentucky	23.3	4.83	1.11	3.9	
Missouri	10.76	2.23	.2	3.5	
Arkansas	4.00	6	.02	.37	
Northern Slave States	$145.05	$29 00	$5.15	$27.14	$1 23
South Carolina	$23.1	$2.23	$.12	$ 2.9	$ .002
Georgia	28.8	2.15	.21	3.15	
Alabama	22.3	1.64	.08	2.95	
Mississippi	24.	1.5		1.61	
Louisiana	21.7	2.68	09	13.7	
Florida	1.75	.4		.75	172
Southern Slave States	$121.65	$10.60	$0.50	$25.06	$0.174
United States	$539.9	$220.72	$26.65	$169.00	$10.3

Estimated values obtained from the forest, including wood for fuel, lumber, and other products—the aggregate values produced by labor and capital in each of the States during the year preceding the census of 1840—the amount to each person, and the amount to each free person, after deducting thirty dollars for the cost of supporting each slave.

STATES.	Products of the Forest		Aggregate values produced.		
	Fuel. *Millions.*	Lumber, &c. *Millions.*	*Millions.*	Amount to each person.	Amount to each free person.
Maine	$1.50	$1.52	$27.74	$55	
New Hampshire	.9	.36	17.04	60	
Vermont	.85	.36	16.8	58	
Massachusetts	2.1	.31	78.44	106	
Rhode Island	.4	.035	12.73	117	
Connecticut	1.	.15	27.15	88	
New York, S. District	1.6	.3	71.42	96	
New York, N. District.	5.0	3.73	109.05	65	
New Jersey	1.2	.3	30.61	82	
Pennsylvania	4.3	.97	119.6	69⅛	
Ohio	3.75	.96	69.3	45⅜	
Indiana	1.4	.57	25.62	37½	
Illinois	1.2	.20	19.51	41	
Michigan	.5	.38	8.54	40	
Wisconsin	.07	.29	2.34	75	
Iowa	.1	.07	1.49	24⅜	
Free States	$25.87	$10.505	$637.38	$65½	
Delaware	.2	.012	5.48	$70	$72
Maryland	1.15	.196	28.396	60	67
District of Columbia	.01		1.89	44	
Virginia	2.5	.52	62.07	50	61
North Carolina	1.4	1.64	32.89	43⅜	50
Tennessee	1.44	.185	31.275	38	40
Kentucky	1.5	.16	34.80	44⅜	49
Missouri	.7	.44	17.83	46½	49
Arkansas	.2	.182	5.37	55	61
Northern Slave States	$9.1	$3.335	$220.001	$47	$53
South Carolina	1.2	.44	29.992	50	75½
Georgia	1.15	.095	35.535	51	66
Alabama	.95	.144	28 064	47½	60
Mississippi	9	.169	28.199	75	125
Louisiana	.9	.058	39.128	111	185
Florida	.1	.024	3.196	59	
Southern Slave States	$5.2	.93	$164.114	$61¾	$91
United States	$40.17	$14.77	$1.021.495	$60	

The estimates made of the value of products, and of the raw materials used, are mostly in accordance with commercial reports; with the returns of the census of the United States of 1850; with the returns of the censuses of 1845, of the States of New York, Massachusetts, and Connecticut; and with the opinions of writers and persons the most competent to judge on such subjects. The results present no apparent inconsistencies which are not easily accounted for. Mining being about twice as productive as farming, and the number of miners in Wisconsin large in proportion to the population, the mining industry of that territory raised the average income of its inhabitants greatly above that of the inhabitants of Indiana, Michigan and the neighboring states. The income from commerce, and from the culture of sugar and cotton, is nearly three times as great as from the culture of tobacco and of grain in the interior and western states. This accounts for the large average incomes in Louisiana and Mississippi, compared with those of all the agricultural states. The commerce of Missouri raises their incomes above those of Tennessee.

These tables exhibit the profits of slavery in a very clear light. They show that slave labor, employed in the culture of cotton in the southern slave States, is more profitable and productive, than free labor employed in agriculture in the free States; and that the culture of sugar in Louisiana must be still more profitable than the culture of cotton. They show also, that the culture of tobacco and Indian corn in the northern slave States is greatly depressed, and much less productive than the culture of cotton at the south, and of wheat, corn, &c., in the manufacturing and commercial States of the north and east.

It needs but a glance at the tables in Sections 14, 15, and 16, to see that both labor and capital employed either in mining, manufactures or commerce, are more than twice as productive as when they are employed in agriculture, except in the culture of sugar and cotton. When the reader takes this into consideration, he need be at no loss for the cause of the incomes of the people of the commercial and manufacturing States of Massachusetts and Rhode Island being about twice as great to each inhabitant, as they are in the agricultural State of Vermont. He will see at once the reason why the incomes of the people of the rich soil of Ohio and the north-western States are so low, when compared with those of the manufacturing and commercial States. He will also see, that though the great Erie Canal, the most magnificent work of the age, has poured much wealth into the city of New York, and perhaps doubled the population, business and wealth of that great commercial emporium, it has at present very little perceptible influence in raising the incomes and increasing the wealth of the inhabitants of the northern district of

New York. This great and splendid work, together with the canals and railroads of Ohio and the western States, have had an influence in dispersing the population, spreading it over a wide surface, and deluding the people with the idea, that nothing but internal improvements, agricultural industry and commercial enterprise, are necessary to make a country wealthy.

On comparing the foregoing tables with those in sections 7, 8, and 9, and more particularly with table C, in section 7, the reader will see that the productive industry of the United States as a whole, compares very favorably with that of France, Holland, and Belgium; and also with that of Great Britain, prior to the nineteenth century. He will see that the productive industry of Massachusetts and Rhode Island exceeds all Europe in proportion to the population, and is equalled only by Louisiana, and perhaps Cuba, and some other sugar and coffee growing countries of the torrid zone.

When the reader contemplates the progressive steps in the productive industry of England, France, and the Netherlands; and reflects that a century since, and before the invention of the steam engine, of the spinning jenny, and of the machinery for rolling iron, all the manufactures of the metals, as well as of cloths, were by hand labor; he need be at no loss for the reason why the productive industry and wealth of those countries was small a century since, compared with what it is now; and why it is now small in France, Ireland, and our agricultural States of the west, in comparison with Great Britain and our manufacturing States.

SEC. 19. *Value of furniture made; and the number, value, and average value of houses erected in each of the States.*

Summary statement of the value of furniture made, and the number of brick and stone, and of wood houses erected in 1840, and the aggregate and average value of the same, according to the returns of the census; with the amounts added for omissions in the valuation, and deducted from the valuation for apparent errors.

STATES.	Furniture.	Houses built. Brick & S.	Houses built. Wood.	Aggregate value.	Average value.	—Deducted. A Added.
Maine	$204,875	34	1,674	$833,067	$487	$100,000A
New Hampshire	105,827	90	434	487,715	930	17,000A
Massachusetts	1,090,008	324	1,249	2,827,134	1,790	60,000A
Boston	329,600	219	173	1,107,450	2,825	
Mass. except Boston	760,408	105	1,076	1,719,684	1,456	
Rhode Island	121,131	6	292	379,010	1,271	
Connecticut	253,675	95	517	1,086,295	1,775	
Vermont	83,275	72	468	344,896	638	

States.	Furniture.	Houses built,		Aggregate value.	Ave'ge value.	—Deducted. A Added.
		Brick & S.	Wood.			
N. Dist. New York	$853,926	589	4,253	$4,204,972	$878	$50,000A
New York city,	916,675	542	59	1,889,100	3,112	
S. Dist. N. Y. except city	201,175	102	886	1,221,772	1,239	
New Jersey	176,566	205	861	1,092,052	1,024	
Philadelphia city & county	547,900	927	138	3,009,633	2,825	
East Dist. Pa. except city	199,526	601	603	817,807	679	
W. Dist. Pennsylvania	403,741	463	1,665	1,512,090	710	
City of Cincinnati	459,000	260	74	1,196,000	2,755	
Ohio except Cin.	302,146	710	2,690	1,080,823	588	*600 000–
Gallia, Geauga, Holmes, and Jackson counties, Ohio	2,300	15	267	57,206	202	
Indiana	211,481	346	4,270	1,341,312	290	100,000A
Clay, Miami, and Randolph counties, Ia.	800	6	401	41,404	102	1,000A
Illinois	84,410	334	4,134	1,725,255	417	340 000–
Michigan	23,494	39	1,280	571,005	435	
Wisconsin	6,945	7	509	212,085	411	
Iowa	4,600	14	483	135,987	272	
Delaware	16,300	47	104	147,350	981	1 500A
City of Baltimore	268,200	213	1	548,400	2,563	
Maryland, except Balt.	37,160	176	591	533,370	699	3,000A
Virginia, East Dist.	195,455	221	1,977	984,227	449	
Virginia, West Dist.	93,936	181	627	383,166	474	
North Carolina	35,002	38	1,822	511,004	274	100,800A
Tennessee	79,600	193	1,098	553,551	429	126,149A
Kentucky	273,350	485	1,757	1,045,172	421	6,000A
Missouri, except St. Louis		203	2,072	854,593	376	175,000A
City of St. Louis		210	130	761,980	2,240	
City of Charleston, S. C.	10,000	94	53	1,059,200	7,205	
S. Carolina, except city	18,155	17	1,541	468,376	300	
Georgia	49,780	38	2,591	937,116	356	244,000A
Alabama	41,671	67	472	489,871	892	250 000–
Mississippi	28,610	144	2,247	1,175,513	491	
New Orleans		201	210	2,231,300	5,429	
Louisiana, except N. O.		47	409	505.644	909	
Arkansas	20,293	21	1,083	360,474	326	*780,000–
Florida		9	306	327,913	1,040	
Dist. of Columbia	125,872	60	33	168,910	1,816	

The foregoing table shows how wealth accumulates in cities, the centres of manufactures and commerce; and enables the business men to live in fine and expensive houses, compared with the cheap and plain dwellings that shelter the farming population.

* The returns for Licking County, Ohio, give seven hundred and sixty-eight thousand and eighty-five dollars as the cost of constructing nineteen brick and stone, and one hundred and fifty-six wood houses. In Pulaski County, Arkansas, the returns show the erection of fourteen brick and stone, and twenty-four wood houses, at an aggregate cost of $867,400. I suppose the error occured in putting down a cypher too much, or in calling dollars and cents all dollars, in some of the subdivisions.

Gallia, Geauga, Holmes, and Jackson, are among the oldest settled counties in the State of Ohio; but they are all agricultural counties, without any large towns or villages; and the average value of the dwelling houses erected in them in 1840, was but $202 each; while the average value of the dwellings built in the manufacturing and commercial city of Cincinnati amounted to $2,755 each. Compare the values of the dwelling houses erected in the agricultural State of Vermont, costing on an average but $638 each, with those erected in the manufacturing State of Massachusetts, exclusive of the city of Boston, costing on an average $1,456 each; and the reader will readily come to the conclusion, that the income of the people of the latter state must be much greater than that of the former. Look at the aggregate value built during the year, and the value of furniture made, and the contrast is equally striking. The population of Vermont was nearly half as great in 1840, as Massachusetts, excepting Boston, and yet the value of houses erected in the latter was about five times as great as in the former, and the value of furniture made over nine times as great. This indicates that the average income of the people of Massachusetts, exclusive of Boston, is about twice as great as that of the people of Vermont, (as stated in section 18;) which enables them to live in houses twice as expensive, to spend twice as much, and yet accumulate wealth twice as fast. What cause can be assigned for this great difference, but the one I have suggested, that one is an agricultural, and the other a manufacturing state? The people of both are equally well educated, and equally intelligent.

If we compare the condition of Great Britain and the value of dwelling houses in the Kingdom at different periods, the result will be still more striking. The rental of the dwelling houses and all other buildings in England and Wales, according to the assessment of the income tax in 1688, amounted to only £1,500,000, and according to Mr. Davenant's estimate to £2,000,000 per annum. In 1815 the rental of the dwelling houses alone in Great Britain amounted to £15,035,000, and in 1843, to £38,888,880, as shown in table A, of section 1, and tables B, and D, of section 4. In 1688, Great Britain was an agricultural country; her mining and manufactures not being much greater in proportion to her population than those of Vermont were in 1840. This is shown in sections 1, 2 and 18, and the reader can compare them for himself. The British did not become very distinguished as a mining and manufacturing people, and superior to the other nations of Europe, until about the year 1780; and their manufactures were small in amount even in 1815, compared with what they were in 1843.

With the exception of a few royal palaces and fine castles of the nobility, the dwellings of the British people in 1688, were plain, humble and comparatively cheap; otherwise the rental would have been estimated higher. Though by reason of high prices, the incomes of the people were as great in 1815 as they have ever been since; yet the taxes and expenses of the government were enormously great, and the amount of wealth then accumulated was much smaller than it was in 1843, as illustrated in tables B, and D, of section 4. At the latter period, the lordly palaces had greatly multiplied among the manufacturing, mining and commercial classes; many of which rivalled in splendor and magnificence, the royal castles and palaces, and exceeded those of the nobility of the previous century. The value of the dwellings of the people of a nation constitute a pretty accurate index of the amount of their wealth. What has caused the immense difference between the value of the dwellings of agricultural England in 1688, and manufacturing England in 1843? Let the reader inquire for himself, and form his own opinion.

During the whole of the seventeenth and eighteenth centuries, Holland was the wealthiest country in the world, far in advance of England. Even down to the time of our revolutionary War, the public revenues of France were nearly twice as great as those of Great Britain; and prior to that time, the French were as wealthy, and perhaps more so, than the British. What has caused this wonderful change? Can any reason be assigned for it, except the power of machinery, and the great extension of the mining and manufacturing industry of Great Britain, coming in aid of, and furnishing the materials for the most extensive commerce which ever existed?

According to my estimates, the same number of persons can now, by the aid of machinery, make about twenty times as much cloth of cotton and wool, as they can by carding, spinning and weaving by hand, in the old method in use prior to 1750. The profits of labor and capital aided by machinery, at present prices of products, are about three times as great as they were a century since. Is it strange, that the people of Great Britain should grow rich by the combined influence of capital, machinery, science and skill in manufactures and mining, and the aid of the markets of half the civilized world ready to buy their products, at prices which afford them three times as much profits and wages, as they could have obtained a century since, and about three times as great as the agriculturists of our new states can now make? Is it strange that by their policy, they should manage to prevent the growth of manufactures in Ireland, in their colonies, in the United States, and in all other countries, preach the doctrines of free-trade, and try to keep all the world dependent on them for the products of their mining and manufacturing ndustry?

CHAPTER XV.

On Free Trade—the circumstances which suggested the outlines of the system—its principles, false assumptions, sophistries, and tendencies—the necessity of regulating commerce, of organizing capital and labor; and the true principles of political economy.

Sec. 1. *Feudal privileges and monopolies in the mechanic arts, manufactures, and commerce in Europe.*

The general tendencies of free trade were pointed out in Section 7, of the last chapter; but the subject has been so much discussed of late years, and has assumed so much importance in the public mind, as to render it expedient to discuss its principles and effects more at length in a distinct chapter.

Of all the principles which have crept into our government, none have been so paralyzing to the industry, and destructive to the interests of the country, as those of *free trade with foreign nations;* whereby the importation of foreign luxuries, and the products of foreign industry have been encouraged at low duties; American laborers deprived in a great measure of the markets of their own country, and the country drained of specie, involved in debt, and kept in a dependent condition. Up to within about half a century since, the government of every country of Europe was in the habit of passing special laws and ordinances, and granting to particular individuals and associations of persons special charters, allowing them exclusive privileges to make and vend particular articles, to do certain things, or to monopolize certain markets. The monopolies granted by these special acts and charters, were almost infinitely various in their character; comprising almost every kind of manufactures, commerce and banking, even the learned professions, and the dissemination of learning and intelligence. In this mode, not only all the offices of the government, and the learned professions, but the banking, commerce and manufactures of each country were monopolized by the families of the nobility, and their friends and dependents, and by wealthy capitalists, who could make an interest with the government. The business of manufacturing of many kinds, being monopolized by a few privileged persons, was associated in the minds of the people, with the personal and feudal privileges and powers of the aristocracy; and became odious to them.

The poor were also restrained by the poor-laws of England, and by acts against vagrancy, from migrating from one county to another, in search of employment. Personal liberty as well as industry, was thus restrained, to the great vexation and injury of the laboring classes.

Domestic as well as foreign commerce was subject to numerous duties, taxes, monopolies, restraints and regulations, made by the feudal aristocracy for their own exclusive benefit; which were extremely oppressive to the laboring classes, and became even more odious to them, than the manufacturing monopolies.

SEC. 2. *The system of monopoly was extended to all the countries of America, which were held in colonial bondage.*

This principle of monopoly was extended to America, and under it, almost the whole Western continent was parcelled out into lordly domains by the crowned heads of Europe, to the nobility and their particular favorites; and the colonists were prohibited all commercial intercourse except with the mother country; and in many cases were prohibited from manufacturing for themselves, and the privilege of manufacturing for them reserved for the mother country. The object of the system was to enable the mother country to monopolize the more profitable employments of commerce and manufactures; to supply the colonists with manufactures at high prices; to confine them to the hard drudgery of agriculture, and mining for gold and silver, to producing raw materials at low prices; and to keep them in debt, poor, and dependent. It was these restrictions upon production and upon their industry, which excited the public mind, and had ten times more effect than the little tax on tea, in bringing about the glorious American revolution.

SEC. 3. *Smith's Wealth of Nations. Its character and effects.*

The Inquiry into the Nature and Causes of the Wealth of Nations, by Adam Smith, was first published in 1776. In this work the author examined critically and philosophically into the theory, practice, and effect of all this system of monopoly; and showed most clearly the inexpediency and injustice of the system of monopoly, so far as production and domestic commerce are concerned. But so far as regards foreign commerce, he was not equally philosophical, clear, or successful. Manufactures and commerce were then in a comparatively infant state, and the materials were few, compared with what we now have, to enable one to deduce, according to the inductive system of philosophy, the true theory of political economy and public policy. His work is filled with important truths, and with many errors and false assumptions, so curiously interwoven with acute reasoning, as to have given direction to the opinions of nearly all the school-men and merely theoretical political economists, from that day to the present. With the single exception of John Calvin's Institutes, perhaps it has had more effect upon the public mind, than any work that has been written since the Koran was penned by Mahomet; though practical statesmen have generally repudiated many of its doctrines.

SEC. 4. *Free production, but not free trade, the true rule.*

It is generally admitted to be a matter of expediency and good public policy, as well as of justice, to allow inventors and authors the exclusive benefit of their own works and inventions for a limited period. With these exceptions, the true rule is, FREE PRODUCTION, BUT NOT FREE TRADE. The cases are very few, however, where domestic commerce should be restricted or regulated by law; but the importation of foreign commodities should in all cases be regulated in view of the condition, circumstances, and natural as well as acquired resources of a nation. The foreign producer and laborer who do nothing to support our government, and often take the specie out of the country for their products, should never be allowed to come into competition on equal terms with our own laborers and manufacturers, whose surplus income goes to swell the capital and support the government of our country. *Adaptation to condition and circumstances may be said to be the great law and corner-stone of political as well as of private economy; the golden rule of government and jurisprudence as well as of morals.*

SEC. 5. *Definition of the word fact.—The rules of political economy should be deduced from facts.*

Dr. Smith's treatise is a very learned and philosophical work, founded on facts which he had been years in collecting; and his theories are mostly deduced from his facts. But he wrote when commerce and manufactures were in their infancy, and before governments commenced collecting accurate statistics of the population, productive industry, wealth, and resources of their respective countries; and he was unfortunately mistaken in many of his facts. A mistake in relation to facts, and the difficulty in ascertaining them with accuracy, is one of the principal causes of man's errors. Mr. Webster defines fact to be, first, any thing done, or that comes to pass; an act; a deed; an effect produced or achieved; an event; second, reality, truth.

Facts comprise not only all the acts of man, and the result of all his acts, but also all the motions, changes, developments, events, and effects produced by causes either physical or spiritual in the whole universe. Facts are therefore the connecting links between cause and effect; and comprise all the effects which have ever been produced in the spiritual as well as the natural, political, and social world. They may be divided into four classes: first, simple or single; second, complex or compound; third, general facts or aggregates of details; and fourth, philosophical facts, or the ordinary current of events produced by natural causes. As all the operations of nature are produced by combinations of causes, no fact can properly be called single, except the acts of man which result from a single operation of the mind, or one volition.

Complex, or compound facts, comprise effects produced by numerous persons, all acting in concert during a considerable space of time. This would include any one evolution of a single corps of an army acting in concert under their commanding officer, though the acts of each individual would be in some measure distinct; and the victory or result of an engagement, however various its character, complex its parts, and numerous the causes producing it, would comprise but one complex fact.

General facts comprise aggregates of details. The population, products, property, and capital, exports and imports, coin, schools and scholars, income and expenditures of the government and people of every country are general facts; they comprise numerous details, and can be ascertained only by carefully collecting, and aggregating those details.

Philosophical facts not only comprise the ordinary current of natural events produced exclusively by natural causes; but also the current of human events, produced conjointly by physical causes, and the free and voluntary agency of man, acting either in concert, or in conflict with each other. In this view of it, M. Guizot made the progress of civilization in Europe, a matter of fact, and the subject of history. The natural tendency of any particular employment, pursuit, course of action or policy, to produce a certain result, and to contribute to increase the comforts, wealth, and well-being of man, or the contrary, may be regarded as a philosophical fact; which must be ascertained by observing great numbers of simple facts, aggregating them together, and thereby deducing causes from effects. When general and philosophical facts are understood with perfect accuracy, there is no great difficulty in deducing from them the uniform laws by which they are produced. Hence the importance of statistics, of facts, of general facts, and philosophical facts, in order to deduce from them the true rules of political economy.

SEC. 6. *Causes of many of the errors into which Dr. Smith fell.*

Adam Smith, I have remarked, was mistaken in many of his facts; that is, in many of the general and philosophical facts on which his reasoning is founded; and it may well be doubted, if he could have had the light which modern statistics throw upon this question, if he ever would have deduced from them the maxims and principles of free trade. He was a philosopher, a man of great learning, great powers of reasoning, and great originality of mind; but a mere scholastic philosopher, a professor, a theoretical, not a practical man. *He was led into many errors by theorizing, without sufficient knowledge of practical business to verify the conclusions deduced from his theories, and to correct them. Like Mr. Walker (late Secretary of the Treasury), he deduced many of his philosophical facts from his theories, instead of deducing his theories from the facts shown by the business and records of the country.* He assumed as a matter of fact, that capital and labor employed in agriculture were more productive than when employed in mining, manufactures, or any other pursuit. Many of his errors arose from reasoning on this false assumption.

The odious monopolies existing in nearly all the countries of Europe, in all matters of production and trade also, made strong impressions on him of the evils resulting from them; and the only remedy which was suggested to his mind, was entire freedom of trade, as well as of production. It is not strange that at that day, his mind was led into such a train of reasoning. All the facts collected by him are consistent with the maxim of FREE PRODUCTION; but they are not all consistent, nor is his reasoning all consistent, with the doctrines and maxims of FREE TRADE between nations. Perceiving this, he made certain exceptions and limitations to the general rule, in the commerce between nations, which have been critically sought out and condemned as inconsistencies and errors, by his disciples and followers, Ricardo, McCulloch, Mill, and others in Great Britain, and by Dr. Wayland, Condy Raguet, Professor Vethake, and many others in this country, and partially so by Mr. Say; and they have carefully excluded from their works all those exceptions, and made them conform strictly to all the abstract rules and assumptions of free trade. By overlooking many of the most important facts of history, omitting all those exceptions, and the soundest arguments as well as the most reliable facts collected by Dr. Smith, and copying all his errors of fact and argument, they have constructed one of the most harmonious and plausible systems of sophistry and error, ever presented to the reading world.

SEC. 7. *Great Britain has capital and capacity to manufacture for the world. Necessary effects of Free Trade.*

For some years past, Great Britain has produced nearly two million tons of iron annually, and spun about six hundred million pounds of cotton. This is nearly equal to the tons of iron produced, and the quantity of cotton spun, in all the other countries of Europe and America. By referring to Sections 4, 6 and 7, of the last chapter, the reader may realize, how small the amount of capital necessary, to employ the immense amount of mining and manufacturing industry of that kingdom, when compared with the value of farming lands and agricultural capital, and the amount invested in palaces and dwellings for the wealthy. By referring to Section 11 of Chapter XI., he may learn how many persons were employed in 1847, in all the factories and mines of the kingdom ; and how few are necessary, with the aid of science and machinery, to accomplish results so truly wonderful.

Perhaps half of the time during the last twenty years (from 1830 to 1850), many of the factories, furnaces, and iron mills, were not in use ; and half of those in use were running short time, not doing more than two-thirds as much as they were capable of doing, because the markets were surfeited and prices depressed. These facts are sufficient to show that Great Britain has the natural resources and physical capacity, by means of machinery, to manufacture for the whole civilized world. Let the reader contemplate the increase in the amount of capital invested in dwelling-houses and railroads between the years 1815 and 1843 (as exhibited in Section 4 of the last chapter, amounting to about £520,000,000 ; more than three times as much as the whole amount invested in mining, manufactures, and the mechanic arts), and he will see at once, that one-third part of that increase invested in mining and manufactures, would have doubled the manufacturing capital of Great Britain, and enabled them to accomplish that object ; if they could have commanded the markets of the world. As their manufactures are better established, and they have a better supply of experienced and skilful laborers than any other nation, they can, as a general rule, undersell every other people ; and they would soon drive the manufacturers of almost every nation out of their own markets, and supply and monopolize the markets of the world, were it not for the tariff laws of France, the United

States, and other nations, regulating and restricting foreign imports, and thereby partially securing their own markets to their own people.

The question is not so much what a nation can produce, but *what they can sell and get their pay for.* MARKETS, *therefore, enter into the question, as the great, yea, the greatest and most important of all the elements of political economy. The important point is to secure a market; to secure the home market first, for their own laborers and manufacturers as far as they may want it, and thereby create a domestic market for their own agricultural products.* MARKETS, I repeat again, are THE GREAT STIMULANTS TO INDUSTRY, AND OF ALL THINGS IN THE WORLD, THEY ARE THE MOST IMPORTANT AND NECESSARY TO SUSTAIN IT. This great truth has been entirely overlooked by the advocates of free trade, and hence have arisen many of their errors.

SEC. 8. *Maxims of Free Trade.*

I have carefully collected the principal maxims on which the doctrines of free trade are based; and have numbered them for the purpose of referring to them conveniently. The first six and the eleventh are taken almost literally from the "WEALTH OF NATIONS." The others are taken in most cases literally, and in some cases they are only abstracts from the Essays on Free Trade, of Condy Raguet, Esq., late of Philadelphia. All, or nearly all these maxims are generally insisted on by the advocates of free trade, as axioms; and many of them are laid down as self-evident truths.

1st. Every individual in his local situation can judge better than the government, or any statesman or lawgiver can do for him, what is the species of industry in which he can employ his labor and capital to the best advantage, in order to produce the largest income.

2d. The study of his own profit and advantage, naturally and necessarily leads every individual to prefer that employment of labor and capital, which is most advantageous to the society, as well as to himself.

3d. All persons find it for their interest to employ their whole industry in a way in which they have some advantage over their neighbors, and to purchase with a part of its produce, or what is the same thing, with the price of a part of it, whatever they have occasion for. The same rule applies to communities or countries; and whether the advantages which one country has over another be natural or acquired, it is in this respect of no consequence. As long as the one country has those advantages, and the other wants them, it will always be more advantageous for the latter, rather to buy of the former, than to make; and for every individual to buy where he can buy cheapest.

4th. That the number of workmen who can be kept in employment by any person or community, must bear a certain proportion to the capital employed, and can never exceed it; that no regulation of commerce can increase the quantity of industry in a society, beyond what its capital can maintain; that all a government can do, is to divert a part of the capital and industry of the community into new channels, without power to increase the aggregate amount of either; and that our industry cannot be diminished by buying of other nations whatever they can produce cheaper than we can, and employing our capital in some other mode.

5th. That all restrictive laws tend to force capital and labor from a more to a less profitable mode of employment, and to render the producing faculties and the industry of the country less productive; and thus they prevent the rapid accumulation of capital and wealth, in which is found the means of affording employment to an increasing population.

6th. That there is in every society an ordinary or average rate of both wages and profit, in every employment; that the amount of labor and capital employed in producing any article determines its cost, by the fixed standard of the rate of wages and profits; that this cost is its natural price; that the producer cannot, for a long period, charge more than a fair remuneration for his labor and capital, because a higher price would invite competition, which would soon reduce the price; that he cannot for a long period charge less, because in this case he would be ruined, and must leave the employment, and thus the number of producers would be diminished, and the value of the product rise to the average rate of profit; and that no domestic competition can bring down prices below the fixed standard, or natural price.

7th. That there can be no such thing as a permanent superiority of one branch of business over another; for if capital and labor employed in agriculture or any other business, were for a great length of time more profitable than if employed in other pursuits, persons would withdraw their capital and leave the latter pursuits, and fly to the former, until the equilibrium would be restored.

8th. That the great fall which has taken place since 1816 in the price of many articles of manufacture, has resulted chiefly from the great improvements in labor-saving machinery, which have progressed not only in this country, but in Europe.

9th. That all high duties exclude a portion of the articles upon which they are laid, by raising their price, or keeping their price from falling, and are thus a tax on the consumer, for the exclusive benefit of the domestic producer, to the full amount of the duties.

10th. That the complaint of the manufacturers of the United States, that the duties are not high enough, is positive proof that foreign fabrics can be imported cheaper than they can be made at home; consequently, that there is a want of consistency in the conduct of those who assert that the tariff system brings down prices.

11th. To give the monopoly of the home market to the produce of domestic industry in any particular art or manufacture, must, in almost all cases, be either a useless or a hurtful regulation. If the produce of domestic industry can be bought as cheap as that of foreign industry, the regulation is evidently useless; if it cannot, it must generally be hurtful.

12th. That commerce is an exchange of equivalents not merely beneficial to one of the parties which carries it on, but to both, by enabling each to exchange with the other those products which he can furnish upon the most favorable terms.

13th. That commerce must be reciprocal; and, consequently, that when one nation restricts its trade with another, and says "I will not buy," it declares in the same words, "I will not sell."

14th. That so far as foreign nations refuse to take our productions, they, *ipso facto*, and without requiring any laws on our part to enforce a retaliation, absolutely deprive us of the power to take their productions.

15th. That foreign commerce is an exchange of domestic products for foreign products, and gives employment to domestic industry, because foreign products can be paid for only with domestic products.

So far as these maxims are correct and true, they are *philosophical facts* as heretofore explained; but so far as they differ from the facts, they are mere *false assumptions. All the truths and principles of political economy are in accordance with, and deducible from facts;* and like the truths and principles of every natural science, they can be ascertained in no other mode. Abstract reasoning on such snbjects is always uncertain; and the conclusions of the mind can never be relied upon, except when they are verified by facts.

SEC. 9. *Critical examination of the maxims of Free Trade.*

1st. The first and second maxims will be examined together. To determine the most advantageous mode of employing labor and capital, requires a survey of the whole country, of all its wants, all its resources and capacities, and all its industry. It is not the duty of governments, to direct the pursuits of individuals, but to collect and disseminate, for the use of the people, information of the productions, wants, commerce, and natural resources of the country, to ascertain what commodities are produced in excess, of what the production is deficient, what new branches of industry are adapted to the condition of the country, and how its industry is affected by foreign commerce; to shape its legislation, in such manner as to promote the industry of the nation, and to encourage the transfer of labor and capital from pursuits in which they are not needed, into those in which they are most needed, in order to supply the wants of the people.

The first maxim implies, or assumes, that each member of the community, including all the most ignorant classes, can determine all these matters more accurately than the general sense and wisdom of the nation collected in the halls of legislation, with the aid of all the records and statistics of the country. Is this assumption true, or is it false? How do the uneducated classes acquire such knowledge? Is it the result of instinct, or of intuition; or how is it acquired? Of what use are schools, seminaries of learning and science, lyceums, libraries, and agricultural societies, if each one of the mass of the people knows more than the united wisdom of the legislative and executive departments of the government. If every man's information and wisdom were complete and perfect, the assumption would be true; but in the present state of knowledge, it is false. If maxims numbered 1 and 2 were true, the industry of every community in the civilized world would be nearly equal in value, in proportion to their numbers; and they would accumulate wealth with nearly equal rapidity. This is proven to be untrue, by all the facts collected in the last chapter.

2d. The second maxim assumes that the virtue as well as the wisdom of every individual is complete and perfect; and that it is impossible for any one to engage in any employment, which is not the most advantageous to the community, as well as to himself. If when Dr. Smith first conceived this maxim, he had looked into some of the grog-shops of London, and contemplated the subject of the manufacture, sale, and effects of intoxicating liquors, in connection with it, he would have perceived its falsity at once. It also implies or assumes that, inasmuch as communities and nations are constituted of individuals, the gain of every individual necessarily increases the aggregate gains of the community. This is true, when individual gains arise from production; but it is not always true, when they arise from trade and commerce. In the latter case, the gain of the merchant is often at the expense of the purchaser and consumer ; and the importer, jobber, and retail merchants who sell foreign goods, often grow rich by the business, when many of the consumers, as well as the manufacturers, and manufacturing laborers of the country, are directly injured by it ; and the aggregate industry of the nation lessened, both in amount and value. The converse of the proposition assumed, is, however, true in all cases ; for nations being composed of individuals, whatever increases the aggregate industry and income of the nation, necessarily increases the income of individuals, and as all pursuits are mutually dependent on each other, the tendency is, to promote the interest of all the industrious classes. For a further commentary on this maxim, see the remarks on maxim numbered 12.

3d. The third maxim assumes that, no matter what employment or pursuit a man may follow, he can either exchange all its products for whatever he may want on fair terms, or can sell them for money at fair prices, and with the price of a portion of them, purchase whatever he may have occasion for. The truth of the maxim depends on the truth of these assumptions, and if they are false either in whole or in part, the maxim is false also. Every man who has a correct knowledge of the condition of the United States, knows that the markets for almost everything produced in the nation, are generally surfeited ; and that it is much easier, with the great natural resources of our country, to produce, than it is to sell at fair prices, and collect the pay. All that we want in this country, to stimulate industry and increase production to almost any extent, are regular markets at fair prices, and sure pay. The principal products of many of the interior districts of the Western and South-western States, are Indian corn, pork and cattle. The corn crop is so superabundant in those districts, that it will scarcely sell at all for money, or for over ten to twenty cents per bushel ; and pork and cattle are equally cheap. See Chapter XII., Sections 33 and 37. In such districts the people cannot pay for many foreign goods, but must clothe themselves coarsely, and have but few comforts, except what they produce themselves ; simply because their markets are too limited, and not equal to their products.

It is of very little consequence to persons who have no means of payment, that foreign products are nominally cheap. Of what consequence is it to the poor peasantry of Ireland, that British goods are nominally cheap, when they are idle half of the time for want of employment, and have scarcely any means of payment ? On the contrary, it makes no difference to buyers generally, how high the nominal prices of domestic goods which they need may be, provided they have a plenty of employment, and can exchange their labor, or the products of their labor, for them, at prices equally high. The true test of cost to the consumer is, not the nominal price, but the comparative ease or difficulty of payment.

The principal reason why one nation can manufacture cheaper than another, is not so much owing to natural advantages and resources, as to those which are acquired. It is owing to inventions, improvements in mechanical science, more perfect tools and machinery, greater skill and experience, and greater facilities for transportation. It is for the interest of every nation adapted by nature to mechanical and manufacturing industry, to adopt such a policy as to acquire these advantages; and the only mode in which it can be effected is, to secure the domestic market, as a field of employment to the domestic laborer and producer, and to diversify employments according to the wants of the people.* Commerce in domestic products is substantially, in a national point of view, a mere exchange of products; and every man who consumes domestic manufactures, pays for them in the products of his own industry. Those things are really the cheapest to the consumer, which he can pay for the easiest, no matter what their nominal price may be; and, in a national point of view, taking a long series of years into consideration, those articles are generally the cheapest, which are produced by domestic industry.

That part of the maxim—that it is for the interest of every individual to buy foreign goods when he can buy them with money nominally cheaper than domestic goods, is not true as a general rule. It is true only so far as it applies to importers, dealers in foreign goods, and persons living on their money, on the interest of loans, and the income of stocks, without labor or business, and who receive no benefit from an increase of the industry and prosperity of the country.

4th. On account of the intimate connection between maxims numbered 4 and 5, I shall examine them together. There is some truth in maxim 4, mixed up with much sophistry, but in number 5 there is nothing but a tissue of false assumptions.

The amount of productive industry in a country, measured by the quantity of its products, is one thing, while its value is a very different thing. This is an important distinction, which Adam Smith and his disciples have entirely overlooked. Perhaps there is no very great difference between the amount of productive industry in proportion to the population in Vermont and Massachusetts; but the difference in value is nearly one half. There

* See on this point Section 6 of Chapter XIII., and Sections 8, 9, 10, 11 and 12 of Chapter VI.

is very little difference also in the amount of industry, between the manufacturing States of Massachusetts and Rhode Island on the one hand, and the fine agricultural States of Ohio and Indiana on the other; and yet the products of the former are more than twice as valuable, in proportion to the population, as those of the latter.

Capital and labor employed in mining, manufactures, and the mechanic arts of almost any description, produce twice as much value as the same amount of capital and labor employed in agriculture.* This being the case, it requires but a grain of common sense to perceive that any regulation of commerce, which tends to divert capital and industry from a less to a more profitable employment, must necessarily tend to increase the value of the productive industry of a country, and to enhance the accumulation of wealth. When the facts are properly presented, this conclusion forces itself upon the mind as a self-evident truth. The assumptions contained in maxim five are, therefore, false, entirely false, and do not embrace a single shadow of truth. Our tariff laws do tend to encourage mining and manufactures, and to divert capital and industry from agriculture to those employments. That they do thereby tend to increase the value of the productive industry of the country, has been generally believed by our sensible and practical men, though very few have been able to understand fully, and to explain clearly, the reasons of their belief, and to point out the fallacies and false assumptions of the doctrines of free trade.

The number of laborers which may be employed in a nation depends on the field of employment, and on the immaterial capital—that is, on the science, knowledge and experience, and skill of the people; and not on the amount of material capital accumulated, and is not in proportion to the amount of capital, as is alleged in maxim four. On the contrary, the effect of the use of machinery, improved tools, and an increased amount of capital, is to enable a given number of laborers to do more, and to bring to market an increased quantity of products; and if the market is limited, the producers employ only so many laborers as are necessary to produce sufficient products to supply the market, and the necessary consequence of an increased amount of capital under such circumstances, is to thrown out of employment a portion of the laborers previously employed. British machinery has not only stopped many factories, forges, rolling mills, and shops in the United States, but it has stopped the domestic wheels and looms also, and it has had a much greater and more depressing

* See on this subject, sections 16, 17, and 18 of the last chapter.

influence in Ireland, in British India, and all the British provinces.

A given number of laborers may accomplish more with a sufficient amount of capital and the best of tools, to keep them all at work to the best advantage, than they can with poor tools and half as much capital as would be useful to them ; but it is not true, as implied in the maxim, that the industry of a people may be increased indefinitely by an increase of capital. The amount of capital, as well as the number of laborers which can be usefully employed, depends on, and is limited by, the field of employment. The people of Holland and Great Britain long since accumulated more wealth and capital, than could be productively employed at home as capital.

It has been generally assumed by the advocates of free trade, and reiterated over and over again, that we have not capital enough in this country to manufacture for ourselves advantageously; that the proper time has not come yet ; that while we have large quantities of rich uncultivated lands, it is the most profitable and advantageous for our people to devote themselves principally to agriculture ; that we should wait until capital and laborers become more abundant ; and that when the proper time comes, manufactures will grow up of themselves, and without the aid of protective duties.

All these positions are a tissue of false assumptions. First: The average amount of capital to each person in each of our old free States, was greater, even in 1840, than it was in England in 1770, and much greater than it was in England in the year 1700; secondly, it is not true that the culture of new land is more profitable than mining and manufactures. On the contrary, the latter are in general twice as profitable as the former ; thirdly, capital never did, and never can, become abundant in an agricultural country without manufactures, for the plain reason, that agricultural pursuits, in countries without manufacturing industry, are not sufficiently productive to admit of much accumulation of wealth ; and, fourthly, it is not true that manufactures ever will grow up of themselves without exertion, and without the fostering care of the government. The population of England was as dense three centuries since, as that of the State of New York is now, and yet the manufacturing and mining industry of the kingdom was very trifling, and scarcely worth naming. It has all grown up during the last two centuries, and mostly during the last eighty years.

Mechanical and manufacturing pursuits do not in general require as much capital, in proportion to the number of persons employed, as farming. The amount of capital invested in agriculture in the United States, including the value of farming land, is more than twice as great in proportion to the number of persons employed, as it is in mining and manufactures The farming capital alone, over and above the value of lands in Great Britain, exceeds the whole amount invested in mining, manufactures, and the mechanic arts, notwithstanding the immense amount and value of the manufactures of that kingdom. It is shown in Chapter III. that mining and the mechanic arts precede agriculture in the progress of civilization. There is no want of material capital in the United States for manufacturing purposes; all that is wanted is, to have capital diverted into the proper channels—an increase of skilful workmen, and our markets better secured to our own citizens. We have now more capital invested in factories, forges, furnaces, rolling mills, and machinery, than is fully employed; and many of them are standing still, because our markets are surfeited with British iron and manufactures to such an extent, that the products of our own citizens cannot find markets, at prices which will enable them to pay the high prices demanded for labor in this country, and continue their business.

The capital of England was small until after the civil wars in the time of Cromwell; though nearly six centuries had elapsed between the Norman conquest and that period, the capital, as well as the population, continued small, and increased very slowly; the increased continued te be slow as long as the capital and industry of the country was mostly confined to agriculture; but since it began to be diverted into mining and manufactures, about the year 1770, productive industry, capital, wealth in houses, furniture, &c., and population, have all increased with railroad speed. It is impossible to accumulate capital very rapidly, while the income of a people remains small. Small incomes are nearly all consumed. The only practical mode for our new States, and some of the old agricultnral States to increase their capital and wealth rapidly, is to divert a part of their industry and capital into mining and manufactures, and thereby increase their earnings. Then, and not till then, they will have a large surplus annually, which may be put into capital, dwelling-houses, and other property.

The subject of numbers six and seven, is thoroughly examined in Chapter XII. on prices, and their false assumptions clearly pointed out. The price of commodities, of labor, of land, the rent of land, and interests or profits of capital, are all governed by the proportion between the demand for them, and the supply in the market. The demand for most things depends not only on the actual wants of a community, but also on their ability to pay for them. The wealth or poverty of a community has, therefore, a great influence on prices.

8th. The facts assumed in maxim number 8, are clearly proven to be untrue, by the records of British commerce. The facts are collected in Chapter XII., sections 26 to 30, to which the reader is referred. So far from the fact assumed being true, it is shown in the sections referred to, that notwithstanding the great improvements in machinery between the years 1750 and 1815, prices were much higher at the latter, than they were at the former period; that the increased demand, not only neutralized the tendency of machinery to reduce prices, but actually raised them; and that nothing reduced them but the tariffs of the United States, France, and other countries of Europe; which built up manufactures in those countries; increased the supply of goods; diminished the demand for British goods; compelled the British producers to pay the foreign duty, or reduce their prices to the amount of it; and also to make a further reduction of prices, in order to retain a portion of the markets, against their new competitors. The advocates of free-trade overlook, and seem blind to the fact, that an increased production in this country tends to reduce prices.

9th. The facts collected in sections 26 to 30 of Chapter XII., also prove that every word of maxim numbered 9 is untrue, with the exception of the first clause of the sentence—That high duties do tend to lessen the importation of the goods on which they are levied, is true; they do not, however, often do it by raising prices of goods which come into competition with domestic products; but, first, by compelling the producer to pay the duties, or rather to submit to such a reduction of price as to be equivalent, or nearly equivalent, to the duties, whereby they diminish his profits, and lessen the object or motive to send his products into the country. Secondly, they tend to encourage and increase domestic manufactures, and thereby lessen the demand of the community for foreign products.

In some cases, where the domestic competition is small, the price is at first raised, but falls again as soon as the protection of the market to the home producer has invited sufficient capital and labor into that department of industry, to aid very materially in supplying the market. To avoid an immediate rise of prices on raising the duties, they should be increased gradually for three or four years in succession, so as to increase the domestic competition, before the highest scale of duties takes effect. For instance, if duties are put on any article at the rate of 25 per cent. the first year, put them at 33⅓ per cent. the second, 40 per cent.

the third, and 50 per cent. the fourth year, and still higher the fifth year, if necessary. All duties should be specific, in order to prevent evasions and frauds. When duties are laid on articles which do not come into competition with domestic products (as on tea and coffee), the usual effect is to raise the price nearly as much as the whole amount of the duty; unless the duties are so high as to lessen the consumption, or some other article is introduced as a substitute. In either of those cases, the demand being lessened, it often happens that the rise in price is not half equal to the amount of the duty—and the practical effect is, to make the producer pay part of the duty, and the consumer a part. These fluctuations in price are governed by the *great laws of demand and supply*, as explained in sections 3 to 6 of Chapter XII. The effect of demand and supply on price, the advocates of free trade have never seemed to understand.

10th. The first part of maxim number 10, is undoubtedly true. By reason of Great Britain having taken the advance in mining and manufacturing of all the nations of the earth; having had practical wisdom enough to protect their own markets (which we have not); having accumulated large capitals, and an immense amount of machinery, by means of great profits when goods were high; having instructed and produced great numbers of skilful workmen; and having a dense population, who must starve or work at such prices as they can obtain, there is no reason to doubt that capitalists can produce many articles at a money price from twenty to fifty per cent. cheaper than they can be produced at present in the United States. But all these advantages, except the last, can soon be acquired in this country, if the domestic market can be secured to the home laborer and producer.

The conclusion, however, drawn in the maxim, that a protective tariff does not tend to reduce prices, is not a legitimate conclusion, as is shown in answer to maxim number 9. Nor does it follow that, because the people of Great Britain can produce at a money price cheaper than we can, that they will do so; when the demand for their products is such, for want of competition, as to raise the market price above the standard yielding fair profits to capitalists, and fair wages to the laborer. Whenever the generosity of British manufacturers shall induce them to sell their products for a profit equal to five per cent. per annum on their capital invested, when the demand is such that they might realize twenty-five per cent., then, and not till then, the conclusion of maxim number ten will be true. The truth is, there is no fixed standard for either wages, profits or prices; all are governed by the rules of supply and demand; and every man sells his products, as a general rule, at the highest prices the market will command.* British manufacturers, like all other classes of men, are selfish beings; and what prices they can afford to sell ofr, and what they will sell for, are very different things. We have had many specimens of their throwing the surplus of their manufactures of cotton, wool and iron into our markets, when they were fully supplied, and selling them at cost, in order to depress prices, ruin our manufacturers, and drive them out of the market, to enable them to monopolize our markets again. But we have had no instance of their selling their goods at cost, or at very low prices, when the supply in the market was deficient, and they had no motive to do so but generosity.

11th. Maxim number 11 assumes that a protective tariff to aid in securing the home market to our own industry, must necessarily be useless, if we can manufacture at as low a money price as the British and French can manufacture for us; and hurtful, if we cannot manufacture as low as their goods can be imported. Both of these assumptions or conclusions are fallacious and false.

As to the first assumption, that it is or would be useless, if we could manufacture as cheap as Great Britain. Let us suppose, for the sake of argument, wages reduced so low in this country, that we could compete successfully in our own markets, though not in theirs, with the British manufacturer. It has been shown that Great Britain has the natural resources, and might, in a few years, by converting her accumulations of capital into manufactures, have the physical capacity, to manufacture cotton, wool, iron and hardware, for the whole civilized world, if she could only command their markets. At the present reduced prices, the income, over and above materials, from capital and labor employed in the forges, iron mills, and factories of Great Britain, amounts to about $400 per annum to each person employed. Such being the case, the profits of manufacturing being so great, if the doors of free trade were thrown open to all the nations cf the earth, the British manufacturers would force their goods into every market, in order to make all the profits in th eir power; and the result would be, that they would divide our market with our manufacturers, and thereby prevent the growth of manufactures in this country, disperse our people, confine them to the less profitable pursuit of agriculture, keep us embarrassed with debt to them, drain us of specie to pay the balance of trade against us, cripple our banking institutions, lessen the industry, and paralyze the energies and enterprise of our country.

* See on this point Sections 3 to 6, and Section21 of Chapter XII.

As I have said before, the question is not so much what so intelligent, active and industrious a people as those of Great Britain and the United States can produce; but *what can they sell at good prices and get their pay for?* Great Britain has the natural resources, and could soon acquire the capacity to manufacture for the world. The natural resources of the United States for mining and manufacturing are, perhaps, still greater; and they have also a territory sufficiently large and fertile to supply provisions for a population of five or six hundred millions. The friends of free trade say we may better confine ourselves mostly to agriculture, and depend on selling our agricultural products to pay for our clothing, iron, hardware, &c. But we already produce more than we can sell, and four years out of five not only our own, but all foreign markets are surfeited with agricultural products of almost every description. It is folly to produce what we do not want and cannot sell. The supposition is, that *wages may be reduced so low in this country, that our manufactures may compete with British manufactures in our own markets, and not in the markets of Great Britain*, or in those of any of the manufacturing nations of Europe; and the result would be, that we never should or could compete with them in their markets. We should be giving them permanently, perhaps, half of our markets for manufactures, and get in return a partial market for our grain and pork, beef, &c., about one year in five. In this mode we should and do employ foreign laborers in preference to our own, and thereby deprive our citizens of profitable employment, and lessen the industry of the nation.

As to wheat and wheat flour, the wheat land of the United States is mostly occupied; and the time is not far distant when we shall have none to export, unless, like the Irish, free trade makes us so poor, that we shall be under the necessity of living on coarse grains, and selling our wheat to the manufacturers of Great Britain and France, to pay for our clothing and other necessaries. We are giving away our markets for the products of the most profitable employments of life; confining ourselves mostly to agriculture, the least profitable of all the departments of human industry; making ourselves dependent on Great Britain and France for many of the necessaries of life; keeping ourselves in a state of colonial dependence, debt and embarrassment; and thus preventing the growth of manufactures in our own country for want of markets sufficiently extensive and stable; and depriving our agriculturists of the benefits of an extensive and secure market for their products at home, without giving them a foreign market of any stability, or much extent and value.

The merchant wants customers who are able to pay, the lawyer wants clients, the doctor patients, the manufacturer wants consumers of his goods, the laborer wants an employer, and the farmer is equally in want of consumers of his produce, who are able to pay for them. A market for their labor, or the products of their labor, is equally necessary for all classes of men, and all departments of industry and business; without which industry languishes, and man becomes indolent; he soon becomes poor also, for want of income. This truth was well expressed by Silas Wright, late Governor of New-York, in the agricultural address written just before his death. He says: "*The active stimulus which urges all forward, excites industry, awakens ingenuity, and brings out invention, is the prospect or the hope of a market for the productions of their labor. The farmer produces to sell; the merchant purchases to sell; and the manufacturer fabricates to sell.*"

A steady and extensive foreign market for vegetables, and most kinds of breadstuffs and provisions, is impossible in the nature of things; on account of the great expense of transportation, and the perishable nature of the commodities themselves. The principal market for food of most kinds, must, therefore, necessarily be a domestic one; and if we give away our market for manufactures, and thus prevent the growth of manufactures in our own country, the farmers of our Western States must remain destitute of good markets; and the income of the West must continue as it is now, from $36 to $45 to each person per annum, while the income of the people of Great Britain and our manufacturing States, will be more than twice as great. But if we secure our domestic markets to our own laborers and manufacturers, and thus build up a large mining and manufacturing interest in this country, we shall thereby improve, increase, and, in fact, create domestic markets for our farmers; we shall also soon have a division of employments in accordance with the wants of the people; shall produce almost everything that we need, and in such quantities as we want; and shall produce nothing in greater quantities than either the domestic or the foreign market demands; and all our wants will be well supplied. In this mode, and in no other, the splendid conception of Adam Smith may be realized, as stated in Section 5 of Chapter XII.

Nor is it a fair conclusion, that duties imposed on imports are useless to the domestic producer and laborer, unless they raise, or keep up prices. They aid in securing the domestic market to domestic producers, and thereby tend to give them full employment. The laws of all the States prescribe the fees of sheriffs, clerks of courts, and many other officers, and in many of the

States, the fees of attorneys are prescribed by law. Does it not make a difference to sheriffs and clerks, whether there are fifty or five hundred suits per year, commenced in their respective counties? Let us suppose attorneys' fees fixed by law at an average of twenty dollars for each suit; would it not make a difference with a lawyer, whether he got at that price, twenty or two hundred suits per year to attend to?

Let us suppose the case of a hotel-keeper with a house, furniture, servants, and accommodations for an hundred persons. Does it not make a difference with him, whether he has daily an hundred guests, or an average of only thirty or forty at the same price per day? Again, let us suppose the case of an iron mill, capable of making ten thousand tons of iron per annum. Does it not make a difference in the amount of profits realized by the owners, and in the amount of wages received by the workmen, whether they make and sell ten thousand tons annually, or can sell, and, therefore, make only five thousand tons at the same prices?

All that is necessary to show the fallacy of the maxim, is to exhibit its practical application.

Let us now examine the other branch of maxim 11; that if we cannot manufacture in this country for as low a price in money as goods can be imported, all tariff laws to restrict importation must generally be hurtful. In the first place a tariff of duties on foreign imports affords the best and easiest mode of collecting revenue to support the Government. Secondly, it aids in securing the home market to the domestic laborer and manufacturer, and thereby stimulates industry, and increases the aggregate incomes of the country. Thirdly, by increasing domestic manufactures, it renders a less quantity of foreign goods necessary to supply the wants of the people, and diminishes the importation of many kinds of goods. And, fourthly, it lessens the importation of foreign luxuries. By these means, it prevents a balance of trade against the country. It is of no importance to a people to have goods offered to them cheap, if they have no means of payment. On the other hand, it is of but little importance how high prices we pay for goods, provided we can pay for them in the products of our own labor at prices equally high. In the latter case, the high prices of the products in which payment is made, balances the nominally high prices of the articles purchased; so that we really buy them on fair terms.

Money is an instrument, and a necessary instrument of domestic commerce; and as Silas Wright well expressed it, "*the farmer produces to sell; the merchant purchases to sell; and the manufacturer fabricates to sell.*" Commerce is the great stimulant to industry; and as domestic commerce cannot be conveniently carried on without money, the exportation of specie to pay the balance of trade which may be against us, tends to paralyze and diminish the industry of the country. Money being fixed capital, and one of the main-springs of industry, whatever regulations of commerce tend to retain it in the country, cannot be otherwise than useful, and cannot be hurtful, as assumed in the maxim.

12. In all commercial transactions, it is most true, that each party obtains what he desires (for the time being at least), more than what he parts with; but that the things exchanged are always of equal value, and the exchange beneficial to both parties, though generally true, is not always so; the maxim is, therefore, untrue, in the general form in which it is laid down by the advocates of free trade. Take, for instance, distilled liquors and wines purchased to be used as a beverage. However wealthy the importer and vender may grow by importing and vending them, it is impossible that they should have any good effect, or be of any real value to the consumer, unless they are used in small quantities as a medicine, in particular conditions of the system. If they are used as a common beverage, in sufficient quantities to produce much effect, the necessary consequence is, that they weaken the judgment and reasoning powers, blunt the conscience and moral sense, and injure the health. Take any foreign luxury, such as silks, satins, fine cloths, pictures and jewelry, fine furniture, fine carriages and equipages; though they may be sold at fair prices, yet, whenever they are purchased by individuals not able to pay for and enjoy them, the purchaser is not benefited, but is actually injured by the purchase, and often ruined by it. Industry and frugality is the road to competence and wealth; while extravagance is the broad way which leadeth to poverty and ruin. Every man should confine his consumption to his circumstances and condition in life; and commerce of every description, both foreign and domestic, should be adapted and confined to the condition and circumstances of the consumer; and whenever it goes beyond this, it is just as profitable to the community for men to jockey horses, or for boys to swap jackets and penknives, as it is for merchants to sell goods. If either party gains, what A gains, B loses, and the time of both parties is lost to the community.

As a general rule, no man should sell the tools and instruments necessary to enable him to carry on his business. The tools, &c., constitute his capital; he should not sell his capital, but only the annual products of his industry. Money has been shown to constitute tools of commerce; it should, therefore, be retained in the country to carry on domestic commerce, and should not be sold to be exported as an article of foreign commerce. It is about as rational for a blacksmith to sell his anvil and bellows, a carpenter his broadaxe and augers, or a shoemaker to sell his awls, as it is for a community not producing the precious metals, to export and sell their coin, the tools of their commerce, to pay for articles of food, dress, or any other species of consumption.

If a man lives in idleness, and pays out his money for food, fuel and clothing, which he might produce, or make himself, though he may purchase at fair prices, yet he is made poorer by the purchase. The same rule applies to nations. Labor is the real source of wealth. Nations, as well as individuals, can grow rich only by producing more than they consume. If they import large amounts of the products of other nations, and consume more in value than they produce, no matter how cheap they may purchase, they must necessarily consume their substance, and grow poor. The seller only and the foreign producer, are benefited in such cases, while the buyer and consumer are injured. The maxim is, therefore, false.

13 and 14. As these maxims cover partially the same ground, I shall consider them together. If all commerce consisted only of a barter of commodities, without any coin to adjust and pay balances, and no debts were contracted, these maxims would be true. But as the supposition is false, the maxims are in the main false also. Every intelligent man knows that specie is constantly exported by countries not producing it, to pay the balances of trade against them.* Even the commercial credit of Great Britain was shaken, and almost destroyed, by reason of the exportation of the precious metals in 1847, caused by the excessive importation of breadstuffs and provisions, during the first few months of FREE TRADE in grain.

It has been shown† that all the colonies of Great Britain, and the greater part of the civilized world beside, are indebted largely to Great Britain; amounting in the aggregate to a sum equal to nearly one-fourth part of all the property in the United States. It seems, therefore, that *Great Britain has refused to buy or take the products of other countries, to an extent sufficient to pay for the goods she has sold to them*; and yet this refusal has not prevented her from surfeiting their markets with her manufactures, and involving them in debt; and she would have involved them still more in debt, if their embarrassments and poverty had not admonished her, that it was prudent to withhold farther credits. These maxims are, therefore, mostly false, though there is some truth in the last clause of maxim numbered 14. Great Britain seldom takes the productions of her colonies, and of agricultural

* See Sections 3 and 12 of Chapter XIII.
† See Section 6 of Chapter XIV.

nations lying in cold climates, to an amount sufficient to pay for the manufactures she sells them ; but she drains them annually of specie to pay part of the balance of trade against them, and involves them in debt beside. The result is, she absorbs all their income which she can get, keeps them poor, prevents them from manufacturing for themselves, and also deprives them of the power to take and pay for her productions, to the full extent which their necessities seem to require. This has been the final effect of her trade with Ireland, with the Canadas, and the other British provinces of North America, and also with the United States ; and such has also been the effect of her trade with India, and with many of the countries of Europe. The foreign imports into the United States during the three fiscal years after the war, ending September 30, 1815, 1816, and 1817, amounted to $337,-000,000. These heavy imports involved the country in debt, paralyzed its industry, and ruined many of the manufacturers, embarrassed all of them, and disabled the people to pay for many foreign goods ; so that the imports during the following three years of 1818, 1819, and 1820, amounted to only about $171,000,000. After the country recovered from its embarrassments under the tariff acts of 1824, 1828, and 1832, and became able to pay, the imports became large under the compromise act—averaging, during the five years from 1835 to 1839, inclusive, about $150,000,000 annually. The same results followed ; the people became embarrassed, and the imports sunk during the next three years, 1840, 1841 and 1842, to an average of less than $112,000,000 per annum. We may expect the same results to follow the large importations under the tariff of 1846.

Those maxims assume what is frequently asserted, that the principles of free trade are in accordance with, and regulated by, the laws of nature ; that they tend to check and prevent excesses, and to cure the evils which they produce. The evils of free trade and of excessive imports, do tend to check themselves by alarming creditors, and destroying the credit of the debtor nation ; but they never tend to repair the injuries they produce. When a patient is prostrated by fever, the vigor of his constitution may be sufficient to stand the shock, and the curative powers of nature may restore him after the fever has run its course. So with countries like Ireland and the British colonies and provinces—constantly depleted by free trade and excessive imports, which paralyze their industry—or, like the United States, often depleted, and occasionally convulsed by an adverse balance of trade. The people, by means of industry and a system of frugality, forced upon them by their circumstances, are enabled to live under, and bear the burthens imposed upon them; but it would be as rational to say in the case of the patient, that the fever cured itself, as it is to say that free trade and excessive imports cure, or repair the evils they produce.

It has been said that all the nations of the earth should be bound together by the ties of commerce, like a band of brothers; that philanthropy and the principles of liberty require us to adopt the principles of free trade, and to import without restriction, and consume the products of the nations of Europe. We open our doors to immigrants, receive and treat them as citizens, employ them, and consume the products of their industry, when they come and reside in our country, and take our products in payment; but neither justice, charity nor liberality, requires us to consume their products, while they remain in Europe, to the prejudice of the best interests of our own country.

15. Maxim number 15 is partly true, and partly false. It is not true, that imports are necessarily paid for with domestic products, whereby domestic industry is increased; they are sometimes paid for in coin, sometimes in bills of exchange on other countries, drawn for the proceeds of products sold to them—sometimes in national, State, city, or corporate bonds, and sometimes a mercantile debt is accumulated.

Foreign products are, to be sure, mostly paid for with domestic products; foreign commerce does, therefore, give employment to domestic industry so far as it opens a foreign market for domestic products, and transports them to it. Suppose it to open a foreign market for domestic products to the amount of ten millions of dollars, all the proceeds of which are paid for in products which do not come in competition with domestic products. In that case, domestic industry is increased to the full amount of the ten millions. If, on the contrary, all the proceeds of such exports are imported in products which come in competition with domestic products, and which might be produced at home, then there is no increase of industry by reason of it; the only effect being to turn domestic industry into a different channel. If half the proceeds are imported in products which do not come in competition with domestic products, and the other half in those that do supersede so much in amount of domestic products, in that case, domestic industry will be increased to the amount of five millions. But if for the ten millions of exports, fifteen millions should be imported, all of which come in competition with, and supersede, so much in amount of domestic products, the balance of five millions being paid in specie, or accumulated in debt, to be paid for in future, the operation would diminish domestic industry to the amount of the five millions.

Sec. 10. *Importance of organizing capital and labor.*

Tariff laws are of but little use, however, except for purposes of revenue, among a people wanting in either intelligence or industry, to manufacture for themselves. Though agriculture requires more capital in proportion to the laborers employed than mining and manufactures, yet there is this difference in them: Two persons, as a general rule, can work on a farm about as advantageously as twenty can. Not so with manufactures. They require a more minute division of employments; and a combination of an extensive capital in many cases, with the labor of a great number of persons, under the direction of one head, and several superintendents of minor departments, in order to make labor and capital the most productive. Such employments must be directed by science, experience, and business talent; and the requisite capacity cannot be commanded without high salaries, which no establishment can afford to pay, unless a large capital and a large number of laborers are employed. *Capital and labor must, therefore, be combined and organized*, in order to prosecute either manufactures or mining to the greatest advantage.

The common law of England, and the local laws and customs of the countries of Europe being generally defective, and not adapted to the management of combined or associated capital, it became necessary to obtain special charters to organize associations of capitalists and laborers, and to regulate the management of their capital and business. These special charters for mechanical, manufacturing, mining, commercial, and many other purposes, have been common in Europe ever since the Crusades; and though many abuses grew out of the exclusive privileges and monopolies unnecessarily granted to them, yet the charters and associations were the mainsprings of nearly all the enterprise, and of the spirit of liberty, as well as of inquiry, invention, and discovery, and of progress in improvement, productive industry and civilization, between the time of the Crusades and the great Reformation of the 16th century; and of much of the improvement and progress made since the latter period. Though the exclusive privileges and monopolies, formed no necessary part of the charters and associations, yet being associated together, and the abuses being prominent, they made a powerful effect on the mind of Adam Smith. He did not discriminate properly between them, but confounded the whole together; and exhibited the evils arising from them in bold relief, as the necessary tendency of the associations themselves. He attributed nearly all the progress of the age to what he called *division of labor;* when in truth it has *resulted from an organization of labor and capital associated or combined, and from the division of employments.*

THE ORGANIZATION AND COMBINATION OF LABOR AND CAPITAL, AND THEIR PROPER REGULATION *may, therefore, be regarded as one of the chief mainsprings of manufacturing and mining industry; equal in importance to the protection of the home market.* By organization of capital and labor, I do not mean its association on the principles of the Fourierism or Communism of France, or of the Shakerism or Owenism of America; nor do I mean a general community of property and income of any kind, among the persons associated. Such associations diminish the motives necessary to induce industry, attention, and frugality, to improve the mind, and develope the capacities of man. They tend to destroy individuality of character; to discourage inquiry and invention, and to check progress. By the organization of labor and capital, I mean their organization under general statutes of incorporation, like those of Massachusetts, and the new statutes of New York, merely prescribing the mode of organization; regulating the management of the associated capital and business; granting no special privileges or exemptions from personal liability to any class or classes of men; limiting the power of the corporation or association, to contract debts; and prescribing proper legal remedies for and against the corporation and the stockholders thereof. In this mode all the advantages of associated capital and labor, and the division of employments are attained; without losing those arising from free competition and the stimulus of individual interest, which are numerous and very great. In order to give the small stockholders their proper influence in the management of the property and business of the association, and to protect their rights against combinations to defraud them, the elections should be conducted on the principles suggested in Chapter V., Section 9. All the laborers should be encouraged to become stockholders. This would increase their care and diligence, and tend to promote frugality and good morals.

Nearly all the heavy manufacturing establishments of New England are the property of numerous persons associated under acts of incorporation; and in most of them, a considerable portion of the stock is owned by the superintendents and persons laboring in them. Almost the whole male population are devoted to some useful employment or business; nearly all the wealthy and most influential men have arisen from the plough, the work-shop, the factory, or the lowest stations in the store or counting-room, and are practical business men. To be out of business and idle, is not considered respectable in Holland; nor is it in New England.

No employment or diversity of employments can render a

whole people equally wealthy. There will necessarily be differences in capacity, differences in energy and persevering industry, differences in frugality, and differences in the amount of favors distributed by the accidents of fortune. Manufactures, and a diversity of employments never, however, make any class of people the poorer; and if they cannot make all equally wealthy, they at least contribute to promote the well-being of every individual in the community.

The inhabitants of Massachusetts and Rhode Island have the largest average annual incomes of any people in the world, with the exception of some slaveholding communities, cultivating sugar, coffee, and cotton; and, perhaps, they are the best specimens as a whole, of a well educated, intelligent, moral, religious, industrious, and highly prosperous people which the civilized world can exhibit. Let those individuals, communities and States, that wish to become prosperous, study their institutions and their history, and follow their example.

CHAPTER XVI.

ON ROADS AND OTHER INTERNAL IMPROVEMENTS, THE MEANS OF COMMUNICATION AND CONVEYANCE IN DIFFERENT COUNTRIES, AND THEIR EFFECTS ON THE INTELLIGENCE AND INDUSTRY OF NATIONS.

SEC. 1. *Posts and Post Offices.*

The establishment of posts, to furnish horses for post-boys or carriers, who carried dispatches for the government, is attributed to Cyrus, who first established them in Persia. They were introduced among the Romans by the Emperor Augustus, and were instituted in France by Charlemagne, about the year 800. Post Offices, for the regular transmission of letters by post-boys, were first instituted by Louis XI. of France, about the year 1470. Like posts, they were originally intended merely to facilitate the conveyance of letters and dispatches for the government; but, soon after their establishment, individuals were allowed to avail themselves of the institution, for the conveyance of letters and dispatches on private business, on paying certain rates of postage for the privilege.

The Post Office was not established in England, until the 17th century. A system of posts was established in England, in the time of Edward the IV., about the year 1481, and Postmasters were appointed; but their business was confined to furnishing post horses to the carriers of the government, and to persons who were desirous of travelling expeditiously, or wished to send extraordinary packets upon special occasions. In 1635, Charles I. established a letter office, for the transmission of letters between England and Scotland; but this extended only to a few of the principal roads; the times of carriage were uncertain, and the Postmasters on each road were required to furnish horses for the conveyance of the letters, at the rate of 2½d per mile. Dr. Brande says this establishment did not succeed, and that at the breaking out of the civil war, great difficulty was experienced in the transmission of letters. At length a Post Office, or a national establishment for the weekly conveyance of letters to all parts of the kingdom, was instituted by Cromwell in 1649.

From the establishment of the Post Office down to the year 1784, the mails were carried, either on horse-back, or in carts made for the purpose. In 1784, (Dr. Brande says), it was usual for the stage coaches, between London and Bath, to accomplish the journey (about 100 miles) in 17 hours, while the post took 40 hours; the comparative rate of travelling of the post and stage coaches, was in about the same proportion on other roads, and that, during that year, the first contracts were made to carry the mails in stage coaches. Even as late as 1730, the mail was sent only three times a week between London and Edinburgh.

As late as the year 1838, the average rate of postage in Great Britain was about 7d., or 14 cents, for carrying a single letter. Postages have been since reduced to one penny per letter, and the most of the mails are carried on railroads, at the rate of from 30 to 40 miles per hour.

The receipts of the Post Office Department have been as follows:—

In England, in			1686,	£ 65,000	sterling.
Great Britain,			1763,	238,999	"
Do.	do.		1800,	1,083,950	"
Do.	do.		1820,	1,993,885	"
Great Britain and Ireland			1820,	2,191,562	"
Do.	do.	do.	1839,	2,467,215	"
Do.	do.	do.	1840,	1,359,466*	"
Do.	do.	do.	1849,	2,165,349	"

The first establishment of Post Offices in the United States, while colonies, was in 1710. The number of Post Offices in the United States, the extent in miles of post roads, and the amount of postages received at different periods, have been as follows:—

Years.	Post Offices.	Post Roads. Miles.	Postages. Dollars.
1790,	75	1,875	37,935
1800,	903	20,817	280,804
1820,	4,500	72,492	1,111,927
1830,	8,000	115,000	1,850,583
1840,	13,868	155,739	4,539,269
1848,	16,159	163,208	4,371,077

* 1840 was the first year after the adoption of the uniform system of penny postage.

Sec. 2. *Roads in ancient and modern times.*

The ancients had but few roads fit for wheeled carriages—very few, indeed, except those made in and about cities, and such as were made in the country for military purposes. All their travelling was on horses, mules, camels and elephants, and the transportation of products was either by the same mode of conveyance, or by water. The invention of paved roads is traced to the Carthaginians. The Romans learned from the Carthaginians; and during the time of Julius and Augustus Cæsar, Rome was made to communicate with all the chief towns of Italy by paved roads; and leading roads were made mostly for military purposes through all the provinces of the empire.

The first roads of artificial construction in England were made by the Romans, while it was a Roman province. A grand trunk road was carried through the country, north and south, and another nearly at right angles to it, from east to west; and the main lines were supplied with many branches. After the fall of the empire, the subject of roads was entirely neglected, the Roman roads were allowed to fall into decay, and no new ones, except about cities, were constructed.

For many centuries, there were no roads in England fit for waggons or carriages—none but rude paths, fit only for foot passengers, and travellers on horse-back. The condition of all the north of Europe was the same, and that of the south of Europe was very little better.

One-horse carts were used some; but, with the exception of Italy and the Netherlands, the general mode of transportation throughout Europe, up to the close of the 16th century, was by pack horses, and mules, or by water. Such is the condition of the roads, and the general mode of conveyance to this day, in Spain, Portugal, Turkey, Mexico, and all South America. Even fuel and provender for horses are generally carried in Mexico on the backs of horses and mules, at the present time.

Every country emerged from barbarism, must necessarily have roads of some kind; but the expense of making a few leading roads only, has ever been paid out of the national treasury in any country. The statute of Philip and Mary (passed about the middle of the 16th century) is said by Mr. McCulloch to be the first legislative enactment in England, in which provision is made for the regular repair of the roads by the people, under the direction of surveyors of the highways, chosen annually in each parish. About the year 1663, the practice was adopted of imposing tolls for travelling on the great roads, to raise funds to improve them, and keep them in repair; the appropriations under the acts of

Philip and Mary, were then applied entirely to the improvement and repair of the cross roads, and the common roads in the country

Sec. 3. *Turnpike roads, Carriages, and Coaches.*

The first turnpike road on which toll was taken, was established in England about the year 1665. Turnpikes were not introduced into the United States until after the revolutionary war, about the year 1790. The roads then in the United States, fit for carriages, and the transmission of the mail, were very few, as is indicated by the few miles (only 1,875) of post roads.

Though chariots and wheeled carriages were invented at an early period, yet those used by the Romans and other ancient nations, and those in use in England and throughout Europe, until after the middle of the 17th century, were mostly one-horse vehicles, generally having but two wheels ; and comparatively few of any kind were used.

Coaches were invented in France about the year 1500, but were not introduced into England until about the year 1553. They were then without springs, which were an invention of a later date. It is said that there were only two coaches in Paris in the reign of Henry II., about the middle of the 16th century. Coaches were first let for hire in Paris about the year 1650.

Stage coaches commenced running in England, for the transportation of passengers, soon after the improvement of the great roads, and the introduction of turnpikes, in the time of Charles II. The first stage coach commenced running between Edinburgh and Glasgow in 1678. So late as the year 1763, there was but one stage coach running between London and Edinburgh, which set out only once a month, and took from 12 to 14 days to run from one city to the other, a distance of 337 miles. I suppose they were not introduced into the United States until the establishment of turnpike roads, which was since the year 1790.

The improvement of the roads, and the introduction of turnpikes and stage coaches, changed the mode of travelling in Great Britain, France, and many other countries, including all Protestant Europe, and also in the United States of America ; but the mode of travelling and transporting products and merchandise, on the backs of horses and mules, still continues the same in Spain, Portugal, Mexico, and all South America, where there are to this day very few roads fit for stage coaches, or even waggons.

There were in England and Wales in 1829, no less than 20,895 miles of turnpike roads, and over ninety-five thousand miles of other roads, used for waggons and carriages, beside about two thousand and five hundred miles of paved streets. There were at the same time 3,666 miles of turnpike roads in Scotland.

Mr. Murray in his geography, speaking of Spain, says, "The main roads, maintained by government between Madrid and the other great cities, are good, and the mails well conducted; but most of the other communications are mere tracks, worn by the feet of mules, which are chiefly employed in the conveyance of goods." I presume there are not one-tenth part, and very likely not one-twentieth part as many miles of roads fit for waggons and coaches in Spain, as there are in either Great Britain or the United States.

France and Germany were no better provided with roads than England, before the introduction of turnpikes, and not so well supplied since that time. Prior to the revolution of 1789, France had a few leading roads between the cities, which were fit for coaches, and but a few. Even at this day, France has less than one-fourth part as many miles of roads fit for coaches or waggons, in proportion to the extent of the country, as Great Britain. The roads of France are divided into royal, departmental, and communal; comprising in the whole, an extent at the beginning of the year 1837, of about 53,320 miles, as stated by McCulloch. The royal roads constitute the great roads of the country. They were constructed by the government at great expense, and their aggregate extent was then stated at about 21,455 miles. The departmental roads are made and kept in repair at the expense of the several departments, and are under the superintendence of the central board of bridges and public highways, which has a head engineer in each department. They are generally good; but the communal roads, which are made by the communes, or local authorities, are subject to no such control. The latter are generally very poor, and often impracticable for carriages.

SEC. 4. *Origin and progress of Canals.*

Some time previous to the Christian era, a canal was made from the Red Sea to the river Nile in Egypt. The great canal of China is said to have been commenced as early as the ninth century. Some small canals were made in Flanders as early as the 12th or 13th century; very many were made in Holland in the 17th century, though they were generally small; those made in the 18th century were much larger; but the largest canals in Holland, those of greatest depth and width, have been made during the 19th century.

The Briare canal, from the Loire to the Seine, (about 38

miles), was the first canal made in France. It was commenced under Henry IV., in the year 1605, and finished about the year 1640. The second one made in France was the canal of Languedoc, which was constructed during the reign of Louis XIV, between the years 1666 and 1681. It is about 170 miles long, 6½ feet deep, and connects the river Garonne with the Mediterranean. The next was the Orleans canal, commenced in 1675, and finished about the year 1720.

France had, in 1840, about 1600 miles of navigable canals, which cost about $60,000,000 ; of which there were made in the 17th century about 250 miles ; in the 18th century about 250 miles ; and in the 19th century, up to 1840, about 1,100 miles.

Peter the Great commenced canaling in Russia the early part of the 18th century. Canals were also made during the 18th century in Prussia, Denmark, and some other countries of Europe ; a greater number of miles of canals were made during the first fifty years of the present century, than had ever been previously constructed.

England is one of the last countries of Europe which engaged in the construction of canals; but at the present time, the canals of Great Britain, exceed those of every other country, except the United States. Mr. Murray makes the following remark in his "Encyclopedia of Geography :" "The interior navigation of England is justly regarded as one of the prime sources of her prosperity. Till the middle of last century, the making of canals did not enter into the system of English economy. In 1755 was formed the Sankey Canal, a line of twelve miles, to supply Liverpool with coal from the pits of St. Helens. The example then set by the Duke of Bridgwater gave a general impulse to the nation. Since that time, upwards of £30,000,000 sterling have been expended in this object. Twenty-one canals have been carried across the central chain of hills, by processes in which no cost has been spared ; all the resources of art and genius have been employed ; every obstacle, however formidable, which nature could present, has been vanquished. By locks, and by inclined planes, the vessels are conveyed up and down the most rugged steeps ; they are even carried across navigable rivers by bridges. When other means fail, the engineer has cut through the heart of rocks and hills a subterraneous passage. Of these tunnels, as they are called, there are said to be forty-eight, the entire length of which is at least forty miles." He states the total length of canals in Great Britain, excluding those under five miles, at 2,581 miles.

There are only two canals of any importance in Ireland. The Royal Canal, 83 miles long, cost £1,420,000 ; and the Grand Canal, 156 miles, cost about £2,000,000.

Though there had been some short canals made in the United States prior to the Erie canal of New York, yet that was the first of much importance. The Erie Canal was commenced July 4th, 1817; first navigated from Utica to Rome, fifteen miles, October 23d, 1819; 280 miles of the eastern part finished, and the first boat passed through it into the Hudson at Albany, October 8th, 1823; and the whole line of 364 miles completed in October, 1825. The original cost was $7,143,789.

There were in the United States, at the end of the year 1845, about 3,450 miles of navigable canals; of which about 3,000 miles, costing about $89,000,000 were in the free States; and about 450 miles, costing about $22,000,000, were in the slave States. With the exception of the Erie Canal, nearly all of them have been made since the year 1825.

Sec. 5. *Railroads and Locomotives.*

Railways are of modern invention. They were at first, (about the middle of the 17th century,) made of timber only, and used to transport coals from the pits in the coal districts of Northumberland and Durham in England, to navigable waters. They were made by laying down parallel tracks of timber with a horse path between them, the wheels being confined upon the beams or rails of timber by flanges projecting from the inside of the tires of the wheels. Soon afterwards double timber railways were invented; one rail being laid upon another, with cross ties or sleepers. The next improvement consisted in the addition of a plate of bar-iron, about two inches broad, and half an inch thick, laid upon the upper surface of the wooden rail, and attached to it by spikes.

The plate railway, or Tramway of cast iron, came into use in the collieries in the north of England about the year 1770. About twenty years afterwards, and after the improvement of making bar-iron by rolling was invented, and bar-iron had become more abundant, the edge-rail of bar-iron was introduced. For many years after their first adoption, edge-railways were confined to the mining districts, and more particularly to the collieries, where they were used to transport the products of the mines to the places of shipment; but this species of road acquired vastly increased importance when passengers and goods began to be transported on it by Locomotive Engines, which took place between Liverpool and Manchester in the year 1830.

The first Locomotive Engine was used on a railroad at Merthyr Tydvil in South Wales in 1804; but the engine and carriage were not so constructed as to be of much practical value. In

1814 one was made which drew a load of thirty tons, at the rate of six miles per hour. Before the Liverpool and Manchester Railroad was completed, the directors offered a premium for the best Locomotive for their road. This stimulated invention, and excited much competition. The time to test the engines was appointed, and took place on the road in October, 1829. Several engines were produced and tried ; the prize was awarded to one called the Rocket, constructed by Mr. Robert Stevenson. On the first trial, this engine attained a speed of fifteen miles an hour, and it ran one mile at the rate of twenty-nine miles an hour. This improvement in Locomotives, opened a new era in railways, and in the mode of transporting both property and persons.

The whole expenditure on railways in Great Britain, up to the end of the year 1830, was only about £4,000,000 sterling. Nothing had then been expended in Ireland.

Statement in round numbers, of the amount of expenditure on railways, in the United Kingdom of Great Britain and Ireland, at the undermentioned periods, and the number of miles opened for use :

		Miles opened.	Total expenditure.
1830,	Dec. 31,		£ 4,000,000
1840,	" "	about 1,100	60,000,000
1845,	June 30,	" 2,343	80,000,000
1849,	Dec. 31,	" 6,031	200,000,000
1850,	Oct.	" 6,621	225,000,000

Of which there were in 1850, in England and Wales, 5,132 miles,
in Scotland, 951 "
and in Ireland, only 538 "

There were also, on the 31st December, 1849, about 1,500 miles of railroad in the progress of construction.

The first train of railway passenger cars in the United States, was put in motion upon the Baltimore and Ohio Railway, which was opened from Baltimore to Ellicott's Mills, a distance of thirteen miles, on the 29th of December, 1829. Two carriages or coaches put on car wheels, were drawn by a single horse, at the rate of from ten to twelve miles per hour.

The charter for the Mohawk and Hudson Railroad Company was granted by the legislature of the State of New York in April, 1826 ; the work was commenced August 12th, 1830 ; and the most of it constructed from Albany to Schenectady, a distance of fifteen miles, during the year 1831, and opened for use that fall. This was the first railroad of much importance made in the United States ; but works were projected and some commenced soon afterwards in nearly every State in the Union.

There were in use in the United States in 1830, less than 100 miles in extent of railways. In 1840, the railways in use were equal to 3,328 miles in extent; of which 1,853 miles were in free States, and 1,472 miles in the Slave States. There were in operation in the Free States in 1845, about 2,942 miles of railways, and in the Slave States 1,763 miles. In 1851, the number of miles in operation in the Free States had increased to over seven thousand, besides over 5,500 in the progress of construction; and in the Slave States those in operation had increased to 2,700 miles, besides over 1,900 miles in the progress of construction. The amount expended in railways, and their appendages and stock upon them, up to July, 1851, in the Free States, was about $247,000,000, and in the Slave States about $55,500,000.

No railroads of much consequence were constructed on the Continent of Europe, prior to the year 1830, and comparatively little was done towards their construction on the continent until since the year 1835.

The railroads of Belgium cost about $20,000,000; the principal lines of which were opened in 1835; their extent is about 350 miles.

There were in operation in France, in 1845, twelve railroads, extending about 518 miles, which cost about $44,500,000; in July, 1851, they had increased to 1,831 miles.

At the end of August, 1844, there were many railroads in the progress of construction in Germany and Prussia, and about 1,100 miles opened for use; in July, 1851, they had increased to about 4,542 miles.

The railroads of Russia, and of all other countries, have been made since the year 1840. The extent of railroads in use in different countries, in 1851, was as follows—in the United States about 10,000 miles; in Great Britain, 6,083 miles; in Ireland, 538 miles; in France, 1,831 miles; in Prussia, Germany and Austria, 4,542 miles; in Belgium about 350 miles; in Russia, 422 miles; in Spain 60 miles; in Canada about 100 miles; in the Island of Cuba, 359 miles; in Panama, 22 miles; and in South America, 30 miles.

Railroads, like common schools for the education of the people, newspapers and periodicals, and the use of machinery for manufacturing, appear to be mostly confined to Protestant communities, and to those on which Catholicism sits loosely and lightly.

SEC. 6. *Steamers, Electric Telegraphs, and Plank Roads.*

The first steamboat of any practical value ever constructed, was the Clermont, built by Robert Fulton, which made her first

22*

trip from New York to Albany in July, 1807, in thirty-two hours, and returned in thirty hours. Boats now (1851) run the same distance (about 150 miles) in from seven to ten hours, and all the lakes, rivers and bays of the United States are covered with steam vessels, which do, perhaps, half or more of all the internal transportation business of the nation. They have not only produced almost a complete revolution in the mode of carrying passengers by sea, as well as on lakes and rivers, but they bid fair to effect a similar revolution in the whole system of maritime warfare also. Their effect is to make mechanical power and science, a substitute for muscular power, in the arts of war, as well as in peace.

The first steamboat used in Great Britain was the Comet—a small vessel of 40 feet keel and 10½ feet beam, with an engine of three horse power, which carried passengers on the river Clyde, in Scotland, in 1811; two years later, the Elizabeth, of eight horse power, and the Clyde of fourteen horse power, were built and used on the same river.

Statement of the number of steam vessels belonging to England, Scotland, and Ireland respectively, and the aggregate amount of tonnage thereof, at the undermentioned periods.

	Number of vessels in			
Years.	England.	Scotland.	Ireland.	Total Tonnage.
1815,	3	5		638 tons.
1820,	17	14	3	3,018 "
1830,	203	61	31	30,009 "
1840,	560	129	79	87,539 "
1844,	679	137	81	113,232 "
1849,	865	166	111	158,729 "

The tonnage of the registered, enrolled and licensed steamboats and steam vessels belonging to the United States, amounted, in 1840, to 202,319 tons; and in 1850, it had increased to 525,946 tons. The number built during the fiscal year, ending June 30th, 1850, was 159.

The first line of ocean steamers intended to cross the Atlantic, was established in 1838. Several lines are now employed between England and the United States, which make their trips regularly, in from ten to fifteen days. The passage has been shortened more than one-half; the usual passage of packet ships at the present time, is from twenty to over thirty days, and it was formerly much longer.

The greatest and most splendid achievement ever made by science, was the application of electro-magnetism to the transmission of intelligence. The Electric Telegraph is an American invention; it was patented by Professor Morse in the year 1840, and first put in operation between Washington and Baltimore in 1844. It will transmit intelligence so much faster than rogues, swindlers and criminals can travel, and send a statement of their offences, and a description of their persons in advance of them, that it is very valuable as an instrument in aiding the police. It is also useful in transmitting commercial intelligence, and has a tendency to destroy the pernicious system of itinerant speculation in produce and merchandize, which was formerly practised, on the receipt of any change in the markets of Europe, or on our seaboard. It will also be of great service to a country invaded by a foreign enemy; as it will transmit information to the government of the movements of the enemy with the speed of lightning, and enable them to concentrate their forces at the point of attack, to repel the invasion. It will, therefore, be of immense benefit to a people acting on the defensive; and will render defensive warfare much more efficient, certain, and less expensive; and make aggressive warfare, or a war for conquest in a corresponding manner, more difficult and dangerous, by requiring a greater number of troops, and greater supplies to meet the concentrated forces of the country attacked. In this view of the subject, it may be of great importance to the peace of the world, and to the cause of civilization.

The electric telegraph is extensively used in the United States, and also in many countries of Europe.

Plank roads were first introduced into Upper Canada about the year 1837, and from thence into Western New York. The first one made in Ohio was commenced in 1846; but they are now very numerous in New York, Ohio, Michigan, and several other States. Being very cheaply built in a new country, where timber is cheap, they have proved to be of great value in proportion to their cost.

SEC. 7. *Productiveness of Canals and Railroads, and their effects.*

The principal canals, and the leading lines of railroad in Great Britain, between their great cities, were at first exceedingly profitable, yielding a net income of from six to twelve per cent. annually. But the roads have been so multiplied, and the business divided among so many canals and railroads, that the business of nearly all of them is necessarily limited to a small territory; and the result is, that the aggregate net income of all the railroads in Great Britain has been reduced to less than three per cent. per annum, on their cost. They have nearly destroyed the value of the stock of the greater part of the turnpike roads, and reduced greatly, the value of the stock of the canals.

Similar effects have been partially developed, and will soon be more extensively felt in the United States. Excessive competition produces substantially the same effects on canals and railroads, as in staging, raising Indian corn, wheat, making pork, or producing any other perishable commodity. If two bushels of corn are produced when only one is needed, the excess will be wasted, or perish, and be valueless to the community; so if two railroads are made where only one is wanted, the capital invested in making the second will be lost to the nation.

Neither the canals nor the railroads of Ireland have ever been profitable investments of capital. The tolls received on the Royal Canal of Ireland, in 1831, amounted to only about £12,700, though it is 83 miles in length, and cost £1,420,000, or nearly as much as the Erie Canal.

Taking into consideration the surface of the country, its productiveness, the small amount of lockage on the Erie Canal, and the fact that it connects the tide water of one of the noblest rivers in the world (the Hudson), one hundred and fifty miles from the ocean, with four great inland seas, and, by means of the canals of Ohio, Indiana, and Illinois (its tributaries), connects the Hudson with the navigable waters of the Ohio and Mississippi rivers, it has greater advantages than any other canal on the globe. Perhaps this is the only canal in our country, which yields a clear income equal to the interest on its cost. The canals of Pennsylvania and Ohio generally, yield less than three per cent. net income on their cost; and some of those of New Jersey, Maryland, Virginia, Indiana and the other States, are like the Royal Canal in Ireland, and pay little more than the expenses of tending them, and keeping them in repair. The canal of Languedoc in France, and most of the other canals in that country, have been equally unproductive.

The main lines of railroad first constructed in New York, New England, New Jersey, and from Philadelphia to Baltimore and Washington, and some few other roads, have proved very profitable to the stockholders. Their profits are mostly derived from the transportations of passengers, carrying the mails, and tolls on valuable merchandise, and but a small proportion of it from tolls on the raw materials of agriculture. The most of the canals and railroads of Pennsylvania have never been very profitable, and there is scarcely a single road or canal south or south-west from the Potomac, which yields a net income equal to the interest on its cost.

The history and effects of canals and railroads seem to establish the following propositions: 1st. That the principal income of all the most profitable railroads in America, as well as in Europe, is derived from carrying passengers, and the transportation of the products of mining and manufacturing industry.

2dly. That the greater part of agricultural products are so cheap in proportion to their weight and bulk, that very few, if any, railroads or canals can yield much profit, if their principal income is derived from the transportation of such articles.

3dly. That canals and railroads aid commerce, and mining and manufacturing industry, much more than they do agriculture.

And, 4thly. That they should follow population and business, and not attempt to penetrate the wilderness in advance of them.

Whether we look to the canals of France, of Ireland, those of New Jersey or Ohio, or any other State or country, the result is the same; those which depend for their income mostly on the transportation of agricultural products have never been found very productive. The products of warm and hot climates, worth from two to fifty cents per pound, can be advantageously transported great distances to market on canals and railroads; and the products of manufacturing industry, which are worth from six cents to six pounds sterling per pound, may be carried the world over on railroads, or on camels' backs, mules or pack-horses, and yet the cost of transportation will bear such a moderate proportion to the value of the article, that the manufacturer may be well rewarded for his industry. Some agricultural products of cold and temperate climates, such as wool, butter, cheese, wheat flour, and salted beef and pork, may be carried great distances on navigable waters to a market, provided they will command a ready sale and high prices; but it is impossible to transport rye, buckwheat, Indian corn, oats, potatoes, and other vegetables, hay, &c., very far on canals and railroads, before the cost of transportation consumes the whole value of the product when brought to market; and the articles which may be profitably taken to a distant market are so few, that it requires a very great extent of country to supply a sufficient quantity of them to make a railroad or canal profitable. The Erie Canal transports nearly all the merchandise consumed, and the agricultural products sent to a distant market produced by many millions of inhabitants. No other work, either of Europe or America, does the business of so numerous a people. It is not strange that the Erie Canal is profitable, when nearly all the other canals and railroads of agricultural countries are unprofitable.

Many railroads and canals, however, which have not proved good investments of capital to the stockholders, have been valuable to the country through which they run, and have increased the value of property to the full amount of their cost. But where two such improvements run near each other, either of which would accommodate the whole country accommodated by the two, though a few villages may be benefited by the second improvement, yet others are injured by the competition, and in the aggregate, no benefit whatever to the nation arises from it. In a comparatively new country, however, like the most of the United States, an expensive improvement may in many districts be nearly valueless at the present time, which may be of great value within the next twenty years, when the country shall have become more populous, and its resources more fully developed.

If the people of a state or country have not sufficient capital to construct a railroad or other improvement, it will not, under ordinary circumstances, improve their condition, to incur a heavy debt, and build it by loans, the burthens of which generally overbalance all the advantages of the work. If foreign capitalists will take stock in an incorporated company, and furnish capital to do the work, the evil will be much less to the community than to do it by loans; but even then, the payment to distant capitalists of the income of the work, serves to drain the country of money, and is no trifling evil. The evils of debt are discussed in Section 11 of Chapter XIII.

Roads, canals, railroads, steamboats, and other means of communication and transportation, serve as instruments and agents to aid production, and to promote both industry and commerce. Mining for iron cannot be prosecuted without facilities for transporting the ore, and fuel to smelt it, to the furnace; and manufacturing establishments must have facilities of collecting and conveying to them the raw materials to be manufactured, and also fuel, as well as facilities at cheap rates, to transport their manufactured products to market. Manufactures and mining (except for the precious metals) cannot be carried on extensively without such facilities; for without cheap transportation, the products cannot be conveyed far enough to command an extensive market. But coarse agricultural products cannot generally be transported very far, with all the facilities which man has been able to invent, before the cost of transportation will equal the value of the product, and leave nothing to the farmer. Mining for iron and coal, as well as manufacturing on a large scale, cannot be carried on without the aid of either navigable waters, canals, or railroads. Hence railroads, and other internal improvements, aid mining and manufacturing industry much more than they do agriculture. And hence the people of agricultural districts have been very generally disappointed, in not deriving as great advantages from canals and railroads as they anticipated, unless they availed themselves of such improvements to introduce manufactures, and thereby create a market at home for their agricultural products.

SEC. 8. *Effect of Steamboats, Railroads, and Electric Telegraphs, in disseminating knowledge among men.*

Turnpike roads, steamboats and railroads have all greatly increased mail facilities, and the circulation of newspapers; and, together with the electric telegraph, have increased the circulation of information, since the adoption of the Constitution of the United States, perhaps ten fold. Railroads also constitute a means of educating the people by travel, and opportunities for observation. Perhaps five times as large a proportion of the people of the United States, of Great Britain, and some other countries of Europe, are accustomed to travel at the present time as were a century since, and each travels four times as much; making the amount of travel twenty times as great, in proportion to the population in 1850, as it was in the year 1750. This subject is illustrated by the recent WORLD'S EXHIBITION, in the CRYSTAL PALACE in LONDON, and the MILLIONS WHO ATTENDED IT. All those things tend to disseminate knowledge among men—to enlighten the masses, as well as to diffuse information among the educated classes, and to promote the cause and progress of civilization.

CHAPTER XVII.

On castes, orders of men, systems of religion, associations, corporations, political parties, and savings banks.

Sec. 1. *Condition of Society, and Castes of the ancient world—the laboring classes uneducated.*

The term Caste denotes the hereditary classes into which the population of Hindostan is divided, according to the religious system of Brama. Traces of the system of caste, which confines employments to hereditary classes, are to be found in the institutions of many countries, and in the history of many more. That the ancient Egyptians were thus divided, is well known; and it is supposed that similar institutions prevailed in the Assyrian empire. According to Plato, the Athenians, in the first ages of their commonwealth, were divided into five classes; priests, shepherds and hunters, ploughmen, mechanics, and soldiers. The tribe of Levi was set aside as a caste, or hereditary order of priests, among the Israelites; and they were supported by tithes.

The ancient Romans, and all the inhabitants of Italy, at the time of the foundation of Rome, were divided into patricians and plebeians. The former possessed nearly all the real estate of the country, and all the learning; the latter were poor and dependent peasants and laborers. Such was the condition of the whole ancient world, with the exception of the Tyrians, Athenians, and a few other commercial nations. Every man was trained to the pursuit of his ancestors, had no other education, and was not fitted for any other calling. The mass of the people were ignorant, and inherited their condition, which it was impossible for them to change. There was no organization of associations among the laboring classes, and no means of forming any; and consequently there was no interchange of opinions, no action in concert, no means of acquiring information, and no means of exercising power, or improving their condition. Education, organization, association, the possession and exercise or power, were all (with few exceptions) confined to the priests and higher castes in some countries, and to the patricians and the wealthy in others.

SEC. 2. *Origin of Associations distinct from the government, and of corporations.*

Though priests, military chieftains, and the members of various kinds of aristocracy, had their associations and assemblies in many countries, yet there were no organized associations among the peasantry and the laboring classes prior to the Christian era. Even in republican Rome, there were no associations among the plebeians or laboring classes, except political parties attached to party leaders; and in imperial Rome, organized clandestine assemblies were prohibited, for fear they might be converted to purposes of sedition. The persecutions of the Christians during the first three centuries, arose in part from the evil reports spread against them, and the credence given those reports, because they violated the law and policy of the government, in holding meetings in the night time to avoid observation, and in uniting together in organized associations.

The Jewish priesthood were an hereditary order, which constituted the principal organization of the Jewish Church. The Christian Churches of the first, second and third centuries were voluntary associations of Christians, who elected their own priests and deacons, and established their own organization independent of, and in defiance of, the government. They were nearly all of the common and laboring classes, without much property, influence, or learning; and their association and organization were probably the first ever firmly established in the world among such a class of people, and independent of the government. Christian Churches continued to be voluntary associations independent of each other, during the first century, and independent of the government, until Christianity became the established religion of the empire, in the fourth century. Laws were then enacted for the government and union of Christian Churches, and to regulate the election of bishops and other officers. The churches then ceased to be voluntary associations, were united with the government, and became ecclesiastical corporations. They were probably the first substantial corporations in the modern sense of the term, ever organized.

From the fourth to the tenth century, there were no associations of consequence, except those for military purposes, and the association of bandits and pirates for robbery and plunder. About the tenth century, Guilds, or voluntary associations and fraternities of merchants and mechanics, began to be formed for mutual aid and protection, in several countries of Europe. Their principal objects were, to regulate and promote their respective branches of handicraft and trade, to check competition and monopolize the markets, as far as practicable, and keep up prices and wages. Municipal powers were acquired by some of the cities and provinces of the western Roman empire, in the fifth century. During the eleventh, twelfth and thirteenth centuries, numerous charters were granted to cities, towns and boroughs in France, England, Spain, Italy, Germany and Netherlands, conferring on them the power of electing their own magistrates, and regulating their own municipal concerns—thus conferring on them the powers of *municipal corporations*, in the modern sense of the term.

Though schools had been established by governments, as well as by individuals in all civilized countries; yet, I apprehend that no schools, colleges or universities were established under charters as corporations, until about the eleventh or twelfth century. During the sixteenth and seventeenth centuries many companies were incorporated in Europe for commercial purposes, and some for banking, but very few prior to the discovery of America. Turnpike companies were first incorporated in the seventeenth century; but, I think, companies to make canals were not incorporated until the eighteenth century, and railroads, mining and manufacturing companies, not until the nineteenth century.

SEC. 3. *Change in the organization of churches in the fourth century.*

The organization and government of Christian Churches were entirely changed after Christianity became the established religion of the Roman empire, in the fourth century. Up to that time, they were voluntary associations of persons who regulated their own government; and in most cases elected their own priests and deacons, but in some instances only confirmed them. During more than a century, the churches were independent of each other. About the middle of the second century, the Grecian churches adopted the political system of confederation, which had been common among the Grecian States, and introduced the system of holding councils, consisting of delegates from many churches. This system of confederation, and holding councils, was soon extended to all the Christian Churches; and the consequence was, that the whole power of legislation, and of electing the higher officers, was assumed and exercised by the councils.

Under Constantine and his successors, laws were enacted to govern the churches, divide the country into dioceses, provide for the election of bishops, and for the appointment of inferior officers. The churches became corporations, the chief powers of which were vested in the bishops and priests; and by means of the greater talents and influence of the bishops, and particularly of the metropolitan bishops, in deliberative councils and conventions, they extended their power and jurisdiction, from time to time; the exercise of increased power was confirmed by precedent and usage, and the government became more and more aristocratic. Four patriarchs were eventually appointed over great divisions of the churches, which resulted in establishing Popery at Rome, about the year 600; and in the gradual expansion of the power of the Pope, and the college of cardinals, during about six centuries, until the Catholic Church finally assumed the established symmetrical and monarchical form, represented in the fourth chapter of these essays.

In this mode, power gradually passed from the uneducated people to the priests, bishops, and patriarchs, until the entire government of the Church, and all the property of religious societies, were concentrated in the hands of the clergy. The clergy then constituted the corporations, and the people ceased to be corporators, and to have any legal interest in the corporations, or in the property belonging to them. The practice of celibacy among the clergy, served to separate them from the people, and came in aid of the clerical corporations, to unite them as an organized order of men, similar in spirit and interest, to the castes of the brahminical priesthood.

SEC. 4. *Protestant Societies, or Churches, and the influence of different systems of religion on the progress of nations.*

Though Protestant Churches are generally corporations, yet they are not mere corporations of bishops and priests, like the Catholic Churches; but corporations in which all the heads of families and adult males of the society, are corporators, and participate more or less in the government and management of the property and secular affairs of the society. The government of some Protestant Churches is purely democratic, and that of all others has some of the elements of republicanism, as is shown in chapter IV.

Christianity, as understood by Protestants, is not a ceremonial, but a spiritual system of religion, which involves a high exercise of the intellectual faculties in the worship of God, and in maintaining the moral relations between members of the Church, and of man with his fellow man. It does not consist in mere passive submission of the mind to forms, ordinances, and doctrines announced by the clergy; but it includes also the active exercise of the intellect in search of truth, and in disseminating it among men. While the passive submission of laymen of the Catholic Church amounts to little more than mere sensibility of soul, leaving the mind nearly inert, the active exercise of the intellect of lay Protestants serves not only to develope and expand the mind, but to spread intelligence through the community. Hence every Protestant Church is a school for the exercise and development of the mind, and for the increase and diffusion of knowledge. The extent, however, of the influence of each church, depends on the education and capacity of its pastor, and on the attention given to the education of the people.

The ecclesiastical dominion of the Catholic Church and clergy, have ever had a restraining and depressing influence upon the human mind, and upon the progress of nations, as is shown in Chapter IV. On the contrary, the free and republican spirit of Protestantism, has encouraged inquiry and education, led to inventions and discoveries, to the advance of science, and to the progress of nations in knowledge, civilization, productive industry, wealth, population, and power. Rome began to sink immediately after the union of Church and State (which was the foundation of Catholicism and Popery), and the world made but little progress at any period, from that time, until the rise of Protestantism. All the inventions and discoveries in science, made during the last three centuries, and all the elements of progress, have originated among Protestant nations, and those which have thrown off the yoke of Popery. The elements of all the progress made by subjects of the Catholic and Greek Churches, have been borrowed.

Pagan worship has generally been limited to mere ceremonies, prayers, ablutions, sacrifices, and consulting auspices. It has had very little to do with either education or morals, and had but little effect, except to fill the mind with superstitions. The Polytheism of the Greeks, Romans, and other flourishing nations of antiquity, had no perceptible influence, either to advance or retard their intellectual and national progress. It left them intellectually free, subject to the instincts, propensities, appetites and passions of human nature, without exercising much influence over their minds or morals.

All the elements and principles of progress must originate in the human mind, or be discovered by it. It is impossible for the mind to be fully developed, and make inventions and discoveries in science, without freedom from restraint; and it is impossible for the mind to be free, in a country where but one system of religion and of religious doctrines is tolerated. All the progress made by the nations of antiquity was made by those which tolerated polytheism. The progress of the Hindoos was arrested by the establishment of Brahmanism and the religious castes of that system of worship; and the progress of the Persians was arrested in like manner, by establishing Magianism as the sole religion of their country. The Mahometans borrowed nearly all the learning they had, and never contributed much to advance the civilization of the world. The feeble polytheism and rationalism of the Chinese and Japanese, have been like the polytheism of Greece and Rome, and have had very little influence, either to advance or retard their progress.

SEC. 5. *Advantages and power of associations, corporations, and associated wealth.*

To accomplish great purposes and objects, means must be used co-extensive with the ends to be attained. The means necessary to accomplish physical objects consist of muscular powers, directed by cultivated intellects, and using material and mechanical instruments. In other words, numerous human agents must act in concert, in many instances for a great length of time, employing a large amount of capital or mechanical instruments, and consuming a large amount of products daily, for their subsistence. Man can accomplish nothing without effort; physical effort, intellectual effort, and the use of capital. To accomplish great moral, political, and religious purposes and enterprises, requires also numerous agents of cultivated minds, who must have the means of subsistence, and capital to defray the expenses of printing and circulating information.

Action in concert by great numbers of persons, with a large amount of capital, can be attained only by governments, or by means of associations properly organized, with numerous officers and agents, whose powers and duties, and the rights of the members are defined, either by law, or by articles of association, which may be enforced by efficient remedies. Corporations, joint stock companies, and organized associations, (except of a political character), were wholly unknown in ancient times. The ancients seem to have had no conceptions of the modern mode of uniting together a great number of individuals to act in concert, and collecting large amounts of capital, by means of corporations and organized associations, to effect great enterprises and objects; and hence all their roads, great improvements and enterprises, were made by governments. The avenues and modes of investing a surplus income in those days, in order to make it productive as capital, were few, compared with what exist at this time in the United States, and in many countries of Europe. Hence in those days, great incomes were generally expended in keeping a large retinue of servants; and there were less inducements to industry and economy, to save and accumulate, than there are at present.

An incorporated trading company has extended the dominion of Great Britain over a large proportion of the richest part of Asia; and a similar company has been the source of the extensive dominion of the Dutch in the East Indies. Nearly all the railroads and turnpike roads, and many of the canals in the United States—all the canals, turnpike roads, and railroads in Great Britain and Ireland, and many of those in other countries of Europe, have been made by incorporated companies, with capitals collected in most instances in small sums, from great numbers of stockholders, the result of little savings from their monthly and annual incomes. Numerous colleges, universities, lyceums, library associations, and other institutions to diffuse knowledge among men, and to spread Christianity and civilization, are established and managed, and the means of sustaining them are collected in like manner. Nearly all the great manufacturing establishments in the United States were established, and are carried on by means of corporations.

The union and organization of Christian societies and the Roman laws regulating their government and the management of their property, probably suggested the idea of municipal corporations, of charters for colleges, for trading and mining corporations, and other great objects of private enterprise. Corporations have furnished the means of uniting individuals, and of combining and managing capital to carry on great enterprises and undertakings, which are beyond the power of individuals. They have thus opened new fields of employment for both labor and capital, contributed to increase the productiveness of capital, to increase the demand for it, and to raise the rate of interest. They have increased the demand for labor, encouraged industry, economy, frugality, saving, and enterprise, and contributed greatly to promote the progress and welfare of many modern nations. They are among the great characteristics which mark the distiction between ancient and modern times. There are very few, however, except ecclesiastical corporations, in Catholic countries, and none among Mahometan and Pagan nations.

SEC. 6. *The Monks, Jesuits, Missionaries, and colonization societies.*

The monastic order was first instituted in Egypt in the fourth century, and was introduced into Italy in the fifth or sixth century. The order of St. Dominic, the Franciscan friars, and some other mendicant orders, were established by the papacy in the 12th and 13th centuries, for the promotion in part of political purposes, and to aid in combating heresy. They have had comparatively little effect, except to withdraw men from industry, and to promote indolence.

The society of Jesuits was established in 1534, to propagate Catholicism, and to counteract the influence of Protestantism. The first principle of the order is perfect submission to the commands of the Pope, and the whole society is under the absolute control of the general of the order, who resides at Rome. The members are made blind instruments in the hands of the General and Pope, to propagate any doctrine or principle, or effect any purpose, which may suit the interest, caprice, or ambition of their superiors. They established many schools and colleges—strove to obtain the direction of education, in order to mould the young mind in submission to popery, and went as missionaries among the natives of America, as well as among the heathen of the old world. They acted every where, and particularly in Protestant countries, as secret emissaries and agents of the court of Rome, communicating to the Pope all the important information they could collect. Their influence was so pernicious, and their intrigues so numerous, that they were banished in the course of the 18th century, from France, Spain, Portugal, and some other Catholic countries, and the order was abolished by Pope Clement XIV., in 1773. It was deemed, however, so important an aid and support of popery, that it was reëstablished by Pope Pius VII., on the fall of Napoleon, in 1814.

The Jesuits have been the most zealous devotees of the court of Rome, and have done more than any other order of men to sustain and spread the principles of Catholicism, and absolute submission to the spiritual dominion of the Pope. They have done much to promote education, and to diffuse some kinds of knowledge; but nothing of any account to extend the domain of science. Their principles are so accommodated to the ends of personal and papal expediency, their reasoning so sophistical and subtle, and the principles of absolute submission taught by them so restraining in their influence, that much of their instruction tends rather to fill the mind with bigotry, than to expand or develope it; and the general effect of their influence has been, to retard the increase and diffusion of religious, as well as political and social knowledge. Not a single mind of great originality and power, has been developed in the society.

The societies formed at different periods, to send missionaries into distant countries, and among the pagan nations of the earth, have had a great influence in spreading the gospel, and diffusing knowledge; but the experience of ages has taught us, that colonists are the most effective missionaries to extend the domain of civilization. The experience of fourteen centuries shows, that it is impossible to convert savages into substantial Christians. They can be Christianized only as they are civilized, taught the arts of peace, and to live in fixed habitations, and by regular industry. In order to Christianize them, you must at the same time improve their physical, mental, and social condition, and elevate them in the scale of civilization. If the interior of Africa shall ever be civilized, it will be by means of colonizing the free colored persons of America upon that continent, and thereby establishing a system of government and social order, and instructing the natives in agriculture, in the mechanic arts, and in the habits and customs of civilized life. The efforts of the Colonization Society have been crowned with great success, which tends to show the practicability of this most desirable object.

SEC. 7. *Political associations and parties.*

The organization of associations furnishes the means of collecting and diffusing information and the opinions of individuals, and of operating upon, and aiding in the formation of public opinion. They not only furnish facilities for individuals, to confer together in relation to their rights and interests, but also to collect arms and means of defence to protect themselves against the oppression of a tyrannical government, or for revolutionary purposes.

The political associations, clubs, and affiliated societies of Paris had a powerful influence upon the French Revolution of 1789, as shown in Section 10 of Chapter I., and similar societies produced the revolutions in France of 1830 and 1848. There have been numerous political unions and associations in Great Britain and Ireland. The most powerful was the great Catholic association, formed in May 1823, and dissolved in March 1829, when its great object, the passing of the Catholic Relief Bill, was attained. The Irish Repeal Association, got up by Daniel O'Connell some years afterwards, enabled him to agitate the people of Ireland for many years; and it finally terminated in a feeble rebellion in 1848.

There have been numerous political associations in the United States, acting in concert with political partiies, to promote party purposes; the most permanent and powerful of which, is the Tammany Society of the City of New York. The power and influence of political parties in this country, has been discussed in Section 9 of Chapter V. of these essays. The democratic party is organised, and has its committees, and holds meetings and conventions in every state, and in nearly every county in every state of the Union. The organization of the whig party is not so extensive, nor so complete and effective, and yet it is a very powerful party.

A complete change has taken place in the organization of parties in the United States since the year 1820. The first State Convention of delegates of the people assembled in the State of New York, to nominate candidates for Governor and Lieutenant-Governor, was in the year 1824, when Dewitt Clinton was nominated for Governor. Previous to that time, candidates for Governor were nominated in caucus, by members of the Legislature of their respective parties; and candidates for President and Vice-President were nominated in caucus by members of Congress. In 1828, the candidates for President and Vice-President of the United States were nominated in some of the States, by State Conventions; and in 1832, for the first time, they were nominated by national conventions. Since that time, many of the State governments have been changed, a greater number of officers are elected by the people, and the candidates for all offices elective by the people, from the President down to county, township, and corporation officers, are all nominated in nearly all the States, by conventions of their respective parties. County conventions are generally composed of delegates appointed by townships and ward meetings; and State conventions of delegates appointed by county conventions and meetings. Mass meetings of the people for political objects, were commenced by the friends of General Harrison in 1836, and became very general throughout the United States in 1840. Numerous mass meetings were assembled by both political parties in 1844, and by the three political parties of 1848.

All these partisan meetings and conventions serve to bring together the people, as well as politicians; more or less discussion is had on political questions; resolutions are passed, drawn up by the leaders, expressive of the general sense of the meeting; the minds of political partisans become more or less committed, and their opinions formed; and public opinion is thus operated upon. This system of organization and party machinery, and these meetings and conventions have increased the force and power of public opinion, and diminished the power and influence of members of Congress, of the State Legislatures, and of the executive officers, of both the national and State governments. Our government has become more popularized; popular influences have increased, and the influence of the administration, and of office-holders generally, has greatly diminished during the last thirty years. How important, therefore, that the mass of the people should be properly educated.

These national and State conventions have become of great consequence; they sometimes comprise more ability than the same parties have in Congress, or their respective State Legislatures; and by means of previous examinations and preparations, and short consultations of committees, they frequently pass upon numerous great and complicated questions, with much ability, and accomplish as much in two or three days, as Congress does in some instances in as many weeks. The contrast is very great, and shows the futility of long debates. But when such conventions attempt to pass hastily upon complicated questions of international law or boundary, and the influence of their resolutions is such as to overcome the action of members of Congress, and control the action of the administration; or when an attempt is made to enforce uniformity of opinion in a political party, and to proscribe all who do not yield their individual opinions, then the influence of such conventions becomes destructive of that freedom of opinion and action, which is necessary to promote the highest good and welfare of a free people.

When the dominant party in Congress cling together, and by means of party discipline, are made to act in concert as one man, each surrendering his own individual opinions to the majority, and the whole acting in accordance with, and in a measure in obedience to, the opinions and decisions of their political friends expressed in a national convention; the result is, that the substantial powers of legislation are transferred from the halls of Congress, where both political parties are represented, and both sides of every question can be presented and discussed, and vested in a convention of only one political party. Congress becomes a mere agent to register and execute the decrees of a partisan convention; and the minority is disfranchised, and deprived of all substantial participation in the legislation of the country. The resolutions of the Baltimore Convention of 1844, seemed to be regarded by the democratic party, as authoritative interpretations of the Constitution, laws and treaties of the United States; more clear, conclusive and binding, than the decisions of the Supreme Court; and the proceedings of that convention have had a greater and more extended influence over the government and welfare of the people of the United States, than the acts of any one Congress which has assembled during the last thirty years.

Sec. 8. *Order of Freemasonry.*

A society of architects or builders was formed in the middle ages, but at what period is not certainly known. The society was liberally patronised by the Popes; it spread through Europe, and the members of it were the principal builders of churches in

Catholic countries. Out of this society, arose the institution of Freemasonry; but the mode and period in which the association became changed from a mere professional fraternity, to a society of persons of all classes and employments, connected by secret symbols, is not known. It is said to have attracted attention as a secret society in Great Britain, and numbered among its members many men of distinction, as early as the 15th century; though Masonic lodges were not introduced into France, Germany, and America, until some time in the 18th century. It has been mostly a convivial and benevolent society; but like many other secret societies, it has been subjected in France, and some other countries, as well as in the United States, to a variety of suspicions; and it is most probable that political aspirants have in some instances availed themselves of the secrecy afforded by it, to promote their schemes and purposes. As a convivial society, its influence has been unfavorable to the cause of temperance. As its members have been comparatively few, its charities and objects few and personal, and the most of its purposes, principles and proceedings secret, it never commanded the public sympathies or confidence, and never exercised much influence over public opinion, or the welfare of the human family, either by example or otherwise.

SEC. 9. *Friendly, or benefit societies.*

Friendly societies, or benefit societies, originated among the manufacturing laborers of Great Britain in the latter part of the eighteenth century. They are founded on the principle of mutual insurance, being voluntary associations of persons contributing to the formation of a general fund, for the assistance of members in sickness, and other occasions of distress. Each member pays an initiation fee, and contributes weekly, monthly, or quarterly, a certain sum while in health, according to their by-laws, and receives from the society a certain weekly allowance when he is incapacitated for work, either by sickness, accident, or old age. It is obvious that nothing can be more unexceptionable than the principle of these associations; and when their funds and business are properly managed, nothing can be more useful to the laboring classes than these societies and savings' banks.

Mr. McCulloch says, "There were enrolled from the first of January, 1793, to the commencement of the year 1832, no fewer than 19,783 such societies, of which 16,596 were in England, 769 in Wales, 2,144 in Scotland, and 274 in Ireland. The societies existing in 1815 are said to have comprised 925,429 individuals."

Sec. 10. *Savings' Banks.*

The want of a safe place of deposit for the earnings not needed for immediate use by the laboring classes, where they would yield a reasonable interest, and from which they could withdraw them at pleasure, has formed one of the greatest obstacles to the formation of habits of economy and accumulation among laborers, in all countries. Banks of issue and deposit do not generally pay interest on deposits; and for laborers to loan their savings to individuals, is not only hazardous, but puts them beyond their reach for immediate use, in case of need. The benefit societies soon accumulated considerable amounts of funds, for which they sought means of safe deposit and investment, where they would draw interest, and yet be convertible into money without difficulty. Out of these wants grew the institution of savings' banks.

Porter, in his Progress of the Nation, makes the following remarks: "The first Savings' Bank was established in 1804 at Tottenham, in Middlesex (England), by Mrs. Priscilla Wakefield, and was called the Charitable Bank. In this bank deposits were received, and five per cent. interest was allowed upon their amount—a rate which left a considerable loss to the benevolent individuals by whom Mrs. Wakefield was joined in the undertaking. The society next formed, of which we have any account, was opened in 1808 at Bath, chiefly through the instrumentality of ladies, for receiving deposits from female servants. The good resulting from these efforts was soon made manifest; and the successful example thus set, was so far followed, that in the year 1817, there were seventy savings' banks in operation in England, four in Wales, and four in Ireland. In that year, acts of Parliament were passed to encourage the establishment of such institutions, and to place the funds under safe-guard of the State. By subsequent acts, the provisions were extended to Scotland, and the Channel Islands." The funds of the savings' banks are mostly invested in public stocks.

The first savings' bank established in the United States, was at Philadelphia in 1816; the next was in Boston in 1817; since that time, such institutions have been established in nearly all the cities of the Northern States.

Condition of the Savings' Banks in Great Britain and Ireland on the 20th of November, in each of the under-mentioned years.

	1830.	1840.	1845.
In England and Wales,			
Number of depositors,	367,812	662,338	865,389
Amount of deposits,	£12,287,606	£20,203,438	£25,930,266
In Wales,			
Number of depositors,	10,204	15,825	18,916
Amount of deposits,	£314,903	£521,918	£618,092
In Scotland,			
Number of depositors,	not stated	43,737	82,203
Amount of deposits,	" "	£538,961	£1,278,929
In Ireland,			
Number of depositors,	34,201	76,155	96,422
Amount of deposits,	£905,056	£2,206,733	£2,921,581
Total No. of depositors,	412,217	798,055	1,062,930
Total amt. of deposits,	£13,507,565	£23,471,050	£30,748,868

The English and Irish banks, other than the savings' banks, do not pay interest on deposits, but all the Scotch banks do, and the greater portion of the laboring population of Scotland, deposite their earnings in banks other than savings' banks; this accounts for the fact of the deposits in the savings' banks being so much less in proportion to the population than in England.

By the act 9 Geo. 4, ch. 92, the interest payable on the deposits is not to exceed £3 18s. 5¼d. per cent. per annum; and when the deposit of any one person amounts to £200, it ceases to draw interest.

Number and condition of the Savings' Banks of France, according to the official reports.

	1834.	1839.
Number of savings' banks and branches,	70	404
Number of depositors,	81,714	310,843
Amount of deposits in francs,	37,015,492	171,057,904
Average deposit for each person,	453	550
Deposits equal in sterling money to	£1,450,000	£6,681,000
Number of depositors June 30th, 1851,		611,000
Amount of deposits June 30th, 1851, in francs,		172,159,000

Statement of the savings' banks in New York, with the exception of one in Poughkeepsie, one in Rochester, and one in Canandaigua, not included:

	Dec. 31st, 1839.	Dec. 31st, 1844.
Number of institutions reported,	8	9
Number of depositors, about	39,000	———
Amount of deposits,	$4,641,284	$8,030,375

Savings' Banks in Massachusetts.

	1843.	1846.	1850.
Number of banks and branches,		38	45
Number of depositors,	42,587	62,893	78,823
Amount of deposits,	$6,900,451	$10,680,933	$13,660,024

The average annual per cent. of dividends of the five years ending with 1850, was 6¼, and the whole expense of managing them in 1850, but $41,680 57. See Amer. Al. for 1852.

The savings' banks in Massachusetts in 1843, were located in thirty cities, towns and villages, embracing a population in 1840 of 284,086 ; the depositors comprising nearly one-sixth part of the entire population of those places. Four of the savings' banks in New York were located in the city of New York, and the others reported, were all in commercial cities.

The deposits in these institutions are mostly made in small sums, by mechanical and manufacturing laborers, females, clerks, and servants. They are either vested in government stocks of some kind, or loaned out to be employed in manufactures or commerce. Many of the manufacturing laborers in the United States have saved enough from their earnings to buy lots, and build very comfortable houses for their families, and to furnish their houses better, and to enjoy more of the comforts of life, than were enjoyed by the nobility of England three centuries since. They have also loaned considerable sums of money to their employers, and to other manufacturers and commercial men ; many of them own a portion of the stock of the establishments in which they labor.

The amount deposited in savings' banks by the laborers of Great Britain, is more than the value of all the personal property in the kingdom in the year 1600. It amounts to nearly one-sixth part as much as all the capital employed in Great Britain, in mining manufactures and the mechanic arts in 1841, and to about half as much as was employed in the United States in 1840 in the same employments, (except milling.) I wish the reader to realize this great fact ; that the manufacturing laborers of Great Britain, in addition to furnishing their houses, buying great numbers of cottages for themselves, and loaning moneys to business men, have actually deposited in savings' banks an amount equal to half the capital invested in the United States in the mechanic arts, mining and manufactures of all kinds, except making flour, oil and lumber.

We have heard the cry repeated year after year in this country, that manufacturing tends to make the rich, richer, and the poor, poorer. These facts should put to the blush all the demagogues who raise such a false cry, for partizan and selfish purposes. The truth is, agricultural laborers who have families and work for hire, seldom save anything beyond the support of their families. They are poor in all countries, and have been so in all ages; but they are much better off now in Great Britain, than they were two or three centuries ago. They are at this day better off in Great Britain, than they are in any of the agricultural countries of Europe. Their earnings are much greater than the earnings of the same classes in any country of either the new or the old world, with the single exception of the United States. Mining and manufactures tend to increase the productiveness of labor; to increase the demand for labor; to increase the wages of labor; to stimulate and increase the industry of a country; to increase the population; to increase the demand for food, and products of all kinds, and the ability to pay for and enjoy them; and to increase the wealth, and the value of real estate, and property of every description. It is true that they make the capitalist richer; but they improve the condition of the laborer also, in a much greater degree, than they do that of the capitalist. They make no man and no classes of men poorer. It is true that the income of the manufacturing classes is much greater in proportion to the capital employed, than that of the farmer; but the income of the latter is much greater in manufacturing States and countries, than it is in those countries which are devoted mostly to agriculture.

SEC. 11. *The independent order of Odd Fellows.*

The order of Odd Fellows originated in Great Britain about the beginning of the nineteenth century. It is a benefit society, having all the general characteristics of the class of societies known as friendly societies, with some of the features, secrets and ceremonies of free-masonry, engrafted upon them. It was first introduced into the United States at Baltimore in 1819. It has since spread through the United States, and the British provinces of North America. On the 30th of June, 1851, the order numbered no less than 2,647 lodges, and 189,512 members in the United States, under the control of thirty-two Grand Lodges, or State jurisdictions. The revenues of the lodges, arising from initiations and weekly dues during the preceding year, amounted to $1,219,664. Of which there was expended,

for the relief of sick and infirm members,	$343,406
for the relief of widows and distressed families,	55,438
for burying the dead,	71,204
and for educating orphans,	10,113
Total for the above purposes,	$480,161

There have been fourteen degrees instituted by the order, as appears by their publications. A portion of the members who have taken the higher degrees, are organized into Encampments. On the 30th of June, 1851, there were 21,030 contributing members reported by the encampments. The revenues of the encampments for the previous year, were reported at $96,562, and the sums paid out for the relief of the sick, widows, orphans, and burying the dead, amounted to $31,044; which are in addition to the sums heretofore stated.

The order of Odd Fellows was at first a convivial society, and, in many instances, became a mere drinking and convivial club; but it has been reformed, and its character changed in this country, and it is now said, that temperance (not total abstinence from all intoxicating drinks) has become an attribute of the order. Each lodge has its committees to look after the sick, and disciplines its members for neglect of duty, and gross immoralities. From every appearance, the institution has become useful and salutary, and contributes to the good order and welfare of society.

Sec. 12. *Temperance Societies, and Sons of Temperance.*

Temperance societies originated in the State of Massachusetts about the year 1825. The State Temperance Society of New York was formed in 1827, or 1828. In a few years, county, town and village societies were formed in all parts of New York and New England; some were formed in other States, and the subject was extensively agitated in all the Northern States, by public addresses, lectures, newspapers, and the distribution of tracts and reports. There was no bond of union among the members, except the common desire to promote the cause of temperance. They adopted a simple pledge, to abstain from the use and sale of distilled liquors as a beverage, and to discourage their use. They had no property in common, no mode of raising any revenues to promote the object, except by voluntary contributions, and no system of discipline.

It was at first supposed, that there was a material difference in principle, and in the necessary consequences, between the use of distilled and fermented liquors, and that if persons abstained wholly from the former, they could use the latter in moderate quantities with impunity. A few years' experience showed the fallacy of this distinction, and satisfied those who gave close attention to the subject, of the necessity of total abstinence from all intoxicating drinks. The most of the societies, after a few years, adopted the total abstinence pledge, which was too rigid to suit the tastes and opinions of a majority of those who had signed the old pledge, and the result was, that a very large proportion of the members abandoned the cause, and many of them relapsed into their former habits. The organization being defective and feeble, without discipline, property, or regular meetings to hold the members together, everything depended on the excitement of the moment—on the interest created by some public address, speech, or lecture. At times a powerful effect has been produced on the public mind, upon public opinion, upon the public tastes and habits, and upon legislation in all the Northern States; and so far as the country and the farming population is concerned, the reformation has been very permanent; but so far as concerns the cities and large villages, the influence was like a spasmodic excitement, which soon passed away, and the most of the people resumed their old habits. Temptations are more numerous in cities and large villages than in the country, and hence the necessity of a more efficient organization. Out of this necessity, arose the order of the Sons of Temperance and the Rechabites.

The order of the Sons of Temperance originated in the city of New York in the year 1842. It is a benefit society, modelled after the order of Odd Fellows, with the addition of a total abstinence pledge, and a system of discipline, adapted to it, with this exception, that there are fourteen degrees (as it is said) in the order of Odd Fellows, and but one in the society of the Sons of Temperance. The Sons of Temperance have no mysteries, ceremonies, or secrets, with which every member is not made acquainted when he is initiated. Meetings are held weekly, and the officers elected for only three months. The members pay weekly or quarterly dues, and are paid a weekly allowance or benefit when sick or infirm, provided their sickness or infirmity is not produced by misconduct after they become members. They have standing committees to attend to the sick, and a regular system of discipline. The amount of their quarterly dues, the amount of benefits, and the sum appropriated for funeral expenses on the decease of a member, depends on the by-laws of each division, subject to certain limitations.

The order has spread throughout the United States, and into Great Britain and the British provinces of Canada, New Brunswick, Nova Scotia, and Prince Edward's Island. There are two grand divisions in the State of New York, one in each of the other States, except California, one in the District of Columbia, and four in the British provinces; all of which are united in the National Division of the Sons of Temperance of North America. At the last annual meeting, held in June, 1851, there were reports from all but two of the grand divisions, showing on the 1st day of April, 1851, 6,069 divisions, 237,984 contributing members; receipts during the previous year amounting to $718,726, and payments of benefits amounting to $194,605.

Though the order is very new, yet many of the divisions are accumulating considerable amounts of funds and property. In this age of the world, not much can be effected without money, or without organization. The property, organization, frequent meetings, and the prospect of sympathy and assistance in case of need, all operate to strengthen the bonds of union among the members. The general organization of local, grand, and national divisions, facilitates the collection of information, and the dissemination of information and sound principles, by means of reports, tracts, temperance newspapers, and public addresses. Its organization, revenues, benefits, benevolence, discipline, numerous meetings, vigilance, and system of operations, make its influence regular, constant and permanent; and render it the most efficient society for promoting the cause of temperance, which has ever been devised, unless the order of the Rechabites is equally so.

Some have classed the Sons of Temperance with the Free-masons and Odd Fellows, as a secret society, and taken exceptions to the order on that account. Though its organization is modelled in many of its features after the order of Odd Fellows, yet it differs materially from that order, and has scarcely a feature in common with Free-masonry. The Sons of Temperance confer no degrees, and have but one class of members. They have no secret ends to attain, no secret principles, no secret objects or purposes; they take no oaths, and no secret pledges. Their principles, purposes, and the substance of their pledges, are all public. They have no secret signs or symbols by which to know each other. Nothing is secret, but their forms and ceremonies, private business, and pass-words, to enable the members only to gain access to their meetings.

The Rechabites is an order of temperance men very similar (as I suppose) to the Sons of Temperance; but I have no definite information in relation to their organization, numbers, or progress.

It is desirable that all these societies should have libraries, to increase their attractions and usefulness, and to disseminate useful knowledge, as well as to occupy the leisure hours of the members, and keep them out of the paths of temptation.

SEC. 13. *Effect of independent associations and churches, on civil liberty, and civilization.*

Large standing armies, and societies under the control of ecclesiastical hierarchies, have always been instruments of despotism, and inconsistent with civil liberty. On the contrary, associations independent of the government, and of any clerical hierarchy, and municipal corporations, have been favorable to liberty. It has been the policy of absolute monarchs to keep their subjects isolated, disunited, and without association as far as possible, in order to keep them weak and helpless, and destitute of the means of communication, combination, and self-defence. They are well aware that, in association and union, there is strength. All the associations allowed by them have been dependent on the government. The priesthood, and the teachers and professors of colleges and seminaries of learning, are all dependent on the government, and made agents and instruments of the monarch, to teach the people, and impress upon the minds of children and youth, the principles of absolutism, and the duty of passive obedience and submission to the government. Russia furnishes a striking example of this policy. The Czar is the head of the Church ; and he and his councils control the appointment of all the higher orders of the clergy. Napoleon adopted the same policy, and reëstablished the Catholic Church in France, as the religion of his empire.

All the members participate, more or less, in the government of voluntary associations ; nearly all the private corporations of this country have a popular form of government ; in municipal corporations and the state governments, all, or a very numerous class of the people, participate ; and hence these associations and institutions are schools of freedom, and bulwarks of civil and political liberty.* But large associations and corporations governed by a central board or council, or by an aristocratic class or order, are liable to the same objections as the centralization of the powers of civil government ; they may be used by the leaders and master spirits as instruments of ambition and despotism.

In large associations, the masses have no means of expressing their opinions, except through their leaders, who manage the proceedings, and mould into form the public declaration of their opinions and principles, to which they become committed. Direction and uniformity, in some measure, are thus given to their opinions ; freedom of thought is checked and restrained, and freedom of will is surrendered to the leaders. The case is very different in small independent associations, were a greater proportion of the members can participate in the deliberations and government.

The mind is improved and developed by activity, competition, comparing different things, and observing the workings and effects of different and independent institutions. Hence the division of

* See on this subject numbers 46 and 51 of the Federalist.

Protestant Christians into several sects, has contributed to the freedom, activity, and development of the minds of the people, and overbalanced (perhaps ten-fold) all the disadvantages arising from numerous sects. The same reasoning applies to all associations of men. I do not think it desirable that a majority of the people of any one nation, State, city, town or village, should belong to any church or denomination of Christians, or to any one association, or order of men. On the contrary, I believe that different churches, different institutions, associations, and orders of men, and corporations for different purposes, all independent of each other, contribute to diffuse knowledge, to encourage freedom of thought and inquiry, to develope and improve the human mind, and to promote the cause of liberty, and the general welfare of man. Churches and associations, which comprise only a minority of the people, influence public opinion and governments by reason only, and leave the reason of others free to combat their errors; while churches and associations, which comprise a large majority of the people, are so powerful as to control public opinion as by authority, and have such an influence over the government as to be able to put down their opponents, and silence opposition. The church and the government, in many Catholic countries, prohibit all associations, even for benevolent and moral purposes, except such as are connected with, and subject to, the Church.

The division of Christendom into several different churches in the sixteenth century, was not only the dawn of religious and civil liberty, but the era from which we may date the causes of a great change in the progress of civilization. God has so constituted man, that, while he is subjected to despotic rules, and his mind is enslaved, his mental faculties remain weak, and only partially developed, and he continues to be a comparatively inefficient being. Countries having despotic governments, have not usually more than half as much productive industry and power as free nations, in proportion to the population.

CHAPTER XVIII.

ON THE ART OF DISTILLATION,—AND ON THE MANUFACTURE, CONSUMPTION, PROPERTIES AND EFFECTS OF FERMENTED AND DISTILLED LIQUORS.

SEC. 1. *On fermented liquors, and the art of distillation.*

IN order to give a correct view of the progress of nations, it is important to treat of the customs, institutions, principles and causes which retard, as well as those which promote it. Distilled liquors should be ranked among the greatest scourges which ever afflicted the human family; and hence their history, character and effects, legitimately form a part of the general subject of these essays

Alcohol is produced by the process of fermentation; but in a state of combination with water and other liquid substances, from which it can be separated and procured in a pure state, only by distillation. We read that Noah planted a vineyard, drank of the juice of the vine, and became drunk. Fermented liquors have been in use among the nations of Europe and western Asia, from a period anterior to authentic profane history; but the art of distillation is a comparatively modern invention, as late as the eleventh or twelfth century. Alcohol is composed of atoms of carbon, oxygen, and hydrogen, in a state of chemical combination produced by fermentation; but when so produced, it is so much diluted with water and other substances in solution, that it will not resist the action of heat and of the atmosphere upon it, and will soon undergo a second fermentation, and be converted into vinegar, unless it is separated from the water and other foreign substances by distillation. Alcohol in a pure state, or any thing approximating to a pure state, is never produced by any process of nature, but by a highly artificial process invented by man.

SEC. 2. *Chemical properties and component parts of Alcohol, Ether, and several other gases and substances.*

All the component parts of Alcohol, like many other compound substances, are useful to man in certain combinations and circumstances, and destructive to life in others.

Statement of the component parts, and the relative number of the ultimate atoms, of which the undermentioned substances, liquids and gases are composed.

	Carbon.	Oxygen.	Hydrogen.	Nitrogen.
Water -		1 atom	1 atom.	
Vinegar -	4 atoms	3 "	3 "	
Sugar -	9 "	8 "	8 "	
Starch -	24 "	20 "	20 "	
Alcohol -	2 "	1 "	3 "	
Ether -	4 "	1 "	5 "	
Quinine -	20 "	2 "	12 "	1 atom.
Camphor -	10 "	1 "	8 "	
Carbonic acid gas	1 "	2 "		
Nitrous oxyd		1 "		1 "
Ammonia, or salts of hartshorn			3 "	1 "

Chloroform is very similar in its effects to ether; it consists of two parts carbon, to one of hydrogen, united with chlorine gas. The most of the volatile oils and essences consist of carbon, hydrogen, and a little oxygen.

The reader will observe that the relative number of atoms of oxygen and hydrogen is the same in the composition of water, vinegar, sugar, and starch; and such is the case with nearly all the food which is conducive to the health of man. He will observe also, that, with the exception of alcohol, all those substances which contain large proportions of hydrogen and carbon combined with a very little oxygen, are used for medicines only; and why should alcohol form an exception to the general rule?

All the above substances constitute chemical combinations; atmospheric air, on the contrary, is a mere mechanical mixture of over three parts nitrogen to one of oxygen. Though nitrogen is taken into the lungs in the air we breathe, yet forming a mere mechanical mixture with oxygen, it is easily separated from it and expelled, and the oxygen only retained, which is the only air that will support respiration and animal life. Carbonic acid gas, on the contrary, is over two-thirds oxygen, yet in as much as the carbon forms a chemical union with the oxygen, the lungs cannot separate them, and when the gas is taken into the lungs in mines and stagnant wells where it collects, life is destroyed in a few minutes. When nitrogen is taken into the lungs in a chemical combination with oxygen in nitrous oxyd, the lungs do not possess the power to separate them; immediate intoxication is produced, and the powers of reason entirely suspended for a few moments, until the lungs are again filled with pure oxygen from the atmosphere.

Hydrogen is a very light, subtle, and highly inflammable substance, only one-sixteenth part as heavy in proportion to its volume as oxygen. When chemically combined with oxygen in water, vinegar, sugar, and starch, the number of atoms of oxygen and hydrogen are equal; but in alcohol there are three atoms of hydrogen to one of oxygen. It is the extra quantity and proportion of hydrogen in alcohol, which gives it a burning taste; and when taken into the stomach, and the component parts separated by the process of digestion, the extra quantity of hydrogen passes into the blood-vessels, and with the blood into the brain, and not being required for the purposes of nutrition, it acts only as a burning and powerful stimulant to the brain, nervous system, and the circulation of the blood, until it is thrown off in the perspiration, or in some other mode.

Carbon is also inflammable, though in a very slight degree, when compared with hydrogen. The facts seem to be well established, that several persons, long addicted to the excessive use of distilled spirits, have been actually consumed by internal combustion. Can there be any reasonable doubt that such sad occurrences were occasioned by the sufferers becoming perfectly saturated with these inflammable substances, the quantity being so great, that it could neither be thrown off by the system, nor assimilated to it?

SEC. 3. *Effect of ether, chloroform, nitrous oxyd gas, and alcohol on sensation, and on the mental faculties.*

Hydrogen taken into the lungs in sulphuric ether or chloroform, operates almost instantaneously, and suspends the powers of sensation; and the nitrogen contained in nitrous oxyd gas, when inhaled into the lungs, produces intoxication in less than a minute.

The first effect of alcohol, is the same as that of tea, coffee, vinegar, or any other active stimulant, taken into the stomach. It operates as a stimulant to the nerves of the stomach, which communicate with the brain, and thus stimulate the whole nervous system. Tea and coffee are soon assimilated to, and combined with the elements of nutrition; but when alcohol is resolved into its original elements, the oxygen, carbon, and a portion of the hydrogen become assimilated with the elements of nutrition, and the extra quantity of hydrogen, which cannot be assimilated, passes into the chyle, and from thence into the blood, and through the heart. Being an extremely subtle and inflammable fluid, it increases the action of the heart and the circulation of the blood, and generally throws the blood with great violence into the arteries and to the head. When the tendency of the blood to the brain is so rapid that the capillaries cannot pass it to the veins as fast as it comes, the arteries of the brain soon become unnaturally full and distended, so that they press upon the soft and pulpy part of the brain, and upon the nerves contained in it; and thus they compress the nerves, and derange the action of the mental faculties, which constitutes *intoxication.* This is proven by the fact that, when a man dies in a fit of intoxication, the immediate cause of death is generally appoplexy; that is, a congestion or accumulation of blood in the brain. It is also confirmed by the fact, that many persons are deranged by congestion, or accumulation of blood in the brain, produced by fever; so that they are insane or partially so, during the paroxysms of fever, and sanity is again restored as soon as the fever passes off for the day, and the equilibrium of the system is restored.

Tea and Coffee operate directly on the nervous system, increase its action, and (as is supposed by some) increase, also, the nervous substance or fluid.* Though they have no direct influence on the heart or the circulation of the blood, yet they do slightly increase the action of the heart, and quicken the circulation of the blood by means of their action on the nervous system, and its influence on the heart. But the extra quantity of hydrogen contained in alcohol passes very soon into the blood, and acts directly upon the heart and the circulation of the blood, as well as upon the nervous system.

The hydrogen of ether or chloroform taken into the lungs, coming in immediate contact with the blood, acts directly upon the blood and heart, and suspends the powers of sensation and volition almost instantly; but taken into the stomach, it acts indirectly and slowly, produces a congestion of the brain, obstructs and deranges the action of the nervous system, suspends, partially, the powers of sensation and volition, and all the powers of the intellect. When a man is intoxicated, both sensation and perception are imperfect, and he neither perceives nor remembers distinctly any thing that he does, or any thing that occurs in his presence. When the increase of blood in the brain is so small as to produce only partial intoxication, the circulation of the blood is unnatural, the pressure upon the nerves irregular, and the effect upon the nervous system is often so great as to excite images in the mind, and trains of thought which pass through the mind rapidly and involuntarily.

* See on this point, Section 17 of Chapter IX.

Alcohol tends to derange the functions of the human system; to produce disease; to stupefy the mind, and particularly the reasoning faculties; to blunt the moral faculties and feelings; to excite the passions, and the involuntary and habitual action of some of the mental faculties, and cause them to predominate over the powers of reason, and to control the will. This tendency is the same, whether the quantity taken be great or small, though if it be very small, the powers of the system may so far overcome it that its effects may not be perceptible. Small quantities of arsenic, or any other poison, may also be taken from day to day, without producing any immediately perceptible effect.

Public speakers often drink to produce an excitement of mind, a greater flow of ideas, and of animal spirits; but the ideas thus excited arise from physical, and not from intellectual causes, from fancy and the imagination, and not from the judgment or the reasoning faculties, and are often more or less wild and incoherent. They are generally images and trains of thought previously existing in the mind, involuntarily reproduced by habit and the association of ideas. Alcohol never yet aided any person either to judge or reason more correctly than he could without it. It may make him a better social boon companion of the hour, but a less safe adviser, and a less trusty friend or agent. The flow of animal spirits, and the agreeable sensations excited by a moderate quantity of alcohol, have contributed to create and keep up the delusion, that it is a cure for every ill, both mental and physical; that it is useful to drink when fatigued, and to prevent fatigue; to drink when cold to warm the body, and when warm to prevent the bad influences of the heat; and to drink to protect the system from winds, storms, damp air, malaria, fevers, and even contagious diseases.

Intoxicating drinks have been made in the United States, and also in many countries of Europe, the means of popularity, as well as the medium of social intercourse. Thousands seem anxious to be called liberal and generous, and to attain that reputation, they strive to drink themselves into favor. Merchants, lawyers, physicians, mechanics, farmers, tavern keepers, and laborers, as well as politicians and gentlemen, nearly all have thought that they must treat their friends and acquaintances with intoxicating drinks, as an evidence of friendship and social feeling; to avoid the reputation of being mean and illiberal; and to acquire the character of being liberal and generous. The temperance reformation has, however, made a great change in public sentiment on this subject, in the greater portion of the free states, within the last twenty years; but the quantity of intoxicating drinks still consumed in the United States, is very large.

SEC. 4. *On poisons, and their operation.*

Dr. Brande says:* Poisons have been divided by Orfila and Christison into irritants, narcotics, and narcotic-acids; the first class including those whose sole or predominating symptoms are those of irritation, or inflammation; the second those which produce stupor, delirium, and other affections of the brain and nervous system; and the third, those of a mixed character.

The chief effects of irritants are upon the alimentary canal; exciting inflammation, and sometimes ulceration, nausea, vomiting, and heat and pain of the stomach.

Narcotic poisons induce a train of symptoms of a very different character; their direct influence is upon the nervous system, and the leading effects produced, are headache, vertigo, confused vision, stupor, convulsions, paralysis and coma. The symptoms of the narcotic-acrid poisons usually consist of those of the two former classes blended. In large doses, narcotism predominates; in smaller, irritation.

1st, *Irritant poisons.* Dr. Christison puts in this class mineral acids, mineral salts, fixed alkalies, alkaline and earthy chlorides, lime, nitre, ammonia and its salts, arsenic and its compounds, mercurial compounds, vegetable acids, &c. 2nd, *Narcotic poisons;* among which he classes opium, poisonous gases, several acids and some other substances. 3rd, *Narcotic-acrid poisons*, among which he enumerates tobacco, hemlock, strychnia, cocculus indicus, alcohol, ether, and several other substances.

Almost all the medicines used in the old system of medical practice are poisons; and if taken in too large doses will soon destroy life; taken in small doses, the narcotic poisons are, in certain conditions of the system, extremely effective and useful, to allay unnatural excitability; and the irritant poisons are in some instances equally useful and necessary, to aid the powers of nature to resist and overcome the obstructions of the system, and the causes of disease. Health depends on a proper balance and equilibrium of all the functions of life; and when the equilibrium is destroyed by disease, a powerful counteracting agent (like an active poison) is often necessary to restore it. But to use such agents when the functions of life are well balanced and acting harmoniously, tends to give an unnatural activity or want of activity to some of them, to derange their action, destroy the equilibrium of the system, and cause disease. There is no reason to doubt, that alcohol, like opium and calomel, is useful as a medicine taken in a proper manner, in certain conditions of the system; but like laudanum and other preparations of opium, it is

* See Brande's Encyclopædia of Science and Art, title Toxicology.

strictly a poison, and will soon destroy life, if taken in large quantities. It would be as rational to take opium or calomel daily through the year when in health, as to take alcohol daily as a beverage, or to take it at any time in health. In either case, the natural tendency is to derange the system, and produce disease.

SEC. 5. *Is it, or is it not immoral, to use intoxicating drinks as a beverage.*

The principal test of the morality or immorality of human action, is its tendency to produce good or evil. Acts, habits, and customs, which tend to produce evil, are not in accordance with the moral laws of nature; and hence they are not moral, but immoral and vicious.* Men do not become drunkards at once; they commence by drinking small quantities of mixed liquors, usually sweetened and diluted with water, and made weak. Their moderately stimulating effects being agreeable, a taste for them is formed, which is strengthened by use, until their use becomes habitual. In process of time, the taste and appetite for them increases, the quantity used is increased, and the result often is, confirmed habits of intemperance. Though the same effects are not produced in every individual, yet the ordinary and natural tendency of their use, is to disturb the proper action of the brain and nervous system, to produce bad habits, indolence, poverty, distress, vice, crime, disease, and premature death. Even when taken by persons capable of resisting this tendency in themselves, in too small quantities to produce intoxication, or to affect the health, their consumption being expensive, without producing any good, is a loss to the consumer, and to the community; which is an evil of itself. Their use by such persons in small quantities, tends also to encourage their general use, and to encourage employments which produce a multitude of evils, and in their best aspect, effect no good.

Men are led into temptation by example, and can be delivered from evil, only by being turned from the path which leadeth to it. We are taught in the Holy Scriptures to pray "*lead us not into temptation, but deliver us from evil.*" Were those words intended as a mere form of speech; or were they designed to announce a general rule of action for the whole human family, through all future time? To what do they apply? Do they refer to any particular evil, or to all the evils, physical, social, moral and political, to which man is subject? Do they not refer to every act and habit of man, which tends to produce evil in its consequences? To what do they refer more clearly, than to the use as a beverage, of intoxicating drinks; which tends to produce such a multitude of evils?

* See on this point sections 4 and 5 of Chapter I.

Are not the words of the prayer equivalent to a divine injunction, declaratory of the moral law—that it is the duty of man to avoid temptation and evil of every character and description? These are questions which every Christian and moralist should examine and determine for himself.

Many Christian churches have come to the conclusion, that the use of intoxicating drinks as a beverage, is immoral, and hence they condemn it as sinful, and make it a matter of discipline. When every Christian church shall have come to the same conclusion, and adopted the same practice; when a dozen or more of the passages of scripture on the subject shall have been poetized, made into divine songs, inserted in hymn books, and occasionally sung in churches, and by children at Sabbath schools; when the subject shall have been poetized in the form of soul-stirring songs, adapted to music for the drawing-room, for concerts, and other places of fashionable amusement; and when the unfermented juice of the grape shall be generally used at the communion table; then the principles and practice of total abstinence will soon become general.

Sec. 6. *Consumption of Intoxicating Liquors in the United States, in* 1810, 1840, *and* 1850.

It appears from the returns of the marshals with the census of 1810, that there were then 14,191 distilleries in the United States; that 22,977,167 gallons of spirits were distilled during the year previous, from fruits and grain, and 2,827,625 gallons from molasses; making an annual product of 25,804,892 gallons, valued at 15,580,040 dollars. In the same year, only 608,843 gallons were exported from the United States, leaving for consumption of that distilled, during the year, 25,196,049 gallons. On the average of ten years from 1803 to 1812 inclusive, 7,512,-415 gallons of foreign distilled spirits were annually imported into the United States, and but 679,322 gallons re-exported.

By the returns of the marshals with the census of 1840, it appears that in 1839 there were distilled in the United States, 41,402,627 gallons of spirits, and that 23,267,730 gallons of beer were brewed. The quantity of spirits imported during the year ending September 30th, 1839, was 3,792,718 gallons; exported 884,992 gallons; excess of imports over exports 2,907,726. The wines imported during the same year amounted to 6,577,219 gallons; of which 348,219 gallons were re-exported, and the balance of 6,229,000 gallons were retained for consumption. There is about two-fifths as much alcohol in a gallon of wine, on an average, of light and heavy wines, as in one of brandy or rum and there is generally about one-eighth part as much alcohol in strong beer as in distilled spirits.

The returns of the census of 1850 show that the products of the distilleries and breweries of the United States, and the materials consumed, during the previous year, were as follows:

Whiskey and high wines made, gallons, . .	42,133,955
Rum distilled, gallons, ...	6,500,500
Ale and Porter brewed, barrels, . . .	1,177,924
Bushels of Indian corn used, ...	11,067,761
Bushels of rye used, ...	2,143,927
Bushels of barley used, ...	3,787,195
Bushels of oats, ...	56,517
Bushels of apples, ...	526,840
Hogsheads of molasses, ...	61,675

The average quantity of distilled spirits annually imported into the United States during the two fiscal years ending June 30th, 1850, was reported at	4,319,501	gallons
And the average quantity exported,	1,361,168	"
Excess of imports over exports annually,	2,958,338	"
The average quantity of wine annually imported in casks, during those years, was	5,573,558	"

And the quantity imported in bottles did not vary much from the whole quantity exported.

Intoxicating liquors are not usually furnished for slaves. Estimating ten gallons of wine, or a barrel of ale, as equal to four gallons of distilled spirits; and estimating the quantity of alcohol and other spirits used for compounding medicines, making varnish, and other mechanical purposes, as equal to half a gallon for each free person, the comparison of the consumption in the United States, at different periods, will be as follows:

	1810.	1840.	1850.
Free population in millions,	6	14.57	20.1
Spirits distilled, in millions of gallons,	25.8	41.4	48.63
Spirits imported, excess of, over exports, in millions of gallons,	6.22	2.9	2.95
Beer brewed, equal in spirits to	73	2.9	4.7
Wines consumed, equal in spirits to	55	2.5	2.22
Making in all, in millions of gallons,	33.3	49.7	58.5
Used for medicinal and mechanical purposes,	3	7.27	10
Consumed as a beverage,	30.3	42.43	48.5
Equal for each person in gallons to	5	2.9	2.4

In 1845 the Detroit City Temperance Society appointed a committee to ascertain and report the amount of crime, pauperism and expenditures arising from the use of intoxicating liquors in that city, during the previous year. A sub-committee was appointed for each ward, to ascertain and report to the general committee, the number of places where liquors were sold in small quantities, and the quantities sold and consumed in the respective wards. Much attention was given to the subject, and great care taken to ascertain, with as much accuracy as was practicable, the quantity sold at each tavern, store, and grocery, in each ward. The following is an abstract or summary statement of the facts and estimates reported by the committee:

Number of places of sale, 171.	Quantity sold.	Amount of sales.
Gallons of distilled liquors sold,	79,850	$93,178
Gallons of wine,	10,000	15,000
Barrels of strong beer,	2,158	25,528
Total amount of sales as estimated,		$133,706

Two-thirds of the distilled liquors, and three-fourths of the beer, are estimated as sold by the glass. The estimate includes the amount sold at retail, by the quart and gallon, by about twenty retail grocery stores, but does not include any sales at wholesale. The population of the city was then about 12,000; and if two-thirds of that quantity was consumed by the citizens, (which is quite probable,) it was equal to over 60,000 gallons of distilled spirits, and exceeded five gallons to each person

The average annual consumption of intoxicating liquors by the whole free population of the United States in 1810, and from that time until 1825, was equal to five gallons of distilled spirits to each person. Being more accessible to all classes of persons, at all hours of the day, in cities and villages, than in the country, we may reasonably estimate that the average quantity then consumed in cities and villages was from six to seven gallons, and in the country, from four to four and an half gallons to each person. The temperance reform produced but little effect in the slave states, until since the year 1840. The reformation among the farming population of New England, New York, Ohio, Michigan, and some other portions of the free states, is now nearly complete; the average quantity of intoxicating drinks consumed by the inhabitants of the cities and villages, and all the other portions of the northern states, has been reduced perhaps about one-third part; some reduction has also taken place in the slave states; and the average quantity to each person consumed in the whole United States, is less than half as great as it was previous to the year 1825.

SEC. 7. *Consumption of intoxicating liquors in Great Britain and Ireland, Prussia, and Sweden.*

Statement made from extracts taken from Porter's Progress of the Nation, of the quantities, in millions of gallons, of domestic and foreign distilled liquors consumed in England and Wales, Scotland, and Ireland, during the undermentioned years; and the average quantity to each person.

	England & Wales. *Millions of gallons.*	Scotland. *Millions of gallons.*	Ireland. *Millions of gallons.*	U. Kingdom. *Millions of gallons.*	Gallons to each person.
1802	7.65	2.	5.44	15.	nearly 1.
1812	7.	1.88	4.28	13.1	.7
1821	7.26	2.56	3.4	13.2	.62
1831	12.1	5.86	8.74	26.7	1.1
1838	12.1	6.38	12.32	30.8	1.1
1841	11.5	6.	6.5	24.	.9
1849	9.1	6.9	6.98	23. *	1.03
1849, foreign distilled liquors consumed,				5.2	

Statement of the number of barrels of strong beer, and of table and small beer consumed in England and Wales on which the duty was paid, during the undermentioned years.

	Strong Beer.	Table and Small Beer.
1801	4,735,574	1,691,955
1811	5,902,903	1,649,564
1821	5,575,830	1,439,970
1829	6,559,210	1,530,419

This statement does not include the beer brewed in private families, on which no duties are paid; the duties being charged, and the account taken, only with reference to the beer brewed for sale. The quantity of malt made at different periods, is stated in section 5 of Chapter IX., from which the reader can estimate the quantity of beer brewed and consumed in each division of the United Kingdom, with a reasonable approximation to accuracy. It requires from three to five bushels of malt, to make a barrel of beer or porter, averaging about three and a half bushels to the barrel; each bushel of malt producing about as much alcohol as is contained in a gallon of rum, and perhaps more.

* There were consumed in 1849, about 23 millions of domestic, and over 5 millions of foreign distilled liquors.

The average quantity of intoxicating drinks consumed by the inhabitants of Scotland appears to be greater in proportion to the population than it is in the United States; but in England it is less. There is no reason to doubt, however, that the quantity consumed in the cities of England is as great as it is in the cities of the United States; but it is much less among the agricultural population and the mechanics in the country, and in villages, than it was in the United States prior to the organization of temperance societies.

Mr. Porter says it was given in evidence before a Committee of the House of Commons in 1743, that the quantity of spirituous liquors made for consumption in England and Wales in 1740, was 15,250,000 gallons, in 1741—17,000,000; and in 1742—19,000,000 gallons. These quantities, besides beer and wine, were consumed by a population of about 6,600,000; there being then about 20,000 houses and shops in London, in which intoxicating drinks were sold at retail. Great changes have taken place in the habits and manners of the people since that time. Porter remarks; "It is at once a consequence of the sobriety of the age, and a help to its continuance, that great numbers of houses have been opened for the sale of cups of coffee and tea at low prices. It is said that there are from 1,600 to 1,800 of these coffee-houses in the metropolis (London) alone, and that they are established and rapidly increasing all over the country." "The charge made at these houses for a cup of excellent coffee, with sugar and milk, varies from one penny up to three pence. There are many houses where the lowest of these charges is made, and which are frequented by 700 to 800 persons daily.

One house in Sherrard street, Haymarket, is mentioned, where the charge is three half pence (three cents,) and the daily customers average from 1,500 to 1,600 persons, of all classes, from hackney coachmen and porters, to the most respectable classes." "The proprietor of another house stated to the committee that he had paid £400 a year for newspapers, magazines, and binding. He said I have, upon the average, 400 to 450 persons that frequent my house daily; they are mostly lawyers' clerks, and commercial men; some of them are managing clerks; and there are many solicitors, likewise highly respectable gentlemen, who take coffee in the middle of the day in preference to more stimulating drink."

Most men desire stimulants of some kind, and the moderately stimulating properties of tea and coffee, which make the mind more active and never tend to derange it, are good substitutes for intoxicating drinks; and have aided greatly to promote sobriety and the cause of temperance. The coffee-houses of England are worthy of imitation in the United States, and it is to be hoped that the time is not far distant, when tea and coffee will be substituted for intoxicating drinks, in all the eating houses and oyster cellars, as well as in the taverns of our cities and villages.

Mr. McCulloch states the population of the Prussian monarchy, in 1837, at 14,157,573; the consumption of spirits annually at from 40,000,000 to 45,000,000 gallons; and that beer and spirits are extensively produced and consumed in all parts of the kingdom. He remarks, "If we take Prussia for a standard, the people of the United Kingdom may be said to be temperate in the extreme; for while the consumption of spirits in Prussia amounts at an average to about three gallons to each individual, the consumption in Great Britain and Ireland is only about three-fourths of a gallon; and we believe that the consumption of beer in Prussia exceeds its consumption in the United Kingdom in a corresponding proportion."

The consumption of distilled spirits is perhaps greater in Sweden, in proportion to the population, than in any other country in the world. The following is extracted from McCulloch's Gazetteer:

"The Swedes are great consumers of ardent spirits; every proprietor and occupier of land has a right to distil spirits; the size of the still, and the amount of the duty, depending on the value of the property. Mr. Stevens states that, in 1829, there were 167,744 stills going, which were calculated to make within the year about 30,000,000 gallons, worth as many rix dollars, and paying a duty of 434,396 dollars." "We understand that but little change has taken place during the last ten years; but taking the consumption at only 25,000,000, and the population at 3,000,000, it gives an average annual supply of eight and a third gallons to every individual, young and old, being about three times the average consumption of the people of Scotland."

Who can number the victims of alcohol? Who can calculate how much it has done to destroy, as well as to debase mankind, and to retard the progress of nations?

CHAPTER XIX.

ON THE GENERAL LAWS WHICH GOVERN THE PROGRESS OF POPULATION; AND ON THE POPULATION OF THE OLD WORLD.

SEC. 1. *On the general laws which govern the progress of population.*

THE remark has been frequently made by writers on population that as a general rule, when population is not affected by war or pestilence, it increases as fast as food increases. It appears to me this rule is not correct; that it attaches quite too much importance to food, to say that human life, the health, strength, activity and longevity of man, depend on food alone. It attaches too much importance also to agriculture, to say that human life depends entirely on food; on the means of subsistence, provided by one branch of industry; and that the products of all others, which we are accustomed to rank as necessaries and comforts of life, do not tend to sustain and promote human life, and to increase population. Such a position is disproved by the whole history of man. The truth is, that in all countries below the 60th degree of latitude, it has generally been more difficult for mankind to provide themselves with clothing, dwellings and lodging of such kind and description as are the best adapted to promote and secure the greatest degree of health, strength and longevity, consistent with the climate in which they resided, than to procure a sufficient supply of such food as is necessary to attain that object. Though food constitutes the most indispensable means of supporting human life, yet food alone comprises but a small part of the means necessary to promote life to such a degree, as to cause a rapid increase of population. The other means necessary have been exhibited in chapter XI.

The increase of population has been more or less checked in almost every country, by considerations of prudence, and by vice, as well as by natural causes. When not affected by wars, population generally increases above the 35th degree of latitude, about as fast as the aggregate amount of the comforts of life increases. The increase, however, cannot exceed, or never has yet exceeded, about three per cent. annually, or thirty-three per cent. in ten years. The ratio of increase is very much affected by early marriages, which are promoted by the frugal and simple habits of an agricultural people; and particularly those settled in a new country. Population is influenced much more by climate, below the 35th degree of latitude, than it is above. Though good and comfortable dwellings, clothing and lodging adapted to the climate, together with a sufficient supply of fuel, have a very great influence upon health, longevity and the increase of population in warm countries; and the progress of population is to some extent in proportion to the increase of the comforts of life in the aggregate; yet no amount of comforts can guard against many of the diseases incident to the decay of vegetation in hot climates, and in the vicinity of marshy lands and stagnant waters. No general rule can be given with accuracy in relation to the causes of the progress of population where the climate has a preponderating influence over all other causes in producing disease. In such countries, like the delta of the river Ganges, and the countries bordering on the Gulf of Mexico, or lying in the valleys of rivers like the Mississippi and Amazon, where the soil is mostly alluvial and very rich and productive, and vegetation abundant, so far as food is concerned, the means of supporting human life are almost unlimited. It is therefore evident that in such countries the supply of food has very little influence upon the increase of population; and though an increase of the comforts of life, and the aid of the medical sciences, may enable man to guard against and resist the influence of the climate to some extent, and may have great influence upon health and the progress of population, yet after all, the influence of climate seems to preponderate over all other causes.

Famines are almost unknown in the present age of the world; and the failure of crops, short crops, and dearths, are much less common than they were in ancient times, or even two or three centuries ago. Modern science and industry have not only increased the products of agriculture, but rendered crops more uniform and certain. The drainage and sewerage of cities, as well as the drainage of countries, is generally much better than it was a century since; and greater attention is paid to cleanliness, and to a sufficient supply of good water. Dwellings are generally better and more comfortable, and cellars better drained. All these causes have tended to check the influence and spread of pestilences and epidemics, to promote health, and produce greater uniformity in the ratio of mortality, and the increase of population, in all civilized countries.

SEC. 2. *Population of the Roman Empire, and of the Roman Provinces, and countries of Europe, at different periods.*

The increase of the population of Italy, Spain and Portugal during the two centuries next before the Christian era, and the two centuries next after it, was probably about twenty-five or thirty per cent. each century; and the ratio of mortality was greater than it is at present; ranging from twenty-five to forty per cent. every ten years, of all the inhabitants above five years of age. The increase of the population of the island of Great Britain at that time, could not have been over ten or twelve per cent. in a century, in time of peace; and the mortality, including periods of famine and pestilence, nearly three times as great as it is now. The decennial increase of the population of Great Britain is now greater than the centennial increase was at any time prior to the Crusades of the twelfth century. From the twelfth to the middle of the eighteenth century, the general ratio of increase of the population of Europe, was only from fifteen to thirty per cent. in a century. These facts will be illustrated by statistics of population.

The Roman Empire, when the greatest in extent, and the most populous, during the third century after the Christian era, has been estimated by Gibbon to have had a population of 120,000,000; about half of whom were slaves. M. A. Moreau de Jonnes, a learned statistician of France, with all the lights of modern science, has recently estimated it at only about 83,000,000, (in his Statistiques des Peuples de l'Antiquité.) The Empire then comprised all southern Europe, western Asia, and northern Africa; and when we take into consideration the vast extent of territory, much of which was very productive; the mild climate of the countries bordering on the Mediterranean Sea, of all others the best adapted to supply the wants of man in a low state of civilization, and enable mankind to multiply and increase in numbers; together with the state of agriculture, and the mechanic arts, and the degree of civilization, which the Romans had attained, it does not seem improbable, that the population was an hundred millions, and perhaps more.

An enumeration of the adult male citizens of Rome was made several times; but no census of any kind was ever taken of the whole Empire, or of the provinces, during the existence of the Republic; nor was there a complete census at any time taken of the whole population of the city of Rome The population of the Republic, and of the Empire at different periods, is the subject of conjecture, and of estimates, founded on the condition and extent of the provinces, and other evidence of a slight character. We have no reliable evidence that the population of the provinces materially declined, until after the government interfered with the religious freedom of the people, attempted to enforce uniformity of opinion, and to suppress heresy as well as paganism, in the fourth century.

Severe edicts were enacted not only against the pagan worship, but also against all heretical sects, including the Manicheans, Arians, Donatists, Nestorians, Pelagians, Eutychians or Monophysites, Monothelites, and Paulicians; all of whom were condemned as heretics, subjected to various penalties and punishments, many of their bishops banished, and great numbers of the people persecuted and compelled to flee their country. The schisms and dissensions among the different sects and factions, and the violence, persecutions and despotism of the government in religious matters, excited tumults, riots, rebellions, civil wars, assassinations, and shocking massacres; which distracted the whole Empire; disturbed industry induced great numbers to emigrate to Persia and other countries for protection; made all the proscribed and persecuted sects enemies to the Roman Government; destroyed the unity of feeling, the martial spirit, and the national pride, which previously existed among the Roman people; and exhausted the empire to such a degree, that it was unable to defend its provinces against either the barbarians, or the Saracens.

The pagans, Donatists and Arians of Africa sought the protection of the Vandals, and aided them in conquering that province in the fifth century. The Arians and pagans also took refuge among the Goths, Burgundians and other barbarians, and aided them in subduing Italy and other European provinces of the empire, in the 5th and 6th centuries; and the Nestorians and Monophysites sought the protection of the Saracens, and assisted them in conquering several of the Asiatic provinces of the empire, in the 7th century.* Before the end of the seventh century, all the Roman provinces of Africa, and the most of the Asiatic provinces, were taken by the Saracens. All the provinces of the Western empire were conquered and devastated by the Northern barbarians, and reduced to the lowest point of population, degradation and poverty. The heretical sects had been mostly extirpated and driven to the Saracens; the doctrines of the Greek Church prevailed in all the provinces of the eastern empire; and the Catholic faith was triumphant in nearly all the

* See on this subject Mosheim's Ecclesiastical History, Harper's ed., vol. I. pages 99 to 190, and page 232—and particularly pages 132, 134, 141, 170, 176, 183, 184, and 190—See also ante section 1, chapter IV.

countries of western Europe; but with few exceptions, all the countries of Europe remained in nearly the same condition of poverty and exhaustion, until after the Crusades, of the 11th century. From that time the mechanic arts, commerce and agriculture began to revive, and population to increase. The increase of population in many countries must have been very large, between the end of the 11th and the end of the 15th century.

From the best evidences we can derive from history, we have no reason to believe that the Roman provinces conquered by the Saracens, declined very much in population, wealth, or productive industry, under their dominion; or that Egypt, the northern provinces of Africa, Asia Minor, Syria, Palestine and Mesopotamia, were much less populous at the time of the Crusades in the twelfth, than they were in the seventh century. But from the moment those countries, Greece, and Turkey in Europe, fell under the dominion and the blighting influence of the indolent, haughty and barbarous Turks, they began to decline rapidly, and have been sinking ever since.

The culture and manufacture of cotton, and many other useful arts, were introduced into Spain and northern Africa by the Saracens; it is said that the mechanic arts and agriculture revived in those countries, and it is supposed that the population increased.

The countries contained in the following table comprise about the same territory as the Roman Empire did. Their extent in English square miles, and population in 1840, are taken from McCulloch's Gazetteer, to which is added an estimate of their population in the 3d, and also at the close of the 7th and 15th centuries:

	Square Miles.	Millions of inhabitants in the y'r			
		200 to 300.	700.	1500.	1840.
Italy, and the Italian Islands,	119,555	14	8	15	22.4
Spain and Portugal, -	219,268	16	10	14	15.8
Switzerland, - -	15,233	.5	.5	1	2.2
France, - - -	203,736	8	5	12	34.1
Belgium and Holland, -	26,814	1	.8	1.6	7.1
England and Wales, -	57,812	2	1.2	3.2	15.9
Turkey in Europe, and Greece,	225,000	15	12	13	10
Turkey in Asia, or Asia Minor, Syria, Palestine, Mesopotamia,	450,000	24	18	15	12
Egypt has arable lands, -	19,000	4.5	3.5	3	2
Morocco, Algiers, Tunis, and Tripoli, -	450,000	15	10	12	12
		100	69	89.8	133.5

Area of the countries of Europe since the fall of Napoleon in 1815, and estimates of the population contained within their present limits at different periods, from the year 1500 to 1850. Lombardy and Venice are included with Italy and its islands. The square miles are stated in thousands, and the population in millions.

	Sq. Miles.	1500.	1600.	1700.	1800.	1840.	1850.
Italy and Islands	119.5	15.	16.5	18.	20.	22.4	24.
Spain and Portugal	219.3	14.	14.	13.5	13.5	15.8	16.
France	203.7	12.	15.	20.5	27.3	34.1	35.8
England and Wales	57.8	3.2	4.3	5.6	9.1	15.9	17.8
Scotland	29.6	.6	.8	1.	1.6	2.6	2.8
Ireland	31.8	1.5	1.8	2.4	5.	8 1	6.5
Holland, or Netherlands	13.6	.6	1.1	1.6	2.	3.	3.3
Belgium	13.2	1.	.9	1.4	3.	4.1	4.4
Prussia	107.9	5.	6.	7.5	10.	14.9	16.5
Denmark	21.8	.8	1.	1.2	1.5	2.1	2.3
Sweden and Norway	292.	1.6	2.	2.4	3.	4.3	4.6
Germany	90.7	6.	7.	8.5	11.	14.5	15.5
Switzerland	15.2	1.	1.2	1.5	2.	2.2	2.3
Austria and Hungary	240.	12.	14.5	18.	23.	31.	33.
Poland	50.7	2.5	3.	3.5	4.	4.5	5.
Russia	1.950.	12.	14.	17.	33.	51.6	57.
Turkey	210.6					9.	9.
Greece and	17.9	13.	13.	12.	11.	.9	.9
Ionian Islands	1					.2	.2
	3.686.3	101.8	116. 1	135.6	180.	241.2	256.9

The military power and prosperity of the Turks was the greatest, the latter part of the sixteenth century, and began to decline soon after. France was disturbed with religious wars and persecutions, during much of the 16th century; but after the passage of the edict of Nantes, in 1598, that kingdom enjoyed tranquillity and prosperity, until its repeal in 1685. The religious wars in Germany, from about the year 1530 to the peace of Westphalia in 1648, partially devastated many portions of the country, and checked the increase of population, in nearly all the kingdoms and states of Germany. The treaty of Westphalia not only secured the blessings of peace, but also the religious rights and privileges of the Protestants in the northern kingdoms. From that period they began to improve, and to increase more and more rapidly, in industry and population. Holland began to flourish soon after the Union of Utrecht in 1579; Great Britain and Ireland, after the revolution of 1688; and Russia, after Peter the Great ascended the throne, in 1689.

SEC. 3. *Population of Italy at different periods.*

The population of Italy, until within a few years past, is more uncertain than that of either France or England. Dr. Morse, in the edition of his Geography published in 1793, says: "Some doubts have arisen whether Italy is as populous now as it was in the time of Pliny, when it contained 14,000,000. It is, however, believed that the present inhabitants exceed that number." "It may not perhaps be extravagant, if we assign to Italy 20,000,000 of inhabitants; but some calculations greatly exceed that number." Mr. McCulloch states it in 1838 at 22,478,192.

Italy and the Italian islands, including Sicily and Sardinia, contain about 119,555 English square miles. It is about twice as large as England and Wales; and being situated in a very mild climate, like all the countries bordering on the Mediterranean Sea, it was much more favorable to health and an increase of population in a comparatively low state of the mechanic arts and of civilization, than England, the north of France, or any other country in a high latitude. The population of Italy in the third and fourth centuries, was perhaps four times as dense, and eight times as great, as that of England and Wales. The Romans lived by agriculture, and subsisted on grain and vegetables; while the Britons were yet in the pastoral state, subsisting on the milk and flesh of their flocks, agriculture being almost unknown among them. Italy was in a state of peace the most of the time for more than two centuries before the Christian era, and more than four centuries afterwards, and yet we have no reason to believe that it increased in population more than thirty per cent. in a century, or doubled in less than about three centuries, during the most flourishing period of the Roman government, either under the Republic or the Empire.

Italy was overrun by numerous hordes of barbarians at several different periods in the fifth century; ravaged, desolated, most of the arts and improvements of civilization destroyed, and the country depopulated, and reduced probably to less than eight millions of inhabitants, or about half its former number. This instance of rapid decline is not without a parallel. The Island of Hayti or St. Domingo, which is about one-fourth part as large as Italy, was estimated to contain a million of inhabitants when discovered by Columbus in 1495; but in consequence of the butchery and oppressions of the Spaniards, who made slaves of the natives, compelled them to labor incessantly in the mines without any regard to their wants and comforts, and without supplying them with sufficient food, the native inhabitants in a single generation declined to less than one hundred thousand. Disease of mind soon preys upon the body, and it often happens that persons accustomed to freedom, or affluence, pine away, and find a premature death, when reduced to poverty, or restrained of their liberty. When nearly all the inhabitants of a country are despoiled of their property, and reduced from a state of comfort to poverty and want, like the Romans in the fifth century, all the objects of life seem to have perished; all the energies of the body, as well as the mind, are soon paralyzed, so that few persons under such circumstances have sufficient energy to provide themselves with the necessaries of life apparently within their power; disappointment and disease of mind, as well as want of food, prey upon them; they become feeble, nervous, and emaciated, and disease sweeps them off by thousands.

Slaves have not the muscular power to labor like freemen. Muscular power depends much on the mind, on the will; and the will is seldom if ever firm, energetic, and powerful, when the person is conscious that some individual, other than himself or his children, will reap the reward of his exertions. Productive industry and security of rights and of property are as necessary to cheer up, encourage and invigorate the mind, as they are to feed and clothe the body, and strengthen it by exercise. Hence the decline of the population of Italy in the fifth century. Comparatively few perished by the sword; few adults perished by positive starvation. Millions, depressed in mind and emaciated in body, perished by disease, and millions of children perished from neglect and want.

Though Italy remained in a very depressed condition until the beginning of the crusades, and recovered very slowly previous to that time, yet it was much more advanced in civilization and all the arts of peace, and more densely populated during the dark ages than either France or England. Perhaps it had 9,000,000 of inhabitants at the commencement of the 12th century, or about five times as many as England and Wales. During the crusades, and shortly after them, many of the arts and products of the east were introduced into Italy, and more particularly into Venice, Genoa, Pisa, Florence and Sicily. The culture and manufacture of silk was introduced in the 12th century, and of cotton in the early part of the 14th century.* From the time of the crusades until some time after the discovery of America, the Italian republics were in the most prosperous and flourishing condition of any part of Europe, with the exception of Flanders, which was perhaps equally so, by reason of the woollen manufacture. During the 12th, 13th, 14th and 15th centuries, the population of Venice, Genoa, Florence and some other parts of Italy, perhaps doubled,

* See Baine's history of the cotton manufacture, chapter IV.

and the population of the whole of Italy increased from about 9,000,000 to 15,000,000.

The discovery of a passage to India and China around the Cape of Good Hope and Africa, diverted much of the trade from the Italian cities, and affected their prosperity very much; and this, together with the religious wars growing out of the reformation, checked the increase of the population during the 16th, 17th and 18th centuries, so that it did not perhaps exceed 20,000,000, as estimated by Dr. Morse, at the close of the 18th century. Since the feudal system was overturned by Napoleon, and the revival of commerce at the close of the wars growing out of the French revolution, there has been a very perceptible increase in the population of nearly all the Italian States; amounting to about 2,500,000, or 12½ per cent. during the first forty years of the present century, making the population in 1840 about 22,400,000

SEC. 4. *Population of Spain and Portugal.*

The population of Spain prior to the present century was much more uncertain than that of England or France. Mr. McCulloch says, "In 1787 the population amounted to 10,268,150, or perhaps 10,500,000, as it is believed on apparently good grounds, that the official returns were below the mark; and since then it has increased nearly two millions." He gives the area at 182,758 square miles, and the population at 12,168,774

The climate of Spain is warm, mild and favorable to an increase of population with a small amount of comforts; some of it is very productive, and the Spaniards, during the 15th and first half of the 16th century, were, next to the Italian States and the Netherlands, the most enterprising of any people in Europe, and quite as much advanced in the mechanic arts and manufactures. It is probable that at the close of the career of Charles V., in the middle of the 16th century, the population of Spain was nearly as dense as that of France, and amounted to from eleven to twelve millions; that the swarms of priests and monks during the despotic reigns of Philip II., Philip III., Philip IV., Charles II., and their successors, together with the combined tyranny of the government and of the Popish Inquisition, reduced the population; that it amounted to about 10,500,000 in 1787, as estimated by Mr. McCulloch; and that since the iron reign of the inquisition and of feudalism was broken by Napoleon, it has increased during the last half century nearly two millions, or about eighteen per cent.

Some have supposed the emigration to America has been the principal cause of the decline of the population of Spain; but this supposition is not correct. According to the statements of McCulloch in his Gazetteer, the whole population of the West

Indics and the continent of America of Spanish descent in 1840, was less than 4,500,000; though those of English and Scotch descent then numbered over 12,500,000.

	1550.	1840.
Inhabitants of Spain, estimated at	11,500,000	12,200,000
Do. in America of Spanish descent,	100,000	5,000,000
Total of Spanish descent,	11,600,000	17,200,000
Inhabitants of Great Britain,	4,400,000	18,000,000
Do. in America of British descent,		10,000,000
Total of British descent,		28,000,000

What a contrast between the relative increase of the two people!

Mr. McCulloch says that, according to the official returns of the census of 1787, the ecclesiastics of all descriptions, including 61,617 monks, 32,500 nuns, and 2,705 inquisitors, amounted to 188,625 individuals, and that in 1833 they amounted to 175,574 individuals, of whom 61,727 were monks, and 24,007 nuns Independent of the depressing influence of the tyranny of the Inquisition, what country could flourish with such an immense army of priests, inquisitors, monks and nuns, devouring their substance? Spain, Mexico, and all the Spanish American states and colonies, have been ruled for centuries by a clerical, landed, and military aristocracy; and no country ever yet flourished under such a dominion, no matter what the form of the government, whether republican, democratic, or monarchical. In the Islands of Cuba and Porto Rico, a more commercial and manufacturing spirit prevails, and predominates over the priesthood and the military; I say manufacturing, because the expense of making sugar, molasses and rum, from the cane, is about as great as the culture of the cane.

Portugal has been depressed by nearly the same causes as Spain. McCulloch states its area at 36,510 square miles, and its population, in 1838, at 3,549,420; the American Almanac for 1852 states the population at the last enumeration in 1841, at 3,412,500. It probably had, during the 16th, 17th, and 18th centuries, from 2,500,000 to 3,000,000 of inhabitants.

Sec. 5. *Progress of the population of France.*

The population of France has been estimated in the table of population of the Roman Empire, and of the countries comprising the Roman provinces, at eight millions in the third century; but five millions at the end of the seventh century, and twelve millions at the end of the fifteenth century; those estimates are intended for the present territory of France, including Corsica.

The province of Lorraine was annexed to France in 1766, with nearly a million of inhabitants, and Corsica in 1768, with about 180,000. The population of France was estimated by the government, on partial enumerations, at 19,669,320 in the year 1700, previous to those annexations; it was subsequently estimated in 1773 at 23,531,000. Several annexations were made during the revolution, and at the peace of 1815, France was allowed to retain Avignon and Venaison on the Rhone, and several other small parcels of territory, with a population of about 700,000.

Mr. McCulloch remarks, "The information with respect to the population of France previously to 1784 is extremely imperfect. But according to the best attainable information, it amounted in 1700 to 19,669,000, and in 1762 to 21,769,000. In 1784 it was estimated by M. Necker at 24,800,000." By the first census, taken in 1801, France, with its increased territory, (comprising 203,736 square miles,) had a population of 27,349,003; and by the official census, taken in 1836, it had increased to 33,540,910.

The climate of France being much colder than that of Italy and Spain, and the country less populous, flourishing and wealthy, was less inviting to the barbarians who ravaged the provinces of the western Roman Empire in the fifth and sixth centuries; and though the decline of the population of France (then Gaul) was very great, it must have suffered much less from the barbarians than Italy and Spain. We have less certain and accurate information in relation to the population of France prior to the eighteenth century, than we have in relation to England. We have reason to believe, however, that while a Roman province, and also in the time of Charlemagne, France was more flourishing, more advanced in civilization, and more populous in proportion to its territory, than England; but from the end of the eleventh to the end of the sixteenth century, there was no great difference in the condition of the two countries, and the population in proportion to the territory was probably very nearly the same. During the reign of Louis XIV., up to the revocation of the edict of Nantes in 1685, France was more flourishing and advanced in civilization than England.

It has been estimated that about 70,000 Huguenots, or French Protestants, were massacred in France, by virtue of secret orders from the king, in 1572. The massacre occurred at the festival of St. Bartholomew, and is known in history, as the Massacre of St. Bartholomew. During the religious persecutions of the first ten years after the revocation of the edict of Nantes, it has been generally estimated that from 500,000 to 700,000 Protestants were massacred and driven out of the kingdom. The Protestants were mostly mechanics, and comprised a very large proportion of the best mechanics in the kingdom. Those persecutions had a very depressing influence upon the industry and business of the nation, and checked the increase of the population.

Population in 1700 as generally estimated,	19,669,000
Increase in 70 years nearly 15 per cent.,	2,831,000
Estimated population of Lorraine, annexed in 1766, and of Corsica,	1,000,000
Estimated population in 1770,	23,500,000
Increase in 14 years nearly 6 per cent.,	1,300,000
Population in 1784, as estimated by the government,	24,800,000
Increase in 17 years nearly 7½ per cent.,	1,849,000
Population of Avignon, Venaison, and other scraps of territory annexed, about	700,000
In 1801, population by the first census,	27,349,000

Statement of the population of France according to the official returns of the census taken in the undermentioned years, with the per cent. of increase, and the total increase during the intermediate periods.

Years.	Population.	No. of Years.	Increase during previous period.	
			Per cent.	Total increase.
1801	27,349,000			
1806	29,107,425	5	6	1,758,425
1816	29,217,465	10		110,040
1821	30,461,875	5	over 4	1,244,410
1826	31,858,937	5	4⅔	1,397,062
1831	32,569,223	5	2¼	710,286
1836	33,540,910	5	3	971,687
1841	34,194,875	5	2	653,965
1846	35,401,761	5	3½	1,206,886
1851	35,781,628	5	1	379,867

The reader will see that the increase of the population was checked during the wars of Napoleon, from 1806 to 1815. This was caused by the conscription, to supply troops for the Emperor, which drained the country of great numbers of its young and middle-aged men. During the previous years, from 1801 to 1806, (which was mostly a period of peace,) the population increased more rapidly than it ever did before; since 1816 the increase has been very regular; and even during the revolutionary period, from 1789 to 1801, the increase seems to have been more rapid than it ever was during any previous period.

The victims of the revolution, from 1789 to 1795, are stated by Alison in a note to the fourteenth chapter of his History of Europe, as follows:

Guillotined by sentence of the revolutionary tribunals:	
Nobles,	1,278
Noble women,	750
Priests,	1,135
All other persons,	15,440
Total guillotined,	18,603
Women died of premature childbirth, estimated at	3,400
Women died in childbirth of grief,	348
Victims under Carrier, at Nantes, estimated at	32,000
Victims at Lyons, estimated at	31,000
Men slain in the civil wars of La Vendee, estimated at	900,000
Women killed in La Vendee, estimated at	15,000
Children killed in La Vendee, estimated at	22,000
Total as above stated and estimated,	1,022,351

This number does not include the massacres at Versailles and several other places, and at the prisons; nor those shot at Toulon and Marseilles. It should be borne in mind, however, that the numbers stated as killed at Nantes, Lyons, and in La Vendee, are but vague and uncertain estimates, which are most likely greatly exaggerated; and that the destruction of human life in La Vendee, was not the direct and necessary effect of the revolution, but was caused by the civil wars excited by the priests, nobles, and other opponents of the revolution, in opposition to the government established by it. When these things are taken into consideration, it appears probable that the real victims of the revolution did not exceed fifty or sixty thousand; that they were less numerous than the victims of the religious persecutions, in 1572, known as the massacre of St. Bartholomew; and that the destruction of human life during the wars of Napoleon was from twenty to fifty times as great.

The revolution broke the shackles of the feudal nobility and of the Catholic priesthood; it set free the human mind, and the industry of the people; and from that time the energies of the people were aroused; they began to improve and to increase in numbers, and nothing but the iron rule and the exhausting wars of Napoleon checked their increase from 1806 to 1816. The policy of the government of encouraging industry, by securing its markets to its own citizens, and the partial freedom enjoyed by the people under the comparatively mild reign of Louis Philippe, enabled France to increase in productive industry and population.* It remains to be seen whether it can increase under the despotic rule of the Dictator, Louis Napoleon.

SEC. 6. *Progress of the population of England and Wales, Scotland and Ireland, and the emigration.*

The population of England according to the official returns, at the time of making Doomsday book after the Norman conquest, about the year 1075, consisted of 300,785 families, estimated by Turner in his history of the Anglo-Saxons, at 1,700,000. This estimate has been adopted by Sir James McIntosh in his history of England, and by other eminent British authors. It is probable that the population of Wales at that time, bore about the same proportion to that of England, as it does now; which would give about 100,000 for Wales, and 1,800,000 for England and Wales. McCulloch in his Gazetteer estimates the population of England and Wales, at that period, at 2,150,000; in 1377 at 2,350,000; in 1575 at 4,500,000; and adopts the estimate of Gregory King, of 5,500,000 in 1696. Hallam in his History of the Middle Ages, says the whole population in 1377 did not much exceed 2,300,000. Murray in his Encyclopædia of Geography estimates the population in 1377 at 2,300,000; in 1575 at 4,500,000; and in 1688 at 5,500,000.

The estimates for the year 1377 are founded on the returns of a poll tax, levied on all laymen over fourteen years of age; and those for 1696, are founded on the returns of a hearth tax. The census of the United States, taken in 1790, was the first enumeration ever taken by a nation of all its inhabitants. The first complete census ever taken of the population of Great Britain, was in 1801; and the same year, the first census was taken of all the inhabitants of France. Other nations of Europe, at later periods, followed the example of the United States, in enumerating all their inhabitants. All previous enumerations were of families, of males capable of bearing arms, of adults, or houses, for purposes of taxation; from which estimates were made of the whole number of inhabitants.

England and Wales contain 57,812 square miles. The Norman conquest in 1066 was easily effected, and was not very destructive to human life. The number of Normans who came into the country during the first nine years after the conquest (up to 1075) perhaps equalled the decrease of the Anglo-Saxon population, by reason of the conquest.

* See Chapter XIII., Section 15, and Chapter XIV., Section 9.

Estimates of the population of England and Wales, at the undermentioned dates; with the per cent. of increase, and the total increase, during the intermediate periods.

Years.	Population.	No. of Years.	Increase during previous period.	
			Per Cent.	Total Increase.
1075	1,800,000			
1200	2,000,000	125	About 11	200,000
1300	2,200,000	100	,, 10	200,000
1400	2,600,000	100	Nearly 20	400,000
1500	3,250,000	100	,, 25	650,000
1600	4,300,000	100	,, 33	1,050,000
1700	5,600,000	100	About 30	1,300,000
1750	6,700,000	50	,, 20	1,100,000
1775	7,500,000	25	,, 12	800,000
1790	8,325,000	15	,, 11	825,000
1801	9,225,000	11	Nearly 11	900,000

There were over thirty years civil war during the fifteenth century, which checked the increase of the population. It was lessened also during the seventeenth century by civil wars and emigration. The number stated for 1801 includes about three-fourths of the 470,598 employed in the army and navy in the United Kingdom.

Scotland had 1,050,000 inhabitants in 1696;* 1,265,380 in 1755; and 1,599,068 by the first complete census taken in 1801.

Estimates of the population of Scotland at the undermentioned dates, and its progressive increase.

Years.	Population.	No. of Years.	Increase during previous period.	
			Per cent.	Total increase.
1200	400,000			
1500	600,000	300	50	200,000
1600	780,000	100	30	180,000
1700	1,040,000	100	33⅓	260,000
1750	1,248,000	50	20	208,000
1775	1,373,000	25	10	125,000
1790	1,508,000	15	nearly 10	135,000
1801	1,658,068	11	,, 10	150,068

The number stated for 1801 includes 59,000 for the Scotch

* See McCulloch's Gazetteer.

employed in the army and navy, or about one eighth of the whole number in the United Kingdom.

IRELAND is said by Mr. McCulloch to contain an area of 31,874 square miles, of which 711⅓ are covered with water. The population was estimated in 1672 at but 1,100,000; in 1731 at but 2,010,221; in 1754 at 2,372,634; and in 1785 at only 2,845,932. But it is impossible, considering the number at subsequent periods, for it to have been so low at those dates. Those estimates are founded on the returns of the hearth money collectors of the number of houses, and they estimated six persons for each house counted in the returns. Their fallacy is shown by the fact that the number in 1785 was estimated at but 2,845,932, and in 1788, 3,900,000; showing an increase of nearly forty per cent. in three years. Dr. Morse estimated the population of Ireland in 1792 at 4,000,000; and Dr. Newenham estimated it in 1805 at 5,375,456. The hearth money collectors returned the number of houses in 1785 at only 474,322; in 1788 at 650,000; and in 1791 at 701,102, which, allowing an average of six persons to each house, would show a population, in 1791, of 4,206,612. The returns for the year 1785, and all prior years, must have been very imperfect. An imperfect census was taken in 1812, from which the population was computed at 5,937,856. The first complete census was taken in 1821, showing a population of 6,801,827.

It is probable that the population of Ireland was less per square mile than that of England and Wales, at the time of its conquest by Henry II. of England in the year 1172, and did not amount in the year 1200 to more than 900,000; in the year 1300 to 1,000,000; in the year 1400 to 1,140,000; in the year 1500 to 1,400,000; and in the year 1600 to 1,750,000. Ireland was mostly a grazing country, without much agriculture, manufactures, commerce or enterprise, until the rise of manufactures in Great Britain the latter part of the 18th century. The Irish were very little affected by the European wars, and very few emigrated until since the close of the wars in 1815. Though a few thousand Protestants were massacred in the rebellion in 1640, yet as emigration from England during the civil wars was great, and none from Ireland, the increase of the population of Ireland during the 17th century was perhaps much greater than that of England, or about 40 per cent.; amounting to 700,000; making the population in 1700 about 2,450,000.

Statements of the population of Ireland, according to the returns of the censuses of 1821 to 1851, and estimates for the previous undermentioned periods, and its progressive increase.

Years.	Population.	No. of Years.	Increase during previous period.	
			Per cent.	Total increase.
1700	2,450,000			
1750	3,100,000	50	25	650,000
1775	3,600,000	25	16⅔	500,000
1790	4,300,000	15	nearly 20	700,000
1801	5,000,000	11	16⅔	700,000
1811	5,830,000	10	about 16⅔	830,000
1821	6,801,827	10	" 16⅔	971,827
1831	7,767,401	10	over 14	965,574
1841	8,175,124	10	about 5⅔	407,783
1851	6,515,784	10	decrease 20	1,659,340

Statement of the population of England and Wales, Scotland and Ireland respectively, and of the Channel Islands of Jersey, Guernsey, Man, &c., according to the returns of the censuses from 1801 to 1851; being estimated for Ireland and the Channel Islands for 1801 and 1811. Also the per cent. of increase during each intervening period, and the emigration.

	Population in 1801.	Increase per cent.	Population in 1811.	Increase per cent.	Population in 1821.
England - - -	8,331,434	14.5	9,538,827	18.	11,261,437
Wales - - -	541,546	13.	611,788	17.3	717,438
Scotland - - -	1,599,068	12.9	1,805,688	15.9	2,093,456
	10,472,048	14.2	11,956,303	17.6	14,072,331
Army and Navy -	470,598	. .	640,500	. .	319,300
Ireland - - -	5,000,000	18.	5,830,000	16.6	6,801,827
Channel Islands -	60,000	. .	74,000	. .	89,508
Total - -	16,002,646	15⅝	18,500,803	15⅓	21,282,966
Emigration partly estimated	. . . . .	. .	80,000	. .	159,465
Natural increase of the emigrants	. . . . .	.	6,000	.	12,500
	16,002,646	16.	18,586,803	16.	21,454,931

	Increase per cent.	Population in 1831.	Increase per cent.	Population in 1841.	Increase per cent.	Population in 1851.
England - -	16½	13,091,005	14.6	15,000,154	12½	17,905,831
Wales -	12⅓	806,182	13.	911,603		
Scotland - -	13.	2,365,114	10.8	2,620,184	10.8	2,870,784
	15½	16,262,301	13.9	18,531,941	12·1	20,776,615
Army and Navy	. .	277,017	. .	209,926		
Ireland - -	13⅞	7,767,017	5¼	8,175,124		6,515,784
Channel Islands	. .	103,710	. .	124,040		142,916
Total -	14·6	24,410,429	10.7	27,041,031	1½	27,435,315
Emigrated -	. .	253,676	. .	703,130		1,684,894
Incr'se of emi'gnts	. .	18,000	. .	49,000		85,000
Convicts transported, about	. .	25,000	. .	30,160	abo't	33,000
	16.	24,707,105	14.	27,823,321	8.1	29,238,209

It is a remarkable circumstance, illustrating the great prosperity and productive energy of every part of Great Britain, that every county of England and Wales increased in population between each decennial period from 1801 to 1841; that every county in Scotland increased in population between the census of 1821 and that of 1831, while seven counties declined in population between the years 1831 and 1841; that England increased from 1801 to 1811 about 14½ per cent.; from 1811 to 1821 nearly 18 per cent.; from 1821 to 1831 about 16 per cent.; and from 1831 to 1841 14½ per cent. Ireland increased from 1790 to 1831 about as fast as England, being from 14 to 20 per cent. every ten years every county but one increasing from the census of 1821 to that of 1831, when the rapid increase is suddenly checked and reduced from 14½ per cent. in ten years, to about 5¼ per cent. from 1831 to 1841. Though there was a large emigration from Ireland from 1830 to 1845, yet there is no reason to believe that the population declined prior to the year 1846. Then commenced the great dearth, excessive mortality, and immense emigration, which reduced the population in five years nearly two millions. There is reason to believe from the reports of the time, and the returns of the census of 1851, that the mortality caused in Ireland, during the years 1846 and 1847, by a want of sufficient food, clothing, fuel, lodging, and other comforts, was from a quarter to half a million.

During the first half of the 18th century, England was an agricultural country, and exported considerable quantities of grain; and during that period, Ireland was a grazing country.

About the year 1767, England began to import grain, and since the year 1780, has imported large quantities annually from Ireland; which furnished employment and the means of procuring the comforts of life to some extent to the Irish, and occasioned a very rapid increase of the population of Ireland from 1780 to 1831. It should be borne in mind, however, that the English market for the agricultural products of Ireland, which furnished employment to the Irish, and was very advantageous to them, and caused them to increase in numbers, after all, only enabled them to subsist, and to breed. While the English have been accumulating immense wealth during the last sixty years, by mining, manufactures, agriculture and commerce, combined; the Irish have been confined mostly to agriculture, and the manufacture of linen; and though they have had all the advantages of FREE TRADE with England, and got British goods FREE OF DUTY in payment for their agricultural products, yet the British have got all the profits, and three-fourths of the inhabitants of Ireland may be ranked among the poorest and most miserable of any people on the earth, having any claims to civilization.

The miseries of the mass of the people of Ireland arise from causes which have been operating for ages, whose influences may be classed in proportion to their magnitude, as follows: First, Catholicism, with its machinery of ecclesiastical government, which keeps the most of the people in ignorance, and unfits them for business, and for all the higher stations and branches of industry. Secondly, the policy of the British Government, in discouraging manufacturing industry in Ireland, and encouraging free trade with Great Britain; whereby the British manufacturer is enabled to supply the markets of Ireland, and to deprive the Irish producer and laborer, of the field of employment and industry, which justly belong to them. Thirdly, a superabundant population; greater than the extent, resources and condition of the country will warrant. Fourthly, absentee-landlords, whose rents being taken from, and spent out of, the country, serve to drain it of the means of supporting its inhabitants, without an equivalent. Fifthly, Episcopacy, with its burthens and oppressing influences. Sixthly, and lastly, the indebtedness of the people to Great Britain, and the constant drain of the means of supporting its inhabitants, to pay for British goods, and the interest on their debts. Though this is put down as a cause, it is only a secondary, not a primary cause; being an effect produced mostly by free trade with Great Britain. The cause assigned as the third, is also greatly aggravated by the causes classed as the first, second and fourth.

The decline of the population of Ireland, between the middle of the year 1846, and the time of taking the census, in March, 1851, must have been over a million and a half. The dearth of 1846 and partial famine of 1847, which produced an excessive mortality, were caused by the partial failure of the potatoe crop. The establishment of free trade in grain in 1846, has reduced the prices of grain and flour in Great Britain about twenty per cent. greatly depressed agricultural industry in Ireland, and rendered it impossible for a large portion of the Irish tenants to pay their rents. These causes have driven them out of the country, and they have emigrated in pursuit of employment, and the means of subsistence, at the rate of about three hundred thousand a year, for some years past. The emigrants are mostly Catholics, of Celtic origin. The greatest part of them come to America, but many of them go to Great Britain, to dig their canals and cellars, grade their rail-roads, and perform the lowest grade of labor. The places of many of them in Ireland, have been supplied by Protestant peasants from England and Scotland, who make more thrifty and better tenants. This will contribute also, to drive out the poor Catholics, and the probability is, that the emigration will continue, until nearly all the Catholic tenants of farming lands have left the country. Very likely, (if the present policy of the government is pursued) the population of Ireland may continue to decline, for ten or fifteen years to come, and until it is reduced to four and a half, or five millions. That is about as many as can find sufficient employment under the present condition of things, and the system of measures adopted by the government. We shall soon have in the United States, a larger population of Celtic Irish descent, than will remain in Ireland.

Emigration.—The emigration from Great Britain and Ireland from 1812 to 1821, inclusive, is stated in the Encyclopædia Americana, on the authority of official reports, ordered to be printed by the House of Commons, as follows:

	To the United States.		To the British Colonies in America.	
From England,	33,608		23,783	
" Scotland,	4,727		19,471	
" Ireland,	30,653		47,223	
		68,988		90,477
				68,988
Total,	-	-	-	159,465

Emigration from Great Britain and Ireland.*

	British N. American Colonies.	United States.	Other Countries & Colon's	Total.
1821	12,470	5,000	2,496	19,966
1822	11,282	5,000	2,490	18,772
1823	8,133	5,000	2,638	15,771
1824	7,311	5,000	2,252	14,563
1825	8,741	5,551	1,681	15,973
1826	12,818	7,063	2,932	22,813
1827	12,648	14,526	1,985	29,159
1828	12,084	12,817	2,402	27,303
1829	13,307	15,678	3,464	32,449
1830	30,574	24,887	1,446	56,907
Total	129,368	100,522	23,786	253,676
1831	58,067	23,418	1,675	83,160
1832	66,339	32,872	3,929	103,140
1833	28,808	29,109	4,610	62,527
1834	40,060	33,074	3,088	76,222
1835	15,573	26,720	2,185	44,478
1836	34,226	37,774	3,417	75,417
1837	29,884	36,770	5,380	72,034
1838	4,557	14,332	14,313	33,202
1839	12,658	33,536	16,013	62,207
1840	32,293	40,642	17,808	90,743
Total	322,465	308,247	72,418	703,130
1841	38,164	45,017	35,411	118,592
1842	54,123	63,852	10,369	128,344
1843	23,518	28,335	5,359	57,212
1844	22,924	43,660	4,102	70,686
1845	31,803	58,538	3,160	93,501
1846	43,439	82,239	4,173	129,851
1847	109,680	142,154	6,436	258,270
1848	31,065	188,233	28,791	248,089
1849				299,498
1850				280,849
Total				1,684,892

* The numbers to the United States for 1821 to 1824 are estimated; the others are taken from the Com. Dict., and the British Almanac.

Convicts sent from the United Kingdom to New South Wales from 1825 to 1831, inclusive, (attested by Porter) - - -	18,652
Do. from 1832 to 1841, inclusive, " "	30,160
Do. estimated from 1842 to 1850 inclusive, -	33,000

The emigration since January, 1847, has greatly exceeded the natural increase of the population of the United Kingdom; and the emigration to the United States has been about as great. The effect is, to diminish the number of laborers in Great Britain and increase them in the United States; and the tendency is, to equalize the price of labor in the two countries, by raising the price of it in Great Britain and reducing it in this country.

Sec. 7. *The Netherlands, or Holland and Belgium.*

During the 13th, 14th and 15th centuries, and the first fifty years of the 16th century, the manufacture of wool was carried on more extensively in Flanders, now Belgium, than in any other country of Europe, and the manufacture of linen and lace was also very extensive. These manufactures, and commerce as their necessary attendant, sprang up in the Netherlands, (including Holland as well as Belgium,) during the time of the crusades in the 12th century; and such were their effects upon the prosperity of the people, and their increase in numbers, wealth, revenues and power, that in the year 1550 the Netherlands was the most flourishing, wealthy and populous, in proportion to its extent, of any country in Europe. Vide ante, section 8 of Chap. viii.

The provinces now comprising the kingdom of Belgium were distracted, ravaged, and in some parts desolated, by the religious wars and persecutions of the Duke of Alva, under Philip II., of Spain, between the years 1566 and 1573. Their manufactures, commerce, productive industry, and the energies of the people were all prostrated, and their numbers greatly reduced; but the seven United Provinces, generally known as Holland, were successful in throwing off the yoke of Spanish despotism, and maintaining their independence. Dr. Morse makes the following remarks in his geography: "In other countries, which are possessed of a variety of natural productions, we are not surprised to find manufactures employed in multiplying the riches which the bounty of the soil bestows. But to see in a country like Holland, large woollen manufactures, where there are scarcely any flocks; numberless artists employed in metals, where there are no mines; thousands of saw mills, where there is scarcely any forest; an immense quantity of corn exported from a country where there is not agriculture enough to support one half of its inhabitants, is what must strike every attentive observer with admiration."

The manufactures of the Hollanders, including ship building, furnished the principal materials and means of carrying on an immense commerce; and their manufactures, fisheries and commerce, with great frugality, were the causes of the accumulation of their great wealth and their increase in numbers; until Holland, with a territory (including a part of Limburg and Luxemburgh, now attached to it,) of about 13,600 square miles, much of it a marsh redeemed from the sea, became by far the richest country in the world, in proportion to its extent and to the number of its inhabitants. The frugality and commercial policy of the Hollanders is vividly pictured by Sir Wm. Temple, (ante, section 16, of chapter xiii.)

Though there were occasionally government as well as individual estimates of the population of Holland, yet I am not aware that there was any complete census ever taken of the population of either Holland or Belgium, until the year 1815. The population of the seven United Provinces, (Holland,) in 1620, is estimated at 1,200,000 in Mr. Grattan's history of the Netherlands, chap. xviii.; and Dr. Morse says in his geography, that it was estimated by the government in 1785 at 2,758,632, but that it was then estimated by M. Pestel at only 2,000,000. But in either case, the population was nearly two centuries in doubling. Perhaps the population declined from 1790 to 1815, under the galling yoke of the French, and the continental system of Napoleon.

The census of 1815 was incomplete. The population of Holland and Belgium and the parts of Luxemburgh and Limburg attached to them, have been stated as follows:

	In 1815.	In 1825.
Holland,	2,118,000	2,360,000
Belgium,	3,424,502	3,653,476
Total,	5,542,502	6,013,476
In 1829, population of Belgium by the census,		3,757,866
In 1846, Oct. 15, do. do.		4,337,196
In Jan. 1838, population of Holland do.		2,913,396
In do. 1848, do. do. do.		3,236,741
In Dec., 1850, estimate for Holland and Belgium,		7,700,000

It should be remembered, that this rapid increase has occurred in the most densely populated countries of Europe, and perhaps in the world; and that the population is still increasing, as industry increases, and has not been checked, as it has in Ireland, for want of employment and the means of subsistence. Holland is increasing in population, with a very small territory, by means of manufactures, commerce and agriculture combined, having no mines. Belgium, with a territory of only 13,214 square miles, (less than one-fourth part as large as the State of Virginia,) by reason of its great mineral resources, has a more complete division of employments among its citizens than Holland; and by means of mining, manufactures, agriculture and domestic commerce combined, with but a trifling amount of foreign commerce, has increased its population since the close of the wars in 1815, with a rapidity truly wonderful. The division of employments among them is so complete, that they produce almost every thing for themselves, and have no occasion to import much, except the products of warm climates; which do not come in competition with, and do not displace and depress any of their own industry. They are not afflicted with the DOGMAS OF FREE TRADE. The system of popular education, established in Holland, was extended over Belgium, during its connection with Holland; the most of the people have had a common school education; and their Catholicism seems to sit very loosely upon them, and does not appear to have exercised much influence in depressing their spirit of independence, enterprise, or genius for manufactures, and other branches of productive industry.

SEC. 8. *Population of Prussia, Denmark, Sweden, Norway and Switzerland.*

In 1657, Prussia was acknowledged by Poland, to be a free and independent State; after making some acquisitions, it was advanced to the dignity of a kingdom in 1700; and a part of Pomerania was not long after added to it. McCulloch remarks, when Frederick the Great ascended the throne in 1740, his disjointed dominions did not contain 2,500,000 inhabitants, who had made but little progress in the arts, or in the accumulation of wealth. In the early part of his reign, he wrested the province of Silesia from the house of Austria; in the latter part of his reign, in conjunction with Russia and Austria, he planned, and partly carried into effect the partition of Poland, acquiring as his share, the western parts of it. By these different acquisitions, Prussia, at the death of Frederick in 1786, had been increased in size nearly one-half; while, owing to the fertility of the country, and the improvements effected in every part of his dominions, after the peace of 1763, the population had increased, according to the Prussian writers, to about 6,000,000.

Prussia acquired by the subsequent partition of Poland, in 1792, and its final dismemberment in 1795, a large extent of territory, and upwards of 2,000,000 of inhabitants. In addition to this, Prussia acquired some small districts of territory in Germany; so that in 1805, according to estimates of Krug, the kingdom had a population of 9,640,000. No accurate census was taken until 1816. Her disastrous contest with Napoleon, in 1806, and the exhausting wars in which she was involved much of the time from 1806 to the peace of 1815, checked, and very likely entirely prevented, any increase of population, during that eventful period. Some additions were made to Prussia by the treaty of peace of 1815, which swelled the territory to 107,641 English square miles.

Population of Prussia, by the first census taken in 1816—	10,349,031
Increase in 9 years to 1825 about 18½ per cent.	1,907,694
Population by the census of 1825,	12,256,725
Increase in 15 years to 1840 about 21½ per cent.,	2,671,776
Population by the census of 1840,	14,928,501
Increase in 9 years, to 1849 about $9\frac{2}{5}$ per cent.,	1,402,686
Population by the census of 1849,	16,331,187

Early marriages are less common in cities than in the country; and less common also in old densely peopled countries, than in new ones. In proportion as the population becomes dense, marriages are generally contracted later in life, and the ratio with which the population increases becomes less, as is exhibited in the foregoing statement of the result of the censuses of Prussia.

The census of 1849 shows that about five-eighths of the inhabitants are Protestants, and three-eighths Catholics. The system of education of Prussia is the most complete, and the mass of the people the best educated, of any in Europe. Education and intelligence have stimulated and directed the industry of the people, made their labor more productive, contributed to increase the means of subsistence, and to increase the population and the prosperity of the nation.

Denmark, with the Duchy of Schleswig Holstein, comprises an area of about 21,856 English square miles.

In 1801, population by the census,	1,527,000
Increase in 33 years, 32.4 per cent.,	506,265
In 1834, population by the census,	2,033,265
Increase in 11 years over 10 per cent.,	205,812
In 1845, population,	2,239,077

The result shows a regular increase of over nine per cent., during each period of ten years, since 1801.

SWEDEN.—Mr. McCulloch says there was a progressive diminution of the population during the disastrous period, from 1800 to 1810; that the population in 1820 amounted to 2,584,690
Increase to 1839, - - - - - - 525,082
Amounting by the census to - - - 3,109,772

NORWAY.—According to the returns of the census of November 1826, the population of Norway amounted to 1,050,132
In 1835, by the census, - - - - 1,194,827

SWITZERLAND.—Dr. Morse says, from the best accounts the cantons of Switzerland then (1793) contained about 2,000,000 of inhabitants. McCulloch states the area at 15,233 square miles, and the population at the end of the year 1837 at - - - - - - - 2,188,000
The American Almanac states it for 1850, at 2,365,286

SEC. 9. *Progress of the population of Russia.*

Russia has gained many accessions of territory and population within a century past; authors sometimes include the whole Russian dominions under the term Russia; at other times they include Poland and all the Russian dominions in Europe; and at others they include only the ancient dominions of Russia in Europe, so that it is often difficult to determine, to what extent of territory their estimates apply. Dr. Morse, in the edition of his geography published in 1793, estimated the territory of European Russia, including the part of Poland then subject to Russia, at 1,194,976 square miles, and the population at 20,000,000, and the population of Asiatic Russia at 4,000,000. Mr. Murray, in his Encyclopædia of Geography, says, "the population of Russia, (meaning all the Russian dominions in Europe and Asia,) which, in 1722, was rated probably too low at 14,000,000, had risen in 1762, to 20,000,000; in 1795, to 36,000,000; in 1818, to 45,500,000, and in 1824, to 50,000,000." But much of this increase was caused by accessions of territory; and all the estimates for periods since 1763 are too high.

Mr. McCulloch states the area of Russia in Europe, including Poland in 1839, at 2,000,000 English square miles, and the population at 49,000,000. It does not appear that a complete census of all the Russian provinces has ever been taken in any one year; though several enumerations have been taken of the provinces, at different periods, and registries of births and deaths have been kept. From the official enumerations and reports at different periods, M. L. De Tegoborski, a privy councillor of the Empire, in a recent work, published during the present year (1852), has stated the population as follows:

Russia in Europe, exclusive of Poland and Finland, in 1840, at 50,231,000; in 1848, at 54,334,000; and in 1850, at 55,500,000. He states the population of Finland, according to the official returns of 1849, at 1,524,000, and estimates them in 1850, at 1,539,000. He states the population of Poland in 1844, according to official reports, at - - - - 4,770,000
and estimates it in 1850, at - - - 5,008,000
Total for the Russian dominions in Europe, in 1850, - - - - - - 62,047,000

He says the population of the Russian dominions in Asia, was estimated by M. Koeppen, in 1838, at 4,638,000; and he estimated it in 1850 at 5,200,000.

The increase seems to have been about one per cent. annually, and over 11 per cent. in ten years, since the commencement of the present century.

Peter the Great ascended the throne of Russia in 1689; and at that time the Russians were in a rude and barbarous state, with very little knowledge of the mechanic arts or agriculture; scarcely any productive industry or employment, but war, hunting, and tending their flocks; destitute of nearly all the comforts of life; and the mortality necessarily so great, that it was impossible for the population to increase more than from ten to twenty per cent. in a century. This great prince did more for the real welfare of his country, than was ever done before by any monarch, in any age of the world. He traveled into Holland and England, spent some time as a laborer in their ship-yards, in learning the art of ship-building, and the mechanic arts of those countries, which he labored to introduce, and finally succeeded in introducing into his dominions; and thereby laid the foundation of the advancement of his subjects in the mechanic arts, agriculture, mining, and commerce; and of the rapid increase of his country in productive industry, the comforts of life, population, wealth and power.

The present territory of European Russia, exclusive of Poland, perhaps contained a population from the beginning of the tenth to the end of the fifteenth century, of from 10,000,000 to 12,000,000 of miserable barbarians. As the inhabitants were a hardy, robust race, without any ideas of luxury, they generally married young, and their simple habits were well adapted to a rapid increase of population, as soon as they acquired comfortable dwellings, and a sufficient supply of clothing and other comforts, to protect them from the severity of the climate. Estimated increase during the sixteenth and seventeenth centuries, twenty per cent., amounting in the year 1700 to 17,000,000. Increase in 50 years to 1750, about twenty-five per cent.

In 1750, estimated population,	21,250,000
Increase in 25 years, 20 per cent.,	4,250,000
In 1775, estimated population,	25,500,000
Increase in 15 years, 15 per cent.,	4,300,000
In 1790, estimated population,	29,800,000
Increase in ten years, 11 per cent.	3,200,000
In 1800, estimated population,	33,000,000
In 1840,	51,600,000
and in 1850,	57,000,000

SEC. 10. *Austria, Germany, and Turkey.*

No census was ever taken of Turkey; and no complete census was ever taken of Germany, and the Austrian dominions, until since the peace of 1815. Germany and Austria have been subjected to so many changes, and consist of so many kingdoms and political divisions, the inhabitants of which have been enumerated at different times, that it is impossible to state the number with accuracy, at any particular period, until very recently. Their population at different periods is estimated in section 2.

SEC. 11. *Population of Asia.*

An estimate has been given in Section 2 of the population in the third century, and at several periods since, of Turkey in Asia, including Asia Minor, Syria, Palestine, and Mesopotamia. McCulloch states the area of Persia at about 450,000 square miles, and estimates the population at from eight to ten millions. There is no reason to doubt that Persia, the valleys of the rivers Euphrates and Tigris, and the countries lying between them, comprising the eastern part of Turkey, were more populous from five hundred to fifteen hundred years before the Christian era, than they have ever been since. Such was probably the case also with Hindostan. There is no reason to believe that there has been any substantial increase for many centuries in the productive industry and population of any of the countries of Asia, except China, the Islands of Japan, some other islands, and the Russian dominions. No census has ever been taken of the population of any country of Asia, and everything on the subject is mere conjecture, and calculation based on very imperfect evidence. Mr. McCulloch has estimated the population of the continent of Asia, at 375,230,000; and the population of the islands, including

Japan, at 54 370,000—making in all, nearly 430,000,000. He has put down the Chinese Empire at 168,000,000, and the Islands of Japan at 25,000,000, which in my opinion are too low estimates, though they differ very little from the estimates of Balbi. The Weimar Almanack, for 1840, states the population of Asia and its islands at over 608,000,000; putting down the Chinese Empire at 252,866,000.

CHINA.—The area of China proper has been generally estimated at about 1,300,000 square miles. Mr. McCulloch estimates it at 1,348,870. The population has been variously estimated at from 150,000,000 to 360,279,897. The latter is said to be the number according to the government census in 1813. Very little credence should be given to any of the official statements, but all persons who have visited China agree that the population is exceedingly dense; and as the whole country lies between the twentieth and forty-second degree of latitude, partly in a warm and partly in a temperate climate, and the territory is nearly half as large as that part of Europe lying below the sixty-second degree of latitude, there is reason to believe that the population is greater than that of Europe at the beginning of the present century, and probably amounts to 200,000,000, and perhaps more. Belgium has over three hundred inhabitants to the square mile; England and Wales about as many; and if we allow China an average of two hundred to the square mile, the population would amount to 260,000,000.

The area of Japan is said to be about 266,000 square miles, or four and a half times as great as that of England and Wales, and the population has been variously estimated at from twenty to fifty millions. It is undoubtedly very great, and quite likely may amount to thirty millions, and perhaps more. Though the Chinese and Japanese have had very little commerce or intercourse with other nations, yet China, in particular, embraces so many degrees of latitude and grades of climate, and its productions are so various and great, its internal improvements and domestic commerce so extensive, and the division of employments among the people so complete, that enough is produced in the country to supply nearly all the real wants of the people without the aid of foreign commerce. The density of the population of China is very conclusive evidence that the productive industry of the Chinese was greater, and the state of the mechanic arts, manufactures and agriculture more flourishing among them, than it was in any country of Europe a century since.

Since the conquest of China by the Tartars, about two centuries since, the country has had almost uninterrupted peace; the people have enjoyed freedom of opinion, and perfect liberty on all matters of religious exercise and worship; and from the accounts of voyagers, travellers, merchants, and missionaries who have visited the country, as well as the official reports of the government, we have reason to believe that the population has increased much more rapidly than that of Europe, and has perhaps more than doubled during the last two centuries. Notwithstanding the impression which generally prevails in this country and in England, that the people of hot climates are so much enervated by the heat as to be naturally feeble and indolent, and unfitted for mechanical and manufacturing labor, or a very high degree of productive industry, it is affirmed by M. Compte in La Traité de Legislation Liv. iii. Chap. xxxii. that the activity and productive industry of the Chinese is much greater in the southern part of the empire, below the twenty-fifth degree of latitude, than it is in the northern part, above the thirty-fifth parallel of latitude.

The Turks first entered Europe about five centuries since, and took Constantinople in the year 1453. We have reason to believe, that the population of Turkey in Europe, including Greece, has declined under their dominion, from 15,000,000 to about 10,000,000; and that the decline of the population of Turkey in Asia, and Egypt, has been still greater.

McCulloch says "except in the article of provisions, no restriction on commerce ever existed in Turkey. All foreign articles may be imported into the Turkish ports, without let or hindrance of any kind, on payment of an import duty of three per cent. ad valorem; and all articles of foreign and domestic growth or manufacture may be freely conveyed all over the empire." The result has been, that the country has been supplied with British goods to the full extent of the ability of the people to pay for them; the domestic manufacturer and mechanic have been undersold, and mostly deprived of the benefits of their own markets; industry has languished, the country is impoverished, and the population has declined.

The British have had dominion over a large portion of Hindostan, for about three-fourths of a century, during which time, the population of Great Britain has more than doubled, and the population of China, and of nearly all the countries of the civilized world, has greatly increased. What evidence have we that either the population or the wealth of Hindostan has increased at all? Six enumerations have been made of the population of Great Britain, during the present century; but no census has ever been taken of British India. Why has it been omitted? During the whole of the eighteenth century, and up to within thirty or forty years past, nearly all western Europe was supplied with cotton goods from Hindostan; but now that country is filled with English goods; prices are reduced so low that the natives can scarcely obtain a subsistence by spinning and weaving by hand; and the consequence is, they are reduced to the most abject poverty and distress. Many branches of manufacturing industry have been almost entirely superceded and destroyed; and there is no reason to doubt that the aggregate industry, wealth and population, have all declined.

Sec. 12. *Population of Africa.*

Less is known of Africa, than of Asia, and the population of the former is still more uncertain than that of the latter. It has been variously estimated at from sixty millions, to over an hundred millions. Balbi estimates it at 60,000,000, Malte-Brun at 70,000,000, and the Weimar Almanac at 101,000,000.

Sec. 13. *By what causes, is population affected?*

The mere form of government seems to have but little influence upon population, though it is much influenced by the measures and policy of the government; climate appears to have less influence upon it than religious bigotry and ecclesiastical dominion; it may increase rapidly in the severe climate and under the stern despotism of the Czar of Russia, or the warm sun and milder dominion of the Emperor of China, and the principles of religious toleration; though it has increased in China under the dominion of the Tartars, and perhaps increased under some of the successors of Mahomet, yet it has sunk under the combined influence of Mahometanism, and Tartaric indolence and stupidity in Turkey. It will increase either with or without slavery, and under any system of despotism, either of government or religion, or both combined, provided they concur in encouraging the mechanic arts, and productive industry; but it will not increase much in the States of the Church, under the immediate civil and religious dominion of the Pope; nor under the dominion of the ecclesiastical, military, and landed aristocracy of Mexico, who pursue a policy tending to discourage the mechanic arts, manufactures and commerce, though all the people may be nominally free, and enjoy the blessings of a republican form of government.

The causes which affect population directly are, first, climate; secondly, the comforts enjoyed by the people; thirdly, early marriages; and lastly, war, pestilence and famine. Government and religion both exercise a great influence in stimulating or depressing industry, and encouraging or discouraging economy, and they thereby increase or diminish the comforts of life, and indirectly exert a powerful influence upon population. The history of the Catholic population of Ireland, and that of the French of Canada, show the effect of early marriages upon the increase of population, and that an increase of population is not a certain indication of the prosperity of a country

As the increase of population depends much on an increase of the comforts of life, which are supplied by industry—it depends on the productiveness of industry—on the skill, intelligence and science of the people, and on public improvements, and the facilities of making exchanges. Though an agricultural people, without education, will increase for a time, as was the case in Ireland from 1750 to 1840, yet a period is soon put to their increase. Agriculture alone cannot support a dense population. Russia has increased rapidly in population during the last hundred years; but that increase will soon be checked, unless common school education is extended to a much larger proportion of the people, and the mechanical and manufacturing industry of the nation is increased. The truth is, there are but few nations whose people have sufficient education, skill and intelligence, for the higher grades of mechanical and manufacturing industry,* and hence they soon attain as dense a population as can be maintained by an uneducated people, depending on agriculture and a rude condition of the mechanic arts.

* See on this subject, Section 8, of Chapter VI.

CHAPTER XX.

ON THE POPULATION OF THE NEW WORLD.

SEC. 1. *Population of the American colonies at different periods.*

THE American Statistical Association has recently published a volume of collections of partial enumerations of the number of militia, and of white adult males, in the New England colonies, and estimates of the population at different periods; which contains the most accurate and full evidence that has ever been collected of their population prior to the census of 1790. The following statements and estimates are mostly made on the authority of that collection.

The Puritans landed on Plymouth rock, December 22d, 1620, made the first white settlement in New England, and founded the Plymouth Colony, which remained an independent colony until 1691, when it was united with Massachusetts.

The first settlements in the Massachusetts colony were made at Salem and Charlestown, in 1628; and at Boston in 1630.

The first settlement in Connecticut was made at Windsor in 1633, by colonists from Massachusetts. A settlement was made at Hartford in 1635, and one at New Haven in 1638, by emigrants from England.

Rhode Island was first settled at Providence by Roger Williams and his associates, who went from the colony of Massachusetts in 1636.

New Hampshire was first settled at Dover and Portsmouth, in 1623. It came under the jurisdiction of Massachusetts in 1641, and did not become a separate colony until 1680, when it had but 209 voters, which showed a population of about 1,250.

Maine was purchased by Massachusetts in 1652, and remained subject to its jurisdiction, until it was admitted into the Union as a State in 1820.

It is observed by Johnson, in his "Wonder-working Providence," that in the period of fifteen years, up to 1643, there had been brought to Massachusetts, 21,200 passengers. More than half of them, it is said, went to other colonies and returned to

Europe. The population of the colony of Massachusetts in 1629 is estimated at only 506, in 1637 at 7,912, and in 1639 at 8,592. The population of the Plymouth colony is estimated in 1624 at 180, in 1633 at 396, and in 1637 at 549.

ESTIMATES OF THE POPULATION OF THE NEW ENGLAND COLONIES.

In	1654.	1665.	1673.
Massachusetts, - -	16,026	23,467	35,644
Plymouth, - -	2,941	5,310	9,410
Connecticut, - -	3,186		23,362
Rhode Island, - -	1,959		
Total,	24,112		68,416

A census was commenced in 1763, and completed in 1765, which showed the population as follows:

	Massachusetts.	Maine.	Total.
Whites, - -	221,329	23,661	244,990
Negroes, - -	4,978	334	5,312
Total, - -	226,307	23,995	250,302

The population was estimated in 1776, by multiplying the number of polls or white males over sixteen years old, by four and a half, and the result was as follows: in

Massachusetts, - - -	286,139
Maine, - - -	47,279
Total white inhabitants, - -	333,418

The population of Rhode Island is stated in Dr. Morse's Universal Geography, as follows:

	Whites.	Blacks.	Total.
1730	15,352	2,633	17,985
1748	29,755	4,373	34,128
1761	35,939	4,697	40,636
1774	54,435	5,243	59,678
1783	48,538	3,361	51,899

Statement of the population of Connecticut, according to the official returns of the censuses taken in 1756, and Jan. 1st, 1774.

	1756.	1774.
Whites, - -	126,975	191,392
Negroes, - -	3,019	6,464
Indians, - -	.617	

Statement of the number of inhabitants in the colony of New York, according to the official reports of enumerations taken in the undermentioned years, as published in the Documentary History of the State.

	Whites.	Negroes.	Total.
1698	15,897	2,170	18,067
1723	34,393	6,171	40,564
1737	51,496	8,941	60,437
1749	62,756	10,692	73,448
1756	83,223	13,542	96,765
1771	148,124	19,883	168,007

The population of New Jersey is stated by Dr. Morse, as follows:

	Free inhabitants.	Slaves.	Total.
1738	43,388	3,981	47,369
1745	56,797	4,606	61,403

It is stated in Gordon's History of Pennsylvania, that in 1684 the colony, including the territory now comprising the State of Delaware, was divided into twenty-two townships, containing seven thousand inhabitants, of whom two thousand and five hundred resided in Philadelphia; and that the population, in 1776, was estimated at about 300,000. The city of Philadelphia, it is said had cause to complain of the great influx of strangers, many of them with families, having no means of support. The number of emigrants to the colony, that arrived during the year, from December, 1728, to December, 1729, is stated in a note at 6,208. As the population is supposed to have increased between the years 1684 and 1776, from 7,000 to about 300,000, the immigration must have been very great.

The first colony settled in Maryland in 1634, consisting of about 200 Roman Catholics. Dr. Morse states the population of Maryland as follows: in 1665 at about 16,000; taxable inhabitants in 1734 at about 36,000; and the whole population in 1755 at 153,564,—consisting of 55,319 free white males; 49,908 free white females; 1,981 white convicts; and 46,356 mulattoes and negroes.

Dr. Morse says the inhabitants of Virginia were estimated as follows: in 1618 at 600; in 1623 at 2,500; in 1640 at 20,000; in 1660 at 30,000; in 1671 at 38,000 whites and 2,000 blacks; in 1681 at 14,000 titheable inhabitants; and in 1703 at 25,023 titheable inhabitants.

Professor Tucker says that according to an official communication from the governor, Sir William Berkly, made in 1671, the population of the colony of Virginia was then 40,000; of whom 2000 were slaves, and 6000 were white indented servants; that the importation of slaves did not exceed two or three cargoes in seven years, but that of servants he estimated at 1500 annually, the most of whom were English, a few Scotch, and fewer Irish.*

Professor Tucker says the population of Virginia in 1744 exceeded 200,000; of which number, from a fourth to a third were slaves; and that the population in 1781 was estimated at over 500,000.

Wheeler in his history of North Carolina states the number of militia in that colony in 1754, at 15,400; which would indicate a white population of about 80,000.

Dr. Morse gives the following numbers as the estimates made at the time, of the population of South Carolina.

In 1700, . .	Whites, 5,500	
1723, . .	Whites, 14,000 . .	Blacks, 18,000.
1765, . .	Whites, 40,000 . .	Blacks, 90,000.

The most of the enumerations, as well as the estimates, made of the population of the several colonies and states at different periods, previous to the census of 1790, are more or less inconsistent with each other, and imperfect; and yet by comparing them together, they afford the most reliable information that is attainable.

Pitkin says the white population of the American colonies (now the United States) were estimated in the year 1700 at 262,000; in 1749 or 1750 at 981,000; and in 1775 at 2,243,-000; and that the slaves and free colored persons at the latter period, were estimated at about 500,000. Dr. Seybert says that in 1775 "the inhabitants of the United States were supposed to amount to 2,389,300 persons of every description." There was an obvious motive on the part of the government at the time of our revolutionary struggle, to magnify the population and strength of the country by large estimates. Many of the estimates of that period are too high to be consistent with the census of 1790, with the census taken in some of the colonies prior to that time, and with the estimates of the population in 1700 and 1750. History attests that the hardships and privations suffered by emigrants to new countries, produce an excessive degree of mortality, and that the ratio of mortality in nearly all the countries of Europe was much greater a century since than it is at present. The deaths exceeded the births annually, in the city of London, until about the year 1790; and such was

* See Professor Tucker's Life of Mr. Jefferson, I., 14.

the case in all the great cities of Europe. The great increase in the comforts of life, the improvements in medical science, and the greater attention to cleanliness, drainage, sewerage, and a plentiful supply of wholesome water, have diminished the ratio of mortality, and accelerated the increase of population during the present century.

With the immense emigration to the United States the most of the time since 1790, the white population has doubled in about twenty-three years, and doubled twice in forty-six years; but the estimates of Mr. Pitkin and of some other writers do not make it double twice in forty-nine years (from 1700 to 1749), though they calculate the increase at over one hundred and twenty per cent. in twenty-six years (from 1749 to 1775), and reduce the increase to less than forty-two per cent. during the fifteen years from 1775 to 1790. Their estimates of the population at different periods are not consistent with each other. It may be said that the revolutionary war checked immigration and the ratio of increase; very likely it did check the natural increase as well as immigration to some extent, and so did the French war (from 1756 to 1763), and so did the Indian wars at an earlier period. If the white population doubled in twenty-six years (from 1749 to 1775), and increased at the same ratio from 1700 to 1749, I see no reason to doubt that it increased about fifty per cent. from 1775 to 1790. On this basis I estimate the increase of the population from 1700 to 1790, or rather deduce the aggregate from the returns of the census of 1790, and distribute the number among the several colonies, according to the several colonial censuses and official estimates, so far as they appear to be consistent and probable.

A large proportion of the emigrants to the southern colonies consisted of indented servants, sent over as agricultural laborers, including some convicts. The emigration to Pennsylvania and the southern colonies was much greater, during the whole of the eighteenth century, than it was to New England and New York, and hence the population of the former increased the most rapidly.

Statement of the white population of the several States according to the census of 1790 ; estimates of it in the years 1700, 1750, and 1775 ; and Mr. Pitkin's statement of the estimates for 1749.

STATES.	1700	1750	Per Pitkin in 1749.	1775	1790
Maine - -	4,000	16,000	200,000 (Maine and Massachusetts)	45,000	96,002
Massachusetts -	66.000	190,000		280,000	373.254
New Hampshire	10,000	30.000	30,000	90,000	141,111
Vermont - -		10,000		40,000	85,144
Rhode Island -	10,000	32,000	35,000	50,000	64,689
Connecticut -	30,000	110,000	80,000	195,000	232,581
New York -	18,000	72,000	90,000	175,000	314,142
New Jersey -	15,000	60,000	50,000	120,000	169,954
Pennsylvania -	15,000	130.000	230 000	275,000	424,099
	168,000	650,000	715,000	1,270,000	1,900,976
Delaware -	5,000	20,000	20,000	35,000	46,310
Maryland -	25,000	90,000	85,000	160,000	208,649
Virginia - -	75,000	200,000	90,000	360,000	442,115
Kentucky -					61,133
North Carolina	8,000	80,000	35,000	200,000	288,204
Tennessee					32,013
South Carolina	7,000	50,000	30.000	90,000	140,178
Georgia -		10,000	6,000	25,000	52,886
	120.000	450,000	266.000	870,000	1,271,488
Total Whites -	288,000	1,100,000	981,000	2,140,000	3,172,464
Free colored, and Slaves -	32,000	220,000		500,000	59,466 697,897
Total -	320,000	1,320,000		2,640,000	3,929,827

SEC. 2. *Population of the several States at each census, from 1800 to 1850.*

The free States, with the exception of California, lie almost entirely north of the thirty-ninth, and mostly north of the fortieth degree of latitude. Slavery forms a clearly defined dividing line across the Union, from east to west. The cultivation of sugar and rice is confined, and that of cotton nearly so, to the southern slave States, lying south of the thirty-fifth degree of latitude; while the cultivation of tobacco is mostly confined to slave States lying north of the thirty-fifth degree of latitude. On account of the difference in climate as well as in the productions of the several latitudes, and in order to ascertain and show the influence of the climate, productions, and local policy and pursuits of different States upon their prosperity and increase in population, I have arranged and classified the States as follows: first, the free States and territories east of the Rocky Mountains; secondly, the slave states lying north of the thirty-fifth degree of latitude, including Arkansas; thirdly, the slave States lying south of the thirty-fifth degree of latitude; and lastly, the States and territories lying west of the Rocky Mountains, including the adjoining territory of New Mexico.

Statement of the white population of each of the States and Territories at each enumeration, from 1800 to 1850.

FREE STATES.	1800.	1810.	1820.	1830.	1840.	1850.
Maine	150,901	227,736	297,406	398,263	500,438	581,863
New Hampshire	182,898	213,390	243,375	268,721	284,036	317,489
Vermont	153,908	216,963	234,861	279,771	291,218	313,411
Massachusetts	416,793	465,303	516,547	603,359	729,030	985,704
Rhode Island	65,437	73,820	79,457	93,6 4	105,587	144,000
Connecticut	244,721	255,279	267,261	289,603	301,856	363,305
New York	556,039	918,699	1,333,445	1,868,061	2,378,890	3,049,457
New Jersey	195,125	226,861	257,458	300,266	351,588	466,240
Pennsylvania	586,098	786,804	1,019,045	1,309,900	1,676,115	2,258,463
Ohio	45,028	228,861	576,711	928,359	1,502,122	1,956,108
Indiana	4,[illegible]77	23,890	145.758	339,399	678,702	977,628
Illinois		11,501	53,837	155,061	472,253	846,104
Michigan		4,618	8,722	31,346	211,560	395,097
Wisconsin					30,749	304,565
Iowa					42,924	191,879
Minnesota						6,038
Total	2,601,525	3,653,225	5,033,883	6,865,730	9,557,068	13,157,351
Under 10 years old	866,486	1,226,314	1,632,427	2,150,712	2,892,742	
Per cent. under 10	33.30	33 57	32.43	31.33	30.268	
NORTH'N SLAVE STATES.						
Delaware	49,852	55,361	55,282	57,601	58,561	71,289
Maryland	216,326	235,117	260.222	291,108	318,204	418,590
District of Columbia	10,066	16,079	22,614	27,563	30,657	38,027
Virginia	514,280	551.534	603,337	694,300	740,968	895.304
North Carolina	337,764	376,410	419,200	472,813	484,870	553.295
Tennessee	91,709	215,875	339,979	535,746	640,627	756,893
Kentucky	179,871	324,237	434,826	517,787	590,253	761,688
Missouri		17,227	56.017	114,795	323,888	592,077
Arkansas			12,597	25,671	77,174	162,068
Total	1,399,868	1,791,840	2.204,074	2,737,384	3,265.202	4,249,231
Under 10 years old	500 544	639,254	771,077	943,562	1,107,521	
Per cent. under 10	35.756	35.70	35.00	34 44	33.93	
SOUTH'N SLAVE STATES.						
South Carolina	196,255	214,196	237,440	257,863	259,084	274,623
Georgia	101,678	145,424	189,568	296,806	407.695	521,438
Florida				18,385	27,940	47,167
Alabama			85,451	190,406	335,185	426.507
Mississippi	5,179	23.024	42,176	70.443	179,074	295,758
Louisiana		34,311	73,867	89,231	158,457	255,416
Texas						154,100
Total	303,112	416,955	628,502	923,134	1,367.435	1,975,009
Under 10 years old	112.285	150.913	222.286	333,456	484,789	
Per cent. under 10	37.00	36 20	35.40	36.17	35.558	
Total Slave States	1,702,980	2,208,795	2,832,576	3,660,518	4,632,637	6,224,240
California (estimated in part in census)						163,200
Oregon						13,087
Utah						11,330
New Mexico						61,530
Total United States	4,304,505	5,862,020	7,866,459	10,526,248	14,189,705	19,630,738
Increase per cent. in the Slave States	33.94	29.70	28.24	29.23	26.56	34.56
Do. in the Free States	36.85	40.37	37.79	36.39	39.21	37.67

Statement of the number of square miles, and of the number of free colored persons, in each of the States and Territories.

FREE STATES & TER'S.	Sq. miles.	1800.	1810.	1820.	1830.	1840.	1850.
Maine - -	32,000	818	900	929	1,190	1,355	1,325
New Hampshire	9,200	856	970	786	604	537	475
Vermont -	9,800	557	750	903	881	730	709
Massachusetts -	8,250	6,452	6,806	6,740	7,048	8,669	8,795
Rhode Island -	1,300	3,304	3,609	3,554	3,561	3,238	3,544
Connecticut -	5,100	5,330	6.453	7,844	8,047	8,105	7,486
New York -	49,000	10,374	25.333	29,279	44,870	50,027	47,937
New Jersey -	7,500	4,402	7,843	12,460	18.303	21,044	23,093
Pennsylvania -	47,500	14,561	22,452	30.202	37,930	47,854	53.323
Ohio - -	39,750	337	1,899	4,723	9,538	17.342	24,300
Indiana - -	36,000	163	393	1,230	3,629	7,165	10.788
Illinois - -	57,000		613	457	1,637	3,598	5.366
Michigan -	59,000		220	174	261	707	2,557
Wisconsin -	54,000					185	626
Iowa - -	51,000					172	335
Minnesota -	83,000						39
Total -	549,400	47,154	78.241	99,281	137,499	170,728	190,698
NORTH. SLAVE STATES.							
Delaware -	2,200	8.268	13.136	12.958	15,855	16.919	17,957
Maryland -	11,150	19,587	33.927	39,730	52.938	62,078	74,077
District of Columbia	60	783	2,549	4.048	6,152	8.361	9,973
Virginia -	66,620	20,124	30,570	36,889	47,348	49.842	53.829
North Carolina	49,500	7,043	10.266	14.612	19.543	22,732	27,196
Tennessee -	40.200	309	1.317	2.727	4,555	5.524	6.271
Kentucky -	40.500	741	1,713	2.759	4,917	7,317	9.736
Missouri -	65.500		607	347	569	1,574	2,544
Arkansas -	55,000			59	141	465	589
Total -	330,730	56,855	94,085	114,129	152,018	174.812	202,172
SOUTH SLAVE STATES.							
South Carolina -	31,750	3,185	4,554	6.826	7,921	8.276	8,900
Georgia -	61,500	1,019	1,801	1,763	2,486	2,753	2,880
Florida -	55,680				844	817	925
Alabama -	52,900			571	1,572	2,039	2,272
Mississippi -	47,680	182	240	458	519	1,366	899
Louisiana -	49,300		7,585	10,476	16,710	25,502	17,537
Texas - -	237,000						331
Total -	585,810	4,386	14,180	20,094	30,052	40,758	33,744
California -	190,000						1,800
Oregon -	341,000						206
Utah - -	188,000						24
New Mexico -	200,000						17
Total of United States		108,395	186.506	233.504	319.56[illegible]	386,293	428,661
Increase per cent.			72.2	25.2	36.6	21.	10.9

Statement of the number of slaves in the different States and Territories, at seven enumerations, from 1790 to 1850.

FREE STATES.	1790.	1800.	1810.	1820.	1830.	1840.	1850.
Maine - -					2		
New Hampshire	158	8			3	1	
Vermont -	17				1		
Massachusetts -							
Rhode Island -	952	381	108	48	17	5	
Connecticut -	2,759	951	310	97	25	17	
New York -	21,324	20,343	15,017	10,088	75	4	
New Jersey -	11,423	12,422	10,851	7,557	2,254	674	222
Pennsylvania -	3,737	1,706	795	211	403	64	
Ohio - -					6	3	
Indiana - -		135	237	190	3	3	
Illinois - -			168	917	747	331	
Michigan -			24		32		
Wisconsin -						11	
Iowa - -						16	
Utah - -							26
Total -	40,370	35,946	27,510	19,108	3,568	1,129	248
NORTH'N SLAVE STATES.							
Delaware -	8,887	6,153	4,177	4,509	3,292	2,605	2,289
Maryland -	103,036	105 635	111,502	107,398	102,994	89,737	90,368
District of Columbia		3,244	5,395	6,377	6,119	4,694	3,687
Virginia -	293,427	345,796	392,518	425,153	469,757	448,987	472,528
North Carolina -	100,572	133,296	[illegible]68,824	205,017	245,601	245,817	288,412
Tennessee -	3,417	13,584	44,535	80,097	141,603	183,059	239,461
Kentucky -	11,830	40,343	80,561	126,732	165,213	182,258	210,981
Missouri -			3,011	10,222	25,091	58,240	87,422
Arkansas -				1,617	4,576	19,935	46,982
Total -	521,169	648,051	810,523	967,122	1,164,246	1,2[illegible]5,332	1,442,130
SOUTH'N SLAVE STATES.							
South Carolina -	107,094	146,151	196,365	258,475	315,401	327,038	384,984
Georgia - -	29,264	59,404	105,218	149,656	217,531	280,944	381,681
Florida - -					15,501	25,717	39,309
Alabama - -				41,879	117,549	253,532	342,892
Mississippi -		3,489	17,088	32,814	65,659	195,211	309,898
Louisiana -			34,660	69,064	109,588	168,452	244,786
Texas - -							58,161
Total -	136,358	209,044	353,331	551,888	841,229	1,250,894	1,761,711
Total United States.	697,897	893,041	1,191,364	1,538,118	2,009,043	2,487,355	3,204,089
Increase per cent.		28.	33.4	29.1	30.6	23.8	28.8*

* The increase of slaves from 1840to 1850 was about 26½ per cent. in the States, exclusive of Texas.

Statement of the relative number of each class of persons in a population of 10,000 in the undermentioned countries.

AGES.	France before 1789. *Annuaire.*	Belgium, 1821. *Annuaire.*	Sweden, 1820. *Marshall.*	Ireland, 1821. *Marshall.*	England and Wales by census of 1821. *Rickman.*	England and Wales by the census of 1841,	Whites in the United States by census of 1840. In the Free States.	In Slave States north of the 35th degree of latitude.	In Slave States south of the 35th degree of latitude.
Under 5,	1,201	1,297	1,307	1,535	1,487	1,324	1,654	1,893	2,008
5 to 10,	981	1,089	1,010	1,355	1,307	1,197	1,373	1,491	1,548
10 to 15,	939	946	894	1,218	1,114	1,089	1,186	1,260	1,254
15 to 20,	897	883	899	1,219	992	997	1,101	1,089	1,031
20 to 30,	1,638	1,680	1,711	1,760	1,574	1,780	1,845	1,738	1,788
30 to 40,	1,404	1,341	1,362	1,150	1,181	1,289	1,198	1,069	1,108
40 to 50,	1,161	1,017	1,087	771	934	959	760	683	651
50 to 60,	892	793	855	600	659	645	458	413	346
60 to 70,	577	604	586	273	456	440	260	232	175
70 to 80,	255	279	240	96	228	216	125	99	68
80 to 90,	50	66	41	23	63	59	36	28	18.7
90 to 100,	4.8	4.9	1	3	5	5	4	4.3	3.2
over 100,	0.2	0.1	0	0.5	0.2	0	0.4	0.7	1.1
Total,	10,000	10,000	10,003	10,003.5	10,000.2	10,000	10,000.4	10,000	10,000
Under 15,	3,121	3,332	3,211	4,108	3,908	3,610	4,213	4,644	4,810
Over 15,	6,879	6,668	6,782	5,895.5	6,092.2	6,390	5,787.4	5,356	5,190

Sec. 3. *Emigration to the United States.*

Official records were not kept regularly of the number of emigrants to the United States, prior to the year 1820. Since that time, the collectors of the customs have been required to make quarterly returns of passengers arriving by sea, in their respective districts; but the returns were often very defective, until since the close of the year 1832. Hutchinson states in his "History of the settlement of the New England Colonies," that the number of Puritans who came over to New England in ten years, next prior to 1640 was about 21,000; but this must have been a mere estimate, and was probably too high.

The first settlement was made in Virginia in 1607, at Plymouth in Massachusetts in 1620, in New York and New Jersey about the year 1620; in Delaware in 1630, and in Maryland in 1634. We may reasonably estimate the emigration to the colonies up to 1640, at thirty-six or thirty-eight thousand; and though the mortality was very great, there is reason to believe, that taking the whole period, the births exceeded the deaths, and that the white population in 1640 was about 40,000; about half of which was in Virginia.* The natural increase of the white population from births alone, independent of immigration, has been on an average about 30 per cent. every ten years, during the present century; doubling in twenty-seven years, and by the aid of immigration, doubling in twenty-three years. The privations and sufferings of the early immigrants being very great, and the mortality among them great, it is not probable that they doubled during the 17th century by natural increase only, short of about forty years.

In 1640, estimated white population - -	40,000
Natural increase in 40 years, to 1680 - -	40,000
immigrants estimated at 1,500 annually - -	60,000
natural increase of the immigrants - - -	28,000
1680, estimated white population - - -	168,000
Natural increase in 20 years, at 50 per cent. -	84,000
immigrants estimated at 1,500 annually - -	30,000
natural increase of the immigrants about - -	6,000
1700, estimated white population - - -	288,000
Natural increase 100 per cent. in 35 years -	288,000
immigrants in 35 years, at 2,500 annually -	105,000
natural increase of the immigrants about - -	45,000
1735, estimated white population - - -	726,000

* See section 1 of this Chapter.

Natural increase in 15 years, about 44 per cent.	320,000
immigrants estimated at 3,000 per year - -	45,000
natural increase of the immigrants, about -	9,000
1750, estimated white population - - -	1,100,000
Natural increase in 25 years 84 per cent -	924,000
immigrants estimated at 3,500 annually - -	87,000
natural increase of immigrants, about - -	30,000
1775, estimated white population - - -	2,141,000
Increase to the census of 1790 over 48 per cent.	1,031,464
1790, white population by the first census -	3,172,464

Dr. Seybert, in his statistical annals of the United States, gives a statement showing that 22,240 passengers arrived in ten of the principal ports of the United States during the year 1817. He estimated the number of foreign emigrants to the United States from 1790 to 1810 at 6,000 annually, on an average. Professor Tucker, in his work on the progress of the United States, concurred in that estimate, and estimated the number arriving from 1810 to 1820, at 114,000.

Statement of the number of emigrants and passengers who arrived in the United States from foreign countries, by sea, during the undermentioned years; distinguishing Americans, or citizens of the United States, from foreigners.*

Years.	Americans.	Foreigners.	Years.	Americans.	Foreigners.
1821	2,405	9,224	1831	977	‡42,100
1822	1,564	7,008	1832	1,155	‡60,000
1823	1,904	6,262	1833	1,279	58,234
1824	1,699	7,861	1834	2,114	64,916
1825	2,670	9,691	1835	3,320	45,444
1826	3,060	10,370	1836	4,029	76,923
1827	2,897	18,756	1837	3,813	79,205
1828	2,749	27,268	1838	3,964	42,731
1829	1,993	15,303	1839	4,171	70,494
1830	1,515	‡39,692	1840	5,810	86,338
	†22,456	151,435		30,654	626,392

* The time is for fiscal years, ending September 30th, from 1821 to 1831, for fifteen months, ending December 31st, 1832; for calendar years, ending December 31st, from 1833 to 1842; for nine months, ending September 30th, 1843; and for years ending September 30th, from 1844 to 1850.

† See Force's National Calendar for 1831, p. 156.

‡ The returns being defective for the years 1830, 1831, and 1832, the numbers for these years are partly estimated, and corrected by the reports of the number arriving at New York. See Hunt's Mag. for December 1849, p. 657.

Years.	Americans.	Foreigners.		Americans.	Foreigners.
1841	5,811	80,642	3 months to Dec. 31st, 1850	5,594	59,976
1842	4.968	106,016			
1843	3,429	53,100			
1844	8,858	75,906	year 1851	29,367	379,461
1845	4,216	115,668			
1846	4,239	154,409			
1847	4,514	234,966			
1848	2,968	226,515			
1849	2,665	296.945			
1850	36,501	278,832			
	78,169	1,622,999			

Forming my own opinion from all the facts which I have collected, and the calculations I have made, and calculating the natural increase of the immigrants during the decennial period in which they arrive, the increase of the white population of the United States from one census to another, by means of immigration and accessions of territory, would be as follows :

1790 to 1800 immigrants estimated by Dr. Seybert 60,000
natural increase to 1800 at 15 per cent. - 9,000

Total from 1790 to 1800 - - - - 69,000
1800 to 1810 immigrants estimated at - - 65,000
natural increase - - - - - - - 10,000
increase by the purchase of Louisiana - - 35,000

Total from 1800 to 1810 - - - - 110,000
1810 to 1820, immigrants by sea - - - 114,000
natural increase - - - - - - - 15,000
immigrants by way of Canada - - - 12,000
Total from 1810 to 1820 - - - - 141,000

The censuses of 1790—1800—1810—and 1820 were taken as of the first day of August; those of 1830—1840 and 1850 were taken as of the first day of June of each year.

Deduct those arriving between the first day of June and the 30th of September 1830, and it would leave only about 130,000 between the census of 1820 and that of 1830; but the records and returns are so defective that I estimate them at 150,000
natural increase about - - - - - 18,000
immigrants by way of Canada - - - 19,000
Spanish inhabitants of Florida, first included - 15,000

Total from 1820 to 1830 - - - - -	202,000
1830 to 1840 foreign passengers about - -	626,000
add half of those that arrived in 1830, about -	20,000
making - - - - - - - -	646,000
Perhaps two-thirds of those that came in 1840, arrived after the census of June 1st. - -	58,000
when they are deducted, it leaves - - -	588,000
increase after their arrival about 10 per cent. -	60,000
excess of immigrants from Canada, over and above those to Canada, as shown in section 5 - -	128,000
Total - - - - - - - -	776,000
Deduct for emigration to Texas, about - -	60,000
leaving an increase of - - - - - -	716,000
1841 to 1850, foreign passengers - - -	1,623,000
add for last part of 1840 - - - - -	58,000
add on account of the acquisition of Texas, California, and New-Mexico - - - -	160,000
natural increase of immigrants - - -	165,000
immigrants by way of Canada - - -	124,000
Total - - - - - - - -	2,130,000
Deduct half that came in 1850 - - -	140,000
and for those that returned - - - - -	50,000
and it leaves the increase from June 1st 1840 to June 1st 1850 by means of immigration and the acquisition of territory - - - -	1,940,000

Sec. 4. *Ratio of the mortality, and of the natural increase of the white population of the United States.*

It must be apparent to the reader on reflection, that the proportion of children in any two countries, where the mortality and average length of human life is the same, is an exact index of the relative increase of the population of each. The proportion of children in countries of about or nearly the same density of population, is also a pretty certain index of the ratio of mortality; for the greater the mortality among adults, the greater will be the per centage of children in the community. Where a census is taken every ten years, the children under ten years old at each enumeration, supply the places of all who have died and constitute the increase during the preceding ten years.

The following table exhibits the aggregate number, and the per centage of children among the white population, at the several periods of taking the census, an estimate of the per centage of deaths, and a statement of the per centage of domestic increase corresponding with such ratio of deaths, during each period of ten years from 1790 to 1840. In these calculations, the deaths of children, which happened between the time of their births and the first census thereafter, are not taken into the account; but when they died after having been once enumerated, their deaths are included in the calculations.

	CHILDREN UNDER TEN YEARS OLD.		Per cent. of deaths for the previous ten years.	Per cent. of decen. increase.
	Number.	Per cent.		
In 1800	1,479,315	34.366	12.4	33.4
1810	2,016,479	34.399	12.3	33.66
1820	2,625,790	33.380	12.2	31.79
1830	3,427,730	32.563	11.5	31.25
1840	4,485,052	31.607	12.4	28.

This illustration shows a gradual decrease in the proportion of children, and also in the natural or domestic increase of the population. The natural decennial increase from 1790 to 1810 was over 33 per cent.; from 1830 to 1840 only 28 per cent.; and from 1840 to 1850 it was only about 25 per cent. This is owing to the fact that, as the country grows older and luxury increases, early marriages are not so common. The ratio of mortality decreased considerably from 1790 to 1830, and was not perceptibly increased by the war of 1812 to 1815; but from 1830 to 1840 it was increased by the Asiatic cholera, by an increased proportion of destitute people from abroad, and by extensive emigrations to very new portions of the country.

The ratio of deaths is found with tolerable accuracy, by numerous calculations founded on supposed ratios of mortality, and approximating to the facts and results shown by the census and reports of immigration; and the ratio of domestic increase and the immigration is adapted to the ratio of mortality with mathematical accuracy, as shown in the following examples.

I. Children under 10 years old by the census of 1800, 34.3667 per cent.

Over ten, 65,6333
If of 100 persons in 1790, there have died 12.4 as estimated, leaving 87.6 alive,—
then as 87.6 : 12.4 : : 65.633 to 9.29 dead,
of the original stock of 74.923 alive in 1790
which taken from 100 shows an increase of 25.077
As 74.923 increase 25.077 : : 100 will increase 33.4
Whites in the United States in 1790, 3,172,464

Whites over ten years old in 1800,		2,825,190
Deaths from 1790 to 1800, at 12.4 per cent.,		393,385
Total,		3,218,575
Deduct those enumerated in 1790,		3,172,464
Leaving for emigrants over 10 years old,		46,111
Total in 1790,	3,172,464	
Domestic increase at 33.4 per cent.	1,059,602	
Foreign emigrants and their children necessary to make the number in 1800,	72,439	
Total by the census of 1800,	4,304,505	
Children of emigrants under 10 years old,		26,328

All the calculations to ascertain the ratio of domestic increase and the number of foreign emigrants and their children under ten years old, are made in the same manner. Only those enumerated at the census next after their arrival, including their children, are included in these calculations as emigrants; those who die before the first census after their arrival are not taken into the account; and at the second and all subsequent enumerations of the people, they are reckoned as citizens, and their children as domestic increase.

II. To determine the ratio of increase from 1830 to 1840, and the increase of our population during that period by means of immigration, estimating the mortality at 12.4 per cent.

Children under 10 by the census of 1840,	31.60 per cent.	
Over 10 years old,	68.40	
Deaths at 12.4 per cent.,	9.68	
of the original stock of	78.08	alive in 1830
Which taken from 100 shows an increase of	21.92	
As 78.08 increase 21.92 : : so 100 will increase 28.	.28	
White population of the United States in 1830		10,526,248
Do. over ten years old in 1840,		9,704,653
Deaths from 1830 to 1840 at 12.4 per cent.,		1,305,254
Total,		11,009,907
Deduct those enumerated in 1830,		10,526,248

and it leaves for immigrants over 10 years old,	483,659
1830, white population,	10,526,248
natural increase at 28 per cent.,	2,947,349
increase by means of immigration,	716,108
1840, white population by the census,	14,189,705
In 1800, white population by the census,	4,304,505
natural increase at 33.66 per cent.,	1,447,797
increase by means of immigrants and their children, and the purchase of Louisiana,	109,718
1810, white population by the census,	5,862,020
Domestic increase at 31.79 per cent.,	1,863,536
Increase by means of foreign immigration,	140,903
1820, white population,	7,866,459
Domestic increase at 31.25 per cent.,	2,458,267
Increase by means of foreign immigration,	201,522
1830, white population by the census,	10,526,248
1840, white population,	14,189,705
Domestic increase about 24⅝ per cent.,	3,501,033
Estimated increase by means of immigration and increase of territory.	1,940,000
1850, white population by the census,	19,630,738

Sec. 5. *The British Provinces of North America.*

The country now known as Canada was discovered, colonized, and settled by the French, by the name of the "Province of Quebec;" conquered by the British in 1759; divided into the two Provinces of Upper and Lower Canada by the British Parliament in 1791; and re-united into one province in 1843. The inhabitants, at the time of the conquest in 1759, exclusive of the native Indians, were entirely French, and are estimated by Mr. McCulloch, in his Gazetteer, as amounting to about 70,000; and that the descendants of these 70,000 French amounted in 1831 to upwards of 400,000; which, he remarks, "is the most rapid increase, probably, of any on record, from births alone." And it undoubtedly is so, if we except our free states, and the case of the Israelites while in the land of Egypt. The Canadian French are almost all plain, frugal, and moderately industrious peasants; of very little intelligence, enterprise, avarice, ambition, or energy of character; mostly possessing a little property; far removed from the vices and luxuries of wealth, and of large cities; contented, cheerful, honest, hospitable and happy. They cling with uncommon tenacity to their ancient prejudices and customs. They are in that condition of all others, best calculated to promote a rapid increase of population. The vices, luxuries, corruptions and excitements of large cities, not only undermine the health and weaken the constitution of man, but contribute to shorten human life, to discourage, and diminish marriages and births, and to check the increase of population. The increase from births is greater in every country among its peasantry or yeomanry, than in its cities; and much of the increase of its cities is by reason of inhabitants from the country, and young men in particular, constantly removing from the country into villages, and from villages into cities.

The Province of Quebec contained in 1783, by enumeration, 113,000 inhabitants, French and English, exclusive of about 10,000 or 12,000 loyalist refugees from the United States, who went to the province during the war of the American revolution. Call the population in 1783, 125,000; of these, probably 110,000 were of French descent, and but 15,000 of English, Scotch, and Irish descent. According to this calculation, the French population increased the first ten years after the conquest, twenty per cent., to 84,000, twenty per cent. the next ten years to 101,000, and at the same rate the last four years to 110,000 in the year 1783. The French population of Canada must have increased nearly twenty per cent. in seven years, amounting in 1790 to 130,000, and at the rate of thirty per cent. each ten years from that time, up to the year 1840; amounting in 1800 to 169,000; in 1810 to 220,000; in 1820 to 286,000; in 1830 to 370,000; in 1840 to 481,000; and in 1844 to 534,000, of whom 518,565 were in Lower Canada. These astonishing results were produced by early marriages, and plain, frugal habits.

Of the 693,649 inhabitants of Lower Canada, according to the census of 1844, 518,565 are stated to be natives of Canada of French origin; 85,075 natives of British origin; 11,886 natives of England; 44,002 natives of Ireland; 13,341 natives of Scotland; 11,943 natives of the United States; 2,353 natives of Continental Europe; and the nativity of the others, 6,484, is not given. There are also several thousand Canadian French in Upper Canada.

Mr. J. D. Andrews, United States consul at St. John, New Brunswick, in his report to the Secretary of the Treasury, bearing date December 10th, 1850, stated the population of Canada as follows:

	Upper Canada.	Lower Canada.
In the year 1676,	—	8,415
1700,	—	15,000
1750,	—	65,000
1784,	—	113,000
1825,	158,027	423,630
1831,	*235,000	511,922
1841,	465,357	*640,000
1848,	723,292	770,000

The population of Upper and Lower Canada is stated by Porter in his Progress of the Nation, at 270,718 in 1806, and at 580,450 in 1824. The population is stated in McGregor's Statistics, as follows :

	In Upper Canada.	Lower Canada.	Total.
1800	10,000	220,000	230,000
1831	234,865	511,922	746,787
1836	372,502	572,827	945,329
1842	486,055	—	—
1848	723,087	768,334	1,491,421

A census was taken in 1831, 1836, 1844 and 1848, and the official returns showed the population as above stated.

The immigration from Europe was comparatively small until after the close of the war in 1815, and was but about 40,000, or a little over 13,000 annually, for three years ending in 1828. It is stated in McCulloch's Gazetteer, title Canada, that "The number of immigrants from the United Kingdom, which landed at Quebec in the nine years ending in 1838, amounted to 263,089 ; of these 165,000 proceeded to the Upper Province; but of the whole number from fifty to sixty per cent. re-emigrated, after a short residence, to the United States. The greatest number which emigrated in any one year was in 1832, when 51,746 arrived at Quebec ; the smallest number was in 1838, when 4992 only reached that port. Within the period spoken of, there were 50,000 estimated to have reached the provinces by way of New York and the Erie Canal ; a like proportion of whom also re-emigrated. (Lord Durham's Rep. pp. 76 and 77.")

* The statements for Upper Canada in 1831 and Lower Canada in 1841, are my estimates from the official returns of other years.

Statements of the population of the undermentioned British Provinces of North America, made on the authority of Mr. Andrews' Report to the Secretary of the Treasury, and McGregor's statistics; some of which are official estimates only, some of them reports of official enumerations, and some of them, at the intermediate periods, are my estimates:

	Nova Scotia.	Cape Breton.	NewBrunswick.	Newfoundland.	P.Edward's Island.	Total.
1764	—	—	—	—	—	13,000
1784	—	—	12,000	—	—	32,000
1800	50,000	2,000	25,000	—	—	100,000
1806	65,000	2,515	32,000	26 505	9,000	135,000
1816	83,000	7,000	—	52,672	—	—
1827	123,878	18,700	81,000	56 000	20,651	300,000
1840	188,000	33,000	156,152	84,000	45,000	506,000
1848	230,200	49,600	200,000	108,000	62,678	650,000

Estimates deduced from the foregoing statements and authorities of the population of Upper and Lower Canada, Nova Scotia, New Brunswick, and other British Provinces of North America, at the undermentioned periods:

	U. and L. Canada.	Nova Scotia and other Prov.	Total.
1800	230,000	100,000	330,000
1810	330,000	155,000	485,000
1820	490,000	230,000	720,000
1831	746,787	340,000	1,086,000
1841	1,105,000	520,000	1,625,000
1848	1,493,000	650,000	2,143,000

The enumerations were generally made in the spring of each year, and do not include many of the immigrants of the years in which they were taken.

Estimated population of Upper and Lower Canada, and the other British Provinces of North America in April,

1800, - - - - - -	330,000
Domestic increase at 30 per cent. to 1810, -	99,000
Increase by means of immigration, - -	56,000
1810, estimated population, - - -	485,000
Domestic increase at 30 per cent. to 1820, -	145,000
Increase by means of immigration, - -	90,000
1820, estimated population, - - -	720,000
Domestic increase at 33 per cent. to 1831, -	237,000
Increase by means of immigration, - -	129,000
1831 estimated population, - -	1,086,000
Domestic increase at 28 per cent. to 1841 -	304,000
Increase by means of immigration, - -	235,000

1841, estimated population, - - -	1,625,000
Domestic increase in 7 years, to April, 1848, at 18 per cent. - - - - - -	292,000
Increase by means of immigration, - -	226,000
1848, estimated population, - - -	2,143,000

Estimating the natural increase of the immigrants between the time of their arrival and the end of the decennial period, at about 10 per cent., and the result would be as follows:

	In 10 years. 1810 to 1819.	In 11 years. 1820 to 1830.	In 10 years. 1830 to 1840.	In 7 years. 1841 to 1847.
Immigrants about,	90,000	129,368	322,465	323,651
Natural increase,	12,000	18,682	40,535	26,400
Total -	102,000	148,000	365,000	350,000
Remained in the Brit. Pro.	90,000	129,000	235,000	226,000
Re-emigrated to U. States,	12,000	19,000	128,000	124,000

The great emigration to Canada during the eighteen years (from 1830 to 1847 inclusive,) was induced in a great measure by the expenditure of large sums of money by corporations, and by the British Government, in making canals and other public improvements, which furnished employment to great numbers of laborers, and gave unusual life and activity to business and enterprise in that country. The Canadians also imported large quantities of wheat during some of those years, from the North-Western States, and sent it to England as Colonial produce, subject to only a nominal duty. The abolition of the corn laws has enabled the Continent of Europe to supply the English markets with wheat, and cut off that trade; the public improvements in Canada are mostly completed; and both of these sources of prosperity to the Canadians are nearly dried up; and they are in a very depressed condition, for want of sufficient markets for their products, and sufficient mechanical and manufacturing industry to supply their own wants.

They import from Great Britain almost everything they use and wear, including much ready-made clothing, boots and shoes; and, under such circumstances, it is impossible that they should be otherwise than poor. Free trade with Great Britain prevents them from manufacturing for themselves; deranges the division of employments; discourages and depresses industry; and hangs upon them like an incubus, exhausting their money, and the proceeds of all their products that will sell, to enrich the manufacturers of England. The lumbering, fur, and fishing business, as well as the expenditure of the public moneys, are of immense consequence to the Canadians; and were it not for these sources of prosperity, they would be nearly as poor as the Irish. Though the ratio of increase of the population has been greater in Canada than in the United States, yet their increase of wealth has barely kept pace with the population, and they are as poor as they were half a century since. They have enjoyed the blessings of FREE TRADE with England all the time; we have only a part of the time. Whenever we have attempted to supply ourselves by our own industry, with the comforts and necessaries of life, we have improved our condition as a people; and during the intervals of free trade and large importations of foreign goods, we have relapsed again into a condition bordering on bankruptcy; while the Canadians have been constantly exhausted, and kept so poor by free trade, as to be unable to get sufficient credit to have even the ups and downs of prosperity and bankruptcy in succession

SEC. 6. *Population of Cuba and Porto Rico.*

Mr. Murray states the population of Cuba in 1775 and 1827, in his geography, (which very nearly agrees with Mr. McCulloch,) as follows:

	1775.	1827.
Whites,	96,440	311,051
Free mulattoes,	19,327	57,514
Free blacks,	11,520	48,980
Slaves,	44 333	286,942
Total,	171,620	704,487

Mr. McCulloch says that by a census in 1791, the population amounted to 272,140; and by the census of 1817, to 551,998, and he estimated it in 1839 at over 900,000.

The culture of sugar and coffee has increased with wonderful rapidity, but has not much more than kept pace with the wants of the commercial world; and therefore prices have kept up much better than the price of cotton. The most important manufactures of Cuba consist of making sugar, molasses, and rum, the preparation of coffee, the making of cigars, the bleaching of wax, and the manipulation of the minor staples of the island. These pursuits furnish profitable employment to great numbers of whites, as well as of slaves, and produced the rapid increase of the white population (partly by immigration, but mostly by natural increase,) indicated in the above table, of nearly twenty-five per cent. every ten years; doubling in about thirty-two years.

The population was about 1,200,000 in 1850.

The area of Porto Rico comprises 3,700 square miles. Mr. Murray says, in his geography, that in 1778 the population was but 70,278; and that it amounted, by the official census of 1830, to 323,838. Mr. McCulloch says that the population in 1788 did not exceed 80,650; it amounted in 1836, according to the official returns, to 358,086.

Statement of the number and classes of the population according to the censuses of the

Years.	1830.	1836.
Whites,	162,311	188,869
Free mulattoes,	127,287	101,275
Free blacks,		26,124
Slaves,	34,240	41,818
Total,	323,838	358,086

Increase of the whites in six years, 26,558, equal to 16⅓ per cent., and the increase of the slaves is over 20 per cent.; while there is scarcely any increase of free colored persons.

SEC. 7. *Population of Mexico.*

Mr. Murray says: "The population of Mexico, which had previously been estimated on the most vague conjecture, has been computed by Humboldt with extraordinary care. He copied from the archives of the viceroy a statement containing the results of an enumeration made in 1793, by which the number was rated at 4,483,529. The census was taken, however, in opposition to those popular apprehensions and prejudices with which such an enumeration is always viewed; and the real amount might be at least a sixth more, or 5,200,000. After carefully comparing the numbers of births and deaths, and observing the progress of agriculture, the increased amount of duties on consumption, and the many new houses every where building, he considered that the population in 1823 might be safely estimated at 6,800,000."

The government took a partial census in 1841, and estimated the population at 7,044,140. It was estimated by Mr. Poinsett in 1825 at 6,500,000; by Mr. Ward in 1827 at 8,000,000; and by M. Chevalier in 1835 at 7,000,000.

M. Humboldt's estimates are entitled to great credit, but the census of 1841 shows that they were too high.

In 1793, estimated population,	-	4,700,000
1800, do. do.	-	5,000,000
1820, do. do.	-	6,000,000
1841, according to official reports,		7,044,140
1850, estimated population,		7,500,000

M. Chevalier estimated the different classes of the population in 1835 as follows:—1st, the Chapetones, or pure Spaniards, 24,000; 2d, the Creoles, or native whites of European descent, 1,300,000; 3d, Indians, or native Mexicans, 3,800,000; 4th, the mixed castes, comprising Mestizoes, Mulattoes, Zambos, Quadroons, and Quinteroons, 1,900,000.

A chart of the population, resources, and condition of Mexico recently published in that country by MM. Lerdo de Tejeda, states the population in 1850 at 7,661,919, divided as follows:

Two-fifteenths, about 1,000,000, of pure European descent.

Four-fifteenths, about 2,000,000, of mixed European and Indian descent.

Nine-fifteenths, or about 4,500,000, of pure Indian descent.

SEC. 8. *Population of the other Spanish American States and Nations.*

The population of the countries of South America is uncertain. A census was taken in Peru in 1803, and in New Granada in 1834. With those exceptions the statements of the population of each and every one of them is either an official or an individual estimate, founded on information more or less imperfect. Within the last twenty years, the population of Buenos Ayres, now the Argentine Republic, has been variously estimated at from 600,000 to 1,600,000; that of Chili from 600,000 to 1,500,000; and that of Bolivia, or Upper Peru, at from about 1,000,000 to 1,700,000. Dr. Morse says that in 1778 there were not more than 80,000 white inhabitants in Chili, and about 240,000 negroes, including those of a mixed race. How can even an approximation to the truth be attained amidst such conflicting evidence

Nature's laws are uniform, and the ratio of deaths and births are very nearly the same from year to year, in the same country, and under similar circumstances. The only method by which any safe conclusions on the subject can be arrived at, is to compare with each other the results of the different censuses, partial enumerations, official calculations, and individual estimates of the population of all these countries, at different periods, and endeavor to deduce from the whole the general ratio of increase. By this method all the evidence can be compared and weighed, and the inconsistencies of different estimates and portions of the evidence can be ascertained. The ratio of the natural increase must be very nearly the same in all Spanish America, except Chili, and the countries lying south of the Torrid Zone, where it is greater than in the others. There has also been more emigration to Chili and Buenos Ayres than to other Spanish

American States. This is owing partly to their commercial advantages, and partly to the policy of the Government.

Population of Peru in 1803, and of New Granada, Ecuador, and Venezuela in 1834, stated in millions, and classified according to their origin.

	Peru. *Per census.*	New Granada. *Per census.*	Ecuador. *Estimate.*	Venezuela. *Offic. statement.*
Whites,	.136	1.058	.157	.2
Indians,	.609	.376	.393	.207
Mixed castes &	.244	.169	.042	.433
Free colored,	.041			
Negro slaves,	.04	.084	.008	.06
Total,	1.07	1.687	.6	.9

The evidence indicates that the natural increase of the white population of Buenos Ayres and Chili is about one and a half per cent. annually, and one per cent. annually in Mexico and the other countries of Spanish America; that the increase of the Mestizoes and other mixed races, is nearly as great; and that the ratio of increase of the pure Indian population is only from one-fourth to half as great. There seems to be no reason to doubt that the aboriginal population of Peru, and of nearly all South America, declined during the first three centuries after the conquest of the country by the Spanish. An estimate of the population of each country is given in Section 12.

SEC. 9. *Population of Brazil.*

The population of Brazil at the beginning of the present century was very vaguely and variously estimated at from one to three millions. Mr. Murray estimated it at 3,000,000: he says that according to an official report made in 1819, and different official statements furnished between the years 1816 and 1818, Brazil then contained 3,617,000 inhabitants.

The importation of slaves has been very great since 1820, until recently. It has been variously estimated from 40,000 to 80,000 annually; and McCulloch says the immigration of whites had been as high some years, as from 8,000 to 9,000.

Malte Brun estimated the population of Brazil for 1830 at 5,340,000; Balbi at 5,300,000; and Murray at about 5,000,000; of which he said about one-fifth were whites, and three-fifths slaves.

Statement of the number of each class of the inhabitants of Brazil, according to the Government reports made from 1816 to 1818, and M. Balbi's estimate for 1830.

	1816 to 1818.	1830.
Whites, - - - - -	843,000	900,000
Mestizoes and Mulattoes, free,	426,000	600,000
Do. do. slaves,	202,000	250,000
Negro slaves, - - -	1,728,000	2,920,000
Free Negroes, - - -	159,000	180,000
Converted Indians, - -	259,000	300,000
Independent Indians and Europeans,		150,000
Total, - - -	3,617,000	5,300,000

Mr. McCulloch estimated the population in 1839 at from 6,500,000 to 7,000,000, and it is estimated in the American Almanac for 1851 at 7,500,000. The evidence indicates that the natural increase of all classes of the free population is about one per cent. annually, and that the slaves increase at nearly the same rate after they become acclimated and accustomed to the galling chains of slavery.

SEC. 10.—*Indian population of the United States.*

Number of Indians in the United States according to the report of the Indian Bureau, prepared by Henry R. Schoolcraft, LL.D.; a part of whom were enumerated from 1847 to 1850, and a part estimated from the returns of Indian agents.

I. Iroquois group, per census in

New York, Oneidas, - - - - -	153
Onondagas, - - - - - -	376
Cayugas, - - - - - -	150
Senecas,* - - - - - -	2,776
Tuscaroras, - - - - - -	285
St. Regis Tribe,† - - - - -	450
Wisconsin, Oneidas at Green Bay, - -	762
West of Missouri, Wyandots, - - -	687
Missouri, Senecas and Shawnees, - -	273
Total Iroquois, - - - - -	5,912

* This includes 55 Senecas at Conawanga, Pennsylvania, and 158 at Neosho, west of Arkansas.

† The number of this tribe is put down in Schoolcraft's notes on the Iroquois at only 260.

II. Algonquin group, per census—

Michigan, 23 bands of Chippewas, - - - -	2,005
Indian Ter. West, 1 do., " - - - - - -	23
On Lake Superior, 6 do., " - - - - - -	1,610
St. Croix Valley, 5 do., " - - - - - -	487
Chippewa Valley, 3 do., " - - - - - -	1,180
Upper Mississippi, 10 do., " - - - - - -	2,706
Rainy Lake, 3 do., " - - - - - -	1,020
Indian Ter. West, 1 do., Ottawas, - - - - -	236
Michigan, 14 do., " - - - - - -	1,706
Do. 1 do., Pottawatamies, - - - - -	63
Ind. Ter. W., Western Algonquins, Sacs and Foxes, Miamies, Pottawatamies, Shawnees, Delawares, &c., 12 tribes, - - - - - - - - -	6,538
Wisconsin, Menomonies, - - - - - - -	416
Total Algonquin group, - - - - -	17,990

III. Dacota group, per census—

West of Miss. River, Omahas, - - - - - -	1,349
" " Ottoes, 2 bands, - - - - -	903
" " Winnebagoes, 20 bands, - - -	2,531
" " Iowas, - - - - - - -	744
Minnesota Ter., Sioux, 7 bands, - - - - - -	1,063
Missouri, Quapaws, - - - - - - - -	271
Total Dacota group, - - - - - - -	6,861

Fragments of tribes in other States

Maine, Souriquois, Passamaquoddies, and Penobscots -	956
Massachusetts—remnants of 12 tribes, - - - -	847
Rhode Island, Narragansetts, - - - - - -	420
Connecticut, Mohegans, - - - - - - -	400
Virginia, Nottoways, mixed with negroes, - - -	40
North Carolina, Cherokees and Catawbas - - -	1,005
South Carolina, Catawbas, - - - - - - -	200
Florida, Seminoles and 4 other tribes, - - - -	348
Total in those eight States, - - - - -	4,216

Other tribes between the Mississippi and the Rocky Mountains, north of Texas and New Mexico, officially estimated.

Chickasaws, - -	9,260	Brought up, -	105,760
Cherokees, - -	26,000	Foxes and Sacs, - -	2,400
Creeks, - -	25,000	Gros Ventres, - -	3,000
Choctaws, - - -	16,000	Kanzas, - - -	1,600
Arapahoes, - -	3,500	Menomonies, - -	2,500
Crows, - - -	4,000	Minitarees, - -	2,500
Aurrickarees, - -	1,500	Pawnees, - - -	17,000
Blackfeet, - - -	13,000	Pottawatamies, - -	3,200
Cheyennes, - -	2,500	Sioux, - - -	14,500
Caddoes, - - -	2,000	Seminoles, - -	1,500
Chippewas, - -	1,500	Shawnees, - - -	1,600
Delawares, - -	1,500	Tetans, - - -	3,000
		About 20 other tribes,	11,976
	105,760		
		Total,	170,536

In Texas, Camanches, - - - - -	15,000
" Apache bands, - - - - - -	3,500
" Parts of 14 other tribes, - - - -	5,600
Total in Texas as officially estimated, - - -	24,100

In New Mexico, Pueblos, - - - - - -	11,180
" Apaches, 7,500, Camanches, 12,000, -	19,500
" Navajoes, 12,500, Utahs, 5,000, - -	17,500
" Ancient Cibolos, north of Gila, - -	20,000
" Umahs of the Colorado, - - - -	6,500
" Other tribes, - - - - - -	17,450
Total in New Mexico as officially estimated, - -	92,130

In Utah Territory, Utahs, - - - -	7,000	
" Other tribes, - - -	4,500	
Total in Utah Territory, - - - - -		11,500

In California, according to the returns of the Spanish missionaries at 18 missions, - - - - -	14,931
Mustees and Mulattoes, - - - - - -	1,300
Wild mountain tribes officially estimated at, - - -	16,000
Total in California as officially estimated, - -	32,231
In Oregon, 59 small tribes estimated at, - - -	22,733
Grand total in the United States and Territories,	388,229

The numbers in New Mexico and north of New Mexico, between the Rocky Mountains and the Indian Territory, west of Arkansas Missouri and Iowa, according to the official estimates, seem quite too large to correspond with the numbers in California, Oregon, Texas, and east of the Mississippi River. The Pueblos are estimated at 11,180; the seventh census since taken shows that there were only 7,712. Judge Houghton and Mr. James L. Collins, who have resided in New Mexico many years, and have had good advantages for acquiring information, estimate the Camanches of New Mexico and Texas at only 12,000. They estimate the Indians of New Mexico, including the Camanches of Texas and the Utahs, who roam into Utah territory, at less than 54,000. Their estimate for New Mexico, Texas, and Utah Territory, is about 57,000 less than that of the Indian Bureau. On comparing the area of the several States and Territories, their relative condition as hunting grounds, the various estimates of the Indian population, taking into consideration their wandering habits, and the liability to estimate the same persons two or three times over, my mind inclines to the conclusion, that the estimate of the Indian Bureau of those in New Mexico and Texas, is too high by more than 40,000; that the estimate for the open country, north of Texas and New Mexico, and east of the Rocky Mountains, is about as much too high; and that the real number in the United States and Territories, is about 300,000.

The number contained in the most of the tribes west of the Mississippi, is mere conjecture; and the number of Indians east of the Mississippi during the seventeenth and the early part of the eighteenth century, was equally uncertain. Many estimates of them have been excessively extravagant and vague. The fears of the early settlers, aided by public rumors, generally magnified the numbers from two to tenfold. It has been estimated that the number in Massachusetts, prior to a traditionary plague in 1617, exceeded 100,000, and that there were 37,000 in the present State of Maine. Dr. Morse estimated that there were in Rhode Island in 1620, from 12 to 16,000; in 1670, about 8,000; and that there were from 35 to 40,000 in Connecticut at the latter period. The number in Massachusetts in 1698, is stated in Dr. Holmes's Annals at 4,168; the number reported by the census of 1765, was 1,569; and the number returned by a recent census, 847, as heretofore stated.

The Indians designated by Mr. Schoolcraft as the Iroquois group, were mostly settled in the State of New York prior to the Revolutionary war, and were generally known as the Six Nations of Indians, and sometimes as the Five Nations.

In 1776, the Mohawks, and a portion of the Cayugas, took sides in the war with the British against the United States, and removed to Grand River in Upper Canada. In 1779, the Rev. Mr. Kirkland, long a missionary among the Oneidas, estimated the Six Nations as containing 6,330 souls ; and said there were comparatively very few children among them.

The most of the Iroquois constituted a confederacy of five tribes from some time in the seventeenth century, and afterwards of six tribes or nations. Mr. Schoolcraft, in his Notes on the Iroquois, published in 1847, says, that "at a conference with the five cantons at Albany, in 1677, the number of warriors was carefully made out at 2,150, giving a population of 10,750 ; that according to Smith's estimate of the warriors in 1756, the whole number of souls was only about 6,000 ; according to Douglass in 1760, only 7,500 ; and according to Colonel Boquet in 1764, about 7,750. Mr. Schoolcraft estimated the descendants of the Iroquois in Canada, at about 2,000. The Iroquois group has been heretofore stated as comprising (in 1848) about 5,912 persons. Deduct 812 for the Wyandots, and the Shawnees included with them, and add the 2,000 in Canada, and it shows that the descendants of the Six Nations of New York Indians, now number over 7000. From these statements it would seem that these Indians have decreased very little during nearly a century past. Mr. Schoolcraft thinks their numbers have been less, but that they have been slowly increasing for many years past, since they have ceased to be engaged in wars, and have turned their attention to agriculture.

Statement of the condition and leading products during the previous year, of agricultural industry of the Iroquois group of Indians, according to the census of 1848, and of that portion of them in the State of New York, according to the census of 1845, as reported by Mr. Schoolcraft. The reports make nine subdivisions in New York in 1845, and fifteen in all in 1848, ten of which were in New York. There were no reports from many of the subdivisions on some branches of industry in 1848.

	Subdivisions reported.	Iroquois group in 1848	New York Indians in 1845.
Whole number of persons,	15	5,912	3,753
Number in New York,	10	3,977	3,753
Marriages during the year,	8	31	36
Births,	13	184	121
Deaths,	13	139	120
Families living by agriculture,	12	768	371
Blacksmiths,	6	10	
Carpenters,	9	27	20
Shoemakers,	5	8	
Number of children at school,	9	613	462
Acres of improved land,	12	30,838	13,867
Indian corn raised, bushels,	12	66,009	35,499
Wheat raised, "	12	13,192	11,508
Potatoes, "	12	16,676	16,681
Oats, "	12	28,736	28,866
Beans and peas, "	12	5,938	954
Butter made, pounds,	11	41,164	20,341
Milch cows,	13	1,303	803
Oxen,	12	774	1,472
Other neat cattle,	13	2,546	
Horses and mules,	13	1,903	948
Sheep,	8	832	839
Hogs,	13	7,115	3,458
Ploughs,	13	737	381
Saw-mills,	7	18	no report
Grist-mills,	3	3	no report

Though the reports are incomplete so far as regards everything but population, yet so far as they go they show that those Indians have made, and are making, considerable progress in industry and civilization, and that they are increasing in numbers.

Statement of the number, condition, and leading products of agricultural industry of the previous year, of that portion of the Chickasaws which had been enumerated in 1849, and the returns published in Mr. Schoolcraft's work ; also of the Western Algonquins, with the exception of the Sacs, Foxes, and Menomonies.

	Chickasaws.	Western Algonquins.
Number of Indians of full blood, . . .	4,260	4,813
Whites and those of mixed blood, white and Indian, ...	627	185
African slaves, ...	2,264	——
Marriages during the previous year,. .	——	191
Births, ...	——	230
Deaths,.	——	294
Families living by agriculture and grazing,	——	773
Blacksmiths, carpenters, and shoemakers,	——	29
Number of children at school, . . .	——	417
Indian corn raised, bushels, . . .	265,351	143,207
Wheat raised, do, ...	4,252	3,202
Potatoes, do, do, ...	63,917	14,332
Oats, do, do, ...	14,402	17,117
Beans, do, do, ...	——	2,149
Horses, ...	5,789	4,946
Neat cattle, ...	14,788	4,748
Sheep, ...	1,148	302
Hogs, ...	24,142	7,813
Value of agricultural implements, . .	——	$42,000

Mr. Schoolcraft has estimated the Indians in North Carolina in 1708, at about 6,000 ; and those in South Carolina, when it was first settled by English colonists, at about 7,000.*

It is said in the report of H. Knox, secretary of war, bearing date, June 15th, 1789, "The whole number of Indian warriors south of the Ohio, and east of the Mississippi, may be estimated at 14,000. Those to the northward of the Ohio, and to the southward of the lakes, at about 5,000. In addition to these, the old men, women, and children, may be estimated at three for every warrior—the whole number amounting to 76,000 souls."†

The secretary of war in his letter to the President, bearing date July 7th, 1789, in relation to a treaty made with the

* See Schoolcraft's Notes on the Iroquois, p. 110 and 156.

† See American State Papers, vol. IV., on Indian Affairs, pp. 13, 38, 39, and 659.

Cherokees, says, "The frequent wars they had with the frontier people of the United States, have greatly diminished their numbers." The commissioners appointed to negotiate a treaty with them in 1785, in the report of Dec. 2d of that year, make the following statement: "We have for the information of Congress collected as near as may be, the number of Indians in the four southern States, and we find the gun men of the Cherokees,

kees,	2,000
The Upper and Lower Creek nations, from an agent who resided seven years in their towns,	5,400
The Chickasaws,	800
The Choctaws,	6,000
Total,	14,200

There are also some remains of tribes settled among these, as Shawanees, Eutchees," &c., &c.

The estimate of the secretary of war in June 1789, is evidently based mostly on the report of the commissioners of Dec. 1785, just referred to, which, judging from the present estimates of those tribes, was too high for the Choctaws, and quite too low for the Chickasaws and Cherokees. The commissioners appointed to negotiate with the Choctaws, in a communication to the secretary of war, bearing date Dec. 18th, 1801, say, "A very few families have commenced the culture of cotton; it is not manufactured by more than twelve in the whole nation, whose population exceeds fifteen thousand."

The report of the secretary of war of June 1789, estimating the Indians at 76,000, did not include those in New England, New York, and other middle States, probably numbering about 10,000, which were not under the jurisdiction of the United States, but were subject to the several States in which they resided. This would swell the whole number then east of the Mississippi River, to about 86,000, the descendants of whom now number over 112,000, according to the enumerations and estimates of the Indian Bureau, as heretofore stated.

The probability is, that the Cherokees and Chickasaws, and perhaps some of those in the northwestern territory, were underestimated, and that there were nearly 100,000 Indians in the United States in 1789. Great numbers of them were destroyed in the various wars waged against them by the United States from 1790 to 1815, and many lives were lost in removing them west of the Mississippi; but there is no reason to doubt that, with these exceptions, all the tribes which have turned their attention to agriculture, have been increasing during the last fifty years.

The tendency of the savage, and particularly the hunter state, is to separate and individual exertion—to isolation and individuality of character, and to produce petty independent tribes. Except for warlike purposes, they resist all efforts for association, union, and confederation of tribes. Hence the want of any regular institutions of government, of religion or education; of any fixed laws, accurate conceptions of morals, of personal rights, and of tribunals to administer justice. Hence individuals and tribes have no conceptions of any remedies for wrongs and injustice, except retaliation, force, violence, and murder. Savage tribes coming in contact, have frequent wars with each other; and after the country was colonized by Europeans, they had frequent wars with the whites. They are an isolated, austere, unsocial people, and have few children, as appears by the works of Mr. Schoolcraft. As they are ignorant of medical science, and suffer great hardships, a very large proportion of their children die young.

The principal causes of the decrease of the Indians in the United States, during the last two centuries, are as follows:

1st. The introduction among them, and the use of intoxicating liquors.

2d. The frequent quarrels, murders, and bloody wars among themselves.

3d. Their wars with the whites.

4th. Frequent sufferings by reason of a want of the necessaries of life; and,

Lastly. Ignorance of medical science.

All these causes, except the first and third, operated with greater force before the settlement of the country by the whites, than they do at present. Though their hunting grounds have been contracted, yet the increased value of their furs, deer and buffalo skins, and the use of agricultural implements and domestic animals, which they have learned from the whites, more than compensate for the loss. The second and third causes have ceased to operate with the colonized tribes, as well as those east of the Mississippi; and the evils of the first, fourth, and fifth, have greatly diminished among those tribes which have fixed habitations, and give their attention to agriculture and grazing.

I see no reason to believe that the number of Indians within the present limits of the United States, east of the Mississippi River, exceeded 200,000 when the European colonists first settled in Virginia, New York, and New England; nor that they exceeded 150,000 at the beginning of the eighteenth century; nor do I see any reason to doubt that the descendants of those

Indians, now numbering about 112,000, may increase to 150,000, and perhaps more, before the close of the present century. It is to be hoped that the time is not far distant, when Congress will unite all the tribes colonized west of Arkansas and Missouri under one government, appoint a governor, judges, and marshals, or sheriffs, for them, and allow them a delegate in Congress, to look after their rights and interests. Union, and a regular system of government, would do more for them than anything else ; which their excessive tendency to independent action will probably prevent them from ever forming, without the aid of Congress. As to the Indians farther west, they must be chastised into submission to the government and laws of the country, and a just regard for the rights of others, before much can be done effectually to learn them habits of regular industry, and the arts of civilization. The missionary cannot effect much without law, the judge, the sheriff, and the soldier.

SEC. 11. *Indians of the British North American Provinces.*

Mr. Schoolcraft, in his Notes on the Iroquois, gives the number of Indians in Canada, from a report of the Canadian parliament, as follows: In Lower Canada, 3,301, and in Upper Canada, 8,862—total, 12,163. This report, he remarks, "is at best but an estimate; and in this respect, the Canadians, like ourselves, are apt to over-estimate."

M. H. Perley, Esq., Indian Agent of the province of New Brunswick, gives the number in that province and Prince Edward's Island, according to a recent census, and estimates it for other provinces as follows :

Indians in New Brunswick per census, - - -	1,427
Do. in Prince Edward's Island per census, - -	297
Do. in Nova Scotia, estimated at, - - - -	1,200
Do. in Newfoundland, estimated at, - - -	900
Do. in Ter. of Labrador, estimated at, - - -	4,000
Add for Canada, per Mr. Schoolcraft, - - - -	12,163
Making a total of, - - - - - - -	19,987

Mr. Perley estimates the Moravian missionaries, and other white settlers among the Labrador Indians, at 1,000. He says the migratory habits of the Indians render it difficult to estimate them, and cause the same persons, in many instances, to be reckoned two or three times over ; and that they have been generally greatly over-estimated. He says the government has no data for even estimating the Indians west of Canada and Hudson's Bay, which I shall put down as a mere conjecture at 20 000.

Sec. 12. *Population of America.*

The population of Patagonia has been estimated at 80,000, and the independent tribes of Indians of Mexico and South America at from 1,000,000, to 1,500,000. The probability is, that these estimates are too high. The enumerations made, and the more accurate information acquired, during the present century, show that nearly all the estimates made of the savage tribes of America, have been entirely too high.

Estimates of the population of America at the under-mentioned periods.*

	1800. Millions.	1820. Millions.	1840. Millions.	1850. Millions.
Mexico,	5.	6.	7.	7.5
Guatemala,				.9
San Salvador,				.3
Nicaragua,	1.25	1.5	1.8	.38
Honduras,				.3
Costa Rica,				.12
Venezuela,	.7	.8	.95	1.05
New Granada,	1.8	2.1	1.8	2.
Ecuador,			.6	.65
Peru,	1.05	1.15	1.3	1.4
Chili,	.65	.8	1.05	1.2
Bolivia,			1.	1.1
Argentine Republic,	1.4	1.8	1.	1.14
Uruguay,			.13	.14
Paraguay,			.2	.22
Cuba,	.6	.6	.9	1.2
Porto Rico,		.3	.38	.4
Total Spanish America,	12.45	15.05	18.11	20.
Brazil,	3.	4.3	6.3	7.4
Guiana,	.12	.14	.14	.14
Other West India Islands,	1.2	1.5	1.8	2.
British Prov. North America,	.33	.73	1.6	2.3
United States,	5.3	9.53	17.06	23.25
Indians in United States,	.3	.3	.3	.3
Indians in Brit. Prov. and Ter.	.04	.04	.04	.04
Other Indians not included above,	1.	1.	1.	1.
Total in America,	23.74	32.59	46.35	56.43

* The estimates for the year 1800 are mostly in accordance with those of Baron Humboldt, in his History of New Spain

CHAPTER XXI.

On the Property and Productive Industry of the United States.—continued from chapter xiv.

Sec. 1. *On the wealth of the several States at different periods, and the amount of property to each person.*

I. Statement of the population of Massachusetts, the aggregate amount of taxable property according to the official valuations, and the average amount of property to each person, at the under-mentioned periods; also the per cent. increase of the population, from one period to another.

Years.	Population.	Increase per cent.	Value of Property.	Amount to each Person.
1790	378,717		$44,024,349	$116
1800	423,245	11.7	72,065,718	170
1810	472,040	11.5	97,949,917	207
1820	523,287	10.9	153,545,171	293
1830	610,408	16.6	208,856,422	642
1840	737,699	20.8	299,880,338	406
1850	994,499	34.8	597,936,995	601

In 1820 Maine was admitted as a State. Prior to that time it was a District, subject to Massachusetts, but it is not included in the foregoing table. The valuation of the property in Massachusetts and Maine, in 1792, and the amount to each person, was as follows:*

	Valuation.	Amount to each Person.
Massachusetts, - -	$44,487,266	$115
Maine, - - -	7,607,132	72

* See American State papers on Finance, vol. I. pages 420, and 443 to 541.

II. Summary statement of the valuation of lands, town and city lots, and dwelling houses, in the several States, made by the assessors of direct taxes levied by the United States, for the years 1798 and 1813;* and the amount to each person,† at each period. Also the valuation of slaves in several of the States in 1813.

	Valuation in Millions in 1798.	Valuation in Millions in 1813.	Amount to each Person.		Valuation of Slaves in 1813.
			1798.	1813.	
New Hampshire	$23.17	$36.96	$132	$165	
Massachusetts, Maine	83.99	149.25	151	204	
Rhode Island	11.06	21.56	160	274	
Connecticut	48.31	86.54	194	326	$0.003
Vermont	16.72	32.75	120	147	
New York	100.88	265.22	187	245	.842
New Jersey	36.44	*98.61	176	376	
Pennsylvania	102.14	*346.63	180	370	
Delaware	6.23	14.22	100	195	.142
Maryland	32.37	106.49	96	274	14.526
Virginia	71.22	no returns.	83		
North Carolina	30.84	58.11	67	100	34.082
South Carolina	17.46	no returns.	54		
Georgia	12.06	"	83		
Kentucky	21.41	"	112		
Tennessee	6.13	28.75	68	93	9.663
Ohio in 1815		*61.35		186	
	$619.93				$59.258

* The States of New Jersey, Pennsylvania, and Ohio, and some others, assumed their taxes for 1813, and hence no valuations were made that year; the sums stated as the valuations of those three States in 1813, were made in 1815.

† As the slaves produce wealth by their labor, and consume the products of industry like other persons, for the purpose of instituting a fair comparison of the condition of the several States, they are not treated as property, but as persons, by whose labor a portion of the wealth of the country has been produced.

III. Summary statement in millions of dollars, of the official valuations of taxable real estate in the State of Virginia, at the under-mentioned periods—

		In 1850.
1st District—6,178,716 acres of land and buildings - - - -		$49.61
The buildings upon it were valued at	$10.92	
Value of buildings on city and town lots - - - -	16.16	
Value of city and town lots, including buildings - - -		28.35
2d District—9,945,362 acres of land and buildings - - -		73.28
Value of buildings on the lands -	12.13	
Value of buildings on city and town lots - - - -	2.74	
Value of city and town lots, including buildings - - -		4.5
3d District—6,527,368 acres of land and buildings - - - -		53.12
Value of buildings on the lands -	8.04	
Value of buildings on city and town lots - - - -	2.88	
Value of city and town lots, including buildings - - -		4.29
4th District—26,644,341 acres of land and buildings - - -		55.74
Value of buildings on the lands -	6.13	
Value of buildings on city and town lots - - - -	3.31	
Value of city and town lots, including buildings - - -		5.77
Total value of real estate and buildings, in 1850 - - - -		274.66
Total value of the buildings only -	62.31	

Total Valuation of real estate and buildings:—

	In 1819.	In 1838.
1st. Tide-water District - -	$71.49	$60.70
2d. Piedmont District - -	78.16	69.02
3d. The Valley District - -	41.17	42.99
4th. The Trans-Alleghany District -	16.06	39.22
Total valuation of real estate and buildings	206.88	211.93

IV. Summary statement in millions of dollars, of the value of the taxable property in the States of Ohio and Kentucky, according to the official valuations made for levying taxes for the year 1850—

	Ohio.	Kentucky.
Lands, buildings, and improvements -	$266,751	$141,720
City and town lots, and buildings -	74,638	32,124
Slaves - - - -		65,190
Other personal property, stocks, moneys, and credits - -	98,487	60,348
Total taxable property, - -	439,876	299,382

The foregoing table shows that the average value of slaves in Kentucky was estimated in 1850 at about three hundred and ten dollars, including old, young, male and female. Table II. shows, that they were valued, in 1813, in Maryland, at about one hundred and thirty dollars, and in North Carolina, at about one hundred and ninety dollars. A comparison of valuations leaves no room to doubt, that lands in those States were assessed in 1813, at their full cash value, and the probability is, that slaves were also assessed at their full average value. Prior to 1790, the average value of slaves was less than one hundred dollars; they have increased in value more than three fold since that time; their average value in the United States at the present time (1852) being about three hundred and seventy dollars. Children a year old are generally valued in Virginia at about one hundred dollars each; those five years old are valued at from two hundred to two hundred and fifty dollars; and in the cotton planting States, they are more valuable than they are in the States bordering on the free States.

V. Statement in millions of dollars, generally in accordance with the returns of the census of 1850,—1st, of the value of farms and plantations in each of the States, including the wood and timbered lands thereon, or connected therewith; 2d, of the value of agricultural tools, implements, and machinery; 3d, of live stock; 4th, of all the lands and real estate, according to the valuations made in assessing state and county taxes; 5th, of all the personal property and effects, except slaves; 6th, the aggregate valuations of personal and real property; 7th, estimate of the true valuations or real amount of personal and real estate, exclusive of the value of Slaves; and, lastly, the average amount of property to each person, of the whole population:—

	Farms.	Agricul. Tools, &c.	Live Stock.	Real Estate.	Personal Estate.	Personal and Real.	Property estimated.*	Amount to each Person.
*Maine -	$54.8	$2.28	$9.7			100.2	$134.	$230
New Hampshire	55.2	2.31	8.87			92.2	103.6	326
Vermont -	59.7	2.79	12.64	57.2	15.7	72.9	92.5	294
Massachusetts -	109.1	3·21	9.64			597.9	597.9	601
Rhode Island -	17.1	.49	1.53	51.1	26.6	77.7	80.5	545
Connecticut -	72.7	1.89	7.46	96.4	22.7	119.1	155.7	420
New York -								
Sn District -	136.3	4.04	13.72	322.3	111.4	433.7	557.2	502
*Nn District -	418.2	18.04	59.85	249.4	44.4	293.8	650.	326
*New Jersey -	120.2	4.42	10.68	153 1			208.	425
*Pennsylvania -	407.9	14.72	41.5			497.0	800.	345
	1.451.2	54.19	175.59				3,379.4	
Ohio - -	358.7	12 75	44.12	337.5	96.8	433.8	504.7	254
Indiana -	136 4	6.7	22.48	112.9	39.9	152.9	202.6	205
Illinois - -	96.1	6.4	24.21	81.5	33.3	114 8	156.3	184
*Michigan -	51 9	2.89	8.			52.8	85.	212
Wisconsin -	28.5	1.64	4.88	21.2	5 5	26.7	42.	137
*Iowa - -	16.6	1.17	3.69	16.9	5 7	22.6	26.	135
Minnesota -	.2		.09				.6	100
	688.4	31.55	107.47				1,017.2	
*Delaware -	18.9	.51	1.85				27.5	300
Maryland -	87.2	2.46	8.			181.5	192.2	329
District Columbia	1.7	.04	.07	12.5	.4	12.9	13 5	267
*Virginia -	216.4	7.02	33.65	274.6			355.	250
North Carolina -	67.8	3.93	17.72	71.7	45.1	116.8	131.6	152
*Tennessee -	97 8	5.36	30.	104.3		185 5	175.	175
Kentucky -	154.3	5.17	29.6	173.9	60.1	234.	234.	238
*Missouri -	63.	3.96	19.77	66.8			120.	175
*Arkansas -	15 3	1 6	6.65	17.2	4.4	21.6	26.	124
	722.4	30.05	147.31				1,274.8	
South Carolina -	82 4	4.13	15.06	105.7	43 4	149.1	153.5	230
Georgia - -	95.7	5.89	25.73	121.6	60 8	182.4	182.7	202
*Florida - -	6 3	·66	2.88				10·9	125
*Alabama -	64.3	5.12	21.69				130.	170
Mississippi -	54.7	5.76	19.4	65.2	19.3	84.5	105.	173
Louisiana -	75.8	11.57	11.15			122.2	136.1	263
Texas - -	16.4	2.13	10.27			27.7	29.5	189
	395.6	35.26	106.18				747.7	
California -	3.9	.1	3.35	16.4	5.6	22.0	22.2	
Oregon - -		.18	1.87					
*Utah - -	.3	·08	.54				.9	79
*New Mexico -	1.6	.08	1.49				8.7	60
	5.8	.44	7.25				26.8	
United States -	3,263.4	151.49	543.80				6.445·9	277

* The estimated amounts of property in the northern district of New York, in the States of Maine, New Jersey, Pennsylvania, Michigan, Iowa, Delaware, Virginia, Tennessee, Missouri, Arkansas, Florida, and Alabama, and also in the Territories, are my estimates,—the other amounts of property stated, including all those in the first six columns of the table, are either official estimates, or official valuations. In every case, where I have made an estimate, I have made it higher than the official valuation.

VI. Estimate of the average and aggregate value of the slaves in the several States; the total valuation of property including slaves, according to the next preceding table, and the average amount to each free person:—

	Value of Slaves.		Value of other Property.	Total Value of Property.	Amount to each Free Person.
	Each.	Aggregate in Millions.	Millions.	Millions.	
Delaware	$300	$0.68	$27.5	$28.2	$316
Maryland	do.	27.01	192.2	219.2	445
District of Columbia	do.	1 1	13.5	14.6	304
Virginia	310	146.48	355.	501.5	526
North Carolina	330	95.17	131.6	226.8	387
Tennessee	330	79.02	175.	254.	333
Kentucky	310	65.4	234.	299.4	386
Missouri	do.	27.1	120.	147.1	247
Arkansas	350	16 44	26.	42.4	260
		458.40	1 274.8	1.733.2	
South Carolina	350	134.74	153.5	288.2	1,016
Georgia	400	152.67	182.7	335.4	647
*Florida	do.	15.72	10.9	26.6	553
*Alabama	do.	137.15	130.	267.1	623
Mississippi	do.	123.96	105.	229.	772
Louisiana	do.	97.91	136.1	234.	857
Texas	do.	23.26	29.5	52.8	341
		685.41	747.7	1.433.1	
Total in the Slave States		1,143,81	2.022.5	3,166,3	

The foregoing tables show that there has been a very great disparity in the relative increase of wealth of the people of the several States. The increase in Massachusetts and Rhode Island has been without parallel in the history of the world; the increase in England and Wales from 1800 to 1815 came the nearest to it. —(See Ante Chapter XIV., Section 7.)

A comparison of the valuations in Table II. with each other, and with the statements in the other tables, induces the belief, that property was generally estimated at its full cash value in 1813, and but little under its cash value in 1798. The restoration of peace in 1815 was succeeded by immense importations of foreign goods, which flooded the country, induced extensive sales on credit, and vast speculations, which inflated the price of lands, and made a false show of prosperity, when it was undermining the industry of the country. These causes produced the extravagant valuations in New Jersey and Pennsylvania in 1815, stated in the table. These causes continued to operate, until the passage of the tariff of 1824; the country became embarrassed, and property began to fall, and continued to fall until 1824. Table III. shows that the real estate in the eastern part of Virginia was estimated at about $20,000,000 less in 1838, than it was in 1819, and it must have been much less in 1824, than it was in 1838. Let the reader reflect upon the general fall of real estate from 1818 to 1824, and satisfy himself of the causes.

While the average amount of property to each person in Massachusetts increased nearly fifty per cent. from 1840 to 1850, the average amount in the agricultural States increased very little. The per cent. of increase of the population from 1840 to 1850, was greater in each of the manufacturing States of Massachusetts, Rhode Island, and New Jersey, than it was in either of the great States of New-York and Ohio. In 1798, the average wealth of the people of Vermont and the northern district of New York, was nearly as great as that of the inhabitants of Massachusetts; at the present time, it is only about half as great. Why this great change in relative condition? This question should excite the earnest inquiry of every reflecting man. The territory of Vermont is about a quarter greater than that of Massachusetts, and the soil much better, and yet the farming lands of the latter are valued at an amount nearly twice as great as those of the former. The rich lands of the north western States are of comparatively small value, for want of manufacturing, industry, and a large manufacturing population, to create a demand for their products. The anticipated benefits of canals and railroads to agricultural communities, without manufacturing or mining industry, have, to a very great extent, proved delusive.

The tables show that there is a much greater amount of wealth in the slave States, than the people of the free States have generally supposed; and that the cotton planting States are at present more prosperous than the agricultural States of the north and northwest. They show that the prosperty of a country depends less on the question between slavery and freedom, than it does on the spirit, habits, and pursuits of the people, and on a proper division of employments, in accordance with their wants, and with the resources of the country. It is idle and absurd for a people to produce what they do not need and cannot sell to advantage, and rely on purchasing of foreigners articles of necessity, which they might learn to produce themselves.

SEC. 2. *Improved Lands and Live Stock of the several States.*

Statement in thousands, of the number of acres of improved lands contained in farms and plantations, and of the number of horses, cattle, and other live stock in the several States, according to the Census of 1850; also the number in the United States according to the Census of 1840:

	Improved Lands.	Hor's.	Mul's	Milch Cows.	Work Oxen.	Other Cattle.	Sheep.	Swine.
Maine, . . .	2,039	42		134	84	126	452	55
New Hampshire, .	2,251	34		94	59	115	385	63
Vermont, . . .	2,591	61	.2	146	48	154	920	66
Massachusetts, . .	2,133	42		130	47	83	189	81
Rhode Island, . .	356	6		29	8	9	44	20
Connecticut, . .	1,768	27		85	47	80	174	76
	11,138	212	.3	618	293	567	2,164	361
S. District of N. York,	2,124 }	447	.9	931	179	767	3,453	1,018
N. District of N. York,	10,285 }							
New Jersey, . .	1,768	64	4.1	119	12	80	161	250
Pennsylvania, . .	8,628	350	2.3	530	61	562	1,822	1,040
	22,805	861	7.3	1,580	252	1,409	5,436	2,308
Ohio, ...	9,851	463	3.4	544	65	749	3,943	1,965
Indiana, . . .	5,046	314	6.6	285	40	390	1,123	2,264
Illinois, . . .	5,039	268	10.6	294	76	541	894	1,916
Michigan, . . .	1,929	58	.1	100	55	119	746	206
Wisconsin, . .	1,045	30	.1	64	43	76	125	159
Iowa, ...	824	38	.7	46	22	69	150	323
Minnesota, . .	5	$\frac{3}{4}$		$\frac{2}{3}$	$\frac{2}{3}$	$\frac{3}{4}$	$\frac{1}{8}$	$\frac{3}{4}$
	23,739	1,172	21.5	1,334	302	1,945	6,981	6,834
Delaware, . .	581	14	.8	19	10	24	27	56
Maryland, . . .	2,798	76	5.6	87	34	99	178	353
District of Columbia,	16	$\frac{3}{4}$		$\frac{3}{4}$	$\frac{1}{8}$	$\frac{1}{8}$	$\frac{1}{8}$	2
Virginia, . . .	10,361	272	21.5	318	89	669	1,310	1,831
North Carolina, .	5,454	149	25.3	222	37	434	595	1,813
Tennessee, . .	5,175	270	75.3	250	86	414	812	3,114
Kentucky, . .	6,068	315	65.6	247	62	443	1,102	2,861
Missouri, . . .	2,925	223	41.5	228	111	446	756	1,692
Arkansas, . . .	781	60	11.6	93	34	165	91	837
	34,159	1,380	247.2	1,465	464	2,695	4,872	12,559
South Carolina, . .	4,072	97	37.5	193	20	564	286	1,065
Georgia, . . .	6,378	151	57.4	334	73	690	560	2,169
Florida, . . .	349	11	5.0	73	6	182	23	209
Alabama, . . .	4,435	128	59.9	228	67	433	372	1,904
Mississippi, . .	3,444	115	54.5	214	83	436	305	1,583
Louisiana, . . .	1,590	89	44.8	106	55	415	110	597
Texas, . . .	639	75	12.4	215	50	637	99	684
	20,907	666	271.5	1,363	354	3,357	1,755	8,211
California, . . .	62	22	1.6	4	5	254	17	3
Oregon, . . .		8	.4	9	8	24	15	30
Utah, ...	16	2	.3	5	5	2	3	1
New Mexico, . .	166	5	8.6	11	12	10	377	7
	244	37	10.9	29	30	290	412	41
United States, . .	112,992	4,328	558.7	6,389	1,695	10,263	21,620	30,314
United States in 1840,		4,335.6		14,971			19,311	26,301

Sec. 3. *Agricultural Products of the several States in* 1849.

Statement in millions, of the number of bushels of wheat, rye, maize or Indian corn, oats, buckwheat, Irish potatoes and sweet potatoes, produced in the several States in 1849, according to the returns of the Census of 1850:

	Wheat.	Rye.	Maize.	Oats.	Buck-wheat	Irish potatos	Sweet potatos
Maine,	.296	.103	1.75	2.18	.104	3.436	
New Hampshire,	.186	.183	1.57	.97	.065	4.305	
Vermont,	.526	.176	2.03	2.31	.209	4.947	
Massachusetts,	.031	.481	2.34	1.16	.106	3.585	
Rhode Island,		.026	.54	.21	.001	.651	
Connecticut,	.042	.600	1.93	1.26	.229	2.689	
	1.081	1.569	10.16	8.09	.714	19.613	
New York,	13.121	4.148	17.86	26.55	3.183	15.398	.005
New Jersey,	1.601	1.255	8.76	3.38	.879	3.207	.508
Pennsylvania,	15.367	4.805	19.83	21.54	2.193	5.980	.062
	30.089	10.208	46 45	51.47	6.255	24.585	.575
Ohio,	14.487	.425	59.07	13.47	.638	5.057	.188
Indiana,	6.214	.079	52.96	5.65	.149	2.083	.202
Illinois,	9.414	.083	57.64	10.08	.184	2.515	.157
Michigan,	4.926	.106	5.64	2.86	.473	2.36	.001
Wisconsin,	4.286	.081	1 99	3.41	.079	1.402	.001
Iowa,	1.530	.02	8.65	1.52	.052	.276	.006
Minnesota,	.001		.02	.03	.001	.021	
	40.858	.794	185.97	37.02	1.576	13.714	.555
Delaware,	.482	.008	3.14	.6	.008	.240	.065
Maryland,	4.495	.226	11.10	2.24	.103	.765	.209
District of Columbia,	.017	.005	.06	.01		.028	.003
Virginia,	11.232	.459	35.25	10.18	.214	1.317	1.813
North Carolina,	2.130	.229	27.94	4.05	.016	.620	5.095
Tennessee,	1.619	.089	52.27	7.70	.019	1.061	2.778
Kentucky,	2.140	.415	58.67	8.20	.016	1.492	.998
Missouri,	2.967	.044	36.07	5.24	.023	.934	.332
Arkansas,	.199	.008	8.89	.65		.194	.788
	25,281	1.483	233.39	38.87	.399	6.651	12.081
South Carolina,	1.066	.044	16.27	2.32		.136	4.337
Georgia,	1.088	.054	30.08	3.82		.227	6.986
Florida,	.001	.001	2.	.06		.007	.757
Alabama,	.294	.017	28.75	2.96		.246	5.475
Mississippi,	.138	.009	22.44	1.5	.001	.261	4.741
Louisiana,			10.22	.09		.095	1.428
Texas,	.042	.003	5.92	.18		.093	1.323
	2.629	.128	115.68	10.93	.001	1.065	25.045
California,	.017		.01			.009	.001
Oregon,	.212			.06		.091	
Utah,	.108		.01	.01		.043	
New Mexico,	.196		.36				
	.533		.38	.07		.143	.001
United States,	100.471	14.182	592.03	146.45	8.945	65.771	38.257
United States in 1839,	84.823	18.645	377.53	123.07	7.291	108.298.060	

Statement in millions, of the bushels of peas, beans and barley, the pounds of rice, tobacco, wool and sugar; and the bales of cotton, of four hundred pounds each, stated in thousands, produced in 1849, according to the returns of the Census of 1850:

	Peas, beans.	Barley.	Rice.	Tobac'.	Cotton.	Wool.	Sugar.
Maine,	.205	.152				1.364	.093
New Hampshire,	.071	.070				1.108	1.295
Vermont,	.105	.042				3.411	5.981
Massachusetts,	.044	.112		.14		.585	.795
Rhode Island,	.006	.019				.13	
Connecticut,	.019	.019		1.27		.497	.051
	.450	.414		1.41		7.095	8.215
New York,	.742	3.585		.08		10.071	10.357
New Jersey,	.014	.006				.375	.002
Pennsylvania,	.055	.166		.91		4.481	2.326
	.811	3.757		.99		14.927	12.685
Ohio,	.060	.354		10.45		10.196	4.588
Indiana,	.036	.045		1.04		2.61	2.922
Illinois,	.083	.111		.84		2.15	.249
Michigan,	.074	.075				2.043	2.439
Wisconsin,	.021	.209				.254	.611
Iowa,	.005	.025		.01		.374	.078
Minnesota,	.010	.001					.003
	.289	.820		12.34		17.627	10.890
Delaware,	.004					.058	
Maryland,	.013	.001		21.41		.480	.048
District of Columbia,	.008			.01			
Virginia,	.522	.025	.017	56.8	3.95	2.861	1.228
North Carolina,	1.584	.003	5.466	11.98	73.85	.971	.028
Tennessee,	.369	.003	.259	20.15	194.53	1.364	.158
Kentucky,	.202	.095	.006	55.5	.76	2.297	.437
Missouri,	.046	.009		17.1		1.616	.179
Arkansas,	.286		.063	.22	65.34	.183	.009
	3.034	.136	5.811	183.17	338.43	9.830	2.087
South Carolina,	1.027	.004	159.93	.07	300.9	.487	.671
Georgia,	1.142	.011	38.95	.42	499.09	.990	1.644
Florida,	.135		1.075	1.	45.13	.023	2.752
Alabama,	.893	.004	2.311	.16	564.43	.657	8.243
Mississippi,	1.073		2.719	.05	484.29	.559	.388
Louisiana,	.162		4.425	.03	178.74	.110	226.0
Texas,	.179	.005	.088	.07	57.59	.131	7.351
	4.611	.024	209.498	1.80	2,130.17	2.957	247.049
California,	.002	.010				.005	
Oregon,	.006					.03	
Utah,		.002				.009	
New Mexico,	.016			.01		.033	
	.024	0.12		.01		0.77	
United States,	9.219	5.163	215.309	199.72	2,468.60	52.513	280 926
United States in 1839,		4.161	80.841	219.16	1,976.2	35.802	155.111

Statement in thousands, of the gallons of molasses made, of the value of the products of orchards, market gardens, and home-made or domestic manufactures, and, in millions, of the pounds of butter and cheese made, and the value of animals fattened for slaughter, during the year ending June 1, 1850, according to the returns of the Census.

	Molasses.	P'ducts orch'ds	Pro. mkt gardens.	H. made manuf's.	Butter.	Cheese.	Animals Fattened.
Maine,	3.1	$343	$122	$514	9.244	2.434	$1,647
New Hampshire,	9.8	248	57	393	6.977	3.196	1,523
Vermont,	6.	315	19	278	11.871	8.730	1,871
Massachusetts,	4:7	464	600	205	8.071	7.088	2,501
Rhode Island,		64	98	26	.995	.316	667
Connecticut,	.7	175	197	192	6.498	5.363	2,202
	24.3	1,609	1,093	1,608	43.656	27.127	10,411
New York,	56.5	1,762	912	1,280	79.766	49.741	13,574
New Jersey,	.9	607	475	113	9.487	.366	2,638
Pennsylvania,	50.6	723	689	749	39.878	2.505	8,220
	108.	3,092	2,076	2,142	129.131	52.612	24,432
Ohio,	308.3	695	214	1,712	34.449	20.819	7,439
Indiana,	180.3	325	73	1,631	12.881	.624	6,568
Illinois,	8.3	446	127	1,156	12.526	1.278	4,972
Michigan,	19.8	133	15	341	7.066	1.011	1,328
Wisconsin,	9.9	5	32	43	3.634	.4	920
Iowa,	3.2	8	9	221	2.171	.21	820
Minnesota,					.001		003
	529.8	1,612	470	5,104	72.728	24.342	22,050
Delaware,		46	12	38	1.055	.003	374
Maryland,	1.4	164	201	112	3.806	.004	1,955
Dist. of Columbia,		15	67	2	.015	.001	9
Virginia,	40.3	177	183	2,156	11.089	.436	7,500
North Carolina,	.7	34	39	2,086	4.146	.096	5,768
Tennessee,	7.2	53	97	3,138	8.139	.178	6,402
Kentucky,	40.	106	293	2,457	9.878	.214	6,459
Missouri,	5.6	512	99	1,663	7.792	.202	3,349
Arkansas,		40	17	638	1.854	.03	1,163
	95.2	1,147	1,008	12,290	47.774	1.164	32,979
South Carolina,	15.9	35	47	909	2.982	.005	1,303
Georgia,	216.1	93	76	1,839	4.64	.047	6,340
Florida,	352.8	1	9	76	.371	.018	515
Alabama,	83.4	15	85	1,934	4.009	.031	4,823
Mississippi,	18.3	50	46	1,164	4.346	.021	3,636
Louisiana,	10,931.2	22	148	139	.683	.002	1,459
Texas,	441.6	12	12	256	2.326	.091	1,106
	12.059.3	228	423	6,317	19.357	.215	19,182
California,		17	75	7	.001		100
Oregon,		1	90		.211	.037	164
Utah,			24	1	.083	.031	68
New Mexico,	4.2	8	7	6		.006	82
	4.2	26	196	14	.295	.074	414
United States,	12.820.8	$7,714	$5,266	$27,475	312.941	105.534	$109,469
U. States in 1839,		$7,257	$2,601*	$29,023	val. $33,787,008		

* Nurseries and florists, in 1839, $593,534.

Statement of other agricultural products returned with the Census of 1850, not included in the foregoing tables:

	Quantity.	Estimated Value.
Wine made,—gallons,	221,248	$221,000
Hay,—tons,	12,839,141	
Clover seed,—bushels,	467,983	
Other grass seed,—bushels,	413,154	
Hops,—pounds,	3,467,574	346,000
Flax,—pounds,	13,391,415	805,000
Flax seed,—bushels,	562,810	
Silk cocoons,—pounds,	14,763	29,000
Beeswax and honey,—pounds,	14,850,627	1,856,000
Hemp,—tons,	35,093	3,150,000

Estimated income of agriculturists in the United States, from labor and capital, employed during the year ending, June 1st, 1850, including the value of improvements* :

	Millions.
Wheat,* 90,424,000 bushels at an average price of 80cts.	$ 72.34
Rye,* 16,781,000 bushels at 50cts.	8.39
Indian Corn,† about 120,000,000 bushels used for food and sold to distil, export, and to use for other than agricultural purposes, at 40cts.	48.00
Oats,* perhaps half, or 67,100,000 bushels sold and used for other than agricultural purposes, at 28cts.	18.79
Buckwheat,* 8,200,000 bushels, at 50cts.	4.10
Potatoes,* 96,360,000 bushels, at 25cts.	24.09
Peas and Beans,* 8,450,000 bushels, at 80cts.	6.76
Barley,* 4,650,000 bushels, at 50cts.	2.33
Rice, 215,000,000 lbs. at 3cts.	6.45
Tobacco, 199,720,000lbs. at 4½cts.	9.00
Cotton, 987,200,000lbs. at 10¼cts.	101.18
Wool, 52,513,000lbs. at 30cts.	15.75
Cane Sugar, 247,778,000lbs. at 4½cts	11.15
Maple Sugar, 33,980,000lbs. at 8cts.	2.72
Molasses, 12,820,000gals. at 20cts.	2.56
Products of Orchards, valued at	7.71
Products of Market Gardeners	5.26
Value of home-made goods, less one-half for materials, &c.	13.73

* Note—One-tenth part of the wheat, barley and rye, and one-twelfth part of the oats, buckwheat, peas, beans and potatoes, have been deducted for seed; and the remaining quantities stated at their estimated average values, at the places of production.

† As to the disposition of the crop of Indian corn, see section 3, of chap. xi. and note on page 275.

	Millions
Butter, 312,941,000lbs. at 14cts.	43.81
Cheese, 105,534,000lbs. at 7cts.	7.38
Value of animals fattened and slaughtered,*	109.47
Value of wine, hops, flax, silk cocoons, bees-wax, and honey, heretofore estimated at,	3.26
Hemp, 35,093 tons at $90	3.15
One-fifth part of the Hay, estimated as sold, and not used by agriculturists, valued at	25.00
Annual increase, of live stock, over and above those killed, 3 per cent. (being the same as the increase of the inhabitants), valued at	16.37
Horses, Mules, &c., raised and sold for purposes other than agriculture, estimated at	5.00
Clearing and Fencing 2,800,000 acres of land at $11	30.80
Draining, and other agricultural improvements	8
Milk and Cream consumed, estimated as worth one-third part as much as the butter and cheese,	17.00
Products of domestic gardens, estimated at	13.00
Eggs and poultry, estimated at	15.00
Total	$657.55

SEC. 4.—*Manufacturing, Mechanical, and Mining Industry of the several States in* 1850.

Statement of the capital and number of persons employed in the United States, in manufactures of cotton, wool, and iron—the value of the raw materials used, including fuel, &c., and the gross value of the products, during the year ending, June 1st, 1850, according to the returns of the census; also the average amount of capital employed, and the net value produced to each person:

	Cotton.	Wool.	Pig Iron.	Castings.	Wrought Iron.
Capital invested (millions)	$74.5	$28.12	$17.34	$17.41	$14.49
Value of products in millions	61.87	43.2	12.75	25.1	16.74
Value of materials do.	34.83	25.7	7.	10.34	9.69
Net value produced do.	27.	17.5	5.75	14.76	7.05
Males employed	33.150	22.678	20.298	23.541	13.178
Females employed	59.136	16.574	150	48	79
Capital to each person	$807	$716	$848	$740	$1.093
Net value produced to each person.	$293	$444	$280	$625	$531

* The returns of the value of animals slaughtered agree substantially with the estimates of animal products consumed, contained in section 3, chap. xi, (page 278,) and show that the estimates of animal products, and the increase of animals contained on page 454, are greatly too high—perhaps too high by forty millions of dollars, considering that the whole value of the corn and oats is estimated in addition.

Summary statement in millions of dollars, of the amount of capital employed in the several States in mining, manufactures, and the mechanic arts, in 1840, and in 1850; also, the value of materials and fuel used, and the value of the products, during the year ending June 1st, 1850.*

	Amount of Capital invested.		Materials and Fuel used.	Value of Products.
	In 1840.	In 1850.		
Maine - -	$7.5	$14.7	$13.5	$24.6
New Hampshire -	9.4	17.9	13.8	24.8
Vermont - -	5.1	5.	4.2	8.6
Massachusetts -	44.1	83.3	85.8	151.1
Rhode Island -	10·7	12.9	13.2	22.1
Connecticut -	14.6	26.1	24.5	48.8
	91.4	159.9	155.	280.
New Yk. { S. Dis.	23.4	48.3	70.2	130.9
New Yk. { N. Dis.	35.6	53.4	63.4	106.8
New Jersey -	13.3	22.2	22.	39.7
Pennsylvania -	44.6	90.6	79.4	147.8
	116.9	214.5	235.	425.2
Ohio - -	14.3	28.4	33.4	62.1
Indiana - -	4.2	7.9	9.3	18.7
Illinois - -	3.4	6.1	9.	16.7
Michigan - -	3.2	6.5	5.6	10.5
Wisconsin - -	.8	3.4	5.3	8.7
Iowa - -	·3	1·21	2.	3.4
Minnesota - -	—	·09	.02	.05
	$26·2	$53.60	$64.62	$120.15

* The returns for 1850, embrace only industrial establishments, the products of which exceed in value $500 per annum. This arises from a defect in the Statute regulating the taking of the census. It is proper to remark, also, that the statements so far as regards many of the States, are taken from the first hasty examination of the schedules, and may be corrected by a revision, and a more careful examination of them. The returns from California and the territories are too uncertain to base any safe conclusions upon them.

	Capital		Materials.	Products.
	In 1840.	In 1850.		
Delaware - -	$1.6	$2.8	$2.8	$4.7
Maryland - -	7.3	14.7	17.3	32.5
Dist. Columbia -	1.	1.	1.5	2.2
Virginia - -	14.4	18.1	18.1	29.6
N. Carolina -	4.	7.7	4.2	9.4
Tennessee - -	5.3	7.	4.7	9.4
Kentucky - -	6.6	14.2	12.5	23.3
Missouri - -	3.1	4.2	12.4	24.2
Arkansas - -	.4	.4	.3	.7
	43.7	70.1	73.8	136.0
S. Carolina- -	3.4	6.	3.9	6.7
Georgia - -	3.	5.8	3.4	6.7
Florida - -	.7	.7	.2	.6
Alabama - -	2.1	3.9	2.1	4.5
Mississippi - -	1.8	1.9	.8	2.7
Louisiana - -	6.8	7.	.3	7.4
Texas - -	—	.6	.4	1.2
	17.8	25.9	11.1	29.8
California - -	—	.6	.8	12.7
Oregon - -	—	.8	.9	2.1
New Mexico -	—	.1	.1	.2
United States -	$296.	$525.6	$541.3	$1,006.1
Deduct the materials - - - -				541.3
Net Value produced by Labor and Capital				$464.8

SEC. 5. *Income from Capital and Industry in the United States, in* 1850.

The returns of the census of 1850 give no information on the subject of commerce and navigation. The census of 1840 states the amount of capital employed in commerce, retail-trade, navigation, and internal transportation, at $390,972,000; which, in connection with the annual reports on commerce and navigation, made by the Secretary of the Treasury, the reports of transportation by canals and railroads, and the reports of Chambers of

Commerce, furnish the only reliable information from which the income from that branch of industry and business can be estimated. The increase in the commerce of the United States, between the years 1840 and 1850, was about equal to the increase of the population. I have estimated the income from commerce, navigation, and transportation, in 1840, at about $169,000,000 ;* add to that sum, one third, and it would give $225,000,000, as the income for the year ending June 1st, 1850.

The returns of the census of 1850 furnish very few returns of the products of the forest and fisheries, which must be mostly estimated from those of the census of 1840. The value of pot and pearl ashes made, is included with the products of manufacturing establishments. The products of the forest, in 1840, including fuel, and excluding pot and pearl ashes, have been valued at about $38,500,000 ; and they may be estimated in 1850, at $50,000,000. The net products of the fisheries in 1840, have been estimated at over $10,000,000, and they may be estimated at that sum for 1850.

	Mil.
Estimated income of the people of the United States, arising from labor and capital employed in agriculture, and on farms, during the year ending June 1st, 1850, brought forward nearly - - - - -	$658.
Income from manufacturing, mechanical, and mining industry, about - - - - - - - -	465.
Income from commerce, navigation, and transportation	225.
Income from the forest estimated at - - - -	50.
Income from the fisheries, estimated at - - -	10.
Total - - - - -	$1,408.

This sum gives an average income to each person in the United States, of nearly sixty-one dollars ; and if the average consumption of each slave does not exceed $30 (which is the largest sum usually estimated), it allows an average income to each free person in the United States, of about $65¾.

After correcting the estimate of the value of animal products, and the increase of animals† over and above the value of the

* See Chap. xiv. sec. 16.

† The returns of the census of 1840 do not include the value of animals slaughtered. This information contained in the census of 1850, enables me to correct my estimate of the income from animals in 1840, and shows that the estimates contained on pages 453 and 454, and carried into the aggregates on page 462, were too high, by not less than forty millions of dollars. More than three fourths of the Indian corn is consumed by animals, and is included in the value of hogs, cattle, and sheep slaughtered.

grain consumed by them, the result will show that the aggregate amount of the productive industry of the United States in 1840, was about $980,000,000 ; which was equal to about $57½ to each person, and about $62 to each free person, after deducting the support of the slaves. On correcting the estimates of the income from animals, it will reduce the aggregate income of the agricultural States, stated on page 462, very considerably, and show the disparity between the average income of the people of the agricultural States of the north, and that of the manufacturing States, greater than it is there stated. The remarks at the end of section 18 of Chap. xiv. (ante pages, 463, 464) apply to the condition of the United States in 1850, and to the census of that year, nearly as well as to the census and year 1840. Cotton was not so high in 1840, as it was in 1850 ; and hence the income of the cotton-planting States ,and the profit of slave labor in them, was greater at the latter, than it was at the former period. The income in 1850, of slave labor in Louisiana, Mississippi, and some other States, exceed the income from free agricultural labor in the north western states, much more than appears from the table on page 462.

Why is it that farming lands in Massachusetts, are worth twice as much as those of the same quality in Vermont and Ohio ; and from three to four times as much as those of the same quality in Indiana, Illinois, Michigan, and Wisconsin ?* Why is it, that the increase of wealth, and particularly of the value of real estate, has been so much more rapid in Massachusetts, than in Vermont, and in the northern District of New York ? Why is it that the average amount of productive industry to each person, is about twice as great in Massachusetts, as it is in Vermont, Ohio, or any of the rich agricultural States of the north-west ? Why is it, then, from 1840 to 1850, the increase of population in Massachusetts and Rhode Island, was from 34 to 35 per cent., and less than 8 per cent. in Vermont ; and that great numbers of persons went from the latter to the former, in search of employment ? Why are all the agricultural countries of the earth, poor, when compared with manufacturing countries ? Why is agricultural Ireland poor, and manufacturing Britain, immensely rich, beyond all former examples, in the history of the world ? How can these results (shown by the censuses of the United States, of 1840, and 1850, and the statistics of other countries), be accounted for ? These are questions which should command the attention, not only of every statesman, but of every farmer, and of every citizen. I cannot account for the facts, for the condition

* See Tables, I, II, IV, and V, in section 1, of this chapter.

of classes, communities, states, and nations, and the different degrees of progress made by them during the last two centuries, and particularly during the last forty years, except on the principles stated and discussed in these essays. Let every man inquire into the causes for himself.

INDEX.

A.

B.

C.

D.

G.

H.

I.

J.

L.

M.

N.

O.

P.

R.

S.

T.

U.

V.

W.

Z.